Trends and Effects of Technology Advancement in the Knowledge Society

Miltiadis Lytras
The American College of Greece, Greece

Isabel Novo–Corti
University of A Coruña, Spain

T0350097

Managing Director:	Lindsay Johnston
Editorial Director:	Joel Gamon
Book Production Manager:	Jennifer Romanchak
Publishing Systems Analyst:	Adrienne Freeland
Development Editor:	Heather Probst
Assistant Acquisitions Editor:	Kayla Wolfe
Typesetter:	Lisandro Gonzalez
Cover Design:	Nick Newcomer

Published in the United States of America by
Information Science Reference (an imprint of IGI Global)
701 E. Chocolate Avenue
Hershey PA 17033
Tel: 717-533-8845
Fax: 717-533-8661
E-mail: cust@igi-global.com
Web site: http://www.igi-global.com

Library of Congress Cataloging-in-Publication Data

Trends and effects of technology advancement in the knowledge society / Miltiadis Lytras and Isabel Novo Corti, editors.
    p. cm.
  Includes bibliographical references and index.
  Summary: "This book brings together academicians, industry professionals, policymakers, politicians, and government officers to look at the impact of information technology, and the knowledge-based era it is creating, on key facets of today's world: the state, business, society, and culture"-- Provided by publisher.
  ISBN 978-1-4666-1788-9 (hardcover) -- ISBN 978-1-4666-1789-6 (ebook) -- ISBN 978-1-4666-1790-2 (print & perpetual access) 1. Information technology. 2. Knowledge management. I. Lytras, Miltiadis D., 1973- II. Corti, Isabel Novo, 1958-
  HC79.T4T74 2012
  303.48'3--dc23
                        2012017817

British Cataloguing in Publication Data
A Cataloguing in Publication record for this book is available from the British Library.

The views expressed in this book are those of the authors, but not necessarily of the publisher.

Table of Contents

Detailed Table of Contents

In this paper, the authors apply models extracted from the Many-Body Quantum Mechanics to understand how knowledge production is correlated to the innovation potential of a work team. This study is grounded in key assumtpions. First, complexity theory applied to social science suggests that it is of paramount importance to consider elements of non-objectivity and non-determinism in the statistical description of socio-economic phenomena. Second, a typical factor of indeterminacy in the explanation of these phenomena lead to the need to apply the instruments of quantum physics to formally describe social behaviours. In order to experiment the validity of the proposed mathematic model, the research intends to: 1) model nodes and interactions; 2) simulate the network behaviour starting from specific defined models; 3) visualize the macroscopic results emerging during the analysis/simulation phases through a digital representation of the social network.

Educational games display great potential as an active form of knowledge transfer. This research field is young, but some patterns in educational game development can be recognized. In this paper, the authors present a new approach to educational game development that overcomes some downsides of more traditional systems. The paper provides the opportunity to create an educational adventure game by using specialized software tool as well as integrating knowledge in that specific game instance. As a result of that process, game definition is created as a form of XML document. On the other side, a web-based interpreter is used to present the adventure game to user in runtime. XML format provides us with platform independency. By use of this tool, the educator gains the ability to create an educational game without programming knowledge, and to reuse some previously created knowledge.

Chapter 3

Ravi S. Sharma, Nanyang Technological University, Singapore

Elaine W. J. Ng, Nanyang Technological University, Singapore

Mathias Dharmawirya, Nanyang Technological University, Singapore

Ekundayo M. Samuel, Nanyang Technological University, Singapore

In this article, the authors explore the definition of a knowledge society and why such a society is desirable in the development of nations. First, this paper reviews the literature on knowledge societies and notes a gap in qualitative approaches which are amenable for framing development knowledge policies. The authors then describe a conceptual framework that depicts a knowledge society in terms of 13 dimensions that span infrastructure, governance, human capital and culture. This framework is validated with published proxy indicators from reputable sources such as the United Nations and the World Bank. In a field exercise, this paper determines the usability of the framework for policy discussion using Singapore, Nigeria, the United States and the United Arab Emirates as the foci of our analysis. The authors conclude by suggesting that such a qualitative framework is useful for policy-makers and other stakeholders to understand that the evolution to a knowledge society is a journey that requires benchmarks, environmental intelligence and an emphasis on the tacit structure of knowledge for sustainable advantage.

Chapter 4

Saad Haj Bakry, King Saud University, Saudi Arabia

Abdulkader Alfantookh, Ministry of Higher Education, Saudi Arabia

Building the knowledge culture is of increasing importance, not only because of its role in providing sound knowledge management and effective knowledge-based economic development, but also because of its support to environment protection, intercultural harmony and human well-being. This paper provides a review of the knowledge culture and its related issues, and introduces a development framework for building this culture. The proposed framework integrates the main knowledge activities of knowledge generation, diffusion and utilization into an activated "Knowledge Circle: KC". It uses the five-domain structure of "Strategy, Technology, Organization, People and Environment: STOPE" to map and interrelate the various issues associated with the knowledge culture. In addition, it adopts the "Six-Sigma" principles, and its continuous process of "Define, Measure, Analyze, Improve and Control: DMAIC" as an approach to the work toward building the target culture. The paper calls for building the knowledge culture, not only at an organization, or a country level, but also at the global level. It provides its KC-STOPE with Six-Sigma framework for this purpose and strongly recommends its use for future development toward building the target culture.

Chapter 5

Adrián Hernández-López, Universidad Carlos III de Madrid, Spain

Ricardo Colomo-Palacios, Universidad Carlos III de Madrid, Spain

Ángel García-Crespo, Universidad Carlos III de Madrid, Spain

Pedro Soto-Acosta, University of Murcia, Spain

Due to increasing globalization tendencies in organization environment, Software Development is evolving from a single site development to multiple localization team environment. In this new scenario, team building issues must be revisited. In this paper components needed for the construction of the Trust Building Process are proposed in these new Global Software Development Teams. Based in a thoroughly state of the art analysis of trust building in organizations, this new process comes to narrow the gap between dynamics of trust building and intrinsic characteristics of global teams. In this paper, the components for Trust Building Process are justified and presented, with the purpose of a future assembly in further publications, leaving testing of this assembly far behind.

Craig Deed, La Trobe University, Australia
Anthony Edwards, Liverpool Hope University, UK

Realising the potential for web-based communication in learning and teaching is challenging for educators. In this paper, the authors examine students' attitudes toward active learning when using an unrestricted blog in an academic context and whether this can be used to support reflective and critical discussion, leading to knowledge construction. The authors collected data using an online survey with questions on student perceptions of the type, frequency and effectiveness of their strategy. Analysis of the data was conducted using Bloom's revised taxonomy. The research indicates that students must have prior familiarity with this form of communication technology to construct knowledge in an academic context. The authors conclude that effective learning will only emerge if informed by the student experience and perspective.

Constanta-Nicoleta Bodea, The Academy of Economic Studies, Romania
Maria Dascalu, The Academy of Economic Studies, Romania
Melania Coman, The Academy of Economic Studies, Romania

This paper examines the factors that influence the quality of training and education on project management. The authors present the results of two questionnaire-based surveys. The goal of the first survey was to find what factors influence the quality of project management education, according to the perspective of trainers, professors, and training providers. The respondents included Chinese and European academics and professionals, such as project managers, software developers, financial managers and professors. The respondents were not only involved in project management training but also served as team members or team managers, thus ensuring a balanced overview of theoretical and practical issues. The goal of the second survey was to explore the definition "quality" to trainees and students. Although there were small differences of perspective, both trainers and trainees have the same approach toward a qualitative project management education.

Jordi Díaz Gibson, Ramon Llull University, Spain
Mireia Civís Zaragoza, Ramon Llull University, Spain
Jordi Longás Mayayo, Ramon Llull University, Spain
Ana Mª López Murat, Ramon Llull University, Spain

This paper describes the inside organization of Educative Networks (ENs) and the aspects that allowed their growth and success in the city of Barcelona, Spain. ENs emerged over the past ten years in Catalonia, Spain, as a way to incorporate social and educative challenges in the territory. These educative proposals are based on the connection between the different educative institutions in the community to tackle social and education challenges in cooperation through transversality and a common project. The intent of ENs is to create synergies between cooperating organizations and coordinate community action to avoid overlap and redundant work. This study shows how these educative structures use context possibilities to improve educative impact and develop a new vision of organizing and conceiving education.

Chapter 9

Lorayne Robertson, University of Ontario Institute of Technology, Canada

Janette Hughes, University of Ontario Institute of Technology, Canada

The authors review all aspects of a Language Arts methods course for pre-service teachers, one which employs a multi-literacies pedagogy (The New London Group, 1996) and is taught at a laptop-based university. The course begins with a deliberate immersion into the complexities of multiple literacies, including digital literacy and critical literacy. The authors outline the course assignments, resources and instructional goals to determine how technology impacts pre-service teacher learning and intended future practice. The qualitative data sources include digital artifacts such as digital literacy stories, book talks that focus on social justice issues, and media literacy lessons. In addition, the researchers draw from cross-program data based on teacher candidate reflections and interviews. The data suggest that both the use of digital technology and a multi-literacies pedagogy can help pre-service teachers reflect on personal experiences to develop literacy teaching and learning practices that have transformative elements.

Chapter 10

Marco Ronchetti, University of Trento, Italy

In this paper, the author proposes a paradigm shift in the way video lectures are used in education. Instead of using them to support traditional teaching methods, the author suggests replacing standard lectures with video lectures, opening a space for a more participatory and interactive form of teaching that supports students in deeper understanding. In this paper, the author reviews the literature, discusses the effectiveness of video lectures, and describes a methodology called VOLARE ("Video On Line As Replacement of old tEaching practices").

Chapter 11

Patrícia Albergaria-Almeida, University of Aveiro, Portugal

José Joaquim Teixeira-Dias, University of Aveiro, Portugal

Mariana Martinho, Escola EB 2,3/S de Oliveira de Frades, Portugal

Chinthaka Balasooriya, University of New South Wales, Australia

The purpose of this study is to investigate if the teaching, learning and assessment strategies conceived and implemented in a higher education chemistry course promote the development of conceptual understanding, as intended. Thus, our aim is to analyse the learning styles and the approaches to learning of chemistry undergraduates with better grades.

This study took place during the 1st semester of the school year 2009/2010. This research was carried out in a naturalistic setting, within the context of chemistry classes for 1st year science and engineering courses, at the University of Aveiro, in Portugal. The class was composed of 100 students. At the end of the semester, the 8 chemistry students with the highest grades were selected for interview. Data was collected through Kolb's Learning Styles Inventory, through Approaches and Study Skills Inventory for Students, through non-participant observation, through the analysis of students' participation in online forums and lab books. The overall results show that the students with better grades possess the assimilator learning style, that is usually associated to the archetypal chemist. Moreover, the students with the highest grades revealed a conception of learning emphasising understanding. However, these students diverged both in their learning approaches and in their preferences for teaching strategies. The majority of students adopted a deep approach or a combination of a deep and a strategic approach, but half of them revealed their preference for teaching-centred strategies.

In this paper, curriculum design and development for computer science and similar disciplines as a formal model is introduced and analysed. Functions of education process as knowledge delivery and assessment are analysed. Structural formation of curriculum design is presented using definitive, characteristic and predictive functions. The process of changes in the discipline is also described and analysed. The authors then develop an algorithm to determine the core of the discipline and functions of the core moving and merging are introduced.

Evaluation is an important measure for quality control in e-learning, which aims at improving a learning environment and adapting it to users' needs, as well as proving values and benefits of a course to financers and participants. However, results and styles of evaluation are subject to the designers', the evaluators' and the participants' individual and socio-cultural backgrounds. This paper examines evaluation from an infrastructure perspective and presents dimensions and parameters for the evaluation of e-learning. The authors take cognitive, epistemological, social and technical infrastructures into account.

Chapter 14

What are the requirements for the Wiki engines to be used collaborative learning activities? Can any general-purpose engine be used? Or is there a niche for an educationally oriented crop of wiki engines? Do these educational wikis need to be integrated within the LMS to frame the collaborative activity within the walls of the virtual classroom, or is it preferable to have an external engine? These questions arise to every teacher who is about to plan a wiki-based collaborative learning activity. In this paper, the authors examine the use of wikis in college courses at three universities. The findings of this research are introduced and adopted as new features in two major open source wiki engines used for education: the Wiki module for Moodle 2.0 (as a Wiki engine embedded inside a LMS) and Tiki as independent full-featured Wiki CMS/Groupware engine.

Chapter 15

M. Zamorano, University of Granada, Spain

M.L. Rodríguez, University of Granada, Spain

A. F. Ramos-Ridao, University of Granada, Spain

M. Pasadas, University of Granada, Spain

The European Space of Higher Education (ESHE) is a new conceptual formulation of the organization of teaching at the university, largely involving the development of new training models based on the individual student's work. In this context, the University of Granada has approved two plans of Educational Excellence to promote a culture of quality and stimulate excellence in teaching. The Area of Environmental Technology in the Department of Civil Engineering has developed an innovative project entitled Application of new Information and Communication Technologies (ICT) to the Area of Environmental Technology teaching to create a new communication channel consisting of a Web site that benefits teacher and student ("Environmental Studies Centre": http://cem.ugr.es). Through this interactive page, teachers can conduct supervised teaching, and students will have the tools necessary for guiding their learning process, according to their capacities and possibilities. However, the material is designed to serve as a complement to the traditional method of attended teaching.

Chapter 16

Ioannis Karavasilis, University of Macedonia, Greece

Kostas Zafiropoulos, University of Macedonia, Greece

Vasiliki Vrana, Technological Education Institute of Serres, Greece

As governments around the world move toward e-governance, a need exists to examine citizens' willingness to adopt e-governance services. In this paper, the authors identify the success factors of e-governance adoption by teachers in Greece, using the Technology Acceptance Model, the Diffusion of Innovation model and constructs of trust, risk and personal innovativeness. Two hundred thirty primary and secondary education teachers responded to an online survey. LISREL then analyzed the data. Model estimation used the maximum likelihood approach, with the item covariance matrix as input. A SEM validation of the proposed model reveals that personal innovativeness, compatibility and relative advantage are stronger predictors of intention to use, compared to trust, and perceived risk. Findings may enhance policymakers' capacities by presenting them with an understanding of citizens' attitudes.

Chapter 17

Aljona Zorina, ESSEC Business School, France

David Avison, ESSEC Business School, France

This paper studies the nature and the importance of the link between macro and micro levels of innovation management in the knowledge society of Denmark, Sweden, USA, India, Russia, and Moldova, suggesting that countries with different levels of knowledge society development have different link types between the macro and micro levels of innovation management. In particular, findings show that countries with a higher level of knowledge society development have a two-way mediation process between the micro and macro levels of innovation management while countries with lower level of knowledge society development tend towards a "one-direction" link. This paper argues that innovation management can only be fully effective through paying attention to this intersection, which is free of biases inherent in each individually. The authors conclude by introducing a "meso-level" indicator for knowledge society development and underline areas of further research in the field.

Kaj U. Koskinen, Tampere University of Technology, Finland
Pekka Pihlanto, Turku School of Economics, University of Turku, Finland

This paper focuses on knowledge management stressing an individual project manager's point of view. First, the authors outline two knowledge management strategies as well as the notion of project manager. The authors concentrate on the project manager's knowledge creation and communication using the so-called theatre metaphor for conscious experience. According to this metaphor, the human brain and consciousness work together like a theatre. With the help of the metaphor, the authors describe and attempt to understand important aspects of the project manager's mental action in the above tasks.

E. Serradell-Lopez, Open University of Catalonia, Spain
P. Lara, Open University of Catalonia, Spain
D. Castillo, Open University of Catalonia, Spain
I. González, Open University of Catalonia, Spain

The purpose of this paper is to determine the effectiveness of using multiple choice tests in subjects related to the administration and business management. To this end the authors used a multiple-choice test with specific questions to verify the extent of knowledge gained and the confidence and trust in the answers. The analysis made, conducted by tests given out to a group of 200 students, has been implemented in one subject related with investment analysis and has measured the level of knowledge gained and the degree of trust and security in the responses at two different times of the business administration and management course. Measurements were taken into account at different levels of difficulty in the questions asked and the time spent by students to complete the test. Results confirm that students are generally able to obtain more knowledge along the way and get increases in the degree of trust and confidence. It is estimated that improvement in skills learned is viewed favourably by businesses and are important for job placement. Finally, the authors proceed to analyze a multi-choice test using a combination of knowledge and confidence levels.

Chapter 20

Kamran Manzoor, University of Engineering and Technology, Pakistan
Umar Manzoor, The University of Salford, UK
Samia Nefti, The University of Salford, UK

Video stabilization is one of the most important enhancements where jittering caused by un-intentional movements is removed. Existing video stabilizer software and tools cannot differentiate between intentional and un-intentional jitters in the video and treats both equally. In this paper, the authors propose an efficient and practical approach of video stabilization by differentiating between an intentional and un-intentional jitter. Their method takes jittered video as input, and differentiates between intentional and an un-intentional jitter without affecting its visual quality while producing stabilized video only if jitter is found to be un-intentional. While most previous methods produce stabilized videos with low resolution, this reduces quality. The proposed system has been evaluated on a large number of real life videos and results promise to support the implementation of the solution.

Chapter 21

Belinda Masekela, University of South Africa, South Africa
Rita Nienaber, University of South Africa, South Africa

In today's global marketplace, organizations are continually faced with the need to change their structures and processes to attain a competitive advantage. Implementation of new technology and information management systems results in inevitable changes in organizational procedures impacting on the people involved. Resistance to change may impact on this process and contribute to failure of this system. Managing change in an effective and efficient manner may negate this impact. This paper compiles a set of guidelines to support change which involves the incorporation of technology in an organization. These guidelines were mapped to a model, the GIC (Guidelines Implementing Change) model comprising all identified factors. These guidelines are utilized to guide the implementation of a new system, while simultaneously evaluating the success of these set guidelines. This research is cross disciplinary, affecting the areas of organizational behaviour, software project management, and human factors.

Chapter 22

David Castillo-Merino, Open University of Catalonia, Spain
Dolors Plana-Erta, Open University of Catalonia, Spain

This paper investigates the constraints for companies to innovate in order to be competitive in the knowledge society. Using a large and original data set of Catalan firms, the authors have conducted a micro econometric analysis following Henry et al.'s (1999) investment model and von Kalckreuth (2004) methodology empirically contrasting the relationship between firms' investment spread over time and their financial structure. Results show that it exits a positive and significant relationship between firms' investment shift and financial structure, emerging financial constraints for more innovative firms. Furthermore, these constraints are higher for micro companies and firms within the knowledge-advanced services' industry. Finally, the authors find that advanced ICT uses by more innovative firms allow them to reduce con-straints of access to sources of finance.

Preface

Today's society is currently being molded by the rapid exchange of knowledge now possible. This has created a new way to examine, explore, and understand human society, now a "knowledge society," and that new understanding will only become more vital for researchers, governments, schools and universities, and any other institution that is established to interact with and support society. The chapters contained in this summation of the inaugural volume of the International Journal of Knowledge Society Research begin the process of widening the communication between researchers actively studying social effects of technology and the government, policy makers, and any reader interested in detailed analysis of today emerging knowledge society.

In Chapter 1, "Quantum Modeling of Social Dynamics," the authors apply models extracted from the Many-Body Quantum Mechanics to understand how knowledge production is correlated to the innovation potential of a work team. This study is grounded in key assumptions. First, complexity theory applied to social science suggests that it is of paramount importance to consider elements of non-objectivity and non-determinism in the statistical description of socio-economic phenomena. Second, a typical factor of indeterminacy in the explanation of these phenomena lead to the need to apply the instruments of quantum physics to formally describe social behaviours. In order to experiment the validity of the proposed mathematic model, the research intends to:

1. Model nodes and interactions;
2. Simulate the network behaviour starting from specific defined models;
3. Visualize the macroscopic results emerging during the analysis/simulation phases through a digital representation of the social network.

Educational games display great potential as an active form of knowledge transfer. This research field is young, but some patterns in educational game development can be recognized. In Chapter 2, "Adventure Game Learning Platform," the authors present a new approach to educational game development that overcomes some downsides of more traditional systems. The paper provides the opportunity to create an educational adventure game by using specialized software tool as well as integrating knowledge in that specific game instance. As a result of that process, game definition is created as a form of XML document. On the other side, a web-based interpreter is used to present the adventure game to user in runtime. XML format provides us with platform independency. By use of this tool, the educator gains the ability to create an educational game without programming knowledge, and to reuse some previously created knowledge.

In Chapter 3, "A Policy Framework for Developing Knowledge Societies," the authors explore the definition of a knowledge society and why such a society is desirable in the development of nations. First, this paper reviews the literature on knowledge societies and notes a gap in qualitative approaches which are amenable for framing development knowledge policies. The authors then describe a conceptual framework that depicts a knowledge society in terms of 13 dimensions that span infrastructure, governance, human capital and culture. This framework is validated with published proxy indicators from reputable sources such as the United Nations and the World Bank. In a field exercise, this paper determines the usability of the framework for policy discussion using Singapore, Nigeria, the United States and the United Arab Emirates as the foci of our analysis. The authors conclude by suggesting that such a qualitative framework is useful for policy-makers and other stake-holders to understand that the evolution to a knowledge society is a journey that requires benchmarks, environmental intelligence and an emphasis on the tacit structure of knowledge for sustainable advantage.

Building the knowledge culture is of increasing importance, not only because of its role in providing sound knowledge management and effective knowledge-based economic development, but also because of its support to environment protection, intercultural harmony and human well-being.

Chapter 4, "Toward Building the Knowledge Culture: Reviews and a KC-STOPE with Six Sigma View," provides a review of the knowledge culture and its related issues, and introduces a development framework for building this culture. The proposed framework integrates the main knowledge activities of knowledge generation, diffusion and utilization into an activated "Knowledge Circle: KC". It uses the five-domain structure of "Strategy, Technology, Organization, People and Environment: STOPE" to map and interrelate the various issues associated with the knowledge culture. In addition, it adopts the "Six-Sigma" principles, and its continuous process of "Define, Measure, Analyze, Improve and Control: DMAIC" as an approach to the work toward building the target culture. The paper calls for building the knowledge culture, not only at an organization, or a country level, but also at the global level. It provides its KC-STOPE with Six-Sigma framework for this purpose and strongly recommends its use for future development toward building the target culture.

In Chapter 5, "Trust Building Process for Global Software Development Teams: A review from the Literature," the components for Trust Building Process are justified and presented, with the purpose of a future assembly in further publications, leaving testing of this assembly far behind.

Due to increasing globalization tendencies in organization environment, Software Development is evolving from a single site development to multiple localization team environments. In this new scenario, team building issues must be revisited. In this paper components needed for the construction of the Trust Building Process are proposed in these new Global Software Development Teams. Based in a thoroughly state of the art analysis of trust building in organizations, this new process comes to narrow the gap between dynamics of trust building and intrinsic characteristics of global teams.

Realising the potential for web-based communication in learning and teaching is challenging for educators. In Chapter 6, "Using Social Networks in Learning and Teaching in Higher Education: An Australian Case Study," the authors examine students' attitudes toward active learning when using an unrestricted blog in an academic context and whether this can be used to support reflective and critical discussion, leading to knowledge construction. The authors collected data using an online survey with questions on student perceptions of the type, frequency and effectiveness of their strategy. Analysis of the data was conducted using Bloom's revised taxonomy. The research indicates that students must have prior familiarity with this form of communication technology to construct knowledge in an academic context. The authors conclude that effective learning will only emerge if informed by the student experience and perspective.

Chapter 7, "Quality of Project Management Education and Training Programmes," examines the factors that influence the quality of training and education on project management. The authors present the results of two questionnaire-based surveys. The goal of the first survey was to find what factors influence the quality of project management education, according to the perspective of trainers, professors, and training providers. The respondents included Chinese and European academics and professionals, such as project managers, software developers, financial managers and professors. The respondents were not only involved in project management training but also served as team members or team managers, thus ensuring a balanced overview of theoretical and practical issues. The goal of the second survey was to explore the definition "quality" to trainees and students. Although there were small differences of perspective, both trainers and trainees have the same approach toward a qualitative project management education.

The objectives of Chapter 8, "The Study of Educative Network Organizations in the City of Barcelona: The Nou Barris District," is to develop a conceptual framework for studying the relationship between Human Resource Activities and Social Capital while underlining the importance that human resource policies play in the management of this variable in a IT environment. Over the past years, several researchers have analysed the relational dynamics that takes place inside and between organizations (concept, mediating and moderating variables, effects, etc.) considering it as a resource capable of contributing to the orientation and the strategic positioning of the organizations, and, as a last resort, to the support of the competitive advantages. Nevertheless, there are very few studies that include evidence about how the effective management of certain characteristics and properties of the network, such as the work dynamics developed or the interaction in the group may be useful for the operation of the work group itself in firms that develop its activity in high-tech sectors.

In Chapter 9, "The Teachers They Are Becoming: Multiple Literacies in Teacher Pre-Service," the authors review all aspects of a Language Arts methods course for pre-service teachers, one which employs a multi-literacies pedagogy (The New London Group, 1996) and is taught at a laptop-based university. The course begins with a deliberate immersion into the complexities of multiple literacies, including digital literacy and critical literacy. The authors outline the course assignments, resources and instructional goals to determine how technology impacts pre-service teacher learning and intended future practice. The qualitative data sources include digital artifacts such as digital literacy stories, book talks that focus on social justice issues, and media literacy lessons. In addition, the researchers draw from cross-program data based on teacher candidate reflections and interviews. The data suggest that both the use of digital technology and a multi-literacies pedagogy can help pre-service teachers reflect on personal experiences to develop literacy teaching and learning practices that have transformative elements.

In Chapter 10, "A Different Perspective on Lecture Video-Streaming: How to Use Technology to Help Change the Traditional Lecture Model" the author proposes a paradigm shift in the way video lectures are used in education. Instead of using them to support traditional teaching methods, the author suggests replacing standard lectures with video lectures, opening a space for a more participatory and interactive form of teaching that supports students in deeper understanding. In this paper, the author reviews the literature, discusses the effectiveness of video lectures, and describes a methodology called VOLARE ("Video On Line As Replacement of old tEaching practices").

In Chapter 11, "Kolb's Learning Styles and Approaches to Learning: The Case of Chemistry Undergraduates with Better Grades," the authors investigate if the teaching, learning and assessment strategies conceived and implemented in a higher education chemistry course promote the development of conceptual understanding, as intended. Thus, the authors' aim is to analyze the learning styles and the approaches to learning of chemistry undergraduates with better grades. This study took place during the 1st semester of the school year 2009/2010. This research was carried out in a naturalistic setting, within the context of chemistry classes for 1st year science and engineering courses, at the University of Aveiro, in Portugal. The class was composed of 100 students. At the end of the semester, the 8 chemistry students with the highest grades were selected for interview. Data was collected through Kolb's Learning Styles Inventory, through Approaches and Study Skills Inventory for Students, through non-participant observation, through the analysis of students' participation in online forums and lab books. The overall results show that the students with better grades possess the assimilator learning style, that is usually associated to the archetypal chemist. Moreover, the students with the highest grades revealed a conception of learning emphasizing understanding. However, these students diverged both in their learning approaches and in their preferences for teaching strategies. The majority of students adopted a deep approach or a combination of a deep and a strategic approach, but half of them revealed their preference for teaching-centered strategies.

In Chapter 12, "Curriculum Design and Development for Computer Science and Similar Disciplines," curriculum design and development for computer science and similar disciplines as a formal model is introduced and analyzed. Functions of education process as knowledge delivery and assessment are analyzed. Structural formation of curriculum design is presented using definitive, characteristic and predictive functions. The process of changes in the discipline is also described and analysed. The authors then develop an algorithm to determine the core of the discipline and functions of the core moving and merging are introduced.

Evaluation is an important measure for quality control in e-learning, which aims at improving a learning environment and adapting it to users' needs, as well as proving values and benefits of a course to financers and participants. However, results and styles of evaluation are subject to the designers', the evaluators' and the participants' individual and socio-cultural backgrounds. Chapter 13, "Evaluation of E-Learning," examines evaluation from an infrastructure perspective and presents dimensions and parameters for the evaluation of e-learning. The authors take cognitive, epistemological, social and technical infrastructures into account.

Chapter 14, "Requirements for Successful Wikis in Collaborative Educational Scenarios," asks what are the requirements for the Wiki engines to be used collaborative learning activities? Can any general-purpose engine be used? Or is there a niche for an educationally oriented crop of wiki engines? Do these educational wikis need to be integrated within the LMS to frame the collaborative activity within the walls of the virtual classroom, or is it preferable to have an external engine? These questions arise to every teacher who is about to plan a wiki-based collaborative learning activity. In this paper, the authors examine the use of wikis in college courses at three universities. The findings of this research are introduced and adopted as new features in two major open source wiki engines used for education: the Wiki module for Moodle 2.0 (as a Wiki engine embedded inside a LMS) and Tiki as independent full-featured Wiki CMS/Groupware engine.

Chapter 15, "An Innovative Educational Project at the University of Granada: A New Teaching-Learning Model for Adapting the Organization of Curricula to Interactive Learning," details an important project from the University of Granada. The European Space of Higher Education (ESHE) is a new conceptual formulation of the organization of teaching at the university, largely involving the development of new training models based on the individual student's work. In this context, the University of Granada has approved two plans of Educational Excellence to promote a culture of quality and stimulate excellence in teaching. The Area of Environmental Technology in the Department of Civil Engineering has developed an innovative project entitled Application of new Information and Communication Technologies (ICT) to the Area of Environmental Technology teaching to create a new communication channel consisting of a Web site that benefits teacher and student ("Environmental Studies Centre": http://cem.ugr.es). Through this interactive page, teachers can conduct supervised teaching, and students will have the tools necessary for guiding their learning process, according to their capacities and possibilities. However, the material is designed to serve as a complement to the traditional method of attended teaching.

As governments around the world move toward e-governance, a need exists to examine citizens' willingness to adopt e-governance services. In Chapter 16, "A Model for Investigating E-Governance Adoption Using TAM and DOI," the authors identify the success factors of e-governance adoption by teachers in Greece, using the Technology Acceptance Model, the Diffusion of Innovation model and constructs of trust, risk and personal innovativeness. Two hundred thirty primary and secondary education teachers responded to an online survey. LISREL then analyzed the data. Model estimation used the maximum likelihood approach, with the item covariance matrix as input. A SEM validation of the proposed model reveals that personal innovativeness, compatibility and relative advantage are stronger predictors of intention to use, compared to trust, and perceived risk. Findings may enhance policymakers' capacities by presenting them with an understanding of citizens' attitudes.

Chapter 17, "Meso Level as an Indicator of Knowledge Society Development," studies the nature and the importance of the link between macro and micro levels of innovation management in the knowledge society of Denmark, Sweden, USA, India, Russia, and Moldova, suggesting that countries with different levels of knowledge society development have different link types between the macro and micro levels of innovation management. In particular, findings show that countries with a higher level of knowledge society development have a two-way mediation process between the micro and macro levels of innovation management while countries with lower level of knowledge society development tend towards a "one-direction" link. This paper argues that innovation management can only be fully effective through paying attention to this intersection, which is free of biases inherent in each individually. The authors conclude by introducing a "meso-level" indicator for knowledge society development and underline areas of further research in the field.

Chapter 18, "The Project Manager in the Theatre of Consciousness: A New Approach to Knowledge Creation and Communication," focuses on knowledge management stressing an individual project manager's point of view. First, the authors outline two knowledge management strategies as well as the notion of project manager. The authors concentrate on the project manager's knowledge creation and communication using the so-called theatre metaphor for conscious experience. According to this metaphor, the human brain and consciousness work together like a theatre. With the help of the metaphor, the authors describe and attempt to understand important aspects of the project manager's mental action in the above tasks.

The purpose of Chapter 19, "Developing Professional Knowledge and Confidence in Higher Education" is to determine the effectiveness of using multiple choice tests in subjects related to the administration and business management. To this end the authors used a multiple-choice test with specific questions to verify the extent of knowledge gained and the confidence and trust in the answers. The analysis made, conducted by tests given out to a group of 200 students, has been implemented in one subject related with investment analysis and has measured the level of knowledge gained and the degree of trust and security in the responses at two different times of the business administration and management course. Measurements were taken into account at different levels of difficulty in the questions asked and the time spent by students to complete the test. Results confirm that students are generally able to obtain more knowledge along the way and get increases in the degree of trust and confidence. It is estimated that improvement in skills learned is viewed favourably by businesses and are important for job placement. Finally, the authors proceed to analyze a multi-choice test using a combination of knowledge and confidence levels.

Video stabilization is one of the most important enhancements where jittering caused by un-intentional movements is removed. Existing video stabilizer software and tools cannot differentiate between intentional and un-intentional jitters in the video and treats both equally. In Chapter 20, "An Efficient System for Video Stabilization by Differentiating between Intentional and Un-Intentional Jitters," the authors propose an efficient and practical approach of video stabilization by differentiating between an intentional and un-intentional jitter. Their method takes jittered video as input, and differentiates between intentional and an un-intentional jitter without affecting its visual quality while producing stabilized video only if jitter is found to be un-intentional. While most previous methods produce stabilized videos with low resolution, this reduces quality. The proposed system has been evaluated on a large number of real life videos and results promise to support the implementation of the solution.

In today's global marketplace, organizations are continually faced with the need to change their structures and processes to attain a competitive advantage. Implementation of new technology and information management systems results in inevitable changes in organizational procedures impacting on the people involved. Resistance to change may impact on this process and contribute to failure of this system. Managing change in an effective and efficient manner may negate this impact. Chapter 21, "A Change Management Framework to Support Software Project Management" compiles a set of guidelines to support change which involves the incorporation of technology in an organization. These guidelines were mapped to a model, the GIC (Guidelines Implementing Change) model comprising all identified factors. These guidelines are utilized to guide the implementation of a new system, while simultaneously evaluating the success of these set guidelines. This research is cross disciplinary, affecting the areas of organizational behaviour, software project management, and human factors.

Lastly, Chapter 22, "Financial Needs for a Competitive Business Model in the Knowledge Society" investigates the constraints for companies to innovate in order to be competitive in the knowledge society. Using a large and original data set of Catalan firms, the authors have conducted a micro econometric analysis following Henry et al.'s (1999) investment model and von Kalckreuth (2004) methodology empirically contrasting the relationship between firms' investment spread over time and their financial structure. Results show that it exits a positive and significant relationship between firms' investment shift and financial structure, emerging financial constraints for more innovative firms. Furthermore, these constraints are higher for micro companies and firms within the knowledge-advanced services' industry. Finally, the authors find that advanced ICT uses by more innovative firms allow them to reduce constraints of access to sources of finance.

Miltiadis Lytras
The American College of Greece, Greece

Isabel Novo-Corti
University of A Coruña, Spain

Chapter 1
Quantum Modeling of Social Dynamics

C. Bisconti
University of Salento, Italy

M. De Maggio
University of Salento, Italy

A. Corallo
University of Salento, Italy

F. Grippa
University of Salento, Italy

S. Totaro
University of Salento, Italy

ABSTRACT

In this paper, the authors apply models extracted from the Many-Body Quantum Mechanics to understand how knowledge production is correlated to the innovation potential of a work team. This study is grounded in key assumtpions. First, complexity theory applied to social science suggests that it is of paramount importance to consider elements of non-objectivity and non-determinism in the statistical description of socio-economic phenomena. Second, a typical factor of indeterminacy in the explanation of these phenomena lead to the need to apply the instruments of quantum physics to formally describe social behaviours. In order to experiment the validity of the proposed mathematic model, the research intends to: 1) model nodes and interactions; 2) simulate the network behaviour starting from specific defined models; 3) visualize the macroscopic results emerging during the analysis/simulation phases through a digital representation of the social network.

INTRODUCTION

In recent years new organizational forms are emerging in response to new environmental forces that call for new organizational and managerial capabilities. Organizational communities, interdisciplinary teams and industry consortia are becoming the governance model suitable to build

DOI: 10.4018/978-1-4666-1788-9.ch001

a sustainable competitive advantage, representing a viable adaptation to an unstable environment. The theoretical framework used in this research is known as complexity science (Clippinger, 1999; Newman, 2003). According to this approach, teams are considered complex adaptive systems (CAS): they co-evolve with the environment because of the self-organizing behavior of the agents determining fitness landscape of market opportunities and competitive dynamics (Lewin, 1999). A system is complex when equations that describe its progress over time cannot be solved analytically (Pavard & Dugdale, 2000). Understanding complex systems is a challenge faced by different scientific disciplines, from neuroscience and ecology to linguistics and geography. CAS are called adaptive because their components respond or adapt to events around them (Levin, 2003; Lewin, 1999). They may form structures that somehow maintain their integrity in the face of continuing change. The components of a CAS may follow simple rules and yet produce complex patterns that often change over time. Organizational teams share many of the characteristics that are used to define a complex adaptive system. A number of methods have been developed in recent years to analyse complex systems. Amaral and Ottino (2004) identify three types of tools belonging to well known areas to physicists and mathematicians: Social Network theory, Quantum Mechanics, Statistical Physics. Many scholars have shed light on some topological aspects of many kinds of social and natural networks (Albert & Barabasi, 2002; Barabasi & Réka, 1999; Newman, 2003). As a result, we know that the topology of a network is a predictable property of some types of networks that affects their overall dynamic behaviour and explains processes such as: the diffusion of ideas in a firm, the robustness to external attacks for a technological system, the optimisation of the relationships among the network components and their effects on knowledge transfer.

Next paragraph introduces the main contribution we rely on to define the model able to recognize the emergence of innovation within organizational teams.

THEORETICAL BACKGROUND

Social Network Analysis (SNA) represents a widely adopted methodological approaches generally applied to the study of organizational networks during the past years (Wasserman & Faust, 1994). SNA is based on a set of methods and tools to investigate the patterning of relations among social actors. It provides a visual and dynamic representation of social and economic phenomena and relies on the topological properties of the networks to measure the characteristics of the phenomena.

The main limitation of SNA is to be mainly a structural method. Its unit of analysis is not the single actor with its attributes, but the relations between actors (e.g., dyads, triads), defined identifying the pair of actors and the properties of theie relation. By focusing mainly on the relations, SNA might underestimate many organizational elements which might influence the ability of an organization to reach its goals. Perceptive measures are sometimes ignored by SNA researchers. What seems to be missing in current SNA research is an approach to study how the individual actors' characteristics change the network configuration and performance. Furthermore, the empirical work on network information advantage is still considered "content agnostic" (Hansen, 1999). Paying attention only to the structural facets of community interactions is like considering all the ties as indistinguishable and homogeneous. In this perspective, actors performing different activities, or involved in different projects are detected simply as interacting members, with no distinction among sub-categories that might change over time. A recent field within SNA is Dynamic Network Analysis, that uses longitudinal data to perform an evolutionary study of the organizational networks

The principle that many natural laws come from statistics brought many physicists to apply the models of statistical physics also to the study of behavioural models and to study the dynamics of generation of the organizational networks. Statistical physics is currently applied to several interdisciplinary fields like biology, information technology, and social sciences, and physicists showed a growing interest for modeling systems also far from their traditional context (Svozil & Wright, 2005).

The idea of describing social phenomena through physics models is older than that of applying the statistical physics. The discovery of quantum laws in collective properties of a community was originally revealed by the frequency of births and deaths or by the statistics of crimes. Then the development of statistics brought scientists and philosophers to rely on it to develop a systemic understanding of apparently casual behaviour of individuals. The emergence of new extended databases and the rising of new social phenomena (e.g., the Internet) translated the idea of applying statistical physics to social phenomena into a concrete effort. If organizational communities are classified as complex systems, their complexity is determined by the amount and interdependence of variables they include, making it hard to describe them in deterministic terms. Complexity also depends on the same actors, who determine with their own characteristics the complexity of the structure. Human behaviour is often unpredictable so that only probabilistic assumptions can be proposed about the outcome of an action. Although it is not fair to refer to human behaviour as a mere quantum phenomenon, some analogies can be used to build a quantum based mathematical structure for the agents. Once the interactions of the agents with the external environment are defined, this structure might help describe social phenomena.

Based on these assumptions, we propose a model of social systems built as a many-body system based on a quantum structure. We base this model on the important relationship between the state(s) of the agents and the interactions typical of the community in which they live.

RESEARCH OBJECTIVES

This research aims to apply models extracted from the Many-Body Quantum Mechanics to describe social dynamics. It is intended to draw macroscopic characteristics of the network starting from the analysis of microscopic interactions based on the node's model. In the aim to experiment the validity of the proposed mathematical model, the research is intended to model nodes and interactions, to simulate and visualize the network behaviour starting from the models.

At the beginning, most of the Social Network Analysis studies focused their attention to study networks of small size. In this case, researchers could rely on a high reliability of the observation related to relational patterns among social actors. Recently, with the rising of online communities and the availability of less-consuming data mining techniques, social scientists became more interested in exploring social networks based on many nodes, where the interaction model was analyzed through inferential statistics techniques. The presence of large networks and the need to conduct the analysis on samples and statistical approximation opened the discussion about the reliability of the results of the observations conducted on social networks.

A discussion about the limitations and drawbacks of different inferential statistical models (e.g., Bayesian Theory) will represent the theoretical basis to suggest new models based on quantum physics principles to model the complex space of the actors and of the interactions among them. Quantum physics is full of complex models of interaction between states described by vectors in representative spaces, resulting in well defined collective states. Representative space is the space where the actor (the body of the system) is defined. The actor definition is provided through the definition of his state, that could be expressed as distribution function named probability strength and related to the real probability distribution of the actor. This probability strength is a vector of the representative space defined as Hilbert space infinite dimension (Albert, 2000). Based on this consideration, the research intends to answer to the following question: "Which model or which models from the quantum physics are suitable to model the behaviour and the evolution of organizational communities?".

RESEARCH METHODOLOGY

Based on the most recent contributions in literature, we will extract the characteristics of the communities operating in an organizational context. We will define a taxonomy based on dimensions like: community purpose, size, degree of physical proximity, leadership and membership, degree of internal diversity, life cycle, sponsorship and degree of institutionalization. We will focus on the relation between actors' behavior and the socio-technical environment in which actors are involved. A description of the methodologies and the tools of inferential statistics will be provided with reference to relational data analysis. In addition to the studies on statistical modeling of social behavior, we will take into consideration scientific contributions related to their physical modeling. The formulation of physical models to explain events and social dynamics is an idea that has spread in recent years, bringing an increasing number of scholars to apply their concepts and techniques of physics to other disciplines such as biology, economics and sociology. In particular, we will focus on the efforts done in the field of econophysics, a new science that studies both the behavior of social actors (individuals, groups, organizations), considered as "particles" of a physical system, and the effect of their interactions on the system.

From Language and Modeling Primitives to the Mathematical Framework

This paragraph describes the features of the processes related to the formulation of 1) language and modeling primitives to describe the social phenomena on the basis of individual characteristics and interactions between individuals; 2) the mathematical framework for building a quantum model of the agent and of the interactions between actors.

As for the first one, we will describe actor's behavior and the social characteristics that will provide input for defining both the logical structure and the abstract language for modeling actors and interactions. In order to create the quantum mathematical model, it is important to initially define which is the space of configurations where the node has to be modeled. This means defining the properties of the node to which precise functions of distribution will be associated. These functions will act both on ordinary spaces and on spaces with suitably defined characteristics. This is done in analogy to the description of particles of a quantum system by a wave function that depends both on the coordinates of the ordinary space, and the coordinates of the spin area. The models and structures that will shape the organizational community will be described by a formal language that can express at the same time the actors' characteristics and those of the entire network, as well as the management of the simulation and related results.

As for the formulation of the mathematical framework for modeling the actor and the possible interactions with other actors, following the paradigm of quantum physics, the process will consist of building an algebraic abstract structure of operators able to describe the characteristics of the actor. Once identified the algebraic space on which to operate, we will define the possible expressions of the interactions involving actors. This phase has an abstract and mathematical nature, so to consider the whole set of possible properties that need to be represented. After this phase we will formulate the model itself, based on the mathematical framework developed earlier. The stages of formulation of the model will follow the typical paradigms of microscopic description of many-body systems. The actor-agent model that we intend to create is based on the specification of its demographic and cognitive attributes along different dimensions, which can be defined in a more or less interdependent way. This opens the way to a vector representation of the state of an agent and a possible tensorial representation of the interactions between agents. This also leads to a vision in which the bonds in which the community is structured emerge from such interactions.

First we define the microscopic variables based on the algebraic structure built in the previous step. Second we will formulate the basic properties of the interactions. In particular, we will take into account interactions of the type "two-bodies", in which actions on multiple configuration spaces are possible ("tensorial forces"). We will also take into account possible three-bodies interactions (initially only the ones having a "scalar nature"). Finally we will build a particular model on which it will be possible to make "ideal" experiments to verify their validity.

CONTEXT OF APPLICATION

In this paragraph we present a first context of application for the proposed model. The goal is to understand how knowledge flows within organizational teams. The unit of analysis in this scenario is represented by inter-organizational communities involving partners and suppliers or R&D teams involved in innovative projects. This application addresses key questions such as: How to correlate knowledge production and innovation potential of a work team? How to support an effective and efficient transfer of knowledge that foster innovation? Based on the previously described limitations of Social Network Analysis to fully recognize innovation dynamics, this scenario addresses also the following issue: how to better identify the agents responsible for the innovation process? Next paragraph describes the interplay between diversity and innovation in organisational settings.

Diversity Drives Innovation

In a complex world, the number and variety of actors in the organization become the measure of its

wealth. A diverse system of complex interactions drives economic and social richness, boosting the emergence of new market niches and opportunities; it also acts as an antidote for nonlinearity and volatility of the rugged landscapes. A 2005 study entitled *The Business Case for Diversity good practices in the workplace* carried out for the European Commission provides empirical evidence that diversity is good for business. Of the 188 companies developing a diversity agenda, 59 percent felt that diversity made the most significant impact upon company image and reputation, attracted more talented employees, and improved stakeholder relationships (European Commission, 2005). Managers in this context have the role of preventing a tight alignment of the company to a niche or to rigid processes, maintaining the capability of the organization to self renew. They have to help to increase the repertoire of adaptive responses, to redefine in each moment the flow of resources (Romano et al., 2009).

As demonstrated by the emergence of business ecosystems, agents co-evolve their capabilities and roles in an economic community supported by interactions among individuals and organizations including suppliers, lead producers, competitors, and other stakeholders. Diversity is the measure of the variety of systems components that grows as the number of agents and interactions increase. Actually the level of diversity of a system is able to enhance the fitting of a rugged landscape. Innovation and diversity are defined in different multidimensional ways by scholars, policy makers, and business leaders. The often divergent nature of these definitions challenged the understanding of the linkages between diversity and innovation. Diversity is usually defined from a policy and legal perspective across demographic dimensions such as age, gender, race, ethnicity, religion and disability (European Commission, 2005). At the same time, it has been proposed a more extended version of this purely demographic definition to better understand the effect of diversity for innovation. For instance, the learning styles and attributes of individuals and communities include different communication styles, professional skills, educational background, personality traits. Based on this background, we define the concept of *innovation potential* as including both demographic and cognitive variables.

In the next section we shall present a mathematical model inspired to quantum game theory. The creation of the model intends to demonstrate the feasibility to describe our application in order to make predictions over several social indicators useful inside the performance measure processes in practice communities.

In order to familiarize the readers to the mathematical framework, next section presents an overview of classic game theory. We refer to outstanding contributions for details and then we present the classic version of our model followed by its quantum version.

Game Theory Recalls

In this section we give a quickly and simple description of the so called Prisoner's Dilemma, on which our model relies on. This game describes a situation in which two people – called players – are imprisoned and kept in different rooms. Both players have two possible choices, called strategies, that are *collaboration* (*C*) or *defection* (*D*). They have no idea of the other player's choice.

The players get their pay-offs depending on their choices. The pay-off indicates quantitatively the personal preference of each player. Each player seeks to obtain from her own choice the best pay-off independently from the choice of other player.

In Figure 1 we have a matricial representation of Prisoner's Dilemma game. If we label the two players *A* and *B*, and identify the set of strategies as *S* = {*C, D*}, we obtain the following Figure:

The player faces a dilemma, since a rational thought in such situation would dictate the players to defect, even if they could both benefit from mutual cooperation. The best individual pay-off

Figure 1. The pay-off matrix for Prisoner's Dilemma game. We can read the figure under two points of view. (E.g.: if the player A collaborates and the player B does not collaborate the pay-off is 0 for player A and 5 for player B. It is evident that the best choice for a single player is to defect when the other player collaborates. If both defect, they get only 1 unit pay-off).

$$
\begin{array}{c}
\text{player B} \\
\begin{array}{cc}
C & D
\end{array} \\
\text{player A}\ \begin{array}{c} A \\ B \end{array}
\begin{pmatrix}
(3,3) & (0,5) \\
(5,0) & (1,1)
\end{pmatrix}
\end{array}
$$

for a player would happen when his position is the defection, while the other one collaborates.

Formally within the game theory the Prisoner's Dilemma game belongs to binary choice matrix game. Generally speaking, a game deals with the following concepts:

- The players, that is the individuals who compete in the game;
- The players' action;
- One player's (pure) strategy, that is a rule (or function) that associates the player's behaviour with the information available to him when he made his choice
- Pay-offs are represented by numbers expressing the players' utilities.

We give several useful definitions to support our model (Von Neumann & Mongerstern, 1953):

- **Definition 1:** A game is called in normal form if it is defined by the triple (N, S, P), where N is the set of N agents or players, $S = \{S_1, S_2, ... S_N\}$ is the strategy space for the N players and $P = \{P_1, P_2, ..., P_n\}$ is the set of payoff functions $P_i, i = 1, 2, ...N$, so that $P_i : S_1 \rightarrow \mathbb{R}$, being $\mathbb{R}$ the set of real numbers.

We give now few definitions without to enter in mathematical details (since it is out of scope of this paper), useful to understand the background theoretical of our model we will introduce in the next sections.

- **Definition 2:** Depending on the information strucure, a game is cooperative or non-cooperative. In the former players are allowed to form binding agreements. In the second game neither do the players cooperate nor do they enter into negotiation for achieving a common course of action.
- **Definition 3:** The players' number and strategies fixed, the solution of a game is the set of moves related to all the rational choices of each player.

An important concept in the framework of game theory is the equilibrium. The version stated by Nash (1950) plays a basic role in game theory:

- **Definition 4:** A (Nash) equlibrium (NE), is a set of strategies such that no player has an incentive to unilaterally change her action. The implicit assumption behind the concept of a NE is the players make their choices simultaneously and independelntly. If P_i is the pay-off function of $i - th$ player the NE is defined by the following condition:

$$P_i(s_1^*, s_2^*, ..., s_i^*, ..., s_N^*) \geq P_i(s_1^*, s_2^*, ..., s_i ..., s_N^*) \tag{1}$$

When the N players are playing the strategy profile $s = (s_1, ..., s_i, ..., s_N)$ the i-th players decision to play s_i instead of s_i^* cannot increase her payoff. A NE thus defines a set of strategies that represents a best choice for each single player if all the other players take their best decisions too. The well-known Nash Theorem (Nash 1950) in game theory guarantees the existence of a set of mixed strategies for finite non-cooperative games of two or more players in which no player can improve his payoff by unilaterally changing her strategy.

Eisert and Wilkens (2000) proposed the Prisoner's Dilemma game in the version based on quantum theory. Therefore the actions are defined by quantum operators acting over the quantum states. As is stated by Eisert and Wilkens (2000) any quantum system can be manipulated by two or more parts and where it is possible to quantify the pay-offs of each moves, can be conceived as a quantum game. In our case we will redefine the pay-off and strategy sets inside the quantum theory.

The Classic Model

Our model is based on the contribution of Berliant and Fujita (2007), who propose a micro-model to explain the knowledge creation process of a population. The key assumptions of their models are:

- The heterogeneity of people in their knowledge status is essential for a successful cooperative creation of new ideas,
- The knowledge creation process affects the heterogeneity of people throught the accumulation of common knowledge.

The result obtained by Berliant and Fujita highlights - in the most general case - that the knowledge creation goes towards the most productive state when the whole population splits in smaller groups in optimal sizes.

Our focus is centered on the theme of the competitive development inside an organizational community where the cultural heterogeneity is fundamental for the innovation creation. The correlation between the knowledge creation process and the innovation creation process suggests us to design our model following the model by Berliout and Fujita. Without providing too many mathematical details (out of scope in this paper, as mentioned above) we give now a more formal description of our model. We imagine that each individual has a *innovation potential* (IP) related to its cultural background and its job experience. The *innovation potential* is actually related to innovation ideas owned by each individual. Depending on the personal, cultural background, it is suitable that two people or a group have similar innovation ideas or different innovation potential. Thus, we can define the following quantitative variable:

- **Definition 5:** Let be $w_i(t)$ the IP of person i at time t. So $w_{ij}^c(t)$ represents the IP common to i and j persons and $w_{ij}^d(t)$ represents the IP of i person no-common to j person. Then it holds the following equations:

$$w_{ij}^d(t) = w_i(t) - w_{ij}^c(t) \qquad (2)$$

$$w_i(t) = w_{ij}^d(t) + w_{ij}^c(t) \qquad (3)$$

$$w^{ij}(t) = w_{ij}^d(t) + w_{ji}^d(t) + w_{ij}^c(t) \qquad (4)$$

The last equation represents the total IP possessed by i and j persons at instant t. During a first period of time we can imagine that each individual produces innovation due to only their owned IP. After this initial time, the choice whether to meet or not the other individuals is important for improving their IP. We have the following definition:

- **Definition 6:** Let $u_{ii}(t)$ the IP growth rate created by person i i at time t due to only its isolate acitivity. Let $u_{ij}(t)$ the IP growth rate when the persons i meets person j.

Following the assumption in, the growth rate of IP during a meeting of person i and j depends on their common IP, the differential IP of i from j and the differential IP of j from i. The rate of creation of innovation is the highest when the proportions of IP in common, as well as the IP exclusive to person i and the IP exclusive to person j are split evenly. The IP in common are necessary to collaboration and communication, while the IP exclusive are necessary to increase the IP. The IP creation process is then governed by the equations:

$$u_{ii}(t) = \alpha \cdot w_i(t) \quad when\ i\ works\ in\ isolation \qquad (5)$$

$$u_{ij}(t) = \beta \cdot \left[w_{ij}^c(t) \cdot w_{ij}^c(t) \cdot w_{ij}^c(t) \right]^{\frac{1}{3}} when\ i\ meets\ j \qquad (6)$$

The parameters α and β are real numbers indicating the proportionality coefficients. The evolution equations for person i are:

$$\frac{dw_i}{dt} = \sum_{j=1}^{N} \delta_{ij} \cdot u_{ij}(t)\ with\ \delta_{ij} = 1\ for\ j \neq i \qquad (7)$$

$$\frac{dw_{ij}^c}{dt} = \delta_{ij} \cdot u_{ij}(t)\ for\ all\ j \neq i \qquad (8)$$

$$\frac{dw_{ij}^d}{dt} = \sum_{k \neq j} \delta_{ik} \cdot u_{ik}(t)\ for\ all\ j \neq i \qquad (9)$$

It is possible, after algebric transformations, to describe the utility functions u_i by the normalized variables m_{ij}^x (with $x = d, c$) defined as:

$$m_{ij}^c = \frac{w_{ij}^c}{w^{ij}} \qquad (10)$$

$$m_{ij}^d = \frac{w_{ij}^d}{w^{ij}} \tag{11}$$

we have

$$u_{ij} = w_i f(m_{ij}^d, m_{ji}^d) \tag{12}$$

Then the evolution equation for function u_i is

$$\frac{dw_i}{dt} = w_i \left[\alpha + \sum_{j \neq i} (1 - \delta_{ij}) \cdot f(m_{ij}^d, m_{ji}^d) \right] \tag{13}$$

where

$$\frac{dm_{ij}^x}{dt} = g(\alpha, f, m_{ij}^d) \tag{14}$$

and δ is the Kronecker symbol.

We refer to Berliant and Fujita (2007) for details of explicit expressions of function f and g. The equation 13 allows the study of system considered. In particular it is interesting to find the equilibrium points of system with respect to the number of individuals and to find the optimum solution related to maximum value of IP. In the general case we have a system of equations like to 13 (for each person). It represents a typical dynamic system whose solution is analytical when the number of individuals fulfill particular properties.

The next step for defining our model is to translate this formalism in the game theory language. As a matter of fact, we can see this dynamic system as a game between N players each one acting in its strategy space. At this level in order to simplify the treatment, we consider the case of two players only. The individuals of dynamic system are our game players. Each player has the same strategy space $S = \{s_1, s_2\}$, where s_1 strategy is the choice of *to not meet* the other player, and the s_2 strategy is the choice *to meet*

the other player. The pay-offs is given by the utility functions u_i. The first term $\delta_{ii}\alpha$ of equation 13 indicates the payoff when each player choice of to not meet the other player and produces in isolation(defection). The second term $(1 - \delta_{ij}) \cdot f$ represents the payoff when a meeting between the players occurs (collaboration). As illustrated in Figure 2, we can think this system as an evolutionary bi-matrix game.

The Quantum Model

In quantum game theory (Easer & Wilkens, 2000), the pure classical strategies D and C correspond to the ortonormal unit basis vectors $|C\rangle$ (collaboration status) and $|D\rangle$ (defection status) of two-dimensional complex space C^2, i.e., the Hilbert space H_i of i-th player. A quantum strategy of a player i is represented as a general unit vector $|\psi_i\rangle$ in his strategic Hilbert space H_i. The whole quantum strategy space H is given by the tensor product of the different individual space $H = \prod \otimes H_i$. In quantum game theory the correlations between the individual strategies are allowed if two quantum strategies are entangled.

Figure 2. The pay-off matrix for the classic model. Similary to Prisoner's Dilemma game we label the players by A and B and the strategies not meet and meet by the D and C capital letters. α is the payoff when both of players produce in isolation; f and f* are the payoff of player A and B respectively when a meeting occurs. The functions f and f* depend on time.

$$
\begin{array}{c}
\text{player B} \\
\begin{array}{cc}
\text{C} & \text{D}
\end{array} \\
\text{player A} \quad
\begin{array}{c}
\text{A} \\
\text{B}
\end{array}
\begin{pmatrix}
(\alpha, \alpha) & (f, f^*) \\
(f^*, f) & (\alpha, \alpha)
\end{pmatrix}
\end{array}
$$

In our case, for a two dimensional game, the Hilbert space is four dimensional with basis vectors $\{\,|\,CC\rangle\,|\,CD\rangle\,|\,DC\rangle\,|\,DD\rangle\,\}$ where indicated by label C and D the status of player's strategy (C for collaboration and D for defection).

The start point is a prior state $|\,\psi_0\rangle = \hat{J}\,|\,XY\rangle$ with X,Y={C,D} and $\hat{J}$ is the entanglement operator. The strategy action of each player i is performed by an unitary operator $U_i(\theta,\phi)$ acting only over the subspace related to player i.

The expected payoff for each player is given by the following equation:

$$w^i = \sum_{kl} w^i_{kl} P^i_{kl} \qquad (15)$$

with w^i_{kl} is the payoff matrix for player i and $P^i_{kl} = |\,\langle XY\,|\,\psi_f\rangle\,|^2$, with X,Y={C,D}, is the probability to observe $|\,\psi_f\rangle = \hat{J}^+ U \hat{J}\,|\,XY\rangle$ in the state $|\,XY\rangle$ where $U = \prod \otimes U_i$.

Starting from equations (15) we can solve the game and discover new stable equilibria that were absent in the classic description. An important application of this theory is to solve the correspondent dynamic replicator equation where it is possible to study the temporal evolution of the populations involved in the system. In our case, we might apply this equation to recognize the shift over time from non-collaborative behaviours to collaborative ones.

The time dependence opens new application scenarios and possible solutions for the game. These aspects will be the core subject of a future paper.

CONCLUSION AND FUTURE RESEARCH

The research aims at satisfying the need of interdisciplinarity that is the basis of all the studies about complex systems. The framework of analysis and simulation that is proposed in this paper relies on the interdisciplinary contributions from physical and mathematical sciences, information technologies and artificial intelligence, statistics and sociology. The application of the quantum model to recognize the deep patterns of behaviour within and across organizational communities can be the basis for the definition of new managerial guidelines. These managerial indications will suggest how to recognize innovation roles and innovation phases in the life-cycle of an organization, by changing over time the weights of mutiple variables: size, culture, hierarchical vs collaborative environment, personality traits, communication channel preferred and so on. Applications of this model might lead to discover new strategic dashboards where traditional business process indicators (also known as key performance indicators, KPI), are integrated with metrics related to informal interactions. We intends to identify hybrid metrics that include both "process and community metrics" to constantly measure the alignment between the evolution of social dynamics and business process performance. To reach this goal, we will study organizational communities involved in innovative business projects and model the nodes' and network's behaviour through the application of the proposed mathematical model. In this way, we aim to create an integrated toolkit for the measurement of hybrid metrics and assess the degree of resonance/alignment between processes' and communities' structure/evolution. This might help managers to modify/improve the business processes to align them with the effective informal structure (measured through the new hybrid metrics).

If you think of a situation in which the chairman or a project manager moves to another position in another company or department, how does this structural change impact the innovativeness of the organization? What variables should we observe to optimize knowledge transfer? The application of the model proposed in this paper aims to address this kind of questions and find new managerial indicators to assess the value of each weighted connection among people and among firms.

After defining and testing the model, we intend to design and implement digital models to provide analysis and forecasts of the evolution of organizational properties. Such simulation models would suggest ways to optimize allocation of resources, information flows and competences' development.

Future research agenda include the application of the mathematical model and the simulation model to new application scenarios.

REFERENCES

Albert, M. (2000). *Quantum mechanics*. New York: Dover Publications.

Albert, R., & Barabasi, A.-L. (2002). Statistical Mechanics of Complex Networks. *Reviews of Modern Physics, 74*, 47. doi:10.1103/RevModPhys.74.47

Amaral, L. A. N., & Ottino, J. M. (2004). Complex networks - Augmenting the framework for the study of complex systems. *The European Physical Journal, 38*, 147–162.

Barabasi, A.-L., & Réka, A. (1999, October 15). Emergence of scaling in random networks. *Science, 286*, 509–512. doi:10.1126/science.286.5439.509

Berliant, M., & Fujita, M. (2007, November). *Knowledge creation as a square dance on the Hilbert cube* (MPRA Paper No. 4680). Retrieved from http://mpra.ub.uni-muenchen.de/4680/

Clarke, F., & Ekeland, I. (1982). Nonlinear oscillations and boundary-value problems for Hamiltonian systems. *Archive for Rational Mechanics and Analysis, 78*, 315–333. doi:10.1007/BF00249584

Clippinger, J. H. III. (1999). *The biology of business. Decoding the natural laws of enterprise*. San Francisco, CA: Jossey-Bass Publishers.

Eisert, J., & Wilkens, M. (2000). Quantum Games. *Journal of Modern Optics, 47*, 2543.

Epstein, J. M., & Axtell, R. (1996). *Growing Artificial Societies*. Washington, DC: Brookings Institution Press.

European Commission. (2005). *The Business Case for Diversity. Good Practices in the Workplace*. Belgium: European Commission (ISBN 92-79-00239-2). Retrieved from http://ec.europa.eu/social/main.jsp?catId=370&langId=en&featuresId=25

Hansen, M. (1999). The search-transfer problem: the role of weak ties in sharing knowledge across organization subunits. *Administrative Science Quarterly, 44*(1), 82–11. doi:10.2307/2667032

Levin, S. A. (2003). Complex adaptive systems: Exploring the known, the unknown and the unknowable. *Bulletin of the American Mathematical Society, 40*(1), 3–19. doi:10.1090/S0273-0979-02-00965-5

Lewin, R. (1999). *Complexity, life on the edge of chaos* (2nd ed.). Chicago: The University of Chicago Press.

Nash, J. F. (1950). Equilibrium Points in N-Person Games. *Proceedings of the National Academy of Sciences of the United States of America, 36*, 48–49. doi:10.1073/pnas.36.1.48

Newman, M. E. J. (2003). The structure and function of complex networks. *SIAM Review, 45*(2), 167–256. doi:10.1137/S003614450342480

Pavard, B., & Dugdale, J. (2000, May 21-26). *The contribution of complexity theory to the study of sociotechnical cooperative systems*. Paper presented at the Third International Conference on Complex Systems, Nashua, NH. Retrieved from http://www-svcict.fr/cotcos/pjs/

Romano, A., De Maggio, M., & Del Vecchio, P. (2009). The Emergence of a New Managerial Mindset. In Romano, A. (Ed.), *Open Business Innovation Leadership. The Emergence of the Stakeholder University*. UK: Palgrave Macmillan.

Stinchcombe, A. L. (1990). *Information and Organizations*. Berkley, CA: University of California Press.

Svozil, K., & Wright, R. (2005). Statistical Structures Underlying Quantum Mechanics and Social Science. *International Journal of Theoretical Physics*, *44*(7), 1067–1086.

Von Neumann, J., & Mongerstern, O. (1953). *Theory of games and econonmic behavior* (3rd ed.). Princeton, NJ: Princeton University Press.

Wasserman, S., & Faust, K. (1996). *Social Network Analysis. Method and Applications*. Cambridge, MA: Cambridge University Press.

This work was previously published in the International Journal of Knowledge Society Research, Volume 1, Issue 1, edited by Miltiadis D. Lytras, pp. 1-11, copyright 2010 by IGI Publishing (an imprint of IGI Global).

Chapter 2
Adventure Game Learning Platform

Miroslav Minović
University of Belgrade, Serbia

Miloš Milovanović
University of Belgrade, Serbia

Velimir Štavljanin
University of Belgrade, Serbia

Dušan Starčević
University of Belgrade, Serbia

ABSTRACT

Educational games display great potential as an active form of knowledge transfer. This research field is young, but some patterns in educational game development can be recognized. In this paper, the authors present a new approach to educational game development that overcomes some downsides of more traditional systems. The paper provides the opportunity to create an educational adventure game by using specialized software tool as well as integrating knowledge in that specific game instance. As a result of that process, game definition is created as a form of XML document. On the other side, a web-based interpreter is used to present the adventure game to user in runtime. XML format provides us with platform independency. By use of this tool, the educator gains the ability to create an educational game without programming knowledge, and to reuse some previously created knowledge.

1. INTRODUCTION

Video game development budgets are already the size of motion picture development budgets, on the order of $20 million to $100 million, with expected revenue for a hit game reaching from $250 million to more than $1 billion (Michael, 2007).

Such fast development has allowed computer games to become more complex, more attractive,

to have rich content and, at the same time, to attract more players. The popularity of computer games has made them an important part of modern society. Because of this, during the last few years, the idea of using games for educational purposes has become more and more popular.

There is also much scientific evidence that supports the claim that games can be helpful during the learning process. During research conducted in 1998. It was noticed that game playing influenced the increase in the dopamine

DOI: 10.4018/978-1-4666-1788-9.ch002

level in organism (the substance that is in charge of memorizing chemical process). The recorded level was twice as high with game players as opposed to the control group. During the game playing, the brain was preparing for the learning process (Koepp et al., 1998).

Our interest in this area of research was triggered by students. Standard teaching methods in the age of multimedia lose their strength daily. For that specific reason we decided to experiment with educational games in order to get students more involved in course activities. We designed a pilot project for game-based learning, V-Strat (Minovic, Stavljanin, & Vico, 2007). V-Strat game logic is very similar to the logic of the old strategic game Risiko. Also, integration between education and mobile devices was an interesting topic for research (Minovic & Stavljanin, 2006). Recently, our efforts have been directed to developing a more formal approach to educational game development (Jovanovic, Starcevic, Stavljanin, & Minovic, 2008), based on our metamodel of multimodal human-computer interaction (Obrenovic & Starcevic, 2004).

This paper describes a software system that enables the creation of educational games. The idea that separates this software from others is a new approach to educational game defining. By separating the roles of game designer and knowledge expert we provide the ability, for both participants in the game creation process, to perform only the activities within their own specialty. The system consists of three parts: knowledge repository, game editor and web – based game interpreter. Learning objects, which are stored in the data repository, represent knowledge. Game editor is used for defining the game world, rules, scenarios, interactions between players and characters, as well as incorporating knowledge into the game. Game interpreter presents the game to a user, creates game interface and monitors communication between the game and the user. Game editor creates a special XML file which contains the game definition and the knowledge definition.

The XML file is then used by the game interpreter to create a game instance.

Paper structure: in the second part, we a give brief explanation of term e-Learning. The third part give basic information about the game-based learning. Next, we define the problem statement. The fifth part gives a short bibliography review. The sixth part presents our solution proposal. Next we give XML scheme for adventure educational game explained in more details, and after that short comparison of existing solutions and proposed solution. The conclusion is given at the end of the paper.

2. E-LEARNING

Term e-learning is more and more in use and it means using modern information and communication technologies in the learning process. During the 80's e-learning was only "computer-based training" and "computer-assisted instruction." But technological progress has given another dimension to the learning process. Today learning has been made possible regardless of time and place. The latest development enables learning on mobile technology.

E-learning is every aspect of learning using electronic media. This type of learning uses network for interaction. This network can be Internet, university network or any other computer network. E-learning has several types of patterns. It can be individual or group. Group can be synchrony, asynchrony and combined.

E-learning, therefore, is an approach to facilitate and enhance learning through both computer and communications technology. Such devices can include personal computers, CDROMs, Television, PDAs, MP3 Players, and Mobile Phones. Communications technology enables the use of the Internet, email, discussion forums, WIKIs, collaborative software, classroom management software and team learning systems.

3. GAME-BASED LEARNING

Digital game-based learning is a novel approach in the area of universities and lifelong learning, and the search for new positioning of the universities in the changing setting of education; gaming is becoming a new form of interactive content, worthy of exploration (Pivec, 2007).

The popularity of computer games led to the creation of educational games. Games are so common in modern society, that they are almost its inseparable part. They are the ideal platform for presenting new content and new technologies – there are millions of players, who consider playing computer games to be fun. Some researches (De Aguilera & Mendiz, 2003) showed that it's not only young people who play games – mature people love playing games, too.

Before we start further analysis, it should be mentioned that scientists think that it's impossible to address negative effects to computer games. There is no scientific proof to support this claim. On the contrary, there are many positive effects, and they all can be measured and documented (De Aguilera & Mendiz, 2003).

Computers and computer networks had great impact on all aspects of society, education among them. Suddenly, there were many good reasons for introducing computers and Internet into educational systems.

One of the first papers with a strong impact on the scientific community was published in 1978. Since then, there has been a lot of research focused on this topic and in the last few years, whole generations of players have joined the research.

It was clear that different types of games have effect on different sets of skills. Platform and action games developed motor coordination and reflexes. Some games helped players to relax. Finally, complex games, like strategies and simulations, had influence on the development of intellectual skills. Authors came to the conclusion that games like Sims can be used as an example of social interaction, while games like Civilization could be used as strategic and historical simulation.

All researches stated that games had positive effect on concentration, the decision – making process, problem solving skills, logical thinking creativity, team work and, of course, computer skills (De Aguilera, Mendiz, 2003). Estallo claimed in his work (Estallo, 1995) that people who play games have more developed intellectual skills than those who don't.

There is much scientific evidence that supports the claim that games can be used for learning. In a research conducted in 1998, it was noticed that playing games stimulated dopamine production – and dopamine is required for the chemical process of learning. People who played games had dopamine levels twice as high opposed to those who didn't play. By playing games, the brain was "primed" for learning (Minovic, Stavljanin, Milovanovic, Miroslav, & Milutinovic, 2008).

One other experiment also led to some interesting discoveries. Two groups of students from the same school were learning the same subject (electrostatic), but one of them had to play an educational game called SuperCharged! during their learning process. The other group used the traditional way of learning. Students from the first group achieved much higher levels of subject understanding than those who learned normally. One thing is particularly interesting: girls who played the game had almost a four times higher level of subject understanding than those who didn't (Squire, Barnett, Grant, & Higginbotham, 2004).

Considering all this, there is a reason to believe that there is a strong connection between different types of games and improvement of a particular skill. Even more interesting are those games that affect intellectual skills. There are several reasons why computer games can be an effective learning platform (Mayo, 2007):

- **Scope.** Usually, many players can participate in a single game, sometimes even millions. This means that much more users could access educational content this way than through a normal learning process.

Figure 1. Communication process in educational game development

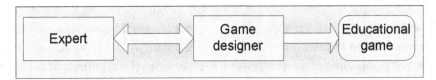

- **Anytime, anywhere.** Games do not require presence in the classroom; they could be played anytime, and thanks to mobile devices, anywhere. At the same time, students already spend a certain amount of time playing games – this is just the upgrade of the existing concept.
- **Interesting.** Game developers create games according to the rules of effective learning and that's what makes them interesting.
- **Brain stimulation.** By playing games, the brain is prepared for learning.

It is better than a regular type lesson. The level of subject understanding is almost 30 percent higher if games are used.

4. PROBLEM STATEMENT

Educational games that are created using traditional methods provide us with many issues. Those games lack the ability of presenting diverse knowledge because the constructing process forces us to determine a specific knowledge that the player will be exposed to. Environment, as a crucial factor in educational games, plays an important role in motivating the player and involving them in the specific matter. In order to get a quality game representation, there must be a strong bond between the environment and the knowledge inserted. Due to the construction process, that bond is usually created during the programming steps. This forced the educator to have programming knowledge in order to build a game, or he had to work with programmers.

The process of game creation required collaboration between the game designer and the knowledge expert (Figure 1). Communication between these two participants is often brought to a halt because of misunderstandings, differences in goals and interests etc. (Minovic, Stavljanin, Milovanovic, Miroslav, & Milutinovic, 2008). The game designer needed programming as well as designing skills.

The result of this collaboration is a game that carries certain knowledge and has one form of presentation. The game environment, game context or the knowledge cannot be reused.

Major issue with the existing solutions is that they focused on only one theme. Educational games were designed with certain knowledge in mind – there was no way to separate knowledge form the game engine and use it in another game. The existing systems also focused on one genre/ type of the game. The whole solution was dedicated to that type of game, so building solution for a different type of game required the repetition of the whole process from the beginning.

The shortcomings of traditional methods presented here drive us towards the development of such a system that would overcome them. We need to find a way of separating roles of our participants so that everyone does the work within their own specialty.

The use of games in education still relies on academic research groups. On the other side, teachers often lack the skills and knowledge to integrate technology effectively into their classrooms (Becker, 2007). This is the reason why there is a need to create a user-friendly environment for teachers who could use the game creation process. It would be a significant improvement if we could develop it in such a way to enable the teachers to create a game independently without the help of a game designer. Also by separating the game environment and game context from the knowledge, we would gain the ability to reuse them according to some other needs.

5. BIBLIOGRAPHY REVIEW

As mentioned before, this research field may still be in the developmental phase, but it does not mean that there are no interesting and effective solutions. Some of the solutions are games focused on solving a particular problem, while other solutions are engines for educational games.

Either way, games are developed with a certain problem in mind. Of course, there are many differences between those games. Each one of them uses its own set of elements to present problems (and knowledge) to the players. Some types of games are more suitable for representing certain types of knowledge than the others. Choosing the right type of game is an important part of the work.

There were several approaches to this problem. Some games are using well-known, popular environments and sets of rules, adapted for purposes of education - for example, the educational game based on "Who wants to be a millionaire?" quiz (Reinhardt & Cook, 2006). It uses all elements of the TV show, but questions are chosen by the teacher.

On the other hand, some games are developed with a certain subject matter in mind, like games for teaching electromagnetism called Supercharged! (Estallo, 1995), or a fantasy adventure game for teaching the basic concepts of programming (Moser, 1997).

Games can also be used for teaching certain skills, or for simulations of real–life events. Game StrikeCOM is a war game used for teaching and researching the development of group process, shared awareness and communication, created by the Center for the Management of Informa-

tion at the University of Arizona (Twitchell, Wiers, Judee, Burgoon, & Nunamaker, 2005). A similar project was initiated by DARPA (Defense Advanced Research Projects Agency) and it resulted in a game called DARWARS (Chatham, 2007) that simulated real-life military operations. Some games focused on learning about cultural facilities, like museums and museum objects and exhibitions (Herminia, 2006).

The existing games and their editors also serve as a good starting point. In some cases, the modification of popular games (game modding) was used for teaching computer science, mathematics, physics and aesthetics (El-Nasr & Smith, 2006). Game design can be used to achieve similar goals to develop problem solving skills and teamwork (Steiner, Kaplan, & Moulthrop, 2006). Some solutions use infrastructure of popular multiplayer on-line games, like Second Life, and combine them with course management systems like Moodle in order to create virtual learning environment (Sloodle, 2008).

Research in this field shows many different approaches. Our research aimed at surpassing the drawbacks of other systems. If a game is developed with a certain subject matter in mind, we actually spend a long and energy and time-consuming process in creating a game whose knowledge or environment will not be reusable. On the other side, simulating a real-life event shows great benefits in the learning process, but it is only aimed at teaching a certain skill. Closest to our solution is using the existing games and their editors. This way one can achieve a certain amount of reusability but still its initial purpose is not education, and that presents us with a lot of limitations.

6. SOLUTION PROPOSED

In order to apply all the principles identified, the first step was to separate the process of knowledge creation from the process of creating game

Figure 2. Modules of game

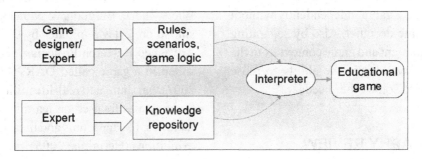

environment and game context. We achieved that by creating two separate software modules, thus gaining the ability to resolve the communication conflict between the game designer and the knowledge expert (Figure 2).

A result of creating environment and game context is a unique form of game definition represented as a specifically structured XML document (Figure 3.). Graphical components are stored separately but the XML document references them

within (Minovic, Milovanovic, Lazovic, & Starevic, 2008).

On the other side, we create the knowledge for use in our game. As seen on picture (Figure 3) software modules for game defining and knowledge creation are separate, thus allowing the Expert and Game designer to concentrate on work within their own specialty.

The game engine can interpret different game instances as long as the game definition is well

Figure 3. Model of the proposed system

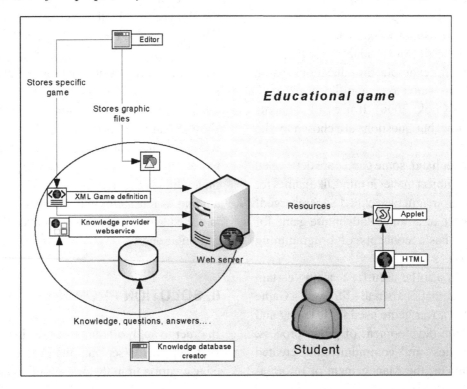

formed. Also, the game engine can interpret different game types such as Adventure, Strategy etc. We would accomplish that with the use of a plug-in pattern that allows us to write the interpretation of different game types separately as long as we override the methods from the specified interface. Our version of game interpreter is web based and uses java applet technology.

Let's try to describe the game defining process by concentrating on a certain game type such as Adventure. Game defining is done with the use of the graphical editor that we developed in Java (Figure 4.). Firstly, we need a game environment in which the game will be played. For this specific game type we use a 2D game environment. Hence we need a background map on which the game will be presented. In order for our interpreter to understand the structure of the map, we need to divide it into regions. The entire map is initially covered with hexagons, and we know the loca-

tion (X,Y) for each of them. Then the user (Game designer) selects hexagonal shapes, thus grouping them into a region. Regions represent the essence of the game play logic. They determine the movement of characters, rules of conduct etc. Also every region contains Non Playing Characters (NPC) that act as enemies, partners and support characters to provide challenges, offer assistance and support the storyline (Merrick & Maher, 2006).

Upon the creation of regions we can make different characters, assign them roles in our game, and make quests and assignments for future players. By advancing through the game, and by solving the quests, the player gains knowledge and learns new concepts.

Since the game logic as well as knowledge is outside the game code we can build a separate layer that will be able to create a game scene based on the user actions. That particular layer's purpose is to know the specific game type struc-

Figure 4. Educational games graphical editor[1]

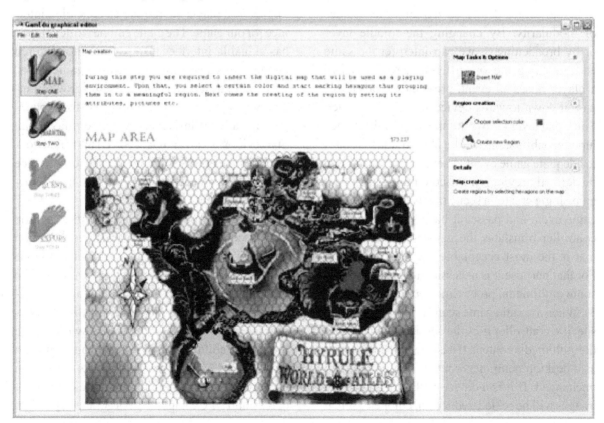

Figure 5. Layered approach to educational game interpretation

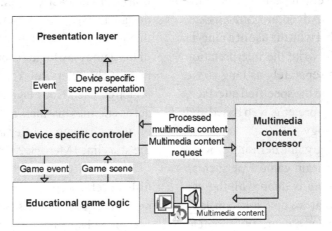

ture and rules of play. Top layer, that is in charge of presentation, has the assignment of reacting to players actions and rising the events to pass towards the game logic. Advantage of extracting the knowledge and game logic outside the program structure enables us to create a middle layer that will provide the service of adapting the content to a specific device.

Architecture described exploits the upsides of modularity. By changing the middle layer or by broadening it, we can interpret the same educational game on different devices. When a player raises an event, presentation layer will pass it down towards device specific controller. Since that layer knows the specifics of the device input capabilities it will be able to translate it in to adequate game event. A set of game events can be defined previously. Based on the game event game logic creates a scene that is the result of the game event and passes it back. Device specific controller translates the game scene to a form that is the most acceptable for a given device. For that purpose it is necessary to use the help of some multimedia processing service (see Figure 5). When a certain game scene is required, device specific controller uses the service of processing the multimedia content. If it is a default device such as a desktop computer, content will be returned unchanged. If it is a device with limited screen, images will be scaled, reduced in color etc. When

device specific controller makes a request for multimedia content it provides the information about the specific needs. If images are in question it provides needed resolution, color etc.

Same scene can be presented differently based on platform limitation. First image shows a scene of starting a new mission in a game run on applet technology (see Figure 6). In order to get the full impact on a player we require an appealing interface for our game. The game engine we developed has skinable interface. By making the required images you can change the way the game looks.

Mobile devices provide an ever-growing industry that promises new foundation for expanding educational influence (Minovic, Stavljanin, Starcevic, & Milovanovic, 2008). This framework provides the ability to easily adapt user interface according to device limitations or the user's special requirements (Figure 7).

Also it is important to state that the specific way of conducting a game varies dependent on device limitations. Since the background map is rather large it can't be presented evenly on mobile device as well as desktop computer applet technology for example. That is why different resources must be used for different devices. Since there is no ability to display background map on mobile device, player must get a sense of location differently. He must be guided by sufficient amount of text, and NPC images to get a good perspective.

Figure 6. Web client game interface

Figure 7. Mobile client game interface

7. CONCLUSION

We presented a new approach to the development of educational games, which should overcome the problem with knowledge integrated into the game. Such embedded knowledge is impossible to reuse, and each new game creation requires a significant amount of effort.

By creating two separate software modules it became possible to resolve the communication conflict between the game designer and the knowledge expert. As a result of such game defining, we create a specially structured XML document that contains game objectives, description, assignments, reference to graphical environment as well as the knowledge inserted from our knowledge repository. Also, with the use of the XML document we can create different game types simply by following a specific XML scheme.

With the use of this software, we hope to encourage teachers and different types of educators to use games as a tool in the knowledge transfer. This will provide students with an alternative to the traditional form of learning, which is much more interesting and more motivating.

Students can also use this system to develop games on their own. The process of creating games will require them to communicate and work as a team, as well as to find a way to adequately provide the knowledge and incorporate it into the game. By doing this they will broaden their knowledge on the subject at hand as well as the knowledge on the games creation.

ACKNOWLEDGMENT

This work is part of a project "Managing intellectual capital", funded by the Ministry of Science and Technology of the Republic of Serbia, contract no 13028-TP.

REFERENCES

Becker, K. (2007). Digital game-based learning once removed:Teaching teachers. *British Journal of Educational Technology*, *38*(7), 478–488. doi:10.1111/j.1467-8535.2007.00711.x

Chatham, R. E. (2007). Games for training. *Communications of the ACM*, *50*(7), 37–43. doi:10.1145/1272516.1272537

De Aguilera, M., & Mendiz, A. (2003). Video games and Education. Computers in Entertainment, 1(1).

El-Nasr, M. S., & Smith, B. K. (2006). Learning through game modding. Computers in entertainment, 4(1), 3B.

Estallo, J. A. (1995). *Los videojugos. Juicios e prejuicios*. Barcelona, Spain: Planeta.

Herminia, W. D. (2006). Play to learn exploring online educational games in museums. In Proceedings of International Conference on Computer Graphics and Interactive Techniques, Boston, Massachusetts. New York: ACM.

Jovanovic, M., Starcevic, D., Velimir, S., & Minovic, M. (2008). Educational Games Design Issues: Motivation and Multimodal Interaction (LNCS 5288, pp. 215-224). Berlin: Springer-Verlag.

Koepp, M., Gunn, R., Lawrence, A., Cunningham, V., Dagher, A., & Jones, T. (1998). Evidence for striatal dopamine release during a video game. *Nature*, *393*, 266–268. doi:10.1038/30498

Mayo, M. J. (2007). Games for science and engineering education. *Communications of the ACM*, *50*(7), 31–35. doi:10.1145/1272516.1272536

Merrick, K., & Maher, L. M. (2006). Motivated Reinforcement Learning for Non-Player Characters in Persistent Computer Game Worlds. In Proceedings of ACM Conference, Hollywood, California.

Michael, Z. (2007). Creating a science of games. *Communications of the ACM, 50*(7), 27–29.

Minović, M., Milovanović, M., Lazović, M., & Starčević, D. (2008). XML Application For Educative Games. In Proceedings of European Conference on Games Based Learning (ECGBL 08), Barcelona, Spain.

Minović, M., & Štavljanin, V. (2006). MOBILE CLIENT FOR MOODLE CMS. In Proceedings of the International conference (IPSI 2006), Belgrade, Serbia.

Minović, M., Štavljanin, V., Milovanović, M., Miroslav, L., & Milutinović, P. (2008). Game-Based Learning Environment. In Proceedings of the International conference(VIPSI 08), Bled, Slovenia.

Minović, M., Štavljanin, V., Starčević, D., & Milovanović, M. (2008). Usability issues of e-Learning systems: Case-study for Moodle Learning Management System. In Proceedigns of the OTM 2008 Workshops (LNCS 5333, pp. 561-570). Berlin: Springer-Verlag.

Minović, M., Štavljanin, V., & Vico, V. *(2007)*. Educative game V-STRAT. *In* Proceedings of the International conference *(*SYM-OP-IS 2007*)*, Zlatibor, *Serbia*.

Moser, R. (1997). A fantasy adventure game as a learning environment: Why learning to program is so difficult and what can be done about. In Proceedings of the (ITiCSE '97), Uppsala, Sweden. New York: ACM.

Obrenovic, Z., & Starcevic, D. (2004). Modeling multimodal Human-Computer interaction. *IEEE Computer, 37*(9), 62–69.

Pivec, M. (2007). Play and learn: potentials of game-based learning. *British Journal of Educational Technology, 38*(3), 387–393. doi:10.1111/j.1467-8535.2007.00722.x

Reinhardt, G., & Cook, L. S. (2006). Is This a Game or a Learning Moment? *Decision Sciences Journal of Innovative Education, 4*(2). doi:10.1111/j.1540-4609.2006.00119.x

Sloodle (Online). (2008). Retrieved from http://www.sloodle.org

Squire, K., Barnett, M., Grant, J., & Higginbotham, T. *(2004)*. Electromagnetism supercharged! Learning physics with digital simulation games. In Proceedings of the 2004 International Conference of the Learning Sciences, Santa Monica, CA. *Los Angeles:* UCLA Press.

Steiner, B., Kaplan, N., & Moulthrop, S. (2006, June 7-9). When play works: Turning game-playing into learning. In Proceedings of (IDC '06), Tampere, Finland.

Twitchell, D. P., Wiers, K., Judee, M. A., Burgoon, K., & Nunamaker, J. F., Jr. *(2005)*. StrikeCOM: A Multi-Player Online Strategy Game for Researching and Teaching Group Dynamics. In Proceedings of the 38th Hawaii International Conference on System Sciences.

ENDNOTES

[1]   A map of Hyrule during the era of The Legend of Zelda: Ocarina of Time taken from the instruction manual.

This work was previously published in the International Journal of Knowledge Society Research, Volume 1, Issue 1, edited by Miltiadis D. Lytras, pp. 12-21, copyright 2010 by IGI Publishing (an imprint of IGI Global).

Chapter 3
A Policy Framework for Developing Knowledge Societies

Ravi S. Sharma
Nanyang Technological University, Singapore

Mathias Dharmawirya
Nanyang Technological University, Singapore

Elaine W. J. Ng
Nanyang Technological University, Singapore

Ekundayo M. Samuel
Nanyang Technological University, Singapore

ABSTRACT

In this article, the authors explore the definition of a knowledge society and why such a society is desirable in the development of nations. First, this paper reviews the literature on knowledge societies and notes a gap in qualitative approaches which are amenable for framing development knowledge policies. The authors then describe a conceptual framework that depicts a knowledge society in terms of 13 dimensions that span infrastructure, governance, human capital and culture. This framework is validated with published proxy indicators from reputable sources such as the United Nations and the World Bank. In a field exercise, this paper determines the usability of the framework for policy discussion using Singapore, Nigeria, the United States and the United Arab Emirates as the foci of our analysis. The authors conclude by suggesting that such a qualitative framework is useful for policy-makers and other stake-holders to understand that the evolution to a knowledge society is a journey that requires benchmarks, environmental intelligence and an emphasis on the tacit structure of knowledge for sustainable advantage.

1. INTRODUCTION

"Does the aim of building knowledge societies make any sense when history and anthropology teach us that since ancient times, all societies have probably been each in its own way knowledge societies?" (UNESCO, 2005, p. 27). In this article, we claim that it does and attempt to support this

DOI: 10.4018/978-1-4666-1788-9.ch003

claim with a conceptual model that articulates why and how this is indeed the case, particularly for the less developed economies. In an environment of globalization and competition, governments at the regional, national, provincial and municipal levels have turned to knowledge as a strategic asset that drives sustainable economic advantage. The value of knowledge is particularly enhanced when it is created, shared and re-used within a critical mass of a society that possesses the requisite absorptive capacity or the ability to understand and apply that knowledge. As Rodrigues (2003) states: "... what is at stake is more than information: it is knowledge, which implies cognitive capacity, learning, cultural patterns and understanding - in a single word, people." (p. 4). We may term such a community of people a *knowledge society*, an integral feature of a knowledge based economy with its consequent higher quality of life and standard of living afforded to its members – a notion that appeals too much of the advanced as well as developing world.

The term knowledge society was first coined by Peter Drucker in 1969 and is often used interchangeably with "Knowledge Based Economy" (UNESCO, 2005). However, a knowledge society is distinct from an information society in that whereas information may be structured or unstructured in being consumed by society, knowledge is almost always transformed with the active participation of the people who comprise a society. When the Organisation for Economic Cooperation and Development (www.oecd.org) defined a *Knowledge-Based Economy* (KBE) as being "directly based on the production, distribution and use of knowledge and information" (OECD, 1996), it was readily adopted and later expanded to also cover the "production, distribution, and use of knowledge is the main driver of growth, wealth creation and employment across all industries" (APEC, 2000). It is generally accepted that a KBE does not rely solely on high technology industries for growth and wealth production, but also requires industries in the economy to be knowledge intensive. This is a Schumpeterian, macro-economic view of leveraging knowledge as a resource for growth and development. It is further implied that the knowledge required by a KBE is wider than purely technological knowledge; also including, for example, cultural, social and managerial knowledge. Hence the community of people and the manner in which they organize themselves play a major role in creating a knowledge society.

In order to create such a knowledge society or economy, the conditions for knowledge-sharing have to be conducive; for example, where knowledge is widely held as a public good with universal access to the community and low entry costs. This is the idea from Joseph Stiglitz (the 2001 Nobel Economist) that knowledge is a "global public good" that is most effective when shared without distribution inequities. As Koichiro Matsuura (2006), UNESCO's Director-General puts it: "An economy based on the sharing and diffusion of knowledge provides an opportunity for emerging nations to increase the well-being of their populations." He goes on to cite the examples of several communities which have transformed themselves into network societies favorable to "knowledge seeking, innovation, training and research". He concludes that knowledge sharing is indeed a powerful tool in both the fight against poverty as well as the key to wealth creation.

Therefore societies have for some time organized themselves in order to achieve a healthy environment of knowledge development, learning and sharing. The characteristics of a knowledge society are that they are part of a knowledge economy; possess high absorptive capacity; have structures and cultures that facilitate frictionless knowledge diffusion and sharing; undergo complex chains of creation, production and distribution including inter-functional collaboration; and are sustainable learning communities with an emphasis on innovation (cf. APEC, 2000; Houghton & Sheehan, 2000; Powell & Snellman, 2004; UNESCO, 2005). If these characteristics can be embraced by the community at large, then, conventional public policy holds that a competitive economy and a higher quality of life is the outcome.

From the academic arena, Powell and Snellman (2004) posit that although the causal factors of a KBE is subject to much discussion and debate, current studies may be classified into three major areas of research: (i) the rise of new science-based industries and their role in social and economic change (ii) sociology and labor economic investigations on whether new kinds of jobs and novel forms of work organizations have emerged in knowledge societies and (iii) managerial focus on the role of learning and continuous innovation inside firms. Alternately, Houghton, and Sheehan (2000) suggest that as society progresses up the value chain of quality and productivity, the role of knowledge as a factor of production and its subsequent influence on skills, learning, organization and innovation are increasingly the determinants of success.

Hence there is considerable agreement that the increasing importance of knowledge and learning is a definitive movement as rapid technological advances have resulted in a highly integrated global marketplace (APEC, 2000; Conceicao et al., 2003; Dolfsma, 2006; Fahey & Prusak, 1998; Houghton & Sheehan, 2000; Powell & Snellman, 2004; Rodrigues, 2002; Soete, 2006; UNESCO, 2005). Economies, which are versatile and can adapt rapidly to the changing environment by exploiting the opportunities offered by the knowledge will prosper while those, which lag behind in knowledge mobilisation, may lose their competitive edge. The central role of knowledge and learning has emerged as a universal public good

and has hence raised challenges for countries in the formulation of public and economic policies.

As advanced and developing economies make the inevitable approach towards knowledge societies, we also witness a movement that is characterized by the amalgamation or transformation of various aspects of society which go beyond the deployment and utilization of technology (for example, communications infrastructure or high capital production facilities) into one that involves institutional and cultural impact as well (Rodrigues, 2003). Such a transformation requires that the creation and measurement of a knowledge society moves beyond the realm of human capital and includes what is known as structural and relational capital (cf. Stewart, 1999; Bontis, 2001; Edvinsson, 2000) wherein the interplay of institutions, infrastructure and culture manifest themselves.

Knowledge (particularly in its tacit form) is difficult to quantify in conventional financial management and hence to justify its value in metrics form. Such intangibility of knowledge and its combination may be explained in terms of Intellectual Capital (IC) shown in Figure 1. More formally, IC refers to the knowledge, skills and technologies used to create a competitive edge

Figure 1. The intellectual capital of a knowledge society

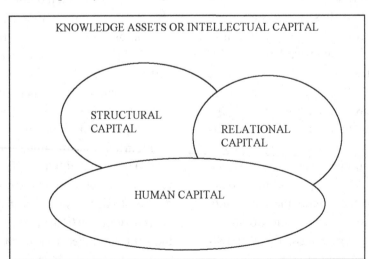

for an organization or community. IC captures the soft and intangible part of the value of business enterprises in addition to the traditional balance sheet (Bucklew & Edvinsson, 1999). The benefits of having substantial IC in a society are: improved productivity, greater innovation, new thinking and of course, and increased economic value. In pioneering work, Stewart (1999) had categorized IC as essentially made up of Human Capital (HC) and Structural Capital (SC) (also including the idea of Customer Capital in the context of a business enterprise). To this, Bontis (2001) - also inspired by Edvinsson (cf. 2000) - had added Relational Capital (RC). HC is the knowledge, skill and experience of the employees within an enterprise; SC is the organizational structure, technology and professional systems which remain within society; and RC (which is often used interchangeably with Social Capital) is the relationship of trust and authenticity that members enjoy within a community. Such a framework applied equally to organisations as well as societies.

The United Nations sponsored World Summit on the Information Society joint declaration on moving towards a knowledge era for all, had put in place infrastructure targets in tele-density, access and training (ITU, 2002) as development goals to grow the SC and HC of developing KBEs. And indeed, in much of the developing world, impressive gains have been made over the past 5 years in achieving universality and affordability in telecommunications services, particularly in the mobile sectors of China, India and Indonesia. Sharma and Azura (2005) have shown that an enterprise-oriented regulatory regime that promotes the build-up of information-communications technologies (ICT) infrastructure is one pillar of this growth. Cultivating user communities is the other pillar. Empowering the mass market with information literacy skills is yet another pillar. They then build on the major trends in the prolific growth of telecommunications in

the major markets of the region and outline some of the best practices that have been adopted by regulators and user communities. These include addressing the digital divide between haves and have-nots in the various communities and summarizing some key challenges for policy makers and private enterprise in the information society with the goal of strengthening the net IC of a knowledge economy and directing efficient investments.

However, it is now known that that access to ICT infrastructure, training and applications is passé. In this article, we seek to understand the dimensions of knowledge societies beyond the obvious ICT and technology base. More specifically, we investigate the critical factors and outcomes of creating and sustaining a knowledge society. In the next section, we review the literature that comprises significant research in the area of knowledge societies, communities and economies. We develop this into a framework for articulating the more significant factors and outcomes that make up a knowledge society. We also interviewed 5 thought leaders for qualitative and anecdotal validation of our model with action research in order to establish its validity. Following this, we sought secondary empirical data for some 20 major economies spanning from the advanced to the developing world in order to test whether these factors and outcomes were associated with national IC measures. To further validate the model for its usability in the field, we used the framework and dimensions in a focus group setting to assess knowledge communities at various stages of economic development and geographic structure – Singapore, Nigeria, the United States and the United Arab Emirates – and discuss policy implications. Finally, we conclude with some thoughts on whether the dimensions offer a means to replicate the development of knowledge societies.

2. LITERATURE REVIEW

Edvinsson (2000, 2003) has pointed out that IC is knowledge that may be applied to yield value and the IC Navigator pioneered by Skandia is an example of a tool that structures, packages, and measures IC – from the tangible financial perspective to the intangible renewal, development and innovation perspective – in order to guide management and reporting knowledge activity in organisations and even nations. In a retrospective review of research in the area of the wealth of nations, Edvinsson (2003) showed that the well-known Skandia Navigator is easily transformed from the corporate to national environment to encompass the following foci: financial (eg., per capita GDP and national debt); market (eg., balance of trade, net IP flows); human (eg., quality of life, health and education levels); process (eg., business leadership, service producing organisations); and renewal and development (eg., R&D expenses, business start-ups). He also cites the work of the pan-European body – Eurostat – as a leader in developing statistical indicators for the new economy which enable a fuller understanding of the knowledge economy and the relationship between intangible assets and socio-economic activity (cf. http://europa.eu.int/en/comm/eurostat/research/retd/sine.pdf). Building on this, Edna Pasher and her associates (cited in op. cit.) have suggested several additions to assess the IC of Israel such as: external debt, international events, openness to different cultures, language skills, teaching effectiveness, freedom of expression, entrepreneurship, risk taking, venture capital funds, immigration and absorption, women in the professional workforce, book publishing, museum visits, alcohol consumption (presumably implying the appreciation of luxuries rather than any manner of addiction), and scientific publications.

Invariably the common thread of most IC measures is the propensity of a society to communicate and share values, and more generically, knowledge. Knowledge sharing is unlikely to be successful unless it is communicated in a manner which is accessible and comprehensible to recipients. Hence there is a need for a common understanding within society on how, when and why knowledge is diffused for a common good. Nahapiet and Ghoshal (1998) call the notion of a common language "the cognitive dimension of social capital". Attributes of the cognitive dimension include a shared paradigm and a common understanding of society's goals. The two other dimensions in the framework are: the "structural" dimension which refers to the formation of both formal and informal networks that enable individuals to identify others with potential resources and the "relational" dimension which addresses issues around trust, shared norms and values, obligations and identification among members of a group. The hypothesis of Nahapiet and Ghoshal is that the cognitive, structural and relational dimensions of a society would ordinarily constitute collective human processing and exploitation of knowledge.

Hence, a knowledge society requires that all three dimensions exist in good measure in order to sustain such a society. However, as Figure 2 depicts, the three dimensions of social capital are not mutually exclusive but interactive. For instance, strong interaction ties among people from different vocations and stratas of society (social dimension) improve intra-society communication, enable information to be shared more freely and create a trusting working environment (relational dimension). In turn, such a relationship helps to create common values and a shared vision (cognitive dimension). Their notion of combination and exchange in order to promote knowledge creation, sharing and exploitation is consistent with the SECI cycle formulated by Nonaka (cf. 2000) and his co-workers.

Nahapiet and Ghosal (1998) define social capital (differently from other IC researchers such as Bontis, Edvisson and Stewart) as "the sum of the actual and potential resources embedded within, available through, and derived from the network of relationships possessed by an indi-

Figure 2. Basis for knowledge creation and exchange

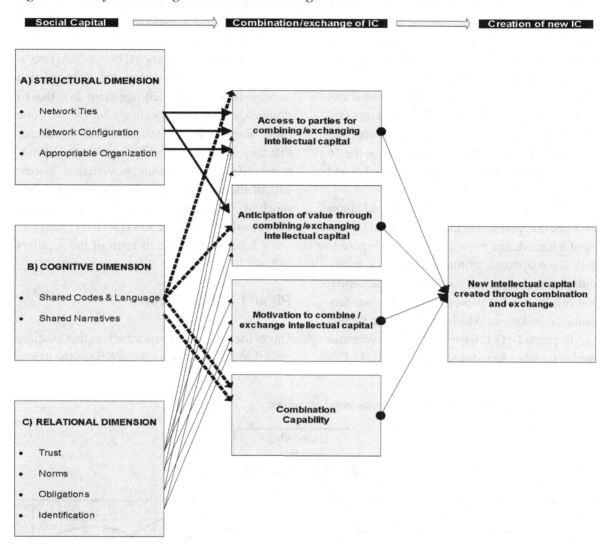

vidual or social unit." Increasing social capital will positively impact four intermediate variables and subsequently foster the creation and sharing of knowledge:-

1. Access to parties for combining or exchanging intellectual capital,

2. Anticipation of value through combining or exchanging intellectual capital,

3. Motivation of individuals to combine/share intellectual capital,

4. Ability of society to change according to the needs of its environment.

Drawing on the synthesis of Edvinsson (2003) of what constitutes the IC of nations and the framework of Nahapiet and Ghoshal (1998) which suggests how knowledge societies organise themselves, a review of the highly-cited literature on the social, structural and relational aspects of knowledge societies was conducted. This was followed by a critical analysis of the related literature from which the authors devised a set of dimensions that contribute towards the formation and evolution of a successful knowledge society. As will be elaborated in the next section which describes the research methodology, this process was and cumulative and iterative. For now, Figure 3 conceptualizes a model that draws from the work of Nahapiet and Ghoshal (*op. cit.*) and operationalises the 4 major philosophical constructs of a knowledge society with some 16 dimensions which may serve as measurable and actionable items for policy-makers.

More specifically, the model in Figure 3 aligns the three components of the "Intellectual Capacity of a Knowledge Society" (shown in Figure 1) with the adaptation of the structural, cognitive and relational aspects of social intellectual capital that results in what is proposed as the four fundamental pillars on which a knowledge society may be created – 1). Infrastructure; 2). Governance (which together form Structural Capital); 3). Human Capital (by nature cognitive); and 4). Culture (which is a part of Relational Capital). Guided by this framework, a review of the related literature has unearthed 13, operational dimensions necessary for creating and sustaining a knowledge society. It is immediately apparent that the 16 dimensions are not mutually exclusive to any one pillar. More specifically, their definitions indicate that they overlap as contributing factors and outcomes of the infrastructure, governance, human capital and culture facets of a knowledge society much like the inter-dependency suggested in the framework of Nahapiet and Ghoshal (1998).

A fuller description of each of the 4 pillars follow.

Pillar 1: Infrastructure

One of the first basic transformations that a society goes through in evolving into a KBE is the nature

Figure 3. A functional framework for knowledge societies

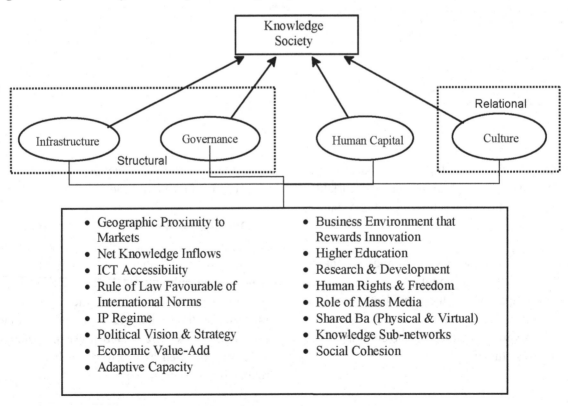

and scope of its investments in infrastructure. Gaps emanating from inefficiencies of knowledge creation, transfer and re-use amongst the citizenry form a great impediment to developing into a KBE (cf. Baquir & Kathawala, 2004; Conceicao et al., 2003; Dvir & Pasher, 2004; Ergazakis et al., 2006). Mansell (2002), for example, suggests that an effective means of eradicating such gaps is to provide an efficient infrastructure which includes more than basic amenities (water, electricity, sewage, transportation, security services, and a currency / stock exchange) to also encompass township planning, advanced systems of education and healthcare, and even networked communities. Hence, efforts to develop knowledge societies do not stop at the level of basic infrastructure as ends in themselves but which benefit society by providing it with the necessary skills and expertise required for functioning in a knowledge intensive economy with speed and value. In other words, structural inefficiencies attributable to power cuts, traffic jams, inadequate schooling, unavailable specialist healthcare, poor financial systems, and so on are not conducive to creating knowledge societies.

Pillar 2: Governance

Governance may be considered to be the effective macro-management of knowledge resources within a society. In order to effectively utilise the typically expensive infrastructure, there has to be appropriate policy measures in place; that is, governmental intervention (at the municipal, provincial or federal level) is necessary to put in place the elements that promote the effective usage of infrastructure and human capital resources – increasingly scare commodities. This is why both Pillars 1 and 2 fall under the Structural Capital of a Knowledge Society. In fact, for societies to move beyond the digital divide and further evolve into a knowledge society, greater policy intervention is needed to harness the potential of classical infrastructure, ICT and new media developments to enable a greater number of citizens to acquire

literacy in the use of knowledge. Whilst by no means unanimous, several studies have alluded to this nexus between governance and the organisation of knowledge economies (Castells, 2000; Dolfsma, 2006; Edvinsson, 2003; Harris, 2001; Kaufmann & Mastruzzi, 2007; Samarajiva & Gamage, 2007; Sharma & Azura, 2006; Soete, 2006; Snowden, 1999; UNESCO, 2005).

Pillar 3: Human Capital or Talent

Much of the literature and studies on development of knowledge societies emphasise the significance of human capital as a key component that gives these societies an edge in competence over others (APEC, 2000; Cheng et al., 2004; Conceicao et al., 2003; Cummings & Teng, 2003; Hamdouch & Sheehan, 2000; Houghton & Sheehan, 2000; Kahin, 2006; Olssen & Peters, 2005; UNESCO, 2005; UNDP, 2007; World Bank, 2006). In fact, many aspiring KBEs understand the importance of managing knowledge gaps and in particular, narrow such gaps between the information rich and poor, because information enriches a society's human capital, which in turn boasts creativity that is essential for the knowledge economy (Olssen & Peters, 2005). Previously, the industrial era saw machines replacing labour, whilst in the knowledge economy, uniquely human (tacit) skills are increasingly in demand (Houghton & Sheehan, 2000). Indeed, "there is a link between human capital and the economic growth of cities" (Cheng et al., 2004, p.100). And this human capital must be kept comfortable in order to be exploitable. The composition of a society's human capital also determines how diversity is viewed. This aspect also goes beyond human capital and capability and touches on the aspect of culture that permeates a society.

Pillar 4: Culture

Culture is indeed the most unique pillar of the four as most societies are already aware of the importance of infrastructural developments; governance and human capital are replicable and transferable, hence culture is the competitive factor that makes a knowledge society unique. According to Ergazakis et al. (2006), some cities have failed to be developed as knowledge cities even as much investment is made towards developing other areas such as transport infrastructures. This implies that greater attention has to be paid to the needs and expectations of the people in KBEs that help improve overall quality of life beyond economic issues (Baqir & Kathawala, 2004; Cohen & Prusak, 2005; Connelly & Kelloway, 2003; Ergazakis et al., 2006; Foray, 2006; Koshland, 2007; Masterman, 1995; Rodrigues, 2002; Sagasti, 2004; Trussler, 1999). Culture also includes attitudes and assumptions about learning, and the objectives of education on the whole. Post World-War II Budapest was a city in which learning was viewed as integral part of living, and soaked in the culture, the city produced a small but impactful band of brilliant scientists, filmmakers, photographers, and engineers (Marton, 2007). An important part of the culture of learning is the sense of adventure of the members of society. A sense of adventure will encourage experimentation, a willingness to think out of the box and to take risks, and this will inevitably lead to knowledge creation.

Using the 4-pillars as the conceptual basis of our understanding of a knowledge society, a review of the relevant literature distilled some 13 operational dimensions that would allow policy analysis and construction. It is claimed in the literature that these are characteristics and features that contribute to the creation and sustainable development of a knowledge society. The detailed manner in which these dimensions were unearthed, justified and validated is described in section 3 on research methodology. In this section, the 16 dimensions are defined with support from the literature in order to justify our postulate that they are essential building blocks of a knowledge society.

Table 1 recapitulates and summarises the 16 dimensions of a knowledge society, the claims of

their contribution to a KBE with corresponding support from the literature, and proxy measures from the authoritative secondary sources.

Recall that the dimensions are suggested as factors and outcomes in the creation and sustenance of knowledge societies. Undoubtedly, there are dimensions that have been suggested in the literature that may have been omitted; for example the centrality of learning and innovation in a knowledge society (Houghton & Sheehan 2000), "failure factors" such as quality of life, arts, culture; the lack of which undermines a knowledge society (Ergazakis et al., 2006), and the participation of women, respect for human resources, and security of normative action (UNESCO, 2005). These possible dimensions were reluctantly deemed less contributory to the framework of infrastructure, governance, talent and culture presented in this article. The frequent criticism is also that the interactive effects of too many independent variables (i.e., the dimensions) cause confusion in the empirical findings of a strong association with the dependent construct (in this case the creation of knowledge societies).

3. EMPIRICAL RESEARCH METHODOLOGY

The empirical methodology adopted in this study was derived from the traditions of information systems research (cf. El Sawy, 2003). Recall that our framework for knowledge societies was operationalised from the conceptual model of Edvinsson (2003) on what constitutes the IC of nations and that of Nahapiet and Ghoshal (1998) which helped formulate our pillars comprising interacting factors as well as outcomes that contribute to the creation of successful knowledge societies. These were mostly distilled from a review of the literature. Some of these dimensions were factors that contribute towards creating a knowledge society (ICT accessibility, expenditure on higher education, R&D) whereas outcomes are the results of

Table 1. Summary of dimensions and support from the literature

Dimension	Claim	References	Proxy Indicators
1. **Geographic Proximity to Markets**	Much of the research into knowledge economies stresses the self-reinforcing advantages of having knowledge producers, suppliers and support services concentrated in a certain geographic area as valuable knowledge may be shared, integrated and transferred through such relationships.	Cheng et al., 2004; Dolfsma, 2006; Foray, 2006; Houghton & Sheehan, 2000	Population; GDP per Capita; Share of Trade in GDP; Global Peace Index
2. **Net Knowledge Inflows**	In an increasing global marketplace of competing KBEs, adequate mechanisms have to ensure that world-class knowledge is diffused into a society.	Dolfsma, 2006; Ergazakis et al., 2006; Foray, 2006; Gupta and Govindarajan, 2000; Hamdouch and Moulaert, 2006; Harris, 2001; Rodrigues, 2002; UNESCO, 2005	Intangible Capital per Capita; FDI Stocks; Net Migration of Skills; Economic Participation of MNCs
3. **ICT Accessibility**	Successful knowledge societies are often well-connected, with broadband Internet content available, accessible and affordable to the mass of organizations and individuals.	Castells 2000; Ergazakis et al., 2006; Mansell, 2002; Sharma & Azura, 2006; UNESCO, 2005	Network Readiness Index; Broadband Internet Subscribers
4. **Rule of Law favourable of International Norms**	The global knowledge marketplace is also characterised by rapid increases in the transactions and flows of capital, talent, services and technology transfer and hence national laws must be harmonised to reflect a common understanding as well as transaparency.	Conceicao et al. 2003; Houghton & Sheehan, 2000; Kahin 2006; Rodrigues 2003	Government Effectiveness; Rule of Law; Global Peace Index
5. **IP Regime**	Intellectual Property Rights (IPRs) regime has to be sound and unbiased because the balance between protecting such IP rights has to be maintained carefully with the need to promote and disseminate the useful knowledge for the advancement of the society.	Dolfsma, 2006; Kahin, 2006; Olssen & Peters, 2005; Powell & Snellman, 2004; UNESCO, 2005	Patents; Share of Citations
6. **Political Vision & Strategy**	Governments' political vision and strategy for growth and development are key factors that are necessary to ensure the success of the evolution towards a knowledge society.	Cheng et al. 2004; Conceicao et al., 2003; Ergazakis et al., 2004; Mansell, 2002; Olssen & Peters, 2005	Political Stability; Regulatory Quality; Control of Corruption
7. **Business Environment Rewarding of Innovation**	A positive business environment would encourage the set-up of more innovative firms, and ease the conduct of knowledge industries, thus furthering society's knowledge creation and dissemination.	Ergazakis et al., 2004; Houghton & Sheehan, 2000	Business Competitiveness Index; Global Competitiveness Index; Ease of Doing Business; Index of Economic Freedoms
8. **Higher Education**	Investments have to be made in order for higher education institutions to stimulate a greater knowledge creation and sharing in societies.	Ergazakis et al., 2004; Foray, 2006; Olssen & Peters, 2005	Tertiary Attainment; Percentage of GDP invested in HE
9. **Research & Development**	A successful knowledge society is one where there is extensive research and development to acquire knowledge and learning for common public good and competitive private advantage.	Edvinsson, 2003; Ergazakis et al., 2006; Koshland, 2007; Shah, 2006	GERD / BERD; R&D Employment per Capita

continued on following page

Table 1. Continued

Dimension	Claim	References	Proxy Indicators
10. **Human Rights & Freedom**	The assurance of the rights of citizens – the right to access data held by public authorities, civil society participation rights, universal participation and universal access to knowledge – is fundamental to the promotion of human development and leads to a greater citizen empowerment and the sharing of information and knowledge.	Ergazakis et al., 2004; Ergazakis et al., 2006; Foray, 2006; Mansell, 2002; UNESCO, 2005	EIU Democracy Index; Voice & Accountability
11. **Role of Mass Media**	The role of a fair, open and responsible mass media cannot be understated in the creation of an informed society capable of making collective decisions in a consensual manner so that it remains inclusive of all potential within.	Federov, 2003; Masterman, 1996; Rice, 2007, personal communication	Voice & Accountability; Press Freedom
12. **Shared *Ba* (Physical & Virtual)**	Knowledge is created when information is put into context … when people gather in a common or virtual apace and share their knowledge to solve a problem, they are providing a shared context to create, validate and share such knowledge.	Baqir & Kathawala, 2004; Nonaka et al., 2000; Dvir & Pasher, 2004	Public and Household Expenditure on Civic Amenities (cultural attractions, entertainment etc); Cafes, theatres and museums per capita
13. **Knowledge Sub-networks**	The diffusion of knowledge through formal networks and links is augmented by exchanges in such informal networks as friendships, professional affiliations and shared disciplines.	Cheng et al., 2004; Snowden 1999	Cultural and Political Links with Advanced Economies through World Organisations and Professional Bodies; Foreign Direct Investments
14. **Economic Value-Add**	The impact of knowledge (and hence non-capital) investments towards a society's growth. Measurement and valuation for investments and growth strategies within a particular society. The ratio of GNP (includes trade) to GDP (i.e indication of what a society consumes and exports abroad).	Sharma et al, 2007	EVA = GDP / GNP
15. **Social Cohesion**	Group solidarity, unity and knowledge involvement of indigenes of a society that result in effectiveness towards the growth and development. Factors such as trust, respect and coordination cements such a cause and makes it yielding.	Green, 2004	Voice & Accountability, Political Stability, Global Peace Index
16. **Adaptive Capacity**	The ability of a society to rise after a fall. How well a society can survive challenges and bounce back to where it was or even better after the crisis – adaptation to change.	Collier, 2008	GDP growth rate (rolling averages growth cycles)

becoming a knowledge society (e.g., economic wealth, quality of life, EVA etc.). As well, almost all the dimensions contribute to more than one of the pillars of a knowledge society. Hence, we note that there is a predominant disposition in each of them and when listed in the order described in the previous section, there is a infrastructure, governance, talent and culture continuum to their membership.

Going forward, the research methodology was conducted over 3 stages. In the first stage, a Delphi Panel of 10 researchers in the area of KBEs were consulted via e-mail for their feedback on the model and the dimensions. They were asked for their judgements on whether the model was comprehensive and relevant. They were also specifically asked for the comments on each of the 16 dimensions – both the definitions as well as their applicability. The dimension "Role of Mass Media" was in fact not derived by the literature but suggested by one of the panellist to the concurrence of the others. EVA, Social Cohesion and Adaptive Capacity were likewise added after much consultation and consensus. Over 3 iterations, a distinct consensus emerged among the Delphi panellists that the model well articulated the contributory factors and outcomes of knowledge societies and that the 16 dimensions were sufficiently comprehensive and parsimonious. On the strength of the grounded theory model formulation, literature search of dimensions and the resulting consensus, we claim face, content and construct validity.

In the second stage, drawing on the infrastructure-governance-talent-culture framework and the operational definitions of the dimensions that were derived in the above-mentioned manner, the research team sourced several reputable, published sources of socio-economic indicators (such as the OECD, ITU, UNDP, UNESCO, WEF, and World Bank) for the availability of reliably collected, accurate and authoritative secondary data that could serve as proxy indicators for each of the dimensions. The major challenge was to match various indicators and measurements with the definitional nuance of each dimension. Since the dimensions themselves were overlapping in some of their meaning and their association with more than one pillar, it was agreed that several proxy indicators could logically measure each dimension and some of these indicators may not be exclusive to a single dimension. Data for about 20 communities spanning various stages of knowledge development was then collected from the relevant secondary databases. Hence, we derived proxies for dimensions that could not be directly measured and in so doing hoped to capture a quantitative snapshot of knowledge societies for later analysis. Here we claim field validity in the sense that these were dimensions that could be used and measured for the purpose of public policy.

During the third stage, in an attempt to derive relevance for policy-makers, a 2-hour focus group workshop with 25 senior graduate students of a course in Knowledge Management Strategies was conducted in order to ascertain the use of such a framework of dimensions in the field. We readily concede that the membership of the focus group as well as the 4 societies of analysis were primarily based on convenience as well as availability. However, we consider the choice defensible on account of their maturity and background knowledge. This was an international group of well-travelled, professionals who were embarking on a mid-career Masters' programme in knowledge management.

Hence, first the model and framework of dimensions was presented as a short seminar. Four distinct societies (Singapore, Nigeria, the United Arab Emirates and the United States of America) were chosen for the policy analysis for convenience as well as interest. They were well-known to our focus group (being subjects of interest as well as familiarity). This made the comparative policy analysis credible as well as meaningful. The focus group participants were then asked to consider each society that they were familiar with and express the society's strengths, weaknesses, opportunities and threats in terms of the 16 dimensions. They were asked to qualify their judgments to their peers in the focus group. Strengths and weaknesses are inward judgements about a society's current knowledge capabilities and shortcomings whereas opportunities and threats were future oriented judgements about the scope of actions available to that society to transform itself. In short, this was a Knowledge-SWOT exercise (Zack, 1999) and will be described further in the discussion section. Finally, the focus group was asked to converge to a rating of each society along the 16 dimensions. In other words, participants were then asked to (subjectively) rate the 4 knowledge societies along the 16 dimensions on a 11-point Likert scale ranging from 0 to 10 (with 5 as the anchored mid-point).

Figure 4. Strength and Opportunity Indices for the four societies

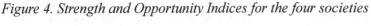

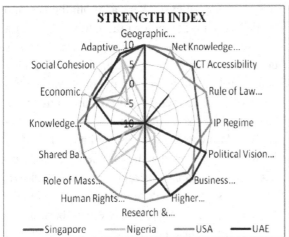

The ratings from the focus group participants were checked for large variances and if within limits, the mean values were computed. In some cases, outliers and missing values were ignored. Consistent with the approach suggested by the pioneering Swedish IC practitioner Lev Edvinsson (2003) and the Peruvian developmental economist Francesco Sagasti (2004), these mean values were plotted in a Kaviat or Radar diagram in order to benchmark various societies for the purpose of qualitative discussion. This is shown in Figure 4 and will be discussed in the next section. More importantly, the resulting chart was used to conduct a general knowledge policy discussion – providing support for our claim of internal consistency and usability in the field.

One major challenge faced in this study was the matching of the 16 dimensions to authoritative and readily-available proxy indicators that captured the definitional and ideological construct of each dimension. We found that in many instances, there was no single proxy indicator that covered the constructs of a dimension entirely. Hence, either several proxy indicators were necessary for a single dimension (see for example dimension 7 in Table 1 which was covered by several indicators such as Business Competitiveness Index; Global Competitiveness Index; Ease

of Doing Business; and Index of Economic Freedoms – each with its own distinct but relevant nuance). As well, there were also proxy measures (for example, Voice and Accountability) that covered more than one dimensions (Human Rights and Freedoms; Role of Mass Media). The identification, selection and combination of these proxy indicators was conducted over several intensive discussions among ourselves and invited experts and was also put to the Delphi Panel for "final form" feedback. It is also worth reiterating that the relationship between the 16 dimensions and 4 pillars is not one-to-one but one-to-many. That is, dimensions contribute to more than one axis on several occasions and perhaps form a less discrete order (as listed above) ranging from infrastructure, governance, talent and culture.

While there have been numerous conceptual studies which have prescribed models and frameworks for the creation of knowledge societies (cf. Baqir & Kathawala, 2004; Chou, 2005; Cummings & Teng, 2003; Ergazakis et al., 2006; Harris, 2001; Kahin, 2006; Mansell, 2002; Sagasti, 2004; Soete, 2006), much fewer have involved the identification and measurement (or collection from secondary sources) of the proxy indicators (or independent variables) that together explain the constituencies of such a knowledge society (cf. ITU, 2007;

OECD, 2007; UNESCO, 2005; for indicators of the information society; the World Bank Knowledge Assessment Methodology, 2007; an annual survey of business competitiveness by the World Economic Forum, 2006; and arguably the most complete characterization of a knowledge society by UNDP, 2007). It was not the stated objective (or otherwise) of our research to obtain a ranking of knowledge societies. Such attempts by the UNDP (2007) and the World Bank (2007) are both exhaustive and well-reported and no benefit can be derived from replicating smaller scale versions of these field investigations.

Hence, with the objective of field testing a qualitative, policy framework for analysing a knowledge society, we report our empirical efforts in the next section.

4. RESULTS AND DISCUSSION

One fundamental challenge in deriving "metrics that gauge the extent to which society has become more dependent on knowledge production" (Powell & Snellman, 2004) is that it is often easier to measure (non-controllable) outcomes than it is to assess the impact of policy parameters which contribute to the development of a KBE. For the purpose of this study, an in-depth, concerted search was conducted on the databases of several high-quality sources such as the Organisation for Economic Cooperation and Development (OECD) for socio-economic metrics, the International Telecommunications Union (ITU) for ICT metrics, the World Economic Forum (WEF) and World Bank for governance, infrastructure and competitiveness rankings, and the United Nations Education Scientific and Cultural Organization (UNESCO) and United Nations Development Project (UNDP) for scientific, educational and cultural data.

Drawing on the above-cited authoritative and relevant secondary sources, we compiled a best fit matching between the 16 dimensions of a knowledge society and available proxy indicators. Table

2 and Table 3 show recent statistics (of the selected proxy indicators) for a representative sample of 20 knowledge societies. These 20 societies were chosen because of the availability of statistics as well as for the reason that their economies ranged across the spectrum of KBE development. The major sources were: ITU[1] (2007), OECD[2] (2007), World Bank[3] (2007), EIU[4] (2007), WEF[5] (2007), Vision of Humanity[6] (2007), Doing Business[7] (2007), Heritage Foundation[8] (2007), Reporters sans frontières[9] (2007). As well, most of the statistics were for the year 2005 unless otherwise stated.

BCI refers to the WEF's Business Competitiveness Index and GCI refers to the WEF's Global Competitiveness Index which are derived by extensive research as well as expert opinions on a host of measures and factors that lead to the competitiveness of an economy. Voice and Accountability (V&A), Political Stability, Government Effectiveness, Regulatory Quality, Rule of Law and Control of Corruption are the five areas of Governance Indicators developed and used by the World Bank (2007) in their Annual World Bank Survey entitled Governance Matters 2007 and is derived from 33 global surveys and rankings (including expert assessments) that represent the largest publicly available resource on governance across countries. More specifically, *V&A* – measures electoral freedoms and free speech; *Political Stability* – measures perceptions of a government's stability; *Government Effectiveness* – measures quality of public services, civil service and public policies; *Regulatory Quality* – measures regulations that allow private sector growth; Rule of Law – measures confidence in laws, police and courts, and the crime rate; and Control of Corruption – measures the extent to which the government keeps corruption in check. These are by far the most used statistics on business and regulatory factors and were adopted as diverse proxy indicators.

NPL Citations refers to references to the non-patent literature. 2006 values for FDI Stocks are given in Millions of US Dollars and are defined as

Table 2. Proxy measures of dimensions for 20 representative knowledge societies

Country	Population[1] (M)	GDP per capita[1] (US$)	Share of Trade in GDP[2] (%)	Intangible Capital per capita[3] (US$)	FDI Stocks 2006 (billion US$)[4]	NRI[5] Rank	NRI[5] Score	Broadband[1] (As % of total Internet subs.)	Government Effectiveness[3]	Rule of Law[3]	Global Peace Index[6] Rank	Global Peace Index[6] Score	Patents[2]	Share of NPL in citations Rank	Political Stability[3]	Regulatory Quality[3]	Control of Corruption[3]
Australia	20.16	32,512	21	288,686	28	15	5.24	35.2	1.89	1.74	25	1.664	22	431	0.87	1.60	1.97
China	1,315.84	1,732	-	4,208	556.9	59	3.68	51.2	-0.09	0.43	60	1.980	18	177	-0.26	-0.28	-0.68
Canada	32.41	34,848	36	235,982	-7.5	11	5.35	80.4	1.94	1.76	8	1.481	28	710	0.94	1.52	1.92
France	60.5	35,158	26.6	403,874	-99.3	23	4.99	71.3	1.47	1.33	34	1.729	17	2356	0.43	1.06	1.40
Germany	82.69	33,877	38.1	423,323	-40.3	16	5.22	53.4	1.51	1.74	12	1.523	-	7111	0.80	1.36	1.92
Hong Kong	7.04	25,239	-	-	51.9	12	5.35	63	1.64	1.47	23	1.657	-	-	1.17	1.86	1.69
Italy	58.09	30,495	26.3	316,045	1.3	38	4.19	38.3	0.60	0.53	33	1.724	13	844	0.29	0.88	0.41
Indonesia	222.78	1,263	-	8,015	-0.2	62	3.59	-	-0.47	0.86	78	2.111	-	-	-1.29	-0.48	-0.87
Japan	128.08	35,592	13.6	341,470	-285.7	14	5.27	44	1.16	1.35	5	1.413	8	13,564	1.01	1.14	1.25
South Korea	48.29	16,309	41.2	107,864	57.6	19	5.14	99.1	1.01	0.78	32	1.719	10	747	0.55	0.77	0.47
Malaysia	26	5,030	-	24,520	25.7	26	4.74	12	1.01	0.57	37	1.744	-	-	0.47	0.49	0.25
Mexico	107.03	7,180	30.7	34,420	189.2	49	3.91	47.7	0.01	0.50	79	2.125	-	16	-0.25	0.35	-0.40
Nigeria	141.4	1,128	-	-	40.3	88	3.23	-	-0.92	-1.38	117	2.898	-	-	-1.77	-1.01	-1.22
Russia	143.5	-	-	5,900	36.7	70	3.54	-	-0.38	0.88	118	2.903	12	56	-0.98	-0.33	-0.78
Singapore	4.35	26,843	-	173,595	77.2	3	5.60	29.5	2.15	1.81	29	1.692	-	-	1.15	1.80	2.25
South Africa	47.43	5,050	-	48,959	32.4	47	4.00	3.9	0.83	0.18	99	2.399	3	38	-0.06	0.51	0.56
Spain	42.69	26,511	28.2	217,300	-1.1	32	4.35	90	1.40	1.11	21	1.633	11	115	0.42	1.24	1.34
Switzerland	7.46	49,191	44.5	542,394	-257.6	5	5.58	62.7	2.05	1.98	14	1.526	-	895	1.34	1.47	2.13
UAE	4.5	24,338	-	-	18.1	29	4.42	24.4	0.55	0.55	38	1.747	-	-	0.59	0.40	1.12
UK	59.67	37,319	28.3	346,347	-433	9	5.45	47.2	1.71	1.63	49	1.898	23	2024	0.33	1.55	1.94
USA	298.21	41,768	13.4	418,009	-396	7	5.54	42.2	1.60	1.53	96	2.317	26	19,222	0.04	1.48	1.57

Table 3. Proxy measures of dimensions for 20 representative knowledge societies

Country	BCI Rank[5]	GCI[5] Rank	GCI[5] Score	Ease of doing business rank[7]	Index of Economic Freedom 2007[6] Rank	Index of Economic Freedom 2007[6] Score	Gross Tertiary Enrollment Rate 2005[2]	GERD % GDP 2005[2]	BERD% GDP 2005[2]	R&D Personnel (per 1000 employment)	EIU Democracy Index (out of 10)[4]	V&A[3]	Press Freedom Rank[9]	Household Expenditure on Recreation & Culture[2] (As % of GDP)	HDI Rank	HDI Score
Australia	13	19	5.29	9	3	82.7	72.20	1.7	0.9	12.3	9.09	1.54	28	6.9	3*	0.957
China	54	54	4.24	83	119	54.0	19.10	1.4	0.8	1.5	2.97	-1.46	163	-	81	0.768
Canada	14	16	5.37	7	10	78.7	60.20	2.9	1.1	12.3	9.07	1.52	18	5.5	6*	0.950
France	10	18	5.31	31	45	66.1	56.00	1.4	1.3	14.1	8.07	1.49	31	5.2	16*	0.942
Germany	2	8	5.58	20	19	73.5	50.10	0.9	1.7	12.1	8.82	1.56	20	5.3	21*	0.932
Hong Kong	17	11	5.46	4	1	89.3	31.40	-	-	-	6.03	0.59	61	-	22*	0.927
Italy	37	42	4.46	53	60	63.4	63.10	1.1	0.5	6.7	7.73	1.06	35	4.2	17*	0.940
Indonesia	59	50	4.26	123	110	55.1	16.70	-	-	-	6.41	-0.16	100	-	108	0.711
Japan	9	7	5.60	12	18	73.6	54.00	3.2	2.3	14.0	8.15	0.98	37	-	7*	0.949
South Korea	24	24	5.13	30	36	68.6	-	2.6	2.2	8.6	7.88	0.78	39	3.7	26*	0.912
Malaysia	23	26	5.11	24	48	65.8	32.40	0.7	-	-	5.98	-0.12	124	-	61	0.805
Mexico	58	58	4.18	44	49	65.8	23.40	0.4	0.2	2.0	6.67	0.19	136	-	53*	0.821
Nigeria	84	95	3.69	108	100	56.0	10.20	-	-	-	3.52	-0.69	55	-	158	0.470
Russia	70	62	4.08	106	120	54.0	68.20	1.3	0.8	14.1	5.02	-0.66	144	-	65	0.797
Singapore	6	5	5.63	1	2	85.7	-	2.2	1.4	11.5	5.89	0.13	141	-	25*	0.916
South Africa	30	45	4.36	35	52	64.1	15.60	0.8	0.5	2.6	7.91	0.74	43	-	121	0.653
Spain	25	28	4.77	38	27	70.9	65.70	1.1	0.6	8.7	8.34	1.12	33	-	19*	0.938
Switzerland	8	1	5.81	16	9	79.1	47.00	2.57	2.1	12.5	9.02	1.61	11	4.9	9*	0.947
UAE	32	32	4.66	68	74	60.4	22.50	-	-	-	2.42	-0.66	65	-	49*	0.839
UK	5	10	5.54	6	6	81.6	60.10	1.89	1.1	-	8.08	1.49	24	7.7	18*	0.940
USA	1	6	5.61	3	4	82.0	82.40	2.68	1.8	-	8.22	1.26	48	6.4	8*	0.948

the Net Foreign Direct Investment Stocks derived by subtracting outward from inward flow. 2003 values for Patents refer to the number of triadic patent families. 2004 GDP Expenditure (GERD) on R&D is calculated as a percentage of GDP. Business enterprise expenditure on R&D (BERD) covers R&D activities carried out in the business sector by firms and institutes, regardless of the origin of funding. 2004 Tertiary Attainment is for the 25-64 (economically productive) age groups and indicates the percentage of the population of that age group with tertiary qualifications (degree, diploma or specialist certification).

Among the less common proxy indicators are the European Community's Migrant Integration Policy Index which uses 140 indicators to measure policies such as workplace rights, permanent residence, family reunions, and anti-racism laws; the Economist Intelligence Unit's Global Peace Index rates countries according to their internal and external conditions for peace which is correlated with income, schooling, level of regional integration; and Reporters without Borders' Press Freedom Index which assesses the plurality and lack of censorship of mass (and perhaps new) media.

Unfortunately, whereas a host of useful measures originated from OECD - such as GERD, BERD and Investment in Knowledge which is defined and calculated as the sum of expenditure on R&D, on total higher education from both public and private sources and on software – such data was limited to the scope of OECD's membership. As well, there was a particular absence of data for the international activities of professional bodies and the knowledge and expertise flows within MNCs.

Finally, as a proxy for all 16 dimensions in composite (the so-called dependent variable), we drew from perhaps the most comprehensive field study of knowledge societies which was conducted by the United Nations Development Program. "The human development index (HDI) is a composite index that measures the average

achievements in a country in three basic dimensions of human development: a long and healthy life; access to knowledge; and a decent standard of living. These basic dimensions are measured by life expectancy at birth, adult literacy and combined gross enrolment in primary, secondary and tertiary level education, and gross domestic product (GDP) per capita in Purchasing Power Parity US dollars (PPP US$), respectively. The index is constructed from indicators that are available globally using a methodology that is simple and transparent [which is shown in Technical Note 1 of the report]. While the concept of human development is much broader than any single composite index can measure, the HDI offers a powerful alternative to GDP per capita as a summary measure of human well-being. It provides a useful entry point into the rich information contained in the subsequent indicator tables on different aspects of human development." (UNDP, 2007, p 225).

In comparison, the World Bank's Knowledge Assessment Methodology (2007) consists of 83 structural and qualitative variables for 140 countries to measure their performance on the 4 Knowledge Economy (KE) pillars: Economic Incentive and Institutional Regime, Education, Innovation, and Information and Communications Technologies. This derives what is called the Knowledge Economy Index (KEI). This overlooks the human aspects of culture and talent which we consider critical and hence we chose the UNDP's HDI over the World Bank's KEI.

The HDI figures marked in Table 2 with an asterisk (*) indicate high human development as defined by the UNDP. We determined the face validity of the HDI score by observing the rankings of the 2007 report. The following were at the top of the world rankings: Iceland, Norway, Australia, Canada, Ireland, Sweden, Switzerland, Japan, Netherlands, France; while (sadly) the following were at the bottom: Congo, Chad, Central African Republic, Mozambique, Mali, Niger, Guinea-Bissau, Burkina Faso, Sierra Leone. This was consistent with the World Bank's (2007) study of the intangible wealth of nations and suggests that the least developed societies of the world were that way primarily because of a lack of national intellectual capital. We also determined the rigor of the exercise from the Technical Notes accompanying the report. In using HDI ranks and scores, we took particular care that the proxy indicators for the 16 dimensions did not derive from identical sources for the avoidance of pre-selection and bias. While we have used the UNDP's HDI rankings with all their limitations, we note that such rankings are skewed towards economically tangible development as opposed to the more holistic but harder to measure objectively idea of concepts such as the utility of infrastructure, governance, talent and culture.

A cursory examination of Table 2 and Table 3 reveal a reasonably strong match between most of the 16 dimensions and conventional notions of what constitutes a knowledge society. Generally, the partial and multiple correlation statistics, in Table 4 and 5 respectively, reveal strong associations among the proxy indicators (and by extension, the dimensions) and between them and the HDI as a composite measure of a knowledge society. More specifically, from Table 5 it is apparent that the following proxy indicators are highly and significantly correlated with UNDP's Human Development Index: GDP per Capita; Intangible Capital per Capita; Government Effectiveness; Rule of Law; Regulatory Quality; Control of Corruption; Democracy Index; Voice and Accountability; and Index of Press Freedom. It is noteworthy that none (save 2) of the dimensions nor their proxy indicators correlated poorly (<0.4) with the HDI scores.

It is also interesting to note that the negative correlations that occur in both Tables 4 and 5 reflect inverse relations between, as an example, population and political stability, regulatory quality, democracy index, index of economic freedom. This is apparent because the countries with higher populations are mostly developing countries (e.g., Indonesia, Mexico) or still controlled

economies (e.g., China, Russia). Share of trade and FDI stocks are also negatively correlated with the HDI – seemingly suggesting that the more reliant a society is in imports (goods, services or capital), the less opportunity it has to develop its indigenous knowledge assets. As well, the apparent inverse correlation between peace index and HDI ranks suggests that "creative tension" is a complex relationship which cannot be explained by the field data that has been examined. (It is otherwise too disturbing to conclude that knowledge societies require some amount of tensions within them in order to develop.) In any case, it bears caution that correlation is not equivalent to causation and that the use of a set of quantitative data, no matter how tediously collected, would not adequately capture what we term as the pulse of a knowledge society.

It is also interesting to note that with few exceptions (for example, population and V&A) there is high co-variance (or interactive effects) among the dimensions, proxy indicators or independent variables. Again, this suggests that the dimensions of a knowledge economy are synergistic and parsimonious – that is, their strengths co-exist in complementary state. The key finding that may therefore be derived from Tables 4 and 5 is that considering the proxy indicators (which interactively measure the 16 dimensions); it is clear that a knowledge society is a multi-faceted construct that cannot be quantified with a single measure. This perhaps explains the extensive measures used in both the HDI and KAM indices.

In order to test the applicability of our policy framework in the field, we next undertook the third stage of the empirical research.

Since one of the major objectives of the present research was to develop a practical framework for policy-makers, we used the 4-pillar model of 16 dimensions to conduct a qualitative discussion of 4 particularly familiar knowledge societies – Singapore, Nigeria, the United States and the United Arab Emirates – as a means of evaluating the model's utility for policy researchers and decision-

Table 4. partial correlations of proxy indicators with hdi score as controlled variable

	1	2	3	4	5	6	7	8	9	10	11	12	13	14	15	16	17	18	19	20	21	22	23	24	25
1. Population	1.00																								
2. Share of Trade in GDP	-0.39	1.00																							
3. GDP per capita	0.85	0.06	1.00																						
4. Intangible Capital per capita	0.92	-0.61	0.75	1.00																					
5. FDI Stocks 2006	-0.82	0.16	-0.94	-0.86	1.00																				
6. NRI Score	-0.69	0.58	-0.26	-0.54	0.16	1.00																			
7. Internet Subscribers	0.90	-0.48	0.58	0.74	-0.48	-0.94	1.00																		
8. Broadband	-0.22	0.82	0.32	-0.26	-0.27	0.77	-0.54	1.00																	
9. Government Effectiveness	-0.64	0.60	-0.18	-0.49	0.09	1.00	-0.91	0.82	1.00																
10. Rule of Law	-0.62	0.59	-0.16	-0.47	0.06	0.99	-0.90	0.82	1.00	1.00															
11. Global Peace Index Score	0.47	-0.99	0.05	0.69	-0.27	-0.55	0.50	-0.75	-0.57	-0.56	1.00														
12. Patents	0.77	-0.27	0.86	0.88	-0.98	-0.11	0.41	0.22	-0.04	-0.02	0.38	1.00													
13. NPL Citation	-0.50	0.96	-0.01	-0.62	0.14	0.77	-0.66	0.90	0.79	0.78	-0.95	-0.21	1.00												

continued on following page

Table 4. Continued

	1	2	3	4	5	6	7	8	9	10	11	12	13	14	15	16	17	18	19	20	21	22	23	24	25
14. Political Stability	-0.89	0.72	-0.53	-0.87	0.54	0.89	-0.94	0.63	0.86	0.85	-0.75	-0.53	0.83	1.00											
15. Regulatory Quality	-0.90	0.65	-0.54	-0.83	0.52	0.92	-0.97	0.62	0.89	0.88	-0.67	-0.49	0.79	0.99	1.00										
16. Control of Corruption	-0.59	0.57	-0.14	-0.44	0.03	0.99	-0.89	0.82	1.00	1.00	-0.53	0.02	0.77	0.83	0.86	1.00									
17. GCI Score	-0.47	0.47	-0.02	-0.28	-0.12	0.96	-0.81	0.81	0.97	0.98	-0.42	0.18	0.68	0.72	0.77	0.98	1.00								
18. Index of Economic Freedom Score	-0.98	0.50	-0.73	-0.88	0.68	0.83	-0.97	0.41	0.79	0.77	-0.54	-0.63	0.63	0.96	0.97	0.75	0.65	1.00							
19. Tertiary Attainment	-0.68	0.86	-0.20	-0.69	0.25	0.91	-0.85	0.86	0.92	0.91	-0.85	-0.27	0.96	0.94	0.92	0.89	0.81	0.81	1.00						
20. GERD	-0.69	0.93	-0.24	-0.78	0.36	0.80	-0.77	0.80	0.80	0.79	-0.93	-0.41	0.97	0.93	0.89	0.77	0.66	0.78	0.97	1.00					
21. BERD	-0.56	0.42	-0.15	-0.34	-0.02	0.97	-0.87	0.74	0.98	0.98	-0.37	0.09	0.64	0.75	0.81	0.98	0.99	0.72	0.80	0.65	1.00				
22. RnD Personnel	-0.06	0.23	0.33	0.17	-0.52	0.74	-0.50	0.73	0.78	0.79	-0.13	0.59	0.43	0.35	0.42	0.81	0.90	0.26	0.53	0.33	0.86	1.00			
23. EIU Democracy Index	-0.90	0.68	-0.53	-0.85	0.53	0.91	-0.96	0.63	0.88	0.87	-0.71	-0.51	0.81	1.00	1.00	0.85	0.75	0.97	0.93	0.91	0.79	0.38	1.00		
24. V&A	0.03	0.33	0.46	0.19	-0.59	0.70	-0.42	0.81	0.75	0.76	-0.23	0.63	0.51	0.32	0.37	0.79	0.87	0.19	0.55	0.37	0.81	0.98	0.35	1.00	
25. Household Expenditure on Culture	-0.72	-0.04	-0.58	-0.39	0.32	0.77	-0.85	0.22	0.73	0.73	0.03	-0.18	0.21	0.63	0.72	0.73	0.73	0.77	0.48	0.33	0.81	0.56	0.68	0.41	1.00

Table 5. Spearman rank correlations of proxy indicators with HDI

Proxy Indicator	HDI Rank	-----	Proxy Indicator	HDI Rank
Share of Trade in GDP	-0.46		Control of Corruption	0.70
GDP per capita	0.89		BCI Rank	0.68
Intangible Capital per capita	0.76		GCI Rank	0.69
FDI Stocks 2006	-0.63		Ease of doing business rank	0.63
NRI Rank	0.69		Index of Economic Freedom Rank	0.68
Internet Subscribers	0.38		Tertiary Attainment	0.69
Broadband	0.27		GERD	0.65
Government Effectiveness rank ind	0.72		BERD	0.45
Rule of Law	0.70		R&D Personnel	0.57
Global Peace Index Rank	-0.63		EIU Democracy Index	0.76
Patents	0.58		V&A	0.80
NPL Citation	0.55		Press Freedom Rank	0.74
Political Stability	0.58		Household Expenditure on Culture	0.58
Regulatory Quality	0.72			

makers. As described in the previous section, we took the mean of focus-group participant assessments of each of the 16 dimensions (dropping outliers and missing values). The first was for net strength (the difference of their strength and weakness assessments) while the second is for net opportunity (the difference of the opportunity and threat assessments). The result of such an exercise was two Kaviat or Radar Diagrams (shown in Figure 4) that served as a means of taking the "pulse of a given knowledge society" that is typically used to understand the developmental stages of various types of knowledge societies and discuss the prescriptive policies for their sustainable growth. In our exercise, the understanding of the model and dimensions, the rating of each society on a standard scale and the ensuing discussion of the qualitative strengths and weaknesses allowed a Knowledge-SWOT analysis (Zack, 1999) which did not serve as a quantitative benchmarking tool but instead as the basis of policy type discussions. It is noteworthy to report that the primary benefit derived from such an exercise was a discernible ability on the part of participants to benchmark and articulate the relative strengths and opportunities is a society and hence provide a policy tool that served to address any gaps in knowledge development policy.

While the use of the framework as a policy tool is beyond the scope of this article and is in fact the subject of a forthcoming one, it is nonetheless useful to note that such qualitative discussions aid the process of policy making. When the Kaviat Diagram from the focus group discussion was benchmarked with the World Bank's Knowledge Assessment Methodology (2007) which derived scores for KEI indicators, it was found to be consistent in terms of what policy-planners understand to be strengths, weaknesses, opportunities and threats of a given society. Whereas a quantitative approach has been used by the Malaysian government to benchmark its 5 yearly performance against OECD economies along 20 or so dimensions ranging from number of computers to ICT investments to expenditure on education to R&D personnel and high tech exports (UNDP, 2007), we suggest that it can be complemented with a richer, more descriptive qualitative analysis using the 16 dimensions as policy parameters.

For the present purpose, however, we are neither plotting a course of developmental policies nor benchmarking the four societies. Our purpose was to test the field validity of our conceptual model in terms of its usability in the field. We may conjecture that the framework developed in this study allows policy-makers the opportunity to benchmark regions, industries or perhaps the competition in an attempt to address structural deficiencies. A Radar Diagram - such as the one illustrated in Figure 4, where A, B, C, D may be regions of a country, industries within a market, or trading blocs - graphically shows the areas of strengths as well as opportunities for the 4 pillars of knowledge societies for policy analyses.

5. CONCLUDING REMARKS

This article has explored what it means to be a knowledge society in an attempt to understand how we may get there. In the process, we have presented a policy framework that would aid planners in discussing and articulating knowledge strategies for economic development. It begs the question – in an era of globalization and competition, are not knowledge and information societies inevitably led by business considerations rather than public policy? Whereas an information society is one which is typically technology-driven (especially with respect to ICT) and one where information is a resource (economic commodity) that promotes wealth and one where information literacy within the society is indispensible in terms of creating conditions for such a society to thrive. A knowledge society is an evolved state which emphasizes the creation and diffusion of knowledge (particularly the cognitive, human element); technology is merely an enabler rather than a driver; and facets such as governance and culture play an important role in its development. Hence, we may conclude that a knowledge society is distinct from an information society in that there is a premium on creation and discovery of the cognitive or tacit kind.

Based on the theory of National Intellectual Capital primarily espoused by Edvinsson (2003), among others, and a view of the structural, cognitive and relational aspects of Intellectual Capital creation within a society, we unearthed the following 16 dimensions from the literature: 1) Geographic Proximity to Markets, 2) Net Knowledge Inflows, 3) ICT Accessibility, 4) Rule of Law Favourable of International Norms, 5) IP Regime, 6) Political Vision & Strategy, 7) Business Environment Rewarding of Innovation, 8) Higher Education, 9) Research & Development, 10) Human Rights & Freedom, 11) Role of Mass Media, 12) Shared Ba (Physical & Virtual), 13) Knowledge Sub-Networks, 14) Economic Value-Add, 15) Social Cohesion, and 16) Adaptive Capacity which spanned the 4 pillars of 1) Infrastructure, 2) Governance, 3) Talent and 4) Culture.

While many proxy measures for the 16 dimensions were available from reliable sources such as the United Nations, World Bank and Organisation for Economic Cooperation and Development, one of the dimensions (Knowledge Sub-Networks) was not amenable to representation in such a manner. Moreover, several of the proxy measures such as population, share of trade, global peace index unexpectedly did not correlate with a composite measure such as the HDI. We cannot conclude an inverse causation. This is a phenomenon that warrants further investigation. Other proxies such as the participation of women in the knowledge sector (cf. UNESCO, 2005) and measures of national happiness (cf. Ezechieli, 2003) did not seem to have a place. We conclude from this that the notion of a knowledge society cannot be easily understood by a set of quantitative measurements and may be in some cases be even negatively correlated. While we note that the intent of composites such as the HDI and KAM is to first define and then track the progress of a knowledge society with statistical indicators, this does not necessarily provide for a rich, qualitative policy framework for discussion and debate. We also caution that a World Bank or OECD notion of what constitutes a knowledge society and how they may be measured (and rated) appear to be symmetric relations and offer limited scope for how policies may be suitably developed.

We reiterate that the usefulness of our conceptual framework of 16 dimensions serves more as a policy instrument than a subjective composite assessment of a society's evolution towards knowledge and growth. As we have seen from our field exercise, the framework complements the HDI and KAM sets of indicators in that it allows policy planners to delve deeper into qualitative discussions about the relative strengths and opportunities inherent in a given society with respect to the 16 dimensions. Perhaps as a suggestion for further research, noting the limits of the focus group, we would suggest reporting field experiences from more extensive and international utilization of the policy framework. Such accumulated experiences would enable a richer body of qualitative knowledge that may be applied in cross-sectional as well as longitudinal ways. The evolution to a knowledge society is undoubtedly a journey that requires benchmarks, environmental intelligence and an emphasis on the tacit structure of knowledge for sustainable advantage. The research reported in this article has attempted to aid such a journey.

ACKNOWLEDGMENT

The authors are part of an informal, irreverent knowledge research factory (styled on the Bourbaki group) at the Nanyang Technological University, Singapore. Ravi S. Sharma is Associate Professor of KM at NTU. Elaine W. J. Ng, Mathias Dharmawirya & Ekundayo M. Samuel are recent graduates of the Masters programme at the Wee Kim Wee School of Communication & Information at NTU and are now knowledge professionals. The findings reported in this article are part of the on-going efforts to develop a formal understanding of knowledge management methods and policies. The authors are grateful to the World Bank, UNDP and EIU for the access to authoritative country data. Many thanks are also due to faculty colleagues for their thoughtful review of an early draft which has led to a much improved paper.

REFERENCES

Ambrosini, V., & Bowman, C. (2001). Tacit knowledge: Some suggestions for operationalization. *Journal of Management Studies, 38*(6), 811–829. doi:10.1111/1467-6486.00260

Baqir, M. N., & Kathawala, Y. (2004). Ba for knowledge cities: A futuristic technology model. *Journal of Knowledge Management, 8*(5), 83–95. doi:10.1108/13673270410558828

Beaulieu, L. (1993). A Parisian café and ten prote-Bourbaki meetings: 1934-35. *The Mathematical Intelligencer, 15*(1), 27–35.

Birkinshaw, J., & Sheehan, T. (2002, fall). Managing the Knowledge Life Cycle. *MIT Sloan Management Review*, 75-83.

Bontis, N. (2001). Assessing knowledge assets: a review of the models used to measure intellectual capital. *International Journal of Management Reviews, 3*(1), 41–60. doi:10.1111/1468-2370.00053

Bucklew, M., & Edvinsson, L. (1999). *Intellectual Capital at Skandia*. Retrieved November 26, 2006 from http://www.fpm.com/cases/el3.html

Castells, M. (2000). The Rise of the Network Society. The Information Age: Economy [nd ed.). New York: Blackwell Publishing.]. *Society and Culture, 1*, 2.

Cheng, P., Choi, C. J., Chen, S., Eldomiaty, T. I., & Millar, C. C. J. M. (2004). Knowledge repositories in knowledge cities: institutions, conventions and knowledge sub-networks. *Journal of Knowledge Management, 8*(5), 96–106. doi:10.1108/13673270410558800

Chou, S.-W. (2005). Knowledge creation: absorptive capacity, organizational mechanisms, and knowledge storage/retrieval capabilities. *Journal of Information Science, 31*(6), 453–465. doi:10.1177/0165551505057005

Cohen, D., & Prusak, L. (2001). *In good company how social capital makes organizations work.* Boston: Harvard Business School Press.

Collier, P. (2007). *The Bottom Billion: Why the Poorest Countries are Falling and What can be done about it.* Oxford, UK: Oxford Univeristy Press.

Conceicao, P., Gibson, D. V., Heitor, M. V., & Stolp, C. (2003). Knowledge and innovation for the global learning economy: Building capacity for development. In Gibson, D. V., Stolp, C., Conceicao, P., & Heitor, M. V. (Eds.), *Systems and Policies for the Global Learning Economy* (pp. 11–43). Westport, CT: Praeger.

Connelly, C. E., & Kelloway, E. K. (2003). Predictors of employees' perceptions of knowledge sharing cultures. *Leadership and Organization Development Journal, 24,* 294–301. doi:10.1108/01437730310485815

Coward, L. A., & Salingaros, N. A. (2004). The Information Architecture of Cities. *Journal of Information Science, 30*(2), 107-118. Retrieved September 1, 2009 from http://zeta.math.utsa.edu/~yxk833/InfoCities.html

Cummings, J. L., & Teng, B. S. (2003). Transferring R&D knowledge: The key factors affecting knowledge transfer success. *Journal of Engineering and Technology Management, 20,* 39–68. doi:10.1016/S0923-4748(03)00004-3

Dolfsma, W. (2006). Knowledge, the knowledge economy and welfare theory. In Dolfsma, W., & Soete, L. (Eds.), *Understanding the dynamics of a knowledge economy* (pp. 201–221). Cheltenham, UK: Edward Elgar.

Dvir, R., & Pasher, E. (2004). Innovation engines for knowledge cities: An innovation ecology perspective. *Journal of Knowledge Management, 8*(5), 16–27. doi:10.1108/13673270410558756

Dyer, J. H., & Nobeoka, K. (2000). Creating and managing a high performance knowledge sharing network: The Toyota case. *Strategic Management Journal, 21,* 345–367. doi:10.1002/(SICI)1097-0266(200003)21:3<345::AID-SMJ96>3.0.CO;2-N

Edvinsson, L. (2000). Some perspectives on intangibles and intellectual capital. *Journal of Intellectual Capital, 1*(1), 12–16. doi:10.1108/14691930010371618

Edvinsson, L. (2003). The Intellectual Capital of Nations. In Holsapple, C. W. (Ed.), *Handbook of Knowledge Management 1 – Knowledge Matters.* Berlin: Springer.

El Sawy, O. A. (2003). The 3 Faces of IS Identity: connection, immersion and fusion. *Communications of the Association for Information Systems, 12,* 588–598.

Ergazakis, K., Metaxiotis, K., & Psarras, J. (2004). Towards knowledge cities: conceptual analysis and success stories. *Journal of Knowledge Management, 8*(5), 5–15. doi:10.1108/13673270410558747

Ergazakis, K., Metaxiotis, K., & Psarras, J. (2006). A coherent framework for building successful KCs in the context of the knowledge-based economy. *Knowledge Management Research & Practice, 4*(1), 56–59.

Ezechieli, E. (2003). *Beyond Sustainable Development: Education for Gross National Happiness in Bhutan.* Unpublished masters dissertation, Stanford University, Stanford, CA. Retrieved December 30, 2007 from http://suse-ice.stanford.edu/monographs/Ezechieli.pdf

Factbook, O. E. C. D. (2007). *Economic, Environmental and Social Statistics.* Retrieved August 20, 2007 from http://lysander.sourceoecd.org/vl=10624761/cl=11/nw=1/rpsv/factbook/

Fedorov, A. (2003). *Media Education and Media Literacy: Experts' Opinions.* Geneva, Switzerland: UNESCO.

Florida, R., & Gates, G. (2001). *Technology and tolerance: The importance of diversity to high technology growth.* Washington, DC: The Brookings Institution.

Foray, D. (2006). Optimizing the use of knowledge. In Kahin, B., & Foray, D. (Eds.), *Advancing Knowledge and the Knowledge Economy* (pp. 9–15). Cambridge, MA: MIT Press.

Green, R. (2004). *Housing, Planning, Local Government and the Regional Committee: Social Cohesion; Sixth Report of Session 2003-2004.* Retrieved November 28, 2008 from http://publications.parliament.uk/pa/cm200304/comselect/cmodpm/45/45.pdf-Gupta, K. A., & Vijay, G. (2000). Knowledge flows within multinational corporations. *Strategic Management Journal, 21,* 473-496.

Hamdouch, A., & Moulaert, F. (2006). Knowledge infrastructure, innovation dynamics, and knowledge creation/diffusion/accumulation processes: a comparative institutional perspective. *Innovation (Abingdon), 19*(1), 25–50. doi:10.1080/13511610600607676

Harris, R. G. (2001). The knowledge-based economy: intellectual origins and new economic perspectives. *International Journal of Management Reviews, 3*(1), 21–40. doi:10.1111/1468-2370.00052

Houghton, J., & Sheehan, P. (2000, February). *A primer on the knowledge economy.* Paper presented at the National Innovation Summit, Melbourne, Australia.

ITU. (2007). *Measuring the information society: ICT opportunity index and world telecommunication/ICT indicators.* Geneva, Switzerland: ITU.

Kahin, B. (2006). Prospects for knowledge policy. In Kahin, B., & Foray, D. (Eds.), *Advancing Knowledge and the Knowledge Economy* (pp. 1–8). Cambridge, MA: MIT Press.

Kaufmann, D., Kraay, A., & Mastruzzi, M. (2007, July). *Governance Matters VI: Aggregate and individual Governance indicators 1996-2006* (World Bank Policy Research Working Paper 4280).

Koshland, D. E. (2007). The Cha-Cha-Cha Theory of scientific discovery. *Science, 317,* 761–762. doi:10.1126/science.1147166

Mansell, R. (2002). From digital divides to digital entitlements in knowledge societies. *Current Sociology, 50*(3), 407–426. doi:10.1177/0011392102050003007

Marton, K. (2007). *The great escape: Nine Jews who fled Hitler and changed the world.* New York: Simon & Schuster.

Masterman, L. (1995). Media Education Worldwide: Objectives, values and superhighways. *Media Development, 2,* 37–51.

Matsuura, K. (2006). Knowledge Sharing – a powerful tool in the fight against poverty. *The Straits Times, 27.*

Nahapiet, J., & Ghoshal, S. (1998). Social capital, intellectual capital and organizational advantage. *Academy of Management Review, 23*(2), 242–266. doi:10.2307/259373

Nonaka, I., Toyama, R., & Konno, N. (2000). SECI, *Ba* and Leadership: A unified model of dynamic knowledge creation. *Long Range Planning, 33,* 5–34. doi:10.1016/S0024-6301(99)00115-6

Olssen, M., & Peters, M. A. (2005). Neoliberalism, higher eduction and the knowledge economy: From the free market to knowledge capitalism. *Journal of Education Policy, 20*(3), 313–345. doi:10.1080/02680930500108718

Powell, W. W., & Snellman, K. (2004). The Knowledge Economy. *Annual Review of Sociology, 30*, 199–220. doi:10.1146/annurev.soc.29.010202.100037

Regis, E. (1991). *Who got Einstein's office?: Eccentricity and genius at the Institute for Advanced Study*. Reading, MA: Addison-Wesley.

Rodrigues, M. J. (2002). *The New Knowledge Economy in Europe: A Strategy for International Competitiveness and Social Cohesion*. Cheltenham, UK: Edward Elgar.

Rodrigues, M. J. (2003). *European Policies for a Knowledge Economy*. Cheltenham, UK: Edward Elgar.

Sagasti, F. (2004). *Knowledge and Information for Development*. Northampton, MA: Edward Elgar.

Samarajiva, R., & Gamage, S. (2007). Bridging the Divide: Building Asia-Pacific Capacity for Effective Reforms. *The Information Society, 23*, 109–117. doi:10.1080/01972240701224200

Shah, S. (2006). *The body hunters: Testing new drugs on the world's poorest patients*. New York: New Press.

Sharma, R. S. (2007). Value-Added Knowledge Management For Financial Performance: The Case of an East Asian Conglomerate. *The Journal of Information and Knowledge Management Systems, 37*(4), 484–501.

Sharma, R. S., & Azura, I. M. (2005). Bridging the Digital Divide in Asia - Challenges and Solutions. *International Journal of Technology. Knowledge and Society, 1*(3), 15–30.

Soete, W. D. (2006). *Understanding the Dynamics of a Knowledge Economy*. Cheltenham, UK: Edward Elgar.

UNDP. (2007). *Human Development Report 2007/2008*. Retrieved December 12, 2007 from http://hdr.undp.org/en/media/hdr_20072008_en_complete.pdf

UNESCO. (2005). *From the Information Society to Knowledge Societies*. Paris: UNESCO Publishing.

World Bank. (2006). *Where is the Wealth of Nations? Measuring Capital for the 21st Century*. Washington, DC: The International Bank for Reconstruction and Development/The World Bank.

World Bank Knowledge Assessment Methodology. (2007). Retrieved April 1, 2008 from http://web.worldbank.org/WBSITE/EXTERNAL/WBI/WBIPROGRAMS/KFDLP/EXTUNIKAM/0,menuPK:1414738~pagePK:64168427~piPK:64168435~theSitePK:1414721,00.html

World Economic Forum. (2006). *The Global Competitiveness Report 2006-2007*. Retrieved August 10, 2007 from http://www.weforum.org/en/initiatives

Zack, M. H. (1999). Developing a Knowledge Strategy. *California Management Review, 41*(3), 125–145.

This work was previously published in the International Journal of Knowledge Society Research, Volume 1, Issue 1, edited by Miltiadis D. Lytras, pp. 22-45, copyright 2010 by IGI Publishing (an imprint of IGI Global).

Chapter 4
Toward Building the Knowledge Culture:
Reviews and a KC–STOPE with Six Sigma View

Saad Haj Bakry
King Saud University, Saudi Arabia

Abdulkader Alfantookh
Ministry of Higher Education, Saudi Arabia

ABSTRACT

Building the knowledge culture is of increasing importance, not only because of its role in providing sound knowledge management and effective knowledge-based economic development, but also because of its support to environment protection, intercultural harmony and human well-being. This paper provides a review of the knowledge culture and its related issues, and introduces a development framework for building this culture. The proposed framework integrates the main knowledge activities of knowledge generation, diffusion and utilization into an activated "Knowledge Circle: KC". It uses the five-domain structure of "Strategy, Technology, Organization, People and Environment: STOPE" to map and inter-relate the various issues associated with the knowledge culture. In addition, it adopts the "Six-Sigma" principles, and its continuous process of "Define, Measure, Analyze, Improve and Control: DMAIC" as an approach to the work toward building the target culture. The paper calls for building the knowledge culture, not only at an organization, or a country level, but also at the global level. It provides its KC-STOPE with Six-Sigma framework for this purpose and strongly recommends its use for future development toward building the target culture.

INTRODUCTION

This section is concerned with providing a background on the work presented in this paper. It defines what is meant by culture, and gives some examples. The multicultural nature of the world and the process of cultural evolution are also taken into account. The importance of knowledge and the emergence of the knowledge culture, as a potential common world culture that supports development and intercultural understanding, are also considered. The work presented in this paper is then introduced.

DOI: 10.4018/978-1-4666-1788-9.ch004

Culture and the Multi-Cultural World

Culture has been viewed by Edward Taylor, the 19th century scholar, as "that complex whole which includes: knowledge, belief, art, morals, law, custom and other capabilities and habits acquired by man as a member of a society" (AAE, 1981). With such complex features, the impacts of various cultures on the world are not always positive, but they can also be negative. Simon Blackburn, a Cambridge university professor, said: "culture gave us the English language, the symphony and the i-Pod; and it also gave us guns, Gulag and Guantanamo bay" (Blackburn, 2008). In these words, Blackburn emphasized the fact that culture can produce both: good and bad outcomes for humanity. On the one hand, the English language, like any other human language is a precious mean for human communication, the symphony is a fine enjoyable art, and the i-Pod is a useful technology. On the other hand, guns are harmful technology products, and Gulag and Guantanamo bay are examples of terrible human detention camps established by the former Soviet Union and the USA respectively.

Looking at the multicultural nature of the world, following the end of the cold war, Samuel Huntington, a Harvard University professor, warned from clash of civilizations, and identified eight main world cultures with different conflict potentials (Huntington, 1996). However, various organizations called for intercultural dialogue toward harmony and pluralism. They emphasized the need for and the feasibility of avoiding, or even preventing such clashes (Bakry & Al-Ghamdi, in press). In addition, the 21st century directions of many higher education (HE) institutions included equipping HE graduates with intercultural competence, that is the ability to move comfortably between different cultures (Bakry & Alfantookh, 2009).

Cultural Evolution and Knowledge

Culture has the feature of being under continuous evolution. It has been considered that this evolution has led to the transformation of human societies from savagery to barbarism, and from barbarism to civilization. The 20th century scholar V. Gordon Child viewed civilization in terms of cultural and technological achievements (AAE, 1981). Both of these achievements are associated, of course, with knowledge activities.

Knowledge, in the present age, has reached an unprecedented volume, an exceptional rate of growth, and an unmatched worldwide sharing and manipulation capabilities offered by the information and communication technology (ICT) and its continuous progress (Bakry, 2005). Although knowledge has always been power, as emphasized by Francis Bacon, who lived in the 16th century (Wikipedia, n.d.), knowledge in our age can perhaps be described as the most important power in our contemporary life. It is inside many good things and unfortunately many bad things too: from useful business products and services to horrible warfare tools; and from mutual respect and understanding to sectarianism and hatred.

Emergence of the Knowledge Culture

The power of knowledge in our contemporary life has produced many new terms and concepts including: "knowledge society"; "knowledge economy", "knowledge management", and "knowledge culture". These terms currently enjoy a wide scale use. For example, the 2001 European summit meeting in Lisbon, emphasized transformation to the knowledge society as a mean for development (European Information Society, n.d.). The World Bank has produced the "Knowledge Assessment Methodology: KAM" for the evaluation of knowledge economy issues in different countries (World Bank, n.d.).

Knowledge management approaches, tools and applications have been addressed and developed by various scholars and organizations (De Burn, 2005; Wiley Media, n.d.). In addition, the issue of building the "knowledge culture" has been addressed within the scope of organizations (Anderson, n.d.; Hauschild, Licht, & Stein, 2001). Furthermore, a Harvard university professor Zbigniew Brzezinski, who was the national security advisor to former USA president Jimmy Carter, recently called for a cultural revolution in the USA, considering the need for knowledge about the world to be diffused among Americans as one of the essential requirements for the country to have a second chance at the world stage (Brzezinski, n.d.).

Knowledge and the Presented Work

The state of knowledge and knowledge activities in the world today affects its different cultures and its intercultural interaction. This has led us to view the world culture as consisting of two main components: a potential positive knowledge-based component that can be called the "common knowledge culture", and a component with different cultures distributed in different parts of the world, as illustrated in Figure 1. The view thinks of the common knowledge culture as a mean, not only for economic development, but also for intercultural understanding and harmony, environment protection, and various other fine virtues that can contribute to the well-being of all people, all over the world.

This paper has two main integrated objectives. The first is concerned with providing a review of the issues associated with the knowledge culture including: the knowledge itself, knowledge management, and knowledge economy. The second is associated with introducing a framework concerned with building the target positive common knowledge culture, considering its various issues. The framework is based on the previously developed knowledge society ecosystem framework of the "Knowledge Circle in the scope of Strategy, Technology, Organization, People and the Environment: KC STOPE" (Bakry, 2008; Bakry & Al-Ghamdi, 2008). It is also associated the "Six-Sigma" approach of development that supports continuous improvement and proactive response to potential change (De Feo & Barnard, 2004; Pyzdek, 2003).

THE KNOWLEDGE CULTURE

The knowledge culture is addressed here through reviews concerned with the following:

Figure 1. A view of the potential positive "common knowledge culture" relative to the different cultures of the world

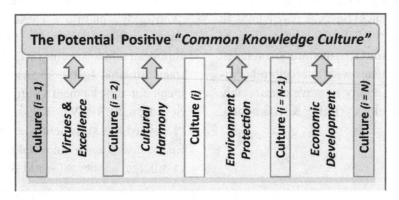

- Knowledge and its related terms and concepts;
- Knowledge culture development issues;
- Knowledge management; and
- Knowledge economy.

In considering the above, explanations associated with different sources have been taken into account.

Knowledge and Related Concepts

In the following, knowledge is addressed in two steps. The first is associated with identifying the lingual meanings of various terms related to knowledge. The second is concerned with presenting the professional concepts of terms directly related to the meaning of knowledge and the meaning of its related issues; in addition to the identification of its basic types.

Knowledge is related to many terms and concepts. It is of course associated with "culture";

and it is also related to "data and information". Through "thinking and intellectualism", information can become knowledge. According to Socrates "virtue and excellence" are among the essential components of knowledge or in other words of positive knowledge (McCall, n.d.). With fine "management" of knowledge, "wisdom" would be a potential precious outcome. In addition, "discovery, creativity, invention and innovation" are concepts associated with knowledge generation. Figure 2 gives the lingual meaning of each of these terms (Webster's New Collegiate Dictionary, 1961); and Figure 3 provides a structure that interrelates these terms and associates them with knowledge.

Figure 4 presents the professional conceptual meaning of both "data and information" (ISO, 1987; KMSL, n.d.), and it also considers different views concerned with what is meant by knowledge (De Burn, 2005; ISO, 1987; KMSL, n.d.; Britannica, n.d.). Figure 5 gives the concepts of three terms concerned with the dynamic nature of

Figure 2. Basic knowledge & related issues: lingual definitions from Webster's [20]

Term	Definition
Innovation	Act of introducing something new
Invention	To bring into being something new
Creativity	The ability to bring into being.
Discovery	To reveal / to disclose
Wisdom	The ability to judge soundly and deal sagaciously with facts as they relate to life and conduct
Management	Act and art to control, conduct and direct affairs
Knowledge	The act or state of understanding
Excellence	The quality of being of great worth
Virtue	Moral excellence
Intellectualism	The doctrine that knowledge is derived from pure reason
Thinking: *Reason*	Exercising the power of judgment, conception, or inference
Information	To give form to knowledge
Data	A group of facts or statistics often used with a sign
Culture	The enlightenment and refinement of taste acquired by intellectual and aesthetic training

Figure 3. Knowledge structure & related issues

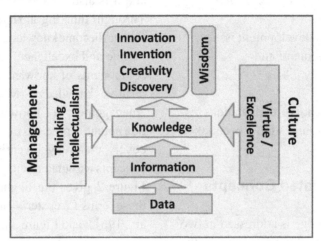

Figure 4. Basic Knowledge issues: professional definitions

Term		Definition	Reference
Data	General	*A representation of facts, concepts, or instructions in a formalized manner suitable for communication, interpretation, or processing by human beings or automated means*	(ISO, 1987)
	Mining	*Analyzing data to identify patterns and relationships so that decision-making processes can be improved*	(KMSL, n.d.)
Information		*The meaning that is currently assigned to data by means of a convention applied to that data*	(ISO, 1987)
Knowledge	Hindu Philosophy	*A word with a range of meanings focusing on a cognitive event that proves not to be mistaken.*	(Britannica, n.d.)
	Origin	*Knowledge is derived from information.*	(De Burn, 2005)
	Elements	*It includes familiarity, awareness and understanding*	
	Resources	*It is gained through experience or study, and results from making comparisons, identifying consequences, and making connections.*	

knowledge, that is: "culture, innovation and management" (AAE, 1981; Webster's New Collegiate Dictionary, 1961; KMSL, n.d.; UK-Idea, n.d.; Wikipedia, n.d.). Figure 6 identifies the three main types of knowledge from the viewpoint of availability, that is: "the explicit knowledge, the implicit knowledge and the tacit knowledge" (Wiley Media, n.d.; KMSL, n.d.).

Knowledge Culture Development Issues

With the above overview of knowledge, we come now to addressing the development of the knowledge culture. For this purpose, four recent publications, on the subject, are taken into account. The first is concerned with building the knowledge culture in Australia through a govern-

Figure 5. Basic knowledge related issues: professional definitions

Term		Definition	Reference
Culture	Social	The complex whole that includes: knowledge, belief, art, morals, law, custom and other capabilities and habits acquired by man as a member of a society	(AAE, 1981)
	Human	Learned behavior acquired by individuals as members of a social group	
	Business	The values and ethos of an organization	(KMSL, n.d.)
Innovation	Wealth creation	A tool for *entrepreneurs* to exploit change as an opportunity & create a resource or capacity for wealth creation.	Peter Drucker (De Burn, 2005)
	Elements	useful innovation = creativity (idea + action) + productivity + marketing	(UK-idea, n.d.)
Management	General	The act of getting people together to accomplish desired goals	(Wikipedia, n.d.)
	Elements	Planning, organizing, resourcing, directing & controlling	
	Resources	Human, financial, technological & natural	

Figure 6. Basic knowledge related issues: professional definitions

Term	Definition	Reference
Explicit knowledge	The knowledge that is articulated in formal language and easily transmitted among individuals both synchronously and asynchronously	Polanyi (Wiley Media, n.d.)
	Information that is formally recorded and stored where people can access it.	(KMSL, n.d.)
Tacit knowledge	Personal knowledge embedded in individual experience	Polanyi (Wiley Media, n.d.)
	The knowledge which cannot be written down	(KMSL, n.d.)
Implicit knowledge	The part of tacit knowledge that can be harvested from its owner and codified to become sharable	Polanyi (Wiley Media, n.d.)
	The tacit knowledge that can be written down, but has not been written down yet.	(KMSL, n.d.)
Michel Polanyi (1966): "Knowledge ranges from explicit to tacit on continuum basis"		

ment education and training plan (MCEETYA, n.d.). The other three are concerned with the knowledge culture at the organization level, and they were prepared by different consulting firms (Anderson, n.d.; Hauschild, Licht, & Stein, 2001;

Providers Edge, 2007). These publications view the knowledge culture from different viewpoints.

The Australian plan (MCEETYA, n.d.) viewed the knowledge culture as the way to the achievement of the information economy, and it empha-

Figure 7. Knowledge culture: "building a knowledge culture", Australia, MCEETYA Project [26]

Issue	Explanation	
Emphasis	*An education and training action plan for the information economy*	
Vision	*Improving outcome of E&T through ubiquitous use of ICT*	
Themes	Innovation	*Creating an innovative society*
	Learning	*Ensuring that all learners achieve their potential*
	Quality	*Improving quality & raising standards*
	Efficiency	*Achieving efficiency through sharing*
	Internationalization	*Capitalizing on the internationalization of education*

sized the use of ICT for this purpose. The plan considered four main themes: innovation, learning, quality, efficiency and internationalization. Further details of the plan are given in Figure 7.

At the organization level, a study for Robbins-Gioia (Anderson, n.d.) considered the knowledge culture to be the implementation of knowledge management practices. It identified this management as the "brain" of the organization; and

considered its function to include: balancing people, processes and tools; and ensuring that experience is leveraged to drive future success. Figure 8 provides further details, including introducing the key drivers and the main elements associated with the required knowledge management.

McKinsey produced another study on the knowledge culture (Hauschild, Licht, & Stein,

Figure 8. Knowledge culture: "building a knowledge culture" Anderson from ROBBINS-GIOIA [12]

Issue	Explanation
Knowledge culture	*Prerequisite: Overhaul processes & overcome organizational biases*
	Implementation of knowledge management practices
Knowledge management	*An organizational "brain"*
	Balancing "people, processes & tools" and ensuring that "experience" is leveraged to drive future success
Key drivers	*Capturing the experience of graying workforce:* tacit K
	Providing a more cost-efficient way of doing business: leveraging K
	Improving corporate agility: K & responsiveness
Elements	*Risk management*
	Configuration & change management
	Procurement management
	Communication management

Figure 9. Knowledge culture: "creating a knowledge culture", McKinsey

Issue	Explanation
Knowledge culture	Knowledge now is the life blood of companies
	Knowledge is more than information
Knowledge management	It is not only building sophisticated IT systems
	Essential for innovation and value creation
Performance	Requirements
Lust of K	Standards, Employee incentives, & Participation: product development & process improvement
Applying K	Overcoming subjectivity of knowledge / Wide range of K application (bench marking, cooperation & market observation)
Distributing K	Capturing tacit knowledge / Training & partnerships (internal & external) / Cross-functional database
Creating K	External inspiration (use of IT channels) / Competition / Innovation support: systematic

2001). It also associated this culture with knowledge management. It emphasized four main requirements for the creation of the knowledge culture: the desire, or lust, for useful knowledge; knowledge application; knowledge distribution; and knowledge creation. Further details of the study are given in Figure 9.

Like the above, Provider Edge addressed the corporate culture in the context of knowledge management (Providers Edge, 2007). It considered this culture to be a prerequisite, or an enabler, to knowledge management; and it identified this management to be about response to rapid change. It elaborated on the knowledge culture through comparisons with past culture and the future creativity culture. For this purpose, it emphasized four main issues: the structure of the organization, its focus, main feature, and basic performance measure. More details are presented in Figure 10.

Knowledge Management

The work reviewed above addressed knowledge management through its consideration of the knowledge culture. It illustrated the interdependence between the two, emphasizing that knowledge culture cannot be achieved without knowledge management. In this section, work specifically concerned with knowledge management is reviewed, in order to provide a comprehensive understanding of the issues involved and consequently of knowledge culture, which is the concern of this paper.

A publication by Wiley media (n.d.) expressed the purpose of knowledge management to be responsiveness and innovation; and it explained its role as leveraging collective wisdom. It addressed its requirements, and in this respect, it identified four main elements: business strategy; leadership, technology and culture. The needed culture is expressed as "faith in collective sharing and thinking". This, of course, emphasizes the concept of "synergy", where the outcome produced collectively by all is much greater than the sum of outcomes produced by individuals. More details are presented in Figure 11.

The basic principle of knowledge management has been stated, by a paper published by the

Figure 10. Knowledge culture: "knowledge management and corporate culture" Providers Edge

Issue	Explanation			
Corporate culture	Suitable corporate culture is a prerequisite for knowledge management to work			
Knowledge management	Knowledge management is about helping an organization to respond to rapid change			
Cultural development	Feudal Culture	Industrial Culture	Knowledge Culture	Creativity Culture
Organization	Territorial	Hierarchies	Networks	Row
Focus	Land	Profit	Customer	Innovation
Feature	Domination Control	Control Responsibility	Responsibility Contribution	Contribution Creativity
Measure	Quantity	Efficiency	Effectiveness	Quality of life

Figure 11. Knowledge management: "What is knowledge management": Wiley Media [11]

Issue	Explanation
Knowledge management	It is the leveraging of collective wisdom to increase responsiveness & innovation
Principles	Requirements
Collective wisdom	Knowledge is connected; it is a collection of multiple experience
A catalyst / response	Knowledge management stimulates action in response to needs
Novelty	Stimulates action in response to need
Elements	Requirements
Business strategy	Development directions
Leadership	Visionary leadership is essential
Technology	An enabler
Culture	Faith in collective sharing & thinking (Comment: "SYNERGY" Outcome produced collectively >> Sum of outcomes by individuals)

"National Library for Health: NHS" (De Burn, 2005), as "creation, sharing and use of knowledge" in the organization concerned. It considered that this management should enable people to have the right knowledge, in the right place and at the right time. It emphasized people's need to understand the knowledge culture; and it identified this culture as the circumstances that "enable or disable needed knowledge activities". Further details are given in Figure 12.

The work of (De Burn, 2005) presents different views of knowledge management expressed

Figure 12. Knowledge management: "ABC-of knowledge management": De Brun from NHS [10]

Issue	Explanation
Basic principle	*Practically all jobs involve "knowledge work", which require knowledge "creation, sharing, and use" throughout the organization*
Knowledge management	Applying the collective knowledge of the entire workforce to achieve specific organizational goals
	Just the knowledge that is most important to the organization
	People should have the *right knowledge*, in the *right place*, at the *right time.*
Elements	Requirements
People	Knowledge culture: *enabling, disabling needed knowledge activities*
Process	Organization functions or operations:
Technology	IT availability & proper use

by individuals and organizations. Three of these views have been chosen for their emphasis on the need for putting knowledge into practical use:

- One view considers that the power of knowledge comes from "transmitting information to make it productive, not from hiding it";
- Another view stresses the need for "converting personal knowledge into an organizational one"; and

- The third view expresses that organizations need to "embody the right knowledge in their products and services".

Figure 13. lists the exact wordings of these views.

Knowledge Economy

The application of fine "knowledge management" in an organization would support the creation of wealth that can be made by that organization. The

Figure 13. Knowledge management: views "ABC-of knowledge management": De Brun from NHS [10]

Viewer	View
Peter Drucker	*Knowledge is power, which is why people who had it in the past often tried to make a secret of it. Power comes from transmitting information to make it productive, not from hiding it.*
Yankee Group	Knowledge management involves efficiently connecting those who know with those who need to know & converting personal knowledge into organizational knowledge
Nonaka & Takeuchi	*The capability of an organization to create new knowledge, disseminate it throughout the organization & embody it in products, services and systems*

"Knowledge Management Specialist Library: KMSL" of NHS (KMSL, n.d.) defines the knowledge economy as "an economy in which knowledge plays a predominant part in the creation of wealth". This reflects the fact that both: knowledge management and knowledge economy are interrelated, and are also associated with the knowledge culture. In this section, various definitions of the knowledge economy are reviewed, together with the main international indicators used to assess knowledge in the economy of different countries.

Figure 14 gives different definitions of the knowledge economy taken from KMSL (n.d.), and from a study published by the work foundation (Brinkley, 2006). These definitions are associated with three main views:

- A general view, expressed by two sources, with both of them associating the knowledge economy with the creation of wealth through knowledge;
- Another view compares knowledge, as a source of economic development, with other economic resources, such as natural resources, and emphasizes that in the

knowledge economy, knowledge takes a greater role than these other resources; and
- A third view, consisting of two definitions, concerned with the scope of the knowledge economy, and with both of them identifying that scope in a broad way that involves not only high tech, but also any business, with knowledge being at the heart of its value.

Collectively, these views identifies the various aspects of the knowledge economy.

Figure 15 lists the seven main issues of the "Knowledge Assessment Methodology: KAM" used internationally to evaluate the economy of different countries from the knowledge perspective (World Bank, n.d.). These include: governance, economic regime, economic performance, education, innovation system, gender, and ICT infrastructure. Each of these issues is identified by an example of its assessment measures, and by the numbers of these measures associated with both: KAM basic evaluation measures, and KAM comprehensive evaluation measures.

Figure 14. Knowledge economy: professional definitions

	Definition	Reference
General view	An economy in which knowledge plays a predominant part in the creation of wealth.	(KMSL, n.d.)
	In the knowledge economy, the creation of knowledge plays the predominant part in the creation of wealth	*From different sources, presented by Brinkley of the work foundation (Brinkley, 2006).*
Relative to other resources	*Knowledge, in the knowledge economy, takes a greater importance as compared with: natural resources, physical capital and low skill labor.*	
Scope	*The idea of the knowledge driven economy is not only related to high tech industries. It describes new sources of competition which can apply to all sectors.*	
	The knowledge society is a larger concept than just an increased commitment to R&D. It covers every aspect of the contemporary economy, where knowledge is the heart of the value added.	

Figure 15. Knowledge economy: Knowledge Assessment Methodology (KAM) [9]

Issues	Measures		Example
	Basic	*All*	
Governance	2	7	*Rule of law*
Economic regime	1	12	*Tariff & nontariff barriers*
Economic performance	2	9	*Human development index*
Education	3	14	*Adult literacy rate*
Innovation system	3	24	*Technical journal articles*
Gender	0	5	*Gender development index*
ICT infrastructure	3	12	*Computers per 1000 population*
(TOTAL)	14	83	*Collective assessment*

The above review has explored the conceptual issues of knowledge, knowledge culture, knowledge management, knowledge economy, and their interrelationships. It is hoped that this has given an insight-view into the various knowledge aspects that need to be considered in building the knowledge culture, not only at an organization level, but also at national and international levels.

A KC-STOPE WITH SIX SIGMA VIEW

The view presented here is concerned with introducing a framework for building and sustaining the required knowledge culture. The principles upon which the target framework is based are presented first. This is followed by elaborations on the basic domains of the scope of the framework, which include: strategy, technology, organization, people and environment.

Framework Development Principles

The development of the target framework is based on the following six main principles.

- **Principle 1:** Transforming the knowledge activities of "knowledge generation, diffusion and utilization" from the state of disintegration, shown in Figure 16, to the state of integration, illustrated in Figure 17. This leads to the formation of the "knowledge circle: KC" (Bakry, 2005) that adheres to the requirements of knowledge management, and supports the development of the knowledge economy.

- **Principle 2:** The consideration of the issues of: "development, innovation, virtue, and excellence". This supports economic development, environment protection and intercultural harmony; and it also leads to the achievement of human prosperity and well-being.

- **Principle 3:** Establishing a well-structured scope of domains that can accommodate the various factors and issues associated with the knowledge culture including: the knowledge circle with both the knowledge management and the knowledge economy considerations. The STOPE scope of "strategy, technology, organization, people and environment" has been chosen for

Figure 16. Separated "knowledge activities": require integration

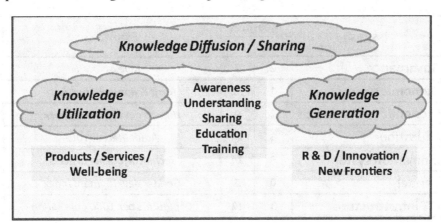

Figure 17. Integration of the knowledge activities

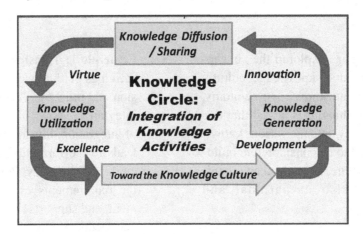

this purpose (Bakry, 2008). Figure 18 illustrates this scope together with the integrated knowledge circle, resulting in a KC-STOPE structure.

- **Principle 4:** Determining a development process for building and sustaining the knowledge culture. The circular, and continuously responsive, Six-Sigma DMAIC process of "define, measure, analyze, improve and control" has been suggested for this purpose. For the implementation of the process, the Six Sigma "team work" approach, with champions, black belts and others can also be used (De Feo & Barnard, 2004; Pyzdek, 2003). Figure 19 considers

the Six Sigma process together with the KC-STOPE structure.

- **Principle 5:** Identification of measures and benchmarks for assessing the state and the development of the knowledge culture. These measures can be based on the STOPE domains, and the KC issues associated with them. KAM issues and indicators can be taken into account (World Bank, n.d.). In addition, future work concerned with such measures for different cases and under different circumstances can be considered.

- **Principle 6:** Making the target framework of generic nature, so that it can be used for

Figure 18. KC-STOPE: basic issues of "knowledge culture"

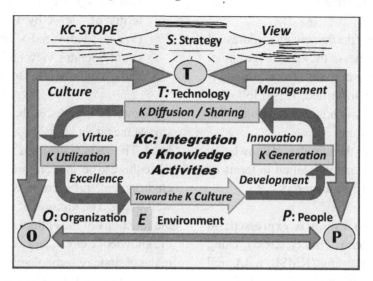

Figure 19. KC-STOPE: with Six Sigma approach for building the "knowledge culture"

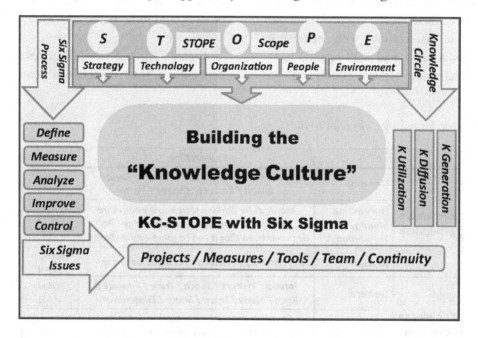

building the positive knowledge culture at an organization level, a country level and of course the global level. For this purpose, the framework should not over-specifies its issues, so that it is not of limited nature, and should not also under-specifies these issues, so that it does not suffer from ambi-guity. The generic nature of the framework would widen its future usability by both: professionals for practical applications, and academics for future investigations and potential extensions.

The "Strategy" Domain

The strategy domain of the framework is addressed here. The main activities of the knowledge circle, which represent the central concern of the knowledge culture, are first identified. This is followed by presenting the vision, mission and objectives of the knowledge culture.

Figure 20 identifies the activities of knowledge generation, diffusion and utilization in terms of different views by different sources.

- **Knowledge generation is expressed:** in basic general terms (Bakry, 2005), using the term of harvesting (KMSL, n.d.), and by associating it with reason (Bakry & Al-Ghamdi, in press);
- **Knowledge diffusion is identified:** also in basic general terms (Bakry & Alfantookh, 2009). in association with acquisition (Wikipedia, n.d.), and with regards to the use of technology (Bakry, 2008); and

- **Knowledge utilization is explained:** in terms of views by Gibran and Drucker (Wiley Media, n.d.), and taking into account Socrates views of considering virtue and excellence (De Burn, 2005).

Figure 21 introduces the vision and the mission of the target knowledge culture at the global level. The vision considers the target benefits of this culture to be: intercultural harmony, protected environment, prosperous economy and human well-being. The mission of the culture considers the functions of the culture to be concerned with the knowledge circle, and associated with the domains of strategy, technology, organization, people and environment. In addition, it emphasizes the development and sustainability of the knowledge culture to be related to the Six-Sigma DMAIC process, and to be based on virtue, wisdom and excellence.

Figure 22 presents the objectives of the knowledge culture. These objectives are concerned with:

Figure 20. Basic knowledge circle activities

Issue		Explanation	Reference
Knowledge generation	General	Research & development: *Discover / Create / Invent / Innovate / Speak / Write*	(Bakry, 2005)
	Harvesting: *Mining / Translation*	*Methods for making tacit knowledge more explicit - getting people's knowledge into documents, so that it can be more easily shared.*	(KMSL, n.d.)
	Reason	*Preparing knowledge for diffusion & use*	(Bakry, in press)
Knowledge diffusion	General	*Inform / Instruct / Teach / Train / Educate / Read / Study / Learn / Share / Edutainment*	(Bakry, 2005)
	Acquisition	*Cognitive processes: perception, learning, communication, association and reasoning.*	(Wikipedia, n.d.)
	Other	*Broadcasting / Publishing / Storing & accessing*	(Bakry, 2008)
Knowledge utilization (use)	Gibran	*A little knowledge that acts is worth more than much knowledge that is idle*	(Wiley Media, n.d.)
	Drucker	*Knowledge for the most part exists only in application*	
	Commitment	*Virtue & excellence*	Socrates (McCall, n.d.)

Figure 21. "Strategy": The proposed vision & mission of the "knowledge culture"

Vision	**Establishing a global knowledge-based culture that enjoys intercultural harmony, protected environment, prosperous economy and human well-being**
Mission	**Meeting the requirements of the vision by integrating and activating the functions of the "knowledge circle: KC", and enhancing it with virtue, wisdom and excellence, considering its interaction with the domains of "strategy, technology, organization, people and environment: STOPE", through following the six sigma approach and its continuous development process of "define, measure, analyze, improve and control: DMAIC".**

Figure 22. The proposed objectives of the "knowledge culture"

Virtues	Excellence	Awareness	Wisdom	Commitment	Will
Virtues & excellence are essential for high moral values and fine achievements.		**Awareness & wisdom are pillars of good management and reliable decision making**		**Commitment & will are source of energy for performance, and continuous development**	
Skills		**Tools**		**Work**	
Communication skills		**Information and Communication Technology: ICT**		**Team work, with collective knowledge**	

virtue and excellence; awareness and wisdom, and commitment and will. They also consider the use of special skills and technology tools; and they emphasize team work.

The "Technology" Domain

The technology domain can be viewed according to two main dimensions:

- The first is concerned with technology, in general; while
- The second is associated with the ICT and the media technology.

With regards to the first dimension, it can be viewed that technology is "knowledge in action". Therefore all types of technology that can generate value and support the vision, mission and objectives of the knowledge culture would be parts of this domain.

Concerning the second dimension, ICT and the media technology are of special importance to the knowledge culture. On the one hand, the production of these technologies would be useful like the production of various other high-tech associated with the first dimension. On the other hand, the wide scale use of these technologies in practically all fields has a special impact on the knowledge culture.

ICT enables information activities of information storage, processing and transfer, to be performed in a manner that enjoys the features of being "faster, cheaper, better, more secure, and with positive difference: FCBSD" (Bakry, 2004). This plays a great role in supporting all knowledge activities of the KC, and consequently in building and sustaining the knowledge culture, as illustrated in Figure 23. In addition, the media technology, supported by ICT, can also play a great role in supporting this culture.

The "Organization" Domain

The organization domain can be viewed according to three dimensions:

- The first is concerned with the knowledge culture at an organization level;
- The second is related to this culture at a country level; while
- The third is concerned with the global or international level.

These three dimensions are of course integrated, where the development of the knowledge culture at any of them would support its development at the others. Of course our main concern is to build and sustain the knowledge culture at the global level which integrates all levels.

At an organization level, the knowledge culture should be viewed through the eyes of the primary and support functions of the organization concerned. This would include, not only the "value chain" of the organization, but also its "value system" that takes its external parties into consideration, as shown in Figure 24 (Bakry, 2004; Porter, 1990). It should be noted here that value should not only be associated with the economic value, but also with virtue and moral values

At a country level, and at the global level, the role of various organizations concerned with knowledge, and associated with knowledge sup-

Figure 23. The use of ICT activates the activities of the KC

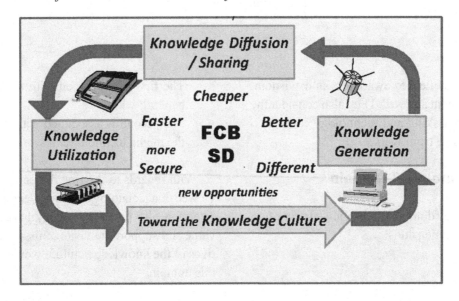

Figure 24. The knowledge culture in an organization: toward further expansion

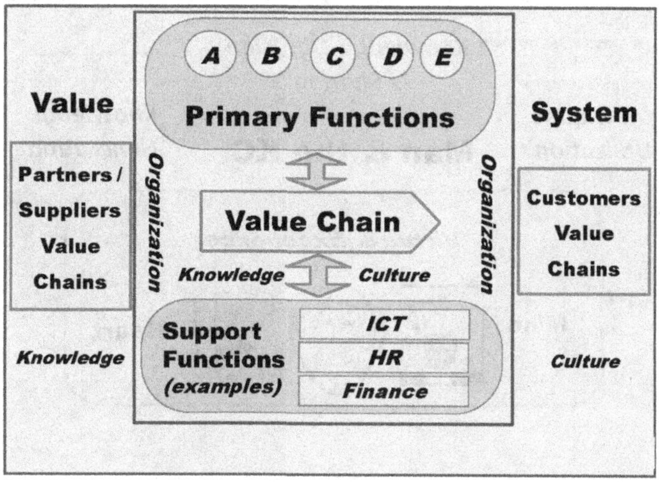

port for different purposes, including intercultural harmony and environment protection, should be emphasized. For example, a recent paper has addressed the national and international organizations concerned with education, and has emphasized their role in the establishment of the knowledge society (Alfantookh & Bakry, in press). Another paper has addressed organizations concerned with intercultural harmony and pluralism, and also emphasized their role in building the knowledge society (Bakry & Al-Ghamdi, in press).

The "People" Domain

Since the subject is knowledge, people would be at its center. In the knowledge culture, not only the minds and intellectualism of people are needed, but also their hearts and enthusiasm (Bakry, 2008). In the above discussion, awareness, virtue and excellence have been emphasized as major knowledge issues. These would be the engine to the sincerity of the heart of people in building the knowledge culture. This view is illustrated in Figure 25.

From building the knowledge culture viewpoint, people can be viewed as associated with three main types:

- Those who may be enthusiastic about participating in building the knowledge culture, and from those the knowledge culture champions and black belts, according to Six-Sigma terms, can be found;
- Those who are intellectually convinced of the objectivity and the noble cause of the knowledge culture, and from those, support and help can be expected; and
- Those who are not interested, or have other views.

It is of course obvious, but useful to be re-emphasized, that while the knowledge culture is needed for people, it also need to be built by people.

The "Environment" Domain

The environment domain represents the conditions surrounding the work needed to build and sustain the knowledge culture. As described above, this work has been associated with the Six-Sigma circular, and responsive to change, process of DMAIC. The conditions surrounding this process would be associated with the following:

Figure 25. Mind "intellectualism" & heart "enthusiasm" in the KC, with "virtue & excellence"

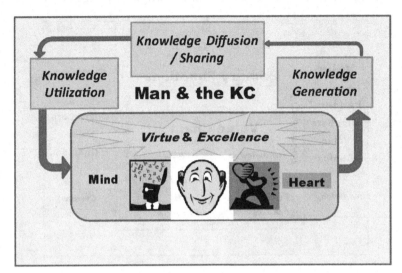

- The conditions associated with the other STOPE domains of: strategy, technology, organization and people;
- The rules and regulations under which the process is executed; and
- The instant management functions performed, including: monitoring, evaluations and directions.

These are illustrated in Figure 26.

CONCLUSION

This paper senses the global need for sound knowledge management, effective knowledge-based economic development, environment protection, intercultural harmony, and human well-being. As

Figure 26. The dimensions of the "environment" domain

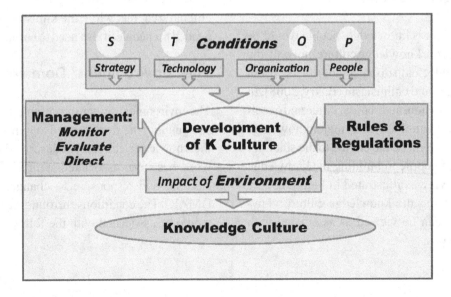

a potential solution to these problems, it advocates the need for building the positive knowledge culture, not only at an organization or a country level, but also at the global level. For this purpose, it reviews the issues involved, and presents its KC-STOPE with Six-Sigma framework as a development tool toward building the target knowledge culture.

The KC considered integrates the main knowledge activities, so that benefits from knowledge can be maximized. Virtue and excellence are recommended to be essential components of knowledge in the KC. In addition, the KC is recommended to be supported by wisdom and fine management. Furthermore, the recommended STOPE structure has the benefit of accommodating the various issues associated with the activities of the KC and their performance, both individually and collectively.

The Six-Sigma principles of identifying projects and assessment measures, and of establishing work teams with champions and black belts, are recommended for the actual development of the knowledge culture. In addition, the Six-Sigma DMAIC process is also recommended to be continuously performed, so that response to change and continuous improvements can be achieved.

Future work using the proposed development tools of KC-STOPE with Six-Sigma framework would be associated with two main integrated directions: further refinement of the framework for different types of situations at different levels; and practical development for specific cases. The paper hopes that organizations and individuals, concerned with knowledge, at different levels, would identify future development projects toward the knowledge culture, and use the KC-STOPE with Six-Sigma framework for this purpose.

REFERENCES

AAE. (1981). *Academic American Encyclopaedia* (*Vol. 5*). Princeton, NJ: Cit-Cz, Arete Publishing Company Inc.

Anderson, A. A. (n.d.). *Building a knowledge culture*. Retrieved September 2008 from www.robbinsgioia.com

Bakry, S. H. (2004, December). Development of e-government: A STOPE view. *International Journal of Network Management, 14*(6), 339–350. doi:10.1002/nem.529

Bakry, S. H. (2005). *Transformation to the Knowledge Society*. Riyadh, Saudi Arabia: King Abdulaziz Public Library.

Bakry, S. H. (2008). *Knowledge Society Eco-System: in watching eyes and hopeful minds*. Riyadh, Saudi Arabia: King Saud University, Knowledge Society Program.

Bakry, S. H., & Alfantookh. (2009). Higher education for the 21st century: reviews and KC-STOPE views. *Evaluation in Higher Education, 3*(2), 87–112.

Bakry, S. H., & Al-Ghamdi, A. (2008, September). *A Framework for the knowledge society ecosystem: a tool for development*. Paper presented at Athens' Knowledge Society Summit.

Bakry, S. H., & Al-Ghamdi, A. (in press). *Cultural pluralism in the context of the knowledge society ecosystem: reviews and views*. Riyadh, Saudi Arabia: King Saud University. *Knowledge Society Program*.

Blackburn, S. (2008). *How are we to think about human nature?* Paper presented at Provost's Lecture Series On being human: 2007-2008, Duke University, Durham, NC.

Brinkly, I. (2006, July). *Defining the knowledge economy*. London, UK: the Work Foundation. Retrieved September 2008 from www.theworkfoundation.com

Britannica. (n.d.). Retrieved October 2008 from www.britannica.com

Brzezinski, Z., (n.d.). *Will American superpower have a second chance* (Tech. Rep.). Duke University, Durham, NC.

De Burn, C. (2005). *ABC of knowledge management*. KMSL: Knowledge Management Specialist Library. Retrieved October 2008 from www.library.nhs.uk

De Feo, J. A., & Barnard, W. W. (2004). *Juran Institute Six Sigma: Breakthrough and Beyond: Quality Performance Breakthrough Methods*. New York: McGrawHill.

European Information Society. (n.d.). Retrieved May 2008 from http://ec.europa.eu/information_society/index_en.htm

Hauschild, S., Licht, T., & Stein, W. (2001). *Creating a knowledge culture*. UK: McKinsey.

Huntington, S. P. (1996). *The Clash of Civilizations and the Remaking of World Order*. New York: Simon & Schuster.

ISO (International Standards Organization). (1987). *Information Processing Vocabulary* (ISO 12382), Geneva, Switzerland.

KMSL (Knowledge Management Specialist Library). (n.d.). *NHS (National Library for Health)*. Retrieved October 2008 from http://www.library.nhs.uk/KnowledgeManagement/

McCall, M. (n.d.). *Leading the good life: lessons from the Greeks*. Paper presented at the Reunion Homecoming, Stanford University, Stanford, CA.

MCEETYA (Ministerial Council on Education Employment Training and Youth Affairs). (n.d.). *An education and training action plan for the information economy: Australia 2005-2007*. Retrieved September 2008 from www.mceetya.edu.au/aboutmc.htm

Porter, M. E. (1990). *The Competitive Advantage of Nations*. New York: The Free Press.

Providers Edge. (2007). *Knowledge management and corporate culture*. Retrieved September 2008 from www.providersedge.com

Pyzdek, T. (2003). *The Six Sigma Handbook*. New York: McGrawHill.

UK-Idea. (n.d.). Retrieved October 2008 from http://uk-idea.co.uk/html/basics.htm

(1961). *Webster's New Collegiate Dictionary*. Springfield, MA: G. & C. Merriam Co. Publishers.

Wikipedia. (n.d.). *Acquisition*. Retrieved September 2008 from http://en.wikipedia.org/wiki/Knowledge_Acquisition_and_Documentation_Structuring

Wikipedia. (n.d.). *Francis Bacon*. Retrieved August 2008 from http://en.wikipedia.org/wiki/Francis_Bacon

Wikipedia. (n.d). *Management*. Retrieved October 2008 from http://en.wikipedia.org/wiki/Management

Wiley Media. (n.d.). *What is knowledge management*. Retrieved June 2008 from http://media.wiley.com/product_data/excerpt/51/18411270/1841127051.pdf

World Bank. (n.d.). *Knowledge Assessment Method (KAM)*. Retrieved May 2008 from http://www.worldbank.org/kam

This work was previously published in the International Journal of Knowledge Society Research, Volume 1, Issue 1, edited by Miltiadis D. Lytras, pp. 46-64, copyright 2010 by IGI Publishing (an imprint of IGI Global).

Chapter 5
Trust Building Process for Global Software Development Teams:
A Review from the Literature

Adrián Hernández-López
Universidad Carlos III de Madrid, Spain

Ángel García-Crespo
Universidad Carlos III de Madrid, Spain

Ricardo Colomo-Palacios
Universidad Carlos III de Madrid, Spain

Pedro Soto-Acosta
University of Murcia, Spain

ABSTRACT

Due to increasing globalization tendencies in organization environment, Software Development is evolving from a single site development to multiple localization team environment. In this new scenario, team building issues must be revisited. In this paper components needed for the construction of the Trust Building Process are proposed in these new Global Software Development Teams. Based in a thoroughly state of the art analysis of trust building in organizations, this new process comes to narrow the gap between dynamics of trust building and intrinsic characteristics of global teams. In this paper, the components for Trust Building Process are justified and presented, with the purpose of a future assembly in further publications, leaving testing of this assembly far behind.

INTRODUCTION

Software Engineering (SE) has evolved steadily since its foundation in the conferences sponsored by NATO Science Committee at the end of the 1960s, and will continue its evolution due to internal improvements and some adaptations brought about external changes (Campbell-Kelly, 2003).

DOI: 10.4018/978-1-4666-1788-9.ch005

One of the most important external changes in today's market is Globalization (Wolf, 2004). This new phenomenon has influenced software evolution and has multiplied the production and demand of software products (Arora & Gambardella, 2004). The SE research has also evolved in order to adopt some Globalization characteristics; as a result, a new field called Global Software Development (GSD) emerged to cover specific aspects of global distributed software development (Gorton

& Motwani, 1996; Karolak, 1998; Herbsleb & Moitra, 2001; Oshri et al., 2007). Simultaneously, many classical software engineering knowledge areas have also evolved following this global trend, i.e., configuration management (Pilatti et al., 2006), requirements engineering (Damian, 2007).

Software development presents three critical dimensions: people, tools and equipment, procedures and tasks, which are held with processes (CMMI Product Team, 2006). These dimensions are present in every software development team, either global or local. Focusing on the people dimension, the relevance of team work has been widely proven (Lister & DeMarco, 1999; Humphrey, 1997; Hilburn & Humphrey, 2002; Sharp et al., 2009, Trigo et al., 2010). Team work in GSD environments presents some aspects that require to be minimized in order to carry a successful software development (Hinds & Bailey, 2003; Poltrock & Engelbeck, 1999): trust (Jarvenpaa et al., 1998), communication (Hinds & Mortensen, 2005), coordination (Cramton, 2001) and unhealthy subgroup dynamics (Armstrong & Cole, 2002). In addition to the critical dimension about people in Software development, trust building has been identified as critical processes for GSD teams' effectiveness (Handy, 1995; Dirks & Ferrin, 2001; Aubert & Kelsey, 2003).

The study of trust in IT environment is a part of studies in human capital; a combination of sociology and politics along with organizational and management science (Coleman, 1990; Putnam, 1993; Huysman & Wulf, 2004), and has a vast applicability to different contexts and levels of analysis, therefore a delimitation of the domain of research is required. Some delimitations made regarding globalization are, for example, team trust (Costa, 2003), GSD team trust (Jarvenpaa et al., 1998); trust in software outsourcing relationships (Oza et al., 2006), trust in alliances (Das & Teng, 1998), trust in GSD teams leadership (Derosa et al., 2004; Barczak et al., 2006), but also presents gaps, i.e., building and maintaining methods in GSD teams trust (Moe & Smite, 2008).

According to Zucker (1986), there are three ways to develop trust in a relationship: characteristics-based trust, institutions-based trust, and process-based trust. Characteristics-based trust represents altruistic sources of social norms and kindness, i.e. membership of professional associations or educational achievements. Institutions-based trust represents the macro altruistic source of social norms, i.e., technical/professional standards. Process-based trust represents the micro altruistic sources of friendship, habituation, i.e. mutual adaptation, learning by doing, routinization.

In this paper, the components for the process-based Trust Building Process (TBP) construction for GSD teams will be presented using a review of trust and trust in GSD research literature as a basis. The work is based on the need pointed out by Moe and Smite (2008) and the dynamic character of trust (Miller, 1992; Lewicki & Bunker, 1996), the different character that trust presents along the growing stages of a business relationship (Shapiro et al., 1992) and the multifaceted character (Lewis & Weigert, 1985). This paper is motivated by the lack of presence of building process of GSD teams trust in research literature as Moe and Smite (2008) pointed out. There are efforts that cover building of trust in virtual teams from a practical standpoint, like Duarte and Snyder (2006), but this valuable model does not cover particularities about software engineering. In a learning environment scenario, Coppola et al. (2004) propose a model for building trust for virtual teams. Thus, TBP covers all software engineering processes and particularities to offer a model in which software development virtual teams can enhance their performance.

This paper has a two-fold purpose, firstly, redefine the construction and maintenance of trust for GSD teams using a formal model of trust definition as a start point, and secondly, define the components required for the process of building trust in GSD teams. The components in the process for trust creation in GSD teams may shed light in this interdisciplinary research area and may establish the start point for an improvement in the creation of trust in these environments.

BACKGROUND

Trust is a four place predicate, someone (trustor) trust something or someone (trustee) in respect to something (competence, intentions), depending on the conditions (Nooteboom, 2002). This predicate extends the conceptualization proposed by Hardin (1993), dividing the context or domain over which trust is conferred into conditions and intentions. From a team-work standpoint, trust refers to which team members trust each others as a team, and is a pillar of effective co-operative behaviors with significant effect on change processes and associated risks (Lewis & Weigert, 1985; Shockley-Zalaback et al., 2000), it also engenders cooperation, reduce conflicts, and increase commitments (Morgan & Hunt, 1994). Despite of being fundamental to the successful formation and growth of any new work team (Shaw, 1997; Senge et al., 1994), its influence in team-work, trust is necessary but not sufficient itself for improving and maintaining team performance (Erdem et al., 2003; Costa et al., 2009). Within a team, each member has a defined role that indicates the capabilities, dispositions, motives and intentions that the he or she has, therefore, the role act as an enabler of trust among team members (Barber, 1983; Meyerson et al., 1996). Trust existence is related to risk existence (Morris & Moberg, 1994), if the trustor does not perceive a probability of loss, there is no room for trust (Yamagishi & Yamagishi, 1994); and interdependence between positive expectations about the intentions and behaviors of the trustee, and willingness to be vulnerable in the relationship with the trustee (Rousseau et al., 1998). From viewpoint level, high-trust groups perform better than low-trust groups (Zand, 1972); while on the other hand, an excess of trust is considered counterproductive for team performance,

for example questioning and creative criticism are keys for team-work improvement (Manz & Neck, 1997). Additionally, team composition may change and new members may be included, in these situations the lack of previous interaction with new members (Kramer, 1999), the difference of individuals' predisposition to trust other people (Gurtman, 1992; Sorrentino et al., 1995), and the team size (Sato, 1988) should be considered as threaten trust factors.

According to Costa (2003), the factors related to trust in teams can be classified into three groups: team composition, work characteristics, and organizational context. In team composition group there are factors such as adequate job skills to perform the allocated tasks, team cohesion, tenure, and preference of working in team contexts. For work characteristics, information required to effectively performing the tasks jointly with the capacity for processing it, functional dependence (Morris & Steers, 1980), and task ambiguity are considered the main factors. According to Rico et al. (2009), task interdependence is a key antecedent for trust development from the beginning to a middle point of the project (Gersick, 1988; Jarvenpaa & Leidner, 1999), which is associated with interaction, communication and information exchange between team members. Finally, organizational context factors group contains management of climate (Costa, 2003) and empowerment of team members.

One specific type of work teams are GSD teams. GSD teams can be characterized as virtual teams according to Martins et al. (2004), which are becoming a standard at work in the current organizational context (Gibson & Cohen, 2003). They have been defined as two or more individuals, who work together with a mutual goal or work assignment, interact from different locations and, therefore, communicate and cooperate by means of information and communication technology (Bell & Kozlowski, 2002). In the case of GSD teams, the goal, work or assignment are related to a software development project. The influence of trust in GSD teams has been treated in research literature from many different standpoints (Jarvenpaa, Knoll, & Leidner, 1998) and distrust has been treated too (Lewicki et al., 1998). Trust is especially vital in GSD teams due to the lack of personal face-to-face interactions. The effects of trust in this kind of teams are, mainly, positive leadership (Kaywort & Leidner, 2002), enthusiasm (Meyerson et al., 1996), predictable communication patterns (Jonassen & Kwon, 2001), and significant social communication (Jarvenpaa & Leidner, 1999). On the other hand, the lack of trust between the team's members may interfere with the effectiveness of individuals contribution to team (Bandow, 2004), reduces the transfer of information between members (Newell & Swan, 2000), moves to individual's goals rather than group's goals (Salas et al., 2005), makes them feel the need to double check work performed by others (Kramer & Tyler, 1996), insecure (Bandow, 2004) and, finally, their productivity and quality decrease to lower levels (Dirks & Ferrin, 2001).

Trust is dynamic (Kanawattanachi & Yoo, 2002; Six, 2003) and is divided in three types: calculus-based, knowledge-based, identification-based (Lewicki & Bunker, 1996). Alternatively, McAllister (1995) defined two types: cognition-based and affect-based, that according to Six (2003), covers the three types defined by Lewicki and Bunker (1996). All of these types depend on the information exchange about the other team members and how it is renewed regularly, so information plays a central role in trust for GSD teams (Holland, 1998). Additionally, the lack of proper technology used by team members to communicate and exchange information may decrease trust (Chubin et al., 2005).

To lose trust is easier than to gain it, consequently trust building should start as soon as the team is created (Janoff-Bulman, 1992; Meyerson et al., 1996) and must be continually monitored. In order to avoid the loss of trust, monitoring has to focus on the communications and feedbacks made on basis (Suchan & Hayzak, 2001; Jarvenpaa

et al., 2004). Team has to minimize the effect of silence and delays due to time differences in communications (Piccoli & Ives, 2003). Also, on the beginning of team building, expectations on team relationships have to be communicated (Bandow, 2004). Trust loss does not mean an increase of distrust in any case. The opposite of trust is not distrust and both can coexist in a relationship; they are separate but linked dimensions (Lewicki et al., 1998). This coexistence is also covered by the existence of a contract in the working distributed relationships; distrust supports the formal contract and addresses expected changes (March & Olsen, 1994), while trust supports the psychological contract and address unexpected changes (Robinson, 1996; Sabherwal, 1999). Therefore, a balance between trust and distrust is required as Lewicki et al. (1998) argued.

GSD teams have to work according to work practices, as any other team. Trust in work starts trusting the method used to produce the assets as mentioned on the 4th level of People-CMM (Curtis et al., 2001). GSD teams have to balance the plan-driven and mutual adjustment in order to set a win-win relationship (Moe & Smite, 2008); also a balance between agility and plan-driven methodologies may be required (Ramesh et al., 2006). Before the apparition of conflicts in team relationship, conflict handling mechanisms have to be established and used when those occur (Jarvenpaa & Leidner, 1999). One of the most frequent GSD team conflict is team performance, but using a constant work monitoring could cause the backside effect, trust losing, so there have to be a balance between structural controls and trust (Gallivan, 2001), eliminating the duplicated controls established because of mistrust on work performance (Kramer & Tyler, 1996). However, monitoring appears to provide team members with information about the actions of other team members, thus enabling actors to coordinate their actions towards team goals, and may also prevent process losses by correcting actions of others (Costa et al., 2009). Besides, the four types of trust should be controlled (Sabherwal, 1999).

Finally, trust has to be maintained, it is not permanent. Rocco (1998) argued that socializing in meetings and team-building activities maintain and strengthen trust in teams. In this direction, the importance of predictable communication patterns for trust maintenance in GSD teams, especially during later stages of a project (Maznevski & Chudoba, 2000; Piccoli & Ives, 2003; Rico et al., 2009). Specifically, face-to-face meetings have been recognized as developers and restorers of trust (Carmel, 1999; Piccoli & Ives, 2003; Bhat et al., 2006). The trust process is basically a learning process (Barber, 1983) in which some risks are taken (Lewis & Weigert, 1985), so learning abilities should be considered (Nooteboom, 2002). Additionally, GSD teams may include people from different cultures, in those cases, familiarization with cultural diversity (Ali-Barbar et al., 2006) and improvement of language skills, written and spoken mostly, are required (Moe & Smite, 2008). All in all, there is not a similar contribution in the current literature. As a first step, trust characteristics and relevant works for building trust in GSD teams have been established (See Appendix 1). Next steps are the definition of components for building it, the calibration of each component, the assembly of components, and finally the calibration of the process. In next section the definition of components is presented, and following steps will be presented in future works.

TRUST BUILDING PROCESS DEFINITION

Once the state of art about the creating trust process has been characterized (see Appendix 1), the TBP can be created. First of all, a formal model of trust has been selected to extend internal processes of trust according to characteristics of trust in GSD teams.

Formal Model of Trust

The selected model is a formal model of trust based on outcomes presented by Bhattacharya et al. (1998). This model allows a calculative evaluation of trust and still psychologically meaningful. The model represents a world of two individuals indicated by index 1 and 2. These individuals can engage in actions (denoted α_1 and α_2), which jointly determine outcomes (denoted x_1 and x_2). The actions (σ_1, σ_2) randomly determine outcomes (x_1, x_2) according to the translation functions (α_1, α_2) which are random. The model also represents a finite set of all possible outcomes of persons (denoted as X_1 and X_2) and a finite set of all possible actions of persons (denoted as A_1 and A_2). The outcomes have consequences on the two parties (denoted μ_1 and μ_2). Additionally, the individuals have conjectures about the actions of the other party, which influence his or her choice of actions, and therefore the outcomes and consequences. The model includes two interaction types of how individuals interact, simultaneous-actions and sequential-actions. In the first one, the two parties act without knowing the specific action of the other party, while in the second one, one of the parties move first and the other party knows for certain which action that party has taken. The second kind is selected for this paper purpose because it fits the sequential interaction characteristic of knowledge work in teams (Mohrman et al., 1995) and the work across time zones factor of GSD that represents a sequential collaborative interaction (Taweel & Brereton, 2006). This type also reflects the existence of start points for interactions. Therefore, the level of trust that person 1 has for person 2, where σ_1^* is person 1's choice of actions, is defined as:

$$T_{1,2} \mid a_1^* = \Pr(\mu_1 > 0 \mid a_1^*) = \sum_{x_1 \in \gamma_1} \Pr(\alpha_1 = x_1 \mid a_1^*)$$
$$= \sum_{x_1 \in \gamma_1} \sum_{a_2 \in A_2} F_1(x_1; a_1^*, a_2) c_1(a_2 \mid a_1^*)$$

On the other hand, the extent to which person 2 trusts person 1 can be shown by:

$$T_{2,1} = \Pr(\mu_2 > 0)$$
$$= \sum_{a_1 \in A_1} \Pr(\mu_2 > 0 \mid a_1)c_2(a_1) = \sum_{x_2 \in \gamma_2} \sum_{a_1 \in A_1} F_2(x_2; a_2^*, a_1)c_2(a_1)$$

and once person 1 has acted, interpersonal trust becomes pure predictability as can be shown by:

$$T_{2,1} = \sum_{x2 \in \gamma_2} F_2(x_2; a_2^*; a_1^*)$$

That represents the evaluation of the uncertainty associated with the relationship between outcomes and actions. It is important to highlight that this definition is focused on single-action outcomes. Finally, it should be considered that this model includes a directional characteristic of

trust (person 1's level of trust in person 2 may be different from person 2's level of trust in person 1).

Formal Model of Trust for GSD Teams

Following the indications of Bhattacharya et al. (1998), characteristics of trust function used for building trust in GSD teams will be a set of possible actions included in the work process, formation of conjectures, relationship between actions and outcomes and feedbacks, along with mechanisms for inducing trust around the term $T_{i,j}$, specifically, affecting the formation and efficiency of conjectures about other's actions, in other words, preparing the GSD team to work in GSD conditions.

GSD team, like any 'normal' software development team, is created after the project kick-off

Figure 1. Schematic structure of model of trust based on outcomes

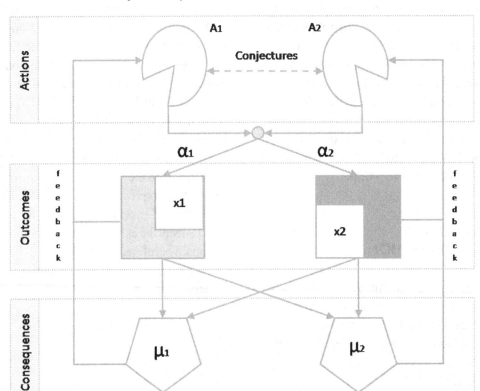

and will go beyond steps and milestones until its finalization (Humphrey, 1999). Before building trust, it should be considered that this task is not free; it takes time, effort and money (Creed & Miles, 1996). It is important to take into account that trust has to be built as soon as a relationship starts in order to achieve high-levels of trust (Jarvenpaa & Leidner, 1999), so team building process represents the best step to begin with the building trust process. According to Holton (2001), standard team building tools can be used to enhance trust in virtual teams. Additionally, during team building process, team members establish their own goals and commitments and the team's ones too, and communicate the expectations (Locke & Latham, 1984; Zand, 1997; Bandow, 2004). With this communications, each team member will know each other's roles, goals and expectations, establishing a start point for mutual learning (Barber, 1983). Moreover, if there is cultural diversity between team members, some familiarization activities are required, mainly focused on language and working culture (Ali-Barbar et al., 2006). At the same time, risk management needs to consider that trust existence is parallel to risk existence (Coleman, 1990; Das & Teng, 1998), therefore, risk management needs to consider situations when trust is at a low level, or even lost, in its management; additionally, high levels of trust have to be considered because these levels may result in a lack of control in processes. Finally, risk management covers with special emphasis failures and risks occurred on past project preventing to occur on current ones, therefore if trust was a failure cause of some past GSD projects then trust has to be managed as a potential risk.

When a team has been created, it chooses the project methodology considering a balance between plan-driven and agile methods (Ramesh et al., 2006; Moe & Smite, 2008). On the one hand, plan-driven methods like Personal Software Process (Humphrey, 1995) or Cleanroom (Prowell et al., 1999), have common characteristics, i.e.

focus on repeatability and predictability, detailed plans, workflows, roles, responsibilities, and work product descriptions, focus on verification and validation, on-going risk management. On the other hand, agile methods, such as Extreme Programming (Beck, 1999) or Scrum (Schwaber & Beedle, 2001), are based on an adaptive and iterative development with frequent inspections and adaptations along with a teamwork culture based on self-organization and accountability. A method for balancing both methods is proposed by Boehm and Turner (2003). This method proposes to take advantage of their strengths and compensate their weaknesses. In order to do that, team members are enhanced to understand their environment and organizational capabilities. Based on this model, GSD teams may reach a balance between agile and plan-driven methods according to GSD characteristics and taking into account risks associated with trust.

Once the team is built, a team socialization process starts under the premise of mutual learning (Barber, 1983). In this process, socialization activities are carried in order to build trust in a gradual and mutual manner (Bhide & Stevenson, 1992). If the project budget allows it and it is not within project restrictions, face-to-face meetings are performed and used as strengtheners and maintainers of trust (Rocco, 2001; Holton, 2001; Costa, 2003; Six, 2003). During this process, activities for improve language skills are performed, if needed, in order to prevent misunderstandings in future communications (Moe & Smite, 2008). These processes are executed if trust evaluation results are not as expected, and secheduled on the project calendar.

During project activities, structural and informal controls may coexist (Lewicki et al., 1998). Taking into account this fact, both informal and structural controls should be established considering that their levels are not related in a strictly inverse manner and that both may coexist (Ring & Van de Ven, 1992; Das & Teng, 1998; Sabherwal,

1999; Lewicki & Bunker, 1996; Bandow, 2004). Inside structural controls, monitoring activities have to be minimized (Jarvenpaa et al., 2004); however, they should be present in order to prevent process losses by correcting others actions (Costa et al., 2009) and established controls should focus on the guarantee of work process and performance (Kramer & Tyler, 1996; Sabherwal, 1999; Moe & Smite, 2008). These controls are also related to risk management as indicators of possible risk occurrence, and the result outputs are inputs for the conflict handling process.

Additionally to the feedbacks defined in Bhattacharya et al. model, that are the base for work process performance, communications are required to maintain trust, and minimize the effect of silence and delays due to time differences (Jarvenpaa et al., 2004; Piccoli & Ives, 2003). Communication should include both, positive and negative, feedbacks in order to eliminate situations such as unknown project state and possible surprises that may lead to distrust (Zand, 1997). Also, team members have to put special interest in communicating the commitments achieved (Jarvenpaa, Knoll, & Leidner, 1998). Communicating commitments achievement increase team cohesion and team culture (Humphrey, 1999).

As long as GSD team interacts, conflicts, confusions, and disagreements emerge as natural parts in the convergence of the creative process of software development (Humphrey, 1999). These includes conflicts related to trust (Jarvenpaa & Leidner, 1999; Six, 2003), that should be taken into account with special care due to the fragility of trust and the easiness to lose it (Janoff-Bulman, 1992; Meyerson et al., 1996). Once a conflict is solved, trust is evaluated and the socialization process is executed. Additionally, conflict handling process related to trust have to be linked with risk management in order to cover the life cycle of trust handling as a risk.

Finally, the evaluation process used in this paper as evaluation for the model presented, may be used as a guide for trust evaluation process. The evaluation of trust has to produce results that indicate that the level of trust that it is supposed to be maintained during team cooperation is actually achieved and maintained. Measurements of trust for this purpose should cover the three levels of trust that exists: calculus-based, knowledge-based identification-based trust (Lewicki & Bunker, 1996). If the expected results are not satisfying, socialization process is executed.

Once the TBP and its parts are defined, the value of trust can be defined for each one of the milestones it has. Before a GSD Team is built, trust can be evaluated with the aid of Battacharya's model, and subsequent evaluation steps are based on their model (Bhattacharya et al., 1998). After the Build GSD Team process, personal actions sets, denoted in model as A_1 and A_2 are reduced because each member will have goals and commitments that will reach with actions covered by the project methodology; this reduced set of actions will be represented by Z_1 and Z_2. Before the team start to work, project methodology is balanced; this balance will be reflected in trust evaluation, reducing the set of actions as noted and has the purpose of establishing a project methodology that fits with GSD and specific project characteristics. In addition, project methodology reduces the random factor of the function that translates actions into outcomes; this is denoted in model as α_1 and α_2 and with project methodology as $\varphi 1$ and $\varphi 2$. Within project methodology, risk management may include trust as a risk factor. This factor can be obtained from trust evaluations done during project life. Next trust evaluations are produced in an iterative cycle of sequential actions that are required to achieve the project success.

The iterative cycle starts with the Team Socialization Process which goal, over building trust, is to fix the conjectures of team members about team and individuals actions required in order for project to succeed; this change is denoted by $k_1(\bullet)$ and $k_2(\bullet)$ and replace $c_1(\bullet)$ and

$c_2(\bullet)$ in Battacharya's model. After the socialization process, team interacts with the purpose of developing software that meets the requirements using a balanced project methodology as base for its actions, commitments and controls. During theses interactions and in addition to feedbacks, communications should help maintaining the set of possible actions that each member has to do. These communications are reflected in the trust evaluation as an external factor that may minimize the level of trust due to the lack of it; this factor will be noted as two variables: $m_{1,2}$ and $m_{2,1}$ that represents the level of communication between members in both directions. As a special communication, commitments are communicated reducing the possible actions of team members; this will be noted with Z'_1 and Z'_2.

During the iterative cycle, conflicts can emerge as a result of an unexpected outcome or action, or a lack of communication or feedback. The Conflict Handling Process has the purpose of handling conflicts from a proactive perspective; that is analyzing consequences (μ_1 and μ_2) and taking actions required to prevent future conflicts like the one handled. After a conflict is handled, trust is evaluated in order to know if the conflict has had an impact in the trust level. If a conflict has lowered the rust level, this could influence the trust level on the next evaluation; that is represented by $t_{2,1}$.

The trust evaluation process is launch after conflict handling process, as mentioned earlier, and at project milestones or at calendar based events. Trust, according to limitations identified in previous steps, can be defined by:

$$T_{2,1} = \sum_{x2 \in \gamma_2} F_2(x_2; z'^*_2; z'^*_1) * (m_{2,1} + t_{2,1})$$

It should be noted that conjectures are not included in this definition. This omission is caused by trust post-action measurements, which disables the possibility of considering conjectures.

TRUST BUILDING PROCESS COMPONENTS

Once trust building has been reformulated, components needed to build trust in GSD teams should be defined. Based on the literature, four components are identified. The first identified component includes face-to-face meetings, team building activities and communicative skills improvement and may be called Prior Social Capital Process. Prior social capital refers to the degree of familiarity among team members either through past work experiences (Goodman & Leyden, 1991) or friendship (Jehn & Shah, 1997); it can be determinant to the trust level at the start of a project: teams with a low prior social capital demonstrate a lower level of initial team trust than teams with high prior social capital (Costa et al., 2009). The second identified component includes familiarization (if there is cultural diversity between team members) (Powell, 1996; Sydow, 1998), communication of expectations, both individual and project expectations, and establishment of goal and commitments for each member and for team (Locke & Latham, 1984; Zand, 1997; Bandow, 2004); this component may be called Build GSD Team Process. Nearly related with this component, the third one is associated with a project methodology using a balance between plan-driven and agile methods (Ramesh et al., 2006; Moe & Smite, 2008), risk management linked with the management of trust during a project (Coleman, 1990; Das & Teng, 1998; Schöbel, 2009), considering trust as a risk factor, and conflict handling if the trust level is threatening project execution (Jarvenpaa & Leidner, 1999; Six, 2003). This third component may be called Project Trust Management Process. The next component is Trust Management Process, which includes evaluation of the trust level between team members and trust climate, feedback between team members (both positive and negative ones) (Zand, 1972; Zand, 1997), communication of commitments (Jarvenpaa,

Figure 2. Proposed Components for the construction of TBP

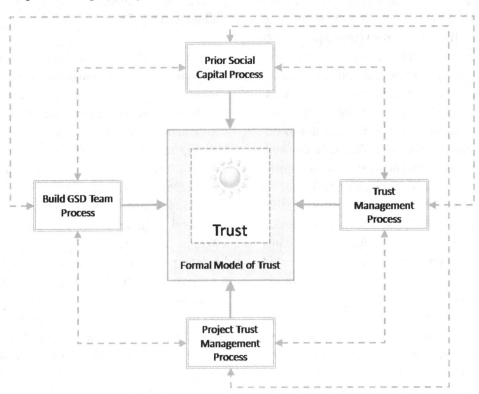

Knoll, & Leidner, 1998), informal controls and structural controls (Ring & Van de Ven, 1992; Das & Teng, 1998; Lewicki et al., 1998; Sabherwal, 1999; Bandow, 2004).

These components may interconnect with each other. For example, in order to improve the trust level and trust climate between members, Trust Management Process may connect with Prior Social Capital Process and Project Trust Management. During the trust evaluation, if measured level of trust is near the one estimated as risk in risk management (Project Trust Management component) then socialization activities are requirement (Prior Social Capital Process). Another example may be produced when team members had not worked together; in this case, Build GSD Team component is connected to Prior Social Capital Process for the members to meet each other and produce a more familiar environment and shared meaning of the project.

The components of the model and its relations, both between them and with Bhattacharya et al. model, are presented on Figure 2. The dot lines represent possible connections between components as described above. The other lines represent feedback relations between components and components of Bhattacharya et al. model; that is: expectations, conjectures, actions, outcomes, feedback, and consequences, and specializations of these components described in the Formal Model of Trust for GSD Teams section.

DISCUSSION

The state of art shows controversy between the relevance of trust and its influence. On the one hand, factors that influence trust and its building in GSD environments are widely recognized in the literature. It should be noted that these factors are also important in more general environments with similar characteristics such as virtual teams and outsourcing relationships too. On the other hand, despite of their recognition and acceptance, the weight of each factor has not been addressed from a practical viewpoint, there are only approaches for its relevance, consequently, the influence of each factor in trust has not been measured as an isolated factor.

The difficulty of trust analysis as a factor that needs to be calculated, and also each factor that influences it, requires using formal models such as the introduced by Battacharya et al. (1998) with the purpose of defining trust in a formal manner instead of textual definitions. This definition has been used as a base for an initial trust definition in GSD environments. It needs to be calibrated with the weight of each factor that is included, namely: communications and conflicts. Additionally, other factors that influence the definition need to be taken into account: i.e., risk management, balance between plan-driven and agile methodologies, team building activities, and socialization activities. In order to formally introduce these factors in the definition, the weight of each one needs to be known. This requirement is similar to calibration performed for dynamic models (Abdel-Hamid & Madnick, 1989) and COCOMO II (Boehm et al., 1995), under the premise that software projects change along its lifecycle, by both its factors and its efforts, and are different in each organization; therefore models require to be calibrated.

CONCLUSION

In the current literature, there are approaches for building trust like in virtual teams, for example, Coppola et al. (2004) presented a case for a learning environment, but there is not a specific one for GSD, neither a more general one for virtual teams. In addition, the lack of studies about the weight of trust and its factors in GSD teams, teams makes impossible the calculation of the trust level

taking into account the influence of each factor, so just a black-box analysis can be carried out. The presented components for building trust in GSD teams may shed light in this opaque process that is widely recognized as important, albeit their construction is not addressed. Moreover, components would create a research base for building trust in GSD teams and add value to common theoretical frameworks about trust (Schiller & Mandiwalla, 2007).

The presented definition of the components for the construction of the process for building trust in GSD, along with the formal model proposed by Battacharya et al. (1998), and its specification to GSD environments, point to a formalization of trust building in GSD environments. These definitions do not cover all the factors, and the weight of each one is not clarified, therefore, it was not possible to perform neither a study of neither each TBP component nor the construction of the process. This represents a promising future work line.

Finally, there are three main future researches that arise from this work. Firstly, the creation of a maturity model for trust specifically in GSD teams is proposed. Once the main key factors have been identified across the literature, the maturity of trust in a team requires to be addressed according characteristics such as its fragility (Meyerson et al., 1996), coexistence with distrust (Lewicki et al., 1998) and cost (Creed & Miles, 1996). Secondly, the identified key components for trust and its building require to be assembled in order to test the influence of each component in the building process. Thirdly, once the components are weighted, a contrast between using the process for building trust and not using it may provide information about the relevance of the process for building trust. Knowledge of the influence of each component before contrasting the process usage becomes relevant due to the independently contrast of each process component as a white-box test. Once all the components are contrasted, a black-box test may be performed.

REFERENCES

Abdel-Hamid, T. K., & Madnick, S. E. (1989). Lessons learned from modeling the dynamics of software development. *Communications of the ACM, 32*(12), 1426–1438. doi:10.1145/76380.76383

Ali-Barbar, M., Verner, J. M., & Nguyen, P. T. (2006). Establishing and maintaining trust in software outsourcing relationships: an empirical investigation. *Journal of Systems and Software, 80*(9), 1438–1449. doi:10.1016/j.jss.2006.10.038

Anderson, A. H., McEwan, R., Bal, J., & Carletta, J. (2007). Virtual team meetings: an analysis of communication and context. *Computers in Human Behavior, 23*(5), 2558–2580. doi:10.1016/j.chb.2007.01.001

Armstrong, D. J., & Cole, P. (2002). Managing distances and differences in geographically distributed work groups. In Hinds, P., & Kiesler, S. (Eds.), *Distributed Work* (pp. 167–186). Cambridge, MA: MIT Press.

Arora, A., & Gambardella, A. (2004). *The Globalization of the Software Industry: Perspectives and Opportunities for Developed and Developing Countries*. Washington, DC: National Bureau of Economic Research.

Aubert, B., & Kelsey, B. (2003). Further understanding of trust and performance in viutal teams. *Small Group Research, 34*(5), 575–619. doi:10.1177/1046496403256011

Bandow, D. (2004). Time to create sound teamwork. *Journal for Quality and Participation, 24*(2), 41–47.

Barber, B. (1983). *The Logic and Limits of Trust*. New Brunswick, NJ: Rutgers University Press.

Barczak, G., McDonough, E., & Athanassiou, N. (2006). So you want to be a global project leader? *Research Technology Management, 49*(3), 28–35.

Beck, K. (1999). *Extreme Programming Explained: Embrace Exchange*. Reading, MA: Addison-Wesley Reading.

Bell, B. S., & Kozlowski, S. W. J. (2002). A typology of virtual teams. *Group & Organization Management, 27*(1), 14–49. doi:10.1177/1059601102027001003

Beranek, P. G., & Martz, B. (2006). Making virtual teams more effective: improving relational links. *Team Performance Management, 11*(6), 200–213. doi:10.1108/13527590510617774

Bhat, J. M., Gupa, M., & Murthy, S. N. (2006). Overcoming requirements engineering challenges: lessons from offshore outsourcing. *IEEE Software, 23*(5), 35–44. doi:10.1109/MS.2006.137

Bhattacharya, R., Devinney, T. M., & Pillutla, M. M. (1998). A Formal Model of Trust Based on Outcomes. *Academy of Management Review, 23*(3), 459–472. doi:10.2307/259289

Bhide, A., & Stevenson, H. (1992). Trust, uncertainty, and profit. *Journal of Socio-Economics, 21*(3), 191–208. doi:10.1016/1053-5357(92)90009-V

Boehm, B., Clark, B., Horowitz, E., Westland, C., Madachy, R., & Selby, R. (1995). Cost models for future software life cycle processes: COCOMO 2.0. *Annals of Software Engineering, 1*(1), 57–94. doi:10.1007/BF02249046

Boehm, B., & Turner, R. (2003). Using risk to balance agile and plan-driven methods. *IEEE computer, 36*(6), 57-66.

Campbell-Kelly, M. (2003). *From airline reservations to Sonic the Hedgehog: a history of software industry*. Cambridge, MA: MIT Press.

Carmel, E. (1999). *Global Software Teams: Collaborating Across Borders and Time Zones*. Upper Saddle River, NJ: Prentice-Hall.

Chubin, D. E., May, G. S., & Babco, E. L. (2005). Diversifying the Engineering Workforce. *The Journal of Communication, 94*(1), 73–86.

CMMI Product Team. (2006). CMMI for Development (Version 1.2) (Tech. Rep. No. CMU/SEI-2006-TR-008). Pittsburgh, PA: Carnegie Mellon University, Software Engineering Institute.

Coleman, J. S. (1990). *Foundations of social theory.* Cambridge, MA: Belknap Press of Harvard University Press.

Coppola, N. W., Hiltz, S. R., & Rotter, N. G. (2004). Building trust in virtual teams. *IEEE Transactions on Professional Communication, 47*(2), 95–104. doi:10.1109/TPC.2004.828203

Costa, A. C. (2003). Understanding the nature and the antecedents of trust within work teams. In Nooteboom, B., & Six, F. (Eds.), *The trust process in Organizations: Empirical Studies of the Determinants and the Process of Trust Development* (pp. 105–124). Cheltenham, UK: Edward Elgar.

Costa, A. C., Bijlsma-Frankema, K., & de Jong, B. (2009). The role of social capital on trust development and dynamics: implications for cooperation, monitoring and team performance. *Social Sciences Information. Information Sur les Sciences Sociales, 48*(2), 199–228. doi:10.1177/0539018409102408

Cramton, C. D. (2001). The mutual knowledge problem and its consequences in geographically dispersed teams. *Organization Science, 12*(3), 346–371. doi:10.1287/orsc.12.3.346.10098

Creed, W. E. D., & Miles, R. E. (1996). Trust in Organizations: A conceptual framework linking organizational forms, managerial philosophies, and the opportunity costs of controls. In Kramer, R. M., & Tyler, T. R. (Eds.), *Trust in Organizations: Frontiers of theory and research* (pp. 16–38). Thousand Oaks, CA: Sage Publications.

Curtis, B., Hefley, W. E., & Miller, S. A. (2001). *People Capability Maturity Model (P-CMM, Version 2.0) (Tech. Rep.).* Pittsburgh, PA: Carnegie Mellon University, Software Engineering Institute.

Damian, D. (2007). Stakeholders in global requirements engineering: lessons learned from practice. *IEEE Software, 24*(2), 21–27. doi:10.1109/MS.2007.55

Das, T. K., & Teng, B. S. (1998). Between trust and control: developing confidence in partner cooperation in alliances. *Academy of Management Review, 23*(3), 491–512. doi:10.2307/259291

DeMarco, T., & Lister, T. (1999). *Peopleware: Productive projects and teams.* New York: Dorset House.

Derosa, D., Hantula, D. A., & D'Arcy, J. (2004). Trust and leadership in virtual teamwork: a media naturalness perspective. *Human Resource Management, 43*(2-3), 219–233. doi:10.1002/hrm.20016

Dirks, K. T., & Ferrin, D. L. (2001). The role of trust in organizational settings. *Organization Science, 12*(4), 450–467. doi:10.1287/orsc.12.4.450.10640

Duarte, D. L., & Snyder, N. T. (2006). *Mastering Virtual Teams* (3rd ed.). San Francisco, CA: Jossey-Bass.

Erdem, F., Ozen, J., & Atsan, N. (2003). The relationship between trust and team performance. *Work Study, 52*(7), 337–340. doi:10.1108/00438020310502633

Gallivan, M. J. (2001). Striking a balance between trust and control in a virtual organization: a content analysis of open source software case studies. *Information Systems Journal, 11*(4,) 277-304.

Gersick, C. J. G. (1988). Time and transition in work teams: toward a new model of group development. *Academy of Management Journal, 31*(1), 9–41. doi:10.2307/256496

Gibson, C. B., & Cohen, S. G. (2003). *Virtual teams that work: Creating conditions for virtual team effectiveness*. New York: Wiley.

Gibson, C. B., & Manuel, J. A. (2003). Building trust: effective muticultural communication processes in virtual teams. In Gibson, C. B., & Cohen, S. (Eds.), *Virtual teams that works: creating conditions for virtual team effectiveness* (pp. 59–86). San Francisco, CA: Jossey-Bass.

Golembiewski, R. T., & McConkie, M. (1975). The centrality of interpersonal trust in group processes. In Cooper, C. L. (Ed.), *Theories of group processes* (pp. 131–185). New York: Wiley.

Goodman, P. S., & Leyden, D. P. (1991). Familiarity and group productivity. *The Journal of Applied Psychology*, *76*(4), 578–586. doi:10.1037/0021-9010.76.4.578

Gorton, I., & Motwani, S. (1996). Issues in co-operative software engineering using globally distributed teams. *Information and Software Technology*, *38*(10), 647–655. doi:10.1016/0950-5849(96)01099-3

Gurtman, M. B. (1992). Trust, distrust, and interpersonal problems: a circumplex analysis. *Journal of Personality and Social Psychology*, *62*, 989–1002. doi:10.1037/0022-3514.62.6.989

Handy, C. (1995). Trust and virtual organizations. *Harvard Business Review*, *73*(3), 40–50.

Hardin, R. (1993). The street-level epistemology of trust. *Politics & Society*, *21*(4), 505–529. doi:10.1177/0032329293021004006

Herbsleb, J. D., & Moitra, D. (2001). Global software development. *IEEE Software*, *18*(2), 16–20. doi:10.1109/52.914732

Hilburn, T. B., & Humphrey, W. S. (2002). Teaching Teamwork. *IEEE Software*, *19*(5), 72–77. doi:10.1109/MS.2002.1032857

Hinds, P. J., & Bailey, D. E. (2003). Out of sight, out of sync: Understanding conflict in distributed teams. *Organization Science*, *14*(6), 615–632. doi:10.1287/orsc.14.6.615.24872

Hinds, P. J., & Mortensen, M. (2005). Understanding conflict in geographically distributed teams: The moderating effects of shared identity, shared context, and spontaneous communication. *Organization Science*, *16*(3), 290–307. doi:10.1287/orsc.1050.0122

Holland, C. P. (1998, April). The importance of trust and business relationships in the formation of virtual organizations. In *Proceedigns of the Organizational Virtualness 2ⁿᵈ*. International VoNet - Workshop.

Holton, J. A. (2001). Building trust and collaboration in a virtual team. *Team Performance Management*, *7*(3-4), 36–47. doi:10.1108/13527590110395621

Humphrey, W. S. (1995). Introducing the personal software process. *Annals of Software Engineering*, *1*(1), 311–325. doi:10.1007/BF02249055

Humphrey, W. S. (1997). *Managing Technical People - Innovation, Teamwork, and the Software Process*. Reading, MA: Addison-Wesley.

Humphrey, W. S. (1999). *Introduction to the team software process*. Reading, MA: Addison-Wesley.

Huysman, M., & Wulf, V. (2004). *Social capital and information technology*. Cambridge, MA: MIT Press.

Janoff-Bulman, R. (1992). *Shattered Assumptions: Towards a new psychology of trauma*. New York: Free Press.

Jarvenpaa, S. L., Knoll, K., & Leidner, D. E. (1998). Is Anybody Out There? The Antecedents of Trust in Global Virtual Teams. *Journal of Management Information Systems*, *14*(4), 29–64.

Jarvenpaa, S. L., & Leidner, D. E. (1999). Communication and trust in global virtual teams. *Organization Science, 10*(6), 791–815. doi:10.1287/orsc.10.6.791

Jarvenpaa, S. L., Shaw, T. R., & Staples, D. S. (2004). Toward contextualized theories of trust: the role of trust in global virtual teams. *Information Systems Research, 15*(3), 250–264. doi:10.1287/isre.1040.0028

Jehn, K. A., & Shah, P. P. (1997). Interpersonal relationships and task performance: an examination of mediating process in friendship and acquaintance groups. *Journal of Personality and Social Psychology, 72*(4), 775–790. doi:10.1037/0022-3514.72.4.775

Jonassen, D. H., & Kwon, H. I. (2001). Communication patterns in computer-mediated vs. face-to-face group problem solving. *Educational Technology Research and Development, 49*(10), 35–52. doi:10.1007/BF02504505

Kanawattanachi, P., & Yoo, Y. (2002). Dynamic nature of trust in virtual teams. *The Journal of Strategic Information Systems, 11*(3-4), 187–213. doi:10.1016/S0963-8687(02)00019-7

Karolak, D. W. (1998). *Global Software Development: Managing Virtual Teams and Environments*. Los Alamitos, CA: Wiley-IEEE Computer Society Pr.

Kaywort, T. R., & Leidner, D. E. (2002). Leadership effectiveness in global virtual teams. *Journal of Management Information Systems, 18*(3), 7–40.

Kramer, R. M. (1999). Trust and Distrust in Organizations: Emerging Perspectives, Enduring Questions. *Annual Review of Psychology, 50*(1), 569–598. doi:10.1146/annurev.psych.50.1.569

Kramer, R. M., & Cook, K. S. (2004). *Trust and Distrust in Organizations: dilemmas and approaches*. New York: Russell Sage Foundation.

Kramer, R. M., & Tyler, T. R. (1996). Whiter trust? In Tyler, T. R., & Kramer, R. M. (Eds.), *Trust in Organizations: Frontiers of Theory and Research* (pp. 1–15). Thousand Oaks, CA: Sage Publications.

Leifer, R., & Mills, P. K. (1996). An information processing approach for deciding upon control strategies and reducing control loss n emerging organizations. *Journal of Management, 22*(1), 113–137. doi:10.1177/014920639602200105

Lewicki, R. J., & Bunker, B. B. (1996). Developing and maintaining trust in work relationships. In Tyler, T. R., & Kramer, R. M. (Eds.), *Trust in Organizations: Frontiers of Theory and Research* (pp. 114–139). Thousand Oaks, CA: Sage Publications.

Lewicki, R. J., McAllister, D. J., & Bies, R. J. (1998). Trust and Distrust: New relationships and realities. *Academy of Management Review, 23*(3), 438–458. doi:10.2307/259288

Lewis, J. D., & Weigert, A. (1985). Trust as a social reality. *Social Forces, 63*(4), 967–985. doi:10.2307/2578601

Locke, E. A., & Latham, G. P. (1984). *Goal-setting: A motivational technique that works*. Englewood Cliffs, NJ: Prentice-Hall.

Manz, C., & Neck, S. (1997). Teamthink: beyond the groupthink syndrome in self-managing work teams. *Team Performance Management, 3*(1), 18–31. doi:10.1108/13527599710171255

March, J. G., & Olsen, J. P. (1994). *Rediscovering institutions: The Organizational Basis of Politics*. New York: Free Press.

Martins, L. L., Gilson, L. L., & Maynard, M. T. (2004). Virtual teams: What do we know and where do we go from here? *Journal of Management, 30*(6), 805–835. doi:10.1016/j.jm.2004.05.002

Maznevski, M. L., & Chudoba, K. M. (2000). Bridging space over time: Global virtual team dynamics and effectiveness. *Organization Science, 11*(5), 473–492. doi:10.1287/orsc.11.5.473.15200

McAllister, D. J. (1995). Affect- and Cognition-Based Trust as Foundations for Interpersonal Cooperation in Organizations. *Academy of Management Journal, 38*(1), 24–59. doi:10.2307/256727

Meyerson, D., Weick, K. E., & Kramer, R. M. (1996). Swift trust and temporary groups. In Tyler, T. R., & Kramer, R. M. (Eds.), *Trust in organizations: Frontiers of theory and research* (pp. 166–195). Thousand Oaks, CA: Sage Publications.

Miller, G. J. (1992). *Managerial Dilemmas: The Political Economy of Hierarchies*. New York: Cambridge University Press.

Moe, N. B., & Smite, D. (2008). Understanding lacking trust in global software teams: A multicase study. *Software Process Improvement and Practice, 13*(3), 217–231. doi:10.1002/spip.378

Mohrman, S. A., Cohen, S. G., & Mohrman, A. M. Jr. (1995). *Designing Team-Based Organizations, New Forms for Knowledge Work*. San Francisco, CA: Jossey-Bass.

Morgan, R. M., & Hunt, S. D. (1994). The commitment-trust theory of relationship marketing. *Journal of Marketing, 58*(3), 20–38. doi:10.2307/1252308

Morris, J. H., & Moberg, D. J. (1994). Work organizations as contexts for trust and betrayal. In Sarbin, T. R., Carney, R. M., & Eoyang, C. (Eds.), *Citizen Espionage: Studies in Trust and Betrayal* (pp. 163–187). Westport, CT: Praeger Publishers/Greenwood Publishing Group.

Morris, J. H., & Steers, R. M. (1980). Structural influences on organizational commitment. *Journal of Vocational Behavior, 17*(1), 50–57. doi:10.1016/0001-8791(80)90014-7

Newell, S., & Swan, J. (2000). Trust and interorganizational networking. *Human Relations, 53*(10), 1287–1328.

Nooteboom, B. (2002). *Trust: Forms, Foundations, Functions, Failures and Figures*. Cheltenham, UK: Edward Elgar.

Oshri, I., Kotlarsky, J., & Willcocks, L. P. (2007). Global Software Development: Exploring socialization in distributed strategic projects. *The Journal of Strategic Information Systems, 16*(1), 25–49. doi:10.1016/j.jsis.2007.01.001

Oza, N. V., Hall, T., Rainer, A., & Grey, S. (2006). Trust in software outsourcing relationships: An empirical investigation of Indian software companies. *Information and Software Technology, 48*(5), 345–354. doi:10.1016/j.infsof.2005.09.011

Piccoli, G., & Ives, B. (2003). Trust and the unintended effects of behavior control in virtual teams. *Management Information Systems Quarterly, 27*(3), 368–395.

Pilatti, L., Audy, J. L. N., & Prikladnicki, R. (2006). Software configuration management over a global software development environment: lessons learned from a case study. In *Proccedings of the 2006 International Workshop on Global Software Development for the Practitioner International Conference on Software Engeneering*, Shanghai, China.

Poltrock, S. E., & Engelbeck, G. (1999). Requirements for a virtual collocation environment. *Information and Software Technology, 41*(6), 331–339. doi:10.1016/S0950-5849(98)00066-4

Powell, W. (1996). Trust-based forms of governance. In Kramer, R. M., & Tyler, T. R. (Eds.), *Trust in Organizations: Frontiers of theory and research* (pp. 51–67). Thousand Oaks, CA: Sage Publications.

Prowell, S. J., Trammell, C. J., Linger, R. C., & Poore, J. H. (1999). *Cleanroom software engineering: technology and process*. Reading, MA: Addison Wesley.

Putnam, R. D. (1993). *Making Democracy Work: Civic Traditions in Modern Italy*. Princeton, NJ: Princeton University Press.

Ramesh, B., Cao, L., Mohan, K., & Xu, P. (2006). Can distributed software development be agile? *Communications of the ACM, 49*(10), 41–46. doi:10.1145/1164394.1164418

Rico, R., & Alcover, C-M., Sanchez-Manzanares, M., & Gil, F. (2009). The joint relationships of communication behaviors and task interdependence on trust building and change in virtual teams. *Social Sciences Information. Information Sur les Sciences Sociales, 48*(2), 229–255. doi:10.1177/0539018409102410

Ring, P. S., & Van de Ven, A. H. (1992). Structuring cooperative relationships between organizations. *Strategic Management Journal, 13*(7), 483–498. doi:10.1002/smj.4250130702

Robinson, S. L. (1996). Trust and breach of the psychological contract. *Administrative Science Quarterly, 41*(4), 574–599. doi:10.2307/2393868

Rocco, E. (1998). Trust breaks down in electronic context but can be repaired by some initial face-to-face contact. In *Proceedings of the SIGCHI conference on Human factors in computing systems*, Los Angeles, CA (pp. 496–502). New York: ACM.

Rousseau, D. M., Sitkin, S. B., Burt, R. S., & Carmerer, C. (1998). Not so different after all: a cross-discipline view of trust. *Academy of Management Review, 23*(3), 393–404.

Sabherwal, R. (1999). The Role of Trust in Outsourced IS Development Projects. *Communications of the ACM, 42*(2), 80–86. doi:10.1145/293411.293485

Salas, E., Sims, D. E., & Burke, C. S. (2005). Is there a "big five" in teamwork? *Small Group Research, 36*(5), 555–599. doi:10.1177/1046496405277134

Sato, K. (1988). Trust and group size in a social dilemma. *The Japanese Psychological Research, 30*(2), 88–93.

Schiller, S. Z., & Mandiwala, M. (2007). Virtual team research: an analysis of theory use and a framework for theory appropriation. *Small Group Research, 38*(1), 12–59. doi:10.1177/1046496406297035

Schöbel, M. (2009). Trust in high-reliability organizations. *Social Sciences Information. Information Sur les Sciences Sociales, 48*(2), 315–333. doi:10.1177/0539018409102416

Schwaber, K., & Beedle, M. (2001). *Agile software development with Scrum*. Upper Saddle River, NJ: Prentice Hall.

Senge, P., Kleiner, A., Roberts, C., Ross, R. B., & Smith, B. J. (1994). *The Fifth Discipline Fieldbook: Strategies and Tools for Building a Learning Organization*. New York: Knopf Doubleday.

Shapiro, D. L., Sheppard, B. H., & Cheraskin, L. (1992). Business on a handshake. *Negotiation Journal, 8*(4), 365–377. doi:10.1111/j.1571-9979.1992.tb00679.x

Sharp, H., Baddoo, N., Beecham, S., Tracy, H., & Robinson, H. (2009). Models of motivation in software engineering. *Information and Software Technology, 51*(1), 219–233. doi:10.1016/j.infsof.2008.05.009

Shaw, R. B. (1997). *Trust in the balance: building successful organizations on results, integrity, and concern*. San Francisco: Jossey-Bass.

Shockley-Zalaback, P., Ellis, K., & Winograd, G. (2000). Organizational trust: what it means, why it matters? *Organization Development Journal, 18*(4), 35–48.

Six, F. (2003). The dynamics of trust and trouble. In Nooteboom, B., & Six, F. (Eds.), *The trust process in organizations* (pp. 196–222). Cheltenham, UK: Edward Elgar.

Sorrentino, R. M., Holmes, J. G., Hanna, S. E., & Sharp, A. (1995). Uncertainty orientation and trust in close relationships: individual differences in cognitive styles. *Journal of Personality and Social Psychology*, *68*(2), 314–327. doi:10.1037/0022-3514.68.2.314

Suchan, J., & Hayzak, G. (2001). The communication characteristics of virtual teams: a case study. *IEEE Transactions on Professional Communication*, *44*(3), 174–186. doi:10.1109/47.946463

Sydow, J. (1998). Understanding the constitution of interorganizational trust. In Lane, C., & Bachmann, F. (Eds.), *Trust within and between organizations* (pp. 31–63). Oxford, UK: Oxford University Press.

Taweel, A., & Brereton, P. (2006). Modeling software development across time zones. *Information and Software Technology*, *48*(1), 1–11. doi:10.1016/j.infsof.2004.02.006

Trigo, A., Varajão, J., Soto-Acosta, P., Molina-Castillo, F. J., & Gonzalvez-Gallego, N. (2010). IT Professionals: An Iberian Snapshot. *International Journal of Human Capital and Information Technology Professionals*, *1*(1), 61–75.

Warkentin, M. E., Sayeed, L., & Hightower, R. (1997). Virtual teams versus face-to-face teams: an exploratory study of web-based conference systems. *Decision Sciences*, *28*(4), 975–996. doi:10.1111/j.1540-5915.1997.tb01338.x

Williams, M. (2001). In whom we trust: group membership as an affective context for trust development. *Academy of Management Review*, *26*(3), 377–396. doi:10.2307/259183

Wolf, M. (2004). *Why Globalization Works*. New Haven, CT: Yale University Press.

Yamagishi, T., & Yamagishi, M. (1994). Trust and commitment in the United States and Japan. *Motivation and Emotion*, *18*(2), 433–465. doi:10.1007/BF02249397

Zand, D. E. (1972). Trust and Managerial Problem Solving. *Administrative Science Quarterly*, *17*(2), 229–239. doi:10.2307/2393957

Zand, D. E. (1997). *The Leadership Triad Knowledge, Trust and Power*. New York: Oxford University Press.

Zucker, L. G. (1986). Production of trust: Institutional sources of economic structure. In Staw, B. W., & Cummings, L. L. (Eds.), *Research in organizational behavior* (pp. 1840–1920). Greenwich, CT: JAI Press.

APPENDIX

Table 1. Characteristics of creation of trust in GSD teams

Trust Characteristic	References
Trust is dynamic.	(Miller, 1992; Lewicki & Bunker, 1996; Kanawattanachi & Yoo, 2002; Six, 2003)
Trust is a fundamental to successful formation and growth of any new work team.	(Shaw, 1997; Senge et al., 1994)
Trust has a strong influence on interpersonal and team behaviour.	(Golembiewski & McConkie, 1975)
Trust process is a mutual learning process.	(Barber, 1983)
Trust tends to develop more naturally in familiar contexts.	(Powell, 1996; Sydow, 1998)
Trust has to be developed in a conscious and gradual manner.	(Bhide & Stevenson, 1992)
Trust development requires interaction, communication and information exchange.	(Warkentin, Sayeed & Hightower, 1997; Williams, 2001; Gibson & Manuel, 2003; Beranek & Martz, 2006).
Trust is associated with risk and risk taking.	(Coleman, 1990; Das & Teng, 1998; Schöbel, 2009)
Trust has to be developed as soon as a relationship starts.	(Jarvenpaa & Leidner, 1999)
Socialize the relationship with meetings and team building activities, in order to maintain and strength trust.	(Rocco, 1998; Costa, 2003; Six, 2003)
Face-to-face meetings develop and repair trust.	(Carmel, 1999; Holton, 2001; Piccoli & Ives, 2003; Bhat et al., 2006)
The participant's expectations have to be communicated to the others. Establish goals and commitments for each team member and for the team as a unit.	(Locke & Latham, 1984; Zand, 1997; Bandow, 2004)
Communications are needed to maintain trust, minimize the effect of silence and delays due to time differences.	(Leifer & Mills, 1996; Jarvenpaa et al., 2004; Piccoli & Ives, 2003)
Effective use of communications on early stages of team's development and projects.	(Senge et al., 1994; Anderson et al., 2007)
Predictable communication patterns are important for trust maintenance in GSD teams, especially during later stages of a project.	(Maznevski & Chudoba, 2000; Piccoli & Ives, 2003, Rico et al., 2009)
Communicate positive and negative feedback.	(Zand, 1972; Zand, 1997)
Feedback on a regular basis to confirm commitments.	(Jarvenpaa, Knoll & Leidner, 1998)
Establish informal controls and structural controls considering that their levels are not related in a strictly inverse manner and that both may coexist.	(Ring & Van de Ven, 1992; Das & Teng, 1998; Lewicki et al., 1998; Sabherwal, 1999; Bandow, 2004)
Balance between plan-driven and agile way.	(Ramesh et al., 2006; Moe & Smite, 2008).
Establish the controls needed for the guarantee of the work process and work performance.	(Kramer & Tyler, 1996; Sabherwal, 1999; Moe & Smite, 2008)
Establish a minimum level of monitoring needed. Replace monitoring by communications and feedback.	(Jarvenpaa et al., 2004; Costa et al., 2009)
Establish mechanism for handling conflicts of trust.	(Jarvenpaa & Leidner, 1999; Six, 2003)
Trust and distrust may coexist.	(Lewicki et al., 1998; Kramer & Cook, 2004; Schöbel, 2009)
Familiarization with cultural diversity growth trust.	(Ali-Barbar et al., 2006)
Language skills influence trust.	(Moe & Smite, 2008)
Building trust is not free; it takes time, effort and money.	(Creed and Miles, 1996)
Proactive style of work favours the increase of trust.	(Warkentin, Sayeed & Hightower, 1997; Beranek & Martz, 2006)

This work was previously published in the International Journal of Knowledge Society Research, Volume 1, Issue 1, edited by Miltiadis D. Lytras, pp. 65-82, copyright 2010 by IGI Publishing (an imprint of IGI Global).

Chapter 6
Using Social Networks in Learning and Teaching in Higher Education:
An Australian Case Study

Craig Deed
La Trobe University, Australia

Anthony Edwards
Liverpool Hope University, UK

ABSTRACT

Realising the potential for web-based communication in learning and teaching is challenging for educators. In this paper, the authors examine students' attitudes toward active learning when using an unrestricted blog in an academic context and whether this can be used to support reflective and critical discussion, leading to knowledge construction. The authors collected data using an online survey with questions on student perceptions of the type, frequency and effectiveness of their strategy. Analysis of the data was conducted using Bloom's revised taxonomy. The research indicates that students must have prior familiarity with this form of communication technology to construct knowledge in an academic context. The authors conclude that effective learning will only emerge if informed by the student experience and perspective.

1. INTRODUCTION

The traditional notion of space and time in which learning and teaching takes place is being redefined partly as a result of the use of new technology (Tinio, 2003). The generation born, regardless of

where, at the turn of the last century has not only accommodated to but influenced the development of information and communication technology (ICT) which surrounds it. They are familiar and entirely at ease with the design of these technologies, unafraid of experimenting with them, and take for granted and get on with doing all that they

DOI: 10.4018/978-1-4666-1788-9.ch006

allow – talking, messaging, playing online games, sharing images, finding things out – often simultaneously. Moreover, most of their learning about it, and how to use it, comes from their peers. ICT and the Social Web especially, is their medium and their metier. It is integral to the world they know and that world is the only one they have known. There is no going back from this position. Indeed, it can only become more firmly established as the norm by subsequent generations, and not just in the UK but worldwide (Melville, para. 91, 2009)

Web 2.0 technologies, sometimes collectively known as the Social Web, are a significant part of this milieu. They have had a dramatic impact on the lifestyles of the current generation of students entering higher education and are already widely incorporated into teaching and learning. Questions have been raised about whether academics are sufficiently adept in their use (Georgina & Olson, 2008; Selwyn, 2007) to be able to provide what some believe could be richer and more pertinent educational experiences as a result of them (Melville, 2009). This paper adds to the growing research in this field by presenting material extrapolated from the student experience in the form a case study.

Blogs provide an environment that potentially supports an active process of thinking and learning (Goh, Dexter, & Murphy, 2007). They allow interactivity and, through the expression and discussion of individual ideas, a forum for learning (Williams & Jacobs, 2004). They can provide a record of conversation and evidence of collaboration that can be used by group members as a basis for thoughtful dialogue (Hanlin-Rowney, et al., 2006) allowing for the development of common meaning to be constructed from multiple perspectives (Marshall, 1995). Blogging is essentially constructivist in nature. It offers students an opportunity to engage in collaborative learning that helps them to solve complex problems in a real life context. It involves negotiation, an appreciation of different perspectives, multiple modes of presentation, nurtures reflectivity and puts the student at the centre of learning. It also readily aligns with Constructionism (a reformulation of constructivism by Papert and colleagues) which, whilst acknowledging the social nature of the learning process, also recognises the importance of person experience in creating knowledge artifacts. (O'Donnell, 2006)

The central question examined in this paper is whether an unrestricted blog space supports reflective and critical discussion leading to the construction of knowledge. An unrestricted blog is one where students are tasked as a group to independently solve a problem through online interaction. It is unrestricted in the sense that there is no input or oversight by a tutor during the discussion process, nor are participants given roles or provided with writing frames. They are responsible for deciding how and when they will interact with each other in the blog environment. In other words, they are required to become active learners, employing a range of behavioural and cognitive strategies to describe, organise and process information through an online discussion. Of course, even within an unrestricted blog there are still definite boundaries determined by the context in which students operate, their understanding of the task, the peer group and teacher expectations. The idea of using an 'unrestricted' space was attractive because it required a learning environment in which students had to personally construct meaning rather than being herded or constrained (Jonassen, Davidson, Collins, Campbell, & Haag, 1995). This method was chosen deliberately because the apparent absence of formalised structure mimics to a certain extent how students engage with messaging and networking sites. This allowed us to explore how experience of virtual personal and group space, with its linguistic shorthand and associations with leisure and informality, supports academic exchange which requires precision and decision making based on evidence. Our role was limited to observing and formally describing how the students made sense of working in this context.

2. METHODOLOGY

A case study approach, as described by Yin (2003), was employed to generate quantitative and qualitative material for analysis. It involved a cohort of approximately two hundred students from La Trobe University in Australia who were in the second semester of their first year of a four year primary teaching degree. They were asked to work in small groups to explore an education related theme using a blog as their principal means of interaction.

While face to face contact was allowed for an initial discussion, to set up the blog and to prepare any final submission, the majority of the work was expected to be done using the blog. Through it students were required to;

1. Discuss and debate
2. Determine cognitive strategies
3. Work together with minimal input from a tutor
4. Make a group decision about any final conclusions or solutions.

No specific training was offered to students on how to engage with each other in this context, particularly in relationship to scholastic discourse, apart the general preparation given in other elements of their studies. This was a intentional to see if they could transfer what they already knew about these behaviours into new virtual territory. We were aware this strategy could threaten the validity of the project if students failed to make the transition from casual to academic users of social networks.

Data collection and analysis was based on the cognitive process dimension based on the revised version of Bloom's taxonomy (Krathwohl, 2002). Constructing knowledge assumes the use of complex, or higher order, cognitive strategies including analysis, evaluation and creativity (Anderson, et al., 2001). This is in line with established practice (Schrire, 2006). Table 1 outlines the categories used for the transcript analysis and to prompt students during the self-reporting of posts.

A second analytical framework was employed to compare transcripts against a four level scale (Table 2) which allowed a judgment made about the overall competence the participants displayed in using blogging to address the task they had been set. The levels are based on the five learning pathway proposed by Kozma and Russel (2005) and are defined in terms of the mastery of behavioural and cognitive skills required for academic blogging.

Competence in this instance has been judged by analysing the participants written postings and the effort made to access, read and respond to group member's posts.

A third component of the data collection process was added in the form of an online (self

Table 1. Categories for transcript analysis and student self-reporting (Based on Bloom's revised taxonomy)

Category	Examples
Remembering	Making a post with a personal opinion or idea
Understanding	Asking clarifying questions
Applying	Extrapolating the group's posts against the task requirements to see if the group is working effectively
Analysing	Finding coherence in the group's posts Distinguish between relevant and irrelevant material, important and less important ideas
Evaluating	Judging the potential effectiveness of an idea Making the decision about which idea is best
Creating	Coming up with alternative ideas or solutions Designing and constructing the final product

Table 2. Novice-mastery levels of academic blogging competence

Level	Behavioural strategies	Cognitive strategies
1 (Novice)	None or minimal postings by any group members	-
2	Group members are familiar with blog environment and post their ideas but do not engage with other group member's postings Group have a strategic orientation in terms of wanting to get task finished quickly and therefore focus on end-product	High number of zero count at each level of Bloom's taxonomy Low level of perceived effectiveness of postings Blog posts do not allow students to engage with complexity of task e.g. SMS text language
3	Group members are familiar with blog environment and post their ideas and engage with other group member's postings Group have a mainly strategic orientation in terms of wanting to get task finished quickly but ensure they focus on the process of knowledge construction	Low number of zero count at each level of Bloom's taxonomy High level of perceived effectiveness of postings Blog posts show attempts at engaging with complexity of task
4 (Mastery)	Group members are familiar with blog environment and make a significant investment in effort to achieve task requirements Group have a deep-learning orientation and expend considerable effort in the process of knowledge construction	Each level of Bloom's taxonomy represented Very high level of perceived effectiveness of postings Blog posts appropriate for complexity of task Reflective posts that show awareness of learning as a result of blog participation

reporting) questionnaire conducted after the task was completed. This was introduced both to collect important contextual data and act as a counterbalance to the two analytical frameworks which rely heavily on interpretation. It focused on:

1. Student familiarity with the technology
    i. If they had regular access to both computer hardware and the internet
    ii. Their familiarity with and frequency of use of Blogs, Wikis, Podcasts, YouTube and other social networks
    iii. When they used email and their familiarity with the protocols associated with this form of communication
2. The types, frequency effectiveness of the post they made when undertaking the blogging task about
    i. Their own ideas
    ii. The ideas of others
    iii. The group's ideas
    iv. The group's progress
    v. The group's achievement
3. The level of engagement with or anxiety about the task in relationship to
    i. How much time they devoted to it
    ii. If it developed them academically of professionally
4. What problems they encountered in;
    i. Making the technology work for them
    ii. Making the group function
    iii. Addressing the task fully
5. What were the perceived advantages of using the blog in relationship to
    i. Providing access to each other
    ii. Helping to develop a common understanding

While student self reports cannot capture the ongoing fine grain detail of cognitive processes and are questionable reliability, they do indicate student propensity for strategy use (Pintrich, 2004).

3. FINDINGS

Students indicated a high level of internet access either at University (98.9%, n = 181) or at their current place of residence (90.6%). They were generally not regular users of Wiki's (10.1% overall gave a positive response to the statement "I use a Wiki regularly", n = 179) and Podcasts (10.6%). They were more regular users of Social Networks (86.6%) or You Tube (62.6%) sites. Students were not regular users of a blog (37.4%), implying that the majority of students were not familiar with the use of blogging as a communication media prior to the task being implemented.

Table 3 shows the transcript analysis and mean scores for student perceptions of the frequency and effectiveness of their use of cognitive strategies. The tables are organised using a revised Bloom's taxonomy, cognitive process dimension.

Notes

a. Based on analysis of a sample of nineteen blog transcripts, the percentage of transcripts with no posts from this category

b. Based on analysis of a sample of nineteen blog transcripts and 582 posts, the percentage of post in this category

c. Mean scores for question 'How frequently did you post ...?' 1 = Never, 2 = Rarely, 3 = Occasionally, 4 = Frequently, 5 = Very Frequently (n = 179)

d. Mean scores for question 'How effective do you think your post was about ...?' 1 = Extremely poor, 2 = Below average, 3 = Average, 4 = Above average, 5 = Excellent (n = 179)

The category of 'evaluating' is used as an example to describe the data. In the context of blogging, evaluating refers to checking the group's ideas against the education literature, critically examining the final product by looking for inconsistencies and fallacies, judging the potential effectiveness of an idea, and making a decision about which idea is best. 15.8% of the transcripts examined had no posts related to this category. Postings that could be categorised as evaluating were only 10.3% of the 582 posts examined. Evaluating was perceived by students as the least frequently used post, and those posts that were made were regarded as being below average to average in terms of their effectiveness. This indicates that students were not adept at making judgments or being critical of other group member's posts. The student perception columns show the most frequently used blogging strategies employed by students were attempting to explain a post in detail and posting a personal opinion or idea. The least frequently used strategies were coming up with alternative ideas, constructing a visual representation to show how the group's ideas might work, and making a criticism of another group member's idea. Students generally regarded the effectiveness of their posts as average to above average. The ranking of the students' perceptions of effectiveness generally follow the same pattern as frequency. For example, the most often used strategies have the highest effectiveness ranking.

Table 3. Summary of transcript analysis and student perceptions

Analytical post category	Transcript analysis		Student perceptions	
	Zero Count [a] (%)	Post Frequency [b] (%)	Post Frequency [c]	Effectiveness [d]
Remembering	10.5	11	3.69	3.85
Understanding	0.5	25.1	3.65	3.74
Applying	63.2	2.9	2.99	3.47
Analysing	5.3	35.6	3.54	3.73
Evaluating	15.8	10.3	2.5	2.79
Creating	5.3	15.1	3.32	3.61

The least frequently used strategy of making a criticism of another group member's idea was the lowest ranked both in terms of frequency of use and effectiveness. It can be seen that the most frequent postings are in the categories that call for less complex cognitive processes. Posting an idea or explanation are less complex processes than making a criticism, connecting ideas to learning theory, or seeking alternative ideas from other sources. The data shows there was a tendency, although not significant, for students to use less complex processes to complete the task requirements.

The Novice/Mastery analysis revealed that of the 19 randomly selected transcripts a significant number were at level 2 or 3. None were in the Novice category and, on the basis of having made posts in each one of the cognitive process dimensions identified in Table 3, twenty per cent were at Mastery level although only one could be truly said to comfortably meet the criteria because of the fulsomeness of all the responses it contained. This was in line with our expectations. This analysis also confirmed that evaluation was the least used and most ineffective strategy employed by participants.

Students were asked an open-ended question about the problems they had experienced when blogging. Four themes were identified during the analysis and the coding shown in Table 4.

Students indicated concerns about continuity and clarity while communicating and discussing ideas in a blog. Although blogging could replicate the interactivity of a face to face discussion, it only became conversational if the group members were able to respond to each other's posts within a reasonable time period. These timing problems meant that the conversation within the blog environment was out of sequence, leading to a perception of confusion. This confusion was also related to the notion that it was difficult to clearly communicate an idea or indeed to explain, analyse, justify and apply the meaning of an idea solely in writing. They perceived it to be an inefficient method of getting an idea across. An academic exchange or indeed any form of conversation in person is a multi sensory experience full of both hidden and explicit meaning. It can facilitate understanding at many different levels very quickly depending on context and the familiarity of the participants with each other. It is however very easy to adopt a voice without colour or timbre when posting in a blog. The very act of writing itself also requires a special kind of forethought and effort. Students remarked that in a blog it

- Requires a lot of fiddling around, rather than just sitting down with your peers and talking about your ideas. (Student 23)
- Is hard to clearly express ideas and understand others (Student 48)
- Is not a real conversation (Student 73)
- Is hard to show excitement and enthusiasm in a blog post (Student 101)
- Means you can't be as honest or open about things (Student 107)

Table 4. Student perceptions of problems when blogging

Themes	% (n = 159)
Writing posts was slower and more confusing than face-to-face communication	19.4
Timing issues; waiting for others to respond to posting, simultaneous multiple postings	17.0
Unable to access or use features of blog, internet problems, uncertainty about how to use blog	15.8
Some group members did not participate, or under-performed	14.5

Note. 33% of students indicated they encountered no problems during this task.

Table 5. Student perceptions of advantages of blogging

Themes	% (n = 171)
Flexibility, allowing contributions to be made at any time and from any space	46.8
A visual process of description, clarification and discussion of ideas over time	21.6
Technology was easy to access and use	18.1
Provided a record of discussion that could act as a reminder of task progress and show contribution of each group member	13.5

Two general solutions were employed to resolve some of the problems encountered when blogging. First, several groups used alternative methods to discuss and complete the task. These included email, phone, Face book and face-to-face meetings. Secondly, some groups used other communication methods, including email and texting, to ensure that all group members were aware when and how the blog was to be used. Students were asked an open-ended question about the advantages they perceived in blogging. Four themes were identified during the analysis and the coding shown in Table 5.

Students perceived that the flexibility of the blog allowed them to communicate and work on the task from any location and at any time. This was particularly important for those who either lived off-campus or who had employment and family issues that limited their availability for face-to-face meetings. Students also appreciated the ease of use of the blog, some describing it as an interesting educational tool. Students perceived the blog as a visual record of the thoughts and discussion of the group. A student could contribute in a thoughtful way, and these ideas could then be considered and discussed by other group members.

The process of writing down ideas also forced students to become more precise in the way they wrote about their ideas.

The following selection of student responses illustrates these points:

- The thoughts of group members are made clear and precise (Student 12)
- A great way to show a conversation and communication between group members (Student 35)
- Blogs force you into writing your ideas and encourages feedback (Student 55)
- Writing our ideas down gave me a much better understanding of learning theories (Student 66)
- You get to think in-depth about your response (Student 91)

Table 6 shows five statements about student effort, interest, involvement and perceptions of challenge and anxiety associated with the blogging task. In terms of rank order, students perceived that the task was interesting and required a significant investment of time and effort, although it did not induce a high level of anxiety.

Table 6. Mean scores for question 'Indicate your level of agreement with each statement'

Statement	Mean score (n = 179)
I invested significant time and effort in this task	4.26
This task was interesting	4.23
Overall I was deeply involved in learning	4.16
This task was challenging	3.89
This task made me anxious	2.59

4. DISCUSSION

Blogs allow students, at any time and from almost anywhere, to think about, post, reflect, analyse and evaluate ideas (Mimirinis & Bhattacharya, 2007; Wu, 2003). In this case, these advantages were appreciated by the students. However the central question of whether the full potential of using a blog in this instance was achieved or not is less clear. While the students found the task interesting and invested both individual and collective effort in it, their use of sophisticated tools including evaluating and creating to critically construct knowledge were less obvious. There are a number of challenges that this study has exposed in relationship to elevating the application of the technology in order to facilitate high order thinking. It has become apparent that the transfer of skills and knowledge of other social networks, the perceived value of engaging in this form of exchange, the challenge of collective analysis, risk to the individual and presumption about prior use all have a bearing on how effective blogging can be in this context.

It was evident that in this study some found it challenging to differentiate between how they functioned in social networks and how to behave in the new virtual territory defined by the blog. Some posts were characterised by the use of what has been referred to SMS or Textese (also known as txtese, chatspeak, txt, textspeak, lol, txtspk, txtk, texting language, or txt talk) in which a form of linguistic shorthand is common. Social and work issues were also deeply intertwined. This casualness at first glance appears to at odds with academic conventions. The straightforward answer to address this issue may be that students need be trained to make the transition from social to scholastic engagement. However this might not be easy to do. The all pervasive nature of the technology has so ingrained these practices into this generation that no reconciliation is possible. They could desert it in higher education unless the apparent mismatch between social and academic use can be addressed. Academics themselves may well be required to make a radical shift in what is perceived as meaningful dialogue and exchange, and perhaps use of language, in order to accommodate student experience of social networks. These networks after all have been and continue to be used very effectively to create communities with a strong common identity which can operate outside the normal boundaries of time and place. They allow contributors to exchange information and test ideas readily. They are however places in which instant answers that are not subject to exacting intellectual or legal scrutiny are sought. Melville (2009) predicts that some from of rapprochement will be essential between social networks used in a rigidly academic way and those employed more to facilitate conversations between virtual friends if they are to have credibility amongst students.

The physical proximity of students to each other could have also undermined our efforts to get them to engage in virtual academic exchange. If they had been in locations which were remote from each other then the number of alternative solutions they could employ to enrich (or in some cases circumvent) the blogging experience may be severely reduced. They could not readily meet in person (as some did) to tease out meaning or develop understanding or even help with how well group members related to each other as colleagues working on a joint academic pursuit. In a sense this gets to the heart of one of the main issues. The benefits of using this form of communication to stay in touch, to arrange meetings or to discuss the latest news, whatever it might be, are highly apparent to what could be termed as the first truly digital generation, but less so in an academic context unless genuine need can be demonstrated. The connection between Web 2.0 for social purposes and helping to develop learning in higher education '...is as yet only dimly perceived by students, and only a little more clearly by staff' (Melville, 2009) There is also a certain inertia that results from traditional notions of what it is like to be at University. The view that personal contact through the tutorial system and meetings with peers are what characterises the experience may be deeply ingrained and difficult to overcome. This may or may not be the reality of modern higher education but this notion is very powerful because it is based largely on what students have been told by others. It also reflects how they were taught in the later stages of their school career.

The students tended to post personal opinions, but struggled to collaboratively analyse or evaluate these opinions in order to construct knowledge. This is consistent with Thomas' (2002) finding that it is difficult to have a written online conversation that is both academic and interactive. Thomas argues that while there may be attempts at online discussion, there is frequently no coherent structure between the posts, and a lack of real collaborative knowledge construction. There are several possible explanations for this variation in cognitive investment which could be associated with the very nature of posting itself and how easily students accommodate to using this virtual environment.

The blogging task reported here involved students working in groups to define or examine a concepts central to their understanding of education. The perception of social risk or uncertainly attached to an essentially constructivist task of this nature could hamper the process of interaction (Hills, 2007). Students may behave in a self-conscious way to avoid embarrassment, exclusion or making a negative impression (Hills, 2007). They may be tempted to perpetuate misconceptions and errors rather than challenging each others ideas (Hancock, 2004; Lizzio & Wilson, 2006). They may feel overwhelmed when using a process where they are required to make autonomous choices about effort or lack the knowledge and skills for effective participation (Ploetzner, Bodemer, & Neudert, 2008). They may also resist becoming deeply involved in collaboratively building knowledge and prefer to remain on the boundary and only exert minimal effort (Lizzio & Wilson, 2006) thus reducing the effectiveness of the process

There is perhaps an assumption on behalf of academics that because students are familiar with online communication they can also use these technologies for academic purposes. For blogs to achieve their potential in terms of the critical construction of knowledge, educators need to explicitly structure the learning experience to match the student context including the appropriate use of the technology; and prepare students to engage in and manage and interpret multiple online conversations.

5. CONCLUSION

The opportunities to test the appropriateness of utilising this form of communication in a real life context offer the researcher much scope to experiment. However, reliability and over generalisation are two issues that the cautious academic must be mindful of when employing a case study. Our approach to this undertaking was fashioned with these two challenges in mind. There are other limitations to this study that also need to be taken into account. The analytical tools were a useful sensitising construct that allowed the basic categorisation of student strategy use in the blog environment. However, we remained mindful throughout of the restrictions of any taxonomy (Chan, Tsui, Chan, & Hong, 2002). For example, this framework is underpinned by the notion that there is an effective and relatively concrete process that can be used as a basis for examining blogging transcripts for levels of behavioural and cognitive strategy use in order to construct knowledge. It focuses on the students' actions rather than any deep analysis of the level of thinking apparent in the outcome. There is also a tendency to consider the act of making a post a relatively artificial process. By artificial we mean a form of exchange that can be technically analysed without consideration of the multi-dimensionality, immediacy, subtly and nuances of face to face communication. However, despite these cautions we believe that it is possible to extract some general principles from this work that it is possible to apply to many different situations in higher education where social networks are to be used in learning and teaching.

Publishing space, including blogs, have great potential to utilise and further develop communication skills, creativity, leadership, technological proficiency and provide opportunities for multiple forms of active learning, collaboration and partnership providing they are used appropriately (Garrison & Vaughan, 2008). We contend that effective e-learning will emerge from considered pedagogical design, informed by the student experience and perspective. It is clear that context and the point of application are equally important as the desired learning outcome.

Learning is complex and dynamic and 'imagining technology' as Melville (2009) refers to it, not only presents users with conceptual and logistical challenges, it requires them to redefine their understanding of time and space in relationship to their work. We agree with Salmon (2005) and Westbrook (2006) that truly meaningful learning will only result in this context if a considered and appropriate pedagogical design that addresses some of the difficulties identified in our exploration of the subject is adopted. Protocols need to be established which guide users when and how to engage with the technology, particularly in relationship to the frequency and nature of their contributions. Addressing the vexed issue of writing which represents evolving thoughts at both an individual and collective level is also paramount. There is already an inbuilt conflict between the language used in other social networks and the language required in this context to develop understanding and refine thinking. Clearly participants in this type of activity need demonstration, persuasion and room to experiment before being

launched into the main event. Instructional design can influence the level of student engagement. To ignore these factors invites failure.

While higher education teachers have readily embraced Web 2.0 technologies it is students who have to make sense of and construct a means of using the technology effectively. Perhaps in our rush to use them we have made too many assumptions about their attitudes and experiences. This work provides encouragement to continue using these technologies but raises enough issues for us to pause for thought. Melville (p. 7, 2009) suggests that tacking this means ensuring that students possess the skills and understanding to search, authenticate and critically evaluate material from the range of appropriate sources, and attribute it as necessary. Allied to this is providing for the development of web-awareness so that students operate as informed users of web-based services, able to avoid unintended consequences. For staff, the requirement is to maintain the currency of skills in the face of the development of web-based information sources

There are undoubtedly a number of different approaches and strategies to achieve the desired outcome in online contexts, some of which can legitimately developed by the students themselves. In this case students were able to exert some control over how the task was completed because the environment in which they're working was not heavily regulated. While this offered the opportunity to be creative the lack of structure can also be problematic when combined with a poor motivation and/or experience. Educators need to provide support and scaffolding during the early phases of the task to overcome this issue. They must also be mindful that support can also stifle intellectual growth because if it is too structured and fails to recognise the contribution an individual makes to his or her own development. Students must be allowed to explore different strategies and construct their own meaning. They must have scope for making choices. While it is important to provide students with a framework to support the development of knowledge processes there is a need to balance providing structure with a working space for students to explore emerging meanings without explicit teacher direction.

Our research provides a reference point for further investigations into student's use of online media in higher education. It would be useful to apply more all encompassing frameworks to transcript analysis that would help to map changes in understanding, identify where new knowledge had been created and the point at which users had started on this metaphorical journey. It may be that larger scale trials could involve some form of simple algorism as well as more qualitative analysis of content.

The certainty is that that Social Web in all its formats is destined to become ubiquitous and universally applied as the technology that hosts it becomes cheaper, faster and takes up far less space. The option to ignore it is not open to those involved in learning and teaching at any level, particularly in higher education, if it is to evolve to successfully meet the challenges of a new century.

REFERENCES

Anderson, L. W., Krathwohl, D. R., Airasian, P. W., Cruikshank, K. A., Mayer, R. E., & Pintrich, P. R. (2001). *A taxonomy for learning, teaching and assessing: A revision of Bloom's taxonomy of educational objectives*. New York: Longman.

Chan, C. C., Tsui, M. S., Chan, M. Y. C., & Hong, J. H. (2002). Applying the Structure of Observed Learning Outcomes (SOLO) Taxonomy on student's learning outcomes: An empirical study. *Assessment & Evaluation in Higher Education, 27*(6), 511–527. doi:10.1080/0260293022000020282

Garrison, D. R., & Vaughan, N. D. (2008). *Blended Learning in Higher Education: Framework, Principles, and Guidelines*. San Francisco: Jossey-Bass.

Georgina, D. A., & Olson, M. R. (2008). Integration of technology in higher education: A review of faculty self-perceptions. *The Internet and Higher Education, 11*, 1–8. doi:10.1016/j.iheduc.2007.11.002

Goh, W. W., Dexter, B., & Murphy, W. D. (2007, March 14-16). *Promoting critical thinking with computer mediated communication technology*. Paper presented at the Sixth IASTED International Conference Web-Based Education, Chamonix, France.

Hancock, D. (2004). Cooperative learning and peer orientation effects on motivation and achievement. *The Journal of Educational Research, 97*(3), 159–166. doi:10.3200/JOER.97.3.159-168

Hanlin-Rowney, A., Kuntzelman, K., Lara, M. E. A., Quinn, D., Roffman, K., & Nichols, T. T. (2006). Collaborative inquiry as a framework for exploring transformative learning online. *Journal of Transformative Education, 4*(4), 320–334. doi:10.1177/1541344606294820

Hills, T. (2007). Is constructivism risky? Social anxiety, classroom participation, competitive game play and constructivist preferences in teacher development. *Teacher Development, 11*(3), 335–353. doi:10.1080/13664530701644615

Jonassen, D., Davidson, M., Collins, M., Campbell, J., & Haag, B. B. (1995). Constructivism and computer-mediated communication in distance education. *American Journal of Distance Education, 9*(2). doi:10.1080/08923649509526885

Kozma, R., & Russel, J. (2005). Modelling students becoming chemists: Developing representational competence. In Gilbert, J. K. (Ed.), *Models and modelling in science education: Visualization in science education*. Dordrecht, The Netherlands: Springer.

Krathwohl, D. R. (2002). A revision of Bloom's taxonomy: An overview. *Theory into Practice, 41*(4), 212–218. doi:10.1207/s15430421tip4104_2

Lizzio, A., & Wilson, K. (2006). Enhancing the effectiveness of self-managed learning groups: Understanding students' choices and concerns. *Studies in Higher Education, 31*(6), 689–703. doi:10.1080/03075070601004309

Marshall, S. P. (1995). *Schemas in Problem Solving*. Cambridge, UK: Cambridge University Press. doi:10.1017/CBO9780511527890

Melville, D. (2009). *Report of an independent Committee of Inquiry into the impact on higher education of students' widespread use of Web 2.0 technologies*. London: Joint Information Systems Committee (JISC)

Mimirinis, M., & Bhattacharya, M. (2007). Design of virtual learning environments for deep learning. *Journal of Interactive Learning Research, 18*(1), 55–64.

O'Donnell, M. (2006). Blogging as Pedagogic Practice: Artefact and Ecology. *Asia Pacific Media Educator, December*(17).

Pintrich, P. R. (2004). A conceptual framework for assessing motivation and self-regulated learning in college students. *Educational Psychology Review, 16*(4), 385–407.

Ploetzner, R., Bodemer, D., & Neudert, S. (2008). Successful and Less Sucessful Use of Dynamic Visualisations in Instructional Texts. In Lowe, R., & Schnotz, W. (Eds.), *Learning with Animation: Research Implications for Design* (pp. 71–91). New York: Cambridge University Press.

Salmon, G. (2005). Flying not flapping: A strategic framework for e-learning and pedagogical innovation in higher education institutions. *ALT-J Research in Learning Technology, 13*(3), 201–218.

Schrire, S. (2006). Knowledge building in asynchronous learning groups: Going beyond quantitative analysis. *Computers & Education, 46*(1), 49–70. doi:10.1016/j.compedu.2005.04.006

Wang, K. T., Huang, Y.-M., Jeng, Y.-L., & Wang, T.-I. (2008). A blog-based dynamic learning map. *Computers & Education, 51*, 262–278. doi:10.1016/j.compedu.2007.06.005

Westbrook, V. (2006). The virtual learning future. *Teaching in Higher Education, 11*(4), 471–482. doi:10.1080/13562510600874276

Williams, J. B., & Jacobs, J. (2004). Exploring the use of blogs as learning spaces in the higher education sector. *Australasian Journal of Educational Technology, 20*(2), 232–247.

Wu, A. (2003). Supporting electronic discourse: Principles of design from a social constructivist perspective. *Journal of Interactive Learning Research, 14*(2), 167–184.

Yin, R. K. (2003). *Case study research: Design and methods* (3rd ed.). Thousand Oaks, CA: Sage.

This work was previously published in the International Journal of Knowledge Society Research, Volume 1, Issue 2, edited by Miltiadis D. Lytras, pp. 1-12, copyright 2010 by IGI Publishing (an imprint of IGI Global).

Chapter 7
Quality of Project Management Education and Training Programmes

Constanta-Nicoleta Bodea
The Academy of Economic Studies, Romania

Maria Dascalu
The Academy of Economic Studies, Romania

Melania Coman
The Academy of Economic Studies, Romania

ABSTRACT

This paper examines the factors that influence the quality of training and education on project management. The authors present the results of two questionnaire-based surveys. The goal of the first survey was to find what factors influence the quality of project management education, according to the perspective of trainers, professors, and training providers. The respondents included Chinese and European academics and professionals, such as project managers, software developers, financial managers and professors. The respondents were not only involved in project management training but also served as team members or team managers, thus ensuring a balanced overview of theoretical and practical issues. The goal of the second survey was to explore the definition "quality" to trainees and students. Although there were small differences of perspective, both trainers and trainees have the same approach toward a qualitative project management education.

1. INTRODUCTION

Project management has become widely known, as the main form of organization in knowledge economy (International Project Management Association, 2006). Project management isn't about quick fixes: the key to success here, as everywhere

else, lies in preparation. A good project manager knows the project management principles, methods and techniques and applies them, always looking for the best outcome of a situation. Some project managers don't need too much training to do that, but others, on the other hand, need tons of training and they never really quite figure out what's the best solution to be applied.

DOI: 10.4018/978-1-4666-1788-9.ch007

Whatever the scope of the work, training and education is a key element to survive in knowledge society, as it facilitates the competences development in professional activities (Demirel, 2009), (Castells & Pekka, 2002; Markkula, 2006; Teekaput & Waiwanijchakij, 2006). Nevertheless, practice has its place in sharpening the work skills, especially in project management (Turner & Simister, 2004). Project managers make decisions which affect not only a project, but a carefully built network of contacts and a carefully promoted image (Gareis, 2007). Consequently, the following questions arise: "Where does the quality of project management education and training lie?", "How can we define project management training and education quality?", "Where should we establish boundaries so as to achieve effective and efficient and fit-for-purpose project management training?", "What should we teach, in order to get a ready-to-go project manager?", "Should the project management education be addressed as input based – provider, trainer, curriculum, or also output based – trainee, beneficiary?". The authors of current paper aimed at finding out the answers to these questions, from two different perspectives: from the trainer and from the trainee point of view. The trainers are professors, project managers invited to take part in training courses or trainings' organizers. The trainees are students who are enrolled in a master programme of project management. The research method used for finding out what quality in project management education is was a questionnaire-based survey.

2. TRAINING THE PROJECT MANAGER

In project management, a training session could aim at developing or improving one of the project manager competences (International Project Management Association, 2006). By developing, we mean that the competence is at its basics or is not there at all. By improving, we mean that, from the documentation received from a candidate, we can assume that some competences exist and we can build on those. A training session could refer to one topic or more, thus having an impact on duration of the training (Kanellopoulos et al., 2006), (Lytras et al., 2008). Although it may seem that we are only approaching technical competences, a balanced percentage of theoretical and practical training, backed up by modern teaching methods (Garcia et al., 2003), could lead to the improvement of behavioral competences, as well.

Having established what training means in project management, the paper will further focus on finding out what makes a project management training to be qualitative.

3. THE QUALITY OF EDUCATION AND TRAINING ON PROJECT MANAGEMENT: RESEARCH METHODOLOGY

The instruments used in current research were two questionnaires. The methodology for the development of the questionnaires was based on the following aims:

1. Development of a questionnaire for assessing the general and specific traits of quality in training on project management;
2. Focusing on the practical aspects of organization and logistics, including technical platform for online education;
3. Stressing on candidate accession / enrolment in a training course / programme;
4. Finding out the needs for the inputs and resources ensured by the training providers;
5. Finding out what the trainers' profiles should be;
6. Discovering the minimum requirements of curriculum;
7. Highlighting what the expectations for the training result are;

The main research question is related to what determines the quality of project management training/ programme. The authors argue on determining a good combination of traditional and modern teaching for the project managers-to-be, who do not have the physical time to attend project management traditional courses / programmes. This combination should be practical enough to offer them a ready-to-go information and also will provide them with a certification or a diploma, which is accepted and valuable by their co-workers and clients.

Both questionnaires have, as units of analysis, the perspective towards quality of project management education, but the subjects are different. For the first questionnaire, the trainers are the questioned subjects. For the second questionnaire, our focus is on the trainees.

The questionnaire addressed to professors, trainers and training providers is structured into two main parts, split into questions about general aspects of education and training and particular questions related to project management education and training. The questionnaire was given to 96 professionals engaged in providing project management education.

The respondents' distribution for the first questionnaire was analyzed from two points of view (see Figure 1):

- *By nationality:* 81% of the responses came from China; the rest were received from Romania, from a number of professionals of different EU nationalities;
- *By profession:* the percentage of project managers who answered the questions is rather low – 8%; the most of the respondents are professors, who are involved in both training on project management, but also as team members or team managers in projects, thus ensuring a balanced overview of both theory and practical issues;

The questionnaire addressed to students is structured into four main parts: questions regarding organization aspects and technical platform, trainee's needs (motivation to participate into an online education programme), trainee's commitment towards the project management educational programme and last, but not least, syllabus and expectations from training providers. The questionnaire was given to 181 students enrolled in a two-year master programme of project management, of which 52 in their 1st year of study and 129 in their last year. The project management master (MIP) takes place in a well-known Romanian university.

The respondents' distribution for the second questionnaire was analyzed from two points of view (see Figure 2):

Figure 1. The respondents' distribution for questionnaire addressed to professors, trainers and training providers

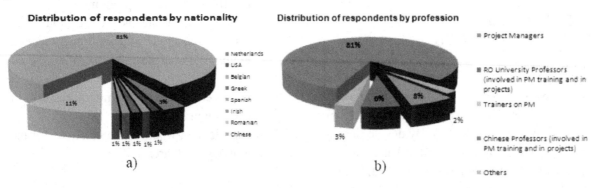

a)   b)

Figure 2. The respondents' distribution for questionnaire addressed to professors, trainers and training providers

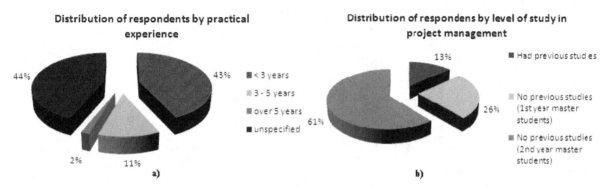

- *By practical experience in project management:* 43% were juniors in project management activities (less than 3 years of experience), 21% had between 3 and 5 years of experience, just 2% of them were seniors (over 5 years of working in project management) and the rest of respondents didn't specify their level of expertise;

- *By experience in project management educational programmes (whether they attended or not other project management courses):* just 13% of them were engaged in previous forms of project management education (occasional workshops, trainings at work, shorter project management courses organized by well-known institutions), but 61% of them were already in the second year of project management master;

4. RESEARCH RESULTS AND ANALYSIS: QUALITY OF PROJECT MANAGEMENT EDUCATION FROM TRAINERS' POINT OF VIEW

The survey made on professors, trainers and training providers revealed important aspects to the quality of project management education. As shown in Figure 3, the selected location for training

is considered important by most respondents – 41 out of the 96. Only 11 say that location is very important, same goes for two who cannot decide. 13 people stated location is not very important, while 27 consider location is neither important, nor un-important. 55 respondents opt for the higher percentage of face-to-face, traditional training. At the extreme, only 14 people consider that open and distance learning (ODL) is more useful than traditional methods (see Figure 4). 24 think an equal split of modern and traditional is useful. Most respondents opt for the network video (52%) and e-platform – 28%. 7% recommend case studies, while only 1% opts for e-tutoring, during and after course delivery (see Figure 5). The majority of respondents opt for the outmost importance of accreditation of training providers (national or international). At the other end, 6 respondents do not care at all about this issue.

National accreditation is seen as very important by 43 respondents, when compared to international – only 41 (Figure 6a). The same trend as above is kept when talking about trainers' accreditation (Figure 6b). The analysis of the questionnaire shows that the importance of accreditation is mostly stressed for the institution, not for the person, but those who opted for 1 in the above questions, also opted for 1 or 2, in the trainers' answers, as well.

Figure 3. The distribution of answers regarding training location

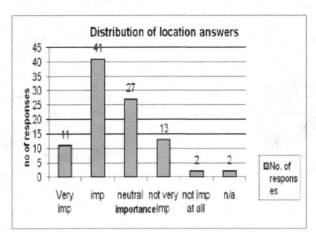

Figure 4. Distribution of answers regarding utility of the ODL methods vs. traditional methods

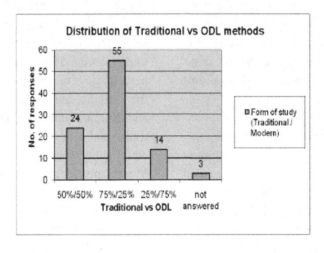

With regard to the characteristics of trainers (see Figure 7), 1 person stated language skills, as being important, while 3 others stated pedagogical skills. 81 interviewees state that it is important for trainers to speak from experience, while 70 consider that the technical expertise is also required. 73 say that it would be important that the trainer is certified as Project Manager. PhD is considered important by 28 people.

Candidate selection is very important for 18 people, and important for 45. This leads to a majority of 63 respondents who think that selection of candidates is an aspect of quality assurance. 25 are neutral about this aspect, while 5 feel that

candidate selection is not important for training quality. Most of the respondents declare themselves in favor of candidate selection. Most important documents required in the candidate file are: CV (very important for 66 respondents), Diplomas, and Employer's references (very important for 39 of them, but completely unimportant for 48), as well as an Application Form.

After our respondents' opinion, the form of addressing the needs of the ones involved in the training activities is the most important factor which determines the quality of the training (see Figure 8). According to the R square value (0.87), the endogenous variables are explained in 87%

Figure 5. Distribution of answers regarding ODL methods

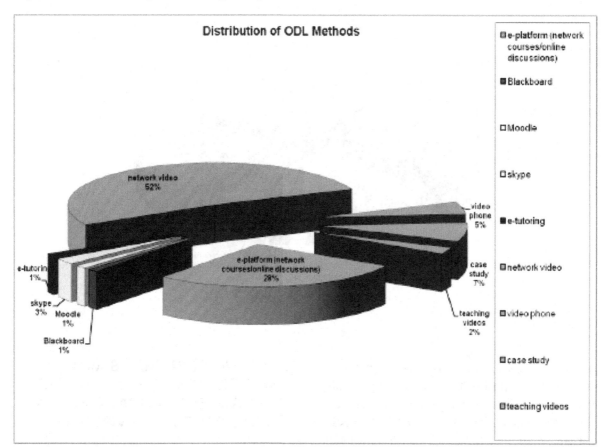

Figure 6. Distribution of answers regarding the provider accreditation a) Distribution of answers regarding the trainer accreditation b)

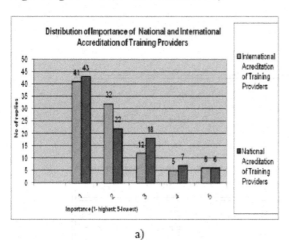

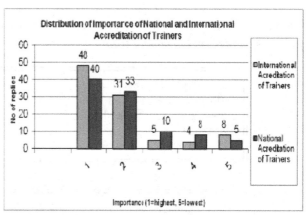

a)

b)

Figure 7. Distribution of answers regarding the trainer characteristics

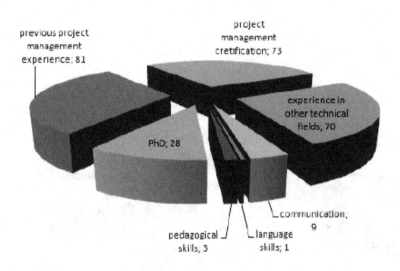

proportion by the exogenous ones, so the quality indicator is positively influenced by people needs, organization accomplishments, trainees' motivation and trainers' skills. The Wald statistic test came to strengthen the idea that all considered variables have an impact on quality. The statistics from Figure 8 was made with EViews tool and Ordinary Least Squares method was applied.

5. RESEARCH RESULTS AND ANALYSIS: QUALITY OF PROJECT MANAGEMENT EDUCATION FROM TRAINEES' POINT OF VIEW

Our second survey revealed different quality attributes of a project management educational programme. Trainees have a stronger preference

Figure 8. Regression output for the multiple regression model regarding the factors which influence quality of project management trainings

Dependent Variable: QUALITY Method: Least Squares Date: 02/03/10 Time: 13:08 Sample: 1 96 Included observations: 96		R-squared 0.870996		
Variable	Coefficient	Std. Error	t-Statistic	Prob.
NEEDS	0.400070	0.037417	10.69215	0.0000
ORGANIZATION	0.135136	0.029024	4.655957	0.0000
TRAINEE_S_MOTIVATION	0.420516	0.072164	5.827203	0.0000
TRAINER_S_SKILLS	0.273471	0.045321	6.034139	0.0000
C	-21.49685	4.632236	-4.640707	0.0000

Figure 9. Students' opinion about flexibility of learning environment

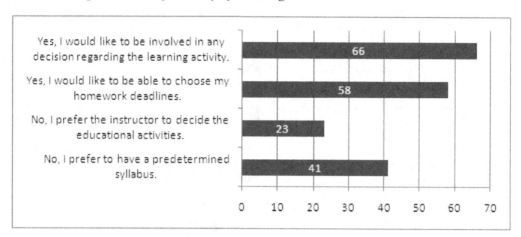

for online education: 93% of the interrogated students answered that the online master programme in project management should continue in the following years, despite its drawbacks. They justified their option by listing some of the reasons for the emergence of e-learning: a way of overcome time constraints, a good surrogate of traditional learning, an efficient method of learning, flexibility, easy access to information, interactivity (Bodea, 2007). Just 2% considered the online platform to be inaccessible, from the technical point of view. Moreover, 14% of them said that the platform is not appropriate, because it hasn't all the technical facilities needed by the users. The high level of computer skills is proved also by the fact that most students don't consider a technical training session necessary prior to using the platform. Still, they consider the face-to-face meetings organized occasionally to be useful enough. Other researches revealed that face-to-face approaches and online approaches have equal significance in educational process. The balance might tilt towards one approach depending on the subject to be taught (Kelly et al., 2007). Although most students have a passive attitude towards online discussions, they consider forums an important ingredient of a successful e-learning platform, because they can easily extract information from what others say.

Most students think that flexibility in learning environments helps them to obtain better results (see Figure 9): they like to choose their learning path or, at least, their deadlines for preparing the homework. This finding is also highlighted by Monolescu & Schifter: they explain the request for flexibility and interaction by the need to feel included. (Monolescu & Schifter, 2000)

The students of a project management educational programme proved to be strong willed: the majority of them enrolled in the programme with the precise scope of improving their knowledge of project management (see Figure 10).

Opposite of professors' and trainers' believes, students don't consider initial selection of candidates to be important for the quality of education: 47% of the ones questioned said that anyone should be allowed in an online master programme of project management, 38% of them stated that an initial check through CV and document revision would be necessary and just 15% of the students admitted that an online test is the proper method for acceptance (see Figure 11). Although they don't have any demands on prerequisites for the courses, they seem to be concerned to improving their knowledge by reading more than it is required in "class": when asked if they searched and used other resources than the one indicated

Figure 10. Students' motivation to enroll in a project management master programme

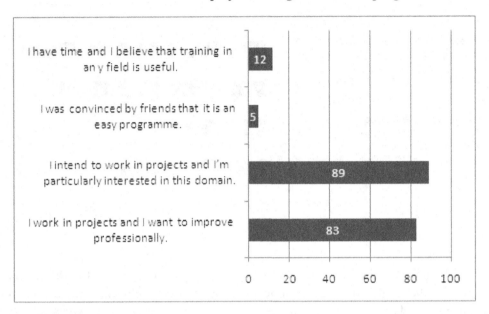

Figure 11. Candidates' selection for enrolling to an online master in project management

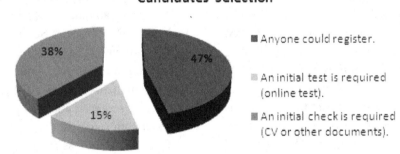

by their instructors, 86 of them answered affirmatively, "often" and "very often", 60 of them were neutral and 26 answered "sometimes" and "never".

Most of our respondents think that the knowledge learned at master can be applied at work (see Figure 12). Unfortunately, 62% of them consider that they don't have the support of their co-workers for improving their knowledge through a master programme. This can affect their learning performance. When asked to list the elements which affect their performance in class, most of them named the degree to which the programme

fulfils their knowledge needs. Other elements were: quality of the education platform, the feedback received from the instructors, the communication to their peers, their desire to learn and to improve professionally, their teachers' behavior and attitude.

The instructor's role is very important to the over-all quality of the education programme, according to 86% of the respondents. This finding is also supported by previous researches (Guardado & Shi, 2007). The main responsibility of the instructor is to offer support for learning activities (explanations, recommendations). Other respon-

Figure 12. Respondents' distribution regarding the extent of knowledge applicability at work

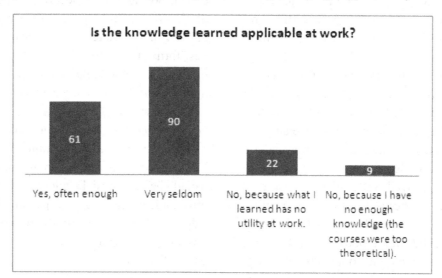

sibilities which were pointed out by the students are: promoting the collaborative learning, monitoring the students' participation, facilitating/ moderating communication, providing well-structured materials, presenting real case studies, implementing strategies for adult education, being actively involved in discussions with the students. 70% of the students prefer communicating with their teacher on the online platform, 24% of them prefer e-mailing and just 6% like face-to-face

discussions. As interactivity is important to 66% of the questioned students, we asked for the most valuable interaction techniques which can be used by a teacher. The following techniques and instruments were identified as being useful: feed-back, open and creative questions, team work, debate subjects, short activities that have a percent in the final grade, online presentations. It is good that students are willing to give feed-back to their teachers, as this "can provide a rich source of

Figure 13. Distribution of answers regarding the importance of Master Accrediation a)Distribution of answers regarding the importance of Master Provider Accreditation b)

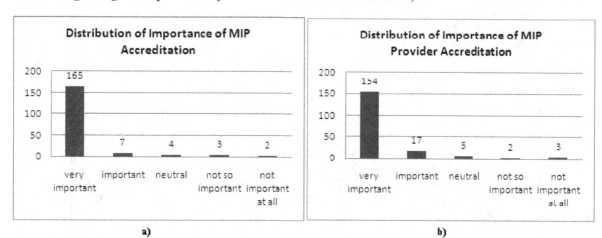

information to help the instructors evaluate specific elements of course design and structure, make revisions, and assess the effects of those changes" (Brew, 2008).

The students are very preoccupied about the accreditation issue: 165 of the subjects said that it was very important for them the fact that their master was a certified programme and 154 militated for the importance of master provider's accreditation (see Figure 13).

Our survey proved that students considered word documents to be most helpful (81 of respondents). The next preferred formats for learning documents are slides and e-books. 22% of respondents don't care about the course format: a significantly amount of this kind of individuals are in the 2nd year of master. According to other answers, we can't say that 2nd year students are less interested in the programme than their younger colleagues, so a more plausible explanation can be the fact that 2nd year students are already used to all kind of electronic materials: the power of adaption to an electronic environment increases gradually (Arbaugh, 2004).

The project seems to be the most suitable form of evaluation, in our respondents' opinions: 73%

of them consider the projects developed at various disciplines to be relevant for their training and 35% of them pointed out the projects to be the best form of evaluation. Other types of evaluation which seemed relevant to the students were multiple-choice tests (33%) or peer reviews (27%).

The responses received from the second survey enlarged our view about quality of project management education and training programmes. Consequently, the regression model from Figure 8 could be improved, by adding at least one extra independent variable: the perspective of considering the quality (from the trainer/ education programme provider or from the trainee/ student point of view).

6. SYNTHETIC RESULTS AND ANALYSIS

We added a dummy variable, ISTRAINEE, to the independent variables from previous regression model (see Figure 8). The new variable can take only two values, depending on the type of quality assessor: trainer or trainee. By inserting a new factor, the impact of trainees' needs and

Figure 14. Regression output for the multiple regression model regarding more factors which influence quality of project management trainings

Dependent Variable: QUALITY Method: Least Squares Date: 02/22/10 Time: 11:05 Sample: 1 277 Included observations: 277		R-squared 0.873362		
Variable	Coefficient	Std. Error	t-Statistic	Prob.
ISTRAINEE	-0.393841	0.395336	-0.996219	0.3200
NEEDS	0.379976	0.022068	17.21840	0.0000
ORGANIZATION	0.137221	0.017347	7.910152	0.0000
TRAINEE_S_MOTIVATION	0.355822	0.040875	8.705106	0.0000
TRAINER_S_SKILLS	0.296807	0.027623	10.74507	0.0000
C	-15.67825	2.572368	-6.094873	0.0000

trainees' motivation is slightly diminished. The second model has a bigger R square (0, 873) (see Figure 14), but the Akaike criterion hasn't been improved much. Thus, one can state that quality of project management education has the same meaning for all involved in the process, trainers, professors, project managers, trainees or students. The concern towards the accreditation of project management programmes is also shared by both trainers and trainees. The criteria for being admitted into such programmes are much fuzzier in trainees' opinion. The students proved to be much more eager to use technology in learning process and accepted very easily the e-learning approaches. This phenomenon is not typical to project management, as other researchers also discovered (Tallent-Runnels et al., 2005; Young & Norgard, 2006).

7. CONCLUSION

According to our survey, we conclude that quality in project management education and training depends on: organization and logistics – a good organization and combination of teaching methods adds value to training (assessed through Session Feedback Forms), the training need addressed – practical solutions, exercises, case studies (assessed through Session Feedback Forms), trainer's skills – pedagogy, languages, knowledge of the field, experience in the field, trainee's commitment and motivation.

Training providers should promote a coaching service for a limited period after the training sessions. Alumni's databases and forums are desirable solutions. Training providers are not responsible for the performance of the graduate at the work place. Training impact should be assessed through feedback forms, after a reasonable period from session graduation. This study can be an important tool in improving quality of project management education, as it identifies the factors which influence it.

ACKNOWLEDGMENT

The authors wish to thank Professor Xiangnan Lu, from Zhejiang University, China for her contribution to the survey.

REFERENCES

Arbaugh, J. B. (2004). Learning to learn online: A study of perceptual changes between multiple online course experiences. *The Internet and Higher Education*, *7*, 169–182. doi:10.1016/j.iheduc.2004.06.001

Bodea, C. (2007). An Innovative System for Learning Services in Project Management. In *Proceedings of 2007 IEEE/INFORMS International Conference on Service Operations and Logistics and Informatics*, Philadelphia. Washington, DC: IEEE.

Brew, L. S. (2008). The role of student feedback in evaluating and revising a blended learning course. *The Internet and Higher Education*, *11*, 98–105. doi:10.1016/j.iheduc.2008.06.002

Castells, M., & Pekka, H. (2002). *The Information Society and the Welfare State. The Finnish Model.* Oxford, UK: Oxford University Press.

Demirel, M. (2009). Lifelong learning and schools in the twenty-first century. *Procedia Social and Behavioral Sciences*, *1*, 1709–1716. doi:10.1016/j.sbspro.2009.01.303

Garcia, A. C. B., Kunz, J., Ekstrom, M., & Kiviniemi, A. (2003). *Building a Project Ontology with Extreme Collaboration and VD&C (CIFE Tech. Rep. #152)*. Palo Alto, CA: Stanford University.

Gareis, R. (2007). *Happy Projects!* Bucharest, Romania: ASE.

Guardado, M., & Shi, L. (2007). ESL students' experiences of online peer feedback. *Computers and Composition*, *24*, 443–461. doi:10.1016/j.compcom.2007.03.002

International Project Management Association. (2006). *IPMA Competence Baseline*. Nijkerk, Netherlands: IPMA.

Kanellopoulos, D., Kotsiantis, S., & Pintelas, P. (2006). Ontology-based learning applications: a development methodology. In *Proceedings of the 24th IASTED International Multi-Conference Software Engineering*, Innsbruck, Austria.

Kelly, H. F., Ponton, M. K., & Rovai, A. P. (2007). A comparison of student evaluations of teaching between online and face-to-face courses. *The Internet and Higher Education*, *10*, 89–101. doi:10.1016/j.iheduc.2007.02.001

Lytras, M. D., Carroll, J. M., Damiani, E., & Tennyson, R. D. (2008). Emerging Technologies and Information Systems for the Knowledge Society. In *Proceedings of the First World Summit on the Knowledge Society*, Athens, Greece.

Markkula, M. (2006). *Creating Favourable Conditions for Knowledge Society through Knowledge Management, eGorvernance and eLearning*. Paper presented at the FIG Workshop on eGovernance, Knowledge Management and eLearning, Budapest, Hungary.

Monolescu, D., & Schifter, C. (2000). Online Focus Group: A Tool to Evaluate Online Students' Course Experience. *The Internet and Higher Education*, *2*, 171–176. doi:10.1016/S1096-7516(00)00018-X

Tallent-Runnels, M.-K. (2005). The relationship between problems with technology and graduate students' evaluations of online teaching. *The Internet and Higher Education*, *8*, 167–174. doi:10.1016/j.iheduc.2005.03.005

Teekaput, P., & Waiwanijchakij, P. (2006). eLearning and Knowledge Management, Symptoms of a Reality. In *Proceedings of the Third International Conference on eLearning for Knowledge-Based Society*, Bangkok, Thailand.

Turner, R. J., & Simister, S. J. (2004). *Gower Handbook of Project Management*. Bucharest, Romania: Codecs Printing House.

Young, A., & Norgard, C. (2006). Assessing the quality of online courses from the students' perspective. *The Internet and Higher Education*, *9*, 107–115. doi:10.1016/j.iheduc.2006.03.001

This work was previously published in the International Journal of Knowledge Society Research, Volume 1, Issue 2, edited by Miltiadis D. Lytras, pp. 13-25, copyright 2010 by IGI Publishing (an imprint of IGI Global).

Chapter 8
The Study of Educative Network Organizations in the City of Barcelona:
The Nou Barris District

Jordi Díaz Gibson
Ramon Llull University, Spain

Jordi Longás Mayayo
Ramon Llull University, Spain

Mireia Civís Zaragoza
Ramon Llull University, Spain

Ana Mª López Murat
Ramon Llull University, Spain

ABSTRACT

This paper describes the inside organization of Educative Networks (ENs) and the aspects that allowed their growth and success in the city of Barcelona, Spain. ENs emerged over the past ten years in Catalonia, Spain, as a way to incorporate social and educative challenges in the territory. These educative proposals are based on the connection between the different educative institutions in the community to tackle social and education challenges in cooperation through transversality and a common project. The intent of ENs is to create synergies between cooperating organizations and coordinate community action to avoid overlap and redundant work. This study shows how these educative structures use context possibilities to improve educative impact and develop a new vision of organizing and conceiving education.

1. INTRODUCTION

The general investigation is developed by the PSITIC[1] research group, and funded by the Municipal Education Institute of Barcelona (IMEB). The Barcelona city government is especially interested in the EN's emergent importance in the social and educational affairs of the city. This article shows the first results and the future research outlets of the initial stage of a research-in-progress.

The academic curriculum of school and the values education of the family have heretofore represented a fractured education, with a shared responsibility between the two institutions. As a matter of fact, today's changing society has

DOI: 10.4018/978-1-4666-1788-9.ch008

brought a collapse of this educational model, setting out the need of rebuilding the construct.

In the actual Spanish context, we find new spaces and actors with a high educative influence. Some of these actors belong to the academic education, integrated in the formal educational system as: Social Services, supporting socially neglected students and families, and advising teachers; pedagogical advising community teams, supporting students with special educative needs, and advising their teachers; linguistic and social cohesion teams, supporting immigrant students with language acquisition; and educational community services, giving educative resources to all the schools in the community.

But other actors are part of the informal education, such as: the media, with several restrictions in children's hours of programming; informal extracurricular activities that reinforce academic and artistic learning; sport clubs, with their educational sports programs; churches' educational projects; libraries, with lecture and scripture programs; families' associations, promoting the relations between families and schools; ludotheques, children's playing centers that provide toys and games to stimulate creative thinking; medical programs, such as drug prevention, sexual health or dental health; the police department, with such educational projects as road safety and surfing the Internet safely; and others.

The coexistence and multiplicity of educational actors in the territory have entailed a diversity of parallel actions, where each institution has developed its project in isolation with minimal interaction. Some consequences of the parallel work are resources overlaps and gaps derived from the lack of coordination. Society faces today the challenge of construction of a global education response. It's necessary to act from a different view, exceeding the individualized action, the sectorization and the mechanism from the educational system.

Educational networking (EN) is shown as an adequate methodological response to attempt such complex educational challenges as school success, school absenteeism, equity, excellence, school-to-work transition, life-long learning, citizen education, and others. We see EN as an alternative organizational model to hierarchical organization charts, capable of equity in institutional integration, and united by a common objective; first, to share needs analysis and projects; second, to coordinate action in a comprehensive way (Longás, Civís & Riera, 2008). Thus, Educative Networks (ENs) are formal associations that have EN as an action method.

EN has become a relevant practice in the development of education in the city of Barcelona. This fact creates a political debate over which is the role of education and social policies organizations, and which is the role of administration. Far away from the improvements in educational results, EN is contributing as well to the strength of citizen participation and educative institutions' cooperation and coexistence, by generating social capital in the city. Halpern (2005) locates institutional cooperation, citizen participation, and social networks as social capital indicators. As well, he establishes education as a clue in the social capital construction, and points out the importance of cooperation between families, school and communities.

Nevertheless, EN is in a praxis construction process, and it becomes necessary to clarify the clue components that characterize its organization. By now, ENs are conceived as complex practices, with some organizational fragilities, and some questions arise over consequences provoked by: the coexistence of different ENs in a territory; their informal and spontaneous characters; their resource overlaps; effects in public education policies; outcomes deriving from different professionals; and the real impact of common actions in the territory.

This article is focused on the approach of the EN organization in the Nou Barris district of Barcelona, going deep into the weaknesses and strengths of its development, and in the principles and variables that constitute EN evolution. Also, this research's first stage intends to validate an analysis methodology for the educative networks study, in order to apply it to the entire city.

2. CONTEXTUALIZATION AND THEORETICAL BACKGROUND

2.1. Epistemological Analysis

Actually, sociology illustrates a new period as a result of the complex interaction between technologies, economics, politics, and culture. The social analysis presents a highly systemic and interdependent context, characterized by the importance of connections for social organization and the fluidity of its structures. In the Knowledge Society, there has arisen a new social structure of the dominant processes and functions: the network era (Castells, 2000). The nets represent the interaction between different nodes in a society based in interconnection logics. The Information and Communication technologies (ICT) represent the architecture and the expansive material of the nets, providing a connectivity that flows at the speed of light, breaking the borders of space and time. This context shows how the action conditions change before they have an opportunity to consolidate, integrating the continuous change in our foundation (Bauman, 2000). This situation results in an unstable existence around everything that was certain before, making liquid everything that was rigid previously.

Fluidity and connectivity set us in the Knowledge Society (Lytras & Sicilia, 2005), a society where people in educative institutions will have to adapt, manage and optimize knowledge in a complex context that demands creativity and innovation to succeed.

Certainly, these social changes that have transformed our environment must determinate the study of social sciences. But connectivity and fluidity are facts difficult to isolate and objectify. The simplicity principle either separates what is linked, or unifies what is diverse (Morin, 1990), in its goal to control its reality version.

The General System Theory (Bertalanffy, 1969) and Complexity introduced by Morin (1990) become suitable epistemological approaches in a reality where the interaction configures the experience. An open system is connected to the enviroment and sensitive to its inputs, and also understands that group properties are superior than all from each part, as a result of the synergies derived from interaction. Recognizing complexity doesn't give us certainty, but makes us aware of the uncertainty of our knowledge.

Focusing on the education discipline, the actual analysis shows an approach to its contextualization, with a significant role played by the connections and interactions with the community environment in order to build an educative community project. It presents an educative action as a complex activity that involves diverse actors and subjects. It becomes necessary in education and training throughout life to adapt to changes and innovation. It also introduces the artificiality of the isolated study of disciplines, opening a door for a transversal and interdisciplinary education, constructed at the same time by different societal areas. The Hierarchical Enterprise, locked up in its local borders, is transformed into an Extended Enterprise without borders, opened and adaptable (Grundstein, 2009).

Certainly, our environment points to a holistic concept of education, where decisionmaking requires a social participation for consensus. Education becomes a process that goes beyond the space of the community, and beyond its time: a life-long learning that takes place everywhere and at every time.

2.2. The Network Metaphor

The social and epistemological analysis projects the idea of interconnexions with the environment and relations between several parts. Castells (1996) defined a net as a group of interconnected nodes, and affirms that functions and dominant processes in our society are organized through nets. These facts set us in a scenario where it becomes easy to use the metaphor of the net to describe a social process. Network is a popular metaphor which is spreading quickly across the social science disciplines (Klijn, 1996; Klijn & Koppenjan, 2000). Without any doubt, the net drawing moves us far away from the isolation of individuality, and represents multiple and diverse connections. Hence, today the concept is used in different fields of society. Social scientists emphasize the role of social networks, professional networks, economic networks, communication networks and governance networks. The Internet irruption as an interconnections and communications platform is the most famous net metaphor.

By the way, we understand that the word is used with a diversity of meanings, not always referring to an accurate concept. This massive use is demonstrated by searching the word –net- in English and Spanish, in search browsers such as Google or Yahoo, obtaining around 6.000.000.000 results. This data becomes relevant in comparison to the data obtained by searching, also in English and Spanish, the word -Obama-, with around 240.000.000 results, or the word -crisis-, with 200.000.000.

With reference to the multiple meanings of the net concept in the Spanish context, we have organized them in four different types of nets that will allow us to situate EN. *Accumulative nets*: a group of parts related simply by common characteristics, but with a minimal interaction. It becomes an informal group that is called net, and some examples are: the –Barcelona Municipal Net-, developed by the Barcelona Province Municipal Department, that integrates all the cities in the province of Barcelona; -the public school net- and -the private school net-, as the Educational Department of Catalonia describes the two school styles. Schools are related by a characteristic, but neither public nor private schools maintain any formal interrelationship.

Distribution nets: They include the idea of connection, but only in one direction. So, different parts are connected to a formal net that provides resources where there is no exchange. Different examples would be: -the electric net- or -Barcelona's water net-, where our homes are connected to obtain electricity and water.

Interconnection nets: Those nets that involve a connection and a bidirectional exchange. The -railway net- connects different territories in both directions; -neural networks- are circuits of neural connections in the peripheral nervous system, and finally; -the Internet- as the net of nets, keep us connected and able to exchange information and to communicate.

Knowledge nets: Have a formal character and contain the characteristics of connection and exchange, but entail a final result from their own exchange and the parts of the net interaction. These groups use connection and exchange as a resource to achieve common objectives, and they require some order and organization between parts. Examples are: –the thematic nets-, as different research groups from Catalonia (Spain) and several countries work together to tackle common research topics. A -network governance- is also a knowledge net that involves a network organization of enterprises or social institutions.

As we have shown, the four types of nets go from low to high levels of interaction and cooperation. We locate ENs in the knowledge nets, according to the networking cooperation between the educational actors in the territory to assume the educative challenges together, creating synergies and optimizing resources.

2.3. Educative Networking

Lastly, we have seen the implementation of several educative programs from local administrations that go beyond the school institution and integrate other educative agents of the community. Some of these are: The Territory Educative Plans, of the Education Department of the Catalonian government; and The Educative City Projects, or The Communitarian Plans, both from the Barcelona's council educative area.

Nevertheless, EN is shown in our context as a fashionable and omnipresent concept. Actually, most of the educative practices that go beyond the institution individuality are called EN, regardless of whether relations or organization are built. Certainly, it becomes an ill-defined and underdeveloped concept. This fact involves the coexistence of several experiences under the fuzzy umbrella of EN, a difficulty in the advancement of the concept definition and in the study of its educational and social impact in the territory.

On the last five years, our research team in PSITIC has been working in the study and definition of the EN concept, with several publications on the topic[2]. From this research on significant EN practices around Catalonia and Paraguay, and taking account the complexity of the social reality, we have defined 6 principles that form the base of this work and all ENs content. These principles have no hierarchy, they feature simultaneously, and are developed in several criteria in order to approach to ENs (Table 1).

Proximity represents the requirement of working for real territory needs. The recognition of professionals, such as people's and educative actors' identities, are clue elements to enhance an EN that avoids technocratic action. It becomes necessary to include all educative agents to achieve social engagement and promote trust and synergies.

Transversality involves a cross-holistic vision of action through all institutions that comprise the net. This concept attempts to bring the institutional interests into common goals that locate citizen needs in the core of the action. It allows a global, integrating and coherent educative response, far away from segmentation, departmentalism and the resources waste from parallel work.

Horizontality describes the net structure as a flat macro-organization with equal decisionmaking power. Far from a hierarchic organization with specialized departments, the transversal work is developed through a basis of equity. This organization facilitates a shared and efficient leadership, where the empowered parts assume leadership roles depending on the specificity of the actions and the context where they take part.

Co-responsibility represents the value where EN is sustained. All institutions take their shared education responsibility, approaching an integral vision of the challenges. Co-responsibility pedagogy succeeds when all educative actors in the network analyze their roles in a critical way, show the interdependency between them and recognize an asymmetric responsibility (Torralba, 2006).

Cooperation is related to the dynamics between actors and involves a positive interdependency as a condition to succeed. The educative agents must understand that they all share the difficulties and challenges, so that everyone contributes their bit. The response will never be complete until everyone participates (Subirats, 2006).

Table 1. EN Principles (PSITIC, 2009)

Principles	Definition concept
- Proximity	- Initial point
- Transversality - Horizontality	- Vision - Structure
- Cooperation	- Relations
- Co-responsibility	- Value
- Proactivity and Projection	- Action

Proactivity and Projection shows the importance of strategic programming. The reflection-action has to be the method to maintain the priorities, accepting the urgencies without losing the shared project objectives. It is focused in a strategic dimension instead of a reactive dimension, involving prevention and future problem solving (Collet, 2009).

3. METHODOLOGY AND PROCEEDINGS

In order to validate an EN analysis methodology, describe weaknesses and strengths of EN development, and the principles and variables that constitute EN evolution, the study raises a qualitative methodology. This is a coherent approach, according to the descriptive nature of the studied object, and to its contextualized reality. The investigation is conceived from the interpretative-hermeneutic paradigm.

The global research is designed in a 4-year timeframe, and is divided in two principal stages. The first stage takes place between January 2009 and January 2010, and involves two clue actions: a theoretical study and construction of an EN analysis methodology, and its implementation and assessment in the study of EN in Nou Barris district. The second stage consists of the study of EN in the other 9 districts in the city of Barcelona (3 per year), where the evaluated methodology is planned to be replicated. This article is focused on the first stage of the investigation.

Nou Barris has been chosen for this first part because of its active citizenship and its high number of citizen associations censed, containing highly relevant EN practices with several years of experience. Nou Barris is located in the northeast of the city of Barcelona and has one of the lowest general rents in the city. It is composed of 13 neighborhoods, with a population of 170.000.

Concretely, the study examines the approach of 10 ENs consolidated in the territory, with more than

3 years of experience, and more than 5 institutions or actors working together. The networks were chosen in cooperation with the city administration educative supervisor. The 10 ENs are: *The Social Educative Commission* in Roquetes neighborhood, and *The Social Educative Commission* in Trinitat Nova neighborhood, both formed by formal and informal educative actors in each community, centered in ages 0-18, detecting educative needs and action planning; *The Social Educative Community Plan* in Verdum neighborhood, with formal and informal actors focused in promoting relations between school-families-community, from 3-16 years; *The 0-18 Nou Barris Net*, composed by all public kindergarten, elementary and secondary schools in the district, and centered in the coordination of the public sector actions; *The 0-33 Education Net*, composed by formal and informal educative actors, focused on ages 3-12 educative actions planning involving school and community; *The Coordinate Families Association from Nou Barris*, focused on promoting dialogue between families and the Council administration; *The "Neighborhood time, educative shared time"* program, formed by families associations, elementary schools and informal actors, and focused on the use of public spaces and resources during after school hours to develop educative activities from ages 3-12; *The Educative environmental plan*, in Canyelles and Roquetes neighborhood, centered in the implementation of community education activities in non-school hours for youth from 12-16 years; *The Children Commission in the north zone*, attending ages from 3-12 and focused on the revitalization of social and cultural activities in school and non-school hours; and finally, *The Youth Commission in the north zone*, attending ages from 12-18, and centered on job orientation and insertion.

The result of the theoretical background study was the construction of an EN Table Analysis. The EN principles had been developed in criteria, as well as in indicators, and had been the basis to create the research questions. The Instruments were developed from the research questions and designed in order to face the investigation objectives. The EN Table analysis and the investigation instruments have been discussed by PSITIC research team and assessed by 2 relevant PHDs[3] at Ramon Llull University, and also have a pilot character to lead in this stage as an assessment and validation (Table 2).

Based on this framework, 3 instruments were constructed by the PSITIC research team. Each instrument is focused in obtaining information about the context reality of EN and the accomplishment grade of the 6 principles, from different supports and different research stages. We understand that the proceeding of the 3 techniques contribute to complement the approach to the research objectives.

After the discussion of the methodological implementation with the chief Department of Education in Nou Barris district, we designed an initial reunion with all actors of each EN. The objective of the general reunion was to present, share and discuss the development of the EN research, and to engage the agents with the main objectives. All the participants were told to extend the information through all their ENs' actors.

The first instrument is a 60-minute semi-structured interview between a researcher and one professional from an institution of each EN studied. The professional interviewed was a clue actor with a leading role in the net organization, and was detected in cooperation with the Department of Education of the district. The interview is composed of 3 parts: a description part, where we ask for descriptive information about the components, the history, results obtained and the evolution of their net; an organization part, where we ask about coordination, communication and

Table 2. EN Table Analysis (PSITIC, 2009)

Principles	Criteria	Indicators
Proximity	-Responding to territorial needs	- Local initiatives inclusion - Shared educative needs analysis - Guarantee the participation of educative actors in the territory
Transversality	- Common objectives - Holistic vision - Citizen in the middle	- Interdisciplinary action - Coordination between actors - Coordination between other administrations - Coordination between other community projects - Cross planning
Horizontality	- Flat organization (non hierarchic) - Shared leadership	- Distributed leadership - Decision-making mechanism - Consensus spaces - Horizontal flow chart
Cooperation	- Positive Interdependency - Synergies creation	- Information and communication flow - Connectivity - Recognition of others' work as an added value - Positive interaction
Co-responsibility	- Engagement - Shared responsibility	- Recognition of own responsibility - Recognition of others' responsibility - Sense engagement
Proactivity & Projection	- Action-reflection - Strategic vision	- Planification spaces - Development of a work plan - Strategic planification -Long term objectives -Evaluation processes - Sustainability planning

decision-making processes, going deep into the principles analysis; and a final opinion part, where they expose their vision and experience about the sustainability, opportunities and weaknesses of their EN.

Once the interviews were done, we proceeded with a second instrument: a questionnaire, administrated to each actor that participates in every EN studied. The questionnaire has 20 items and combines 17 categorized and 3 opening response questions. Therefore, we demanded narrow and systemized information from the actors of each institution forming the net, and also some extra considerations or opinions regarding the EN development. The questionnaire is administrated in a soft online format through email to facilitate the data collection process.

Lastly, the third instrument takes part in a final moment of the research. It is 2 focus groups, planned to complement each other: one focus group with the 3 education directors in the district education department and the research team, in order to check and complete the field work planning; and one with the leading actors interviewed and the research team, to check and complete the pre-final results and conclusions.

The participating sample is composed of the 10 interviews with the leading actors of all the ENs studied; 37 questionnaire answers representing 50% of the possible actors; and 2 recorded focus groups of about a 90-minute time-frame. The data has been analyzed by the research team with the informatics support of ATLAS.TI 6.0.

4. RESULTS

The information analysis shows some significant categories of strengths and weaknesses that ENs face in their organization of cooperative work, achievement of objectives, and their sustainability. Table 3 contains the categories arranged in order of importance.

Starting with EN strengths, the totality of the organizations studied find that ENs contribute to a collective higher power and impact of the educative actions, rather than individual and parallel practices. They also affirm that sharing problems bent to a union and a shared response. Almost all of the ENs affirmed that EN improves community identity in professionals and in citizens as well; at the same time, it breaks down suspicion between institutions, creating confidence. A remarkable consensus exists in the ENs' confirmation that EN promotes educative community engagement and citizen participation. Finally, half of the ENs think that one of the main EN strengths is the professional enrichment achieved by working with other institutions in the community. They assert that collegial interaction involves learning by and with others sharing experiences, and knowing other ways of facing the same challenges, enriching and empowering their own institution.

Continuing with EN weaknesses, all ENs understand that volunteer participation in EN is a difficulty that causes instability in the net organization. Although some of its members as educative technicians assign part of their time for

Table 3. Strengths and weaknesses of the EN in Nou Barris district, Barcelona

Strengths	Weaknesses
- Higher power of the actions	- Voluntary character
- Pertinence feeling and community identity	- Different professional rhythms
- Suspicion breaking	- Low political recognition
- Participation promotion	- Temporary teachers
- Professional enrichment through cooperation	- Temporary school directors
	- Different engagement levels
	- The collaboration fact

networking, most of the professionals do so by volunteering, by personal or institutional conviction, dedicating hours of their time off. They also remark upon the difficulties of working with different professionals, such as psychologists, teachers, social educators, pedagogists, sociologists, and others, in order to share a work rhythm to follow a schedule. Half of the ENs affirm that temporary teachers and directors in the public schools cause several difficulties in the sustainability of the projects. However, almost half of the actors believe that low levels of political recognition to EN with certain trajectory, restrict their evolution. They assert the need of formal recognition to add power to EN decision-making, in order to consolidate the structures. There is a remarkable consensus in the statement that if EN agreements and decisions are not materialized, people and actors stop participating. Another weakness noted by a minority of actors is the different levels of engagement of EN members. They affirm that this fact affects the efficiency of EN in the achievement of objectives. Finally, a minority of actors detect some difficulties for several professionals to work in cooperation. They assert that professionals are not used to cooperate in their own institution, and become a problem in sharing vision and actions.

The results concerning the theoretical principles analysis show that the EN totality responds to the Proximity principle, working as a priority for the inclusion and participation of all agents in the territory. From Transversality, we ascertain that all of the ENs have some reunions or assemblies that get together all ENs commissions or work teams. They all plan common objectives, but only a minority create a cross program. Most of them maintain some punctual contact with other ENs, and only a few cooperate in some topics. In the Horizontality principle, we affirm that all ENs are constituted as flat organizations, but only half of them have structured schedule with defined functions. We ascertain that all EN analyzed has the role of a professional that energizes the work and is responsible for such administrative requirements

as the information flow, redacting conclusions on reunions, today's agenda mailing, remanding reunion dates, and others. From Co-responsibility, we find that professionals admitted their shared commitment with other actors. But we find some ENs where some actors affirm their disagreements with the common objectives or the actions. In the Cooperation principle, we confirm that most of the ENs consider others essential, affirming that cooperation has promoted trust and identity. A minority assert that some actors are dispensable because of their low level of engagement. All ENs use the phone and the Internet as primary interaction tools, but only half have webpages and intranet. In Proactivity and Projection, we find that all created a work plan, but only a minority of the plans had a strategic vision. Half of ENs assessed their programs and projects focusing on results, but only a minority assessed the work processes as EN. Finally, all confirm that EN has improved through years of experience.

5. CONCLUSION AND RESEARCH OUTLETS

Analyzing the initial stage results, we have defined 2 weakness levels that affect EN evolution and sustainability. The first level pertains to temporary teachers, temporary school directors, and low political recognition, and is considered as context difficulties. This first level directly affects a second level related to the network action, consisting of voluntary character, different professional rhythms, different engagement levels, and cooperative work. In order to improve the EN in the city, the action planned to reinforce the EN must be focused on the context difficulties. Thus, the city government should attempt improvements at the first level. A necessary initial and available step is to recognize and reinforce these macro-organizations, participating in and empowering their cooperative work. This recognition can be the basis of EN evolution from a voluntary to a professional activity, facilitating an inter-professional schedule and common rhythm, in order to strengthen its importance in social and educative action in the territory. In the near future, we will go in-depth and define what the government role has to be in EN in order to overcome educative challenges in cooperation.

The fact that a majority of ENs have affirmed the breaking of suspicion as one of the main EN strengths is surprising. The negative enouncement set us in a remote and isolated environment in the different educative institutions in the territory. Ignorance generates suspicion, and this turned out to be the first challenge to work in cooperation: trust building. EN becomes essential in the creation of trust in the community, leading meeting spaces, allowing people to get to know each other, sharing projects and starting to construct a common vision.

The theoretical analysis has shown different levels of EN. This fact allows us to confirm EN as a complex process based on the in-depth application of the 6 EN principles. So, ENs represent the formal organization created in basis of EN, and EN evolution process is developed in the compliance of the indicators defined in EN table analysis.

The analysis of initial stage results ascertains some complex elements that represent a graduation of EN process. Therefore, we detect an emotional dimension that graduates the quality of the process and contributes to ENs consolidation. The EN emotional dimension relates EN strengths to EN theoretical principles in different moments in its evolution. The approach to EN principles grows at the same time and through interaction, but we state a certain order in its development that sets the cohesion of the network organization. As ENs advance in the emotional dimension, trust and engagement between its members are generated.

As we see in Figure 1, the initial stage is clue in the EN emotional development. ENs that are configured from real needs, and all institution members share this perception, go in-depth into Proximity and allow a stable basis for its growth. This background permits an environment of getting to know one other, inter-relating the institutions and professional members. The establishment of common objectives, and the institutions' commitment to the sense of the network, constitutes the approach into Co-responsibility. This sense of commitment allows an in-depth approach to Cooperation, generating EN engagement and

Figure 1. EN quality graduation

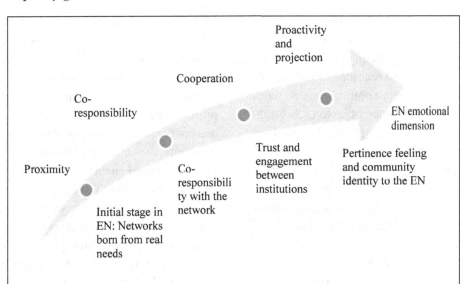

building trust between institutions. Finally, the engagement and trust improve the cohesion of the structure and permit a chance to go in-depth in Proactivity and projection. In this environment it becomes optimum to create an EN strategic organization method. At the same time, it contributes to a pertinence feeling to the net, and to build a community identity based on participation. This process allows a connected work feeling to the net and contributes to advancement in the EN quality. It becomes important for the second stage of the study to enrich the research of the EN emotional dimension and graduation process.

We confirm our suspicions concerning the Transversality principle, with indicators as Cross planning or Interdisciplinary action. The principle approach becomes a difficult challenge for professionals, because it involves a deep cultural change that goes from individual work to cooperative need. As well, its development demands some context changes that affect the educational system organization stiffness. ENs set a need based on context flexibility in order to empower the adaptation to changes. Moreover, it becomes a contradiction that some educative policies demand Transversality while they continue with strict, mechanical and hierarchical flow charts with specialized departments.

The near-future study of this principle is a clue challenge and a research outlet in EN understanding. In addition, it is necessary to examine the approach to how some successful ENs think and plan through a cross-institution and holistic vision of needs and actions, setting the citizen in the middle.

Finally, it becomes necessary to investigate some questions about EN. For example, what are the consequences of EN coexistence in the territory? Which are the EN e-learning needs to enhance connectivity? What do ENs have to do to succeed? What educational benefits do ENs achieve? And lastly, what is the impact of the EN in the territory's social capital? These questions become essential to improve the cooperative

respond of the nowadays education challenges, and will be the core of the research aims in its development in the next three years.

REFERENCES

Bauman, Z. (1999). *Modernidad líquida*. Buenos Aires, Argentina: Fondo de Cultura Económica.

Bauman, Z. (2006). *Vida líquida*. Barcelona, Spain: Paidós Iberica.

Bauman, Z. (2007). *Els reptes de l'educació en la Modernitat líquida*. Barcelona, Spain: Arcàdia.

Bertalanffy, L. (1969). *General System Theory: Foundations, Developement, Applications*. New York: George Braziller.

Castells, M. (2000). *The Rise of the Network Society. The Information Age: Economy, Society and Culture (Vol. 1)*. Malden, MA: Blackwell.

Civís, M., & Riera, J. (2007). *La nueva pedagogía comunitaria. Un marco renovado para la acción sociopedagógica interprofesional* (1st ed.). València, Spain: Nau Llibres.

Collet, J. (2009). *El treball socioeducatiu en xarxa: una breu proposta de marc conceptual. Congrés de Formació per al Treball en Xarxa a la Universitat. Complexitat, corresponsabilitat i construcció del coneixement*. Retrieved from http://www.fbofill.cat/trama/pdfs/congres/marc_conceptual_treball_xarxacollet.pdf

Essomba, M. (Ed.). (2009). *Treball en xarxa a la formació dels professionals en educació. Col·lecció Finestra Oberta, 52*. Barcelona, Spain: Fundació Jaume Bofill.

Grundstein, M. (2009). GAMETH®: A Constructivist and Learning Approach to identify and locate crucial knowledge. *Int. J. Knowledge and Learning*, 5(3/4), 289–305. doi:10.1504/IJKL.2009.031227

Halpern, D. (2005). *Social Capital*. Cambridge, UK: Polity Press.

Klijn, E. H. (1996). Analyzing and Managing Policy Processes in Complex Networks: A Theoretical Examination of the Concept of Policy Network and Its Problems. *Administration & Society, 28*(1), 90–119. doi:10.1177/009539979602800104

Klijn, E. H., & Koppenjan, J. F. M. (2000). Public Management and Policy Networks – Foundations of a Network Approach to Governance. *Public Management, 2*(2), 135–158. doi:10.1080/146166700411201

Longàs, J., Civís, M., & Riera, J. (2008). Asesoramiento y desarrollo de redes socioeducativas locales. Funciones y metodología. *Cultura y Educación, 20*, 303–324. doi:10.1174/113564008785826330

Lytras, M. D., & Sicilia, M. A. (2005). The Knowledge Society: a manifesto for knowledge and learning. *Int. J. Knowledge and Learning, 1*(1/2), 1–11. doi:10.1504/IJKL.2005.006259

Mangione, G., Anna, P., & Salerno, S. (2009). A collaborative vision for generating available learning experiences. *Int. J. Knowledge and Learning, 5*(3/4), 306–317. doi:10.1504/IJKL.2009.031201

Morin, E. (2004). *Introducción al pensamiento complejo*. Barcelona, Spain: Gedisa.

Rhodes, R. A. W. (1997). *Understanding governance - policy networks: Governance, reflexivity and accountability*. Buckingham, UK: Open University Press.

Schön, D. (1998). *El profesional reflexivo. Cómo piensan los profesionales cuando actúan*. Barcelona, Spain: Paidos.

Sorensen, E., & Torfing, J. (2004). *Making Governance Networks Democratic. Center for Democratic Network Governance*. Retrieved from http://www.ruc.dk/upload/application/pdf/7c331b9c/Working_Paper_2004_1.pdf

Subirats, J., & Albaigés, B. (Eds.). (2006). *Educació i comunitat. Reflexions a l'entorn del treball integrat dels agents educatius. Col·lecció finestra oberta*. Barcelona, Spain: Fundació Jaume Bofill.

Torralba, F. (2006). *La responsabilitat asimétrica dels agents educatius sustenta la pedagogía de la coresponsabilitat*. I Tribuna.

World Bank. (2000). *Attacking poverty: opportunity, empowerment, and security*. Retrieved from http://siteresources.worldbank.org/INTPOVERTY/Resources/WDR/overview.pdf

ENDNOTES

[1] PSITIC is a research group in Social Pedagogy and Informational and Communication Technologies, at Ramon Llull University, Barcelona (Spain). More information is available at our website: http://recerca.blanquerna.url.edu/psitic/

[2] In this website you can consult some of them: http://grups.blanquerna.url.edu/XarxesEducatives/

[3] Dr. Tomàs Andrés Blanch & Dr. Miquel Àngel Prats Fernàndez

This work was previously published in the International Journal of Knowledge Society Research, Volume 1, Issue 2, edited by Miltiadis D. Lytras, pp. 26-37, copyright 2010 by IGI Publishing (an imprint of IGI Global).

Chapter 9
The Teachers They are Becoming:
Multiple Literacies in Teacher Pre-Service

Lorayne Robertson
University of Ontario Institute of Technology, Canada

Janette Hughes
University of Ontario Institute of Technology, Canada

ABSTRACT

The authors review all aspects of a Language Arts methods course for pre-service teachers, one which employs a multi-literacies pedagogy (The New London Group, 1996) and is taught at a laptop-based university. The course begins with a deliberate immersion into the complexities of multiple literacies, including digital literacy and critical literacy. The authors outline the course assignments, resources and instructional goals to determine how technology impacts pre-service teacher learning and intended future practice. The qualitative data sources include digital artifacts such as digital literacy stories, book talks that focus on social justice issues, and media literacy lessons. In addition, the researchers draw from cross-program data based on teacher candidate reflections and interviews. The data suggest that both the use of digital technology and a multi-literacies pedagogy can help pre-service teachers reflect on personal experiences to develop literacy teaching and learning practices that have transformative elements.

1. INTRODUCTION

Our Language Arts teaching methods course focuses on multiple literacies including digital literacy, critical literacy and media literacy. Our "students" are teacher candidates engaged in this one-year teacher Pre-service program. We provide this course at a laptop university – one with an emerging presence in the field of digital pedagogies. Each of the teacher candidates is assigned a laptop for the duration of the program. In the first section of the paper, we outline the context of the course, our instructional goals, and the theoretical framework that we have used to evaluate our instruction. Next, we describe our investigation to determine how, and to what degree technology

DOI: 10.4018/978-1-4666-1788-9.ch009

has enhanced our students' ability to grasp and teach key constructs. As one of our key goals in the program is to encourage beginning teachers to think critically about their practice and become change agents, we also analyze our students' reflections and their practice teaching lessons to seek evidence of "transformative" elements. We conclude with a discussion of the implications of our findings.

1.1 Literacy and Technology

We are preparing teacher candidates to teach in a digital age; accordingly, our language and literacy course goes beyond the traditional notions of reading and writing print text. Teacher candidates engage with new digital media regularly in their out-of-school lives and we want them to be familiar with the out-of-school digital practices of their future students. We are aware that because of gaming, MSN, blogs, Face book, and the like, our teacher candidates possess skills that up to this time have been largely untapped in the classroom context. We work from an "asset model" that assumes that using new technologies can work as a benefit to literacy instead of as a deficit (Mackey, 2002). We realize also that multimedia technologies require new teacher skills and competencies if education is to remain relevant (Kellner & Share, 2007).

Garrety and Schmidt (2008) outline emergent and distinct genres of digital storytelling and see that each genre addresses a different function and purpose. They identify *reflective practice* digital stories as a genre that encourages Pre-service teachers to apply higher-order thinking such as meta-cognition in order to grasp and synthesize more difficult concepts. We consider also that digital technology has transformative possibilities – it has the potential to assist teachers and students to make positive changes to their world. Cummins (2000) proposes that the usefulness of technology in education should be judged not only by the degree to which knowledge is transmitted and skills are built but also by the "social pur-

poses to which these skills and information will be applied" (p. 536). He sees that some educators are "uncritical" in embracing technology in education, while others take the opposite stance and are dismissive of technology in education. His stance is a middle position which he explains as, "IT [Information Technology] can and should be employed to develop insight among students about human relationships at both individual and societal levels and to increase students' linguistic and intellectual power to effect positive changes in these human relationships" (p. 536). Because we agree that technology in education has this transformative potential, our Language Arts methods course begins with a focus on digital media and multiple literacies and the possibilities that they present for teaching about social justice.

1.2 Beginning in Complexity and Making a Difference

We begin our Literacy Methods course by immersing our students in the complexity of multiple literacies (Bearne, 2003; Cope & Kalantzis, 2000; Kress, 2003, Lankshear & McLaren, 1993; Mayer 2008). Here we include media literacy, critical literacy, computer literacy and digital literacy. Immersing our teacher candidates in complexity is a deliberative design (New London Group, 1996) and we see ourselves as designers of intentionally-complex learning processes. We ask our students at the outset to consider the study of "literacies," not "literacy" and to engage with multiple literacies while recognizing how literacies are constructed socially through our experience, culture and education. Core teaching methodology topics such as authentic assessment, lesson planning, unit planning and resource selection are learned by our teacher candidates while considering the rich context of the complexities of their own lives, the lived experiences of their peers, and the life circumstances of their future students. We were curious to see how teacher candidates would respond to the immediate immersion into the complexity of multi-literacies and the challenge to consider their colleagues' realities and lived experiences as they defined "literacy."

2. A MULTI-LITERACIES PEDAGOGICAL FRAMEWORK

Based on a consideration that schools do have a role to play in building societies, the New London Group (1996) proposes a multi-literacies pedagogy which encompasses considerations about teaching, learning and the role of schools in a rapidly changing world. They identify that learning's fundamental purpose is to ensure that, "students benefit from learning in ways that allow them to participate fully in public, community and economic life" (p.60) and they propose four underlying pedagogical components: situated practice, overt instruction, critical framing and transformed practice. *Situated practice* refers to pedagogy that immerses the learner in meaningful practices within a learning community. *Overt instruction* is described as interventions by the teacher that guide and support. *Critical framing* helps the learner to study literacies within the context of history, culture, politics and ideologies – acknowledging the cultural location or privilege of some discourses and information. *Transformed practice* refers to change evidenced as the learners attempt and reflect on new practices. Embedded within these four components is a socio-cultural, socio-constructivist approach to literacy which we infuse into our methods course. In the sections that follow, we explain how each of these four pedagogical elements is realized in our teaching methods course.

2.1 Situated Practice: Digital Literacy Stories

The first assignment is the creation of a digital story that introduces their peers and professors to the significant literacy events in the teacher candidates' lives. We employ a simple technology format (e.g., Photo Story or Moviemaker) to encourage them to layer their story-telling with multiple media and modes (such as pictures, text, background music, narration, and shifting focal points). This first assignment is complex in its media but also in its duality; it positions them as producers of media as well as consumers of media. We encourage them to find meaning in their own literacy experiences. The stories are rich, personal and insightful as these future teachers describe new knowledge about literacy and literacy teaching; we invite but do not require them to share their digital stories with their peers. We ask them to reflect and seek deeper meaning from both the production and the viewing, considering how literacies develop within a global context of education and society's constructed realities of advantage and difference.

This first assignment has multiple purposes: a) to help them understand their own literacy story so they can see what has shaped them toward the teachers they want to become, b) to better understand the literate lives of their students, and c) to learn how to use multiple forms of media to convey a personal message. New media offer them multiple means of expression such as gestural, aural, visual and spatial, as well as linguistic (Jewitt, 2008; New London Group, 1996; Gardner, 1993). We guide them to see how they can influence an audience as producers of media. The new media also allow them to write and create for an extended audience. We find that our students' digital stories are more often shared with family and friends than print-based text.

Finally, we position them to examine and to reflect on the mosaic that is offered to them by viewing, hearing and experiencing the literacy and life experiences of their peers. Through this process, we encourage them to seek deeper meanings - not just about literacies, but about how these media representations of education and experience can help us to examine our notions of advantage, disadvantage, social difference and the complex routes through which learners come to "know."

2.2 Overt Instruction: Identifying Disadvantage and Privilege

We ascribe to the need for intervention on the part of the professor to provide learning activities that will help the learner gain explicit information and develop within a community of learners (New London Group, 1996). Course readings and resources are carefully selected to build future teachers' capacity to look beyond the literal meaning of texts and embrace complexity. When we read a story or model instruction based on a commercial resource, we ask them to observe what/who is present or missing; to evaluate the text's complete meaning and the author's intent; and to focus on issues of fairness, equity, and social justice. The first "read-aloud" text is chosen to represent a range of persons and situations that are traditionally "missing" in school resources. We begin with the picture book "All the Colors of the Earth," a representation of children of every ethnicity with some bi-racial families. As they deconstruct the book, the teacher candidates note that "race" is never mentioned – instead children are grouped by hair type or skin colour. We introduce the notion of "race" as a social construction and follow this activity with a discussion of "White Privilege: Unpacking the Invisible Knapsack" (McIntosh, 1998). Our teaching goal with these first two resources is to immerse our teacher candidates deeply in conversations about issues of privilege, difference, representation, assumptions of neutrality, and marginalization. We are providing them with a meta-language through which they can view the resources that they will choose in their practice teaching and in their future Language Arts classrooms.

We also introduce them to teacher research that describes classroom implementation of the discourses of social justice, equity and diversity. We begin with research on teaching critical literacy

in a first grade classroom (Leland, Harste & Smith, 2005) and a resource on how to support students in literature discussions about social justice (Moller, 2002). We then move into discussions about how to include literature that represents diverse family structures (Gilmore & Bell, 2006). In doing so, we model the social justice teaching strategies that are detailed in the course readings. This provides opportunities to talk about situated practice, overt instruction, critical framing and teaching that is transformational (New London Group, 1996).

2.3 Critical Framing: "Make a Difference" Book Talks

For their second assignment, we require them to select books for their future students and discuss the approaches they would take with the books to teach social justice in their future classrooms. The selected readings for this portion of the course promote a philosophy that teachers can "make a difference" for students. We encourage the teacher candidates to think about their developing teaching practice but also to frame their pedagogy within an understanding of the social, political, cultural and ideological systems at work in education and society (New London Group, 1996). We introduce them to a framework of critical literacy practice that has four dimensions: a) disrupting the commonplace; b) interrogating multiple viewpoints; c) focusing on sociopolitical issues; and d) taking action and promoting social justice (Lewison, Flint & Sluys, 2002).

The teacher candidates select a book that has a clear social justice, diversity or equity issue or message and prepare a "digital book talk" explaining how they would use this book in their future classrooms. Again, the assignment is multi-modal and technology-centric. For some it is their first venture using digital video to provide a message to their future students. As part of this assignment, they are required also to investigate research around the intersections of social justice, equity and diversity concepts in classroom practice. This is another step on the journey to becoming teachers who are change agents. At the same time, we encourage them to assess critically the resources they have selected, consider how the social justice issues in the text have been represented, and interrogate whether or not they agree with the author's treatment of the issue.

2.4 Transformed Practice: Critical Media Literacy Lessons

The final course assignment is the creation of critical media literacy lessons that they will use in future classrooms with their students. We begin with discussions about the ubiquitous presence of media and the dangers of a compliant and uncritical public. We emphasize that media teaches values, beliefs and behaviour that we often absorb unconsciously and uncritically. We ask them to consider the number of people who follow movie stars' Twitter blogs, and the impact of that level of saturation around topics such as when or where that movie star is shopping. We believe that the omniscient presence of media in our society requires us to develop critical media literacy skills that both empower students to understand media messages and to produce media (Kellner & Share, 2007). One of the challenges that we face in this mode of instruction is that our teacher candidates are the first generation of teacher candidates to learn the skills of media construction and deconstruction. In their future schools, they will be building their own media literacy skills alongside their future students.

Kellner and Share (2007) outline four approaches to media education. An early media literacy approach is a protectionist stance which focuses on the fear of media (for example, media violence and its impact on children) and the dangers of media manipulation. The second approach is to examine media as an art form, looking at the aesthetic components of media. Kellner and Share discuss that they have problems with an approach that looks at the technical but does not address

the problems of reproduction of "hegemonic representations" (p. 7). The third approach is media literacy which includes the idea of multiple literacies but does not include the political aspects of closely examining literacy and education to observe who is present and who is missing, or who has voice in mass media messaging. This third approach is one that is not likely to lead to a reconstruction of media messages. The fourth approach they espouse is critical media literacy, which responds to some of the shortcomings of the other three approaches.

Our critical media literacy approach includes discussions about the societal realities of culture, gender, race, social class, abilities and sexuality – geared toward a goal of teaching an understanding of larger notions of power and control, privilege, and hegemonic norms. We try to immerse our teacher candidates in both the analysis and the deconstruction of digital media as well as the production of digital media. We introduce them to four key concepts for media literacy: that media are constructions; that audiences negotiate meaning; that media have commercial implications; and that media messages convey ideologies (Media Awareness Network, 2006). We want our students to begin to see also that technology holds strong potential to help students critically analyze their media-dense worlds. We then ask them to apply these understandings to the production of media literacy lessons. In doing this, we are asking them to transfer their new understandings about media toward their future teaching practice. In this way, we hope that they are able to show us "that they can design and carry out, in a reflective manner, new practices embedded in their own goals and values" (New London Group, 1996, p. 22). This is a significant challenge to a teacher-in-training: to grasp the essence of critical literacy and to find ways to engage themselves and their future students in critical media literacy practices.

Our central research question is to determine if and how our deliberative strategies for their learning in this Language Arts methods class have impacted our students. In particular, to investigate how technology and a multi-literacies framework impact teacher candidate learning. As researchers of our own practice, we next identified elements that would indicate that teacher candidates' learning in this methods course had resulted in transformative pedagogy.

3. METHODOLOGY

Labbo and Reinking (1999) observe that, rather than asking whether or not technology is transforming instruction, we might be better served by asking ourselves under which conditions this is most likely to happen. They suggest that if the goal of research on technology and literacy is to inform practice, then research that examines a specific pedagogical goal and looks at its multiple realities holds promise. We focused our research on our specific teaching context and the data generated by our teacher candidates to determine if and how they demonstrated transformative elements in their practice teaching.

We are fortunate that the program affords us multiple data sources to review in our efforts to analyze and weigh evidence of progress toward a stated goal of transformative teaching. First, we have the digital stories and digital book talk presentations of all of the teacher candidates who gave us permission to use their digital work in our research. As a second data source, we asked the teacher candidates to send us a digital reflection of their thoughts on the process of working on the digital story and viewing others' digital stories. We now have three years of these reflections from more than a hundred teacher candidates. Following the course, we invite them to participate in interviews and to send us examples of how they have used the digital assignments in their practice teaching in schools.

During the summer between our course offerings, we undertook a content analysis (Berg, 2004) of these data sources. First, we analyzed our own

practice using the New London Group (2006) multiple literacies framework. Next we identified what we would consider to be "transformative elements" or indicators that our teacher candidates would be taking meaning from our courses and applying it in other contexts. We then analyzed our students' output data from the perspective of whether or not the work they produced had transformative elements. Some of the "look fors" in the data set were the following:

- How do teacher candidates respond to instant immersion in multiple literacies?
- Is there evidence that our students are moving toward or away from complexity and multiple meanings?
- Are our teacher candidates taking new knowledge and skills (such as technology) and using them in new ways?
- Do they value elements of this course enough to replicate them in new settings?
- Is there evidence that they are introducing elements of critical pedagogy (such as questioning voices, silences and representations) into their own teaching practice?

In the section that follows, we have presented our key findings.

4. FINDINGS

4.1 Repurposing the Digital Stories

The reflections of the teacher candidates indicate that unanimously, they thought that the digital literacy assignment was a worthy assignment and that they wanted to employ digital story creation with their own future students. We discovered that many had already taken the digital story assignment and repurposed the concept in their own practice teaching sessions in a multiple ways: to consolidate student learning on a topic; to present stories to engage the class; to engage their own students in guided and shared writing; and to feature the students' own voices in presentations for parents or for assemblies. Others had used the software to introduce themselves to the class or to say goodbye when their practice teaching ended. One teacher candidate indicated that she had used a digital story to introduce critical media studies, but in general, while we found ample evidence of repurposing the digital story, there was less evidence of repurposing the digital story for critical purposes such as this.

One teacher candidate used the digital story to help students understand the level of preparation that goes into a presentation. She explains,

I wanted students to understand the preparedness that goes into a presentation....When creating my digital story for Language Arts, I quickly discovered the process and the steps it took in order to create a short digital story. I guess I wanted the students to realize this.

When asked why she chose this medium on her practicum, she explains,

The first reason was that I wanted to incorporate what I had learned about technology at [the university] somehow in my practicum. I found that the digital story technology was easy to use and I was very comfortable with it...The second reason for using a digital story was that I thought the students would like it. It is my experience that children enjoy seeing themselves portrayed, whether in drawings, photographs or film. This seemed to be a natural extension. The children could see and hear themselves on a piece of digital art.

Another teacher candidate writes:

I can think of a variety of ways that this program [digital story] can be used in the classroom...[It] can be used to help the teacher get to know the students in his/her class and at the same time help the students in the class get to know one another. I

think this software presents a wonderful opportunity for students to construct brief autobiographies and then present them to the class.

Through this project our teacher candidates in general said that they had "discovered" the importance of allowing students to use a variety of modes of expression. One teacher candidate wrote, "I believe sound is such a strong factor in portraying a message. I saw the stories as a mini movie almost - one of which almost brought me to tears because the selection of words, song, and pictures really connected well to convey an overall feeling." The project helped them develop a conceptualization of the teaching of narrative, one that encourages lifting the story from the printed page.

Another teacher candidate reported:

I have used movie maker many ways in my Grade 6 classroom. Not surprisingly, many of my students were quite adept at using software that was even more complicated than Movie maker. I first introduced Movie maker through an "I am from" digital poem activity. Students were asked to pick pictures/videos that matched with their lines from the poem. ... I found it to be a very engaging tool for my students.

Several of the teacher candidates shared with us student work that was produced during their field placements. In each case these digital files were accompanied by excited email messages full of pride, like this representative message:

The kids LOVED it. They laughed and giggled and wanted to see it again and again. Their faces LIT up. ☺ We had to do two photo-stories for each class, as there are 20 kids in each class... [Associate Teacher] will be putting them up on her website for the parents to have and will also be showing it to the parents of her classes before their holiday concerts next week.

4.2 Reflecting on the "Digital" in Digital Stories

As anticipated, some teacher candidates reflected that initially they found the instant immersion into a digital multiple literacy assignment somewhat intimidating while others found that it presented a unique and engaging challenge. What emerged from our research was the finding that the feelings of anxiety and pressure were short-lived and quickly replaced with increased feelings of confidence and expertise. While many teacher candidates expressed that they felt a range of emotions as they undertook this task, this quote is representative:

I was fairly overwhelmed with apprehension and worry when we were assigned this digital literacy story. I had absolutely no idea how people put these works of art together ...I am so happy that I chose to do [it] because it will be a keepsake forever. I experienced a whirlwind of emotions when preparing for the project...I laughed, I cried, I reflected, and I shared my past.

No teacher candidates indicated that the digital medium was restrictive - rather, they consistently indicated that it created more spaces within which to present their ideas. They saw the digital elements of the assignment as powerful and enabling. One teacher candidate describes it this way, "The first time you showed us a digital story...I was AMAZED and EXCITED. I was MOVED! I could not wait to do my own photo-story." A common comment was that the digital story opened up more spaces for expression than pre-digital storytelling. One teacher candidate explains that the digital story "allowed me to convey parts of myself that I otherwise may not have been able to express." Another writes,

Telling the story in Language Arts was especially wonderful because it provided a different form of expression for me. I am socially shy sometimes, *and would not have opened up as much telling a verbal story as I did in telling a visual and verbal story...*

For another, the medium of the digital story allowed her a fuller expression. She explains,

I found the key difference in telling a digital story compared to telling stories verbally was the medium. It allowed me to tell more intimate details of my story. As I incorporated technology I could separate myself from the story somewhat. The verbal aspects of the story were spoken into a microphone so although there was an implied audience there was no possibility of an immediate response. I felt more secure telling a personal story in this manner. Using photographs and music in my story helped me to set a mood and convey emotions I otherwise would have been unable to do.

Another teacher candidate indicated that for her the digital story allowed a special connection with the audience. She explained,

[T]he main difference was the ability to create empathy with my audience... By using a digital story, emotions and details are represented and experienced through the senses visually in the pictures and heard in the music. The audience is naturally drawn into the story and therefore able to "feel" or experience the message the author intended to share. This is why I feel using a digital story creates ability for the audience to "empathize" or truly experience what the author feels about the story.

4.3 Looking into their Souls: Sharing the Digital Stories

Many teacher candidates commented that the real power of the digital story assignment was in the viewing of their peer's digital stories. When discussing the viewing of others' stories, one teacher candidate wrote, "I believe that it gave me a look into their souls." Another wrote powerfully about the emotion of viewing his peers' digital stories,

We, as a group, learn to appreciate the individuals that we have become because they've exposed themselves in a way that makes them vulnerable. Safety among a group of 'strangers' is a huge issue for many people. Emotion tends to be the last thing that people will expose to people they do not know. I personally felt privileged to be able to view the literacy lives of most of our classmates.

In a similar vein, one teacher candidate wrote candidly about an "aha" moment for her when she reconstructed her own unconscious notions about English as a second-language (ESL) learners:

Listening to my peers share their literacies stories was also invaluable to me as a future educator. Their stories helped me understand more clearly the various struggles and situations that can make learning language so difficult and intimidating. It was very powerful for me to be able to recognize that a lack of English is NOT a lack of knowledge.

Not all of the teacher candidates' felt positive emotions with respect to the digital story sharing. One wrote that she viewed the literacy stories to see if others had struggled with literacy as she had and saw, "to my horror, most people in our class loved literacy, which is amazing but left me uncomfortable about sharing." This particular teacher candidate also feared reading out loud, a fear which we found to be a recurrent message across the literacy stories.

A significant finding for this research was the learning potential that was realized through the viewing of each others' stories and the written reflections. Teacher candidates realized from their peers' successes and struggles with literacy that their future students will come to the classroom with varied experiences and abilities. Through the digital stories, the teacher candidates "saw" the need for differentiated instruction.

4.4 The Teacher I Want to Become

Following the digital literacy story presentations, the teacher candidates completed two assignments: a reflection on the process of creating and viewing the digital story; and a book talk using social justice literature for children. We first examined the written reflections, finding numerous unintended yet serendipitous outcomes of the digital stories which hint at the teachers our students are becoming. Several teacher candidates wrote that the digital medium gave them increased confidence in talking about experiences with their peers without fear of rejection. This spilled over into other aspects of their teacher preparation experience. One teacher candidate wrote about the support her peers gave her after she presented her digital story. She states, "As a result of this support, I now feel more comfortable talking to my peers about other aspects of my life."

Teacher candidates repeatedly referred to the digital stories as "eye-opening", indicating new learning and new awareness. One wrote,

Watching these stories and listening to these different views opened my eyes to the idea that there may be a variety of views on literacy within my own classroom. I know to now ensure that there can be a variety of views within a classroom in every area, not only those pertaining to literacy and that I must ensure to acknowledge those differences.

As a result of the digital stories, the teacher candidates seemed to come naturally to some conclusions about future education practices. They indicated that they learned from their peers' successes with literacy and with their peers' struggles. One teacher candidate summed up the digital story assignment in this way:

I view this assignment as a gift to me and my future students. I will carry the insights that I gained through this exercise into my classroom. It is my hope that my classroom will be a place where

people are inspired and captivated. However, it will not be me doing all of the captivating; rather my students will also be captivating me and each other with their wonderful ideas.

The "Make a Difference" book talks provided ample evidence for us that our teacher candidates were able to plan learning activities that would include social justice elements. In their lesson descriptions, teacher candidates included many transformative comments such as this one,

Since many cultural stereotypes are ingrained in our society, our social justice teaching should focus on eliminating these perceptions with early intervention in our schools. In fact, we have an ethical obligation to expand our children's horizons, to socialize them into the global culture which represents our new reality.

Another teacher candidate wrote that she learned from the exercise that introducing social justice topics was much easier than she had expected. She described her insights about including a book that gives "a gentle" introduction of the concept that families include gay families. She stated her intent to include the book "One Dad, Two Dads" (Valentine, 1994) as part of a larger unit that looks at family. She concludes that books about gay families are not about being gay but they are about the things that many families do, such as raising children, caring for pets and family celebrations. This is evidence of her repurposing the technique from her Language Arts class, and applying critical analysis and reflection about the teacher she wants to become. Once again we found that the teacher candidates were comfortable combining the social justice picture books and technology, as evidenced in this comment:

Well I used a lot of the strategies and ideas that you gave us in class for my language/literacy lessons. I also introduced books on social justice and

my AT loved it. She really enjoyed the book "The Other Side". I also did a Photo Story on Peace for the school assembly with my grade 4 classes, and all the students loved it. The principal and staff were so amazed with it and with what I could do with technology.

4.5 Media Literacy Lessons

One of the findings related to the teacher candidates' media literacy lesson plans was that they did use technology in innovative and wide-ranging ways to teach media literacy. Many used video and YouTube and similar innovations in their media literacy lesson plans. One teacher candidate wrote a lesson on product placement in movies and used movie clips to teach the concept of overt and implied messages in media. Another collected media clips of commercials depicting competing political candidates. In her lesson students were encouraged to deconstruct how each of the candidates "positioned" himself or herself in their commercials. She introduced the concepts of bias and position to her students. She encouraged the class to consider how the message had been constructed and why different students received the messages of the commercials differently. Another teacher candidate used screen captures to discuss the issue of internet pop-ups with a primary class. In the media lesson, he discussed privacy and internet safety issues, and he used the lesson to introduce the topic of persuasive language as something that is used to influence people or persuade them to make a purchase. Other lessons designed by the teacher candidates focused on helping their future students see that advertisements are "selling a lifestyle" or "selling happiness." In one representative lesson, the teacher candidate helps her students to see the differences among the terms: "pitch," "product" and "audience."

Another explains how she used a digital story produced by her own students to introduce a unit on media literacy. She explains,

In grade one the students have to think about "Purpose and Audience" for their media literacy unit, so I wanted the video to be an introduction for this unit... The kids were beyond excited seeing themselves on the TV and so eager to do even better work if it was going to end up on video! They were very engaged, but yet they were still able to make connections to the curriculum. After watching the video and discussing who might see it (teachers, peers, parents, etc) and the purpose (a gift for the students from myself, a way to remember their year) the students were able to transition into a conversation on other videos, TV shows, commercials. From there they were able to begin to deconstruct why commercials are created (to sell stuff) and further their knowledge in the area of media literacy.

Some teacher candidates used digital materials available on the internet from the "Dove" commercial series to show how the computer can change a model's appearance. They introduced the terminology "unrealistic body image" and "unreasonable thinness" to the students, then lead students to engage in a critical examination of body image as it is portrayed in magazine ads. They encouraged their students to see that body image in advertising presents a false sense of how an average person looks and that this is done purposefully to promote sales.

This teacher's reflection captures his grasp of the media literacy – multiple literacies connection and provides evidence of transformative pedagogy:

I think that think they are developing a variety of literacy skills. They are learning what is media literacy and all the other aspects around it. I think for a lot of students the digital world plays as much prominence as does the real world. As alarming as this might be it is what I have seen, for example Face book. I think by focusing on digital media in the classroom we are helping students learn how to be critical about what they are viewing

and absorbing as "digital consumers." ... As part of media literacy, my students created their own graphic novel using "Comic Life" on the iMACs. Many of my students were really excited and eager to use it and learn about it because it was very relatable for them. I had many students who were very excited to show off their skills in Photoshop and help their peers who needed help ... technology is another way of communication for them.

5. DISCUSSION

Designing this language arts and literacy program has caused us to reflect on our practice and make important decisions about how we model critical digital pedagogy. The new media that infuse our program are excellent teaching and learning tools, but we want the focus the power of these new media to prepare teacher candidates to "make a difference" as they teach in a digital age.

Labbo & Reinking (1999) remind us that the research-to-practice studies can help us examine how technology transforms instruction, the barriers to transformation, and what can be done to enhance the positive effects of technology-supported transformative teaching. In our research we have determined that in the Pre-service classroom the use of multiple literacies, including digital literacy, can be an empowering pedagogy for new teachers. Our teacher candidates will practice their craft in a world that is "media saturated, technologically dependent, and globally connected" (Kellner & Share, 2007). The teacher candidates must learn how to use technology, produce technology, and question technology; they are the future of critical literacy education. We see evidence that the creative, innovative and intelligent ways they use technology are spilling over into their classroom practices during their field placements. They indicate that they understand the importance of using digital technology to interrogate the world, as well as providing more spaces for both students and teachers to demonstrate their creativity, thinking and learning.

According to Harste (2003) "the redesign of curriculum begins with reflexivity; the self-reflective interrogation and critique of what it is we have been doing" (p. 11). Our findings from this investigation remind us of the important elements of a multi-literacies pedagogy (The New London Group, 1996). Teacher candidates who are given opportunities for authentic situated practice, but who are also given support through overt instruction and critical framing can demonstrate transformative elements in their teaching. We are reminded by our teacher candidates' comments that our role as teacher educators is to model compassion and the creation of safe places for our teacher candidates to learn to absorb the complexities and often unsettling viewpoints that will become evident when spaces are opened for counter-cultural discourse.

We know that many of today's teacher candidates bring a different understanding of digital technology to their professional learning and growth that stems from their prior experience. In most cases they have already developed a level of digital expertise similar to the students of their future classrooms. The questions remain however "To what purpose is this digital capacity being directed?" and "How do we help them further develop the nascent new multiple literacy skills for use in the teaching and learning of language arts?" In providing our Language Arts methods class as a forum to blend these experiences we feel that teacher candidates can make powerful contributions to the digital literacy development of their students. These teachers have gained experience and knowledge to motivate their future students based on their students' interests and digital knowledge – this will help them delve into future literacy activities on a deeper and more critical level.

At the same time, we acknowledge that we are still exploring ways to use multi-literacies in a pre-service Language Arts teacher preparation program. We encourage others to share their explorations with the transformative potential of new media and a multi-literacies pedagogy.

REFERENCES

Bearne, E. (2003). Rethinking literacy: Communication, representation, and text. *Reading Literacy and Language*, *37*(3), 98–103. doi:10.1046/j.0034-0472.2003.03703002.x

Berg, B. (2004). *Qualitative Research Methods for the Social Sciences* (5th ed.). Boston: Pearson Education.

Cooling, W. (2005). *All the colours of the earth*. Frances Lincoln Ltd.

Cope, B., & Kalantzis, M. (2000). *Multiliteracies: Literacy learning and the design of social futures*. London: Routledge.

Cummins, J. (2000). Academic language learning, transformative pedagogy and information technology: Towards a critical balance. *TESOL Quarterly*, *34*(3), 537–548. doi:10.2307/3587742

Gardner, H. (1993). *Multiple Intelligences: The Theory in Practice*. New York: Basic Books.

Garrety, C., & Schmidt, D. (2008). The evolution of digital storytelling: from enhanced oral tradition to genres for education. In K. McFerrin et al. (Eds.), *Proceedings of Society for Information Technology & Teacher Education International Conference 2008* (pp. 916-921). Chesapeake, VA: AACE. Retrieved from http://www.editlib.org/p/27289

Gilmore, D., & Bell, K. (2006). We are Family: Using Diverse Family Structure Literature with Children. *Reading Horizons Journal*, *46*(3), 1–24.

Harste, J. (2003). What do we mean by literacy now? *Voices from the Middle*, *10*(3), 8–11.

Jewitt, C. (2008). *Technology, Literacy and Learning: A Multimodal Approach.* New York: Routledge.

Kellner, D., & Share, J. (2007). Critical Media Literacy, Democracy, and the Reconstruction of Education. In Macedo, D., & Steinberg, S. R. (Eds.), *Media Literacy: A Reader* (pp. 3–23). New York: Peter Lang Publishing.

Kress, G. (2003). *Literacy in the New Media Age.* London: Routledge. doi:10.4324/9780203164754

Labbo, L., & Reinking, D. (1999). Negotiating the multiple realities of technology in literacy research and instruction. *Theory and Research into Practice, 34*(4), 478–492.

Lankshear, C., & McClaren, P. (1993). *Critical literacy: Politics, praxis, and the postmodern.* Albany, NY: State University of New York Press.

Leland, C., Harste, J., & Smith, K. (2005). Out of the Box: Critical Literacy in a First-Grade Classroom. *Language Arts, 82*(4), 257–268.

Lewison, M., Flint, A. S., & Van Sluys, K. (2002). Taking on critical literacy: The journey of newcomers and novices. *Language Arts, 79*(5), 382–392.

Mackey, M. (2002). An Asset Model of New Literacies. In Hammett, R., & Barrell, B. (Eds.), *Digital Expressions: Media Literacy and English Language Arts.* Calgary, Alberta, Canada: Detselig Enterprises Ltd.

Mayer, R. (2008). Multimedia Literacy. In Coiro, J., Knobel, M., Lankshear, C., & Leu, D. (Eds.), *Handbook of Research on New Literacies.* New York: Lawrence Erlbaum Associates.

McIntosh, P. (1988). *White Privilege: Unpacking the Invisible Knapsack.* Retrieved from http://www.nymbp.org/reference/WhitePrivilege.pdf

Moller, K. (2002). Providing Support for dialogue in literature discussions about social justice. *Language Arts, 79*(6), 467–476.

New London Group. (1996). A Pedagogy of Multiliteracies: Designing Social Futures. *Harvard Educational Review, 66*(1), 60–92.

Selber, S. (2004). *Multiliteracies for a Digital Age.* Carbondale, IL: Southern Illinois University Press.

Valentine, J. (1994). *One Dad, two Dads, Brown dad, Blue dads.* Los Angeles, CA: Alyson Wonderland.

This work was previously published in the International Journal of Knowledge Society Research, Volume 2, Issue 1, edited by Miltiadis D. Lytras, pp. 38-49, copyright 2010 by IGI Publishing (an imprint of IGI Global).

Chapter 10

A Different Perspective on Lecture Video–Streaming:
How to Use Technology to Help Change the Traditional Lecture Model

Marco Ronchetti
University of Trento, Italy

ABSTRACT

In this paper, the author proposes a paradigm shift in the way video lectures are used in education. Instead of using them to support traditional teaching methods, the author suggests replacing standard lectures with video lectures, opening a space for a more participatory and interactive form of teaching that supports students in deeper understanding. In this paper, the author reviews the literature, discusses the effectiveness of video lectures, and describes a methodology called VOLARE ("Video On Line As Replacement of old tEaching practices").

1. INTRODUCTION

When the incandescent light bulbs were first introduced, they simply replaced combustion-based lighting systems. Combustion-based lamps however had their own requirements: they could not be placed close to the ceiling because it would have been dangerous. Moreover they had to be easy to reach for maintenance (e.g. for refilling). Hence they were typically placed at mid height on the walls of the rooms: a position that is far from optimal for their main purpose (i.e. lighting the room), but that was dictated by a compromise among contrasting needs. It took years until people realized that a better place was on the ceiling, in the middle of the room. Although the constraints were not there anymore, they had remained in people's head. The same pattern can be found over and over with almost all the technologies: it takes time until we are able to exploit their full potential, because we remain prisoners of the so-called "paradigm paralysis", i.e. the inability to see beyond the current models of thinking.

DOI: 10.4018/978-1-4666-1788-9.ch010

The claim we make in the present paper is that there is the opportunity to shift our current teaching paradigm by exploiting video lectures in a quite innovative way. Most people agree that teaching needs a paradigm shift: the traditional learning model based on frontal lectures held in class has been highly criticized because of the passive role played by the students. Constructionist (see Ally, 2008, for a general discussion of learning theories), and more recently, connectivist (Siemens, 2005) approaches have been suggested as possible alternatives. It is however not so easy to start a transition toward these innovative and presumably more effective teaching styles. Many hurdles make the switch difficult. For instance it is not easy to apply the new paradigms to large audiences: it is generally necessary to split the class in smaller groups guided by tutors (either in presence or on-line), which means that the delivery of a course becomes significantly more expensive.

Temporal limitations also create hurdles that make it difficult to abandon the *status-quo*: teachers often need almost all of the lecture slots to deliver the content. The belief that a constructivist approach is more time-consuming may be wrong but it is widespread. This factor is another significant obstacle to a methodological transition. Time is in fact a precious resource.

Also, many teachers think that students need to have some background knowledge and a basic understanding of the problem domain before they can effectively engage in problem-solving or collaborative learning. Classical on-line course in fact follow a standard pattern: first they deliver knowledge, and then they proceed to sections where the students are supposed to be more active (e.g. by doing exercises that should assess their degree of understanding). Many blended approaches can also be mapped to the same pattern: first knowledge is delivered (typically on line) and then collaborative or constructive approaches are taken in non-virtual sessions.

In the present paper we suggest a methodology that should make it easier for teachers that presently use a traditional, frontal approach to migrate to a (at least) more interactive teaching style. Information and Communication Technology (ICT) plays, in our approach, a fundamental role in allowing such a change. We focus on academic teaching rather than on the processes that take place in other forms of education (such as primary and secondary schools, and adult learning) although the same principles could probably and at least partly be adapted for these cases, with different implementations. The methodology we propose has been successfully experimented by the author with success on a small scale, and a larger scale experiment is presently in progress. The idea is to rethink the use of video lectures so as to create a new didactic space in class. In the rest of this paper we shall first recall the origin and evolution of video lectures and discuss their pedagogical effectiveness. Then we shall introduce our methodology, present the results and the related work before concluding.

2. VIDEO LECTURES

2.1 Historical Perspective

The use of videos for teaching dates back to the VCR days, when it became easy and cheap to record home videos and copy them on cassettes. The possibility of using digital video for distance education was envisioned already in the early Web days, when F. Tobagi (1995) built at Stanford a prototypical architecture for distributing digital video lectures. The digital approach was obviously superior to its analogue precursor in terms of ease of distribution of the didactic material, asynchronous and multiple simultaneous accesses. Moreover it was promising in terms of possibility of interlinking the learning resources.

Actual deployment of video-streaming in teaching followed shortly, when Hayes et al. (1998) substituted a VHS based system for delivering lectures to a geographically remote place (from USA to France) with a digital alternative. Initially they only transmitted an audio stream with synchronized power point images, but soon thereafter the video was transmitted. The video, produced with a technique called chroma key[1], included both the teacher and the slides.

In the same years the German Teleteaching project, originally envisioned in 1995, started delivering results, as reported by Hilt and Kuhmünch (1999). The project focused mostly on synchronous events, but some attention was given also to the asynchronous scenario. Three cases were considered: the "Remote Lecture Room Scenario", in which lectures were transmitted live via the Internet to lecture rooms at the partner universities, the "Remote Interactive Seminar" (much more interactive since a discussion between the participating actors usually took place after each talk) and the "Interactive Home-Learning", in which students running Linux or Windows 95/98 on their PC watched lectures from home via an ISDN Internet connection.

In those years the main challenge was to overcome the problems caused by Internet bandwidth, as discussed by Fong and Hui (2001). The other problem at the time was the choice of the optimal software for performing video-streaming, the main competitors being RealVideo, Apple QuickTime and Windows Media Video (see McCrohon, Lo, Dang, & Johnston, 2001). None of these solutions was really cross-platform (supporting at least Linux, Windows and Apple OS), and hence many opted for the storage in multiple formats. Later also Adobe Flash Video entered into the arena, offering universal support. The situation is still in evolution, as Microsoft recently responded with its Silverlight platform in the attempt to make some previously Windows-only products portable also to other platforms, while at the same time the refusal of Apple to bring Flash on the iPhone broke the universality of a technology that had carved an important niche as "the" truly cross-platform solution.

After the time of the pioneers and early adopters, big players have been coming onto the scene. University of California at Berkeley is offering full courses through a dedicated You Tube channel[2]. Apple started a dedicated section in their iTunes platform that is called "iTunes U"[3] and offers academic video-lectures visible on the iPhone, some iPods, Mac and PCs. The OpenCourseWare initiative at MIT (Abelson, 2008) includes video lectures and seminars[4]. These initiatives open interesting questions. One is whether such open offering is not in contrast with the fact that students pay high tuition fees, while the same lectures are visible for free on the Web. The MIT answer[5] gives an important hint: "Our central value is people and the human experience of faculty working with students in classrooms and laboratories, and students learning from each other, and the kind of intensive environment we create in our residential university". One could also argue that the certification of the learning process is part of the added value that the institution provides. Another very relevant question is "how valid are video lectures from a pedagogical point of view?" The answer needs an articulated discussion, to which we dedicate the next section.

2.2 Evidence of the Pedagogical Validity of Video Lectures

Several authors have dealt with the issue of assessing advantages and problems of the video-lecture as a pedagogical tool.

Ronchetti (2003a) adopted video lectures as a support to traditional teaching, and investigated which were the advantages perceived by the students. A first obvious result was that students appreciated the possibility to recover lectures lost due to forced absence (illness, work or other time-frame incompatibility) and the ability to better organize their time, deciding not to be present at some lecture (elective absence). Less obvious advantages emerged as support of students who regularly frequented the course, and did not consider video lectures as an alternative to class, but rather as an interesting new tool to complement their traditional learning. They appreciated the possibility of:

- Reviewing some critical point (cases of poor understanding of a section due to concentration drop, excessive speed in an explanation or intrinsic difficulty);
- Reviewing (portion of) lectures as a confirmation that their understanding is correct;
- Checking the correctness of notes taken during a lecture.

The relevance of direct access to a particular point of a lecture for reviewing only a few minutes is also supported by the analysis performed by Zupancic and Horz (2002). According to Soong et al. (2006) "recordings enable them to access parts of lectures which they do not understand". The possibility to quickly navigate the lecture is therefore an essential feature (and this is one of the aspects that makes digital recording deeply different from more traditional VHS-based videos, the other being the ease of access via download).

Lauer et al. (2004) evaluated the effectiveness of some aspects of the user interface of video-lecture based systems. These elements emerged as important:

- Sound quality
- Good readability of the accompanying slides, annotation and clips
- The possibility to have also a local copy of the learning material (as opposed to being able to only view in streaming mode)
- The possibility to navigate the lecture both by slide title and by a time-bar
- The availability of text search (keyword or full text)

Obviously the quality of service of the streaming has a relevant impact on users' perception of the video content, and hence on their satisfaction and on the overall system usability (Chen, Ghinea, & Macredie, 2006).

Anecdotic evidence of the effectiveness of videos has been reported by several authors. Ronchetti (2003a) reports that students who did not pass the exam at the first call made (later) an intense use of the video lectures – meaning that they help exactly those students who need more support. Zupancic and Horz (2002) report a strong increase of system usage right before the exams, which also suggests a form of just-in-time support. Zhang et al. (2006) showed that students using video lectures achieved significantly better learning performance than those in other settings, and also reported a higher level of learner satisfaction.

Bennett and Maniar (2008) discussed the efficacy of video lectures. They tried to offer a balanced view, presenting positive and negative aspects. Their review is not conclusive, as they cannot support their personal opinions with a scientific evaluation, so that the matter remains unanswered. Moreover, in their review they mix two different aspects: effectiveness of videos as teaching tool (e.g. using videos for showing scientific experiments) and effectiveness of recorded video lectures. This confusion is prototypical: in literature, very often, different aspects get mixed. Another frequent mistake in literature is the extension of results obtained in a given domain to nearby area, where their holding may be questionable.

Recent work tends to be mostly positive in evaluating the success of video lectures, as shown by the following anthology:

- "92% of students who access the video-streamed lectures ... agreed that this was a useful learning resource" (McCrohon et al., 2001)
- "Students find an added value in having a multimedia version of the traditional lecture, especially if provided through a tool that has a well-thought user interface" (Ronchetti, 2003b)

- Video lectures-based "distance education was at least as good as traditional classroom instruction" (Reisslein, Seeling, & Reisslein, 2005)
- For a good majority of students, "a distance learning course without on-line lecture would compromise learning" Chung (2005)
- "Students have benefited from accessing video recorded lectures" (Soon et al., 2006)
- Video lectures "are indeed adequate alternatives to live lectures for engineering students" (Maness, 2006)
- "The use of video (in the absence of the teacher) in teaching primary school pupils is as effective as when the teacher uses the real objects in teaching Agricultural and Environmental Sciences" (Isiaka, 2007)

Looking further in the past instead, early experiments report an inferiority of remote lectures when compared to in-classroom lectures (see Hilt & Kuhmünch, 1999). The reasons mentioned were the unfamiliarity of the technological equipment, the poor audio quality and a merely sufficient visual quality of the slides in the whiteboard. Obviously in these years most technical issues have been fixed, the bandwidth has increased, and probably today's student are more used to videos over the net.

Not all the problems have however disappeared. On the negative side, in a distance-learning context that was heavily based on video lectures, and hence fully without class activity, the students reported insufficient interaction with the instructor and insufficient interaction with fellow students. Also, the students quite frequently reported the required self-discipline as the least liked aspect of distance education (Reisslein et al., 2005). This basically means that video lectures are an essential ingredient, but they do not suffice. This point of view is reinforced by the quite innovative work presented by Brown and Liedholm (2004). They start from the consideration that students exhibit

different cognitive styles, but unlike other lines of research focusing on system personalization, they rather offer students a spectrum of possibilities (textbook, video lectures, practice quizzes, problems, text slides, lecture slides) so that each student can choose the learning strategy that better suits her/him. They monitor and observe students behaviour during the learning process, and finally they draw conclusions on the relative usefulness of every single resource type. Their results show that video lectures were very valuable for 77% of the students, with more than 50% of the students considering them one of the two most valuable tools.

Demetriadis and Pombortsis (2007) brought evidence that "e-lectures can be safely used as students' introductory learning material to increase flexibility of learning, but only within a pedagogically limited perspective of learning as knowledge acquisition (as opposed to construction)".

The format of video lectures has also been investigated, e.g. by comparing the effectiveness of the combination "video + slides" as opposed to an "audio + slide" format. Results present some contradiction. According to Berner and Adams (2004), who conducted a randomized controlled trial to assess the relative importance of these two modalities, adding video to an audio presentation does not lead to greater satisfaction or greater learning. Moreno and Mayer (2000) stated: "students learn better when the instructional material does not require them to split their attention between multiple sources of mutually referring information". Their work is sometime used as an argument against the standard video-lecture + slide format, as reported e.g. by Krüger (2005), who extrapolated Moreno and Mayer's results, considering that in video lectures there are two screen areas competing for the viewer's attention: the video and the slide. They concluded that this leads to the "split-attention effect".

On the opposite front, McCrohon et al. (2001) report that 83% of the students preferred video streaming to audio streaming. Fey (2002) argues that video does not increase understanding or retention, but is favoured by most people due to emotional reasons. According to the German instruction psychologist Glowalla (2004), learners show a better concentration in front of a video than in a classroom, while the audio + slide version favours less the concentration, and is perceived as more boring. Data obtained by Reisslein et al. (2005) confirm that students felt that the web-carried video helped them to stay focused during the instruction.

We think one should be very careful when interpreting Moreno and Mayer's results. In fact, their experimental work is mostly concerned with generic multimedia rather than with the specific case of video lectures. A video-lecture if fact mimics so closely the real-world experience (with the lecturer, and an often large projected slide that is not necessarily near to the speaker) that students might find this "split" a natural feature, and hence not suffer of the "split-attention effect". On the contrary, video + slides is probably better than audio + slides for a few reasons:

- Viewing the speaker (at least for a portion of the lecture) gives a sense of familiarity that helps getting emotionally more involved;
- Watching the video helps keeping concentration
- In the cases in which the blackboard is used by the teacher to complement the content of the projected slides the video gives a clear advantage: that content is lost if one only relies on audio.

Another relevant issue is whether all types of video lectures are equally effective. This issue is well addressed in a very interesting paper by Fritze and Nordkvelle (2003). They analyze the difference between a live lecture, a video-lecture and a lecture in videoconference. It should be noted that by video-lecture they mean a lecture given in front of a camera, without the presence of a real class:

we shall call this a "synthetic" lecture, because in most cases in literature "video lectures" are actual recordings of live lectures (i.e. lectures given in front of a real audience, and not created on purpose for distance learning). They studied live lectures, synthetic lectures and lectures in videoconference by analyzing the language employed, the examples used, the rhetoric figures, the presence of humour. Their results show that the synthetic lectures lose many of the immediacy qualities of the live lecture. They consider the presence of humorous situations, types of examples, the impact of (recorded) questions and answers, linguistic style. In summary, synthetic lectures are more serious, stringent and linear, with the de-personalized and distanced used of examples and humour. The trust building is more based on authority in synthetic lectures, whilst in the live-lecture model the speaker builds personal trust primarily as an educator. Our interpretation of these findings is that recorded live lectures are pedagogically more effective than the "synthetic" ones.

Overall, there is a strong body of evidence that video lectures are effective and useful for delivering content, especially in the form of recording of live lectures.

3. METHODOLOGY

We started our considerations by asking ourselves: "But if video lectures are good enough for supporting knowledge transfer – which is what frontal lectures often are about – what is the sense of repeating every year the same set of lectures? Can't we find a better way to use the time we spend in class with the students?". The answer was very simple: "Yes, let's record the standard lectures, and let's use the recordings to replace the frontal lecture. Then, let's transform class in an interactive arena where we can help the students". In the present section we shall formalize this intuition.

3.1 Postulates

Our starting postulate is that the students' activity can be divided into three phases:

- KA: Knowledge acquisition
- DU: Deeper understanding
- KC: Knowledge consolidation.

During the first phase, the student is exposed to the theory and ideas. In the DU phase the student "digests" the material, interiorizes the concepts, and creates his own models, establishing the main links with his previous knowledge. The third phase consolidates the understanding and applies it to cases (e.g. through exercises).

Obviously this is an approximation, as multiple cycles may take place. For instance, during the KC phase the student may discover discrepancies (e.g. caused by misunderstandings and misconceptions) that trigger another pass through the second phase or even elicit the need for a review of the material used in the KA phase.

As a second approximation, we assume that each of the three phases lasts approximately an equal amount of time. We know that deeper and deeper understanding levels occur throughout life, and that knowledge consolidation may be a slow process that goes even beyond the lifetime of a course, but we believe our approximations provide a reasonable and pragmatic working hypothesis.

In the European Union, one academic year corresponds to 60 credits of the ECTS (European Credit Transfer and Accumulation System) credits, and it is equivalent to 1500–1800 hours of study irrespective of standard or qualification type. Institutions are free to decide how many of the 25 hours-per-credit are delivered in presence, and how many rely on individual study: on the average however approximately one third of the time is spent in class, while two thirds correspond to individual (or group) unsupervised study. Courses based on laboratory are an exception, and they may have a different time allocation: for example two

thirds of the time may be spent in the lab, and the rest of it is used to produce reports. Laboratory courses are by definition already based on "learn by doing", so that we do not need to deal with them. We focus our attention on more theoretical courses, where only one third of the total time is spent in class, and which are more likely to suffer from the "frontal teaching syndrome".

In the frontal lecture style most – if not all – the time spent in class with the teacher is devoted to passing knowledge to the student. The teacher focuses on the first part of the learning cycle (KA). The action is mostly limited to the "illustration" of the concepts and practices. During the rest of the time the student is on his own. The operations he needs to perform are internalizing and consolidating the understanding, remembering topics and techniques, putting into practice the acquired knowledge (e.g. by doing exercises). Although in some cases there are lectures devoted to exercises, students are mostly left alone in these very critical phases. In particular, the DU phase is the one where discussion would be most useful; yet the traditional approaches provide here very limited help (such as teacher's office hours). Group study is a succedaneum – but it is typically left to the students' initiative.

3.2 VOLARE Methodology

Our idea is to get much more teacher involvement during the DU phase. The teachers' time is however a finite (and expensive) resource: hence to move resources to this phase, it is necessary to subtract them elsewhere (i.e. from KA). The idea in not new: Collard et al. (2002) devised a strategy to encourage students to use the textbook, learning material before the lecture. Online pre-lecture assignments were used to provide structured motivation for students to begin learning material before coming to class. Collard et al. report that they were successful in getting students to prepare for lecture on a regular basis. Also, they claim that students felt positively about it. Obviously the idea of using pre-lecture readings is not a new one: many teachers have tried to apply it (e.g. in high-school), but it is usually not really effective, nor it can be assumed to completely fulfill the KA phase.

Our proposal is far more radical. The methodology we propose is named VOLARE: "Video On Line As Replacement of old tEaching practices". In our approach, all the time in class should be spent supporting the DU phase. To do so, we need to free the teacher from the KA duties. The key element is to virtualize the presence of the teacher in the KA phase. We achieve that through usage of video on line. Here we are using the results discussed in section 2.2, i.e. that the quality of the experience provided by a recorded frontal lecture is comparable with the lecture itself – at least for the KA phase.

Students are required to view the video before coming to class: the time in class is then fully devoted to discussions, collaborative activities, guided exercises, and strong interactions among students and teacher.

The video contains a traditional lecture, possibly given by the very same teacher. Although it is certainly possible to use as material for the KA phase some of the many educational videos that are available for free (e.g. on iTunes-U, or in the MIT Open-Courseware initiative), there are important advantages when a teacher uses his own recorded lectures. In first place, the teacher can convey exactly his own view, and give his own perspective and imprint to the course. The second benefit is that the teacher has a stronger sense of "ownership" of the course. It is certain matter of teaching styles, but for instance even when PowerPoint slides are available for a standard course, many teachers prefer to at least adapt them to better reflect their view. Similarly, we believe that using one's own videos would, at least for those teachers, is better than rely on other material.

Obviously such choice implies a non-trivial requirement: the teacher must have recordings of his previous lectures. Again, there are cost, time and effectiveness issues to be considered.

One possible option is to prepare videos e in a neutral environment ("synthetic lectures"), in front of a video camera (and possibly with an "art direction"). The second option is to record real lectures given in the classroom. The first option is generally more costly, but more importantly we recall that it is also worst than recorded real lectures, as proven by Fritze and Nordkvelle (2003) (as we discussed in section 2.2). In fact "synthetic lectures", although polished and professionally looking, are generally... rather boring! The main reason is that in a sterile environment the teacher has no feedback from real students. In class instead the teacher has constant responses from the students – even if they do not speak. He can see the faces, understand if he has being boring, if students need to be cheered up with a mot of spirit, if anything needs to be repeated using yet another metaphor or by using one more example. Recording "on the field" is an essential requirement to make the learning experience though the video most similar to the one that is available in class. Moreover, this solution also dramatically reduces costs, at least because it does not require a teacher to perform extra activity. There is freely available software (as e.g. the LODE system[6]) that even allows self-recording and publishing (without external assistance).

We envision the transition from frontal teaching to VOLARE as a progressive process: during one academic year (some of) the lectures are recorded, and then they are used during the next year. Initially the recording can be limited to a few lectures, so that the VOLARE methodology can be introduced gradually.

The VOLARE methodology responds to the critics of video lectures, by using them only for KA, and fully compensates the lack of interaction during the video-lecture by providing strong interaction in class throughout the DU phase. Moreover, moving the KA phase on the video offers advantages respect to the traditional frontal lecture in terms of flexibility and of the possibility of reviewing portions of a lecture, which certainly favour a better comprehension.

4. ASSESSMENT

In order to test our ideas, we used the VOLARE methodology in a lecture during academic year 2008-09. Here we summarize the encouraging results that were reported elsewhere (Ronchetti, 2009). Given the success of the experiment, during the academic year 2009-10 a whole course involving approximately 100 students is being based on the proposed methodology. We expect to be able to publish our results soon.

As far as our first experiment is concerned, our starting point was the availability of lectures of an introductory programming course that were recorded in a.y. 2006-2007. The course is about object oriented programming, and the programming languages that are used to introduce and discuss the concepts are Java and C++ (with more emphasis on the first one). An especially challenging lecture was the one on the Java Collections framework, which makes a heavy use of the fundamental concept of Interface, which was new to the students. At the right time, instead of giving the frontal lecture on Java Collections we decided to require the students to take that lecture through the available videos of a previous edition of the course before coming to class.

The time in class was later used for a collective discussion. The teacher inquired about the key points, verified the students' understanding, and explained some issues. The teacher's impression was excellent: it really looked like most students had reached a deeper understanding of the key concepts through this interactive session. To be able to verify in a quantitative manner these impressions, students were required to go through an anonymous survey on the web. They had to express their agreement/disagreement with a set of sentences. Out of the approximately 60 students who were present in the classroom, 38 decided to respond to the questionnaire. A large majority of the students (ranging between 70 and 90%) stated that:

- Watching video lecture is not boring
- The methodology does not cause a work overload
- Discussions in class are useful and allow better understanding, deeper grasp of concepts, more active participation.

Students had the possibility to add free comments. Most comments were in line with the above findings, but two were skeptical about the applicability of the methodology to the whole course (as opposed to one single lecture), while one expressed a preference for a traditional setting, arguing that "it is more serious and more suited to an academic environment" (which we tend to interpret as an expected "resistance di innovation"). Overall, the results went beyond our expectations, and we are very curious to see the outcome of the larger scale experiment that is presently in progress.

Given the limited extent of the experiment, it was impossible to judge if, beyond the perception, the methodology actually achieves better results in terms of better students' performances. We shall try to investigate this aspect during the larger-scale experiment that is being presently run.

5. RELATED WORK

Lage et al. (2000) proposed a methodology that they called "Inverted classroom" that is a precursor of VOLARE. According to them, "inverting the classroom means that events that have traditionally taken place inside the classroom now take place outside the classroom and vice versa". Their approach is hence aligned with the general idea of the pre-lecture readings. VOLARE makes a more explicit use of modern technology and harvests the decade of experiments performed on on-line video lectures.

Independently, Foertsch et al. (2002) came to a similar idea. Online lectures are used to substitute traditional lectures with more laboratory sessions. The outcome was that "the replacement of live lectures with online lectures and Team Labs significantly enhanced the usefulness, convenience, and value of the course for the majority of students".

Day and Foley (2006) performed an experiment that is similar to what we propose; the main difference with VOLARE is that they used "canned lectures". Although they were not able to fully control all possible variables in the experiment, students who followed the video + class mode outperformed those following traditional lectures.

6. DISCUSSION AND CONCLUSION

A limitation of the VOLARE approach is that videos must be available in order to apply the methodology, and a strong emphasis is on the fact that videos must be recordings of real lectures delivered in class. Since this process spans over at least two academic years (one for recording and one for using the recorded videos), it is feasible only for the courses in which the content does not dramatically change from one year to the next. This is actually the case for most basic courses, where content may even remain almost exactly the same for (at least) a few years. Also, if the class is composed by only a small number of students, then the teaching/learning pace may be different in different years because of statistical fluctuations in the students' preparation and ability. If the number of students is relatively large (i.e. at least 50 or 60 students), as it often happens in basic courses, the statistical differences between different years are however not to be significant.

Evolution of the course however need not be frozen: a reasonable scenario could be that (after the bootstrap) every year a portion of the lecture (say on third) is given "in vivo" and re-recorded (allowing for content update and modification), while for the other two thirds VOLARE is applied. Of course this is just an example, as the percentage of content modification can be freely varied.

The VOLARE idea has been experimented by the author during the academic year 2008/09 on a relatively small scale (one lecture), and a larger experiment (one whole 50-hours course) is presently in progress. Results of the first test of the methodology has been reported elsewhere show that the students' feedback on the experiment was embarrassingly encouraging. It showed that students perceived it as effective and that it actually brought to a more interesting teaching.

REFERENCES

Abelson, H. (2008). The creation of OpenCourseWare at MIT. *Journal of Science Education and Technology*, *17*(2), 164–174. doi:10.1007/s10956-007-9060-8

Ally, M. (2008). Foundations of Educational Theory for Online Learning. In Anderson, T. (Ed.), *The Theory and Practice of Online Learning* (2nd ed.). Athabasca, CA: AU Press.

Bennett, E., & Maniar, N. (2008) *Are videoed lectures an effective teaching tool?* Retrieved May 15, 2009, from http://stream.port.ac.uk/papers

Berner, E. S., & Adams, B. (2004). Added value of video compared to audio lectures for distance learning. *International Journal of Medical Informatics*, *73*, 189–193. doi:10.1016/j.ijmedinf.2003.12.001

Brown, B. W., & Liedholm, C. E. L. (2004). Student Preferences in Using Online Learning Resources. *Social Science Computer Review*, *22*(4), 479–492. doi:10.1177/0894439304268529

Chen, S. Y., Ghinea, G., & Macredie, R. D. (2006). A cognitive approach to user perception of multimedia quality: An empirical investigation. *International Journal of Human-Computer Studies*, *64*, 1200–1213. doi:10.1016/j.ijhcs.2006.08.010

Chung, Q. B. (2005). Sage on the Stage in the Digital Age: The Role of Online Lecture in Distance Learning. *Electronic Journal of e-Learning, 3*(1), 1-14.

Collard, D., Girardot, S., & Deutsch, H. (2002). From the Textbook to the Lecture: Improving Prelecture Preparation in Organic Chemistry. *Journal of Chemical Education, 79*, 520–523. doi:10.1021/ed079p520

Day, J., & Foley, J. (2006). Evaluating web lectures: a case study from HCI. In *Proceedings of CHI 2006 – Experience Report – User Centered Design for Learning and Education* (pp.195-200).

9Demetriadis, S., & Pombortsis, A. (2007). e-Lectures for Flexible Learning: a Study on their Learning Efficiency. *Educational Technology & Society, 10*(2), 147–157.

Fey, A. (2002). Audio vs. Video: Hilft Sehen beim Lernen? Vergleich zwischen einer audio-visuellen und auditiven virtuellen Vorlesungen. *Lernforschung, 30*(4), 331–338.

Foertsch, J., Moses, G., Strickwerda, J., & Litzkov, M. (2002). Reversing the lecture/homework paradigm using eTEACH web-based streaming video software. *Journal of Engineering Education, 91*(3), 267–274.

Fong, A. C. M., & Hui, S. C. (2001). Low-bandwidth Internet streaming of multimedia lectures. *Engineering Science and Education Journal, 10*(6), 212–218. doi:10.1049/esej:20010601

Fritze, Y., & Nordkvelle, Y. (2003). Comparing Lectures – Effects of the Technological Context of the Studio. *Education and Information Technologies*, 327–343. doi:10.1023/B:EAIT.0000008675.12095.7a

Glowalla, U. (2004). Utility and Usability von E-Learning am Beispiel von Lecture-on-demand Anwendungen. In *Entwerfen und Gestalten*.

Hayes, M. H. (1998). Some approaches to Internet distance learning with streaming media. In *Proceedings of the Second IEEE Workshop on Multimedia Signal Processing*, Redondo Beach, CA.

Hilt, V., & Kuhmünch, C. (1999). New Tools for Synchronous and Asynchronous Teaching and Learning in the Internet. In *Proceedings of ED-MEDIA* (pp. 975-980).

Isiaka, B. (2007). Effectiveness of video as an instructional medium in teaching rural children agricultural and environmental sciences. *International Journal of Education and Development using Information and Communication Technology, 3*, 105-114

Krüger, M. (2005). Vortragsaufzeichnungen–Ein Querschnitt über die pädagogischen Forschungsergebnisse. In *Proceedings of the DeLFI Workshop*.

Lage, M. J., Platt, G. J., & Treglia, M. (2000). Inverting the Classroom: A Gateway to Creating an Inclusive Learning Environment. *The Journal of Economic Education, 31*(1), 30–43.

Lauer, T., Müller, R., & Trahasch, S. (2004). Learning with lecture recordings: key issues for end-users. In *Proceedings of the IEEE International Conference on Advanced Learning Technologies* (pp. 741-743).

Maness, J. M. (2006). *An evaluation of library instruction delivered to engineering students using streaming video.* Issues in Science and Technology Librarianship.

McCrohon, M., Lo, K., Dang, J., & Johnston, C. (2001). Video Streaming of Lectures Via the Internet An Experience. In *Proceedings of ASCILITE 2001 - The 18th Annual Conference of the Australasian Society for Computers in Learning in Tertiary Education*, Melbourne, Australia (pp. 397-405).

Moreno, R., & Mayer, R.-E. (2000). A Learner-Centred Approach to Multimedia Explanations: Deriving Instructional Design Principles from Cognitive Theory. *Interactive Multimedia Electronic Journal of Computer-Enhanced Learning, 2.*

Reisslein, J., Seeling, P., & Reisslein, M. (2005). Video in distance education: ITFS vs. web-streaming: Evaluation of student attitudes. *The Internet and Higher Education, 8*, 25–44. doi:10.1016/j.iheduc.2004.12.002

Ronchetti, M. (2003a). *Has the time come for using video-based lectures over the Internet? A Test-case report.* Paper presented at CATE - Web Based Education Conference, Rhodes, Greece.

Ronchetti, M. (2003b). Using the Web for diffusing multimedia lectures: a case study. In *Proceedings of ED-MEDIA* (pp. 337-340).

Ronchetti, M. (2009). Using video lectures to make teaching more interactive. In *Proceedings of the International Conference on Interactive Computer Aided Learning ICL-2009.*

Siemens, G. (2005). Connectivism. A learning theory for the digital age. *International Journal of Instructional Technology & Distance Learning, 2*(1).

Soong, S. K. A., Chan, L. K., & Cheers, C. (2006). Impact of video recorded lectures among students. In *Proceedings of the 23rd Annual Ascilite Conference: Who's learning? Whose technology?* (pp. 789-792).

Tobagi, F. (1995). Distance learning with digital video. *Multimedia, 2*(1), 90–93. doi:10.1109/93.368609

Zhang, D., Zhu, L., Briggs, L. O., & Nunamaker, J. F. Jr. (2006). Instructional video in e-learning: Assessing the impact of interactive video on learning effectiveness. *Information & Management, 43*, 15–27. doi:10.1016/j.im.2005.01.004

Zupancic, B., & Horz, H. (2002). Lecture recording and its use in a traditional university course. In *Proceedings of the 7th Annual Conf. on Innovation and Technology in Computer Science Education ITiCSE '02* (pp. 24-28). New York: ACM.

ENDNOTES

[1] http://en.wikipedia.org/wiki/Chroma_key

[2] http://www.youtube.com/user/UCBerkeley

[3] http://www.apple.com/education/mobile-learning

[4] http://watch.mit.edu/

[5] Goldberg. C. Auditing Classes at MIT, on the Web and Free. New York Times (2001)

[6] http://latemar.science.unitn.it/LODE

This work was previously published in the International Journal of Knowledge Society Research, Volume 1, Issue 2, edited by Miltiadis D. Lytras, pp. 50-60, copyright 2010 by IGI Publishing (an imprint of IGI Global).

Chapter 11
Kolb's Learning Styles and Approaches to Learning:
The Case of Chemistry Undergraduates with Better Grades

Patrícia Albergaria-Almeida
University of Aveiro, Portugal

Mariana Martinho
Escola EB 2,3/S de Oliveira de Frades, Portugal

José Joaquim Teixeira-Dias
University of Aveiro, Portugal

Chinthaka Balasooriya
University of New South Wales, Australia

ABSTRACT

The purpose of this study is to investigate if the teaching, learning and assessment strategies conceived and implemented in a higher education chemistry course promote the development of conceptual understanding, as intended. Thus, our aim is to analyse the learning styles and the approaches to learning of chemistry undergraduates with better grades.

This study took place during the 1ˢᵗ semester of the school year 2009/2010. This research was carried out in a naturalistic setting, within the context of chemistry classes for 1ˢᵗ year science and engineering courses, at the University of Aveiro, in Portugal. The class was composed of 100 students. At the end of the semester, the 8 chemistry students with the highest grades were selected for interview. Data was collected through Kolb's Learning Styles Inventory, through Approaches and Study Skills Inventory for Students, through non-participant observation, through the analysis of students' participation in online forums and lab books.

The overall results show that the students with better grades possess the assimilator learning style, that is usually associated to the archetypal chemist. Moreover, the students with the highest grades revealed a conception of learning emphasising understanding. However, these students diverged both in their learning approaches and in their preferences for teaching strategies. The majority of students adopted a deep approach or a combination of a deep and a strategic approach, but half of them revealed their preference for teaching-centred strategies.

DOI: 10.4018/978-1-4666-1788-9.ch011

1. INTRODUCTION

This paper is based upon a growing body of work shaped by a research project aiming to promote the advancement of the scholarship of teaching and learning (SoTL), through the implementation of classroom research, at the University of Aveiro, in Portugal (Albergaria Almeida, 2010; Almeida, Teixeira-Dias, & Medina, 2010). In the last decades, SoTL emerged as a fundamental concept to the development of good teaching practices in higher education (HE) and, consequently, to the enhancement of the quality of student learning. At this point we are investigating the learning styles and the approaches to learning of chemistry undergraduates with better grades.

Presently one of the main aims of HE is the development of the critical, reflective and creative thinking. These competencies can be achieved through the stimulation of students' active (Meltzer & Manivannan, 2002), deep (Entwistle, McCune, & Walker, 2001) and integrated learning (Kolb, 1984). In this essay we will refer to the teaching, learning and assessment strategies that were designed and implemented in the chemistry course for 1st year students in order to stimulate divergent thinking. Moreover, we will discuss how the students with better grades perceived these strategies and we will also examine the Kolb's learning styles and learning approaches of 1st year chemistry students with better grades.

Thus, by conducting this study we intend to investigate if the teaching, learning and assessment strategies conceived and implemented promote the development of conceptual understanding. The specific aims of this study are as follows: (i) to identify and characterise Kolb's learning styles and approaches to learning of chemistry undergraduates with better grades; (ii); to characterise the study habits of chemistry undergraduates with better grades; (iii) to identify the conceptions of learning of students with better grades, and (iv) to discuss the influence of learning, teaching and

assessment methods on approaches to learning and Kolb's learning styles of chemistry undergraduates with better grades.

The sections that follow present a brief literature review on learning and teaching chemistry in HE, on Kolb's learning styles, and on approaches to learning. Later, the methodology is described in detail. Finally, findings, conclusions and limitations are discussed.

2. OVERVIEW OF THE LITERATURE

2.1 Learning and Teaching Chemistry

Science disciplines operate at distinct levels, some of which are not observable (Johnstone, 1991, 1993). Treagust (2007) suggests that this can be particularly important in the teaching and learning of chemistry, since many concepts are abstract and unfamiliar to students. According to Johnstone (1991), learning of chemistry is a matter of learning about its representation at different levels, which can describe (macro level), represent (symbolic level) and explain (micro level) chemical phenomena, as shown in Figure 1.

The macro level refers to the phenomenological, or what can be perceived by senses without the assistance of instruments. This level usually is concerned with concrete information, such as references to students' everyday experiences. The symbolic level refers to pictorial representations, models, symbols and computational and algebraic forms. The micro level refers to abstract information, that can only be perceived with the aid of instruments or that which is abstracted by inference from chemical processes. For instance, this level comprises the particulate level, which can be used to describe the movement of electrons, molecules, particles or atoms (Johnstone, 1991; Mbajiorgu & Reid, 2006; Treagust, 2007).

153

Figure 1. Three levels of chemistry concept representation (Johnstone, 1991)

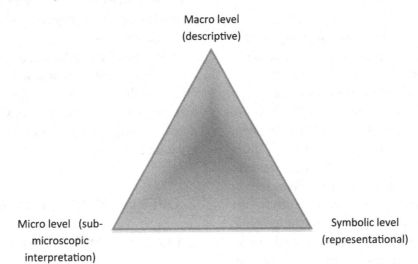

2.2 Kolb's Learning Styles

Chemistry is important as an independent disciplinary field and also as interdisciplinary since it provides a singularly significant understanding of our material world at the micro level, and it shares important connections with many other disciplinary fields, such as biology, electronics and physics. Chemistry is present in all aspects of our everyday life. In this regard, chemistry is a particularly practical disciplinary field and is continuously experiencing change as significant progresses are achieved.

Thus, it is crucial to alter the traditional chemistry courses that solely emphasise algorithmic problems (Mbajiorgu & Reid, 2006), and underline the importance of approaching and discussing open-ended problems (along with algorithmic exercises), both individually and group based (Johnstone, 1991, 1993). Problem solving has shown to be highly effective in enhancing quality thinking, attitudes, generating enjoyment and motivation and addressing issues where chemistry can be recognised and applied in real-life situations. It also constitutes an opportunity to promote genuine understanding. The highlighting on understanding is central in terms of developing a genuine competency.

Kolb's experiential learning theory (ELT; Joy & Kolb, 2009; Kolb, 1984; Kolb & Kolb, 2005; Yeganeh & Kolb, 2009) is one of the best-known educational theories in HE. The theory is called *experiential learning* to emphasize the central role that experience plays in the learning process; it is based on the notion that understanding is not an inflexible element of thought but is formed and re-formed through experience. ELT defines learning as "the process whereby knowledge is created through the transformation of experience. Knowledge results from the combination of grasping and transforming experience" (Kolb, 1984, p. 41).

According to the ELT, there are two primary axes that lie behind the cycle: an *abstract-concrete dimension* and an *active-reflective dimension*. These lead to the main dimensions of the learning process, corresponding to two distinctive ways by which learning takes place. The first refers to the ways in which new information or experience is grasped, and the second to how that which is perceived is then processed or transformed. The ways students perceive or grasp experience ranges from immersing themselves in the experience using their senses, feelings and knowledge in a concrete way (CE) to thinking abstractly about matters, using logic and reason (AC). Having perceived the experience, students need then to understand it through transforming it. Here individuals differ in their preference for doing so, either through active experimentation (AE) or by watching and reflective observation (RO) (Yeganeh & Kolb, 2009). Kolb (1984) identifies four learning styles with specific characteristics: accommodating, diverging, assimilating and converging (Table 1).

Yeganeh and Kolb (2009) suggest that because of the genetic background, the life experiences, and the demands of the environment, students develop a preference for learning in a particular way. The preferred style reflects only a tendency and students may adopt different learning styles in different situations, although they tend to favour some learning behaviours in preference to others.

Kolb (1984, 1999) proposes that it is possible to cluster disciplines based on predominant learning styles of their students. Different academic fields would favour different learning styles. As stated by Kolb (1981, p. 234), "Over time... selection and socialisation pressures combine to produce and increasingly impermeable and homogeneous disciplinary culture and correspondingly specialised student orientation to learning". Table 2 illustrates this distribution.

2.3 Approaches to Learning

The HE literature suggests that approaches to learning might be a useful mode of conceptualising different ways in which students experience a learning context. Marton and Säljö's (1976)

Table 1. Main characteristics of each Kolb learning style

Learning style	Strengths	Dominant learning modes
Accommodating	Carrying out plans and tasks that involve them in new experiences	CE and AE
Diverging	Imagination and generation of ideas	CE and RO
Assimilating	Creating theoretical models and making sense of distinct observations	AC and RO
Converging	Practical applications of ideas	AC and AE

Table 2. Distribution of disciplinary areas according to students' learning styles (adapted from Kolb, 1984, 1999)

Accommodating	**Diverging**
Marketing	Literature
Finances	Languages
Management	Music
Administration	Theater
Architecture	Psychology
Education	Nursing
Government	Social Work

Converging	**Assimilating**
Computer sciences	Chemistry
Environmental Science	Zoology
Chemical engineering	Biochemistry
Electrical engineering	Physics
Mechanical engineering	Mathematics
Civil engineering	Law
Medicine	Sociology

original study allowed distinguishing two approaches to learning: deep and surface. Each one is characterised by a specific intention which leads to qualitatively different learning outcomes. The main features of each learning approach are presented in Table 3.

In the deep approach, the intention to extract meaning produces active learning processes that involve relating ideas and looking for patterns and principles on the one hand, and using evidence and examining the logic of the argument on the other. This approach also involves monitoring the development of one's own understanding (Entwistle et al., 2001). In the surface approach, in contrast, the intention is just to cope with the task, which sees the course as unrelated bits of information which leads to much more restricted learning processes, in particular to routine memorisation.

In 1978, Biggs identified a third learning mode: the strategic approach, which is predominantly influenced by assessment. Learners adopting this approach are motivated by a desire to succeed and will use processes that they believe will most likely to achieve high grades.

3. THE PRESENT STUDY

The "Questions and Answers in Chemistry" project is based within a programme for 1st year students in sciences and engineering, at the University of Aveiro, in Portugal. This work relies upon the belief that it is possible to:

Table 3. Main features of deep, surface and strategic approach (Entwistle et al., 2001)

Deep Approach Seeking meaning
Intention – to understand ideas
Relating ideas to previous knowledge and experience
Looking for patterns and underlying principles
Checking evidence and relating it to conclusions
Examining logic and argument cautiously and critically
Being aware of understanding developing while learning
Becoming actively interested in the course content
Surface Approach Reproducing
Intention – to cope with course requirements
Treating the course as unrelated bits of knowledge
Memorising facts and carrying out procedures routinely
Finding difficulty in making sense of new ideas presented
Seeing little value or meaning in either courses or tasks set
Studying without reflecting on either purpose or strategy
Feeling undue pressure and worry about work
Strategic Approach Reflective organising
Intention – to achieve the highest possible grades
Putting consistent effort into studying
Managing time and effort effectively
Finding the right conditions and materials for studying
Being alert to assessment requirements and criteria
Gearing work to the perceived preferences of lectures

1. Enhance SoTL through the implementation of classroom research projects involving science university teachers and educational researchers;

2. Promote active, integrated and deep learning in chemistry through student-centred teaching approaches, namely by the encouragement of question-asking between teachers and students.

With this in mind, an action research project aiming to promote student-centred teaching approaches, and ultimately to enhance SoTL, is being developed with 100 chemistry students, in full collaboration between an educational researcher from the Education Department, and a professor from the Chemistry Department.

Following the suggestions of Mbajiorgu and Reid (2006), the teaching, learning and assessment strategies at the chemistry course for 1st year students were conceived, designed and implemented in order to support integration (Kolb, 1984) and foster deep learning (Entwistle et al., 2001). It was our intention that students' perceptions of the learning environment should be centred on the need for conceptual understanding. These strategies comprised several formats, such as:

1. *Small pauses during lectures* to encourage students' oral questions. In the middle of the lesson, the teacher stopped lecturing for two or three minutes, and invited the students to think about or to discuss the class topics with their colleagues. At the end of the break, students had the opportunity to raise oral questions. If the students felt more comfortable, they could write their questions instead, and the teacher would answer orally at the beginning of the next lesson.

2. *Teacher's written questions* during lectures to facilitate the organisation of teaching and learning and to serve as a role model to students. For instance, throughout the 'Water' topic, the teacher presented seven-teen written questions. These had diverse degrees of difficulty and served different functions. Some instances of the written questions drawn from our project are:

How can you describe the polarity of a water molecule?

Why are there substances that are gaseous, others are liquids and others are solids?

In the absence of gravity, why are water drops exactly spherical?

3. **Practical laboratory sessions** were conceived in order to promote the development of concepts and understanding and not merely as a handmaid of lectures. Having this in mind, these sessions were used for problem solving and development of concepts, as advised by Mbajiorgu & Reid (2006). In laboratory classes, the students have opportunities to: (a) identify the main objectives of the work; (b) identify and overcome any conceptual and practical difficulties encountered; (c) plan and execute the work; (d) record and discuss the results and observations in their lab book; (e) answer the questions raised in their laboratory manual (e.g. *Comment the title of this laboratory task, Is it possible to determine the percentage of copper recovery? How?*), and (f) raise oral or written questions. For instance, one of the practical activities proposed to students was:

   ○ **Viscosity of liquids:** compare the viscosity of several liquids and water at different temperatures. Consider an air bubble moving in the ascending sense in two liquids with different viscosities. In which liquid does the air bubble move faster? Using this principle, plan and execute experiments for comparing the viscosity of (a) water and diethyl ether; (b) water at several temperatures; (c) oil and water.

4. **'Questions and answers in Chemistry' online forum** to encourage and facilitate students' questioning. Students could use this tool to raise written questions related to the topics taught during lectures and practical laboratory sessions. The teacher answers all questions within two days, also on the online forum. All questions and answers are available to all chemistry students.

5. **'Problem-based cases' online forum to encourage students to ask questions and suggest** possible explanations for the phenomena proposed by the teacher. This kind of activity also aimed to enhance the discussion between students. One of the problem-based cases proposed to the class is shown in Figure 2.

In order to promote the alignment between teaching, learning and assessment (Biggs, 1999), the following assessment strategies were considered:

1. **Multiple-choice test** due to the large number of students in the chemistry course;

2. **Participation in the two online forums** considering both the number and the quality of the participation;

3. **Performance in practical laboratory work** considering both students' performance in practical classes and the content of the lab book.

3.1 Research Questions

According to Case and Marshall (2009), the way students perceive the learning context significantly influences their use of a specific approach. Then, in a chemistry course intentionally conceived and designed to promote higher-order thinking, *do students with better grades adopt a deep approach? Or is it possible to obtain high grades*

using a strategic or a surface approach? It also known that chemistry' students exhibit a tendency to adopt an assimilator style (Kolb, 1984). So, *do chemistry students with better grades possess an assimilator learning style?*

4. METHOD

4.1 Participants

The main sample was composed of 100 undergraduate students (56 female, 44 male; mean age 19 years old) who were tackling foundation chemistry, although following different degree programs, such as physics, environmental engineering and materials engineering; this class did not include students following a chemistry degree program. For this particular research, the eight chemistry students with the highest grades (all over 75%; Table 4) were selected and then analysed in a deeper way.

4.2 Data-Gathering

Data were gathered by means of observation of all Chemistry classes, students' interviews, documental analysis and the administration of the Portuguese version of the Learning Styles Inventory (Kolb, 1999) and the Portuguese version of the ASSIST (Valadas, Gonçalves & Faísca, 2009).

Non-Participant Observation

Throughout one semester, from September to December 2009, all the Chemistry classes were audio-recorded. Observation grids for every class were completed by an educational researcher, who was present at all classes. This way, all the interactions between the students and the teacher, as well as all the interactions between students were registered. Gillham (2000) stresses the importance of observation by mentioning that

Table 4. Main features of the eight students with the highest grades

Student (pseudonym)	Degree program	Age	Gender
Carlos	Physics	18	Male
Ricardo	Materials engineering	19	Male
Liliana	Environmental engineering	19	Female
André	Physics	19	Male
Fábio	Physics	19	Male
Bruno	Physics	18	Male
João	Environmental engineering	18	Male
Pedro	Physics	19	Male

through observation it is possible to observe what people actually do, and not what they say they do.

Kolb's Learning Style Inventory and Approaches and Study Skills Inventory for Students

Kolb's Learning Styles Inventory (LSI; Kolb, 1999) is one of the most prominent and extensively disseminated instruments used to determine individual learning preferences. LSI measures the relative emphases of each one of the four modes of the learning process (CE, RO, AC and AE), and the relationship between abstract and concrete (AC-CE), active and reflective modes (AE-RO). Kolb's LSI was adapted to a Portuguese context by Goulão (2001).

Approaches to learning were assessed with the use of the Approaches and Study Skills Inventory for Students (ASSIST; Tait, Entwistle, & McCune, 1998). The ASSIST was adapted to a Portuguese context by Valadas et al. (2009).

Both inventories were administered during a session with the researcher. The researcher explained the purpose of this activity as part of a research project which aimed to improve chemistry students' learning. The students were invited to write their names on the inventories sheet since the purpose of this activity was to relate their learning style and their approaches to learning to their grades. They were given the opportunity to know the results from the inventories and discuss the implications, since the inventories were not anonymous.

Interviews

As mentioned earlier, eight students were chosen in consideration of their grades. These eight students displayed the better grades at the end of the 1st semester. Students were interviewed individually in a quiet, private room within the building dedicated to the teaching of first year students of Science and Technology. During the interviews students were asked to reflect on their experience of the course (teaching and learning strategies, chemistry contents, assessment methods, study habits). All interviews were semi-structured and audio-recorded. Afterwards, the interviews were transcribed verbatim and content analysis was carried out.

Documental Analysis

Data such as course assessments, participation in online forums, and lab books were also gathered from these eight students. These data were also analysed and content analysis was conducted.

4.3 Data Analysis

Data from multiple sources (transcripts of classroom discourse from audio-recordings, transcripts of audio recorded interviews, field notes, results of both inventories, course assessments, lab books and records of students' participation in online forums) were analysed in relation to each other; this served to triangulate the data and to help enhance the credibility of the findings and assertions made (Lincoln & Guba, 1985).

5. FINDINGS AND DISCUSSION

5.1 Kolb's Learning Styles of Students with Better Grades

The results of the LSI for the eight students show that these learners fall into two camps: assimilating (7 students) and accommodating (1 student). As shown in Figure 3, only one of these students presents a clear preference for AC and AE, being a converger. The other seven students were identified as assimilators, showing a preference for grasping information through AC and processing it through RO. These results concur with those obtained by Kolb (1984, 1999) and Nulty and Barret (1996) (see Table 1), suggesting that the typical chemist is an assimilator. Assimilators usually possess the abilities to create theoretical models, to compare alternatives, to define problems and to formulate hypotheses (Kolb, 1984).

However, as referred earlier, these students are not following a chemistry degree program. The 7 assimilators are studying other scientific areas, such as physics (n=4), materials engineering (n=1) and environmental engineering (n=2), as shown in Table 4. Kolb (1984, 1999) and Nulty and Barret (1996) also associate physics with the assimilating style. In what concerns the other disciplinary fields (environmental engineering and materials engineering), these are usually

related to the converging style. This style shares the preference for AC with the assimilating style.

The student with a convergent style is following a physics degree program. As referred earlier, this discipline is associated to the assimilating style (AC and RO). However, this student presents a clear preference for AC and AE. If considering the group of eight students with better grades, Fábio was the one with lower marks. It is possible that this student had to struggle more to obtain better grades, since his learning style was different from the one usually associated to chemistry.

Even if the assimilating style is characterised by a clear tendency to theory and models, five of these students related their preference for practical classes. Though expressing this preference, these students were aware of the importance of both kinds of classes:

I know that both kinds of classes are important… but I prefer laboratory classes because I can apply what I am learning in lectures… I guess I prefer practical classes because I am more involved in class than in lectures… (João)

I really like to touch the instruments and the materials… and I enjoy to plan my work… so I prefer practical classes… But of course… I know that I would not be able to conduct the practical tasks without the knowledge from lectures. (Liliana)

One student, Ricardo, presented a clear preference for lectures:

Lectures! I prefer lectures because I think that the laboratory tasks are too easy… maybe it is because I already have performed these tasks or others that were similar during high school… well, I like lectures and practical classes, but I think that I learn more in lectures… there is a bigger challenge in lectures… even when the teacher is teaching a topic that I have already studied in high school, there is always a lot of new informa-

tion... so, I really enjoy lectures because I learn a lot! (Ricardo)

Bruno and Carlos, enjoyed equably both kinds of classes:

It's not easy to say which one I prefer or which one I like the most... I think that both are fundamental to chemistry: I cannot conduct the practical work without knowing the theory, and the theory by itself is not important too... So, I cannot say that I prefer lectures or practical classes, because both are equally significant and both are important to me. (Bruno)

It is also relevant to observe the position of Bruno's and Carlos' styles in the learning style chart presented in Figure 3. Bruno and Carlos – the students with highest grades - appear as assimilators, but their data points are close to the centre of the grid, when comparing with their colleagues. This position indicates that these students' learning styles are quite balanced. The more balanced the learning style is, the more the students are able to deal with diverse learning tasks, requiring different learning abilities (Kolb & Kolb, 2005).

5.2 Approaches to Learning of Students with Better Grades

The results of the ASSIST, including conceptions of learning, learning approaches and preferences for different types of courses and teaching, are presented in Table 5.

Building on Säljö's (1979) research, Marton, Dall'Alba and Beaty (1993) identified and characterised six conceptions of learning: (a) increasing one's knowledge, (b) memorizing and reproducing, (c) applying, (d) understanding, (e) seeing something in a different way and (f) changing as a person. This list of conceptions is hierarchical, increasing in both extent and depth from (a) to (f). The first three are related to a surface approach and reveal a conception of learning as reproducing knowledge. The last three are evidence of deep learning and represent a view of learning involving understanding and personal development.

The eight students showed a conception of learning associated with a deep learning approach. During interviews, all the students remarked that it was important to memorise and apply knowledge, but all agreed that learning could not be, and should not be, only memorizing and applying. For instance, João said that:

Table 5. Main features of the students according to the ASSIST

Student	Conception of learning	Learning approach	Different types of courses and teaching
Carlos	seeking meaning	strategic	supporting understanding
Ricardo	seeking meaning	deep	supporting understanding
Liliana	seeking meaning	deep	transmitting information
André	seeking meaning	deep	transmitting information
Fábio	seeking meaning	surface	transmitting information
Bruno	seeking meaning	deep	supporting understanding
João	seeking meaning	deep	transmitting information
Pedro	seeking meaning	deep	supporting understanding

Learning... is not only memorising, because when we try to memorise we don't learn anything... eventually we forget what we memorise (...) learning is to understand the meaning of things... I think this is the most important feature of learning... the most important is to understand, if we comprehend we can connect ideas and even if we forget something, we can relate what we know and move ahead... (João)

All students emphasised the role of understanding in the learning process. Bruno and Carlos went beyond this and also stressed the importance of questioning and critical thinking in the learning process:

Learning is to gather information and knowledge in a way that allow us to reflect about it and reach new conclusions or ask new questions, in order to gather more information... it is a cycle because it is always repeating itself: the more information and knowledge we have, the more knowledge we need to have to answer our own questions about the knowledge we have acquired before... it is like a spiral... it has no end. (Bruno)

Learning is innate... we are all used to learn, but we never think about what we do when we are learning (...) I think that it is fundamental to have critical thinking... everyday we are exposed to a huge amount of new information, and we must be critical... select this information, think about it... we must have critical sense... (Carlos)

Five students adopted a deep learning approach (Liliana, André, João, Ricardo and Pedro); two used a strategic approach (Carlos and Bruno) and only one was identified as a surface learner (Fábio).

Carlos and Bruno were identified as strategic learners through the ASSIST; the interviews showed that these students associated the strategic approach with a deep approach. This seems to be the most successful way to cope with the learning and assessment tasks in this course, since these

learners were the ones with the highest grades. One of the main concerns of the strategic learners is the organisation of time. About this Carlos said that:

I save a lot of time going to lectures [these are not compulsory] because I learn a lot more paying attention to the teacher then studying on my own afterwards (...) and I also take notes of other details explained by the teacher and that are not in the PowerPoint presentations... this way, it is easier to study

These two students also take into account the demands of practical classes, considering both the preparation of practical tasks (before the class) and the execution of the task (during the class). As mentioned by Bruno:

I prepare each task before the class because, this way, it is easier to complete the practical work... First I read the information on the manual, and I get a broad idea of the task... I took a lot of time thinking and writing. So, I have to optimise this and preparing the task at home helps me to save time in class (...) At home, before the class, I read the manual, I take notes, and I write some parts of the report, like the aims, the procedure, the abstract and the security measures. In the class, I take into account what I have learned in lectures, and I try to relate this knowledge to the practical task.

When asked about his participation on the online forums, Carlos emphasised the challenge of discussing chemically day life situations. In Figure 4, we present a short excerpt of a discussion about the problem-based case "acid rain" (Figure 2). The first student to approach this topic was Pedro (a deep learner). He asked an integration question, a kind of question typical of deep learners (Almeida et al., 2008), that was promptly answered by Ricardo (also a deep learner) and by Carlos (a strategic-deep learner).

Figure 2. Problem-based case about acid rain

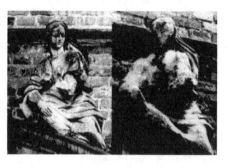

Problem-based case "Acid rain"

Having in mind your knowledge about acids and basis, ask questions or propose possible explanations for the following phenomenon:

Marble and limestone are the most used materials in the construction of buildings and monuments. Both marble and limestone are composed by calcium carbonate $(CaCO_3)$, *differing only in the crystalline structure*. Even if both are known by their high durability, buildings and monuments build with marble and limestone are gradually eroded through the action of acid rain. *How can we explain this phenomenon?*

(More information about acid rain available in: Atkins, P. and Loretta, J. (2005). *Chemical Principles – The Quest for Insight* (3rd Ed.). New York: W. H. Freeman and Company. p. 396)

Figure 3. Distribution of the eight students according to LSI

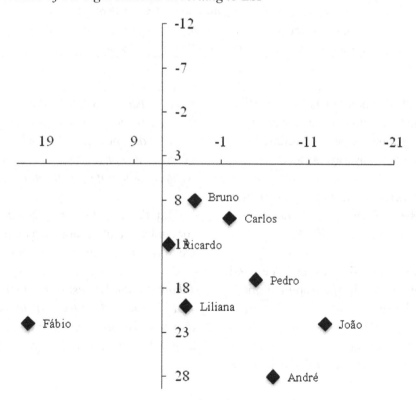

Figure 4. Example of an interaction moment between students, in one of the online forums

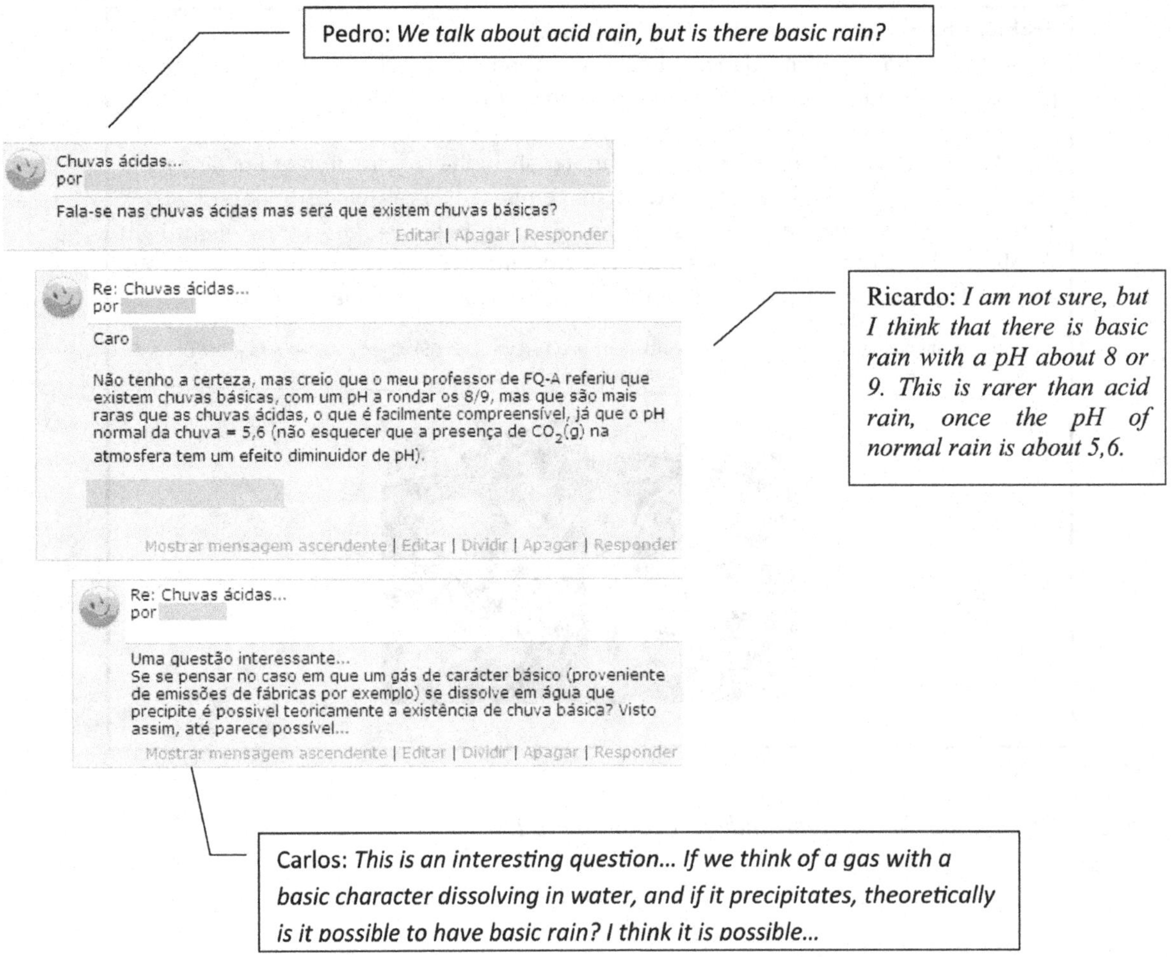

Pedro: *We talk about acid rain, but is there basic rain?*

Chuvas ácidas...
por

Fala-se nas chuvas ácidas mas será que existem chuvas básicas?

Editar | Apagar | Responder

Re: Chuvas ácidas...
por

Caro

Não tenho a certeza, mas creio que o meu professor de FQ-A referiu que existem chuvas básicas, com um pH a rondar os 8/9, mas que são mais raras que as chuvas ácidas, o que é facilmente compreensível, já que o pH normal da chuva = 5,6 (não esquecer que a presença de $CO_2(g)$ na atmosfera tem um efeito diminuidor de pH).

Mostrar mensagem ascendente | Editar | Dividir | Apagar | Responder

Ricardo: *I am not sure, but I think that there is basic rain with a pH about 8 or 9. This is rarer than acid rain, once the pH of normal rain is about 5,6.*

Re: Chuvas ácidas...
por

Uma questão interessante...
Se se pensar no caso em que um gás de carácter básico (proveniente de emissões de fábricas por exemplo) se dissolve em água que precipite é possível teoricamente a existência de chuva básica? Visto assim, até parece possível...

Mostrar mensagem ascendente | Editar | Dividir | Apagar | Responder

Carlos: *This is an interesting question... If we think of a gas with a basic character dissolving in water, and if it precipitates, theoretically is it possible to have basic rain? I think it is possible...*

All the students that participated in these discussions said that the bonus on the final grade was an interesting stimulus, but also referred that they would participate anyway, because:

We don't have this kind of activity in other courses and it is interesting to discuss ideas and situations like this with our colleagues... (Pedro)

In what concerns the final exams, deep and strategic learners agreed in their opinion about the multiple choice test:

Sometimes people think that it is easier because it is a multiple choice test... I don't think so. We really must know and understand everything because we must choose only that answer. It is not like an open question, where we can write everything and escape from those aspects that we don't dominate... (Liliana)

But, these students also agree that it is easier for students that do not prepare properly for the exam to reach acceptable grades:

I think this kind of test is good for those students that do not study a lot... if they are in a lucky day, they can pass the exam... but I think it is not so good for me... because I want to have higher

grades and I feel that I would perform better if it was an exam with open questions (Carlos)

Fábio was the only surface learner. He did not participate in the online discussions and did not attend all classes, because "*it was not compulsory*". About the exams, he expressed an opinion quite different from his peers:

I like this kind of test... sometimes it is a bit confusing because the options are quite similar, but if we study we can have a good grade.

About his study habits, Fábio added that:

We have a lot of tests in the same week... it is not easy to study all days... I know I should do this, but... I only study about two days before the exam... once I had chemistry in high school it is not so difficult for me, and I can do this...

Even if the eight students have a conception of learning that is associated with a deep approach, and if the majority of learners adopt a deep or strategic approach to learning, their preferences in what concerns types of teaching are divided: four students show a preference for types of teaching that emphasise the transmission of information, while the other four prefer teaching strategies that enhance understanding (Table 5).

6. CONCLUSION, LIMITATIONS AND FURTHER RESEARCH

From this study it is clear that it is possible to create a learning environment focused on conceptual understanding. This research shows that, with appropriate and diversified strategies, stimulus and motivation, students can enhance their interest and engagement with learning chemistry and, consequently, adopt a deep learning and obtain higher grades. This concurs with what was reported by Entwistle and Peterson (2004, p. 422): "University teachers using approaches indicating a student-oriented approach to teaching and a focus on student learning (as opposed to a transmission approach) are more likely to have, in their classes, students who describe themselves as adopting a deep approach in their studying".

From the eight students selected, seven were identified as assimilators, the learning style associated to the archetypal chemist. Carlos and Bruno, both identified as balanced learners (Kolb & Kolb, 2005) were also characterised as strategic-deep learners. It seems that these learners are at a higher level of development, having the ability to display different abilities, according to the demands of the learning environment. We believe that it is worth to analyse, with a larger sample, the possible existence of a relationship between the balanced style (Kolb, 1984) and the strategic approach (Entwistle et al., 2001), when this is associated with a deep approach to learning. This could enhance the relationship already established between these two distinct theories of learning styles (Almeida et al., 2008).

Having in mind one of the suggestions proposed by several students, during the second semester the exams also included open questions, in which students were asked to raise questions or explain specific situations. It is our intention to compare the grades of this small sample of students during the 1st semester (multiple choice tests) with their grades on the 2nd semester (multiple choice tests with open questions).

Due to the specific context and to the small number of students interviewed, it is not possible to generalise the results. Thus, one of our purposes for future research is to develop a similar study with a larger sample of students, as well as with students with different kinds of grades (from the lower to the highest marks). We also intend to clearly specify the kind of strategies conceived, as well as the context in which these were implemented, in order to promote discussion about the kind of teaching, learning and assessment strategies that can be used to promote deep learning.

7. REFERENCES

Albergaria Almeida, P. (2010). Scholarship of teaching and learning: an overview. *Journal of the World Universities Forum, 3*(2), 143–154.

Almeida, P., Pedrosa de Jesus, H., & Watts, M. (2008). Developing a mini-project: students' questions and learning styles. *Psychology of Education Review, 32*(1), 6–17.

Almeida, P., Teixeira-Dias, J. J., & Medina, J. (2010). Enhancing the Scholarship of Teaching and Learning: the interplay between teaching and research. *International Journal of Teaching and Case Studies, 2*(3/4), 262–275.

Biggs, J. (1978). Individual and group differences in study processes. *The British Journal of Educational Psychology, 48*, 266–279.

Biggs, J. (1999). *Teaching for Quality Learning at University*. London: SRHE and Open University Press.

Case, J., & Marshall, D. (2009). Approaches to learning. In Tight, M., Mok, K. H., Huisman, J., & Morphew, C. C. (Eds.), *The Routledge International Handbook of Higher Education*. New York: Routledge.

Entwistle, N. J., McCune, V., & Walker, P. (2001). Conceptions, styles and approaches within higher education: analytic abstractions and everyday experience. In Sternberg, R. J., & Zhang, L. F. (Eds.), *Perspectives on Cognitive, Learning and Thinking styles* (pp. 103–136). Mahwah, NJ: Erlbaum.

Entwistle, N. J., & Peterson, E. R. (2004). Conceptions of learning and knowledge in higher education: relationships with study behaviour and influences of learning environments. *International Journal of Educational Research, 41*, 407–428. doi:10.1016/j.ijer.2005.08.009

Gillham, B. (2000). *Case study research methods*. London: Continuum.

Goulão, M. F. (2001). *Ensino aberto à distância: cognição e afectividade*. Unpublished PhD thesis, Open University.

Johnstone, A. H. (1991). Why is science difficult to learn? Things are seldom what they seem. *Journal of Computer Assisted Learning, 7*, 75–83. doi:10.1111/j.1365-2729.1991.tb00230.x

Johnstone, A. H. (1993). The development of chemistry teaching: a changing response to changing demand. *Journal of Chemical Education, 70*(9), 701–705. doi:10.1021/ed070p701

Joy, S., & Kolb, D. A. (2009). Are there cultural differences in learning style? *International Journal of Intercultural Relations, 33*, 69–85. doi:10.1016/j.ijintrel.2008.11.002

Kolb, A., & Kolb, D. A. (2005). Learning styles and learning spaces: enhancing experiential learning in Higher Education. *Academy of Management Learning & Education, 4*(2), 193–212.

Kolb, D. A. (1981). Learning styles and disciplinary differences. In Chickering, A. W.,(Eds.), *The modern American college*. San Francisco: Jossey-Bass.

Kolb, D. A. (1984). *Experiential Learning: experience as the source of learning and development*. Englewood Cliffs, NJ: Prentice Hall.

Kolb, D. A. (1999). *The Kolb Learning Style Inventory version 3*. Boston: Hay Resources Direct.

Lincoln, Y. S., & Guba, E. G. (1985). *Naturalistic Inquiry*. Newbury Park, CA: Sage.

Marton, F., Dall'Alba, G., & Beaty, E. (1993). Conceptions of Learning. *International Journal of Educational Research, 19*(3), 277–300.

Marton, F., & Säljö, R. (1976). On qualitative differences in learning: I. Outcome and process. *The British Journal of Educational Psychology, 46*, 4–11.

Mbajiorgu, N., & Reid, N. (2006). *Factors Influencing Curriculum Development in Chemistry.* Hull, UK: Higher Education Academy Physical Sciences Centre.

Meltzer, D. E., & Manivannan, K. (2002). Transforming the lecture-hall environment: The fully interactive physics lecture. *American Journal of Physics, 70*(6), 639–654. doi:10.1119/1.1463739

Nulty, D. D., & Barrett, M. A. (1996). Transitions in students' learning styles. *Studies in Higher Education, 22*(3), 333–345. doi:10.1080/03075079612331381251

Säljö, R. S. (1979). *Learning in the learner's perspective. I. Some common-sense conceptions (Rep. No. 76).* Gothenberg, Sweden: University of Gothenberg.

Tait, H., Entwistle, N., & McCune, V. (1998). ASSIST: A reconceptualisation of the approaches to studying inventory. In Rust, C. (Ed.), *Improving student learning: improving students as learners.* Oxford, UK: Oxford Brookes University.

Treagust, D. (2007). General Instructional Methods and Strategies. In Abell, S. K., & Lederman, N. G. (Eds.), *Handbook of Research in Science Teaching* (pp. 373–392). Mahwah, NJ: Lawrence Erlbaum Associates Publishers.

Valadas, S., Gonçalves, F., & Faísca, L. (2009). Approaches to studying in higher education Portuguese students: A Portuguese version of the approaches and study skills inventory for students. *Higher Education, 59,* 259–275. doi:10.1007/s10734-009-9246-5

Yeganeh, B., & Kolb, D. (2009). Mindfulness and experiential learning. *OD Practitioner - Journal of the Development Organization Network, 41*(3), 13-18.

This work was previously published in the International Journal of Knowledge Society Research, Volume 1, Issue 3, edited by Miltiadis D. Lytras, pp. 1-16, copyright 2010 by IGI Publishing (an imprint of IGI Global).

Chapter 12
Curriculum Design and Development for Computer Science and Similar Disciplines

Igor Schagaev
London Metropolitan University, UK

Elisabeth Bacon
University of Greenwich, UK

Nicholas Ioannides
London Metropolitan University, UK

ABSTRACT

In this paper, curriculum design and development for computer science and similar disciplines as a formal model is introduced and analysed. Functions of education process as knowledge delivery and assessment are analysed. Structural formation of curriculum design is presented using definitive, characteristic and predictive functions. The process of changes in the discipline is also described and analysed. The authors then develop an algorithm to determine the core of the discipline and functions of the core moving and merging are introduced.

1. INTRODUCTION

Computer Science is a relatively new and fast growing discipline for teaching. It absorbs different theoretical and technical results from different disciplines and creates a fusion which penetrates and influences many aspects of human life. Computer Science is, in fact, the theoretical base for the fastest ever growing area of technological development, that of Information Technology (IT). At first glance, Computer Science as a discipline should absorb its own technical applications (IT), but previous attempts to do this failed.

This work attempts to form a logical *core* of *curriculum design* for computer science and similar disciplines. Initially, the main terms used are defined and the role of education as a very important driving force in the improvement of life for the society at large is identified (Section 2); then existing models of *curriculum develop-*

DOI: 10.4018/978-1-4666-1788-9.ch012

ment and their drawbacks are briefly discussed (Section 3). Curriculum design as *information processing* is then analysed (Section 4) and further developed by the introduction of three main functions in discipline construction: *definitive, characteristic* and *predictive* (Section 5). The *core* of the discipline, the way of its selection and its main features: *moving* and *merging*, are analysed and discussed (Section 6) and finally further work and open problems in the further development of our approach are presented (Section 7).

2. SCIENCE, KNOWLEDGE, SKILLS, CURRICULUM: DEFINITIONS AND CLASSIFICATIONS

The main terms used in this study are general and have a variety of meanings which depend on the human activity that they may be used for. It is, therefore, necessary to define the specific meaning of these terms for the work presented here. Complete description of each term can be found in The New Penguin English Dictionary (2001).

- **Science:** 1. The study, description, experimental investigation and theoretical explanation of the nature and behaviour of phenomena in the physical and natural world; 2. Branch of systematized knowledge of study.
- **Knowledge:** 1. Information, understanding acquired through learning or experience; 2. The total body of known facts or those associated with a particular subject; 3. Justified or verifiable belief, as distinct from opinion *(Phil)*.
- **Skills:** Special abilities in particular field acquired by learning or practice.
- **Curriculum:** The courses offered by an educational institution or followed by an individual or group;
- **Latin:** running, course, course of study, programme

- **Computer Science:** Study of the construction, operation, and use of computers

A more holistic approach to the word *curriculum* assumes that it should be placed between the *aim of education* and the *learning outcome*, where the *aim* is "what we want to achieve" and the *learning outcome* is "what we are able to measure". A major question raised here about the *learning outcome*, as this term assumes to express in one sentence the result of education, is whether we can actually do this!? This term will not be used here and its applicability is out of the scope of this work.

Curriculum design was analysed by Aristotle: "For the formal nature is of greater importance than the material nature" (Jeans, 1930) and Confucius: "He who learns but does not think is lost; He who thinks but does not learn is in great danger", clearly identifying the necessity of reflecting on what one has learned.

The idea of this work is to build an algorithm of *Curriculum design* and development for *Computer Science* disciplines using our own recent theoretical results and experience during the re-development of an existing module within the Faculty of Computing of the London Metropolitan University.

The terminology shows that *Science* differs from *Knowledge* by the indirect introduction of *the Subject* (an agent) to receive *Knowledge*. In spite of its well-deserved recognition, the Penguin Dictionary has, in our opinion, a serious mistake in the definition of the word *Knowledge* by using the too general and absolutely not essential in this context term *Information*. Long discussions on the interrelations of this term are presented in the number of books written by N. Wirth, E. Dijkstra, W. Turski and others. Our opinion about the relation between *knowledge* and *information* is shown below and the efficiency of this description is further elaborated below:

Knowledge = Information + Algorithm of its Application

Curriculum, in turn, is just another name for the program of study. Just like any other program it must be complete, efficient and reliable in order to provide *Education* in the selected area or discipline. The cycle of education is completed when its outcome has been returned back to the society (Figure 1). The roles of the main agents (student and teacher), are analysed here in the framework of the education process.

As shown in Figure 1, feedback is the main measure of teaching success. During teaching the lecturer is the main *deliverer* of the products:

Knowledge and *Skills*. The main *consumer* or *customer* is the student. The cycle of education is completed when *a customer* returns his/her results back to the society and, therefore, becomes *a deliverer*.

Confucius indirectly confirms the usefulness of this kind of modelling when he presented a measure of success for education by the production of better men after education: "a goal is to create gentlemen who carry themselves with grace, speak correctly, and demonstrate the integrity of things". The model presented here goes a step further with the teacher becoming the main *manufacturer* and *deliverer* of *Knowledge*, while the student changes his/her role from *consumer* during the learning

Figure 1. 'Return the results of education to society' algorithm

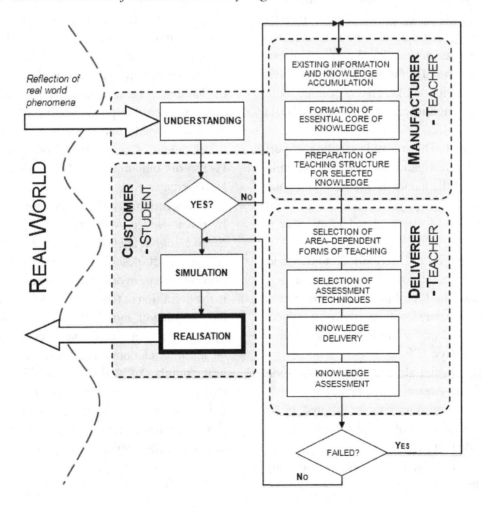

process to a *deliverer* after it, when s/he returns back to society new experiences from the results of education, while Confucius claims only that teacher is "a transmitter and not maker".

Any discipline of Computer Science assumes a certain amount of *Knowledge* and *Skills* in some proportion which plays a very important role in discipline design, and therefore, curriculum development. *Skills* are different from *Knowledge* in the definitions presented above as they concern a special ability, not a wide understanding of the area. A good argument in favour of this differentiation is the variation in the area of application – *Skills* are concerned with the application of particular *Knowledge* or experience in a specific, well known environment, whereas *Knowledge* is about the application of experience and learning outcomes in an uncertain and wide environment. This separation is important in further discipline structure and its curriculum development.

The equation $K+S$ = *Successful Application* presents *Knowledge (K)* and *Skills (S)* as essential components of education. Rigorous separation of K and S helps to balance discipline structure by means of using the most appropriate instruments of the teaching/learning circle: lectures, tutorials, practicals, courseworks, as well as various assessment techniques. Three main but different types of segments (modules) of Computer Science as discipline are presented in Figure 2.

Case A refers to areas within the discipline of Computer Science such as Algorithm Design and Problem Solving, Software Engineering, Network Technologies, Theory of Programming, Discrete Math, Theory of Data Bases, etc. Case B refers to areas such as Human Computer Interaction, Computer Aided Design, Computer Graphics, etc. Case C refers to areas such as Web Design, HTML, Java, Visual Basic, Modula-2, Pascal, Applications of Data Bases, etc.

In disciplines where $K > S$ the discipline must be built with a wide area of knowledge, be more abstract and, where possible, general in order to show the limits of the existing knowledge, as well as its place in the context of science. Areas of discipline which fall within this scenario require much more active lectures and seminars in the pure academic meaning of these words.

In disciplines where $K < S$ there should be more concern for deeper and practical aspects of one narrow area of skills and also of the applicability of these skills. Areas of discipline which fall within this scenario require many more practical sessions with small introductions of elementary or essential theory.

There is no doubt that the *curriculum* for these different cases should have different structure and forms.

The invention of measurement and efficiency of teaching and progress of learning by the use of the so-called Learning Outcomes (LO) caused both serious criticism and scepticism amongst practitioners. Indeed, when considering that 11 from 15 modules in Computer Science have nearly

Figure 2. Ratio of knowledge and skills in computer science disciplines; the blue (darker) segment presents knowledge.

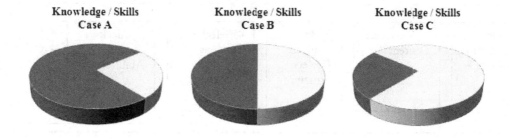

identical LOs and with all others being pretty much similar the immediate question which arises is: what do these LOs actually mean? Neither the structure of the discipline, nor its context and success of understanding can be described in two or three sentences.

It is clear from the above that new research is required in the area of structuring of knowledge delivery and derivation of schemes in order to measure the result of discipline delivery. The research work presented here focuses on schemes of knowledge delivery and assessing and in this context *Curriculum Development.*

3. MODELLING OF EDUCATIONAL PROGRAM DEVELOPMENT

Three very complex entities are involved in the process of education: *Science, Science Deliverer* (Lecturer) and *Science Consumer* (Student). Various authors such as Toohey (1999), Ramsden (1992) and Diamond (1989) described the main elements of the course design process, their interrelation in time and their logical order. The most cited author (Ramsden, 1992) presents the generalized model as is shown in Figure 3.

This model (Figure 3) suffers from poor logic: student characteristics are placed before content determination; goals and objectives, which are much more general terms and wider in meaning, are placed after determination of the context; teaching and assessment methods are selected based on goals and objectives; implementation and evaluation requires "adjustment" as necessary, but with no indication as to the meaning of the phrase "as necessary". More logical might be the sequence presented in Figure 4.

But even this "logicalisation" (Figure 4) cannot change the comments on the applicability, usefulness and efficiency and their measurement in the course design process. Both models shown in Figures 3 and 4 are too general to be useful. Beyond this, neither Toohey's (1999), nor Ramsden's (1992) or Diamond's (1989) models even mention the resource dependence of the discipline and possible ways of its delivery.

Figure 3. A typical model of the course design process (Ramsden, 1992)

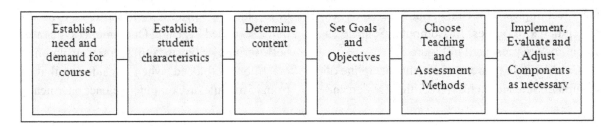

Figure 4. Modified model of course design process

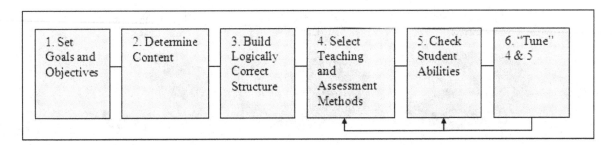

We must add that the context of the discipline should be involved, embedded and reflected in and during the *curriculum design process*. These arguments make obvious the need to develop a new model of the discipline and, therefore, curriculum design. The order is important: at first, one has to develop *a discipline*, and *then* the way of delivery. Below is such a sequence of discipline development:

- Determination and definitions of the main elements in the discipline
  - Description of connections between definitions
  - Selection of main features of definitions
- Analysis of the schemes for discipline delivery (either existing, or new)
- Specification of discipline delivery main elements
  - Course structure
  - Assessment instruments
  - Performance issues and scheme of its measurement

Recent papers by Schagaev (1990, 2001) and Schagaev et al. (2001) concern a development of the *Theory of Information Processing,* described at the level of the main categories and resources. In these papers, *input information* goes through an algorithm (processing), *new information* is created on the way and *the result* is produced and delivered. The process *of Learning* can also be analysed as *Information Processing* and vice versa: *The Processes of Teaching and Learning are in fact one entity - Information Processing.*

4. CURRICULUM DEVELOPMENT AS INFORMATION PROCESSING

By accepting this point of view we could apply terms and results from the *theory of information processing* for various aspects and areas of pedagogy – in this case to the processes of discipline and curriculum development. This means that principles of classification for information systems can help build a course of learning with the highest possible understanding as well as a measure of this understanding.

The next important issue relates to the analysis of all possible resources necessary to form a *discipline* and its *curriculum*. Rigorous classification of resources and ways of their use and processing should be built to form the framework for all further steps.

The delivery of *Knowledge* is a process of transforming a student from a state without *Knowledge* to another state, where the *Knowledge* obtained can be assessed and confirmed. The process of assessment can differentiate those students with the required level of *Knowledge* and those without. A well-known sequence of steps to deliver knowledge includes:

a. *Knowledge* delivery,
b. Delivery of practical (application of knowledge),
c. An assessment.

All steps in this sequence should be completed at the right time and in such a manner that the system (University) should notice neither a fault nor the process of its elimination. Students are involved in all these steps. Some may not understand some elements and/or may not be able to "process" information when delivered in the course, but can catch up during the course. The passing of an assessment will then confirm a student as successful in acquiring the required level of knowledge. In some cases, however, expected failure, lack of confidence or change of interest may cause a student to change his/her course. Such cases will not be considered here due to the uncertainty and existing elements of subjectivity that such cases entail.

In reality, many more steps (in the *Knowledge Delivery Algorithm*) are needed to eliminate malfunctions and avoid student failures or even their withdrawal from a course. These actions depend on the various functions and features of learning and the teaching processes, their roles and "power" to provide knowledge for the students.

A Knowledge Delivery System can be analyzed as an information processing system using first order philosophical categories such as *matter* and *time*. For *Knowledge Delivery* it is *structure* and *time*. More importantly, the main function of *Knowledge* (information) delivery must be considered at the first level of description, together with matter (structure) and time (see Figure 5).

The levels shown in Figure 5 describe the structural core of the system to deliver *Knowledge*. While *first order* categories present reflections of our understanding (they exist in the mind only), the *second order* descriptions (hardware, software) present real world objects as *executive elements* for the first order categories.

In general, the above mentioned sequence of steps to deliver knowledge should be completed

in proper time and in such a manner that an "average" student could cope with and be able *to continue* learning. At the same time we have to pay attention to the following sensible comments:

1. Time spent on exams and tests, in fact, is excluded from learning;
2. This sequence does not match IT use;
3. There is no direct evidence that lectures delivered were transformed into Knowledge until the assessment was completed and passed.

The first statement suggests that the time of learning and the time of assessment (tests, exams) are separated for the student and is usually wrong to expect that under pressure of a possible failure the student continues to learn during the assessment.

The second statement suggests that knowledge delivery uses IT in one-way, and assessment uses IT in another. Knowledge delivery primarily

Figure 5. Classification of resources to deliver Knowledge

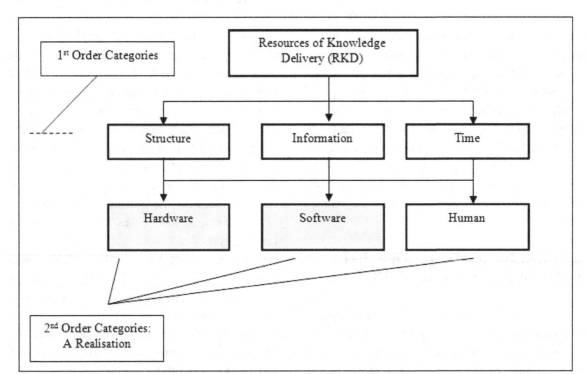

concerns presentation aspects, while the use of IT in assessment is often based on multiple-choice questions.

The third statement suggests that even the best developed and presented lectures can be unclear for students with different background. It becomes visible only during exams, and by then it is too late.

What options and resources do we have when creating a discipline and curriculum suitable for efficient teaching and learning? Again, according to Schagaev (1990, 2001) and Schagaev et al. (2001) these are *structure*, *time* and *information*. At the same time, it is clear that testing time (assessment) should be eliminated from the algorithm of knowledge delivery (see statement 1 above) even though without assessment it will be impossible to receive feedback on the quality of education, either at the macro level – from the society at large (see Figure 1) or from the university. To resolve this issue well-known hardware design techniques of self-checking developed by Carter (1996) could help and should be used. In our case the most important feature of self-checking is *concurrency*, or near concurrency, with functioning and *self-checking* even though the term *self-checking* in pedagogy has a one-to-one synonym: *self-assessment*. The difference lies in

the quality of self-assessment which is very weak in comparison with self-checking as described by the Boolean logic function. As far as resources for *knowledge delivery* are concerned *time* cannot be counted, as it is beyond our control. Figure 5 can therefore be transformed as shown in Figure 6.

The two blue boxes above present Information Technology elements, which can be involved in the process of *Knowledge* delivery. We believe that further progress in the theory of *Knowledge Delivery* should be found in the selection of the principles and also in finding ways to load and reload it on the IT resources.

5. PRINCIPLES OF CURRICULUM DESIGN

By direct analogy with Schagaev (1990, 2001) and Schagaev et al. (2001) the *Knowledge Delivery System* must realize three closely connected functions: *Definitive*, *Characteristic* and *Predictive*.

A *Knowledge area* has to have a *Definitive Function (DF)*, in which terms and concepts are called and nominated. DF answers the question "What is it"? The second function describes the interrelations between *Definitions* and *character-*

Figure 6. Classification of resources to deliver knowledge excluding time

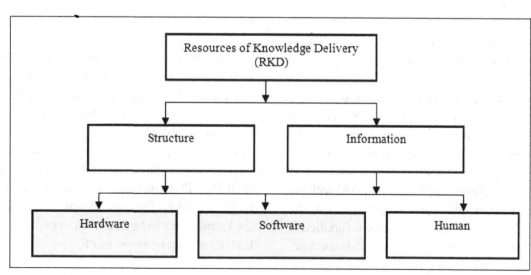

ises them and is called the *Characteristic Function (CF)*. *CF* answers the question "how are these definitions connected"? The *Predictive Function (PF)*, in turn, answers the question "What if"? Knowledge of DF and CF and their application are essential elements here. Application of definitions and characterisation of their interrelations enables the *use* of elements that have just been learned and predicts their behaviour.

But what is the core for the successful organisation of a learning process for one discipline and what is it for another? According to Schagaev (1990, 2001) and Schagaev et al. (2001) the success of learning is the formation of a strong *PF* in the selected area of *Knowledge - discipline* and holds true for both new and well established disciplines. The success of *PF* depends on concurrent observation and satisfaction of two conditions:

- The first condition is accuracy, precision in the selection of the aim pursued, with analysis of a new or existing subject domain and the key required feature - some kind of aim integrity.
- The second condition, not less important, is the internal structure of the course: rigorous approach in the construction and introduction of terms and concepts inside the course, as well as its assessment procedures.

To summarise, the requirements on the formation of a new curriculum note:

1. Any discipline, as an introduction of a theory, should be considered from the point of view of performance of three interconnected functions: *Definitive, Characteristic* and *Predictive*.
2. The discipline must be constructed with the strict principle of aim integrity, i.e. with the selection of the single feature (predictive function) necessary to achieve and maximise.
3. Each phase of introduction, presentation and detailed analysis of a discipline development

must be rigorously analysed. Otherwise, the success of the course built around this discipline will be problematic.

4. Only really essential features and details of the analyzed discipline objects and phenomena must be included. For example, the course of computer science as information processing system should be discussed in terms based or directly connected with information; a course describing distributed systems and networks should present in some way categories of dimensions directly connected to these kinds of systems, as well as basic relative terms.

The applicability of the three functions mentioned above is the key to successful discipline and curriculum development. Essentially, the resources available should be analyzed, including any new technologies such as information processing. IT involvement in the process of course construction should be considered from the beginning. Here, we try to analyse the process of knowledge delivery from the point of view of three interrelated functions: DF, CF, PF and algorithm of learning, using the approach from Schagaev (1990, 2001) and Schagaev et al. (2001).

Consider the sequence of functions discussed above:

$$DF \rightarrow CF \rightarrow PF$$

At first one delivers definitions (DF) and then their interrelations (CF). The algorithm of learning completes when a learner has acquired the skill in the subject to predict the behaviour of the elements presented in the course, and PF exists. The power of prediction (PF) means understanding of the course material by the student. The bigger an individual PF is the better the student knowledge is. PF should be formally measured. Growth of the knowledge can be described as evolution and transition from nowhere to PF:

$$Nowhere\ and\ Nothing \rightarrow DF \rightarrow CF \rightarrow PF$$

This evolution can be analysed and terminated when PFs > PFtr, (indices s: student and tr: threshold). Threshold indicates the required level of understanding, proven by assessment through analysis of predictive functions developed in the student's mind.

If a full set of definitions exists in a discipline it can count towards some development of DF. The question how to build DF of the subject has its own importance and requires special research and elements essential for this paper will be introduced further.

Suppose for now that a teacher has prepared the DF of the course, or it's part, and is ready to deliver it (*Nowhere and Nothing* → DF). The first iteration of learning will then consist of the delivery of DF from teacher to student. Once the student absorbs the essential definitions required for the understanding of the lecture material information from the course segment DF is completed and s/he is ready to learn further. Connections of elements – terms in the subject denote (determinate) CF: DF → CF.

In math CF is an essential set of formulae, in language course – grammar, etc. If we can deliver to a student an explanation on how terms of the course are connected then we can assume that CF (Characteristic Function) does exist. Then the process of learning goes to another phase:

$$DF \rightarrow CF \rightarrow PF$$

In a discipline, as a whole, it is impossible to expect that DF has to be learned as a whole before a student starts to understand CF also as a whole. Therefore, there must be a way to break DF and CF down properly into logical pieces.

To build well-balanced "golden" shape segments of DF one has to build as correct sequence of several DF_i in a curriculum as a whole:

$$DF = \{DF_1,..DF_i,..DF_n, DF_u\}, i = 1,n$$

During the learning process a sequence of DF_i for i = [1,n] should be accompanied by a proper sequence of $\{CF_i\}$ with some shift in time, as presented in Figure 7. Any overlap in time with the delivery of DF_i and CF_i is acceptable and even useful. The length of overlap should be selected regarding the level and ability of students. Also, the size of a particular DF_i might be determined by a student's ability for learning. For good students any particular F_i might be bigger than for weaker students. This is especially important due to some recent political initiatives such as that for 'universities for all'.

We denote DF_u and CF_u as universal (complete) functions for the discipline. Having DF_i and CF_i provides a possibility *to build* in the discipline or its part a predictive function: PF_i; for the whole discipline, having DF_u and CF_u enables to build PF_u for the discipline in the student's mind. Neighbourhood DF_i and DF_{i+1} might not be intersected

Figure 7. Sequence of knowledge delivery

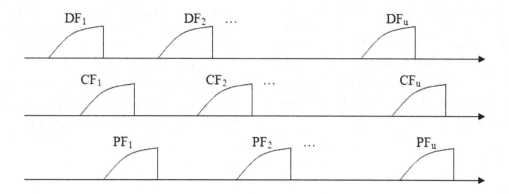

(for the poor organised curriculum), but for the discipline as a whole a unification of all elementary definition (DF$_i$) takes place:

$$DF_1 \ldots \cup \ldots DF_i \cup \ldots DF_m \ldots \cup \ldots DF_n = DF_u$$

The form of the curve for DF$_i$, CF$_i$ and PF$_i$ could also be different as well as the length of their intervals and would be defined by the features of the discipline and the personal preferences of the deliverer. It is not clear as yet what defines the form of curve and the length of the triangles except of the student and teacher abilities. It is, however, clear that the total workload of delivery of DF$_i$ is a sum of workloads to deliver all elements as shown in the equation below:

$$W\left(DF_i\right) = \int\limits_{t_i}^{t_{i+1}} \frac{dDF_i}{dt}$$

where: t_i and t_{i+1} define the interval of delivery for DF$_i$.

In a similar way, the total workloads to deliver CF and PF are shown below:

$$W\left(CF_i\right) = \int\limits_{t_i}^{t_{i+1}} \frac{dCF_i}{dt}$$

$$W\left(PF_i\right) = \int\limits_{t_i}^{t_{i+1}} \frac{dPF_i}{dt}$$

Naturally, discipline delivery should be done smoothly, with well-balanced functions of DF$_i$, CF$_i$, and PF$_i$ as mentioned above. But proper management of their delivery seems to be a subject of special research, and includes human computer interaction aspects and specific features of the learning subject.

6. CURRICULUM CORE

To build the core of a curriculum on a subject a set of Definitive Functions {DF} and one of Characteristic Functions {CF} must be constructed. The {DF} should contain the set of terms, in the same way as the Glossary of a book does, and the {CF} should contain the set of topics describing how definitions are connected, in the same way as the Index of a book does.

By combining terms from the Glossary with the Index we have a semi-automatic procedure to form a set of essential questions required for *Assessment*. Up to now, except for pure math disciplines, the proper formation of a set of essential questions was hardly known. There is no doubt that statistics should be obtained to analyse the relevance of these questions to the core of the curriculum. Additionally, a logical sequence of the questions should be arranged for the *assessment*, as well as for the process of delivery of the discipline. It is clear that even a semi-automatic procedure might be quite useful, as it reduces teacher's workload in formation of assessment and, at the same time, guarantees quality. In one extreme there is a fully automated option in formation of *assessment* by direct programming of a set of terms and a set of questions. But this approach requires further research and approbation. In another extreme, a "manual" application of this algorithm should be taken.

If the *core* of the subject does exist, it does not mean that questions and terms taken from one book or lecture notes do relate to the core. Personal preferences of a teacher can be so high that they may completely mislead students and should be avoided. Thus, several books on the same subject from different authors could be selected and a *joint* Glossary {DF$_j$} of terms, which includes terms that belong to at least one glossary from the analysed books and lecture notes, could be organised thus creating an *essential* Glossary $\{DF_e\}$ of terms which includes those terms only common to all Glossaries. Formally these two sets of glossaries are described as follows:

$$DF_j = DF_1 \cup DF_2 \ldots \cup DF_{n-1} \cup DF_n$$

$$DF_e = DF_1 \cap DF_2 \ldots \cap DF_{n-1} \cap DF_n$$

Building a set of questions around an essential glossary DF_e forms an essential set of questions CF_e and, in fact, complete as a whole a formal preparation of assessment. DF_e and CF_e combined form a core of the discipline assessment.

The core of the curriculum and its features present us with a special interest. Above we discussed in brief some elements of the algorithm *how to define a core*. Here we discuss features of the *observation* and *behaviour* of the core. We discover two phenomena in behaviour of the core – *moving core* and *merging core*.

A *moving core* occurs when curriculum design (and re-design, as this is a permanent process due to the appearance of new books, new papers and other sources of information) shows growth when using some descriptive elements (DF_i) and decrease of use for some others. This change of intensity in the use of different areas of the core is shown in Figure 8 by a different intensity of blue colour.

This process of movement can lead to the separation of a discipline into several new disciplines. This separation should be detected early before it happens, as the discipline can loose its predictive function (PF) and become obsolete – theory can become very advanced to be practical (pure math case) and vice versa – practice can be developed much faster than theory and thus theory becomes almost useless, having only a descriptive function (networking). In the first example, knowledge does not connect with skills and is therefore hardly applicable to the society at large; in the second example, the technological development has big advances in comparison with theoretical adaptation of the technological results. Both cases are very inefficient in terms of the model about the role of education presented in Figure 1. Keeping in mind this model, education should be effective from the point of view of improvement to the quality of life, and thus the early detection of the process of *moving* core seems to be important.

On the other hand, the *merging of several cores* can be caused by serious inventions, practical demand or revolution in technology, which accelerate the involvement of different disciplines into fusion as shown in Figure 9 where Computer Science is used as an example. The main reason of this fusion is the growth of Predictive Function resulting in the applicability of a new discipline to society.

Figure 8. Moving core of curriculum

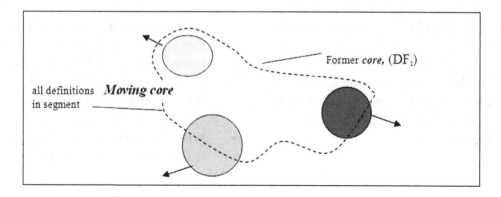

Figure 9. Merging of several cores

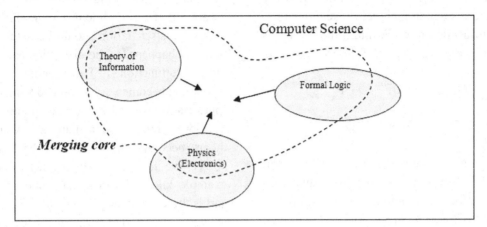

Such processes and their detection are pretty complex but understandable and their algorithmisation and programming do not look impossible. This is a perfect area for the use of IT to assist the teacher to assemble the correct elements for the core of the discipline.

In the long run, these two processes can help detect changes in scientific areas related to the discipline automatically and assist the teacher to almost automatically adjust the curriculum and assessment to these changes. There is hope here that artificial intelligence (AI) and IT can be involved much more in the formation, correction and adjustment of curriculum for any scientific or technical discipline.

7. FURTHER WORK

The next step in this work is the development of assessment as part of curriculum development with analysis of its features and a new approach: *Multiple Choice Answers Approach* (MCAA) will be introduced along with the scheme for its realisation. This approach will enable us to achieve better reliability, validity and consistency of knowledge delivery.

Analysis of distributions of results obtained during the approbation period of the use of MCAA in assessment practice will also be presented. Further development will include analysis of the Penalty function and its possible forms in order to create an applicable library, suitable for practitioners. Further use of set theory should formalise development of essential sub-dictionaries and questionnaires for any selected discipline.

Development of the algorithm of accumulation and selection of elements for questions and for glossaries as well as further extension of this algorithm for the formation of essential questions to achieve iterative and full understanding of the course or discipline (predictive function) seems to be a good challenge for further research.

There are also some open questions about the structure of the discipline and should be clarified. More specifically, what does it mean

- If the Index in the module is much bigger than the Glossary: $(\{DF_u\} > \{CF_u\})$?
- If the Index in the book is much smaller than the Glossary $(\{DF_u\} < \{CF_u\})$?
- When the index and the Glossary are equal $(\{DF_u\} = \{CF_u\})$?
- When the index and the glossary are mixed, ie not separated $(\{DF_u\} \cup \{CF_u\})$?

8. CONCLUSION

This work attempted to form a logical *core* of *curriculum design* for computer science and similar disciplines. Initially, the main terms used (science, knowledge, skills, curriculum and computer science) were defined and the role of education as a very important driving force in the improvement of life for the society at large was identified.

Existing models of *curriculum development* were briefly discussed and were found to be of a very generic nature. Their drawbacks were also identified as being applicability, usefulness and efficiency, and their measurement in the course design process. Curriculum design as *information processing* was then analysed and further developed by the introduction of three main functions in discipline construction: *definitive, characteristic* and *predictive*.

The *core* of the discipline, the way of its selection and its main features: *moving* and *merging*, were also analysed and discussed. The automatic formation of Glossary, Indexes, tracing their modifications, formation of assessment procedure and its realization was shown to be one of the roles of IT. The two processes (moving and merging) were shown to be able to help detect changes in scientific areas related to the discipline automatically and assist the teacher to almost automatically adjust the curriculum and assessment to these changes.

REFERENCES

Carter, W. (1996). *Digital Designing with Programmable Logic Devices*. Englewood Cliffs, NJ: Prentice Hall. ISBN: 0133737217

Diamond, R. (1989). *Designing and improving courses and curricula in higher education: A systematic approach*. San Francisco: Jossey-Bass.

Jeans, J. (1930). *The Mysterious Universe*. New York: Macmillan.

(2001). *Penguin*. The New PENGUIN English Dictionary.

Ramsden, P. (1992). *Learning to Teach in Higher Education*. London: Routledge. doi:10.4324/9780203413937

Schagaev, I. (1990). Yet Another Approach to Classification of Redundancy. In *Proceedings of the IMEKO Congress*, Helsinki, Finland (pp. 485-490).

Schagaev, I. (2001). Redundancy Classification For Fault Tolerant Computer Design. In *Proceedings of the 2001 IEEE Systems, Man, and Cybernetics Conference*, Tuscon, AZ.

Schagaev, I., & Buhanova, G. (2001, July). Comparative Study of Fault Tolerant RAM Structures. In *Proceedings of the IEEE DSN Conference*, Goteborg, Sweden.

Toohey, S. (1999). *Designing Courses for Higher Education*. Buckingham, UK: The Society for Research into Higher Education & Open University Press.

This work was previously published in the International Journal of Knowledge Society Research, Volume 1, Issue 3, edited by Miltiadis D. Lytras, pp. 17-32, copyright 2010 by IGI Publishing (an imprint of IGI Global).

Chapter 13
Evaluation of E-Learning

Bernhard Ertl
Universität der Bundeswehr München, Germany

Katharina Ebner
Universität der Bundeswehr München, Germany

Kathy Kikis-Papadakis
Foundation for Research and Technology – Hellas, Greece

ABSTRACT

Evaluation is an important measure for quality control in e-learning, which aims at improving a learning environment and adapting it to users' needs, as well as proving values and benefits of a course to financers and participants. However, results and styles of evaluation are subject to the designers', the evaluators' and the participants' individual and socio-cultural backgrounds. This paper examines evaluation from an infrastructure perspective and presents dimensions and parameters for the evaluation of e-learning. The authors take cognitive, epistemological, social and technical infrastructures into account.

1. INTRODUCTION

E-learning has evolved intensively over the past decade technologically as well as concerning its scope. E-learning means the acquisition and use of knowledge distributed and facilitated primarily by electronic means (Learnframe.com, 2005). Beginning with text based measures that were presented on media like CDs only 10 to 15 years ago, e-learning nowadays use all possible electronic media and hardware to serve the learner with multimedia, virtual and personalized contents. This enlargement – technologically and

with regard to content – poses new challenges on evaluators. They relate mainly to the rapid development of e-learning and the associated changes in infrastructures (Ertl, Winkler, & Mandl, 2007) as well as in missing experiences in the applicability of the new technologies for beneficial learning. Both aspects emphasize the need for appropriate quality management that can be established by thorough evaluation.

Stockmann (2000) defines four possible results of an evaluation: to get insights into a project and receive data necessary for decisions, to get control over a project and to be able to make refinements, to establish a dialogue between different stakeholders, e.g. financiers, providers and the target

DOI: 10.4018/978-1-4666-1788-9.ch013

group, and to legitimize costs and sustainability of a program. In sum, evaluation means to exactly define and measure a product's or programme's usefulness and worth (Reinmann-Rothmeier, Mandl, Erlach, & Neubauer, 2001).

In the field of e-learning, evaluation mainly focuses on the quality of the learning environment and on learners' negotiation in and with the learning environment. Thereby, evaluation has two main purposes: To improve and to adapt the learning environment to learners' needs (which combines the functions of insight and control) and to prove the quality of the learning environment and its values and benefits for financiers and participants (legitimization). Regarding the first aspect, Mandl and Hense (2007) emphasize the importance for evaluators to learn about the particular functions and effects of a learning environment to realize learners' best benefits. We will elaborate on this in the further sections of this paper. However, also the second argument has special weight: given the costs of research and development as well as purchase of an e-learning environment or program, money plays a role for especially two stakeholders. The one is the company that is offering the environment or product on the education market and the other are companies and organisations that buy and apply it (Haben, 2002). As profit-organisations are interested in satisfactory cost-benefit-relations, the producer may be interested in knowing how well one performs with its product and will try to test it or to get evaluation data to confirm the product's quality (Harhoff & Küpper, 2002). Furthermore, the purchaser might be interested in information about the usefulness of the implementation of the product or environment in terms of learning results (Harhoff & Küpper, 2002): Human resources divisions in companies are responsible for implementation of and reporting on the usefulness of methods and measures offered to the company's employees and are obliged to choose measures that support the organisation's overall success (Sonntag, 2002; Knyphausen-Aufseß, Smukalla, & Abt, 2009).

Another reason to broaden the efforts in evaluating e-learning is the growing market: not only the quantity of e-learning measures and products evolved strongly during recent years, but also the array of recipients increased intensively: young adults with academic qualification take master-programs at distance universities to qualify themselves during they are in job (Schnurer, 2005), undergraduate students have the choice to study at home without attending presence courses, adults without higher formal qualification try to educate further while taking e-learning-courses of private institutions (Erlach, Hausmann, Mandl, & Trillitzsch, 2002) and so on. Having this in mind, it might not only be scientific interest but mere practical need to evaluate e-learning further.

Taking a collaborative perspective on e-learning and its evaluation, we may have to deal with some additional peculiarities (Resnick, Levine, & Teasley, 1991). According to this perspective, learning is more than the pure cognitive act of knowledge acquisition - it includes the participation in cultural practices (Sfard, 1998) and the enculturation in a community (Lave & Wenger, 1991).

In this contribution, we will first have a look on the goals of an evaluation. Then we will focus on evaluators and show which perspectives designers of an e-learning environment, participants of a course, and external experts have towards evaluation. After that, we'll describe two styles of evaluation, a process oriented one (formative evaluation) and a product oriented one (summative evaluation), and will then give a short overview of possible methods convenient to formative or summative evaluation demands. Finally, we will deal with dimensions and parameters for evaluating e-learning and discuss policy impacts of evaluation.

2. GOALS FOR EVALUATION

Evaluation may have different goals, and program-particular goals may influence the issues of the evaluators to ask, the methods to chose, and the dimensions to consider. In general, there are two goal-categories; the one relates to a (continuing) refinement and optimisation of the learning environment, and the other relates to prove the quality of the learning environment.

The traditional focus in evaluation is in general – that means independently from e.g. the media that is chosen to transfer knowledge on the learner – the assessment of the learning success. The results might be an indicator as well as an impulse for both above mentioned goal-categories. The assessment of the learning success relates to the inherent pedagogical concern to support learning and development. Therefore, the overall evaluation indicators are the learners' changes regarding their knowledge, e.g. declarative, procedural and contextual knowledge (De Jong & Ferguson-Hessler, 1996) as well as behaviour changes (Kirkpatrick, 1994). Considering the special form and media that is applied in the e-learning context, another goal has to be considered in evaluation e-learning: efficiency and effectiveness during and because of learning electronically (de Witt, 2005). Therefore, both indicators – effectiveness and efficiency – have to be assessed in evaluating e-learning as well.

Beyond these two broader goal categories, there is a variety of perspectives taken by evaluators stemming from different disciplines which lead to specific sub-goals. Harvey, Oliver, and Smith (2002) emphasize the goal to ensure the quality of instruction, organizational benefits, and cost-effectiveness. They discriminate therefore three different focuses: One focus is on instructional design and teaching methods, a second focus is on the organization and participants, and the third focus is on costs and benefits. Furthermore, they also distinguish between different layers of evaluation which comprise of the assessment of the measure, the assessment of outcomes related to learning goals, and the application of contents and organizational outcome (Henninger & Balk, 2001).

With respect to the evaluation of e-learning, goals for evaluation may also be to ensure the accessibility and interoperability of a learning environment (Kollias, 2007) or to prove the compliance with technical standards (e.g. SCORM; Buendia Garcia & Hervas Jorge, 2006).

Furthermore, the goal of evaluation in e-learning may also be to certify an environment for a particular standard, e.g. according to ISO 9126 (see Abran, Khelefi, Suryn, & Seffah, 2003), which requires the evaluation of functionality, reliability, usability, efficiency, maintainability and portability (Chua & Dyson, 2004).

3. EVALUATORS

The goals of an evaluation also relate to the issue which evaluators are chosen. Evaluators may be internal or external with respect to the institution which offers e-learning (see Hense & Mandl, 2006; König, 2000). Thereby, internal evaluators may be either the developers of an e-learning course themselves (which is called self-evaluation), or they may come from other departments within the organization or they even from come from outside the organizations. Usually, evaluators are experts. This means that the particular goals for an evaluation may specify the particular fields to be analyzed and may invite experts from different fields to be involved in the evaluation.

Hense and Mandl (2006) emphasize advantages and disadvantages of self-evaluations. Considering their advantages, self-evaluations are easy to handle (see also Harvey et al., 2002). Thereby, the developers and designers of a course do the evaluation by themselves. They are reviewing parts of the course to see if everything is working as expected, if contents are correct and if the course meets their own expectations. They are usually very familiar to the peculiarities of their course and this allows a focus on the specific aspects that are necessary for further course development. Due to these advantages, self-evaluations often take place in an early stage of the course development, particularly if there is only little time and results are needed quickly (see Hense & Mandl, 2006). Besides this, Tergan (2004) emphasizes the importance of self-evaluations as one aspect of quality ensurance for providers of e-learning.

In contrast, external evaluations may be more objective and more reliable, because they usually use standardized methods and external evaluators are less involved in the development process (see Hense & Mandl, 2006). They may have also more heterogeneous individual and disciplinary backgrounds than the developers and therefore may be able to discover socio-cultural traits and stereotypes, which may underlie the design of a course. Furthermore, they may also have some particular expertise which is not available in a course development team. For example, one could imagine that a course is evaluated by content experts who analyse if the content is state of the art. Besides that, they may also evaluate if the content is encultured for participants of a particular target group.

A peculiarity in evaluation is course participants as evaluators. They are experts for the perception of the target group, because they are a part of it. Thus, a course could be evaluated by (test) participants who could give insights in the usability of the learning environment and the comprehensiveness of the content (with respect to the target group). Henninger and Balk (2001) report that teachers may have reservations about participants' evaluations, because they attribute them only few knowledge about course design and deny them skills for valid evaluation. However, course participants can reveal the course acceptance (Mandl & Hense, 2007) and identify particular difficulties with and preferences for a course. Furthermore, they could disclose how far they estimate course contents as valuable and applicable.

4. STYLES OF EVALUATION

Talking about goals for evaluation and evaluators in the last both sections, we implicitly also talked about two styles of evaluation - a process oriented one and a product oriented one. The process oriented one is called *formative evaluation,* the product oriented is called *summative evaluation* (see Scriven, 1980). According to Fitzpatrick, Sanders, and Worthen (2003), formative evaluation provides information for program improvement. With respect to learning, Fricke (1997) relates this to the evaluation of learning processes. Formative evaluation takes place during the course application and its development. By analysing learners' pace for example within the learning environment, evaluators seek for knowledge about the learners' learning process to discover their needs and make target group specific improvements. They try to discover and resolve problems and find aspects for the optimization of a learning environment.

Summative evaluation aims at providing information for serving decisions about program adoption, continuation or expansion (see Fitzpatrick et al., 2003). According to Scriven (1991), summative evaluation serves to provide evaluative conclusions for any other reasons besides development. In some cases, this may prove the effectiveness of a course. By this, financiers, participants and designers can see that the course offers a special value and that customers are satisfied with the course. Fricke (1997) relates summative evaluation to learning as an assessment of learning outcomes and knowledge transfer. In this context, many evaluators use the Kirkpatrick model (Kirkpatrick, 1994), which describes four levels of evaluation: The first level relates to learners' pure reaction to the learning material, the second to their learning results, the third to the behavioural changes in the workplace and the fourth to business results. Using the model (Kirkpatrick, 1994), one can analyse how sustainable the effects of a measure have been. Particularly the third level concerning behavioural changes can give hints about how far an e-learning course had effects with respect to learners' enculturation. Summative evaluation can be done quite statically by a one time analysis and it usually takes place at the end of a course. Besides learning outcome and transfer, it may also evaluate learners' acceptance of the learning environment. However, a concluding quality analysis by experts or an ISO certification may also be a kind of summative evaluation.

Formative and summative evaluations are two styles of evaluation that may be applied either independently or combined. Fitzpatrick et al. (2003) propose a model for program evaluation. In this model, formative evaluation is primarily important at the beginning of the course development (see Figure 1). However, it loses importance during several iterations of a course. In contrast, summative evaluation has only a marginal importance at the beginning of a course development. However, its importance increases with each iteration of the course and finally provides a basis for the decision about running the course once again or not.

Methods to apply in formative and/or summative evaluation are diverse. The common methods known and applied in the social sciences fit to either formative or summative evaluation best. There may be, for example some kind of field experiment to test a prototype of an e-learning course. However, experiments and quasi-experiments are seldom possible in real life even if experiments in the laboratory allow accompanying the learner's development and learning process without disturbing influences and so lead to valuable insights into processes and outcomes of a course. Laboratory experiments suit formative evaluation quite well in order to implement changes after the experiment. Besides experiments, collecting data about the learning process is also possible by observing the learner, course, or program during the productive phase. Another way besides experiments and observations to keep track of the learners' experiences is interviewing individual learners or discussing in groups of learners (Lamnek, 2005).

Observations and interviews are mainly qualitative nature and allow exemplary and punctual insights into a course by providing the perspectives of some individuals. Quantitative methods, which allow for more generalization, may be appropriate

Figure 1. Relationship between formative and summative evaluation across life of a program according to Fitzpatrick et al. (2003)

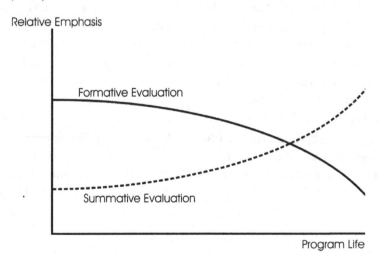

to evaluate e-learning as well. Questionnaires, for example, may be distributed to all participants after the course or program, measuring not only the learners' satisfaction with the learning environment (or its usability) but learning transfer as well (see Kirkpatrick's model (1994) for evaluation, level 2, introduced above). Longitudinal designs with more than one point of measurement are necessary to sharpen the validity of these results and guarantee to survey the transfer in the best possible way. Furthermore, the introduction of a control group can provide insights in the effects of a particular treatment (Bortz & Lienert, 1998). Additionally, correlative evaluation studies should include independent variables that may serve as moderators and/or mediators on learning success: section 5.1 will mention the learners' prior knowledge to an e-learning course that has impact on the grade that new content may be acquired. Also, the learners' technical skills in interacting with the e-learning environment play an important role for the acquisition of knowledge or skills during the course or program (Dobson, 1999). It should also be tested if individual learning strategies play a role in a specific instructional design as it has impact on how new information is processed and how appropriate the design is for a single learner (Mandl & Friedrich, 2005); collecting data about learning preferences, general motivation as well as learners' self-efficacy (Fetaji & Fetaji, 2009) should serve as base to differ evaluation results that are contained as independent variables. Suitable models must be developed or adapted to make an evaluation study to more than a mere self-rating of satisfaction or a knowledge test (e.g. Measure-outcome-Inventory, see Kauffeld, Brennecke, & Strack, 2009, and multi-dimensional approach, see Bell & Farrier, 2006).

5. DIMENSIONS AND PARAMETERS FOR EVALUATION

There are many different approaches helping to identify dimensions to consider for an evaluation.

Their application depends upon the specific goal of an evaluation. Henninger and Balk (2001) emphasized instructional, organisational and economical aspects, Buendia Garcia and Hervas Jorge (2006) focused on technical aspects and Abran et al. (2003) on the ISO 9126. Of course, such dimensions are important for evaluation, because they evaluate the framework of a course and prerequisites for an economical and technical success.

In this paper, we will have a closer look to issues which may be important from a socio-cultural perspective. Therefore, it is necessary to consider different contexts of an e-learning measure. Tergan and Schenkel (2002) distinguish four different contexts, which are relevant for e-learning scenarios: an individual context, which relates to the learner, the application context, which relates to the content, an educational context, which comprises of the instructional design, and a technological context, which comprises of learning technology and media. However, this model omits the collaborative aspect of e-learning. Lakkala (2008) suggests a framework of pedagogical infrastructures. She suggests to classify, to design and to evaluate the elements of technology-based collaborative learning according to a cognitive, an epistemological, a social and a technical infrastructure.

Using this framework for evaluation, each of the dimensions describes different parameters to evaluate. The cognitive dimension relates to learners' cognitive prerequisites and evaluates if learners have the knowledge, skills and strategies which are necessary for working in the learning environment. The epistemological dimension relates to the content and evaluates the quality and structure of the content, its implementation and its effects on the learners. The social dimension is related with sociability which comprises of facilitation and tutoring, and learners' opportunities to have social interactions and finally the technical dimension deals with the usability of the learning environment and support for learners' technical problems. In the following, we will describe exemplarily these dimensions in more detail.

5.1 Cognitive Dimension

The cognitive dimension relates to the issue how far learners have the *learning prerequisites* and appropriate *learning strategies* to work within the learning environment. In contrast to the epistemic dimension, which mainly focuses on aspects of the target group, this cognitive dimension focuses on the individual learner.

The evaluation of *learners' prerequisites* is essential for running an e-learning course. Fricke (1997) calls this input analysis. This helps to characterize and define a target group and particular learning goals. The most obvious prerequisite is a learner's individual prior knowledge (see Ertl, Kopp, & Mandl, 2005; Shapiro, 2004). The knowledge about how learners with different levels of prior knowledge perform in a learning environment can be an important aspect for specific facilitation and the tailoring of the learning environment (see Stark & Mandl, 2002).

One specific prerequisite are individual learning strategies (see Mandl & Friedrich, 2005; Pintrich, Smith, Garcia, & Mckeachie, 1993). E-learning allows many different learning scenarios ranging from drill and practice-exercises to case based learning scenarios and inquiry. These different learning scenarios also require different *learning strategies* to benefit of the learning environment. Learners of different educational backgrounds may also differ with respect to their strategies and therefore they may be important to evaluate.

Learning prerequisites
- Does the learning environment enable learners to activate their existing knowledge?
- How does the learning environment prevent cognitive overload?
- How much prior knowledge do the students have about the subject being taught?

Learning strategies
- Which learning strategies and processes are encouraged within the environment?
- To what extent are the learners supported in these strategies?

To what extent does the learning environment enable learners to take control of their own learning?

5.2 Epistemological Dimension

The epistemological dimension relates to the structure and implementation of the content. This dimension should cover three parameters, the issue about the *correctness and appropriateness* of the content, the issue of the presentation of the content (*didactical design*) and the issue of learner perception of the content (*acceptance*).

The parameter of *correctness/appropriateness* is crucial for the development of learning material. It is obvious that designers should take care not to teach wrong facts. Different approaches to explain certain phenomena should be categorized as approach rather than as evidence. Furthermore, the appropriateness of content for the target group may be important to consider. Appropriateness of the content may relate on its level of difficulty as well as on learners' social and cultural context.

The parameter of the *didactical design* evaluates which instructional efforts are made to facilitate learners' knowledge construction (Tennyson, Schott, Seel, & Dijkstra, 1997). Evaluating the didactical design, one can make conclusions about the appropriateness of the teaching methods. The evaluation of the didactical design may comprise of several aspects, e.g. the theoretical foundation of the learning environment, goals for the learners, curriculum integration and motivation.

The parameter of *acceptance* relates to the issue how learners perceive the contents and the teaching methods (Bürg & Mandl, 2005; Davies, 1989). The acceptance of a learning environment is of particular importance for its success, because if learners don't accept a learning environment, they would hardly use it beneficially.

- **Correctness/Appropriateness**
  - Which specific knowledge will be imparted?
  - Which didactical content will be realised?
  - Which types of knowledge sources are used within the environment?
  - Who is the target group?
  - Are the content and learning goals congruent?
  - Is the content such, that learners are able to theoretically and actively apply it to their own personal situation?
  - Are the situations addressed in the environment authentic?
  - Is the content up-to-date?
  - Is the content presented in an adequate depth?
  - Is the content presented in a coherent way?
  - Are foreign/new words explained in an adequate way?
  - Is the number of sources adequate?
  - Is the content appropriate for different political/religious/ethnic views?

- **Didactical design**
  - Is the learning environment based upon a particular educational theory?
  - If so, is it well designed?
  - Is the didactical design of the learning environment appropriate?
  - Which concrete learning goals are formulated?
  - Is the learning material well integrated into the curriculum?
  - Does the content of the environment encourage learners to actively solve problems independently?
  - Does the content engage the learners emotionally?

  - Does the content allow users to make mistakes and learn from them?
  - Do images/animations clarify textual relationships?
  - Does the content direct the learners' attention to certain essential aspects?
  - Does the learning environment increase the students' level of motivation?

- **Acceptance**
  - Would the participants recommend the learning environment to friends/colleagues?
  - Are the participants satisfied with the content?
  - Did the learning environment meet the learners' expectations?

5.3 Social Dimension

With respect to the social dimension, the focus should be on *facilitation/tutoring* and *sociability*.

Facilitation/tutoring is an important parameter, because it may cover several aspects. It may evaluate tutor support for learners' content specific problems, e.g. if learners have difficulties with comprehension, as well as the moderation and guidance through learners' collaborative work (Schweizer, Pächter, & Weidenmann, 2001). E-learning environments may be subject to particular group phenomena (e.g. lurking, flaming, illusions of consensus; Weinberger, 2003) and a tutor's intervention may be an important mean for the success of the collaborative work.

Sociability relates to the issue how far learners perceive the learning environment as a social medium (Kreijns, Kirschner, & Jochems, 2002). This may be important for learning environments which requires learners' commitment over a longer period of time. Ensuring the learner's commitment is in the focus of social validity as well which is an important quality criteria in diagnostics. Social validity makes the diagnostic aspect of a situation to an "acceptable one" and is achieved through transparency (in terms of background information about the evaluation situation), the learner's participation, his information, and feedback (Schuler & Stehle, 1983). In sum, it can be seen as fairness of the situation. Social aspects of evaluation are important and must not be neglected. The sociability of the learning environment may have effects on the drop off rates of a course and therefore it is important to evaluate.

- **Facilitation/tutoring**
  - To what extent do the users receive support in their use of collaborative learning methods?
  - Are the learning processes and outcomes shared between and transparent to the learners as a group?
  - Do the tutors and pupils have set roles and tasks?
  - How are these roles combined?
- **Sociability**
  - If the learning environment includes a combination of face-to-face and electronic teaching, how well are these aspects integrated into each other?
  - Is there a positive social environment within the learning groups?

Are there chances for learners' socializing?

5.4 Technical Dimension

Regarding the technical dimension, *usability* and technical *support* should be evaluated.

The parameter of *usability* is important for evaluation, because it reveals if the learning environment provides particular problems for learners when working within. Usability is defined as "the extent to which a product can be used by specified users to achieve specified goals effectively, efficiently and satisfactory in a specified context of use" (FORTH, 2010). Usability describes how easy a product or media can be used. It considers the satisfaction of the user who wants to fulfil a

specified task with the aid of the product. It is a multidimensional property of a system or user interface (Nielsen, 2003). Thus, Usability may cover several aspects. Considering e-learning in first line, it should particularly focus on the computer literacy of the target group.

The parameter of *support* receives importance because many e-learning environments use proprietary media format and rely on particular player software. Furthermore, streaming contents rely on high-performance streaming servers, which should be placed in an appropriate network structure. Learners may experience technical problems and need therefore technical support.

- **Usability**
  - Are the learning tools appropriate and adequate?
  - Do the students have a sufficient level of media competence to navigate the learning environment?
  - How is the use of technology organised?
  - Is the usability and screen design of the environment such that a user can easily navigate the environment and find what they are looking for?
  - What kind of media will be used?
- **Technical support**
  - How adequate is the technical support offered to the users?
  - What are the reaction times of technical support?

How far is technical support subject to different national or religious holidays in different countries?

6. SUMMARY

Evaluation is an important aspect of any e-learning project. There are different issues to consider, e.g. which style of evaluation to use, which evaluators to chose and which aspects to evaluate, depending upon the overall goal of the evaluation. Taking a socio-cultural perspective, evaluation should focus on participants' background and differences in attitudes, values and stereotypes. Even evaluation methods may be influenced by social-cultural issues, because different methods are accepted differently from country to country depending upon the culture's openness to evaluation in general and its familiarity with diagnostic methods.

The paper first gave a general definition of evaluation. It then pointed out that evaluation goals might be quite heterogeneous: instructional design and teaching methods, the organization and participants, as well as costs and benefits may be of interest and specify the evaluation outcomes learning goals, application of contents and organizational outcomes. The article then described the difference between internal and external evaluation and emphasized advantages and challenges for each approach. Formative and summative evaluation was introduced and adequate methods for each of the two perspectives were commended. Different parameters for evaluation then were in the centre: a thoroughly conducted evaluation from a social-cultural perspective must not ignore to consider a cognitive dimension (learner perspective), an epistemological dimension (structure and content of medium), a social dimension (interaction between learner and facilitator), and a technical dimension (usability and technical support).

Schaumburg (2008) emphasizes that evaluations can be substantially better if they take place in an early stage of development already to prevent inefficient developments, if they ask questions which are oriented on the goals of development, if they consider the particular context of a course and if they take different perspectives into account, e.g. deciders and developers, teachers and learners, and directly involved persons as well as external experts.

In the future, the knowledge about evaluation of e-learning must be sensitively transferred onto a socio-cultural perspective which may be a challenge for scientists, evaluators and practitioners.

7. OUTLOOK

This paper focused on evaluation mainly on the level of course implementation and thereby allows continuous optimization and quality assurance. As we mentioned before, evaluation may also be decision-oriented. CIPP-models which analyze context, input process and product (see Stufflebeam, 1978) can furthermore provide insights on a macro level with respect to how far particular measures, e.g. e-learning courses have an impact on organizational development. Such analyses take the step beyond aspects of a particular course towards the integration of e-learning and its penetration of a developing knowledge society. As knowledge societies aim at new forms of learning, e.g. by changing lecture models (Ronchetti, 2010) or implementing educative networks (Diaz Gibson, Civis Zaragoza, Longas Mayayo, & Murat, 2010), it is important to explore the values and benefits of such approaches. However, there is the need for high quality project management (Bodea, Dascalu, & Coman, 2010) and thorough evaluation of each single measure.

ACKNOWLEDGMENT

Parts of this contribution were funded by EU (LLP-Program, Projects EFELSE 147760-LLP-2008-GR-KA1-KA1NLLS and PREDIL 141967-2008-LLP-GR-COMENIUS-CMP), DAAD and IKY (Project D0813016 resp. Agreement number 136 IKYDA 2009: Comparative study on gender differences in technology enhanced and computer science learning: Promoting equity).

REFERENCES

Abran, A., Khelefi, A., Suryn, W., & Seffah, A. (2003). Usability meanings and interpretations in ISO standards. *Software Quality Journal, 11*, 325–338. doi:10.1023/A:1025869312943

Bell, M., & Farrier, S. (2006). Measuring Success in e-Learning - a Multi-Dimensional Approach. *Electronic Journal of e-Learning, 6*, 99-110.

Bodea, C.-N., Dascalu, M., & Coman, M. (2010). Quality of project management education and training programmes. *International Journal of Knowledge Society Research, 1*, 13–25.

Bortz, J., & Lienert, G. A. (1998). *Kurzgefaßte Statistik für die klinische Forschung*. Berlin: Springer.

Buendia Garcia, F., & Hervas Jorge, A. (2006). *Evaluating e-learning platforms through SCORM specifications*. Paper presented at the IADIS Virtual Multi Conference on Computer Science and Information System (MCCSIS 2006).

Bürg, O., & Mandl, H. (2005). Akzeptanz von E-Learning von Unternehmen. *Zeitschrift für Personalpsychologie, 4*, 75–85. doi:10.1026/1617-6391.4.2.75

Chua, B. B., & Dyson, L. E. (2004). Applying the ISO 9126 model to the evaluation of an e-learning system. In R. Atkinson, C. McBeath, D. Jonas-Dwyer, & R. Phillips (Eds.), *Beyond the comfort zone: Proceedings of the 21st ASCILITE Conference*, Perth, Australia (pp. 184-190).

Davies, F. D. (1989). Perceived usefulness, perceived ease of use and user acceptance of information technology. *Management Information Systems Quarterly, 13*, 319–339. doi:10.2307/249008

De Jong, T., & Ferguson-Hessler, M. G. M. (1996). Types and qualities of knowledge. *Educational Psychologist, 31*, 105–113. doi:10.1207/s15326985ep3102_2

De Witt, C. (2005). E-Learning. In Hüther, J., & Schorb, B. (Eds.), *Grundbegriffe Medienpädagogik*. Munich, Germany: Köpäd.

Diaz Gibson, J., Civis Zaragoza, M., Longas Mayayo, J., & Murat, L. (2010). The study of educative network organizations in the city of Barcelona: The Nou Barris district. *International Journal of Knowledge Society Research, 1*, 26–37.

Dobson, M. (1999). Information enforcement and learning with interactive graphical systems. *Learning and Instruction, 9*, 365–390. doi:10.1016/S0959-4752(98)00052-8

Erlach, C., Hausmann, I., Mandl, H., & Trillitzsch, U. (2002). Knowledge Master - a collaborative learning program for Knowledge Management. In Davenport, T. H., & Probst, G. J. B. (Eds.), *Knowledge management case book. Siemens best practices* (pp. 208–227). Erlangen, Germany: Publicis KommunikationsAgentur GWA.

Ertl, B., Kopp, B., & Mandl, H. (2005). Effects of an individual's prior knowledge on collaborative knowledge construction and individual learning outcomes in videoconferencing. In Koschmann, T., Chan, T.-W., & Suthers, D. D. (Eds.), *Computer supported collaborative learning 2005: the next 10 years* (pp. 145–154). Mahwah, NJ: Lawrence Erlbaum Associates.

Ertl, B., Winkler, K., & Mandl, H. (2007). E-learning - Trends and future development. In Neto, F. M., & Brasileiro, F. V. (Eds.), *Advances in Computer-Supported Learning* (pp. 122–144). Hershey, PA: Information Science Publishing.

Fetaji, B., & Fetaji, M. (2009). e-Learning Indicators: a Multi-Dimensional Model for Planning and Evaluating e- Learning Software Solutions. *Electronic Journal of e-Learning, 7*, 1-28.

Fitzpatrick, J. L., Sanders, J. R., & Worthen, B. R. (2003). *Program Evaluation: Alternative Approaches and Practical Guidelines*. Boston: Pearson.

FORTH. (2010). *Definitions & Glossary*. Hellas, Greece: Author.

Fricke, R. (1997). Evaluation von Multimedia. In Issing, J. K., & Ludwig, P. (Eds.), *Information und Lernen mit Multimedia* (pp. 402–413). Weinheim, Germany: Beltz.

Haben, M. (2002). E-Learning in large German companies - most of the concepts are not effective. *Computerwoche, 30*, 12–16.

Harhoff, D., & Küpper, C. (2002). *Akzeptanz von E-Learning. Eine empirische Studie in Zusammenarbeit von Cognos und dem Institut für Innovationsforschung, Technologiemanagement und Entrepreneurship*. Munich, Germany: INNOtec.

Harvey, J., Oliver, M., & Smith, J. (2002). Towards effective practitioner evaluation. An exploration of issues relating to skills, motivation and evidence. *Journal of Educational Technology & Society, 5*, 3–10.

Henninger, M., & Balk, M. (2001). *Integrative Evaluation: Ein Ansatz zur Erhöhung der Akzeptanz von Lehrevaluation an Hochschulen*. Munich, Germany: Ludwig-Maximilians-Universität.

Hense, J., & Mandl, H. (2006). *Selbstevaluation als Ansatz der Qualitätsverbesserung von E-Learning Angeboten*. Munich, Germany: Ludwig-Maximilians-Universität.

Kauffeld, S., Brennecke, J., & Strack, M. (2009). Erfolge sichtbar machen: Das Maßnahmen-Erfolgs-Inventar (MEI) zur Bewertung von Trainings. In Kauffeld, S., Grote, S., & Frieling, E. (Eds.), *Handbuch Kompetenzentwicklung* (pp. 55–79). Stuttgart, Germany: Schäffer-Poeschel.

Kirkpatrick, D. (1994). *Evaluating Training Programs: The Four levels*. San Francisco: Berret-Koehler.

Knyphausen-Aufseß, D., Smukalla, M., & Abt, M. (2009). Towards a New Training Transfer Portfolio: A Review of Training-related Studies in the Last Decade. *Zeitschrift für Personalforschung, 23*, 288–311.

Kollias, A. (2007). *Framework for e- learning contents evaluation*. Heraklion, Greece: Foundation for research and technology.

König, J. (2000). *Einführung in die Selbstevaluation*. Freiburg, Germany: Lambertus.

Kreijns, K., Kirschner, P. A., & Jochems, W. (2002). The sociability of computer supported collaborative learning environments. *Journal of Educational Technology & Society, 5*, 8–22.

Lakkala, M. (2008). *The pedagogical design of technology enhanced collaborative learning*.

Lamnek, S. (2005). *Qualitative Sozialforschung*. Weinheim, Germany: Beltz.

Lave, J., & Wenger, E. (1991). *Situated learning: Legitimate peripheral participation*. New York: Cambridge University Press.

Learnframe.com. (2005). *About e-learning*. Retrieved from http://www.learnframe.com/aboutelearning

Mandl, H., & Friedrich, H. F. (Eds.). (2005). *Handbuch Lernstrategien*. Göttingen, Germany: Hogrefe.

Mandl, H., & Hense, J. (2007). Lässt sich Unterricht durch Evaluation verbessern? In Schönig, W. (Ed.), *Spuren der Schulevaluation. Zur Bedeutung und Wirksamkeit von Evaluationskonzepten im Schulalltag* (pp. 85–99). Bad Heilbrunn, Germany: Klinkhardt.

Nielsen, J. (2003). *Usability 101: Introduction to Usability*.

Pintrich, P. R., Smith, D. A. F., Garcia, T., & Mckeachie, W. J. (1993). Reliability and predictive validity of the motivated strategies for learning questionnaire (MSLQ). *Educational and Psychological Measurement, 53*, 801–813. doi:10.1177/0013164493053003024

Reinmann-Rothmeier, G., Mandl, H., Erlach, C., & Neubauer, A. (2001). *Wissensmanagement lernen. Ein Leitfaden zur Gestaltung von Workshops und zum Selbstlernen*. Weinheim, Germany: Beltz.

Resnick, L. B., Levine, J. M., & Teasley, S. D. (Eds.). (1991). *Perspectives on socially shared cognition*. Washington, DC: American Psychological Association. doi:10.1037/10096-000

Ronchetti, M. (2010). A different perspective on lecture video-streaming: how to use technology to help change the traditional lecture model. *International Journal of Knowledge Society Research, 1*, 50–60.

Schaumburg, H. (2008). *Die 5 Ws der Evaluaion von E-Learning*.

Schnurer, K. (2005). *Kooperatives Lernen in virtuell-asynchronen Hochschulseminaren. Eine Prozess-Produkt-Analyse des virtuellen Seminars "Einführung in das Wissensmanagement" auf der Basis von Felddaten*. Munich, Germany: Department Psychologie, Institut für Pädagogische Psychologie. Ludwig-Maximilians-Universität.

Schuler, H., & Stehle, W. (1983). Neuere Entwicklungen des Assessment-Center-Ansatzes – beurteilt unter dem Aspekte der sozialen Validität. *Zeitschrift für Arbeits- und Organisationspsychologie, 27*, 33–44.

Schweizer, K., Pächter, M., & Weidenmann, B. (2001). A field study on distance education and communication: Experiences of a virtual tutor. *Journal of Computer-Mediated Communication, 6*.

Scriven, M. (1980). *The logic of evaluation*. Iverness, UK: Edgepress.

Scriven, M. (1991). *Evaluation Thesaurus*. London: Sage.

Sfard, A. (1998). On two metaphors for learning and the dangers of choosing just one. *Educational Researcher, 27*, 4–13. doi:10.2307/1176193

Shapiro, A. M. (2004). Prior Knowledge Must Be Included as a Subject Variable in Learning Outcomes Research. *American Educational Research Journal, 41*, 159–189. doi:10.3102/00028312041001159

Sonntag, K.-H. (2002). Personalentwicklung und Training. Stand der psychologischen Forschung und Gestaltung. *Zeitschrift für Personalpsychologie, 2*, 59–70. doi:10.1026//1617-6391.1.2.59

Stark, R., & Mandl, H. (2002). *"Unauffällige", "Vorwissensschwache", "Unmotivierte" und "Musterschüler": Homogene Untergruppen beim Lernen mit einem komplexen Lösungsbeispiel im Bereich empirischer Forschungsmethoden*. Munich, Germany: Ludwig-Maximilians-Universität, Lehrstuhl für Empirische Pädagogik und Pädagogische Psychologie.

Stockmann, R. (2000). Evaluation in Deutschland. In R. Stockmann (Ed.), *Evaluationsforschung. Grundlagen und ausgewählte Forschungsfelder* (pp. 11-40). Opladen, Germany: Leske + Budrich.

Stufflebeam, D. L. (1978). An introduction to the PDK book. Educational evaluation and decision-making. In Sanders, J. R., & Scriven, M. (Eds.), *Educational Evaluation: Theory and Practice* (pp. 128–150). Belmont, CA: Charles A. Jones Publication, Wadsworth Publishing Company.

Tennyson, R. D., Schott, F., Seel, N. M., & Dijkstra, S. (1997). Instructional Design: International Perspectives: *Vol. 2. Solving instructional design problems*. Mahwah, NJ: Lawrence Erlbaum Associates.

Tergan, S.-O. (2004). Realistische Qualitätsevaluation von E-learning. In Meister, D., Tergan, S.-O., & Zentel, P. (Eds.), *Evaluation von E-Learning. Zielrichtungen, methodologische Aspekte, Zukunftsperspektiven* (pp. 131–154). Münster, Germany: Waxmann.

Tergan, S.-O., & Schenkel, P. (2002). Was macht Lernen erfolgreich? Evaluation des Lernpotenzials von E-Learning. In Hohenstein, A., & Wilbers, K. (Eds.), *Handbuch E-Learning*. Köln, Germany: Fachverlag Dt. Wirtschaftsdienst.

Weinberger, A. (2003). *Scripts for computer-supported collaborative learning*. Munich, Germany: Department Psychologie. Ludwig-Maximilians-Universität.

This work was previously published in the International Journal of Knowledge Society Research, Volume 1, Issue 3, edited by Miltiadis D. Lytras, pp. 33-43, copyright 2010 by IGI Publishing (an imprint of IGI Global).

Chapter 14
Requirements for Successful Wikis in Collaborative Educational Scenarios

Marc Alier Forment
Technical University of Catalonia, Spain

Maria Jose Casañ
Technical University of Catalonia, Spain

Xavier De Pedro
University of Barcelona, Spain

Jordi Piguillem
Technical University of Catalonia, Spain

Nikolas Galanis
Technical University of Catalonia, Spain

ABSTRACT

What are the requirements for the Wiki engines to be used collaborative learning activities? Can any general-purpose engine be used? Or is there a niche for an educationally oriented crop of wiki engines? Do these educational wikis need to be integrated within the LMS to frame the collaborative activity within the walls of the virtual classroom, or is it preferable to have an external engine? These questions arise to every teacher who is about to plan a wiki-based collaborative learning activity. In this paper, the authors examine the use of wikis in college courses at three universities. The findings of this research are introduced and adopted as new features in two major open source wiki engines used for education: the Wiki module for Moodle 2.0 (as a Wiki engine embedded inside a LMS) and Tiki as independent full-featured Wiki CMS/Groupware engine.

INTRODUCTION

Research Framework and Methodology

The use of wikis in education is of a potentially huge value: wikis can be applied to foster collaborative work, to promote project based learning experiences, to open the work conducted in classroom to the world, to facilitate information exchange between groups and educational institutions, etc. The possibilities are practically endless (Augar, Raitman, & Zhou, 2004; Educause Learning Initiative, 2005; Fountain, 2005; García Manzano, 2006). So, using wikis as environments for educational activities allows new pedagogical scenarios, which are pursued by many educators worldwide in the context of collaborative learning (Dillenbourg, 1999). But since a Wiki engine is a tool, we might want to be sure that we are using the right one for the job.

DOI: 10.4018/978-1-4666-1788-9.ch014

The main question we want to address in this paper is: what kind of wiki application we need in order to host the educational wiki experiences? Or in other words: what are the requirements for a Wiki engine to be suitable to host collaborative learning activities, which successfully facilitate faculty and students with their respective tasks? This paper exposes the conclusions and insights obtained after a 6-year research period conducting the following activities:

- Using Wikis for collaborative learning activities in college courses (degree and master) on different specialties and on 3 different Universities (UOC, UB and UPC).
- Analyzing the feedback from students, the quality of the work and the usage logs.
- A participative observation process within the 2 Open Source communities 'Moodle' and 'Tiki Wiki CMS/Groupware' (also known as "Tiki"), engaging in conversations about teaching using wikis and improvement the wiki engines with teachers, administrator and developers.
- Developing improvements to the Wiki engines, submitting the code to the community and being exposed to the feedback and evaluation.
- Making sure our research is actually being taken advantage of, by committing actual code to the official releases, after an approval process, which sometimes involves votes in the community (Moodle case), or by means of the wiki way of making software (Tiki case).

Two Alternative or Complementary Approaches: Internal or External Wiki

An educational institution has to choose between two basic ecosystems (or set them both ready complementarily, offered as alternatives for their faculty): the first one is to use a wiki engine em-bedded and highly integrated inside the Learning Management System (LMS), host of the "virtual campus" of the educational institution, such as Moodle (http://moodle.org), Sakai (http://sakai.org) or Dokeos (http://dokeos.org), among the free software solutions. The second option is to use a vertical wiki application (such as Tiki or MediaWiki), a stand-alone full featured Wiki CMS/Groupware web application or just a powerful wiki engine, respectively, to conduct a fairly free wiki experience outside of the boundaries of the educational institution.

In both cases, basic conclusions from previous works have to be taken into account as premises in order to ensure the effective use of wikis in Education. These include:

a. WYSIWYG (What You See Is What You Get) is not necessarily a "must" feature because basic wiki markup seems to be easy enough to understand and use even for primary education pupils (Désilets, Paquet, & Vinson, 2005).

b. The main handicaps that prevent users from having a successful activity seem to be the lack of motivation and usability (Kickmeier-Rust, Ebner, & Holzinger, 2006).

c. Our experience indicates that students usually don't participate much (if any) in wikis if there is no grading "retribution" for that participation. This is similar to what has been reported for professional sites where potential contributors don't see its worth, provided the institution hosting the wiki does not offer any benefits to make up for the time spent contributing (Giordano, 2007).

d. In order to enhance their learning, students need "on time" feedback for their individual contributions in the class or the workgroup (Diamond, 2004). Teachers, on the other hand, need tools that facilitate the task of quickly providing objective feedback, assessment, and grading of groups and individuals alike (De Pedro, 2007).

The authors of this paper did not choose one ecosystem, but took parallel lines of work within the Moodle (LMS bound) and the combined ecosystem of the standard institutional LMS with additional Tiki installations for specific cases where more features and versatile wiki engines where needed.

Benefits and Drawbacks of Each Approach

Some benefits and drawbacks arise from any of these two contrasted options. Some of them will affect the possibilities to establish certain teaching, assessment and grading strategies.

The managers of educational institutions will prefer the use of wiki integrated in the LMS, provided it complies with the basic features and selection criteria commonly requested (Schwartz, Clark, Cossarin & Rudolph 2004). The main reasons are pretty obvious: out of the box integration of user authentication and authorization, plus the fact that the wiki is integrated in the LMS structure (course, categories, permissions and roles, tags, search features, course information, access logs, etc). Moreover, the corporate image is preserved due to the use of the institution "theme/skin", color scheme, etc.

This way the wiki becomes part of the institution's portfolio of educational software tools, and educators can be instructed on how to use it in their courses. So everything is kept under control for the educational site managers. Some examples of this type of wiki would be the Wiki Module packages for Moodle (eWiki, the default wiki engine for installations up to branch 1.9, included), dfWiki, nWiki or ouWiki (Moodle, 2010a); RWiki: Sakai Wiki Tool (Sakai, n.d.), or CoolWiki extension for Dokeos (Dokeos CoolWiki, n.d.).

The embedded Wikis are usually more limited in features compared to some full featured and mature Wikis (CosmoCode, n.d.). Under some pedagogic scenarios, or technical requirements in some specific areas, simple wikis seem to be lacking (Choy & Ng, 2007; De Pedro, 2008). Sometimes there is the need to receive RSS feeds or email notification of changes on multiple pages from some student groups on long term collaborative work, in order to help to provide prompt feedback whenever needed (Mutch, 2003). Some other times, there is the need to allow multimedia rich content on the wiki pages of the students (artistic type of courses, animations for scientific lessons, mathematic formulae, etc.). And in some cases, the teacher needs some higher degree of permission handling for pages and categories of pages, in order to easily define whatever complex settings for pedagogic activities, visual editing of tables or linked spreadsheets and concept maps, so that those wiki-based activities simply work on their particular pedagogic strategy (Lindsay, 2008). Therefore, some specific criteria beyond the basic ones used by other institutions must be taken into account, in order to successfully set the pursued pedagogic scenario and high level technical (De Pedro, 2008).

Thus, teachers who are more engaged in innovative activities or pedagogic scenarios might feel that the integrated wikis commonly available inside LMS platforms are less versatile than what they need for their teaching. Some of them have reported feeling handicapped, because they were unable to add on the fly new courses or workspaces beyond the initial course wiki, or they could not grant access to users outside the institution. For seminars, conferences, postgraduate and other special courses, this is a daily issue, and that's why many external wikis (or even full external LMS sites) can be commonly found on the Internet (pbwiki.com, wikilearning.com, wikispaces.com, to name a few), alongside their base institutional campus sites.

When working inside the institutional wiki, and once motivated to contribute, students tend to behave with more caution. They are more reluctant to rush into a wiki page and change content. Thus, the pedagogical experience of participation in an open wiki is contaminated by an excess of formalism and aspirations to excellence. Students usually do not dare contribute to high quality content, but often do not mind doing so to an external wiki were non students can also contribute, such as in Wikibooks from the Wikipedia Foundation, where excellence can be achieved by peer reviewing and fearless collaboration (Sajjapanroj, Bonk, Lee, & Lin, 2008). However, student contributions on those environments increase the difficulty for teachers to easily review them, and to provide in-context feedback without dispersing comments on too many different environments, with all the inconveniences this may cause (Choy & Ng, 2007).

The use of external wiki engines requires an extra effort for integrating user authentication and synchronization systems. Sometimes the adopted solution consists of creating separate accounts for the students in a completely separated application administered by the teachers (like in the experiences behind, see De Pedro et al., 2006; De Pedro 2006a, 2006b; De Pedro, 2007), sometimes hosted in a desktop computer in the teacher's office (Bernat Claramunt, personal communication).

As examples, we can cite the case of MediaWiki installations which are fully external to the main LMS (the most common case everywhere in the world), or partly integrated within installations of Moodle (Moodle, 2009a), or Dokeos (Dokeos MediaWiki, n.d.), for instance, even if some integration issues are well known (De Pedro, 2008; Left, n.d.). Elsewhere, Tiki Wiki CMS/Groupware (or "Tiki", in short, formerly known as Tikiwiki) has been chosen as the wiki engine besides the main LMS installation: several departments at University of York, UK (Davies, 2004); all faculties in Bages University Foundation, Spain, alongside their Dokeos based campus (http://wiki.fub.edu vs. http://virtual.fub.edu); several departments at University of Barcelona (De Pedro, 2006a, 2006b).

There are also some extreme cases where the institution adopted the external wiki site (such as Tiki Wiki CMS/Groupware), with its companion's built-in features to act as Content Management System and Groupware site (including specific modules to act as an LMS). In fact, Tiki was already highly ranked by international institutions when evaluating portal systems including wikis (Catalyst IT, 2004). Some examples of this type of institution are Harbor City International School (Minnesota, USA; http://torch.harborcityschool. net), Trinity School Insite (Cheshire, UK; http:// trinitysch.org.uk/insite), Colegio María Virgen (Madrid, Spain; http://www.cmariavirgen.org), and University of Strathclyde (UK) and Stanford University using a modified version of Tiki called "LauLima" (http://www.didet.ac.uk).

The last and most recent case is a mixed approach: the Open University of Catalonia, Spain (http://www.uoc.edu) already started for their 2008/09 course, a dual approach were teachers are be able to use either the integrated wiki engine in their main LMS sites (based on Moodle, among others), as well as a separate and customized Tiki installation for cases where faculty needed higher degree of features and more complex pedagogic scenarios (Begoña Gros, personal communication).

Learning in Wikis: Assessment, Feedback and Grading

Assessment and feedback of the student learning process in wikis are very delicate tasks, which can be used by students to enhance their teaching, and especially when they include enough oral or written individual feedback on their performance, beyond simply grading their activity. The quality of a wiki page or set of pages is usually the result of a combined work of several students. But not all them necessarily deserve the same grade, nor need the same feedback on their individual contributions for the common document. Some students fake edits, abuse copy and paste, or alter their participation in other ways. So, it is important to state the size and type of contributions that each student performs on wiki-based learning activities.

Most wiki engines, due to their general purpose design, do not consider tagging the type of student contributions, do not allow rating by teachers or student peers, do not facilitate the task of submitting written feedback on students' single edits, nor include a grading feature linked to the course grade book. A wiki engine aspiring to be useful for educational scenarios needs to provide a way to easily track and assess each student's individual contributions, to easily report prompt feedback on them, and should allow grading the participation in the wiki, while transferring this information to the course grade book. When the wiki engine is not integrated in the LMS, then it should provide an easy way of exporting the action log of all student contributions, tagged by student, group, category and time, in order to facilitate the assessment and provide objective information for written feedback or oral tutorship by the teachers.

Moodle, An LMS that Wanted to Integrate a Wiki

Moodle is an Open Source community of more than 350,000 members that releases a Free and Open Source Software (FOSS) LMS available in 75 languages with more than 14,000.000 students in 160 countries. When someone goes for the first time to the Moodle main page, they are greeted by the welcome phrase:

Moodle is a course management system (CMS) - a free, Open Source software package designed using sound pedagogical principles, to help educators create effective online learning communities.

Digging into these principles (Moodle, 2009b) and more formal writings (Dougiamas, 1998; Dougiamas & Taylor, 2003) we receive a briefing into the "social constructionist pedagogy" that can be summarized in 4 points: (1) "Constructivism", people actively construct new knowledge as they interact with their environment; (2) "Constructionism", learning is particularly effective when constructing something for others to experience;

(3) "Social Constructivism", when a social group is constructing things for one another, each member is also learning about how to be a part of that culture, on many levels, (4) "Constructed behavior", looks into the motivations of individuals within a discussion. A "separate behavior" tries to remain 'objective' and 'factual', while a "connected behavior" is a more empathic and subjective approach. Ultimately, the "Constructed behavior" is sensitive to both of these approaches and is able to choose either of them as appropriate to the current situation.

All these deep pedagogical principles, taken from philosophy, sociology and psychology, have been distilled by the Moodle founder Martin Dougiamas, into 5 rules that are easier to apply (Moodle, 2010b):

All of us are potential teachers as well as learners - in a true collaborative environment we are both.

We learn particularly well from the act of creating or expressing something for others to see.

We learn a lot by just observing the activity of our peers.

By understanding the contexts of others, we can teach in a more transformational way.

A learning environment needs to be flexible and adaptable, so that it can quickly respond to the needs of the participants within it.

Thus, the design of the Moodle LMS is focused on a "virtual classroom" as the main object where the teacher has full power of administration and instructional design. Moodle focuses on hosting activities (where students do things and share experiences) rather than delivering contents to be mechanically consumed by students.

This suggests that the underlying philosophy of using wikis in educational activities is very compatible with the Moodle design and what Moodle stands for in pedagogy.

Therefore, it comes as no surprise that many teaching institutions around the globe decided to use Moodle as their main LMS site, in some cases, even after closely comparing it to Sakai (Wittke & Granow, 2007). We discuss two specific cases below, regarding the two biggest universities in Catalonia, which in the past years chose Moodle as their main Campus: the Technical University of Catalonia ("UPC", from its initials in Catalan) and the University of Barcelona ("UB"). In the first case, some lecturers opted to improve the solution of an integrated Wiki engine inside Moodle, and in the second case, some lecturers opted to invest resources to improve some versatile external wiki for their educational requirements, outside the main institutional LMS's, which were lacking many needed features, by the time when Moodle was not officially supported.

The UPC Case: The Birth of a Contribution to the Project

In 2004 the Technical University of Catalonia (UPC), Spain, migrated to Moodle for their LMS to host 34,000 students in grade and post grade studies. Moodle has an embedded wiki engine, but thousands of courses since its start, only 3 instances of that wiki have been enabled.

However, there is a team of teachers at UPC who are using wikis and doing research about it, though, they simply use other wiki engines in unofficial installations. In 2003 the group led by Marc Alier (one of the authors of this paper) (Alier & Barceló, 2005) started using Mediawiki. Mediawiki is a very solid application, easy to use and with a huge of amount of documentation available. Its markup language is very easy to learn and both students and teachers adopted it very quickly. The first experience was a big success. The students adopted it automatically and got quite enthusiastic about the use of the wiki.

Teachers encouraged them to use the wiki also for off topic purposes. A special page named "promenade" was spontaneously used to discuss about music, movies, the Internet and other aspects of the university life. Both students and teachers visited this page and the quality of the research reports was remarkable and so the results in the exams; the students actually learned a lot. Teachers realized that they had succeeded at building a learning community.

However, the experience also exposed that Mediawiki software is not designed for this kind of experiences since its code is very difficult to hack in. This reason triggered the change of platform to Moodle.

Moodle is not a Wiki software, it is a course oriented LMS that has an embedded Wiki activity module, developed several years ago from a slightly modified version of the standalone "erfurtWiki" (http://erfurtwiki.sf.net, eWiki for the purpose of this document). This means that eWiki in Moodle is only one tool among others like Forum, Glossary, Quiz, Task and a lot more. Taking advantage of eWiki, a separate Moodle course was created for each sub group, and instead of creating one wiki for all the students, a separate eWiki activity was created for each team and topic of research and subgroup. This revealed to be an unsuccessful approach; because UPC teachers simply bumped into Moodle using all the tools they found at reach without thinking how this would affect the learning design.

The results weren't so good. Students found Moodle easy to use, and the incorporation of the forums as communication tool was welcome. But the eWiki module was not as powerful and easy to use as Mediawiki. The analysis of the results showed up that the excessive fragmentation of the workspace (subgroups, separate Wiki activities) did not help to create a sense of learning community, and the lack of usability of the eWiki led to a number of teams choosing to elaborate their reports in a text processor and simply upload them to their wiki page as an attachment (Figure 1).

Teachers learned from that experience, and they decided to keep on "Moodling". After a thorough analysis of the eWiki module (usability

Figure 1. Histogram of editions (frequency) per page (versions) using the Moodle eWiki module versus using DFWiki. In the first experience, the most popular option was to attach a PDF file or to simply copy and paste the report from a text processor. Using DFWiki, students adopted the Wiki as a true collaborative tool: more pages and more active where created.

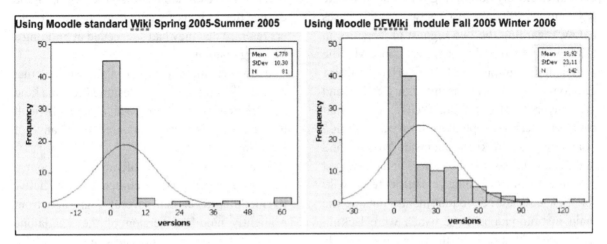

and code), they decided to develop from scratch a new wiki module for Moodle with two main purposes: (1) to have a wiki engine at least as versatile as an embedded Mediawiki engine inside Moodle LMS, so that they would have the best of two worlds: the high class wiki engines and the LMS integration; and (2) to have a framework where they could easily add new features according to their pedagogical requirements.

This group of teachers shared their code and open sourced it since the beginning: modules "DFWiki", for Moodle 1.5, and "NWiki", for Moodle 1.6 and beyond (http://www.dfwikilabs. org). In 2008, after 4 years of maintaining this module ("NWiki"), the Moodle Community chose it to be the official wiki engine in the next stable release: Moodle 2.0, expected in mid-2010 (http:// docs.moodle.org/en/Roadmap).

Moodle 2.0 Wiki Features

The new Wiki Module to be released in Moodle 2.0 and back ported to 1.9 branch, includes the following features:

- "Multiple markup wiki". Moodle 2.0 Wiki allows the page creator to choose from several markups: Mediawiki plus Creole 1.0 markup (Sauer, Smith & Benz 2007), the native DFWiki markup (a subset of Mediawiki's with simplified tables), efurtWiki markup for backwards compatibility, and the Moodle internal HTML editor plus wikilinks.

- Import/Export features. Moodle courses can be saved and restored via backups, Moodle 2.0 Wiki allows to export the wiki contents to a single XML file, and import them in another wiki activity (to merge two wiki contents for example) or in another course in another Moodle server. Another feature is the possibility to export the content to HTML, PDF and some experimental export plug-ins such as Tiddlywiki export (http://moodle.tiddlyspot.com) and OpenOffice Writer import/export.

- Customizable Blocks inside the wiki activity (Figure 2). Moodle design includes Blocks: small micro web applications that the teacher can place in both sides of the

Figure 2. Moodle NWiki blocks. Depending on the purposes of the use of the wiki activity the teacher can choose from several useful blocks with key live information about what's going on in the wiki.

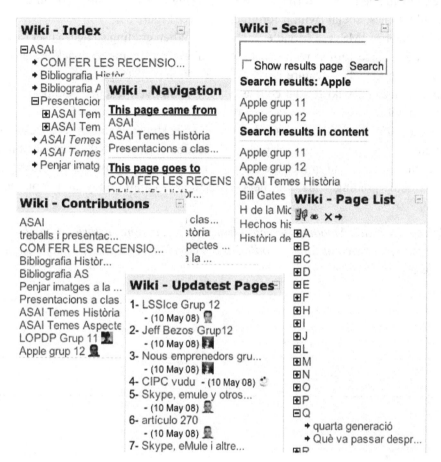

Moodle screen. Moodle 2.0 Wiki provides a number of blocks with useful information and functions such as:

- ○ Dynamic tree index (from the first or the current page). The teacher can choose which of these blocks to enable in their wiki.
- ○ Wanted pages.
- ○ Orphaned pages.
- ○ Alphabetical page list.
- ○ Search engine.
- ○ Page synonyms.
- ○ New page block: a small form to create a new page. The creation of this small form was a very requested feature in the Moodle.org forums.

- ○ Latest contributions list.
- ○ Page ranking. The teacher can enable votes in the wiki pages. The following block shows the ranking.

Moreover, like Mediawiki, the Moodle 2.0 Wiki implements discussion pages and allows two page comparison views: line by line (also like Mediawiki) and inline changes.

The activity (editions and page views) in Moodle 2.0 Wiki instances is logged in the Moodle reporting system, so the teacher can easily track the student's participation in the wiki. This is a common need when using Wikis in educational scenarios (Choy & Ng, 2007; De Pedro, 2007).

Moodle's course design is customizable. There are several available built in formats like a weekly schedule, topics, social (with a forum as main activity), Scorm, IMS, etc Moodle 2.0 Wiki include a wiki course format with a wiki as the main course activity. This feature is very relevant because by using a wiki format course Moodle becomes a wiki.

Finally, Moodle 2.0 Wiki incorporates a redesigned assessment and grading feature. Each page can be assessed and graded. And grades are set according to a Moodle grading scale. Teachers

or students (if they are allowed) can grade pages through a small combo box in the bottom of the page (Figure 3).

When grading a page, a user can give one line of feedback. This feedback is added into the discussion page (Figure 4).

Moreover, teachers and peers can rate single editions with a symbol (+, = or -), as well as giving the student a line of feedback (Figure 5). The feedback is sent to the students through Moodle internal messaging system (that pipes into the students email if they are not online).

Figure 3. Wiki activity inside Moodle. The main features (discussion, historic, administration and the wikipage navigator) are offered as tabs. Moodle 2.0 Wiki implements an auto table of contents and section edit with locking to manage concurrency).

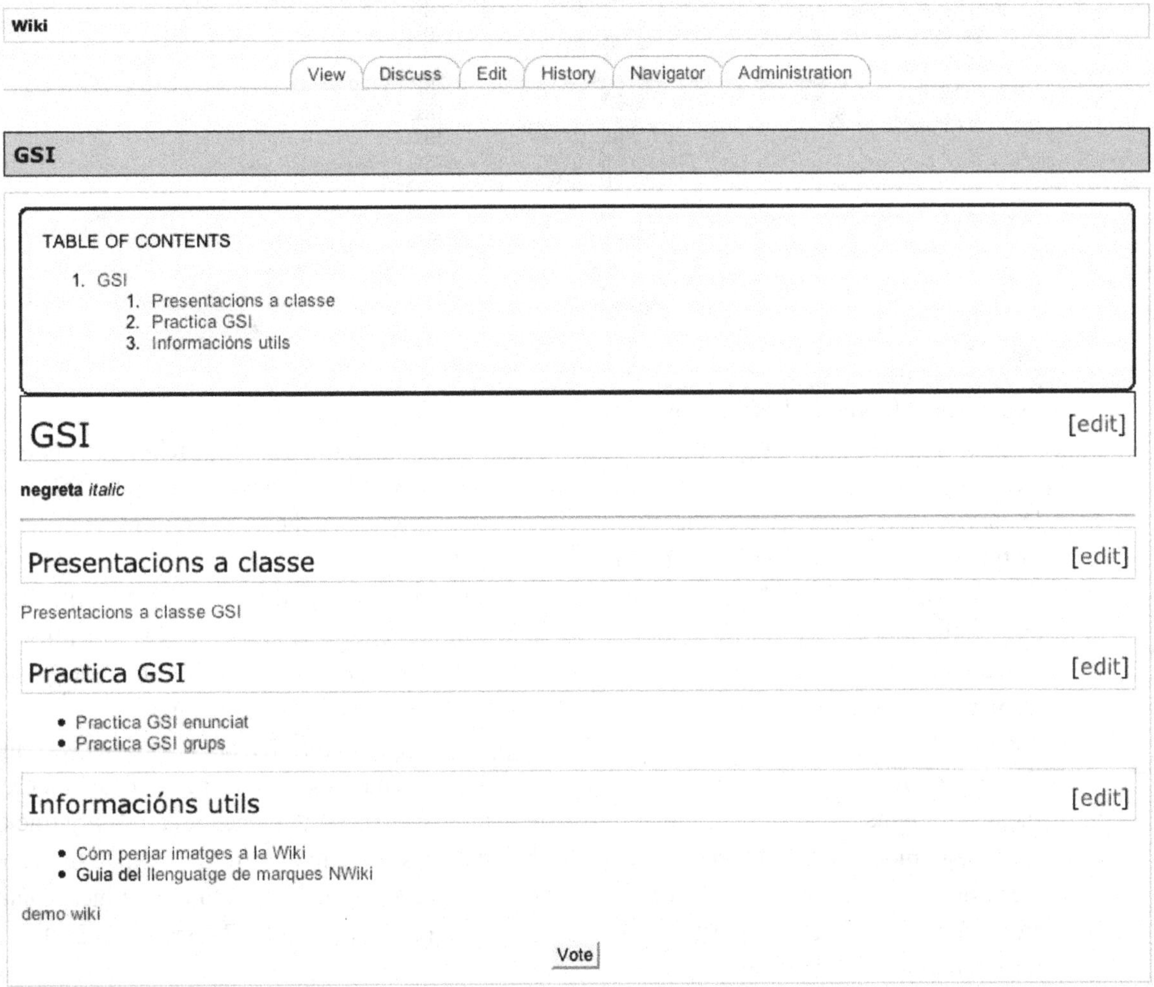

Figure 4. Each wiki page can be graded by teachers and even students if peer review is enabled. The grade can belong in any of the scales defined in Moodle. The feedback line is appended to the discussion page, and also stored in the assessment database tables.

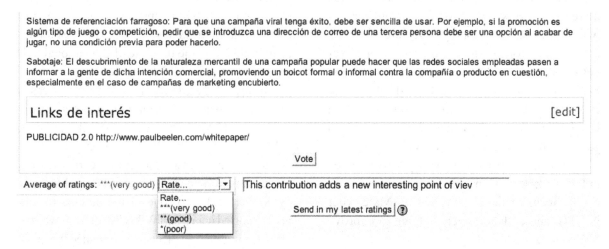

Figure 5. A student receives a feedback message due to the rating of his contribution to a wiki page.

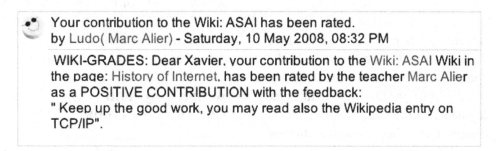

Finally the teacher has access to a special page where he can see all the information about the pages where a student has participated in: page editions, views and received ratings. In this page, the teacher can give an overall grade for the student's contributions to the whole wiki activity and send it to the course's grade book (http://docs.moodle.org/en/gradebook).

The UB Case: Several Wikis, Plus Tiki Enhancements for Education

The University of Barcelona (UB), the oldest and biggest university in Catalonia, Spain, decided to adopt Moodle as its main campus later than the other Catalan universities which are using it. In 2006-2007, a pilot phase for the adoption of a new Virtual Campus based on Moodle was deployed, which meant that in June 2007, almost 300 courses were added to the campus with 400 teachers and 11,000 students.

In 2007/08 the Moodle campus was open for all grades and Masters, some postgraduate courses and Ph.D. Programs (http://campusvirtual.ub.edu). It meant the enrollment of up to 4,500 teachers and 70,000 students, using Moodle version 1.7.x. The official Wiki engine was NWiki for Moodle 1.7.x. There were some critical issues stated by teachers on that installation, the five most important of which were (Lluïsa Núñez, personal communication): (1) there was no notice on edition conflict, (2) there was no way to have notification emails or RSS feeds sent when pages changed, (3) there was no Wiki action log for student activity within Moodle's student report feature, (4) some issues with wrong permissions arose when a user belonged to several wiki groups, and (5) some wiki novice teachers got confused when they chose WYSIWYG html editors and realized that it did not allow big files, and while copying and pasting from text editors, html was not cleaned.

The virtual campus team led by Lluïsa Nuñez in UB is working alongside other teams with the NWiki team of developers, led by Marc Alier in UPC, and collaboratively helping to improve NWiki software.

At the same University of Barcelona, there exist some other institutional LMS deployments with their own wiki engines for different reasons. In 2007/08 a separate installation of Moodle and its wiki were set up for special courses for staff and research groups (http://cvformacio.ub.edu). In this case, Moodle 1.8.x + NWiki were used, as a test ground for production of the new features, in small deployments. On another case, some joint Masters programs like the MSc Bioinformatics for Health Sciences (University Pompeu Fabra / University of Barcelona) are using their own Moodle installation with eWiki in 2006 (http://damocles.imim.es/moodle/). A research group of innovations in teaching called GrindoFI (http://www.ub.es/grindofi/) also has its own Moodle 1.9.x site (http://ganglion.fisiologia.ub.es/moodle/), with an external wiki engine running MediaWiki (http://ganglion.fisiologia.ub.es/wiki). At Pedagogy faculty, they have another separate Moodle installation for trials and staff formation (http://siurana2.ird.ub.es/), where they were testing and using eWiki, DFWiki and NWiki. Finally, there are at least 6 more separate Moodle installations within the University of Barcelona which might have used or tested wiki engines for production with their students or department colleagues: one teacher in Pharmacy (Officinalis.com); some teachers in Physiology from the Faculty of Medicine (http://www.fisiologia.net/curs/); the Laboratory of Interactive Media (http://moodle.lmi.ub.es/); the Faculty of Biblioteconomy and Documentation (http://bd.ub.es/intranet/); the FINT Group, and Pedagogy (http://fint.doe.d5.ub.es/moodle/); and the Institute of Educational Sciences (http://161.116.7.109/moodle/).

On top of that, there have been many cases of teachers using Wiki engines external to the institutional LMS's, such as EconoWiki, TSWiki, MMwiki (powered by "Awki" wiki engine; http://awkiawki.sf.net). In addition, much earlier a group of lecturers from the University of Barcelona lead by Xavier de Pedro (one of the authors of this paper) started using Tiki Wiki CMS/Groupware in 2004 for innovation projects to enhance the quality of teaching on "blended learning" pedagogic scenarios (Garrison & Kanuka 2004)). Those publicly funded projects were UniWiki, AWikiForum, CarpeTiki, Arcòtic (De Pedro 2006b), which survived the early and slow process of Moodle adoption at University of Barcelona.

"Action Log" and "Contribution Types"

Between 2004 and 2007 some features were enhanced and others added in order to ease the task of using a powerful and versatile external wiki engine in addition to the former, full-featured virtual campuses at the University of Barcelona. Basically they are composed of two core features coded in Tiki 2 (http://doc.tikiwiki.org/Tiki2): "Action log" and "Contribution" features (http://doc.tikiwiki.org/Action+log, http://doc.tikiwiki.org/Contribution), plus one external optional package, called AulaWiki (http://edu.tikiwiki.org).

The main difference from the previous NWiki approach reported previously is that teachers focused the enhancements towards allowing the students to select the contribution types of the editions they were performing each time, either on wiki pages, discussion pages (called "comments" section, in Tiki), or forums, blogs and spreadsheets (Figure 6).

Figure 6. Wiki page in Tiki opened for edition showing the type of contribution selector, which had to be selected at each edition

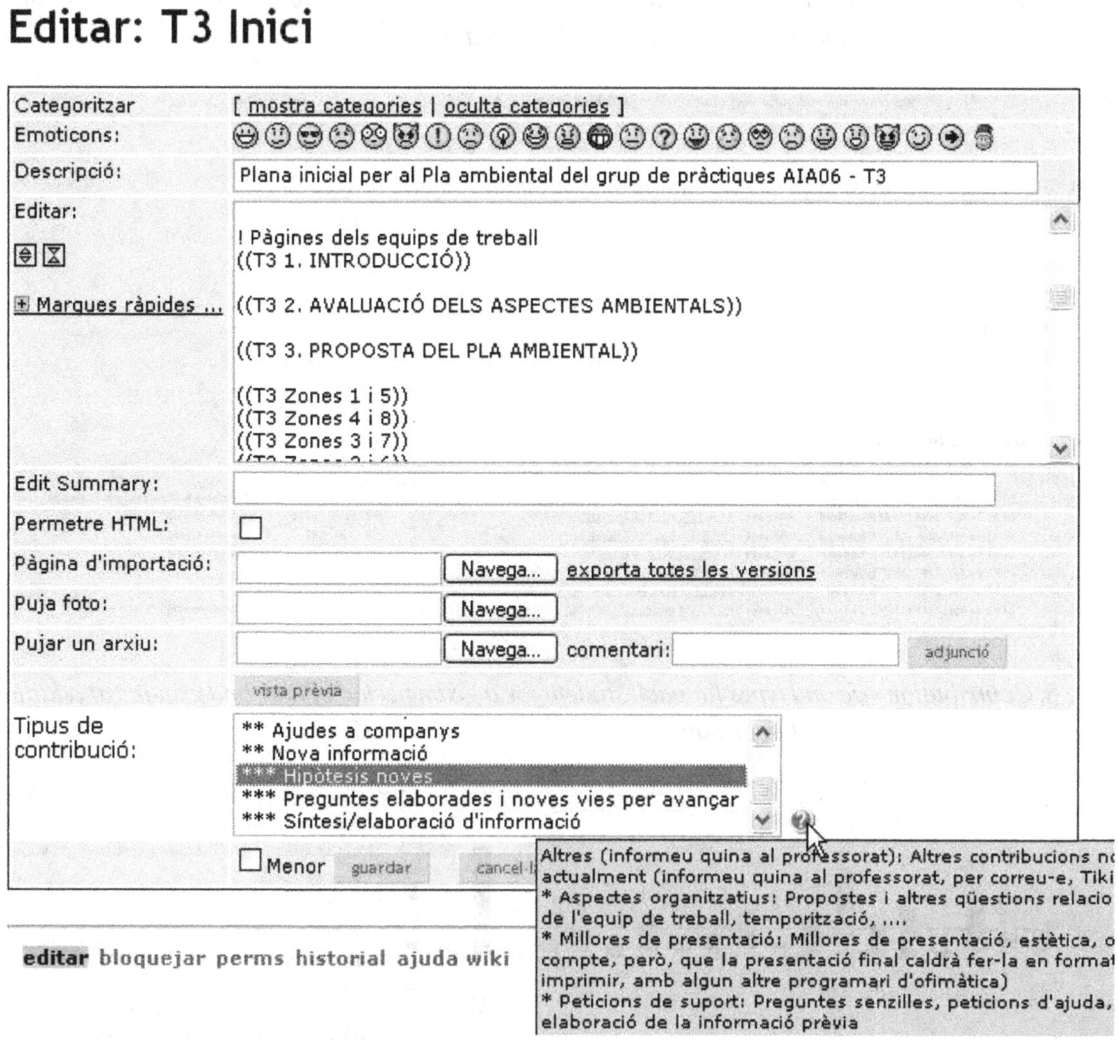

Editar: T3 Inici

Other students with appropriate permissions and teachers could review at any time the amount of contributions from the Action log (Figure 7).

Additionally, graphical reports on individual students or whole groups could be produced at any time, showing clearly in some simple bar charts the necessary information to substantially improve the quality of the feedback with single students or in groups in the scheduled mid-term tutorships (Figure 8). More information on those enhancements was the main focus of previous

works freely available on the Internet (De Pedro, 2006b; De Pedro 2007), and thus, it will not be covered.

CONCLUSION

Some balance has to be achieved between the need for more features in an educational wiki, and its usability for its users (students, but also teachers, some of whom are even more novice to new

Figure 7. Action log interface in Tiki showing the filter options and the corresponding results underneath, including the amount of information (in bytes) added or deleted by means of each action aside with their type of contributions as selected by the students. Type of contributions could be edited by faculty when appropriate to adjust them more to what students did in reality.

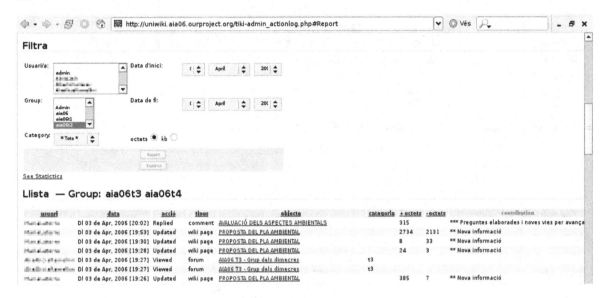

Figure 8. Contribution size and types for each student for a given period of time and group: (a) additions of information, (b) deletions of information.

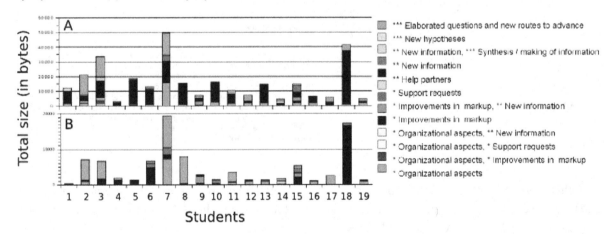

technologies than their pupils). Some educational institutions opt for an integrated wiki engine in their main LMS site. In some other cases, either the institution or the lecturers opt for setting their own external wiki sites for maximum control and a more complete feature set. In both cases, in order to have a successful engine that helps students and teachers in their daily life, the wiki engine should include some mechanism to rate editions and pages or to classify student contributions in types. This mechanism has to take into consideration several aspects:

- The quality of pages or size and type of single contributions in these pages.
- The participation of each student in each edition.
- The possibility of having a review being not only a number or a letter, but also some extended form of written feedback.
- The page or edition evaluation being just a part of the whole activity grade, which is what the teacher sends to the course's grade book, in cases of integrated Wiki engines such as the Moodle Wiki module.

ACKNOWLEDGMENT

Our thanks to Begoña Gros and Lluïsa Núñez for providing feedback on the usage of the Institutional Learning Management Systems on their respective campuses (UOC and UB, respectively). In addition, the feedback gathered from the virtual campus team in the experiences with Moodle 2.0 Wiki conducted in University of Barcelona helped to complete the requirements for the evolution of this wiki engine.

This work has been funded by Google, and the Spanish Ministry of Science and Innovation with the project: TIN2010-21695-C02-02

REFERENCES

Alier, M., & Barceló, M. (2005). An application of social constructionism and open source. In Mendez Villas, B., Gonzalz Pereira, J., & Mesa Gonzalez, J. A. (Eds.), *Recent research developments in learning technologies* (pp. 1170–1175).

Augar, N., Raitman, R., & Zhou, W. (2004). Teaching and learning online with wikis. In *Beyond the comfort zone: Proceedings of the 21st ASCILITE conference* (pp. 95-104).

Catalyst IT. (2004). *Technical evaluation of selected portal systems.*

Choy, S. O., & Ng, K. C. (2007). Implementing wiki software for supplementing online learning. *Australasian Journal of Educational Technology*, *23*, 209–226.

CosmoCode. (n.d.). *Wikimatrix.* Retrieved July 5, 2010, from http://www.wikimatrix.org

Davies, J. (2004). *Wiki brainstorming and problems with wiki based collaboration.*

De Pedro, X. (2006). Cómo evitar el 'café para todos' al evaluar trabajos en grupo, y de paso, estimular el aprendizaje reflexivo: resultados preliminares en el marco del proyecto awikiforum. In *Entorns col·laboratius per aprendre: comunitats virtuals d'aprenentatge.*

De Pedro, X. (2006). Estimulación y evaluación del aprendizaje 'experiencial-reflexivo' del alumnado mediante la formulación explícita del tipo de contribuciones.

De Pedro, X. (2007). New method using wikis and forums to evaluate individual contributions in cooperative work while promoting experiential learning: results from preliminary experience. In *Wikis at work in the world: open, organic, participatory media for the 21st century* (pp. 87-92).

De Pedro, X. (2008). *Informe sobre wikis en educació per a la Universitat Oberta de Catalunya.*

De Pedro, X., Rieradevall, M., López, P., Sant, D., Piñol, J., Núñez, L., et al. (2006). Writing documents collaboratively in higher education using traditional vs. wiki methodology (i): qualitative results from a 2-year project study. In *Libro de comunicaciones del 4° congreso internacional de docencia universitaria e innovación.* Retrieved from http://cidui.upc.edu

Désilets, A., Paquet, S., & Vinson, N. G. (2005, October 17-18). Are wikis usable? In *Proceedings of the 2005 international symposium on Wikis* (pp. 3-15).

Diamond, M. (2004). The usefulness of structured mid-term feedback as a catalyst for change in higher education classes. *Active Learning in Higher Education, 5,* 217–231. doi:10.1177/1469787404046845

Dillenbourg, P. (1999). What do you mean by collaborative learning? In Dillenbourg, P. (Ed.), *Collaborative-learning: Cognitive and Computational Approaches* (pp. 1–19). Oxford, UK: Elsevier.

Dokeos CoolWiki. (n.d.). *CoolWiki extension for Dokeos LMS.* Retrieved July 5, 2010, from http://www.dokeos.com/extensions/index.php?section=tools&id=33

Dokeos Mediawiki. (n.d.). *Integration of Mediawiki in Dokeos.* Retrieved July 5, 2010, from http://www.dokeos.com/wiki/index.php/Integration_of_mediawiki

Dougiamas, M. (1998). *A journey into constructivism.* Retrieved July 5, 2010, from http://dougiamas.com/writing/constructivism.html

Dougiamas, M., & Taylor, P. C. (2003). Moodle: Using learning communities to create an open source course management system. In *Proceedings of the EDMEDIA 2003 conference.*

Educause Learning Initiative. (2005). *7 things you should know about... wikis.*

Fountain, R. (2005). *Dossiers technopédagogiques: wiki pedagogy.* Retrieved July 5, 2010, from http://www.profetic.org/dossiers/dossier_imprimer.php3?id_rubrique=110

García Manzano, A. (2006). *Blogs y wikis en tareas educativas.* Retrieved July 5, 2010, from http://observatorio.cnice.mec.es/modules.php?op=modload&name=News&file=article&sid=378

Garrison, R., & Kanuka, H. (2004). Blended learning: uncovering its transformative potential in higher education. *The Internet and Higher Education, 7,* 95–105. doi:10.1016/j.iheduc.2004.02.001

Giordano, R. (2007). An investigation of the use of a wiki to support knowledge exchange in public health. In Proceedings of the 2007 International ACM Conference on Supporting Group Work.

Kickmeier-Rust, M., Ebner, M., & Holzinger, A. (2006). Wikis: do they need usability engineering? In *M3 – Interdisciplinary aspects of digital media & education* (pp. 137-144).

Left, P. (n.d.). *Integrating Moodle and Mediawiki.* Retrieved July 5, 2010, from http://www.verso.co.nz/learning-technology/35/integrating-moodle-and-mediawiki/

Lindsay, J. (2008). *Wikis that work. Practical and pedagogical applications of wikis in the classroom.* Retrieved July 5, 2010, from http://julielindsaylinks.pbwiki.com/Wikis-that-Work

Moodle. (2009a). *Moodle development: wiki.* Retrieved July 5, 2010, from http://docs.moodle.org/en/Development:Wiki

Moodle. (2009b). *Moodle docs - philosophy.* Retrieved July 5, 2010, from http://docs.moodle.org/en/Philosophy

Moodle. (2010a). *Moodle forums thread about NWiki, and ouWiki.* Retrieved July 5, 2010, from http://moodle.org/mod/forum/discuss.php?d=89653

Moodle. (2010b). *Moodle docs – pedagogy.* Retrieved July 5, 2010, from http://docs.moodle.org/en/Pedagogy

Mutc, A. (2003). Exploring the practice of feedback to students. *Active Learning in Higher Education, 14,* 24–38. doi:10.1177/1469787403004001003

Sajjapanroj, S., Bonk, C., Lee, M. M., & Lin, M. G. (2008). A window on wikibookians: surveying their statuses, successes, satisfactions, and sociocultural experiences. *Journal of Interactive Online Learning, 7,* 36–58.

Sakai. (n.d.). *Sakai wiki tool (rwiki)*. Retrieved July 5, 2010, from http://confluence.sakaiproject.org/confluence/display/RWIKI/Home

Sauer, C., Smith, C., & Benz, T. (2007). Wikicreole: a common wiki markup. In *Proceedings of the 2007 International Symposium on Wikis* (pp. 131-142). New York: ACM Press.

Schwartz, L., Clark, S., Cossarin, M., & Rudolph, J. (2004). Educational wikis: features and selection criteria. *International Review of Research in Open and Distance Learning*, 5.

Wittke, A., & Granow, R. (2007).*Why German universities choose Moodle instead of Sakai.*

This work was previously published in the International Journal of Knowledge Society Research, Volume 1, Issue 3, edited by Miltiadis D. Lytras, pp. 44-58, copyright 2010 by IGI Publishing (an imprint of IGI Global).

Chapter 15

An Innovative Educational Project at the University of Granada:
A New Teaching–Learning Model for Adapting the Organization of Curricula to Interactive Learning

M. Zamorano
University of Granada, Spain

A. F. Ramos-Ridao
University of Granada, Spain

M.L. Rodríguez
University of Granada, Spain

M. Pasadas
University of Granada, Spain

ABSTRACT

The European Space of Higher Education (ESHE) is a new conceptual formulation of the organization of teaching at the university, largely involving the development of new training models based on the individual student's work. In this context, the University of Granada has approved two plans of Educational Excellence to promote a culture of quality and stimulate excellence in teaching. The Area of Environmental Technology in the Department of Civil Engineering has developed an innovative project entitled Application of new Information and Communication Technologies (ICT) to the Area of Environmental Technology teaching to create a new communication channel consisting of a Web site that benefits teacher and student ("Environmental Studies Centre": http://cem.ugr.es). Through this interactive page, teachers can conduct supervised teaching, and students will have the tools necessary for guiding their learning process, according to their capacities and possibilities. However, the material is designed to serve as a complement to the traditional method of attended teaching.

DOI: 10.4018/978-1-4666-1788-9.ch015

1. INTRODUCTION

In recent years the working world demands greater abilities and practical skills, so in addition to theoretical knowledge, universities should develop in their students skills such as leadership, decision making or the ability to work in a multidisciplinary team. To achieve these extra goals, universities should include teaching-learning models that encourage the student body to analyze, discriminate, classify and synthesize the information they receive (King, 2005). In order to promote teaching-learning models that give students a more active role, developing abilities as decision making and analysis, the European Union (EU) has defined the new framework of the European Space of Higher Education (ESHE), based on the establishment of the European Credit Transfer and Accumulation System (ECTS) and defined as a student-centred system with the required student workload geared toward achieving the objectives of a programme specified in terms of learning outcomes and competences to be acquired. The concept of credit should take into account the total workload that a student must carry out to overcome individual subjects and attain the knowledge and skills set out therein, including both the hours of attendance and the effort that the student must devote to studying and preparing for examinations: for example, tutorials, seminars, practical work and non-attendance learning (Arias, 2003; Font, 2003). The adoption of ECTS demands a new approach to teaching methods, and therefore a revision of curricula and subjects. Since the Spanish Royal Decree 1125/2003 (Generalitat de Catalunya, 2003a) establishes the European credit system and the system of qualifications in university degrees, the Spanish University System is immersed in the process of reforming the curricula of higher education for adaptation to the new educational models.

Using new Information and Communication Technologies (ICT) in teaching models lends enormous potential to the support of an advanced teaching-learning process and to the student´s experience -both theoretical and practical- assuming the responsibility of his/her learning (Aragones et al., 2006; Löfström & Nevgi, 2008). Websites or Web portals help knowledge organisation by improving collaborative activities and facilitating knowledge acquisition, the sharing of ideas, and collaborative work (Jones et al., 2006). The Bologna Declaration, signed in 1999, marks a turning point in the development of European higher education; but it does not mention the importance of the virtual dimension (Moon et al., 2007). Later on the European Commission became aware of the important current social and educational role of new technologies, adopting the first multi-annual programme (2004 to 2006) for the effective integration of information and communication technologies (ICT) in education and training systems in Europe (eLearning Programme) through Decision No 2318/2003/EC of the European Parliament and the Council (Gavari, 2006). The overall objective of the programme is to support and further develop the effective use of ICT in European education and training systems, as a contribution to quality education and as an essential element of their adaptation to the needs of the knowledge society in a lifelong learning context (European Parliament, 2003). Many educational institutions have adopted e-learning systems to complement traditional teaching in various disciplines in recent years (Jarvela & Hakkinen, 2002; Shin et al., 2002; Lau & Mak, 2005). In comparison to the traditional methods of teaching that emphasize using the classroom, e-learning can provide an environment that lifts the restrictions of time and space in knowledge delivery and capture. With the advance of computer infrastructures and the Internet, the use of Information Technology (IT) for teaching and learning has vastly increased the flexibility and effectiveness of knowledge delivery. In a typical e-learning system, IT components include computer graphics, animation, multimedia effects, and databases. In addition, Internet applications such as e-mail and chat room facilities are incorporated into the cyberplatform for learning. The Website or Web portal in the context of higher education adopts teaching methodology based on the e-learning concept, that is, providing educational programs and learning systems using a computer or other electronic device to provide educational materials (see Aragones et al., 2006; Gavari, 2005). The Website is understood as a virtual place in which all contents of a subject useful for the students could be provided: curricular organization, contact information about teachers and students, teaching materials, and a variety of resources (Web, multimedia, etc.), as well as useful tools for communication between students and teachers, and among students themselves (chats and forums). This space can be seen as a Virtual Classroom where the learning process that takes place in a traditional classroom is emulated and enhanced.

The normative framework of the Spanish University emphasizes the goal of improving the quality of the university system as a whole and of every one of its aspects. This entails greater efficacy, efficiency and responsibility, so as to further excellence in education and research with more efficient use of public resources. Improving the quality of all the areas of university activity is fundamental for preparing the professionals that society needs. The development of research projects, the preservation and transmission of culture and the promotion of a critical scientific presence, based on merit and rigor, are also essential as a reference for Spanish society (Generalitat de Catalunya, 2001; Generalitat de Catalunya, 2003c). Within this framework, the University of Granada maintains its fundamental goal of imparting quality teaching directed toward the full and critical education of students and their preparation for exercising professional activities. Likewise, the institutional goals for quality in teaching will be specified through the elaboration and execution of programs geared towards evaluation, improvement of instruction,

educational innovation and excellence in teaching (Generalitat de Catalunya, 2003b). The University of Granada has thus far developed two Plans of Educational Excellence that include initiatives in innovation, education, practical support and degrees, as well as and services for evaluation, to improve teaching quality and student training, following principles established by its Statutes and Spanish legislation regulating high education. The first Plan for Educational Excellence of the University of Granada was approved by the Governing Council of the University in 2001. Its goal was to promote a culture of quality and stimulate excellence in teaching; it was conceived as an instrument for developing the UGR's institutional policy on evaluation, improvement and innovation. This plan coordinated 24 actions, set out in three major programs:

• The Evaluation Program,
• The Program for Improvement and Innovation and
• The Program for Excellence in Teaching.

Four years after the approval of the UGR's First Plan, the needs deriving from new objectives, the laws regulating university activity, the challenge of European convergence, and the expectations generated in light of the importance of bringing objectives up to date altogether underlined the need to formulate a second Plan. As a consequence, the UGR put forth a proposal to continue actions of the previous plan and develop additional ones by means of a new plan that integrates and coordinates nine programs (Governing Council of the University of Granada, 2005):

• Adaptation and improvement of educational offerings,
• Adaptation and development of the teaching model,
• Innovation in teaching,
• Improvement in teaching quality,
• Faculty training,

- Excellence in teaching,
- Evaluation of degrees, services and management units,
- Option and user satisfaction studies and
- Analytical studies.

The third and fourth programs correspond to a strategic line of teaching under an innovative model, and propose measures for stimulating the connection between research and teaching, for encouraging innovation and coordinating measures for improvement in response to the needs proposed in the evaluation processes. This paper summarizes an innovative teaching experience developed within the Department of Civil Engineering (Area of Environmental Technology), at the University of Granada. The experience comes under the guidelines of the European Space of Higher Education with respect to interactive learning based on the development of a new teaching-learning model that, on the one hand, uses a Website in the teaching-learning process, and on the other hand, exemplifies adaptation of the curricula of a pilot subject. Results and conclusions of the experience could be applied to other subjects in the aim to reform the curricular organization of higher education and adapt it to the new educational models that include e-learning in the Area of Environmental Technology at the University of Granada.

2. MATERIALS AND METHODS

In the context of the third program of the second Plan for Educational Excellence of the University of Granada, the Area of Environmental Technology, within the UGR Department of Civil Engineering, has developed an innovative educational project entitled *Application of New Information and Communication Technologies (ICT) in the Area of Environmental Technology Teaching*. This novel project was undertaken by professors at the University of Granada during the academic year 2007/2008. It has introduced e-learning in the teaching-learning process, with due respect for the students' leading role. To this end, a new teaching-learning model was designed and implemented in view of the ESHE guidelines, and accordingly resorting to ICT in order to create a new communication channel that consists of a Web portal or Website that benefits both parties: teachers and students. An underlying consideration of e-learning characteristics was necessary for the adaptation of curricular organization to create a new learning experience. For the purpose of testing the teaching-learning model described here, a pilot experience was launched through the subject *Solid Waste Treatment, Handling and Recovery* (as part of the Environmental Science degree). This required adaptation of the subject to incorporate and execute the educational reforms in the new contextual process of the subject.

The educational process consists of two elements: teaching, focused on the professor, and learning, focused on the student. Depending on the closeness to one element or the other, we may distinguish two basic teaching-learning theories: objectivism and constructivism (Albano et al., 2006). Under the first, learning is teacher-centred and seen as the simple transmission of knowledge from the teacher to the student, who has a passive role of receiving information without interacting with the teacher, with other students or with other sources of knowledge. This model is extensively seen in Spanish universities, mainly as a consequence of the great number of students. Under the second theoretical model, knowledge is instead constructed by the individual, that is, learning is student-centered and seen as a personal and active construction of one´s own knowledge. Some authors (Calvo de Mora, 2006) hold that the best option should include both elements in a balanced way. The teaching-learning model underlying the design of our subject followed this option. The study described here formulated a model that uses a teaching-learning platform designed to lay the foundations for the next generation of e-learning;

in any case, this tool will be regarded as complementary to the traditional method of 'teaching presence', because balance in the participation of teacher and student is considered essential for the proper development of the learning process. The use of a web platform urges students to acquire skills such as self-organization and planning ability, and to grasp the dynamic, complex, evolving nature of systems in nature and society (Fuchs, 2007). In order to create an effective teaching-learning experience, the project was based on the fundamental system analysis and design principles shown in Figure 1.

In a learning context, current Learning Management approaches follow the same static and predefined representation of knowledge and the view of 'getting the right information to the right person at the right time'. Strong emphasis is placed on how to centralise and standardise the learning experience. Most learning contents today are designed, authored, delivered and managed via the centralised Learning Management Systems (LMSs), Learning Content Management Systems (LCMS), Course Management Systems (CMS) or Content Management Systems (CMS) such as CLIX, WebCT, Blackboard, Moodle, ATutor, ILIAS, Plone or Drupal as static-packaged online courses and modules (Chatti et al., 2007). Version 1.8 of (free) CMS Moodle was used in this project. It was designed to help educators create online courses with opportunities for rich interaction. Its open source license and modular design mean that people can develop additional functionality.

The decision to choose this software was based on our commitment to provide a reliable system with development possibilities; on the one hand Moodle is a free, open-source alternative to commercial courseware that is widely used in universities around the world; and its large client/developer base and optional commercial development and support make it an optimal choice. Yet at the same time Moodle's many features, including forums, quizzes, assignments, and glossaries, lend Site Generator users great functionality, making easier

Figure 1. Design principles for an effective teaching-learning

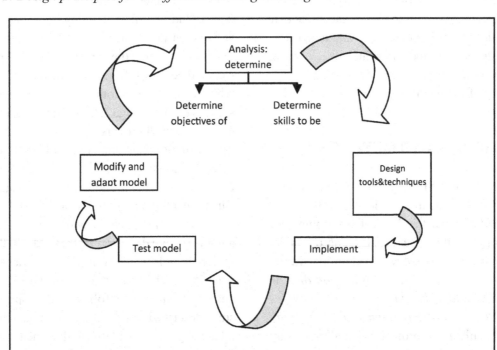

the use of the e-learning platform by teachers that are not experts in communication and information technologies. Moodle runs without modification on Unix, Linux, FreeBSD, Windows, Mac OS X, NetWare and any other systems that support PHP, including most webhost providers. Data is stored in a single database. There are many dimensions regarding interoperability for e-learning systems. Moodle's interoperability features include: authentication, using LDAP, Shibboleth, or various other standard methods (e.g. IMAP); enrollment, using IMS Enterprise among other standard methods, or by direct interaction with an external database; quizzes and quiz questions, allowing import/export in a number of formats: GIFT (Moodle's own format), IMS QTI, XML and XHTML (NB although export works very well, import is currently not complete); resources, using IMS Content Packaging, SCORM, AICC (CBT), LAMS; integration with other Content Management Systems such as Postnuke (via third-party extensions); syndication using RSS or Atom newsfeeds; external newsfeeds can be displayed in a course, and forums, blogs, and other features can be made available to others as newsfeeds. Moodle also has import features for use with other specific systems, such as importing quizzes or entire courses from Blackboard or WebCT.

3. RESULTS

The degree in Environmental Sciences began to be taught at the University of Granada in 1994, within the range of degrees issued by the Faculty of Science. It responds to the needs of professionals who are trained specifically with a view to the environment, and who are capable of co-ordinating activities with other multidisciplinary professionals, managers and citizens having more specific fields of activity. A pilot project has been conducted for four years in order to introduce ESHE foundations in this degree. This meant

a reformulation of the curricula of subjects and teaching-learning models. The optional subject *Solid Waste Treatment, Handling and Recovery* is considered to provide students with the necessary skills to determine negative environmental impacts as a consequence of inadequate waste management, and employ techniques designed to implement actions to minimize these impacts. Its characteristics are summarized below.

The overall objective of this subject is the student´s training in the field of waste management. In order to achieve this overall objective, the following specific targets were taken into account:

- To know basic concepts related to municipal waste impacts and their characteristics,
- To apply waste classification and labelling rules,
- To know basic principles which should guide waste management actions,
- To classify collection and transport waste options and apply design criteria,
- To be knowledgeable in waste reuse, recovery, recycling, valorisation and final disposal in landfills and apply design criteria to construct and operate treatment plants,
- To minimize the negative impacts of waste treatment plants,
- To promote environmental education related to waste management, and
- To understand the waste legislative framework and waste management competences.

The skills to be acquired by the student are established as follows:

- Quality of work,
- Ability to analyse and synthesize,
- Practical exercise resolution,
- Organization and planning ability,
- Oral and written communication,
- Teamwork,
- Critical reasoning and
- Decision making

To achieve the objectives and skills considered in the methodology calls for, firstly, a revision of the curricula of the subjects. The subject was therefore structured into two main parts: theory and practice. The first comprises theoretical contents including practical aspects of waste management, with part of these contents included in the e-learning process using an ad hoc Website. Secondly, it was necessary to adapt to the e-learning model; in this case, the elements used to modify and adapt were based on contents, time, order, assessment, interface and so on (Burgos et al., 2007). Adaptation focused on student, teachers and the set of rules, adopting input from the different stakeholders. The final goal for all was to arrive at the best fit for personalized learning objectives. The description of an adaptive learning flow is mainly based on the four designed tools analyzed below.

The content of theoretical lessons had to be modified to accommodate the new objectives of the subject, as well as the new skills that are expected to be acquired by the students. These lessons are characterized by a lower degree of teacher-student interaction, so they are designed primarily as a method of unidirectional transfer of knowledge from teacher to students. However, part of this knowledge was facilitated using a Website designed for the experimental educational project, including complementary documentation, web links, multimedia resources (videos and photos) and self-evaluation tests.

Problem Seminars are lessons entailing problems with a smaller number of students who work on practical contents individually in class: (i) to acquire scientific and technical knowledge outlined in theoretical lessons, to complete their understanding and deepening, for which several practical activities are undertaken, and (ii) to serve as the natural forum for sharing students doubts in developing practical exercises.

Practical seminars are a natural forum in which each group exposed their work to the rest of the students, acting as a bridge between theory and problem lessons. These seminars seek to promote equal capacity for analysis, synthesis, critical thinking, oral and written expression of foreground, and teamwork.

The *Environmental Teaching Center Website* (ETCW) was designed to be an innovative communication channel between teacher and students, as well as a mode of access to educational materials and bibliography. This teaching-learning virtual platform provides educational material updated daily; here the student can have the class notes and the exercises before the teacher explains them in class; it can interact with the student to solve all kinds of doubts, raising issues for discussion in forums and chats, and promoting participation of students and teachers. In the pilot experiment carried out, the ETCW was also used as a Virtual Classroom to deliver part of the theoretical knowledge of the program, applying basic principles of e-learning and providing self-knowledge and independent alternative action for the students. Finally, and considering the teacher standpoint, another possibility offered by this tool is the control of access of students to each facet of the Website, making it possible to control the level of participation and the use of this virtual tool individually.

The Internet address http://cem.ugr.es permits access to the ETCW homepage, which contains all the subjects taught in the area of technology for the Environment; they are classified by degrees and postgraduate teaching. This page was designed using a Moodle template, customizing it for the area of technology Environment at the University of Granada. The homepage features various specific resources and tools: calendar, upcoming events, etc. It is also used to provide news of general interest to the different users of the platform. Students taking different subjects register themselves at the beginning of the semester, entering their personal data. Afterwards, the ETC administrator, according to the official registration list, gives confirmation. The students can not access their subjects until obtaining this confirmation of registration from the administrator. This is a simple operation involving no difficulty for either the student or the administrator. The homepage of the pilot subject Solid Waste Treatment, Handling and Recovery was customized by its professor. Here three main areas are identified:

- **General.** Affording information about the subject: characteristics, objectives, agenda, consulting books, evaluation criteria, etc. There are also links to the professor´s personal homepage and a link to the chat, to facilitate student-teacher communication to solve and clarify doubts.
- **Main body.** This space collects and develops the thematic blocks and structure of the educational program. It provides the student with materials for the development and monitoring of the subject. The resources and materials in each block include: notes on theory, practical exercises, Web resources, multimedia resources (including

videos and photos), legislation, and other documentation.
- **Workshop.** This area annexes documentation from work performed by the students and set out in the workshops.

In order to implement all the techniques and adaptations required to cover ESHE and e-learning foundations, we undertook a subject review involving contents, working groups and teaching methodology. In the case of theoretical lessons, only one group was authorized by the University board of administration. In the case of the seminar there were four problems; the teacher finally divided the theoretical group into eight to study development. At any rate subject planning was based on the student's personal work as the axis of the learning process, and they had to learn how to work daily with the teacher as guide and help, providing information and/or showing the sources where they could get it. Figure 2 shows resources available through the ETC and the number of times, in percentages, that the students used them.

Figure 2. Resources disposal in ETC and number of times, in percentage, that students have used them

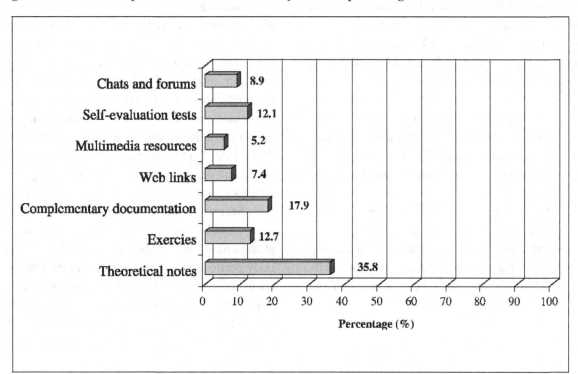

The Website was basically used to download class notes and complementary documentation, while multimedia sources with videos or links to related webs saw low participation. These results suggest that students encounter considerable difficulties in adapting to the learning models based on workload, as the University of Granada teaching-learning models are traditionally focused on objectivistic learning theory, mainly as a result of the large number of students.

In order to evaluate our model, two separate results were analysed: on the one hand, students' knowledge and skills; and on the other, students' opinion about the experience. First it was necessary to define an adaptative evaluation that considers the actual contents, tools, objectives and skills defined in the subject. At Spanish universities, skills and knowledge acquired by students are evaluated in a range between 0 and 10. In the case of values that are equal to or higher than 9, knowledge and skills acquired by students are classified as high or outstanding; if values are between 7 and 9, the degree of assimilation of knowledge is classified as notable; and between 5 and 7 low to acceptable; marks lower than 5 show poor skills and assimilated knowledge, in which case students do not pass the subject. The evaluation of students of pilot subjects accounts for the following four marks, affected by different weights shown in parenthesis:

- Results from an individual test which includes theoretical contents and resolution of several exercises (30%)
- Individual exercises done in practical seminars (40%)
- Work in groups and the oral presentation by each member of the group (20%)
- Individual work of the students, including participation in lessons, use of chats, self-evaluation test and other resources of the Website (10%).

In order to carry out a continuous evaluation of the knowledge and skills acquired by students using the Website, self-evaluation tests are available to allow the students to know their deficits, also allowing the professor to explore the progressive student learning, or directing the need to clarify the most frequently observed issues. Taking into account the above criteria, the results obtained in the academic year 2007/2008 were analyzed, in light of the fact that subject monitoring is quite high because only 5.79% of registered students (121) did not follow the subject. Meanwhile, assimilation of knowledge and skills by students show an average value that is classified as remarkable, with an average mark of 6.66, and 93.39% of students passing the subject. Figure 3 shows the marks of the different parts of the subject; as we can see work and monitoring carried out by students were quite good, although the final marks of individual exams show values that are rather low if compared with the rest of the marks; and only 25.5% of students passed the exam. The results of the students' evaluation point to major difficulties regarding the students´ adaptation to the model of teaching based on student workload.

In order to learn the students' opinion about this experience, a questionnaire was designed and placed on the subject homepage to provide information in relation to the students' degree of satisfaction about the ETC, the usefulness of the materials and sources provided, and the most important problems of the teaching-learning model as defined. The 13 questions were rated from 1 to 5 (1 minimum satisfaction and 5 maximum degree of satisfaction) and grouped in 2 blocks, one about the platform in general and the other one on subject evaluation. The questionnaire was made available to students for 20 days, at the end of the course; 52.1% of the student body participated in this aspect. Figure 4 shows the average score and standard deviation for each question of the survey. We may conclude that the use of the Website was considered positive, although its design and presentation were more

Figure 3. Average, maximum, minimum marks and standard deviation

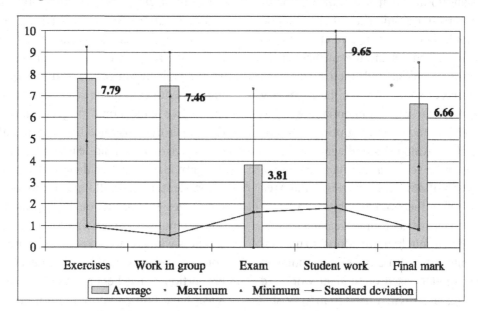

Figure 4. Average, maximum, minimum marks and standard deviation obtained in the survey for assessment of the project

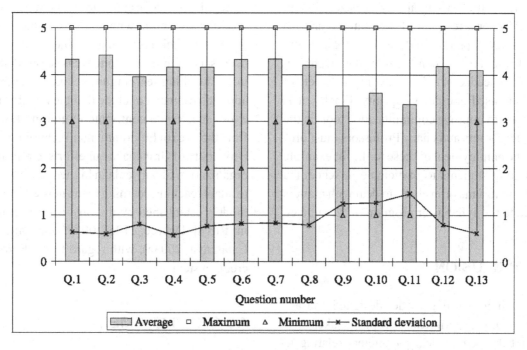

poorly appraised; subject evaluation is fairly good (question 13), yielding values over 3; the sources rating worse were the use of chat rooms and forums, self-evaluation and student-teacher communication, most probably as a consequence of problems involving connection problems and also the inexperience of teachers in this type of technology, pointing to a need to promote the use of chat rooms and forums that would offer a somewhat more personal monitoring of the subject. Teachers should improve their own education in ITC to guide students in the use of these technologies and be familiar with their advantages and disadvantages so as to make the necessary changes in curricula subjects in optimal ways to implement ESHE and e-learning principles (Albano et al., 2006; Antón & Zubillaga, 2005).

This experience served as the starting point in implementation of new technologies in the Area of Environmental Technology subjects; accordingly, it helped us to detect some weaknesses that can be amended through future efforts. In the first place, students show difficulties in adapting to the teaching model based on student workload and e-learning, signalling a need to modify students' learning process, making them better able to assimilate theoretical contents and develop practical skills as well, including the capacities to discriminate, classify and synthesize. This, in turn, calls for a revision of the material and resources developed to guide learning, especially virtual resources. Secondly, improved technical media are needed in order to avoid wasted effort and underused computer capacity. Finally, it is necessary to improve communication tools in the Website, forums and chats. Professors must promote the employment of these tools, for example by inviting students to participate in scheduled events, in forums or in chats, to deal with matters related to the syllabus or program of the subject.

4. CONCLUSION

The teaching-learning model designed and applied in this experimental proposal takes into account the pedagogical parameters relating to student workload, considering the new European Credit concept. These elements are essential for the optimisation of a learning process that develops, in the students, skills demanded by today's working world. Some of these skills are analysis, the capacity of synthesis, ability to work in a multidisciplinary team, fluid oral and written communication, and the capacities of decision making, self-organization and planning. To this end, some revision of the program and curricula of the subjects is necessary, directed to designing student-centred education and training. The innovative educational project summarized in this paper demonstrates that Moodle allows for the design of a teaching-learning virtual platform that provides educational material, interacts with the student to solve all kinds of doubts and raising issues for discussion in forums and chats, and promotes the participation of students and teachers who are non-experts in information and communication technologies. In general, a large proportion of teachers and students, in Spain at least, have limited knowledge of computer science; therefore, Moodle's varied features, including forums, quizzes, assignments and glossaries, provide desirable functionality. This experience is only the first such application of new technologies in conjunction with teaching in the Area of Environmental Technology subjects. It is now necessary to improve some weaknesses detected in the teaching-learning model as designed and applied. We may conclude that the results of this experience could contribute to guiding teachers from the Area of Environmental Technology at the University of Granada in our efforts to reform the organization of curricula in higher education and to adapt teaching-learning to the new educational models established by the Spanish Government in Royal Decree 1125/2003 (Generalitat de Catalunya, 2003a), with regard to the European credit system.

ACKNOWLEDGMENT

This work has been funded by the Office of the Vice President of Planning, Quality and evaluation Professor at the UGR. The work of the first and third authors was supported in part by the Junta de Andalucía (Research Project TIC-02913). The work of the second and fourth authors was supported in part by the Dirección General de Investigación del Ministerio de Ciencia y Tecnología (Research Project MTM2005--01403) and by the Junta de Andalucía (Research group FQM/191). An earlier version of this paper was presented at the 1st World Summit on Knowledge Society, Athens, Greece; 24-28 Spetember 2008.

REFERENCES

Albano, G., Gaeta, M., & Salerno, S. (2006). E-learning: a model and process proposal. *International Journal of Knowledge and Learning*, *2*, 73–88. doi:10.1504/IJKL.2006.009680

Antón, P., & Zubillaga del Río, A. (2005). *Teacher training for the deployment of ICT as a support to new models derived from the European Space of Higher Education (ESHE)*. Paper presented at the First ICT meeting in the Spanish University at a Distance (UNED).

Aragonés, R., Saiz, J., Portero, A., Rullan, M., & Aguiló, J. (2006). Teaching Innovation Experience following European Space of Higher Education Guidelines in Digital Design Teaching. *Revista Latinoamericana de Tecnología Educativa*, *2*(15), 203–222.

Arias, M. (2003). *The European Higher Education Area: An opportunity for development through multi-disciplinary learning and technology*. Retrieved from http://www.usal.es/~ofeees/ARTICULOS/MarioAriasOliva%5B1%5D.pdf

Burgos, D., Tattersall, C., & Koper, R. (2007). How to represent adaptation in e-learning with IMS learning design. *Interactive Learning Environments*, *2*(15), 161–170. doi:10.1080/10494820701343736

Calvo de Mora, J. (2006). Teaching focused on students' work. *Revista de la Educación Superior, 128*. Retrieved from http://www.anuies.mx/servicios/p_anuies/publicaciones/revsup/index.html

Chatti, M. A., Jarke, M., & Frosch-Wilke, D. (2007). The future of e-learning: a shift to knowledge networking and social software. *International Journal of Knowledge and Learning*, *3*(4-5), 404–420. doi:10.1504/IJKL.2007.016702

Commission on Communication Education and Training. (2010). *The success of the Lisbon Strategy hinges on urgent reforms*. Retrieved from http://europa.eu/legislation_summaries/education_training_youth/general_framework/c11071_en.htm

Contero, M., Naya, F., Company, P., & Saorín, J. L. (2006). Learning Support Tools for Developing Spatial Abilities. *International Journal of Engineering Education*, *22*, 470–477.

de Catalunya, G. (2001). Law 6 stablishing University Spanish System. *Official Journal of the Spanish State*, *307*, 49400–49425.

de Catalunya, G. (2003a). Royal Decree 1125 establishing the European credit system and the system of qualifications in university degrees. *Official Journal of the Spanish State*, *224*, 34355–34356.

De Prada, E. (2006). Adapting to ECTS through the creation and use of a web page. *RELATEC*, *5*, 235–249.

Dumort, A. (2002). Guiding Principles of The Virtual European Space of Higher Education. *Revista Electrónica Teoría de la Educación*, *7*, 185–197.

European Parliament. (2003). Decision No 2318 of the European Parliament and of the Council of 5 December 2003 adopting a multiannual programme (2004 to 2006) for the effective integration of information and communication technologies (ICT) in education and training systems in Europe (eLearning Programme). *Official Journal of the European Union. L&C*, *327*, 45–68.

Font, A. (2003). *European Space of Higher Education (ESHE)*. Paper presented at the 9th Conference of Law Faculties Deans in the Spanish Universities.

Fuchs, C. (2007). Towards a dynamic theory of virtual communities. *International Journal Knowledge and Learning, 3*, 372–403. doi:10.1504/IJKL.2007.016701

Gavari, E. (2006). Guiding Principles of The Virtual European Higher Education. *Revista Electrónica de Teoría de la Educación. Educación y cultura en la Sociedad de la Información, 7*(2), 185-197.

Generalitat de Catalunya. (2003b). Decree 325 approving Statutes of the University of Granada. *Official Journal of Andalusian autonomous region Government, 236*, 25745-25776.

Generalitat de Catalunya. (2003c). Law 15 approving the Andalusian University System. *Official Journal of Andalusian autonomous regional Government, 251*, 27452-27474.

Governing Council of the University of Granada. (2005). *Plan for Educational Excellence 05-08*. Retrieved from http://www.ugr.es/~vicinnova/plancalidaddocente05-08.html

Jarvela, S., & Hakkinen, P. (2002). Web-based cases in teaching and learning-the quality of discussions and a stage of perspective taking in asynchronous communication. *International Journal of Interactive Learning Environments, 10*, 1–22. doi:10.1076/ilee.10.1.1.3613

Jones, N. B., Provost, D. M., & Pascale, D. (2006). Developing a university research web-based knowledge portal. *International Journal of Knowledge and Learning, 2*, 106–118. doi:10.1504/IJKL.2006.009682

King, W. R. (2005). An androgogy model for IS and management education. *International Journal of Knowledge and Learning, 1*(3), 186–209. doi:10.1504/IJKL.2005.007756

Lau, H. Y. K., & Mak, K. L. (2005). A Configurable E-Learning System for Industrial Engineering. *International Journal of Engineering Education, 21*, 262–276.

Löfström, E., & Nevgi, A. (2008). University teaching staffs' pedagogical awareness displayed through ICT-facilitated teaching. *Interactive Learning Environments, 16*, 101–116. doi:10.1080/10494820701282447

Moon, Y., Sánchez, T., & Durán, A. (2007). Teaching Professional Skills to Engineering Students with Enterprise Resource Planning (ERP): an International Project. *International Journal of Engineering Education, 23*, 759–771.

Shin, D., Yoon, E. S., Park, S. J., & Lee, E. S. (2002). Web-based interactive virtual laboratory system for unit operations and process systems engineering education. *Computers & Chemical Engineering, 24*, 381–385.

Veron, D. T., & Blake, R. L. (1993). Does problem-based learning work? A meta-analysis of evaluative Research. *Academic Medicine, 68*, 550–563. doi:10.1097/00001888-199307000-00015

This work was previously published in the International Journal of Knowledge Society Research, Volume 1, Issue 3, edited by Miltiadis D. Lytras, pp. 59-70, copyright 2010 by IGI Publishing (an imprint of IGI Global).

Chapter 16
A Model for Investigating E-Governance Adoption Using TAM and DOI

Ioannis Karavasilis
University of Macedonia, Greece

Kostas Zafiropoulos
University of Macedonia, Greece

Vasiliki Vrana
Technological Education Institute of Serres, Greece

ABSTRACT

As governments around the world move toward e-governance, a need exists to examine citizens' willingness to adopt e-governance services. In this paper, the authors identify the success factors of e-governance adoption by teachers in Greece, using the Technology Acceptance Model, the Diffusion of Innovation model and constructs of trust, risk and personal innovativeness. Two hundred thirty primary and secondary education teachers responded to an online survey. LISREL then analyzed the data. Model estimation used the maximum likelihood approach, with the item covariance matrix as input. A SEM validation of the proposed model reveals that personal innovativeness, compatibility and relative advantage are stronger predictors of intention to use, compared to trust, and perceived risk. Findings may enhance policymakers' capacities by presenting them with an understanding of citizens' attitudes.

INTRODUCTION

The pressure of globalization, changes in technology, the de-regulation in economic and social life are nowadays changing personal lives, business methods and relations between governments and citizens (Gupta, 2004). Citizens expect from governments to deliver better, faster and cost-effective services, to become more transparent, to reduce discretionary decision making and introduce simpler methods and procedures (Singh, 2007). Democratic governments feel the tremendous pressures (Singh, 2007), the direct threat of being thrown out of power if they do

DOI: 10.4018/978-1-4666-1788-9.ch016

not perform (Gupta, 2004), and the importance of implementing e-governance and are moving forward in e-governance development (Panagis et al., 2008). Governments need to understand that e-governance is much more than technical issues (Lau, 2004). A mix of technological, administrative, social, human, legal disciplines must be created (Biasiotti & Nannucci, 2004) and several organizational changes are required, in which skills in management, communication, and legal issues play a key role (Joia, 2006). Up to now governments' are driving the development agenda of e-governance and their investment in electronic services based on their understanding of what citizens need and without measuring what increases citizens' willingness to adopt e-governance services. Mofleh and Wanous (1999, p. 1) wrote "Governments must first understand variables that influence citizens' adoption of e-Government in order to take them into account when delivering services online".

The implementation of e-governance transforms theories and practices of public administration (Fang, 2002). Governments develop transaction-oriented application sites in order to allow interaction with citizens, offer information on services regulations, procedures, forms; perform public service electronically; and automate and execute administrative processes (Buckley, 2003; Elsas, 2003). The main advantages presented by e-governance to public administration are paper reduction; transaction efficiency; and improved governance (Joseph & Kitlan, 2008). Greek education system is centralized, by means that the Ministry of National Education lifelong learning and Religious Affairs formulates and implements the educational policy (Giamouridis, 2006; Massialas, 1981). The education system is also characterized by "intense bureaucratization, strict hierarchical structures, extensive legislation (polynomy) and "formalism" (Koutouzis et al., 2008, p.1). Effective development of educational e-governance websites and effective adoption by teachers in Greece may combat the common prob-

lem that bureaucratic systems address as the loss of paper, the destruction of data, and inconsistent data entry (Joseph & Kitlan, 2008). Regarding transaction efficiency savings of time and money are important factors to predict potential usage of e-governance services (Gilbert et al., 2004) and all sectors in public administration can benefit from reduced costs and time efficiencies. Improved governance requires an integrated, long-term strategy built upon cooperation between government and citizens (Johnston, n.d.). E-governance facilitates a more joined-up style of government (Gunter, 2006), involves citizens in the decision-making process (UNESCO, 2007), enhance decentralization, accountability and transparency (IDRC, 2007), and gain greater public confidence in the policymaking process (Norris, 2000). In Greece 150,798 teachers are permanent civil servants, according to Ministry of Education lifelong learning and Religious Affairs (http://www.ypepth. gr) and they represent a percentage of 40.69% of permanent civil servants in Greece. Adoption of e-governance websites by teachers is voluntary and can be viewed as evidence that teachers perceive them as a superior choice, extracting value from them, to the traditional paper-based, face-to-face and phone consultation services.

In order to explain and analyze the factors influencing the adoption and use of computer technologies several models have been proposed. They take into consideration attitudes, beliefs and intentions as these are important factors in the adoption of computer technologies (Bagozzi et al., 1992). The theory of reasoned action (TRA) (Fishbein & Ajzen, 1975); the Technology Acceptance Model (TAM) (Bagozzi et al., 1992; Davis, 1980) the theoretical extension of the TAM (TAM2) (Venkatesh & Davis, 2000); the Diffusion of Innovation (DOI) (Rogers, 1995) are well accepted models and have also been used to predict user acceptance in the field of e-governance.

The study investigates factors that determine the adoption of educational e-governance websites by teachers of primary and secondary education in Greece. The term "educational e-governance websites" refers to the webpages of Greek School Network, the Ministry of Education, Lifelong Learning and Religious affairs, websites of Regional Primary and Secondary Education Administrations, and websites of Primary and Secondary Education Administrations. It uses constructs from the Technology Acceptance Model (TAM) and Diffusion of Innovation (DOI) and integrates the constructs of trust and risk in the model. It measures intention-to-use e-government websites. Intention to-use has been found to be a strong predictor of actual system usage in the IS literature (Colesca & Dobrica, 2008). The study uses an online survey to record teachers; opinions and attitudes. It analyzes the data using a refinement procedure, controlling reliability and validity, and validates the proposed model using Structural Equation Modeling.

TECHNOLOGY ACCEPTANCE MODEL

TAM was developed by Davis (1980) and Bagozzi et al. (1992) and is an extension of the TRA. TRA is a model from social psychology which is concerned with the determinants of consciously intended behaviors (Malhotra & Galletta, 1999). According to TRA salient beliefs and their normative beliefs are important predictors of a person's behavioral intention. TAM has also strong behavioral elements (Bagozzi et al., 1992). A person's actual system usage is mostly influenced by his or her behavioral intentions toward usage and are influenced by the perceived usefulness and perceived ease of use of the system. Attitudes can be used to predict behavior with considerable success under appropriate conditions (Petty & Cacioppo, 1981). Fundamental constructs in TAM are: Perceived ease of use and perceived usefulness. Perceived ease of use is defined as "the degree to which a person believes that using a particular system would be free of physical and

mental effort" and perceived usefulness of the system as "the degree to which a person believes that using a particular system would enhance his or her job performance" (Davis, 1980, p. 320).

Numerous empirical tests have shown that TAM is a parsimonious and robust model of technology acceptance behaviors' (Al-adawi et al., 2005, p. 5) in a wide variety of IT across both the levels of expertise (Gefen, 2002), and across countries (Taylor & Todd, 1995b). This is the major advantage of TAM, the fact that it can be extended when new technologies are introduced by using domain-specific constructs. TAM was used in order to explain user's behavior toward the World-Wide-Web (Koufaris, 2002; Moon & Kim, 2001); consumer attitudes and satisfaction with the e-commerce channel (Devaraj et al., 2002); intention to use on line shopping (Vijayasarath, 2004); technology acceptance decisions by professionals (Yi et al., 2005); user acceptance of object-oriented technology (Lee et al., 2003); and acceptance of an on-line learning system (Saade & Bahli, 2005).

Previous studies have used TAM to investigate factors that affect citizens' adoption of e-governance services. Colesca and Dobrica (2008) analyzed the case of Romania using TAM and they argue for the inclusion of trust, quality and satisfaction as attitudinal constructs on the basis of the e-government context. Al-adawi et al. (2005) proposed a conceptual model of citizen adoption of e-government which integrates constructs from the TAM and trust and risk literature. Using a variation of TAM also, TAM, TAM2, and DOI theory, and trust were used by Sang et al.(2009) to build a parsimonious yet comprehensive model of user adoption of e-Government. The findings of the study have shown that the determinants of the research model, perceived usefulness, relative advantage, and trust were supported. Jaeger and Matteson (2009) examined the relevance of the TAM for e-Government websites at federal government level in the United States through an exploratory research study. TAM alone was not able to explain issues of technology adoption related to e-Government. Additional factors, such as costs and technology maturity considered as well.

TRUST AND RISK IN E-GOVERNANCE

Trust is central to daily interactions, transactions, and practices and is considered as a crucial enabler in e-governance adoption (Al-adawi et al., 2005; Belanger & Carter, 2008; Colesca, 2009; Huang et al., 2006). "Trust makes citizens comfortable sharing personal information, make online government transaction, and acting on e-Government advices" mentioned Alsaghier (2009, p. 295). Yet, citizens do not trust e-governance. The trust problem could be due to many critical factors such as the impersonal nature of the online environment, the use of technology, security issues and the uncertainty and risk of using open infrastructures (AlAwadhi & Morris, 2009; Browne, 2001).

Previous researches have tried to found the connection between trust and TAM (Gefen et al., 2003a, 2003b; Pavlou, 2003; Wu & Chen, 2005). Gefen et al. (2003a) found out that trust is an antecedent of perceived ease of use and perceived usefulness and influences behavioral intention to use. Pavlou (2003) claimed that trust is one of the factors that influence perceived usefulness and Wu and Chen (2005) that trust is considered as an important antecedent of intention to use and attitude.

Teo et al. (2009) examined the role of trust in e-government success. In their model there are two dimensions of citizen's trusting beliefs toward an e-government Web site—trust in government and trust in technology. Colesca (2009) identified age, perceived usefulness, perceived quality, perceived concerns, perceived organizational trustworthiness, trust in technology, propensity to trust and years of internet experience as the factors that affect citizens' trust in e-governance. Five con-

structs, namely, disposition to trust, familiarity, institution-based trust, perceived website quality, perceived usefulness and perceived ease of use were used by Alsaghier (2009) to conceptualize trust in e-government.

Perceived risk is defined as "the citizen's subjective expectation of suffering a loss in pursuit of a desired outcome" (Warkentin et al., 2002, p. 160) and gives the trust dilemma its basic character (Al-adawi et al., 2005). Trust is needed only when uncertain situations exist. According to Pavlou (2003), in e-commerce perceived risk is composed of behavioral and environmental uncertainty. Behavioral uncertainty arises because online service providers have the chance to behave in an opportunistic manner by taking advantage of the impersonal nature of the electronic environment. Environmental uncertainty exists mainly because of the unpredictable nature of the Internet. Belanger and Carter (2008) claimed that the same happens for e-government. Previous research has discussed the role of trust in reducing the risk as well the role of perceived risk in reducing users' intentions to exchange information and complete transactions (Pavlou, 2003; Warkentin et al., 2002). E-governance websites are site is much more than an information technology interface and are open to the public and accessible from anywhere in the world. "Different types of risks and uncertainties prevail in online transactions" mentioned Teo et al. (2009). For these reasons Al-adawi et al. (2005) claimed that perceived risk must be considered to explain citizens' intention to use e-governance websites. Thus, trust and risk are significant notions that should be investigated to understand citizens' adoption of e-governance.

DIFFUSION OF INNOVATIONS THEORY

The Diffusion of Innovations (DOI) theory (Figure 2) was developed by Rogers (1995) in order to explain how an innovation diffuses through a society. "An innovation is an idea, practice, or a phenomenon perceived to be novel by an individual or a community" (Singh, 2008, p. 1227) and diffusion is defined "as the process by which an innovation is communicated through certain channels over time among the members of a social system" (Rogers, 1995, p. 10). E-governance services can be considered as an innovation as they are perceived to be novel by citizen, and are delivered via the Internet (communication channel) to citizens, a community of potential adopters (Singh, 2008). An innovation creates a kind of uncertainty which is important in the diffusion (Lehmann, 2004). Rogers (1995) identified five attributes that affect the rate of diffusion namely relative advantage, compatibility, complexity, triability and observability. Relative advantage is defined as "the degree to which an innovation is perceived as better than the idea it supersedes". Compatibility, as "the degree to which an innovation is perceived as consistent with the existing values, past experiences, and needs of potential adopter". Complexity is the "degree to which an innovation is perceived as difficult to understand and use". Triability is the "degree to which an innovation may be experimented with on a limited basis" and finally observability is the "degree to which the results of an innovation are visible to others".

Previous studies considered DOI for investigation of e-governance acceptance and integrated it with other models (Carter & Bélanger, 2005; Patel & Jacobson, 2008; Sang et al., 2009). Sang et al. (2009) based of previous researches (Agarwal & Prasad, 1998; Carter & Bélanger, 2005) claimed that relative advantage, compatibility and complexity are more important than others in predicting intention to use a technology. Moreover complexity construct in the DOI is often considered as perceived ease of use construct in the TAM and triability and observability have no strong correlations between them and users' attitude toward IT adoption. Therefore they included only

relative advantage and compatibility constructs in their research model. Sang et al.'s (2009) views were adopted in this paper.

THE STUDY

In order to explore the factors that determine the adoption of educational e-governance websites of teachers in primary and secondary education in Greece, based on the aforementioned literature TAM, DOI, trust and risk are integrated to propose a model of user adoption of e-governance. According to Huang's et al. (2006) research model personal innovativeness influences the attitude toward e-governance adoption. Agarwal and Prasad (1998) developed a modified TAM based on the idea that personal innovativeness positively moderates the relationship between the perceptions of relative advantage, ease of use, and compatibility and the decision to adopt an innovation. Construct of personal innovativeness is integrated to the proposed model.

Consequently in the unified model, the following hypotheses are tested (Figure 1):

- **H1.** Trust in e-government websites has an effect on perceived Risk.
- **H2.** Perceived ease of use has a direct positive effect on Perceived usefulness.
- **H3.** Perceived risk has a direct effect on Attitude towards use.
- **H4.** Perceived risk has a direct effect on Intention to use.
- **H5.** Trust in e-government websites has a direct effect on Attitude towards use.
- **H6.** Trust in e-government websites has a direct effect on Intention to use.
- **H7.** Perceived ease of use has an effect on Attitude towards use.
- **H8.** Perceived ease of use has an effect on Intention to use.
- **H9.** Perceived usefulness has a direct effect on Attitude towards use.

Figure 1. The basic Technology Acceptance Model (adapted from Jaeger & Matteson 2009)

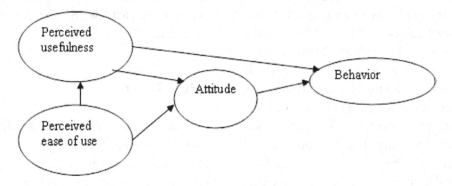

Figure 2. Diffusion of Innovations theory

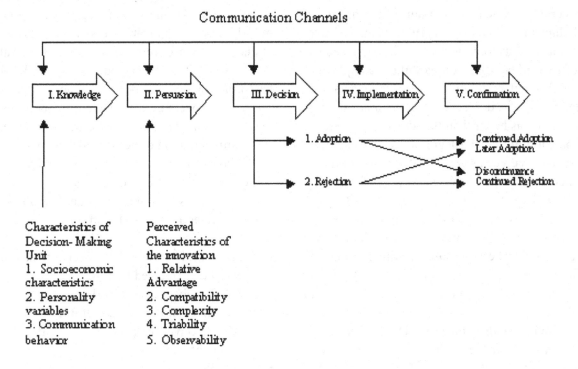

- **H10.** Perceived usefulness has a direct effect on intention to use.
- **H11.** Personal innovativeness has an effect on Attitude towards use.
- **H12.** Personal innovativeness has an effect on Attitude towards use on intention to use.
- **H13.** Compatibility has an effect on Attitude towards use.

- **H14.** Compatibility has an effect on intention to use.
- **H15.** Relative advantage has an effect on Attitude towards use.
- **H16.** Relative advantage has an effect on Intention to use.
- **H17.** Attitude towards use has a direct effect on Intention to use.

METHODOLOGY

An empirical research study was conducted using an online survey. Internet users have been chosen to be surveyed. The reason is that lack of e-Government usage focus primarily on the "digital divide" (Mofleh & Wanous, 1999). Colesca (2009, p. 32) wrote: "nonusers haven't favorable attitudes towards the use of electronic services in relation with the governmental agencies". Therefore, the research does not investigate people who are electronically incapable of accessing services.

A link to the main webpage of the Greek School Network (http://www.sch.gr) notified users of the website about the online questionnaire website. Users willing to participate visited a tailor made web site and responded to the questionnaire. The data were recorded to a database. The Greek School Network offers e-mail accounts (username@sch.gr form) and fully personalized access to education staff. In order to ensure that the responder was a teacher, the e-mail of the responder was recorded. From all questionnaires that were received only those of username@sch.gr form were admitted. Finally, 230 completed and usable questionnaires were received.

The questionnaire used in this study was adopted from previous studies. Five point Likert scales are used ranging from strongly disagree to strongly agree. The questionnaire consists of eight parts: 1) Trust in e-governance websites, 2) Perceived Risk, 3) Perceived Ease of Use, 4) Perceived Usefulness, 5) Innovativeness, 6) Compatibility, 7) Relative advantage, 8) Attitudes towards use, 9) Intention to use.

A pilot study using an extended questionnaire containing all the scales proposed in the literature review was conducted by administering the questionnaire to 50 primary and secondary education teachers. Finally, for each construct the scale presenting the largest Cronbach's alpha was decided to be included in the final questionnaire, since Cronbach's alpha provides the lower-bound

estimate for the Composite Score Reliability, which is eventually used in the analysis of the resulting questionnaire (Table 1).

FINDINGS

Reliability and Validity of the Instrument

LISREL 8.8 was used to analyze the data using the maximum likelihood approach, with the item covariance matrix used as input.

Confirmatory Factor Analysis was used for model refinement. Testing the measurement model involves examining the convergent validity, discriminant validity, and internal consistency of the constructs. Reliability and convergent validity of the measurements are estimated by the item factor loadings, Composite Reliability, and Average Variance Extracted (Fornell & Larcker, 1981).

Convergent validity refers to the extent to which the items under each construct are actually measuring the same construct. Two methods were applied to assess convergent validity. First, item reliability was examined for each item, which suggested that the factor loading of each item on its corresponding construct must be higher than 0.55 (Teo et al., 2009). All items had a loading above the suggested threshold. Convergent validity was assessed by examining the average variance extracted (AVE) for each construct. The AVE for a construct reflects the ratio of the construct's variance to the total variances among the items of the construct. The average extracted variances are all above the recommended 0.50 level (Hair et al., 1998; Teo et al., 2009) (Table 2).

Discriminant validity refers to the extent to which a given construct differs from other constructs. As all items loaded more heavily on their corresponding constructs rather than on other constructs, discriminant validity was satisfied. Further, the square roots of all AVEs were larger

Table 1. Items used

Trust in e-governance websites
adopted by Teo et al. (2009) Constructs also tested in pilot study: Colesca & Dobrica (2008); Sang et al.(2009)
1 e-government Web sites are trustworthy
2 e-government Web sites are seem to be honest and truthful to me
3 e-government Web sites can be trusted
Perceived Ease of Use
adopted from Carter & Bélanger (2005). Constructs also tested in pilot study: Colesca & Dobrica (2008); Sang et al.(2009) ; Shih (2004); Teo et al. (2009)
1 Learning to interact with a state government Website would be easy for me.
2 I believe interacting with a state government Website would be a clear and understandable process.
3 I would find most state government Websites to be flexible to interact with.
4 It would be easy for me to become skilful at using a state government Website.
Perceived Usefulness
adopted from Wangpipatwong et al. (2008). Constructs also tested in pilot study: Colesca & Dobrica (2008); Sang et al.(2009); Shih (2004); Teo et al. (2009)
1 Using e-Government websites enables me to do business with the government anytime not limited to regular business hours.
2 Using e-Government websites enables me to accomplish tasks more quickly.
3 The results of using e-Government websites are apparent to me.
4 Using e-Government websites can cut travelling expense.
5 Using e-Government websites can lower travelling and queuing time.
Risk
adopted from Belanger & Carter (2008)
1 The decision of whether to use a state e-government service is risky
2 In general, I believe using state government services over the Internet is risky
Attitudes towards use   adapted from Shih (2004). Constructs also tested in pilot study: Huang et al. (2006)
1 I like to use government websites
2 It is pleasure for me to use government websites
3 It is desirable for me to learn how to use government Website
Intention to use   adopted from Carter & Bélanger (2005) . Constructs also tested in pilot study: Al-adawi et al. (2005) ; Belanger & Carter (2008); Huang et al. (2006); Sang et al.(2009)
1 I would use the Web for gathering state government information.
2 I would use state government services provided over the Web.
3 Interacting with the state government over the Web is something that I would do.

continued on following page

than correlations among constructs, thereby satisfying discriminant validity. Table 3 shows that all the inter-construct correlations are below 0.9. Also the estimated correlation between all construct pairs is below the suggested cutoff of 0.9 and this implies distinctness in construct content or discriminant validity (Gold et al., 2001; Teo et al., 2009). As shown in Table 2, Composite Reliabilities are above the threshold of 0.7. Overall, the measures in this study are reliable and valid.

Table 1. Continued

Trust in e-governance websites
4 I would use the Web to inquire about state government services. **Personal innovativeness** adapted from Huang et al. (2006), 1 I find it stimulating to be original in my thinking and behavior. 2 I am challenged by ambiguities and un-solved problems. **Compatibility** Adopted from Sang et al. (2009). Constructs also tested in pilot study: Carter & Bélanger (2005) 1 I think using e-Government systems would fit well with the way that I like to gather information from government agencies. 2 I think using e-Government systems would fit well with the way that I like to interact with government agencies. 3 Using e-Government systems to interact with government agencies would fit into my lifestyle. 4 Using e-Government systems to interact with government agencies would be compatible with how I like to do things. **Relative advantage** adopted from Sang et al. (2009). Constructs also tested in pilot study: Carter & Bélanger (2005) 1 Using e-Government systems would enhance my efficiency in gathering information from government agencies. 2 Using e-Government systems would enhance my efficiency in interacting with government agencies. 3 Using e-Government systems would make it easier to interact with government agencies. 4 Using e-Government systems would give me greater control over my interaction with government agencies.

Table 2. Composite Reliability (CR), and Average Variance Extracted (AVE)

	Composite Reliability (CR)	Average Variance Extracted (AVE)
Personal Innovativeness	0.77	0.63
Trust in e-governance website	0.93	0.83
Perceived Risk	0.91	0.83
Perceived Ease of Use	0.87	0.64
Perceived Usefulness	0.93	0.74
Compatibility	0.91	0.74
Relative advantage	0.89	0.68
Attitudes towards use	0.89	0.75
Intention to use	0.92	0.76

Table 3. Inter-construct correlations

	Trust in e-governance website	Perceived Risk	Perceived Ease of Use	Perceived Usefulness	Innovativeness	Compatibility	Relative advantage	Attitudes towards use
Perceived Risk	0.36							
Perceived Ease of Use	-0.20	-0.49						
Perceived Usefulness	0.41	0.40	-0.30					
Innovativeness	0.41	0.39	-0.36	0.62				
Compatibility	0.41	0.51	-0.41	0.59	0.56			
Relative advantage	0.40	0.45	-0.32	0.64	0.55	0.71		
Attitudes towards use	0.49	0.44	-0.37	0.64	0.60	0.64	0.65	
Intention to use	0.48	0.46	-0.41	0.57	0.67	0.70	0.66	0.73

THE MODEL TESTING

The first step in model testing is to estimate the goodness-of-fit of the research model (Figure 3). Recommended fits are suggested from previous studies (Bagozzi & Yi, 1988; Hair et al., 1998) goodness-of-fit index (GFI), Adjusted Goodness of Fit Index (AGFI), normed fit index (NFI), non-normed fit index (NNFI), comparative fit index (CFI), and the root-mean-square error of approximation (RMSEA) as the indices for evaluating the overall model fitness. The chi-square test provides a statistical test for the null hypothesis that the model fits the data, but it is too sensitive to sample size differences, especially where the sample sizes exceed 200 respondents (Fornell & Larcker, 1981). Bagozzi and Yi (1988) suggested a chi-square per degrees of freedom instead. All of the fit indexes indicate that the structural model has a good fit: Chi-square/d.f. ($\leq$ 3.0) = 2.39, GFI ($\geq$0.80) = 0.82, AGFI ($\geq$0.80) = 0.80, NFI ($\geq$0.90) = 0.96, NNFI ($\geq$0.90) = 0.97, RMSEA ($\leq$0.08) = 0.078, CFI ($\geq$0.90) = 0.98. The second step in model estimation is to examine the path significance of each hypothesized association in the research model and variance explained (R^2) by each path. The standardized path coefficients, and explained variances of the structure model are presented in Figure 1. In the presence of Personal Innovativeness, Compatibility, and Relative advantage, the findings reveal somewhat different properties compared to those reported in previous studies (Zafiropoulos et al., in press).

While in Zafiropoulos et al. (in press) trust is found to have an effect on both the attitude towards use and the intention to use, findings from this study do not support the same properly (Figure 1). It seems that both Trust and Perceived Risk, have no significant effect on either attitude towards use or to intention to use. Therefore, although hypothesis H1 is supported, hypotheses 3, 4, 5, and 6 are not supported. Regarding the negative effect β=-0.49 of Trust to e-government websites on Perceived risk, a possible explanation would

be that people, who trust governmental agencies, actually trust the employees who work there. Thus people who declare that they trust the government probably have high trust levels to the civil servants with whom they communicate and have good interpersonal relations. Using e-government practices, those people, might be afraid that they will lose this interpersonal relation with the civil servants, and this situation may increase perceived risk for the citizens. Dashti et al. (2009, p.3) mentioned: "A key distinction between public servants working in government and those working in e-government lies in their level of visibility and direct contact with the public, which in turn influences how much the public trusts them".

Further, concerning the effects originating from Perceived ease of use and Perceived Usefulness, the findings suggest that the original TAM model partially fits the data. Perceived ease of use affects Perceived usefulness (β=0.66) and has a direct effect on attitude towards use (β=0.23), but it does not have a significant direct effect on intention to use. Therefore, Perceived ease of use only has an indirect effect (γ=0.1782) on intention to use, and H8 is partially supported. On the other hand, Perceived usefulness has direct effects on both attitude towards and Intention to use (β=0.16 and β=0.27 respectively). Finally, it seems that Personal innovativeness, Compatibility and Relative advantage have direct or indirect effects on attitude towards use or intention to use, but with only one of them each time. This means that when they have a direct effect on attitude they don't have an effect on intention and vice versa. In detail, Personal innovativeness has a direct effect on Attitude towards use (β=0.16), but not a significant effect on Intention to use. However, it does have a small indirect effect (γ=0.0528) to intention via the effect to Attitude towards use. Thus H11 and H12 are supported (the second through an indirect effect). Compatibility has only a direct effect to Intention to use (β=0.25) and has no effect on Attitude towards use (H13 not supported, H14 supported). Finally,

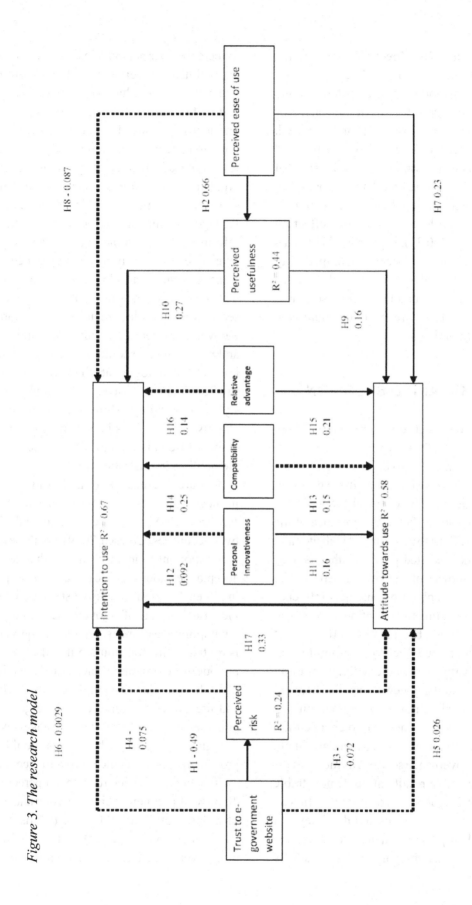

Figure 3. The research model

Relative advantage has a direct effect on Attitude towards use (β=0.21), but not to Intention to use. The second is only indirectly affected by relative advantage through the effect of Attitude on Intention (γ=0.0693). Thus H15 and H16 are supported, at least partially. Overall, considering direct and indirect effects of the variables and the sizes of the indirect effects, it seems that Compatibility is the most important predictor of Intention to use. Attitude towards use has a direct effect on Intention to use (β=0.33), supporting H17. This effect is larger than the effect of Compatibility but still it is comparable to it. Overall, first Attitude towards use, second Perceived usefulness and third compatibility are the three significant predictors of Intention to use.

CONCLUSION AND DISCUSSION

The findings show that in the presence of three new parameters (Personal Innovativeness, Compatibility and Relative advantage) Trust and Perceived Risk lose their predictive power. Considering the multidimensional properties of the model, this means that in the presence of the three variables, Trust to government websites and Perceived Risk predicted power is absorbed by the predictive power of the new variables. The three new key variables are constructs influencing directly or indirectly intention to use and attitudes towards use, but it is Compatibility that has an overall strong effect to intention to use. Personal innovativeness is the willingness of an individual to try out any new. Some teachers are more willing to take a risk by trying out innovation, whereas others are hesitant to change their practices. Highly innovative teachers are likely to consider e-governance services as more favorable and its tangible results more demonstrable to them. So it is crucial to contact them first to try out e-governance services and then they can disseminate their positive experiences to others. Government can also train and educate teachers

to increase their personal innovativeness. Teachers will use e-governance services more if they understand their value over the existing systems and will use them if it helps them to work more efficiently. The introduction of e-governance will not automatically create improved governance unless it is based on policies to promote the effective utilization of technology. Therefore governments should communicate to citizens the relative advantages of using online services from retrieving information to completing transactions. High levels of compatibility are also associated with increased intentions to adopt e-governance services that mean teachers who consider e-governance services compatible to their lifestyle intend to use e-governance services. This is a cultural theme and governments should invest in campaigning internet technologies at all stages of everyday life from business to leisure and emphasize work style compatibility. Moreover, government can classify civil servants into training groups, as to deliver different skills to different actors within the public administration arena.

Culture, welfare state, and political system influence the usage of e-governance (Patel & Jacobson, 2008) and citizens' behavior differs between countries (Colesca, 2009). For these reasons it is important to identify factors that determine acceptance under specific circumstances prevailing in each country and give strategic insight to increase the usage of e-governance. Additionally, the importance of measurement of e-governance is rooted in the contribution that the former can provide to monitor the efficiency and effectiveness of public spending . The findings give some clues and directions for planning effective e-government practices and could assist policy-makers with the first guidelines about which areas should be improved in order to enhance e-governance services.

Teachers in Greece represent a percentage of 40.69% of permanent civil servants and 16.38% of all civil servants in Greece (Ministry of Interior, http://www.ypes.gr). Adoption by them of e-governance has the potential to change the way that education administrations organizations carry out their tasks. Governments capitalize on the unique benefits of online services, explaining relative advantage to teachers work and promoting their use as a status of innovation, and indicating the services' congruence with a teachers' lifestyle. Further exploration and integration of additional adoption constructs is needed in order to develop a more comprehensive, yet parsimonious model of e-Governance adoption. Even though the study offers the first piece of evidence on e-governance website adoption by teachers, the recommendations would be helpful in developing and implementing new e-governance plans.

Although the original TAM fits the data fairly well, the findings suggest that by taking into account new variables, new conclusions arise that differ from previous ones. Further analysis is needed to clarify the interconnections among the variables.

REFERENCES

Agarwal, R., & Prasad, J. (1998). A Conceptual and Operational Definition of Personal Innovativeness in the Domain of Information Technology. *Information Systems Research, 9*(2), 204–215. doi:10.1287/isre.9.2.204

Al-adawi, Z., Yousafzai, Z., & Pallister, J. (2005). *Conceptual Model of citizen adoption of e-government.* Paper presented at the Second International Conference on Innovations in Information Technology.

AlAwadhi, S., & Morris, A. (2008). The Use of the UTAUT Model in the Adoption of E-government Services in Kuwait. In *Proceedings of the 41st Hawaii International Conference on System Sciences* (pp. 1-11). Washington, DC: IEEE Computer Society.

Alsaghier, H., Ford, M., Nguyen, A., & Hexel, R. (2009). Conceptualising Citizen's Trust in e-Government: Application of Q Methodology. *Electronic. Journal of E-Government, 7*(4), 295–310.

Bagozzi, R. P., Davi, F., & Warshaw, P. (1992). Development and Test of a Theory of Technological Learning and Usage. *Human Relations, 45*(7), 659–686. doi:10.1177/001872679204500702

Bagozzi, R. P., & Yi, Y. (1988). On the evaluation of structure equation models. *Journal of the Academy of Marketing Science, 16,* 74–94. doi:10.1007/BF02723327

Belanger, F., & Carter, L. (2008). Trust and risk in e-government adoption. *The Journal of Strategic Information Systems, 17*(2), 165–176. doi:10.1016/j.jsis.2007.12.002

Biasiotti, M. A., & Nannucci, R. (2004). Teaching egovernment in Italy. In R. Traunmóller (Ed.), *Proceedings of the Third International Conference* (pp. 460-463). Zaragoza, Spain: EGOV.

Browne, C. (2001). *Saudie –Commerce Conference Lauded by Major Saudi Industry Experts, ITP.*

Buckley, J. (2003). E-service quality and the public sector. *Managing Service Quality, 13*(6), 453–462. doi:10.1108/09604520310506513

Carter, L., & Bélanger, F. (2005). The Utilization of E-Government Services: Citizen Trust, Innovation and Acceptance Factors. *Information Systems Journal, 15*(1), 5–25. doi:10.1111/j.1365-2575.2005.00183.x

Codagnone, C., & Undheim, T.A. (2008). Benchmarking eGovernment: tools, theory, and practice. *European Journal of ePractice, 1*(4).

Colesca, S. E. (2009). Increasing e-trust: a solution to minimize risk in the e-government adoption. *Journal of Applied Quantitative Methods, 4*(1), 31–44.

Colesca, S. E., & Dobrica, L. (2008). Adoption and use of e-government services: The case of Romania. *Journal of Applied Research and Technology, 6*(3), 204–217.

Dashti, A., Benbasat, I., & Burton-Jones, A. (2009, July 13-14). Developing trust reciprocity in electronic government: The role of felt trust. In *Proceedings of the European and Mediterranean Conference on Information Systems 2009*. Retrieved March, 25 2010, from http://www.iseing.org/emcis/EMCIS2009/ Proceedings/Presenting%20Papers/C16/C16.pdf

Davis, F. (1980). Perceived Usefulness, Perceived Ease of Use, and User Acceptance of Information Technology. *Management Information Systems Quarterly, 13*, 318–341.

Devaraj, S., Fan, M., & Kohli, R. (2002). Antecedents of B2C channel satisfaction and preference: Validating e-commerce metrics. *Information Systems Research, 13*(3), 316–333. doi:10.1287/isre.13.3.316.77

Elsas, A. (2003). Integration of e-government and e-commerce with web services. In R. Traunmuller (Ed.), *EGOV 2003* (LNCS 2739, pp. 373-376). Berlin: Springer.

Fang, Z. (2002). E-Government in Digital Era: Concept, Practice, and Development. *International Journal of the Computer, the Internet and Management, 10*(2), 1-22.

Fishbein, M., & Ajzen, I. (1975). *Belief, attitude, intention, and behavior: An introduction to theory and research*. Reading, MA: Addison-Wesley.

Fornell, C., & Larcker, D. F. (1981). Evaluating structural equation models with unbearable and measurement error. *JMR, Journal of Marketing Research, 18*, 39–50. doi:10.2307/3151312

Gefen, D. (2002). Customer Loyalty in e-Commerce. *Journal of the Association for Information Systems, 3*, 27–51.

Gefen, D., Karahanna, E., & Straub, D. (2003a). Trust and TAM in online shopping: an integrated model. *Management Information Systems Quarterly, 27*(1), 51–90.

Gefen, D., Karahanna, E., & Straub, D. (2003b). Inexperience and experience with online stores: the importance of TAM and Trust. *IEEE Transactions on Engineering Management, 50*(3), 307–321. doi:10.1109/TEM.2003.817277

Giamouridis, A. (2006). Policy, Politics, and Social Inequality in the Educational System of Greece. *Journal of Modern Greek Studies, 24*(1), 1–21. doi:10.1353/mgs.2006.0004

Gilbert, D., Balestrini, P., & Littleboy, D. (2004). Barriers and benefits in the adoption of e-government. *International Journal of Public Sector Management, 17*(4/5), 286–301. doi:10.1108/09513550410539794

Gold, A. H., Malhotra, A., & Segars, A. H. (2001). Knowledge management: an organization capabilities perspective. *Journal of Management Information Systems, 18*(1), 185–214.

Gunter, B. (2006). Advances in e-democracy. *Aslib Proceedings: New Information Perspectives, 58*(5), 361–370.

Gupta, M. P. (2004). *Promise of E-Governance: Operational Challenges*. New Delhi, India: Tata McGraw-Hill.

Hair, F. Jr, Anderson, R. E., Tatham, R. L., & Black, W. C. (1998). *Multivariate data analysis* (5th ed.). Upper Saddle River, NJ: Prentice Hall.

Huang, S.-Y., Chang, C.-M., & Yu, T.-Y. (2006). Determinants of user acceptance of the e-Government services: The case of online tax filing and payment system. *Government Information Quarterly, 23*(1), 97–122. doi:10.1016/j.giq.2005.11.005

IDRC. (2007). *From e-Government to e-Governance: a paradigmatic shift.* Retrieved April 4, 2009, from http://www.idrc.ca/en/ev-115662-201-1-DO_TOPIC.html

Jaeger, P. T., & Matteson, M. (2009). e-Government and Technology Acceptance: the Case of the Implementation of Section 508 Guidelines for Websites. *Electronic. Journal of E-Government, 7*(1), 87–98.

Johnston, M. (n.d). *Good Governance: Rule of Law, Transparency, and Accountability.* Retrieved April 30, 2010, from http://www.unpan.org

Joia, L. A. (2006). A Framework for Developing Regional E-Government Capacity- Building Networks. *Information Technologies and International Development, 2*(4), 61–73. doi:10.1162/154475205775249328

Joseph, R., & Kitlan, D. (2008). *Key Issues in E-Government and Public Administration.* Retrieved April 30, 2010, from http://old.igi-global.com/downloads/excerpts/reference/IGR5202_1YPRPC8baU.pdf

Koufaris, M. (2002). Applying the Technology Acceptance Model and flow theory to online consumer behavior. *Information Systems Research, 13*(2), 205–223. doi:10.1287/isre.13.2.205.83

Koutouzis, E., Bithara, P., Kyranakis, S., Mavraki, M., & Verevi, A. (2008). Decentralizing Education in Greece: In search for a new role for the school leaders. In *Proceedings of the CCEAM 2008 Conference.* Retrieved April 20, 2009, from http://www.emasa.co.za/files/full/H2.pdf

Lau, E. (2004). Principaux enjeux de l'administration ιlectronique dans les pays membres de l'OCDE. In *Revue Franηaise d'Administration Publique* (*Vol. 110*, pp. 225–244). Paris: Icole Nationale d'Administration.

Lee, S., Kim, I., Rhee, S., & Trimi, S. (2006). The role of exogenous factors in technology acceptance: The case of object-oriented technology. *Information & Management, 43*(4), 469–480. doi:10.1016/j.im.2005.11.004

Lehmann, K. (2004). *Innovation Diffusion Theory.* Retrieved April 3, 2010, from http://www.grin.com/e-book/80117/innovation-diffusion-theory

Luo, G. (2009). e-government, people and social change: A case study of China. *Electronic Journal of Information Systems in Developing Countries, 38*(3), 1-23.

Malhotra, Y., & Galletta, D. (1999). Extending the Technology Acceptance Model to Account to Account for Social Influence: Theoretical Bases and Empirical Validation. In *Proceedings of the 32nd Hawaii International Conference on System Sciences.*

Massialas, V. (1981). *The Educational System of Greece.* Washington, DC: U.S. Government Printing Office.

Mofleh, S., & Wanous, M. (1999). Understanding Factors Influencing Citizens Adoption of e-Government Services in the Developing World: Jordan as a Case Study. *Journal of Computer Science, 7*(2), 1–11.

Moon, J.-W., & Kim, Y.-G. (2001). Extending the TAM for a World-Wide-Web context. *Information & Management, 38*(4), 217–230. doi:10.1016/S0378-7206(00)00061-6

Norris, P. (2000). *Digital Divide?* Retrieved March, 12, 2009, from http://ksghome.harvard.edu /~pnorris/acrobat/ digitalch6.pdf

Panagis, Y., Sakkopoulos, E., Tsakalidis, A., Tzimas, G., Sirmakessis, S., & Lytras, M. D. (2008). Techniques for mining the design of e-government services to enhance end-user experience. *International Journal of Electronic Democracy, 1*(1), 32–50. doi:10.1504/IJED.2008.021277

Patel, H., & Jacobson, D. (2008). Factors Influencing Citizen Adoption of E-Government: A Review and Critical Assessment. In W. Golden, T. Acton, K. Conboy, H. van der Heijden, & V. K. Tuunainen (Eds.), *Proceedings of the 16th European Conference on Information Systems,* Galway, Ireland (pp. 1058-1069).

Pavlou, P. A. (2003). Consumer Acceptance of Electronic Commerce: Integrating Trust and Risk with the Technology Acceptance Model. *International Journal of Electronic Commerce, 7*(3), 69–103.

Petty, R. E., & Cacioppo, J. T. (1981). *Attitudes and Persuasion: Classic and Contemporary Approaches.* Dubuque, IA: Wm. C. Brown Company Publishers.

Rogers, E. M. (1995). *Diffusion of innovations* (4th ed.). New York: Free Press.

Saade, R., & Bahli, B. (2005). The impact of cognitive absorption on perceived usefulness and perceived ease of use in on-line learning: an extension of the technology acceptance model. *Information & Management, 42*(2), 317–327. doi:10.1016/j.im.2003.12.013

Sang, S., Lee, J.-D., & Lee, J. (2009). E-government adoption in ASEAN: the case of Cambodia. *Internet Research, 19*(5), 517–534. doi:10.1108/10662240910998869

Shih, H.-P. (2004). Extended technology acceptance model of Internet utilization behavior. *Information & Management, 41*(6), 719–729. doi:10.1016/j.im.2003.08.009

Singh, M., Sarkar, P., Dissanayake, D., & Pittachayawan, S. (2008). Diffusions of e-government services in Australia: Citizens' perspectives In W. Golden, T. Acton, K. Conboy, H. van der Heijden, & V. K. Tuunainen (Eds.), *Proceedings of the 16th European Conference on Information Systems,* Galway, Ireland (pp. 1227-1238).

Singh, V. (2007, December 28-30). Full Circle of Governance: How to Leverage Age Old Organic Structure of Governance. In *Proceedings of the 5th International Conference on E-governance,* Hyderabad, India. Retrieved November 28, 2009, from http://www.iceg.net/2007/books/3/2_281_3.pdf

Taylor, S., & Todd, P. (1995a). Assessing IT usage: The role of prior experience. *Management Information Systems Quarterly, 19*(4), 561–570. doi:10.2307/249633

Taylor, S., & Todd, P. (1995b). Understanding Information Technology usage: A test of competing models. *Information Systems Research, 6*(2), 144–176. doi:10.1287/isre.6.2.144

Teo, T., Srivastava, S., & Jiang, L. (2008). Trust and Electronic Government Success: An Empirical Study. *Journal of Management Information Systems, 25*(3), 99–131. doi:10.2753/MIS0742-1222250303

The Economist Intelligence Unit. (2009). *E-readiness ranking 2009.* Retrieved March 12, 2009, from http://www-935.ibm.com/services/us/gbs/bus/pdf/e-readiness_rankings_june_2009_final_web.pdf

UNESCO. (2007). *E-governance capacity building.* Retrieved April 23, 2009, from http://www.unesco.org/ webworld/e-governance

United Nations. (2008). *UN e-government survey 2008: From E-Government to connected governance.* Retrieved April 23, 2009, from http://unpan1.un.org/intradoc/groups/public/documents/UN/UNPAN028607.pdf

Venkatesh, V., & Davis, F. (2000). A theoretical extension of the technology acceptance model: Four longitudinal field studies. *Management Science, 46*(2), 186–204. doi:10.1287/mnsc.46.2.186.11926

Vijayasarath, L. (2004). Predicting consumer intentions to use on-line shopping: the case for an augmented technology acceptance model. *Information & Management, 41*(6), 747–762. doi:10.1016/j.im.2003.08.011

Wangpipatwong, S., Chutimaskul, W., & Papasratorn, B. (2008). Understanding Citizen's Continuance Intention to Use e-Government Website: a Composite View of Technology Acceptance Model and Computer Self-Efficacy. *Electronic. Journal of E-Government, 6*(1), 55–64.

Warkentin, M., Gefen, D., Pavlou, P. A., & Rose, G. (2002). Encouraging Citizen Adoption of eGovernment by Building Trust. *Electronic Markets, 12*(3), 157–162. doi:10.1080/101967802320245929

Wu, I.-L., & Chen, J.-L. (2005). An extension of Trust and TAM model with TPB in the initial adoption ofon-line tax: An empirical study. *International Journal of Human-Computer Studies, 62*, 784–808. doi:10.1016/j.ijhcs.2005.03.003

Yi, M., Jackson, J., Park, J., & Probst, J. (2005). Understanding information technology acceptance by individual professionals: Toward an integrative view. *Information & Management, 43*(3), 350–363. doi:10.1016/j.im.2005.08.006

Zafiropoulos, K., Karavasilis, I., & Vrana, V. (in press). Exploring E-governance by Primary and Secondary Education Teachers in Greece. *International Journal of Electronic Democracy.*

This work was previously published in the International Journal of Knowledge Society Research, Volume 1, Issue 3, edited by Miltiadis D. Lytras, pp. 71-86, copyright 2010 by IGI Publishing (an imprint of IGI Global).

Chapter 17

Meso Level as an Indicator of Knowledge Society Development

Aljona Zorina
ESSEC Business School, France

David Avison
ESSEC Business School, France

ABSTRACT

This paper studies the nature and the importance of the link between macro and micro levels of innovation management in the knowledge society of Denmark, Sweden, USA, India, Russia, and Moldova, suggesting that countries with different levels of knowledge society development have different link types between the macro and micro levels of innovation management. In particular, findings show that countries with a higher level of knowledge society development have a two-way mediation process between the micro and macro levels of innovation management while countries with lower level of knowledge society development tend towards a "one-direction" link. This paper argues that innovation management can only be fully effective through paying attention to this intersection, which is free of biases inherent in each individually. The authors conclude by introducing a "meso-level" indicator for knowledge society development and underline areas of further research in the field.

INTRODUCTION

In this paper we address a number of questions related to the problems of innovation management in knowledge society development. What makes innovation management so important for sustainable development of the knowledge society?

DOI: 10.4018/978-1-4666-1788-9.ch017

Does the macro level of innovation management presented at government initiatives and programs for research and development solve the problem? Alternatively, should the problem of sustainable knowledge society development be left at the micro level of organizational innovations and organizational capacity for new knowledge creation? Although both the micro and macro levels are clearly important, we suggest that the answer comes most of all from the intersection of these levels which serves the profitability of both.

The macro and micro levels of innovation management have been studied by many authors including Porter, Nonaka and Takeuchi, Dovila, Senge, Bell, and Toffler (we will refer to some of their contributions later). However, the intersection of these two levels, the mechanism of their connection and its influence, has scarcely been studied. We argue that this is often the reason why even the best innovation strategies of private sector and the most ambitious government projects underachieve.

This paper studies the link between the macro and micro levels of innovation management and underlines its particular importance for successful knowledge society development. According to the research framework of the paper presented above, we formulated our main research questions as following:

- *What are the nature and the importance of the link between the macro and micro levels of innovation management in the knowledge society?*
- *How do these levels communicate in countries having different degrees of knowledge society development?*

The conceptual scheme of the research is presented in Figure 1.

The paper is organized as follows. The first section describes the macro and micro levels of innovation management in the framework of its two main domains: theoretical and practical. The second section reflects on the nature and the main types of the meso level of innovation management. A research model is constructed which compares the degree of knowledge society creation in Denmark, Sweden, the USA, India, Russia, and Moldova. This model shows the type of link between the macro and micro levels of innovation management in these countries. After this analysis, a discussion of the results is provided. This is supported by some examples illustrating the nature of the intersection link in these countries. The paper concludes with the arguments elucidating on the importance of the meso level of innovation management and suggests avenues for future research in the field.

THE MACRO AND MICRO LEVELS OF INNOVATION MANAGEMENT

Innovation Management in the Knowledge Society

The process of *innovation* is defined as the development and implementation of new ideas by people who over time engage in transactions with others within an institutional context (Van de Ven,

Figure 1. Innovation management in the knowledge society

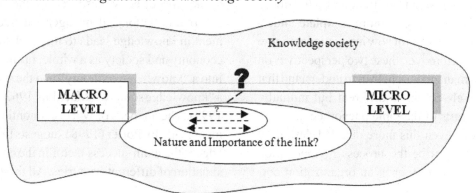

1986). The definition of *innovation management* implies managing the factors that facilitate and inhibit the development of innovations (Van de Ven, 1986). However the above definitions describe the process of innovation creation in a very general way and, consequently, are dependent on the level and context to which they are applied.

In this paper we define several levels of innovation management applied in the context of new knowledge and innovation creation. We refer to innovation management at the *macro level* as a macro economic framework realized in various national and international programs and initiatives of innovation and new knowledge creation assisting in the successful development of a knowledge society. Such programs as "Electronic Europe" and the "Lisbon Strategy" of the European Union, and the "Agenda for Action" and "E-Government Strategy" of the United States can be seen as examples of innovation management at the macro level. We refer to the *micro level* of innovation management as to the micro economic framework associated with the process of managing organizational capacity for innovation and new knowledge creation on the organizational level (which can be seen in such indicators as utility patents, R&D investment, level of firm's capacity for innovation and new technology absorption) as well as with the extent of a firm's staff training. A detailed discussion of theoretical and practical domains of both levels is made in the following section.

We suggest that the above division of the "innovation management" definition into the micro and macro levels gives a more complete understanding of the process of how innovations emerge in a country. Moreover, these two perspectives on innovation management help us to understand that the two levels comprise different but mutually dependent parts of the same phenomenon.

However, even this more detailed definition will fail to describe the process of innovation creation in a country or in an organization cor-

rectly if we do not take into account the specific context of its emergence. The development of innovation management proceeds in the conditions of a specific, complex, and dynamic environment. This includes the dimensions of social, cultural, economic, political and institutional transformation dependent on new knowledge creation and transmission.

THE MACRO AND MICRO LEVELS OF INNOVATION MANAGEMENT IN THE KNOWLEDGE SOCIETY

In general, the framework of both macro and micro levels of innovation management can be divided into two domains: theoretical and practical. Below we refer to the main ideas as well as to some practical implementations of the levels (see Table 1).

Macro level. The idea that new knowledge and innovation creation is necessary for successful economic development has been proposed by many authors. Thus, Schumpeter (1961) put the first stepping stone towards the development of Innovation Theory. He argued that the fundamental impulse for economic growth comes from entrepreneurs, who, looking for irrational ways of making profit, create innovations and technological change. Kuznets (1966) argued that economic growth comes through increasing knowledge and expanding its application. Some authors also suggest that expanding knowledge use is one of the most effective resources of the firm in the area of production and management. Such investment in knowledge leads to major change in the economy and society as a whole, turning the first into a "knowledge economy" and the second into a "knowledge society" (Machlup, 1962; Drucker, 1999). The analysis of world economic development made by Porter (1998) suggests that knowledge is the main success factor in the competitive situation of different countries. All these theories

Table 1. Main domains of macro and micro innovation management in the knowledge society

Domains of the macro and micro levels of innovation management		Common basis of the ideas
Macro	**Theoretical domain:** Schumpeter, Kuznets, Bell, Keynes, Porter, Drucker	• Innovation and knowledge at the macro level are important and even necessary for sustainable economic development. • The process of innovation management and knowledge creation needs special strategic action, initiative and standards.
	Practical domain: Lisbon strategy, Agenda for action, National programs of information society creation; projects and actions of the WSIS, WSIK, AIS, UNCSTD.	
Micro	**Theoretical domain:** Nonaka, Takeuchi, Sullivan, Dosi, Drucker, Senge, Milner, Dovila	• There is a strong coherence between innovation management and a firm's competitive advantage. • Innovation strategy, human resource management, information strategy and R&D create a firm's competitive advantage and defines its success.
	Practical domain: Firm's innovation strategy, human resource management, information strategy and R&D	

indicate a dependence of economic growth at the macro level to innovation development and effective knowledge use.

The *practical domain* of innovation management at the macro level becomes apparent in many international and national strategic programs. Thus, the main goal of the United Nations *Information and Communications Technologies Task Force* lies "in addressing core issues related to the role of information and communication technology in economic development and eradication of poverty and the realization of the Millennium Development Goals" (Information and Communication and Technologies Task Force, 2006). Since 2000 the creation of the economy based on knowledge has been announced by the European Union. This development in strategic programs is referred to as the *Lisbon Strategy*, aimed at world innovation leadership of Europe, and *Electronic Europe (2000-2010)*, with a budget of about 100 million Euros. It consists of a number of separate programs aimed at R&D, computerization in the spheres of economy and management, an increase in the level of education and the adoption of lifelong learning ("Europe's Information Society, Lisbon Review, 2008). Similar programs also exist at national levels in other countries, being a part of their strategic programs of sustainable socio-economic development. These include the

National Innovation Initiative (National Innovation Initiative Interim Report, Innovative America, 2004) in the USA; *Strategy of the development of information society in the Russian Federation* and *Electronic Russia* (Strategy of the development of information society in the Russian Federation, 2007) in Russia; and the *National Strategy on Information Society Development – e-Moldova –* and *E-Governance* in Moldova (National Strategy on Information Society Development "e-Moldova", 2003).

International organizations and projects that have this macro element include the World Summit on the Information Society (WSIS), World Summit on the Knowledge Society (WSKS), World Economic Forum (WEF), United Nations Commission for Science and Technology Development (UNCSTD), Association for Information Systems (AIS), and many others. These organizations help to develop international standards and provide support to international and national initiatives of innovation creation.

Micro level. The *theoretical domain* of innovation and knowledge management at the micro level has been studied by a number of authors. Thus Nonaka and Takeuchi (1995) studied human capital and the transformation of information into knowledge, which may lead to a firm's competitive advantage. Porter (1998) argued that a firm has two sources of competitive advantage: cost reduction and product differentiation. In both, innovation management can be of great use. Dixon (2000) studied how knowledge management turns to prosperity and Rodriguez-Ortiz (2003) described the quality model of knowledge management for R&D organizations.

We refer to the *practical domain* of innovation and knowledge management at the micro level as the firm's innovation strategy and its ability to transform R&D investment, human capital and information into competitive advantage.

We can see that the results of the analysis, presented in Table 1, suggest that at the macro level innovation and knowledge creation are regarded as necessary for sustainable economic development of the knowledge society and the creation process demands special strategic programs. At the micro level innovation management participates in a firm's competitive advantage creation. Both these are complementary and mutually dependent: the macro level of innovation management creates the right business environment, whilst the micro level of innovation management creates the innovation and new knowledge necessary for the development of the knowledge society as a whole. This mutual dependence forms *the meso level* of innovation management. We propose the definition of this level and reasons of its particular importance for successful knowledge society development in the conclusion part of the paper.

STUDIES ABOUT THE INTERSECTION OF THE MACRO AND MICRO LEVELS OF INNOVATION MANAGEMENT

Although the ideas of the macro and micro levels of innovation management have been studied by many authors the mechanisms of intersection and mutual dependence between the two have not been studied to the same extent. Most of the studies refer either to the macro or to the micro levels and ignore precise mechanisms of their interconnection. There are some earlier works indirectly pointing to this interconnection (Beath, 1989; Rhodes & Heidari, 1994) and some more recent studies measuring the strength of the link (Griliches, 2000; Okubo, 2006). A summary of the ideas investigating on the interconnection of the macro and micro levels of innovation management is presented in the Table 2.

Beath (1989) proposed that the micro level strategies of firms doing R&D may be influenced by the macro strategies of government defining the existence of patent systems. He argued that there exist two different R&D strategies of the firm. The first one is adopted by the firm if its rival is not doing R&D. In the case when the firm faces no effective rivalry from its competitor, its decision to undertake R&D will depend only on its profit incentive. In the case when a firm faces effective R&D competition, its incentive to un-

Table 2. Studies and domains of the meso level of innovation management

Domains of the meso level of innovation management	Common basis of the ideas
Theoretical domain: **Beath, Griliches, Rhodes and Heidari, Okubo et al.**	• Government can influence the micro level creating special frameworks for innovations. • Recent studies support the idea that R&D has a spillover effect: spillovers are greater than private returns.
Practical domain: Business investment in research and development, the quality of scientific research institutions, the extent of collaboration in research between universities and industry, patenting per capita, and the protection of intellectual property and innovation stimulation through government procurement.	•

dertake R&D investment is the competitive incentive. The necessary condition for these investments is the existence of the patent system to protect innovations (Beath, 1989). This is also supported by the study of Rhodes and Heidari (1994). They argue that as governments create R&D policies, they also determine market structure. Patent protection seeks to reward innovation according to the cost of R&D. Government subsidies, taxes, and alliances with universities and research institutions can deliver significant, measureable, and distinctive improvement in R&D productivity and return. But governments will do so only if their policies are designed with care and if they select research projects that offer real technological opportunity (Rhodes & Heidari, 1994). Both findings lead us to the notion that R&D investments of firms are influenced not only by internal factors.

Recent studies also support the idea that R&D has a spillover effect. The existing literature generally finds that spillovers are greater than private returns. Thus Griliches (2000) concludes that the excess return of R&D to a firm is 10%, whereas the social return, which includes private returns, is 25%. Okubo et al. (2006) examine many different studies, and conclude that the private return is 26% and the social return 66%.

Among other recent studies aware of the strong link between the macro and micro factors are studies about transformational government as an evolutionary stage of e-Government. They refer to a radical restructuring and re-engineering of the internal and external business processes of the public sector in order to achieve severe cost cuttings and increased efficiency (Layne & Lee, 2001; Gemini, 2007; Murphy, 2005; Parisopoulos, 2009).

The importance of innovations and the need for improving the main factors influencing their creation is also analyzed in many international documents aimed at practical implementation. One of the most important documents of this kind, which 27 European countries agreed to, is the "Lisbon Strategy".

According to the official document of the "Lisbon Strategy", the Lisbon Review 2008: *"Innovation is critical, especially for those countries that have moved very close to the technology frontier, as is the case of most EU countries. These countries must have the necessary framework to ensure that they are at the forefront of innovation in products and processes.... In particular, this dimension is captured in the index using measures such as business investment in research and development (the EU has set a goal of 3% of GDP for R&D spending), the quality of scientific research institutions, the extent of collaboration in research between universities and industry, patenting per capita, and the protection of intellectual property and innovation stimulation through government procurement"* (Europe's Information Society. 2010 in context: ICT and Lisbon Strategy, 2008, p.4). Analysis of these findings and documents leads us to the conclusion that the meso level can play a very important and even a crucial role in the successful development of the both macro and micro levels of innovation management.

In the following section we analyze the possible link types which potentially can exist between the macro and micro levels of innovation management and then look at the research model defining the meso level types of innovation management in different countries.

THE MESO LEVEL OF INNOVATION MANAGEMENT AND ITS MAIN TYPES

The question about the most rational relationship between the macro and micro levels of innovation management suggests different views and paradigms about the nature of the meso level of macro and micro levels of innovation management. We propose a classification explaining the nature of the meso level of innovation management by referring to the possible types of relationship which can exist between the two levels and the extent of their development. Following this clas-

Figure 2. Weak link between macro and micro levels of innovation management

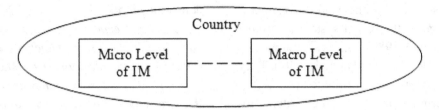

sification four different types of intersection link between the macro and micro levels of innovation management can be proposed.

- **Type 1.** There is no link between macro and micro levels of innovation management, or the link is very weak (see Figure 2). We would not expect to have this situation in a modern economy, especially at the level of innovation management (IM) development, as the intersection of macro and micro environment is both strong and inter-dependent.

- **Type 2.** The interaction of macro and micro levels of innovation management comes mostly from the micro level (see Figure 3). This type of interaction means that the economic model of the country is close to the pure market economy, the so-called "laissez faire" market. In this model, government's initiatives are weak and innovation management at the macro level does not exist or exists only in paper form. Innovation management at the micro level comes most from firms and organizations which are monopolies or oligopolies.

Another example of this type of link could be a case where general level of firms' innovation management and staff training is well developed but the macro level of innovation management lacks government attention and special programs of innovation and knowledge creation in a country.

In this model innovation management will not develop fully. In those spheres where there is no visible profit for firms and organizations (healthcare, public education, environmental security, safe product utilization) and which are usually controlled by government functions, innovation management either will not exist at all or will exist at a very elementary level.

- **Type 3.** The interaction of macro and micro levels of innovation management comes mostly from the macro level (see Figure 4). In this situation there exists a strong motion coming from government and/or international organizations to create national programs of information and knowledge society creation, initiatives to develop knowledge communities, etc. On the other hand, individual economic and social players do not

Figure 3. The link comes from micro level of innovation management

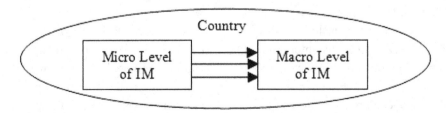

Figure 4. The link comes from macro level of innovation management

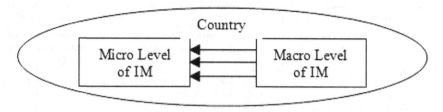

Figure 5. The intersection comes from both micro and macro levels

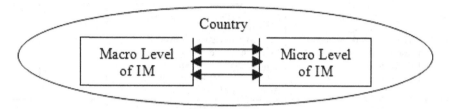

have a developed level of innovation management. This may occur because of some ideological restrictions which can exist in the society, because of the inappropriate economic, political, tax or legal conditions, or when participants of the micro level have low levels of education, are not interested in the development of innovation management, etc. An example of this type of interaction could be seen in the Soviet Union when government had well developed programs of innovation creation in the military and technological spheres; but at the same time, market conditions and separate programs of innovation management for firms were not developed. Another example of this type of link may be seen in the developing countries which have only recently accepted national programs of knowledge society creation but where the conditions for full and comprehensive implementation of innovation management at the micro level are not developed enough and need further elaboration.

- **Type 4.** The interaction of macro and micro levels of innovation management

comes from both macro and micro levels (see Figure 5). In this situation innovation management is well developed both at the macro level (in the form of active national and international programs, creating special conditions for their implementation) and at the micro level (in the form of successful and comprehensive innovation strategies of firms).

In the next section we will apply this classification to the comparison of the degree of knowledge society creation in different countries. Our objective is to see whether the nature of the meso level of the innovation management changes at different degrees of knowledge society development.

RESEARCH MODEL DEFINING THE MESO LEVEL TYPE OF INNOVATION MANAGEMENT IN DIFFERENT COUNTRIES

We have chosen the examples of Denmark, Sweden, United States, India, Russia and Moldova as

Table 4. Summary table defining the levels of innovation management in different countries

Country	Macro Level		Meso Level	Micro Level		Type of the Inter-section
	NRI	Programs of knowledge society creation	Characteristics of macro and business environment *	Companies spending on R&D	Capaci-ty for innov.	
1.Denmark	1	"Electronic Europe" "Lisbon Strategy", The framework programs for research and technological development	Intnt[+] users (per 100 inhabitants) 58.23 Laws relating to ICT 1 Efficiency of legal framework 1 E-government readiness index 2 Venture capital availability 8 Financial market sophistication 13 Availability of latest technologies 5	5.47	5.54	**4**
2.Sweden	2	"Electronic Europe" "Lisbon Strategy", The framework programs for research and technological development	Intnt users (per 100 inhabitants) 76.97 Laws relating to ICT 5 Efficiency of legal framework 5 E-government readiness index 1 Venture capital availability 7 Financial market sophistication 7 Availability of latest technologies 1	5.71	5.88	**4**
3.United States	4	"Agenda for action", "E-Government Strategy" The framework programs for research and technological development	Intnt users (per 100 inhabitants) 69.1 Laws relating to ICT 12 Efficiency of legal framework 30 E-government readiness index 4 Venture capital availability 1 Financial market sophistication 5 Availability of latest technologies 6	5.81	5.44	**4**
4.India	50	"National policy for ICT development", Government initiatives and laws support-ing ICT development	Intnt users (per 100 inhabitants) 5.44 Laws relating to ICT 36 Efficiency of legal framework 34 E-government readiness index 91 Venture capital availability 29 Financial market sophistication 33 Availability of latest technologies 31	4.15	4.01	**3**
5.Russia	72	"Strategy of the development of information society in the Russian Federation", "Electronic Russia"	Intnt users (per 100 inhabitants) 18.02 Laws relating to ICT 82 Efficiency of legal framework 103 E-government readiness index 57 Venture capital availability 60 Financial market sophistication 86 Availability of latest technologies 96	3.42	3.4	**2-3**
6.Moldova	96	"National Strategy on Infor-mation Society Development – "e-Moldova", E-Gover-nance, National Program for Schools Informatization	Intnt users (per 100 inhabitants) 17.36 Laws relating to ICT 90 Efficiency of legal framework 110 E-government readiness index 82 Venture capital availability 108 Financial market sophistication 105 Availability of latest technologies 125	2.48	3.01	**1-2**

*In cases where it is not mentioned specifically, the indexes show the position of the country among 127 countries which were included in the Networked index annually survey.

Intnt[+] - Internet

The following section discusses the differences and similarities between the countries and their meso level types of innovation manage-ment more precisely.

a theoretical sample of countries having different levels of knowledge society development. Table 4 presents the research model of the paper. To increase the comparability of the quantitative indicators used in the research we selected them from the Global Information Technology Report (2007-2008). This report includes 67 parameters of the economy, tech-nology and socio-technological readiness in a country and is annually published by the World Economic Forum and INSEAD for 134 countries worldwide. To ensure that we compare countries with different degree of knowledge society development we have created a theoretical sample of three groups:

- "Leaders" group (Denmark, Sweden, United States);
- "Middle"/ "Coming to the middle" group (India, Russia);
- "Far below the middle" group (Moldova).
- **Macro Level:** The authors propose to evaluate the macro level of innovation management with the following indicators:
  - **The Networked Readiness Index (NRI):** is the summarized index of the Global Information Technology Report. The index has been published since 2002 by the World Economic Forum (WEF) and INSEAD. The 2007-2008 values of the Networked Readiness Index (2007-2008) for Denmark, Sweden, United States, India, Russia and Moldova are presented in Table 3.

    In this paper we take the NRI as a suitable measure for characterizing the degree of knowledge society development at the macro level for the majority of countries.
  - **National and international programs of information society creation:** characterizes the macro level innovation management and shows whether the knowledge society and innovation development is taken into account in national strategies and programs.

    In Table 4 the macro level of innovation management is described by the country's national and international strategies of information and knowledge society creation and by its

position according to the Networked Readiness Index ranking proposed by the World Economic Forum. Such macro programs as "Lisbon Strategy", "Electronic Europe", "Agenda for action" and those similar in other countries are key to successful knowledge society development as they stimulate a special environment where new knowledge and innovations are created, spread and dissimulated.

- **Micro Level:** In the research model the micro level of innovation management in a country is characterized by such indicators as "Companies spending on R&D" and "Capacity for innovation":
  - **Companies spending on R&D:** this index on the micro side comes from the World Economic Forum Executive Opinion Survey 2006-2007 and shows the capacity of national firms to invest in research and development (R&D). These create innovations according to a 7 step scale. Thus, for the R&D index, "1" means that companies do not spend money on research and development, "7" means that companies "spend heavily on research and development relative to international peers" (World Ranking for Companies Spending on R&D, Global Information Technology Report, "Company spending for R&D" index, 2007-2008).
  - **Capacity for innovation:** the index also comes from the World Economic Forum Executive Opinion Survey 2006-2007 and characterizes how companies in a country obtain technology (1 = exclusively from licensing or imitating foreign companies, 7 = by conducting formal research and pioneering their own new prod-

ucts and processes) (World Ranking for Companies Spending on R&D, Global Information Technology Report, "Capacity for Innovation" index, 2007-2008).

However, there are a number of indictors which cannot be attributed only to the macro or micro level and correspond to the interaction of both. Thus, the meso level of innovation management is presented by the characteristics of the countries' business environment, which show the real effectiveness of the macro and micro levels.

- **Meso Level:** The meso level of innovation management indicates the result of the interaction between the macro and micro levels' in a country. At the same time its characteristics show how effective the above macro programs work in reality and how they can directly influence firms' abilities to create innovation programs at the micro level. In Table 4 the meso level is presented by the following indicators:
  - **Number of Internet users per 100 inhabitants;**
  - **Laws relating to ICT:** laws relating to the use of information and communication technologies (electronic commerce, digital signatures, consumer protection) are (1 = nonexistent, 7 = well developed and enforced) (World Ranking for Capacity for Innovation, Global Information Technology Report, "Laws relating to ICT" index, 2007-2008).
  - **Efficiency of legal framework:** characterizes the legal framework in a country for private businesses to settle disputes and challenge the legality of government actions and/or regulations (1 = is inefficient and subject to manipulation, 7 = is efficient and follows a clear, neutral pro-

cess) (World Ranking for Capacity for Innovation, Global Information Technology Report, "Efficiency of legal framework" index, 2007-2008).
  - **E-government readiness index:** assesses e-government readiness based on website assessment, telecommunications infrastructure, and human resource endowment (World Ranking for Capacity for Innovation, Global Information Technology Report, "The E-Government Readiness Index", 2007-2008).
  - **Venture capital availability:** characterizes the conditions when entrepreneurs with innovative but risky projects can generally find venture capital in a country (1 = not true, 7 = true) (World Ranking for Capacity for Innovation, Global Information Technology Report, "Venture capital availability" index, 2007-2008).
  - **Financial market sophistication:** The level of sophistication of financial markets in a country is (1 = lower than international norms, 7 = higher than international norms) (World Ranking for Capacity for Innovation, Global Information Technology Report, "Financial market sophistication" index, 2007-2008).
  - **Availability of latest technologies:** the latest technologies in a country are (1 = not widely available and used, 7 = widely available and used) (World Ranking for Capacity for Innovation, Global Information Technology Report, "Availability of latest technologies" index, 2007-2008).

The choice of the macro, meso and micro level characteristics was made by the authors' evaluation aimed at choosing the best indicators using the descriptions following the definition given above. However, the authors suggest that a more complete, comprehensive and analytical description of the levels of innovation management in the knowledge society should be done by further research in the field.

The summarized description of the innovation management levels for Denmark, Sweden, USA, India, Russia and Moldova is given in Table 4. The meso level characteristics provided in the table show real differences in innovation management between various countries. For example, the macro and micro levels of innovation management in Denmark, Sweden and the USA seem to be rather similar to each other: all the countries have developed programs supporting new knowledge and innovation creation and the indicators of companies spending on R&D and organizational capacity of innovations are situated close to each other according to the networked index survey. Nevertheless, such indicators of the meso level of innovation management development as "Laws relating to ICT", "Efficiency of legal framework", "Financial market sophistication" and "Availability of latest technologies" differ strongly in these countries.

FINDINGS AND DISCUSSION: ANALYSIS OF THE TENDENCIES

In the previous section we compared the macro, micro and meso levels of innovation management in Denmark, Sweden, the United States, India, Russia and Moldova. This section discusses the results of the comparison and summarizes them in Figure 6.

Analysis of the research model built in the previous section and presented in Table 4 shows that the following four groups of countries having different meso level types of innovation management can be defined:

Countries with the interaction level of innovation management coming from both the macro and micro levels. These countries include Denmark, Sweden and the USA. Table 3 shows that Denmark, Sweden and the USA have the fourth type of intersection link between the macro and micro levels proposed in the previous section. These countries have a highly developed meso level of innovation management, through having different national programs of innovation creation and different company structure of spending on R&D. The micro level of innovation management in these countries is characterized by high level of

Figure 6. Meso level in countries with different degrees of the knowledge society development

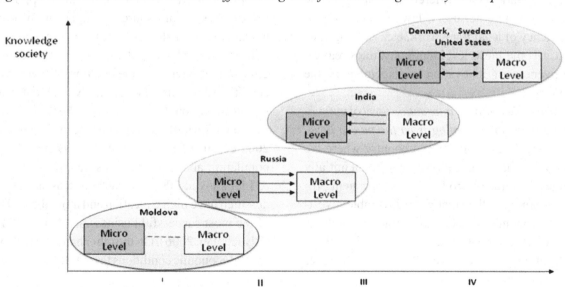

Table 3. The Networked Readiness Index 2007-2008 for some countries

Ranking	Country	Index	Group of the theoretical sample
1	Denmark	5.78	"Leaders"
2	Sweden	5.72	
4	United States	5.49	
50	India	4.06	"Middle"/ "Coming to the middle"
72	Russian Federation	3.68	
96	Moldova	3.21	"Far below the middle"

firms' capacity for innovation and high percentage of companies spending on research and development. The macro level of innovation management in these countries shows active national and international programs of innovation and knowledge society development. These are countries having leading positions in many indicators necessary for successful knowledge society development (see, for example, the full list of "The Networked Readiness Index" 67 parameters, 2007-2008).

However, inside this group we can also find some interesting differences and peculiarities of development. For instance, the indicators of the macro and the micro levels of Denmark and Sweden are very close to each other (see Table 4). At the macro level these countries even share many international programs. Nevertheless the meso level of innovation management in Sweden and Denmark shows different indicators for the number of Internet users, laws related to ICT, efficiency of legal framework, etc. This suggests that it is the meso level that constitutes real effectiveness of innovation management at the country.

Countries with the interaction level of innovation management coming from the macro level. India is a clear example of a country where the development of innovation management initially comes from the macro level. A government program aiming at the creation of favorable investment, economic, tax and administrative conditions for IT development started in 1970s, when about 60% of the population was illiterate (Kochova &

Sucharev, 2001). In 2000 India exported software to 95 countries of the world (62% in the USA and Canada, 23.5% in the EU and 3.5% in Japan); in 2001 there were 24 Indian companies among 44 companies of the world having the highest SEI CMM certification (5th level) (Kochova & Sucharev, 2001). According to the NRI 2007-2008 ranking India was at 50th place and had rather high indicators of the micro and meso levels of innovation management, especially "Efficiency of legal framework", "Venture capital availability", "Financial market sophistication" and "Availability of latest technologies" (see Table 4).

Countries with the meso level of innovation management coming from the micro level. Russia is an example of a country having the meso level of innovation management coming from the micro level. The sources of innovation management development in Russia are to some extent opposite to the corresponding sources of Indian innovation management. Historically Russia is a country with a high level of population education and low government interest in the creation of favorable conditions for social innovation development. The strong educational system built in the time of the Soviet Union still has its results: according to the 2002 census of Russian statistics, 99.5% of the population above age ten was literate (Domsch & Lidokhover, 2007) and 80% of Russian businessmen have high education and more than 40% of the most successful businessmen have a PhD (Blyachman, 2006). On the other hand the lack of special economic conditions favorable for innovation development cause such problems as "brain drain", low share of R&D in GDP and a lack of private capital in innovative and high technological sectors (Blyachman, 2006). According to the NRI 2007-2008 ranking Russia was at 72nd place and had rather low indicators of the micro and meso levels of innovation management (see Table 3). Like India, Russia also has macro programs of knowledge society development but its positions in the micro and meso level are much lower than those of India, especially for such indicators as "Efficiency of legal framework" (82 and 36 places correspondently), "Venture capital availability" (60 and 29 places correspondently), and "Availability of latest technologies" (96 and 31 places correspondently). Further development of the knowledge society in Russia depends greatly on the government's ability to create favorable conditions for the appropriate micro and meso levels of innovation management development.

Countries such as Russia and India have the average of their indicator "Companies spending on R&D" (see Table 4) lower than the average of organizational capacity in these countries. Such a disproportion might well indicate deterioration of equipment. The micro level of innovation management in those countries needs particular support and stimulation from the macro level.

Countries with a weak link between the macro and micro levels of innovation management. Moldova is an example of a country which has a weak link between the macro and micro levels of innovation management. This results in the low extent of the macro, micro and meso levels development. The country occupies 96th place in the NRI ranking (see Table 3). Despite Moldova having some programs of information and knowledge society development officially announced at the macro level (like "National Strategy on Information Society Development – "e-Moldova"), the micro and the meso level of innovation management

have quite low indicators (96th place according to the NRI ranking in Table 4).

However, the above classification describes a dynamic process and should be regarded as a *tendency* of innovation management development in the countries.

In general, we can conclude with two main results shown by our model.

1. The first result shows that the countries with different levels of knowledge society development have different link types between the macro and micro levels of innovation management. Thus the countries which have high levels of knowledge society development according to the NRI also have a strong and developed link between the macro and micro levels of innovation management. On the other hand the meso level of innovation management in the countries which have middle and low levels of knowledge society development according to the NRI (India, Russia and Moldova) tend towards a "one-direction" link between macro and micro levels of innovation management, which corresponds to the types 1-3 of the proposed models.

2. The second result shows that the meso level of innovation management can be a real objective indicator of knowledge society development. The indicators of the macro and the micro levels of innovation management can be very close to each other (as the examples of Denmark and Sweden described above). Countries like Denmark and Sweden (as well as many others in the European Union) can have many international macro programs in common. Their indicators of the micro level of innovation management development like the number of companies spending on R&D and the general amount of

money invested in the innovation policy can also be very close. Nevertheless the meso level of innovation management showed the real differences in their policies and knowledge society development. The example of Moldova discussed above also shows how biased the macro level of innovation management can be if taken as an indicator of the knowledge society development.

CONCLUSIONS: THE IMPORTANCE OF THE MESO LEVEL INDICATOR FOR THE KNOWLEDGE SOCIETY

In this article we make an analysis of the macro, micro and meso levels of innovation management in countries having different degrees of knowledge society development. The research shows that countries with different levels of knowledge society development have different link types between the macro and micro levels of innovation management. Countries with higher level of knowledge society development (Denmark, Sweden, USA) have a two-way mediation process between the micro and macro levels of innovation management while countries with lower level of knowledge society development (India, Russia and Moldova) tend towards a "one-direction" link.

Examples shown in this study illustrate how biased macro and micro indicators of innovation management can be if taken separately. This research suggests that there is a substantial need for the introduction and development of the meso level indicator of innovation management in order to evaluate success and failure of the knowledge society adequately. We define *the meso level of innovation management* as the level created by the macro and micro levels' interplay and describing the availability of the country's specific environment to generate, proceed and transmit new knowledge and innovation creation.

We suggest that the meso level indicator of innovation management is important for a sustainable knowledge society development because:

1. Innovation management is the foundation of the knowledge society, necessary for the creation and application of new knowledge to occur. However, looking at innovation management only from the macro or micro point of view would mean accepting one-sided information instead of analyzing comprehensively by recognizing the existence of both levels which the meso level of innovation management can give.

2. The meso level indicator does not depend on the traits of different strategies and models of knowledge society creation which are applied in different countries and as a result are measured by different indicators based on the country's specific priorities and heterogeneities.

3. The indicators of the meso level of different countries prove to be more useful for comparison purposes than the relevant macro or micro indicators. For example, the indicators of the macro and the micro levels of Denmark and Sweden shown in Table 4 are very close to each other. At the macro level these countries even share many international programs. Nevertheless the meso level of the innovation management in Sweden and Denmark show different indicators for the number of Internet users, laws related to ICT, efficiency of legal framework, to give only some examples. Despite the fact that the US has better indicators of the micro level of "Companies spending on R&D" when compared to Sweden and Denmark, and all three countries have strong macro programs of knowledge society development, the meso level of the USA is less strong in such indicators as "Laws relating to ICT", "Efficiency

of legal framework" and "Availability of latest technologies". So we can see that the real state of the countries' innovation creation cannot be described only with the help of macro or micro levels of innovation management but needs an indicator of the meso level.

4. The meso level of innovation management can also serve as an important indicator of the ability of horizontal innovations development. Horizontal innovations (also called bottom-up innovation and innovation by users) are technical or service innovations derived from the practice of active users and spread in the interchange networks adopted by these users. Horizontal innovations are very important for effective knowledge society creation as they develop independently from traditional top-down vertical innovations and react better to the social needs of people. However horizontal innovations are much more sensitive to the appropriate level of the intersection innovation management development. While vertical innovations can be rather successful when only macro or micro level of innovation management is developed, horizontal innovations demand the existence of both. For example, for the

Wikipedia project, one the most known successful cases of horizontal innovation, the country's interest in ICT and legal framework development, appropriate Internet speed and number of Internet users of certain educational level were necessary to form the nebula of contributors and make the whole project possible.

Our main conclusion is that the meso level of innovation management is important because it combines strategic and governmental macro programs of innovation creation proposed at the macro level with firms' individual strategies of innovative competitive advantage creation at the micro level thus showing the real effectiveness of a country's macro and micro levels in innovation creation (Figure 7).

The findings described in this paper will assist in estimating the real effectiveness of strategic programs aimed at innovative environment and knowledge society creation. They can also be helpful to a firm deciding on an appropriate innovative strategy. Being aware of not only the declared programs and government initiatives but also the results that these initiatives create, a firm can understand the consequential possibilities and limitations of a specific innovative strategy and

Figure 7. Innovation management in the knowledge society

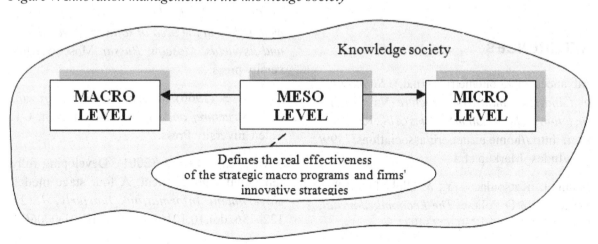

choose the strategy most advantageous for a specific environment. However to generalize the findings obtained in the paper further, research with larger samples is necessary.

Possible limitations of this study lie in the choice of appropriate indicators describing the macro, micro and meso levels of innovation management. One of our research goals was to show the importance of the meso level of innovation management and further discussion on the choice of relevant indicators for every level is needed. Another limitation of the study is the use of only one global source of statistics (Networked Readiness Index). However the objective of this paper was to elucidate on the nature of the meso level of innovation management and shows its potential importance for sustainable knowledge society development. The authors see the comparison of various statistical and measurement systems and choosing the best indicators and measurement system for the levels of innovation management description is a separate complex problem demanding further research and economic and social debates.

Further development of the research could elucidate on the choice of indicators relevant to serve as appropriate measurement of the meso level of innovation management and on the nature and the importance of the link between the macro and micro levels of innovation management in the knowledge society.

REFERENCES

Advances in Econometrics. (n.d.). *Stimulating and Analyzing Industrial Structure* (Vol. 10). *Association for Information Systems (AIS)*. Retrieved from http://home.aisnet.org/associations/7499/files/Index_Markup.cfm

Beath, J., Katsoulacos, Y., & Ulph, D. (1989). Strategic R&D Policy. *The Economic Journal, 9*(9), 74–83. doi:10.2307/2234071

Blanke, J., & Geiger, T. (2008). *The Lisbon Review 2008: Measuring Europe's Progress in Reform.* Washington, DC: World Economic Forum.

Blyachman, L. (2006). Innovation system as social institute of postindustrial information economy. *Problems of Modern Economics, 3*(15). Retrieved from http://creativeconomy.ru/library/prd442.php

Dixon, N. (2000). *Common Knowledge: How Companies Thrive by Sharing What They Know.* Boston: Harvard Business School Press.

Domsch, M., & Lidokhover, T. (2007). *Human Resource Management in Russia.* Cornwall, UK: MPG Books LTD.

Drucker, P. (1999). *Management Challenges for the 21st Century.* New York: Harper Business.

Europe's Information Society. (2010). *In context: ICT and Lisbon Strategy. Lisbon Review (2008).* Retrieved from http://ec.europa.eu/information_society/eeurope/i2010/ict_and_lisbon.htm

Griliches, Z. (2000). *R&D: Education, and Productivity: A Retrospective.* Cambridge, MA: Harvard University Press.

Information and Communication and Technologies Task Force. (2006). *UN Substantive session.* Retrieved from http://www.unicttaskforce.org/perl/documents.pl

Kochova, S., & Sucharev, A. (2001). *India: head for the world leadership in the IT area. Government policy in the area of software development and its yields. Moscow, Russia.* Moscow: University press.

Kuznets, S. (1966). *Modern Economic Growth: Rate, Structure, and Spread.* New Haven, CT: Yale University Press.

Layne, K., & Lee, J. (2001). Developing fully functional e-government: A four stage model. *Government Information Quarterly, 18*(2), 122–136. doi:10.1016/S0740-624X(01)00066-1

Machlup, F. (1962). *The Production and Distribution of Knowledge in the United States*. Princeton, NJ: Princeton University Press.

Murphy, J. (2005). *Beyond e-government - the world's most successful technology-enabled transformations, Executive Summary, MP Parliamentary Secretary Cabinet Office Report*. Retrieved from http://www.localtgov.org.uk

National Innovation Initiative Interim Report, Innovative America. (2004). Retrieved from http://www.goalqpc.com/docs/reports/NIIInterimReport.pdf

National Strategy on Information Society Development. *"e-Moldova"*. (2003). Retrieved from http://www.mdi.gov.md/info21_en/

Nonaka, I., & Takeuchi, H. (1995). *The Knowledge Creating Company*. New York: Oxford University Press.

Okubo, (2006). *R&D Satellite Account: Preliminary Estimates*. Washington, DC: Bureau of Economic Analysis.

Parisopoulos, K., Tambouris, E., & Tarabanis, K. (2009). Transformational Government in Europe: A Survey of National Policies. In *Proceedings of the Second World Summit on the Knowledge Society (WSKS 2009)* (pp. 462-471).

Porter, M. (1998). *Competitive Advantage: Creating and Sustaining Superior Performance*. New York: Free Press.

Porter, M. (1998). *The Competitive Advantage of Nations*. New York: Free Press.

Rhodos, G., & Heidari, A. (1994). Research and Development Competition and Development of Market Structure. In Christopher, A. (Ed.), *Advances in econometrics*. Cambridge, UK: Cambridge University Press.

Rodriguez-Ortiz, G. (2003). Knowledge Management and Quality Certification in a Research and Development Environment. *Computer Science*, 89-94.

Schumpeter, J. (1961). *The Theory of Economic Development*. New York: Oxford University Press.

Strategy of the development of information society in the Russian Federation. (2007). Retrieved from http://www.kremlin.ru/text/docs/2007/07/138695.shtml

The Networked Readiness Index. (2007-2008). Retrieved from http://www.weforum.org/pdf/gitr/2008/Rankings.pdf

United Nations Commission for Science and Technology Development (UNCSTD). Retrieved from http://www.unesco.org/webworld/telematics/uncstd.htm

Van de Ven, A. (1986). Central Problems in the Management of Innovation. *Management Science, 32*(5). doi:10.1287/mnsc.32.5.590

Wauters, P., Nijsken, M., & Tiebout, J. (2007). The user challenge: benchmarking the supply of online public services. In *Proceedings of the 7th measurement*. European Commission. *World Economic Forum (WEF)*. Retrieved from http://www.weforum.org/en/index.htm

World Economic Forum. *Global Information Technology Report*. (2007-2008). Retrieved from http://www.insead.edu/v1/gitr/wef/main/analysis/choosedatavariable.cfm

World Ranking for Capacity for Innovation, Global Information Technology Report. (2007-2008). *Laws relating to ICT Index*. Retrieved from http://www.insead.edu/v1/gitr/wef/main/analysis/showdatatable.cfm?vno=2.27

World Ranking for Capacity for Innovation, Global Information Technology Report. (2007-2008). *Efficiency of legal framework Index*. Retrieved from http://www.insead.edu/v1/gitr/wef/main/analysis/showdatatable.cfm?vno=2.3&countryid=552

World Ranking for Capacity for Innovation, Global Information Technology Report. (2007-2008). *The E-Government Readiness Index*. Retrieved from http://www.insead.edu/v1/gitr/wef/main/analysis/showdatatable.cfm?vno=6.19&countryid=552

World Ranking for Capacity for Innovation, Global Information Technology Report. (2007-2008). *Venture capital availability Index*. Retrieved from http://www.insead.edu/v1/gitr/wef/main/analysis/showdatatable.cfm?vno=1.4&countryid=552

World Ranking for Capacity for Innovation, Global Information Technology Report. (2007-2008). *Financial market sophistication Index*. Retrieved from http://www.insead.edu/v1/gitr/wef/main/analysis/showdatatable.cfm?vno=1.41

World Ranking for Capacity for Innovation, Global Information Technology Report. (2007-2008). *Availability of latest technologies Index*. Retrieved from http://www.insead.edu/v1/gitr/wef/main/analysis/showdatatable.cfm?vno=1.42

World Ranking for Companies Spending on R&D, Global Information Technology Report. (2007-2008). *Company spending for R&D Index*. Retrieved from http://www.insead.edu/v1/gitr/wef/main/analysis/showdatatable.cfm?vno=5.31&countryid=552

World Ranking for Companies Spending on R&D, Global Information Technology Report. (2007-2008). *Capacity for Innovation Index*. Retrieved from http://www.insead.edu/v1/gitr/wef/main/analysis/showdatatable.cfm?vno=8.2&countryid=552

World Summit on the Information Society (WSIS). (n.d.). Retrieved from http://www.itu.int/wsis/index.html

World Summit on the Knowledge Society (WSKS). (n.d.). Retrieved from http://www.open-knowledge-society.org/summit.htm

This work was previously published in the International Journal of Knowledge Society Research, Volume 1, Issue 4, edited by Miltiadis D. Lytras, pp. 1-19, copyright 2010 by IGI Publishing (an imprint of IGI Global).

Chapter 18
The Project Manager in the Theatre of Consciousness:
A New Approach to Knowledge Creation and Communication

Kaj U. Koskinen
Tampere University of Technology, Finland

Pekka Pihlanto
Turku School of Economics, University of Turku, Finland

ABSTRACT

This paper focuses on knowledge management stressing an individual project manager's point of view. First, the authors outline two knowledge management strategies as well as the notion of project manager. The authors concentrate on the project manager's knowledge creation and communication using the so-called theatre metaphor for conscious experience. According to this metaphor, the human brain and consciousness work together like a theatre. With the help of the metaphor, the authors describe and attempt to understand important aspects of the project manager's mental action in the above tasks.

INTRODUCTION

Project management is the dynamic process of leading, co-ordinating, planning, and controlling a diverse and complex set of processes and people in the pursuit of achieving project objectives (Pinto & Kharbanda, 1995). That is, the successful management of projects is both a human and a technical challenge, requiring a far-sighted strategic outlook coupled with the flexibility to react to conflicts and problem areas as they arise on a daily basis. This means that a project manager participates continuously in ongoing processes of evaluating alternatives for meeting an objective, in which expectations about a particular course of action impel him or her to select that course of action most likely to result in attaining the objective. In other words, a project manager is a participant in uninterrupted situations where new knowledge is created and communicated.

DOI: 10.4018/978-1-4666-1788-9.ch018

However, in a project work context knowledge creation and communication is often a complex task. This is due to the fact that the individuals involved in project planning and deliveries are often a set of diversely thinking people with different needs and opinions. Therefore, the personality of a project manager plays an important role in how the project is executed.

Thus, it is obviously very important to know how a project manager's knowledge creation and communication processes are structured and how they function. Therefore, the goal of this conceptual paper is to describe the project manager's knowledge creation and communication processes with the help of the theatre metaphor presented by Baars (1997) (see also Pihlanto, 2009). In the pursuit of this goal the following discussion first describes in principle two different knowledge management strategies. Then follows a description of the concept of project manager. After that follows an illustration of the notions of knowledge creation and communication. Then the discussion deals with the concept of working with metaphors, and particularly our analytical tool - the theatre metaphor. And then follows the main content of this article – an analysis of the project manager's knowledge creation and communication processes.

KNOWLEDGE MANAGEMENT STRATEGIES

Depending on the type of company and industry, different strategic approaches can be utilised in adopting a knowledge management strategy (Haggie & Kingston, 2003; Joia, 2007). Hansen, Nohria, and Tierney (1999) propose codification- and personalisation strategies as alternative ways by which companies can develop their knowledge management strategies. They suggest, for example, that the companies producing customised solutions to unique problems – as many technological project deliveries are – should use

the information technology to help people to communicate. Nevertheless, actual problem solving should often take place with the help of personal interaction (e.g., Jonassen, 2006).

Codification strategies are heavily based on technology and they use large databases to codify and store knowledge. The rationale of a codification strategy is to achieve 'scale in knowledge reuse' (Jashapara, 2004). This means that after completion of a project, companies will retrieve key pieces of knowledge from the assignment and create 'knowledge objects' to store valuable knowledge such as key solutions to problems. This knowledge is stored in knowledge repositories so that other projects and individuals in the company can use the same material for their projects. This means that there is little room for creativity and innovation in this approach and they are likely to be discouraged. Instead, the tried and tested methods of problem solutions are promoted. This is what the projects operating in mechanical project work environments (Koskinen, 2004) is utilised: a solid knowledge management approach based on previous knowledge without the potential risks of innovation. In this case, codification strategies are clearly aligned with the company's business strategy focused on efficiency, cost savings and cost leadership.

Personalisation strategies are less about technology and more about people. Companies which function in organic project work environments are more interested in developing people through brainstorming exercises and face-to-face communication and gaining deeper insights into problems. They place considerable emphasis on knowledge sharing, either by face-to-face interaction, or over the phone, by e-mail or via videoconferences (Hansen, Nohria, & Tierney, 1999). The focus is on networking within the company and through dialogue developing creative solutions for unique problems. Knowledge sharing, mentoring and the use of creative and analytical skills are keys to this approach. In this sense, a personalisation is in alignment with the business strategy focused on differentiation through innovative solutions. Knowledge is then closely tied to the people who have developed it and is shared mainly through direct face-to-face contacts. The chief purpose of computers is to communicate knowledge, not to store it. (cf., Koskinen, 2004, 2005)

However, regardless of utilised knowledge management strategy in a company and project work in general the role of project managers is construed in terms of knowledge creator and communicator. In the following section the concept of project manager is analysed in more details.

PROJECT MANAGER

Project managers have always run their projects according to three criteria: cost, time, and quality. All other considerations are often regarded as subordinate. This approach, however, has not been successful for any of these criteria, let alone for the entire project (e.g., Bubshait & Farooq, 1999). This is due to the fact that project managers traditionally have not given much significance to a very important criterion – people. Yet, people and the way of dealing with them greatly affect the outcomes of projects. This means that neglect or mismanagement of project stakeholders can significantly affect the cost, time, and quality of project. Therefore we can conclude that successful project managers recognize the importance of people, because they know that without people and their competencies no project would exist in the first place. People are the initiators, developers, and users of any project.

Project managers should ideally also take a significant role in the change process by engaging in personal transformation, and become coaches and facilitators serving others. Sustainability and continuity of knowledge creation initiatives are much more prevalent in organisations where leaders who lead by learning are fully engaged in the process. However, project managers may be unaware that their behaviour is inconsistent with what they espouse. They cannot see themselves and they need others to help them to do this.

Thus, the project manager must understand personality traits that he or she needs in order to gain the respect from his or her team members. According to Leslie and van Velsor (1996), there are four personality traits of ineffective managers: poor interpersonal skills (being insensitive, arrogant, cold, aloof, overly ambitious), unable to get work done (betraying trust, not following through, overly ambitious), unable to build a team, and unable to make the transition after promotion.

According to Pinto and Kharbanda (1995), a consensual project management style is wasted, unless the members of the team have access to and are able to collect necessary knowledge. This means that the effective project manager must have good interaction relationships with four groups of people, namely interaction relationships with customers, subordinates, peers, and superiors, i.e. project stakeholders (Figure 1).

If a project manager is unable to structure activities and change, he or she is negated and leadership ceases to exist (e.g., Nonaka & Peltokorpi, 2006). Moreover, the project manager influences the attitudes and behaviour of not just one project team member, but all project stakeholders (e.g., Parry, 1998).

Fortunately, nowadays project management has begun to emphasise behavioural management over technical management, and situated leadership has also received more attention (e.g., Lytras & Pouloudi, 2003). Effective interpersonal relations have also become an important contributory factor in creating and communicating knowledge between the project stakeholders. Project managers now need to be able to talk with many different people in many different functions and situations.

However, to be able to share useful knowledge, the project manager has to create it effectively. A basic condition for this is that he or she understands the conditions of mental processes

Figure 1. Four interaction relationships of the project manager (Adapted from Pinto & Kharbanda, 1995)

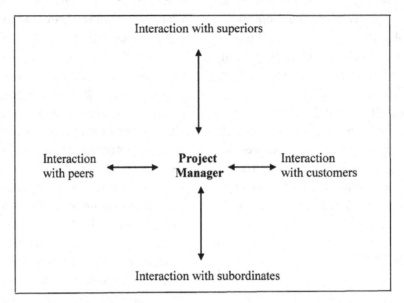

by which knowledge creation and communication are realised in a human mind. So next we concentrate on the nature and structure of these mental processes.

KNOWLEDGE CREATION AND COMMUNICATION

The individual people – project managers in our case – use *meaning* as their basic form of knowledge creation. All kinds of knowledge a project manager acquires, understands and creates is represented in the form of meanings. As a means for forming meanings they use their *consciousness* i.e. their thinking processes or mind. (e.g., Luhmann, 1986; about meanings and consciousness in connection of the so-called holistic concept of man, HCM, see Rauhala, 1986, 1988; Pihlanto, 2000, 2002).

The basic mode of knowledge creation, i.e., consciousness, is defined in the following way: psychical-mental activities constitute, in the form of recurring processes, the consciousness of a project manager. An object in a special situation,

for example a task in a project, provides the consciousness with a meaningful content. A meaning emerges in the consciousness as this content becomes referred to the object located in the situation in such a manner that the project manager understands what the object implies (Pihlanto, 2000, 2002). This means that a project manager can understand an object only in terms of meanings. The network of all meanings accumulated in the consciousness is called the *worldview* of an individual (in psychological terms, worldview is about the same as "memory"). The worldview is recurrently redefined as new meanings emerge on the basis of new contents from one's situation.

Everything in this process occurs in terms of *understanding*, which means that a project manager interprets phenomena and objects located in his or her situation in terms of their 'being something'. Understanding is complete only after a meaning is generated. In the consciousness, a continuous restructuring of meanings occurs as a project manager actively acquires or passively gets impulses from the situation, e.g. creates new knowledge.

What an individual project manager brings to the knowledge creation and communication situation has an important influence on what he or she can learn from another individual. This means that a project manager's personal worldview profoundly influences the way by which he or she experiences the situation at hand. "…although it is the individual who learns, this individual is one who has a language, a culture, and a history…" (Usher, 1989, p. 32). Thus, a project manager's personal worldview affects, for example, how he or she commits to the task at hand, and what he or she can in the first place understand about the knowledge communicated to him or her. People always learn in relation to their worldviews or what they have learned before.

Knowledge communication actually means transfer of knowledge between the worldviews of individuals, and to be transferred genuinely, knowledge must be understood in the consciousness of the receiving party (Pihlanto, 2000, 2002; Koskinen & Pihlanto, 2006). These personal worldviews are derived from the individuals' previous experiences, i.e., previous understanding, which is stored into their worldviews in the form of meanings. This previous understanding is acquired from the social and cultural environments or situations of the persons, and it is partly forged by the individuals' own awareness and efforts. It contains pre-suppositions and assumptions that the individuals have developed in the past. These contents of worldviews are not something about which the individuals can readily give a comprehensive account, and part of it is even totally unconscious, but can still influence the person's behaviour.

All relevant knowledge within a project is within the worldviews of the individuals involved. Therefore, it is critically important to understand how well the people involved know the rough contents of the other project stakeholders' worldviews. This is due to the fact that although people do not always behave congruently with what they say, they do usually behave congruently with the contents of their worldviews – i.e., their earlier experiences and the ways of reacting typical to them.

For instance, intuitive problem solving is not based on individuals' linear cause-consequence thinking, but on creative and surprising reformulations of the contents of their worldviews. A person's intuitive skills are dependent both on the context at hand and on how he or she is able to process the contents of his or her worldview.

Indeed, many projects are dependent on knowledge that is not in the open possession of all project team members (cf., Jones & Smith, 1997). Studies on project management have also demonstrated a lack of learning in projects (Ekstedt et al., 1999) that can be connected to decoupling and separation. The ambition to decouple a project from other projects can contribute to the difficulty of communicating knowledge and competencies developed in other projects (Bengtsson & Eriksson, 2002). However, in any case, knowing what others know is a necessary component for co-ordinated action to take place (e.g., Clark, 1985; Krauss & Fussell, 1991). Therefore, individuals working for a project should effectively communicate with each other by a number of different means, such as face-to-face conversations, telephone, electronic mail, ordinary mail, etc. (e.g., Koskinen, 2003). The effects on problem solving, decision-making, and better understanding of technical issues are perceived as the most valuable effects of knowledge communication.

WORKING WITH METAPHORS

The concept of metaphor for describing approaches to knowledge creation and communication has gained support from many authors (e.g., Tsoukas, 1991). By helping individuals to frame meaning, metaphors provide them with a unique way of portraying the world.

Thus, using metaphors is a distinctive method of affecting perception. It is a means for individuals grounded in different contexts and with different experiences to understand something intuitively through the use of imagination and symbols without the need for analysis or generalisation. Metaphors are a special kind of meanings in a person's worldview. Through metaphors, people put together what they know in new ways and begin to express what they know but cannot yet say exactly. As such, metaphor is highly effective in fostering direct commitment to the creative process in the early stages of knowledge creation.

Indeed, a metaphor can merge two or more different and distant areas of experience into a single, inclusive image or symbol, what Black (1962, p. 38) has aptly described as "two ideas in one phrase." By establishing a connection between different things that seem only distantly related, metaphors set up a discrepancy or conflict.

In the following, we outline a specific metaphor called the theatre metaphor for conscious experience suggested by Baars (1997). We also relate the concepts included in the metaphor with those of the holistic concept of man. By describing consciousness and brain as being structured and functioning like a theatre, we can demonstrate how the project manager actually creates and communicates knowledge. Usually the project manager is regarded as a "black box", which means that we cannot analyze the details of his or her knowledge creation and communication processes within a project work context, and therefore, neither can we deeply understand the real problems of these activities.

THE THEATRE METAPHOR

The Stage of the Theatre

The theatre metaphor describes the functioning and nature of certain brain modules and the consciousness (the mind), which are essential for an individual's thinking processes – knowledge creation included. The basic idea of this metaphor is that the human brain and consciousness work together like a *theatre*. A central feature of this metaphor is that the conscious experience of a person is strictly limited by capacity. According to the theatre metaphor, conscious experience is realized on the "stage of the theatre, in the spotlight of attention," while the rest of the stage corresponds to the immediate working memory (Baars, 1997, pp. 41-42).

What happens under the spotlight of the stage corresponds fairly well with a person's understanding process – in our case the project manager's – in his or her consciousness as presented in the holistic concept of man. Thus, all the conscious meanings formed in the consciousness from objects in the situation, are born "on the lit spot of the stage" (see Figure 2).

The Players on the Stage

In the theatre metaphor, the *players or actors* appearing under the spotlight of the stage are defined as the contents of conscious experience. Conscious contents emerge when the spotlight of attention falls on a player on the stage. Keen competition and cooperation occur between the different players trying to reach the stage. The players are of three origins: *inner and outer senses, and ideas*. Inner senses introduce such players as visual imagery, inner speech, dreams and imagined feelings. Inner speech is what a person hears himself or herself saying, and visual imagery is what a person sees with the "mind's eye." Outer senses produce seeing, hearing, feeling, tasting and smelling sensations about different objects. Ideas consist of imagined and verbalized ideas as well as fringe consciousness and intuitions (Baars, 1997, pp. 43-44, 62-93).

Applying the terms of the holistic concept of man, all these players are types of *meanings* appearing in the consciousness of a project manager. Outer sensations are meanings formed from objects located in the situation at hand. Inner speech and imagination correspond to meanings usually

Figure 2. The theater metaphor for conscious experience (Adapted from Baars, 1997)

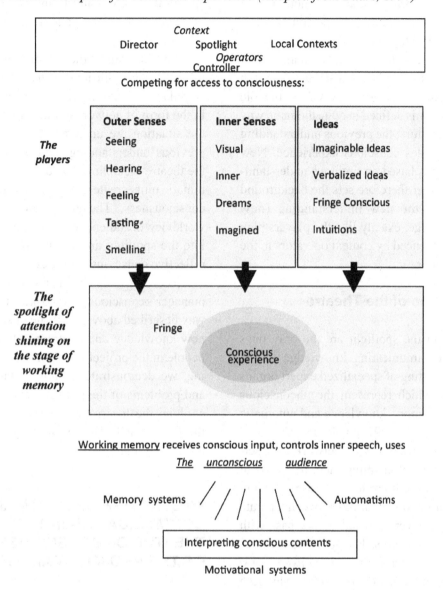

recalled from the worldview, i.e., created before and scrutinized anew at a later time. Inner speech-type meanings are "heard" in speech form in the consciousness. Correspondingly, visual imagery represents meanings experienced in a visual form and fringe images are a feeling-type of meanings.

Context Operators

Behind the scene there are executive processes – *context operators* – such as *director*, *spotlight*

controller and *local contexts*. They set the background against which the "brightly lit" players play their roles. Context is defined as any source of *knowledge* that shapes conscious experiences, without itself being conscious – but if violated it becomes conscious (Baars, 1997, pp. 115-118). Local contexts may be called the scenery of the stage.

Baars (1997) does not clearly separate *director* and *spotlight controller*. Therefore, we apply these concepts synonymously using the term *director*.

The director performs executive functions and maintains long-term stability in a person's experiences (Baars, 1997, p. 142).

In terms of the holistic concept of man, *context operators* refer to certain unconscious content in the project manager's worldview. That is, the role of the worldview is defined in quite the same way as context operators: the previous understanding shapes and guides conscious experience. New understanding is based on previous understanding, and the latter therefore sets the background against which the new understanding (new meanings) emerge, exactly like the players play their roles influenced by context operators in the theatre metaphor.

The Audience of the Theatre

The players in the spotlight are the only ones capable of communicating knowledge to the *audience* consisting of specialized expert organs in the brain, which represent the unconscious resources of memory, knowledge and automatic mechanisms (Baars, 1997, pp. 44-45). Members of the audience share a vast network connecting each to another, enabling them to carry out routine tasks without consciousness. It is likely that these routine collaborations between separate automatic units were created in the past with the aid of consciousness. The audience includes *memory systems, interpreting conscious contents, automatisms,* and *motivational systems*, which are triggered when their "calling conditions" appear: for instance, a visual experience may trigger a linguistic analysis or object recognition (Baars, 1997, pp. 44-46).

To sum up, the connection between the stage and the audience functions as follows: the spotlight selects the most important events on the stage, which are then communicated to the audience consisting of unconscious routines and knowledge sources. The audience may hiss or applaud, asking to hear more or less from any given player. Audience members can also exchange knowledge

among themselves and form coalitions to bring other messages to the stage (Baars, 1997, pp. 42, 46-47).

Thus, in terms of the holistic concept of man, the audience is located in the worldview – the cumulative inventory of previous understanding in the form of networks of meanings. Objects in the situation are understood in relation to this previous understanding, which is according to the theatre metaphor, stored in the "separate automatic units created in the past with the help of consciousness." The unconscious contents of the worldview or audience can sometimes be retrieved into the spotlight and dealt with by mental and reflective conscious activities.

According to the theatre metaphor, the project manager's consciousness and brain function in the way described above, while he or she is creating new knowledge and communicating it to other people in the project work setting. In the following, we demonstrate in more detail the nature and problems of the project manager's work by applying the theatre metaphor – complemented in the above way by the terminology of the holistic concept of man.

KNOWLEDGE CREATION AND COMMUNICATION IN THE THEATRE OF CONSCIOUSNESS OF THE PROJECT MANAGER

With the help of the theatre metaphor it is possible to understand the anatomy of knowledge creation and communication in quite an different way than applying, for instance, the common *Homo economicus* metaphor, according to which the project manager is a pure rational stimulus-response type individual.

According to the theatre metaphor, everything that a project manager can be aware of is called *players,* which appear in the spotlight of attention on the *stage* of working memory. According to the holistic concept of man, the players simply represent *meanings* formed in the consciousness and stored into project manager's worldview.

The players are in a competitive relationship with each other while trying to reach the spotlight. The project manager becomes aware of the winning players, but he remains unconscious of losers. Consequently, as a project manager is creating knowledge, in principle, players of all three origins –inner and outer senses, and ideas – are struggling together to get in.

The starting point for a project manager's knowledge creating process may be a player called an *idea*, which the manager imagines in his or her consciousness (mind) – or in the spotlight of attention – and tries to elaborate better and better.

Into this process enter also such *inner sensations* as visual imageries, inner speech, dreams and imagined feelings concerning the task at hand in a project work: the project manager hears inner speech and imagines things with the "mind's eye". Inner speech may correspond to a real conversation, containing arguments and counterarguments, with the help of which the manager may test ideas and prepare to answer the comments presented by other project stakeholders.

Because project work is essentially a team activity enterprise, the project manager's knowledge creation cannot happen in a vacuum: already at the beginning of the knowledge creation process players from outside – i.e., inputs by *outer senses* - enter on the stage. These include observations based on different kinds of written sources, but also comments, questions and answers by the project team members and other people involved whom the manager is dealing with (see Figure 1). These players may represent, for instance, facts, but also pure opinions, perhaps even very emotionally laden. Anyway, all these represent inputs – meanings – to the project manager's knowledge creation process.

Players provided by inner and outer senses do not play their role among themselves only, but like in a real theatre, participants such as the *director* have their say on the play. This means that in a manager's mind there is a "control unit", which makes choices and presents objections as to the suggestions appearing as players on the stage. In addition, the *scenery* defines the contexts in which the "brightly lit" players appear and play their roles. The scenery represents the project manager's source of contextual knowledge, which is located in his or her worldview. Even if more or less unconscious, it shapes the project manager's conscious experience in the knowledge creation process.

For instance, while reading a project cost report, many contextual factors shape the manager's opinion about it – for example, what is the general financial situation of the company, how the project has thus far met its budget, what have been the project manager's experiences about budget matters in previous projects, how well does the manager trust team members' cost behaviour, etc. A multitude of this kind of contextual factors frame the project manager's attitudes towards every new piece of knowledge, and this, in turn, reflects on his or her knowledge creation and communication. Therefore, the same input of an outer sense may result in quite a different piece of knowledge (player) in different project contexts.

Further, an additional source of influence affecting the players on the stage – called *audience* – is present in a project manager's knowledge creation. It represents certain unconsciously functioning modules in the brain. The audience analogy comes from the fact that also in a real theatre players communicate knowledge (the lines) to the audience, and, on the other hand, the audience influences the players by its reactions.

In the theatre metaphor, the audience comprises memory systems, interpretations, automatisms and motivational systems, which all offer highly individual and as such also potentially surprising inputs to the process of creating knowledge, i.e. the players on the stage – all this controlled by the director and under the influence of contextual aspects called the scenery.

For instance, the project manager's visual experience (e.g., a report or a look on a project team member's face) in a project meeting may trigger a linguistic analysis, object recognition or emotional response in the manager's brain. The manager himself or herself does not have to be aware of these processes, only the resulting conscious reaction – a new player (meaning) appears in the spotlight. The team members may be surprised of the manager's reaction, because the reason for it resides deep in the manager's audience or worldview.

Quite analogously with the above description of the project manager's knowledge creation, it is possible to present how the manager *communicates* the new piece of knowledge to project team members and other interested parties. In fact, as may have become evident from the above, communication cannot be totally separated from the knowledge creation phase, because knowledge creation needs input also from project team members and other outer sources.

CONCLUSION

Our basic message through this article is that without a proper understanding of the real nature of the human actor, it is hard for the project manager to understand the behaviour of the other project stakeholders and organisational actors – he or herself included, and cannot therefore succeed in the project implementation in the best possible way. The theatre metaphor is an option for gaining this kind of understanding. It provides a possibility to approach the project manager's knowledge creation and communication on a decisively deeper level than is common in management studies, because the former is based on the results of modern brain research.

The concept of the holistic concept of man, for its part, provides some complementing insights into a project manager's knowledge creation

behaviour. It stresses that a project manager's knowledge creation in realised in the manager's consciousness or mind in the form of meanings. From this point of view, knowledge and its basic elements are simply *meanings* created in a project manager's consciousness by mental processes.

Perhaps the most important individual finding produced by the theatre metaphor is the notion of the *spotlight* of conscious experience. It clearly demonstrates the limitations of human experience and consciousness. This means that a project manager and also other project stakeholders are aware of only a very limited amount of knowledge, i.e., they are able to deal with conscious meanings only of a few objects at a time. It is important to notice that the people involved in a project work do not adopt all knowledge offered to them: when a project manager communicates with people, he or she tries to get a message to appear as meanings – i.e., players – into the spotlight of their attention. Therefore, only when this message is assessed well enough by the people, it enters into the spotlight, and, consequently, they understand it – and only then the aim of the message has been completed.

As all project stakeholders' brain and consciousness function in the way like in a theatre, it is easy to imagine how challenging tasks project management, knowledge creation and communication are. In particular, the great relevance of unconscious – a kind of instinctive – processes represented by context operators and audience suggested in the theatre metaphor, testify that human activity has typically coincidental and subjective features. Consequently, the project manager and other people involved are by no means invariably conscious, easily anticipated and always rational actors as it is usually assumed in the literature and also in practice.

Of course, the project manager has to some degree of free will to assess the "suggestions" of the hidden brain modules, but can never totally master all phases of his or her knowledge creation process. This, of course, applies also to the other people involved. Therefore, the manager in charge of the project must be constantly aware of this problem area and try to critically control his or her knowledge creation process, as well as try to understand and forecast other stakeholders' reactions.

Finally, it should be realised, however, that the coincidental nature of the human brain is not only a problem for the project manager, but it also means a potential for creativity, which is a key resource in project management.

REFERENCES

Anantatmula, V. S., & Stankosky, M. (2008). KM criteria for different types or organisations. *International Journal of Knowledge and Learning, 4*(1), 18–35. doi:10.1504/IJKL.2008.019735

Baars, B. J. (1997). *In the Theater of Consciousness. The Workspace of the Mind*. Oxford, UK: Oxford University Press. doi:10.1093/acprof:oso/9780195102659.001.1

Bengtsson, M., & Eriksson, J. (2002). Stickiness and leakiness in inter-organizational innovation projects. In Sahlin-Andersson, K., & Söderholm, A. (Eds.), *Beyond Project Management* (pp. 81–107). Malmö, Sweden: Liber.

Black, M. (1962). *Models and Metaphors*. Ithaca, NY: Cornell University Press.

Bubshait, A. A., & Farooq, G. (1999). Team building and project success. *Coastal Engineering, 41*(7), 34–38.

Clark, H. H. (1985). Language use and language users. In Lindzey, G., & Aronson, E. (Eds.), *Handbook of Social Psychology* (pp. 179–231). New York: Random House.

Ekstedt, E., Lundin, R. A., Söderholm, A., & Wirdenius, H. (1999). *Neo-institutional Organising: Renewal by Action and Knowledge in a Project-intensive Economy*. London: Routledge.

Haggie, K., & Kingston, J. (2003). Choosing your knowledge management strategy. *Journal of Knowledge Management Practice, 4*. Retrieved from http://www.tlainc.com/jkmpv4.tm

Hansen, M. T., Nohria, N., & Tierney, T. (1999). What's your strategy for managing knowledge? *Harvard Business Review, 77*(2), 106–117.

Jashapara, A. (2004). *Knowledge Management. An Integrated Approach*. Upper Saddle River, NJ: Pearson Education Limited.

Joia, L. A. (2007). Knowledge management strategies: creating and testing a measurement scale. *International Journal of Learning and Intellectual Capital, 4*(3), 203–221. doi:10.1504/IJLIC.2007.015607

Jonassen, D. (2006). Accommodating ways of human knowing in the design of information and instruction. *International Journal of Knowledge and Learning, 2*(3/4), 181–190. doi:10.1504/IJKL.2006.010991

Jones, O., & Smith, D. (1997). Strategic technology management in mid-corporate firm: The case of otter control. *Journal of Management Studies, 34*(4), 511–536. doi:10.1111/1467-6486.00061

Koskinen, K. U. (2003). Evaluation of tacit knowledge utilization in work units. *Journal of Knowledge Management, 7*(5), 67–81. doi:10.1108/13673270310505395

Koskinen, K. U. (2004). Knowledge management to improve project communication and implementation. *Project Management Journal, 35*(2), 13–19.

Koskinen, K. U. (2005). Learning that took place in office equipment retailers during a technological discontinuity. *International Journal of Learning and Intellectual Capital, 2*(4), 408–421. doi:10.1504/IJLIC.2005.008100

Koskinen, K. U., & Pihlanto, P. (2006). Competence transfer from old timers to newcomers analysed with the help of the holistic concept of man. *Knowledge and Process Management, 13*(1), 3–12. doi:10.1002/kpm.245

Krauss, R. M., & Fussell, S. R. (1991). Perspective-taking in communication representation of others' knowledge in reference. *Social Cognition, 9*(1), 2–24.

Leslie, J. B., & van Velsor, E. (1996). *A look at Derailment Today: North America and Europe.* New York: SYMLOG Consulting Group.

Luhmann, N. (1986). The autopoiesis of social systems. In Geyer, F., & van der Zouwen, J. (Eds.), *Sociocybernetic Paradoxes* (pp. 172–192). Beverly Hills, CA: Sage Publications.

Lytras, M. D., & Pouloudi, A. (2003). Project management as a knowledge management primer: the learning infrastructure in knowledge-intensive organizations: projects as knowledge transformations and beyond. *The Learning Organization, 10*(4), 237–250. doi:10.1108/09696470310476007

Nonaka, I., & Peltokorpi, V. (2006). Visionary knowledge management: the case of Eisai transformation. *International Journal of Learning and Intellectual Capital, 3*(2), 109–209.

Parry, K. W. (1998). Grounded theory and social process: A new direction for leadership research. *The Leadership Quarterly, 9*(1), 85–106. doi:10.1016/S1048-9843(98)90043-1

Pihlanto, P. (2000). *An actor in an individual situation: The holistic individual image and perspectives on accounting research* (Series Discussion and Working Papers 4). Turku, Finland: Publications of the Turku School of Economics and Business Administration.

Pihlanto, P. (2002). *Understanding Behaviour of the Decision-maker in an Accounting Context. The Theater Metaphor for Conscious Experience and the Holistic Individual Image.* Turku, Finland: Publications of the Turku School of Economics and Business Administration.

Pihlanto, P. (2009). *Decision-Maker in Focus. The Holistic Individual in the Theater of Consciousness.* Köln, Germany: Lambert Academic Publishing.

Pinto, J. K., & Kharbanda, O. P. (1995). *Successful Project Managers: Leading Your Team to Success.* New York: Van Nostrand Reinhold.

Rauhala, L. (1986). *Ihmiskäsitys ihmistyössä* [The Conception of Human Being in Helping People]. 3rd ed. Helsinki, Finland: Gaudeamus.

Rauhala, L. (1988). Holistinen ihmiskäsitys (Summary: The Holistic Conception of Man). *Journal of Social Medicine*, 190-201.

Tsoukas, H. (1991). The missing link: a transformational view of metaphors in organizational science. *Academy of Management Review, 16*(3), 566–585. doi:10.2307/258918

Usher, R. S. (1989). Locating experience in language: Towards a poststructuralist theory of experience. *Adult Education Quarterly, 40*(1), 23–32.

This work was previously published in the International Journal of Knowledge Society Research, Volume 1, Issue 4, edited by Miltiadis D. Lytras, pp. 20-31, copyright 2010 by IGI Publishing (an imprint of IGI Global).

Chapter 19
Developing Professional Knowledge and Confidence in Higher Education

E. Serradell-Lopez
Open University of Catalonia, Spain

D. Castillo
Open University of Catalonia, Spain

P. Lara
Open University of Catalonia, Spain

I. González
Open University of Catalonia, Spain

ABSTRACT

The purpose of this paper is to determine the effectiveness of using multiple choice tests in subjects related to the administration and business management. To this end the authors used a multiple-choice test with specific questions to verify the extent of knowledge gained and the confidence and trust in the answers. The analysis made, conducted by tests given out to a group of 200 students, has been implemented in one subject related with investment analysis and has measured the level of knowledge gained and the degree of trust and security in the responses at two different times of the business administration and management course. Measurements were taken into account at different levels of difficulty in the questions asked and the time spent by students to complete the test. Results confirm that students are generally able to obtain more knowledge along the way and get increases in the degree of trust and confidence. It is estimated that improvement in skills learned is viewed favourably by businesses and are important for job placement. Finally, the authors proceed to analyze a multi-choice test using a combination of knowledge and confidence levels.

INTRODUCTION

The number of students attending higher education institutions has more than doubled in Europe during the last twenty-five years. The resulting flow of graduates on the labour market may justify

DOI: 10.4018/978-1-4666-1788-9.ch019

the doubts expressed about these young people's career prospects, given the present economic and social trends (Guégnard, 2008). One of the central issues in higher learning today is the certification of knowledge by universities. In addition to the core mission of knowledge production and transmission, the University must respond to changing education and training needs occasioned by the knowledge economy and society, among which are: increased scientific and technical education, and the need for cross-curricular competencies and lifelong learning opportunities (Rodríguez, 2005).

This paper aims to deepen the study of the concept and measurement of knowledge, especially in this type of knowledge that is acquired in order to get more training. This training usually takes place by definition in professional training schools.

Technical or professional knowledge is acquired through different means and is not an objective of this study to determine the sources through which knowledge can be transmitted to facilitate learning. The aim of this work is to test a system to assess the specific knowledge to be transmitted to achieve a minimum requirement, while at the same time introduce a system of quality assessment, based on the concept of confidence of knowledge. In this sense, test an evaluation system to determine the degree of utilization of a subject related to investment analysis in accordance with the two parameters mentioned, such the level of knowledge gained in a particular field and the level expressed confidence about the answers.

It is important to note that despite the efforts made so far, has not yet been possible to find a comprehensive and effective system that allows students to assess themselves at the beginning and end of a training process so that measurable manner can be shown the progress achieved in each of the aspects evaluated. This could be one of the possible outcomes of this project as well its contrasting by the faculty at the university level.

Definition and Assessment of Knowledge

We start from the classical definition of knowledge as justified true belief. Usually talking about a real and true answer is difficult and complex. So, it has replaced the concept of true by "right" somehow to suggest that such knowledge is recognized

among the group that is grouped so it is ready to establishing rules on a particular subject area.

The term professional is used here according with *the International Standard classification of occupations (ISCO):* "Professionals increase the existing stock of knowledge, apply scientific or artistic concepts and theories, teach about the foregoing in a systematic manner, or engage in any combination of these three activities".

Regarding to Finance and Administration, Department managers plan, direct and coordinate the internal administration or financial operations of the enterprise or organization, under the broad guidance of the directors and chief executives, and in consultation with managers of other departments or sections.

Concerning the knowledge, we have a phenomenal challenge as is to establish the rules by which we must reward certain kinds of knowledge and penalize others, taking into account the two parameters previously expressed: the level of knowledge through its approximation to the correct answer and the confidence level showed. However, it is necessary to emphasize that not all knowledge is valuable to the company, but that kind of knowledge called critical or crucial. Crucial knowledge is knowledge (explicit or tacit) that is essential for decision-making processes and for the progress of support and value-adding processes (Grundstein, 2009)

To be useful to a person, the knowledge must not only be acquired, but also retained or remembered (Hunt, 2003). In professional life there are many occasions when it is necessary to demonstrate not only that they have some knowledge but it is necessary to implement them, share them with others, colleagues, subordinates, bosses, etc. ..,. Elements as interaction, cooperation, credibility, confidence and commitment are recognized in the literature as elements that strengthen the relationship between the organization and consumers, making them more stable with time (Serradell-Lopez et al., 2009b), in all these cases the degree of assurance on the statements and responses manifested as one of the attributes most valued by managers and professionals affiliated companies. National culture can influence in all these relations, for instance, in countries with Lower individualism index, more importance is attached to training and use of skills in jobs (Serradell-Lopez et al., 2009a).

The aim of this work focuses on linking the assessment of learning outcomes from a mixed perspective. Making use of a multiple choice questionnaire will assess the degree of acquired expertise combined with the confidence placed by people who answer the questionnaire. Confidence-based learning has been used extensively in some specific knowledge areas such medical courses Gardner-Medwin and Gahan (2003), but as we know, it hasn't been studied in areas related with financial concepts.

In today's multiple-choice tests if an incorrect answer is selected, then it is interpreted simply that the person does not know the answer, i.e., is uninformed. This inference is misleading. Specifically, the person may be extremely sure that the incorrect answer which he selected is correct and, thus, may be misinformed– which is much worse than being uninformed (Hunt, 2003). In this sense, it helps to visualize schematically the four situations that can arise combining correct-incorrect answer and security – insecurity in the response (Morales, 2008).

Our goal is to get as many students as possible placed in the first quadrant (science) that corresponds to the maximum of knowledge and trust,

and at the same time reducing the other quadrants, especially the third quadrant (delusion), which corresponds to the minimum knowledge and maximum confidence, and in which knowledge is expected to be more damaging to business. As expressed in the preceding paragraphs.

RESEARCH DESIGN

In general, we distinguish between two types of tests: tests training (formative assessment) and evaluative tests (summative assessment). Regarding summative assessment, confidence-based marking places a premium on careful thinking and on checks that can help tie together different facets of knowledge. Thereby, it encourages deeper understanding and learning (Bryan & Clegg, 2006, p. 148).

However, in this article and following the work of Gardner-Medwin (1998) and Gardner-Medwin and Gahan (2003), from the standpoint of learning the evidence seems most effective when they are voluntary and have no impact in terms of academic score, so it is filled in completely voluntary (formative assessment) on the part of students and the commitment by part of the academic direction of not being used to impose a different score, and that the only purpose was purely scientific.

The final version of the test contains 20 questions with for alternative answers where one and only one was correct. A typical answer would content: "above all" or "none of the above". In addition and with each of the questions, the student would answer the degree of confidence in the response.

The questions were contained in four blocks of homogeneous content. Each block contained five questions, two of which corresponded to level 1 (basic), two questions corresponded to level 2 (intermediate level) and one question to level 3 (advanced).

Table 1. Four situations of knowledge and confidence

	With confidence	**Without confidence**
Correct answer	Science	Uncertainty
Incorrect answer	Delusion	Ignorance

In total, therefore, the breakdown by level of difficulty of the 20 questions was: 8 questions of level 1, 8 questions of Level 2, and 4 questions of level 3, linked to the knowledge area of investment analysis, which is part of the curriculum of the Administration and Management degree.

The student profile in this degree is a working person, over the age of 30 years and with family responsibilities. We haven't taken into account in the study variables of gender, although studies such as Koivula et al. (2001) found differences in the responses by gender. In this study, we considered the processing of data in aggregate form.

The test was designed to evaluate the work done during the whole course. An important aspect of the questionnaire is that it was distributed in two different time moments: at the beginning and at the end of the course. The first questionnaire was completed before performing any academic activity. The second questionnaire, which contained exactly the same questions, was completed at the end of the year coinciding with the usual period of examinations. There was zero feedback on the outcome of both questionnaires, and there weren't any comments on the contents of the questions and the possible score of the exercises performed.

Open University of Catalonia is a virtual university so we decided to distribute the test through electronic form, which assured the absence of errors in transcribing data. At the same time, automatic annotations were included on the time spent by each student on completing the assigned test. We believe that the use of electronic test can be an advantage for its realization. Also corresponds to the daily and habitual use of technology in organizations. With the widespread use of ITs, global or virtual teams have become a reality. Some authors, analyzing the ability and willingness to cooperate, suggest that ITs increase teamwork integration in two ways, firstly facilitating and speeding knowledge transfer, both tacit and explicit and secondly, reinforcing the levels of trust and confidence that normally develop in face to face meetings (Serradell-Lopez et al., 2009b).

At an early state, the objectives of the research proposed and discussed in the following paragraph are:

1. Is there a difference in the degree of confidence in the responses in the two periods?
2. Does it match the degree of difficulty of the questions provided by teachers with lower levels of confidence in the answers?
3. What is the difference in final grade between the final examination from the traditional view and this method?

From a total of 606 students, 101 respondents filled out the first questionnaire, and 67 students filled the second. Producing a response rate of 16,7% and 11% respectively. In the next section, we will analyze the results of the study.

DATA AND ANALYSIS

As stated earlier, each question in the questionnaire included another question about the degree of security and confidence in the response variable using a Likert-type scale, with five values, on which the value 1 indicated "Extremely unsure", 2: "Very unsure", 3: "Somewhat sure", 4: "Sure" and 5: "Extremely sure".

To verify the above proposals we have proceeded to a data analysis using the t test for equality of means.

Analysis of the Degree of Confidence in the Answers in the Two Periods

Table 2 shows the main descriptive statistics of the analysis.

The security expressed in the responses of period 1 equals 1,80 (36,08 / 20), being the period 2 of 3,32 (66,49 / 20). Furthermore, this difference shows up as significant. Increased confidence in the response between the two pe-

Table 2. Mean, standard deviation and T-test results of the degree of confidence in the answers

	Period	N	Mean	Std. Deviation	t-value	p-value
Confidence	Per. 1	101	36,0891	15,26637		
	Per. 2	67	66,4925	13,36365		
T-test					-13,271	0,000 <, 05

riods is 84,45%. This increase is explained by the normal monitoring of the course by students.

Analysis of Levels of Difficulty

This section analyzes the responses according to the level of difficulty a priori established by the faculty. The results show that the difficulty of the questions selected by the teacher adapts to the difficulty level set. The higher the difficulty the greater the uncertainty expected in the response. Furthermore, decreases by security levels. The security level used corresponds to the average of each level (Table 3).

The ANOVA analysis performed shows significant differences between the averages of the three levels (Table 4).

Final Score Differences between the Final Examination from the Traditional View and the Confidence-Based Method

In order to analyze the differences between the two systems we have analyzed the responses of the 67 students who answered the questionnaire at the end of the course.

In this section, we proceed to compare the distribution of scores depending on the methodology used for evaluation. We will use an analysis using two methodologies. In the first methodology, we use the traditional approach, with two alternatives: using a global score and a score based on difficulty levels.

In the second approach will use the system based on confidence in the response, as in the previous case, broken down into two parts: using a global score and the score based on difficulty levels.

Table 3. Mean and standard deviation of confidence between levels

Confidence	Period	N	Mean	Std. Deviation	Minimum	Maximum
Level 1	Per. 1	101	2,0532	,86482	,25	4,25
	Per. 2	67	3,5243	,72111	1,88	5,00
	Total	168	2,6399	1,08411	,25	5,00
Level 2	Per.1	101	1,8119	,78235	,38	3,75
	Per.2	67	3,2351	,73711	1,75	4,75
	Total	168	2,3795	1,03430	,38	4,75
Level 3	Per.1	101	1,2921	,88746	,00	4,00
	Per.2	67	3,1045	,86509	,00	5,00
	Total	168	2,0149	1,24886	,00	5,00

Table 4. Anova test of confidence between levels

		Sum of Squares	df	Mean Square	F	Sig.
Level 1	Between Groups	87,163	1	87,163	132,608	,000<0,05
	Within Groups	109,112	166	,657		
	Total	196,275	167			
Level 2	Between Groups	81,586	1	81,586	139,525	,000<0,05
	Within Groups	97,067	166	,585		
	Total	178,653	167			
Level 3	Between Groups	132,310	1	132,310	171,386	,000
	Within Groups	128,152	166	,772		
	Total	260,463	167			

1. **First approach**
   a. **Global score:** In the traditional system to calculate, the final grade will apply a positive point for each correct answer and -0,33 points for each incorrect answer. Given that, the maximum points are 20. The points needed to pass the test will be 10 points. The distribution is:

   Pass: 64 out 67 (with a score equal or higher than 10 points out 20)
   Fail: 3 out 67

   The distribution of results is the following: Score A (maximum score)

Table 5. Score by levels

	Number of students	
	Fail	Pass
Pass Level 1	2	65
Pass Level 2	9	58
Pass Level 3	13	54
Only Level 1	64	3
Only Level 2	66	1
Only Level 3	67	0
Level 1 and Level 2 Only	58	9
Level 1 and Level 3 Only	61	6
Level 2 and Level 3 Only	66	1
Level 1, 2 and 3	20	47

47 students, Score B (medium score) 16 students, and Score C: low score: 4 students

   b. **Score by levels:** In this section, we have proceeded to analyze the results from the standpoint of overall mark, but separating the three levels of difficulty. Therefore, no student can pass the subject without at least have passed level 1, which corresponds to the basic level of knowledge (Table 5).

In summary:

Score A: Students who complete all three levels: 47 students

Score B: Students who complete two levels (including necessarily the first): 15 students (9 beyond the first and second and 6 exceed the first and third).

Score C: Students who complete the first level: 3 students

Comparing with the traditional system without levels, only two students who passed the subject as this system did not do so in the tiered system. These are two students who, despite having a good overall fail the first level.

2. **Second approach. Confidence level analysis.**
   a. **Global score:** Following Sainsbury and Walker (2008), we have used the

next method to calculate the weight of correct and wrong answers considering confidence:

- Correct answer = 1 x (security level)
- Wrong answer = -0,5 x (security level)

There are other more complex methods to calculate the value of correct and incorrect answers, see for instance the work of Bryan and Clegg (2005), but in this case, the score proposed with their own words is "…in principle motivating but is hard to remember and understand". In our study, at no time the students were informed of the assessment of right and wrong answers. The value of trust in the answers has a range of [-50, 100], which is distributed in the following way:

- **Level 1:** [-20, +40], as expected from a total of 8 questions out of 20. Pass score= +20
- **Level 2:** [-20, +40], as expected from a total of 8 questions out of 20. Pass score= +20
- **Level 3:** [-10, +20], as expected from a total of 4 questions out of 10. Pass score= +10

Applying the methodology (confidence-based learning), the pass score needed is a confidence value of + 50.

Only 8 students are able to pass the subject in a comprehensive manner, using the confidence level in the response. The confidence level of the 8 students who passed the test as a whole is 59,31 (corresponding to an average of almost 3 points), while the confidence level of other students is 25,7 points (This corresponds to an average of just over one point). In the next section, we will proceed to the combined analysis of confidence in the response together with the levels of knowledge proposed.

b. **Score by levels:** At this point, we already have more information on the level of accumulated knowledge by students. However, we know nothing of the actual distribution of ratings; therefore proceed to analyze the results using the level of confidence in the answers and the three levels of knowledge (basic, intermediate and advanced).

Table 6 presents the number of students that pass each level and a combination of its with a minimum of confidence on each level (+20 points for levels 1 and 2, and +10 for level 3).

No student is able to overcome the three levels of knowledge. Only 11 students showed an intermediate level and a total of 14 students show a basic level (9 students pass level 1 and 2, and 2 students pass levels 1 and 3); a total of 14 students pass level 1. From the above data can make the distribution of knowledge levels: basic (C), intermediate (B) and advanced (A)

- ○ **Score A:** 0 students
- ○ **Score B:** 11 students
- ○ **Score C:** 14 students

From this moment comes the work of the responsible of the course that must be capable of managing such data in order to correct any malfunctions. Does the level required in the course is basic, intermediate or advanced? Confidence in the answers is within preset limits at the time of course design? The answer to these questions will allow us to properly assess these results. This exam corresponds to an introductory course that has continuity in other subjects and will allow us to better design the learning path of students.

SUMMARY AND CONCLUSION

In this paper, we have tried to verify changes in the degree of confidence in the response of a group of students at the Bachelor's degree in Business Administration and Management of the Open

Table 6. Knowledge by levels

	Number of students
Only Level 1	14
Only Level 2	4
Only Level 3	6
Level 1and Level 2 Only	9
Level 1and Level 3 Only	2
Level 2 and Level 3 Only	0
Level 1, 2 and 3	0
None of the above	32
Total	67

University of Catalonia. It has highlighted the importance of evaluate adequately the knowledge gained by students and the need to provide this knowledge-based guidelines on confidence and trust, the most cherished values of the companies at present.

On this basis, we have designed a multi-choice questionnaire with 20 questions and 4 possible answers. The respondents were students who voluntarily participated in the work, applied to the subject of investment analysis. These results allow us to state that the degree of confidence in the response increases dramatically at the end of the period (from 1,8 to 3,32, representing an increase of 84%). Since this, difference clearly significant. In terms of confidence level used (a variable Likert with 5 positions) the value would be located near 1,8 to a value less than "Very unsure" as that 3,3 would be located in "Somewhat sure".

In a second step, we have proceeded to analyze the three different levels of difficulty of the questions. From the data, we can say that the greater the difficulty a priori established by teachers, the lower the level of confidence achieved. At level 1 (basic), confidence average goes from 2 to 3,5 (an increase of 75%), at level 2 (intermediate), the average goes from 1,8 to 3,2 (increase of 50%), whereas at level 3 (advanced), the average goes from 1,3 to 3,1 (an increase of 138.5%). The use of difficulty levels shows that the perception of teachers is consistent with the results, and also

presents a potential for the development of new educational elements based on the degree of difficulty of the subjects studied.

Finally, we have proceeded to analyze the results that answered 67 students at the end of the course using a combination of levels of knowledge and levels of confidence in the answers. We believe that the use of confidence levels in the answers should be complemented by using the levels of knowledge. From the results we believe that the tests based on the combination of confidence in the responses and the breakdown by level of knowledge are tailored to the requirements that companies make to universities in modern times. Levels of knowledge will enable us to manage those courses by the desired results a priori, in the subject design phase. That is, can discriminate between students who are well aware of what they know and what they don't know, adapted to the quadrant of "science" that we mentioned in previous sections. At the same time, the students are better able to recognize the results and to obtain greater satisfaction with the outcome of their efforts, and gives stronger evidence to develop their own study skills and decision making.. Again, knowledge is shown as an important element in higher education, combined with the confidence level will allow us to develop more and better courses, tailored to the needs of enterprises and the development of competencies and skills for professionals of the future.

Between the advantages, as shown by Gardner-Medwin and Gahan (2003) confidence-based marks improved the statistical reliability of the exam data as a measure of student performance, compared with conventional marking. This method also doesn't have any bias with gender compared with traditional test.

We further consider an alternative that may be suitable for use in automated evaluation and that the approach used is interesting and with high value in the area of management and business administration. Different variants may arise in the future with its use for academic assessment.

REFERENCES

Bryan, C., & Clegg, C. (2006). *Innovative Assessment in Higher Education*. New York: Routledge.

Gardner-Medwin, A. (1998). Updating with confidence: Do your students know what they don't know? *Health (San Francisco)*, *4*, 45–46.

Gardner-Medwin, A. R., & Gahan, M. (2003). *Formative and Summative Confidence-Based Assessment* (pp. 147-155). Paper Presented at the 7th International Computer-Aided Conference, UK.

Grundstein, M. (2009). GAMETH®: a constructivist and learning approach to identify and locate crucial knowledge. *Int. J. Knowledge and Learning*, *5*(3/4), 289–305. doi:10.1504/IJKL.2009.031227

Guégnard, C., Calmand, J., Giret, J.-F., & Paul, J.-J. (2008). Recognition of Higher Education Graduates' Competences on European Labour Markets. *Céreq –. Training & Development*, *83*, 1–8.

Hunt, D. P. (2003). The concept of knowledge and how to measure it. *Journal of Intellectual Capital*, *4*(1), 100–113. doi:10.1108/14691930310455414

ISCO. *Standard classification of occupations*. (n.d.). Retrieved January 14, 2010, from http://www.ilo.org/public/english/bureau/stat/isco/index.htm

Koivula, N., Hassmén, P., & Hunt, D. P. (2001). Performance on the Swedish Scholastic Aptitude Test: Effects of Self-Assessment and Gender. *Sex Role*, *44*(11/12).

Morales, P. (2008). *Corrección de las pruebas objetivas teniendo en cuenta el nivel de seguridad en las respuestas*. Retrieved January 1, 2010, from http://www.upcomillas.es/personal/peter/otrosdocumentos/NivelSeguridad.pdf

Rodríguez, L. (2005). *Libro Blanco sobre los estudios de grado en Economía y Empresa. Aneca*. Retrieved January 10, 2010, from http://www.aneca.es/media/150292/libroblanco_economia_def.pdf

Sainsbury, E. J., & Walker, R. A. (2008). Assessment as a vehicle for learning: extending collaboration into testing. *Assessment & Evaluation in Higher Education*, *33*(2), 103–117. doi:10.1080/02602930601127844

Serradell-Lopez, E., & Cavaller, V. (2009a). National culture and the secrecy of innovations. *Int. J. Knowledge and Learning*, *5*(3/4), 222–234. doi:10.1504/IJKL.2009.031197

Serradell-López, E., Jiménez-Zarco, A. I., & Martinez-Ruiz, M. P. (2009b). Success Factors in IT-Innovative Product Companies: A Conceptual Framework. *Communications in Computer and Information Science*, *49*, 366–376. doi:10.1007/978-3-642-04757-2_39

This work was previously published in the International Journal of Knowledge Society Research, Volume 1, Issue 4, edited by Miltiadis D. Lytras, pp. 32-41, copyright 2010 by IGI Publishing (an imprint of IGI Global).

Chapter 20

An Efficient System for Video Stabilization by Differentiating between Intentional and Un–Intentional Jitters

Kamran Manzoor
University of Engineering and Technology, Pakistan

Umar Manzoor
The University of Salford, UK

Samia Nefti
The University of Salford, UK

ABSTRACT

Video stabilization is one of the most important enhancements where jittering caused by un-intentional movements is removed. Existing video stabilizer software and tools cannot differentiate between intentional and un-intentional jitters in the video and treats both equally. In this paper, the authors propose an efficient and practical approach of video stabilization by differentiating between an intentional and un-intentional jitter. Their method takes jittered video as input, and differentiates between intentional and an un-intentional jitter without affecting its visual quality while producing stabilized video only if jitter is found to be un-intentional. While most previous methods produce stabilized videos with low resolution, this reduces quality. The proposed system has been evaluated on a large number of real life videos and results promise to support the implementation of the solution.

INTRODUCTION

In the current modern world, video enhancement is steadily gaining importance because of the increasing dominance of digital media. One of the most important enhancements is video stabilization in

DOI: 10.4018/978-1-4666-1788-9.ch020

which jitters caused by un-intentional movements are removed. Today we are in the world where mobile phones are in the access of almost every person. Even a layman has his personal cell phone and video cameras are becoming an integrated part of mobile phones. Almost every cell phone has a video camera integrated on it. Due to the lack of stability in human anatomy, the video filmed by cell phone camera will naturally be a jittered video. For example, if a person is making video from his mobile camera in a moving car or if he is running then the corresponding video will be a jittered video due to unstable platform (his hand). Video stabilization is not only required for mobile equipment but has very vast applications like video cameras mounted on the vehicles in motion (as in the case of small unmanned aerial vehicles) experience severe jitters due to different hurdles or wind pressure. The corresponding videos taken from these cameras will be shaky and have to be preprocessed before analysis. So an efficient video stabilization system is required which can produce good quality stabilized videos and should be cheap in the context memory usage and processing power.

A major problem of current software video stabilizers is that they cannot differentiate between an intentional and an un-intentional jitter in the video. Therefore, they treat both the intentional and the un-intentional jitters equally. Another major problem is of missing image areas that appear in compensating the jittered frames. Many methods had been proposed to tackle this problem like one proposed method was to trim the video frames but this approach is not good as it reduces the original video resolution.

In this paper, we propose an efficient and practical approach of video stabilization that produces stabilized videos by compensating the loss of information in the jittered video frames. Most previous methods produces stabilized videos but with low resolution thus reduces quality of the video sequence, our method without affecting the quality of the video can produce full-frame stabilized video by *temporally* filling missing frame parts. The method works by gathering required missing information from the neighboring frames and then locally aligning it to complete the lost information in the jittered frame. In addition our system can also differentiate between an intentional and an un-intentional jitter so that only the un-intentional jitters can be operated.

Experimental results are included from real life situations and result shows the efficiency of the proposed system.

The proposed algorithm can be used in real time applications, due to the low memory usage and low computational complexity. To achieve full frame video stabilization with compensation to the lost information in the jittered frame, rudimentary replication is proposed and background segregation is proposed to differentiate between an intentional and an un-intentional jitter. These techniques are explained in the coming sections.

BACKGROUND

In the last decade, many methods for video stabilization have been proposed. There are three types of image stabilizers currently available (Robert, n.d.): Digital Image Stabilization (DIS), Optical Image Stabilization (OIS), and Mechanical Image Stabilization (MIS). Digital Image Stabilization (DIS) systems controls image stability by using electronic processing. But this system is not efficient because if there is a large motion of object in any frame then the system becomes fool in believing it as camera vibration so attempt to stabilize it and thus cause blurring and distorts picture quality.

The Optical Image Stabilization (OIS) system, manipulates the image before it gets to the Charge Coupled Device (CCD), unlike to the above explained Digital Image Stabilization (DIS) system, where image first hits the CCD. But this system makes the lens very complex and very susceptible to damage (Canon Digisuper 100xs, n.d.).

Mechanical Image Stabilization (MIS) not just stabilizing the image but involves stabilizing the entire camera. A device called "Gyros" is used in this type of stabilization (iMultimedia, n.d.; Kimura, 1985). But they are not suitable for energy sensitive imaging applications because they are heavy and consume more power.

Figure 1. Process model of "an efficient system for video stabilization by differentiating between intentional and un-intentional jitters"

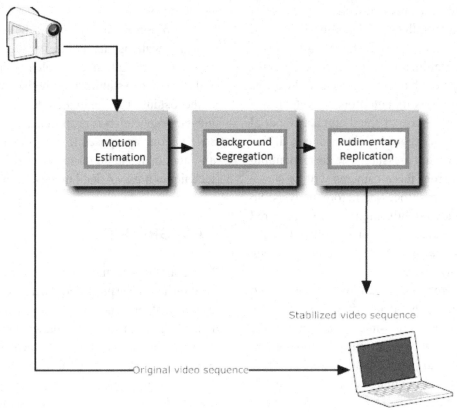

To compensate the aforementioned drawbacks, we propose a practical and robust approach of video stabilization that enhances the quality of jittered video by removing the unwanted jitters from the video stream. Our proposed system can also differentiate between an intentional and an un-intentional jitter in the incoming video frames.

SYSTEM DESIGN

Many methods for video stabilization have been reported over the past few years. Most proposed methods compensate for all motion (Morimoto & Chellappa, 1996; Irani, Rousso, & Peleg, 1994; Hansen, Anandan, Dana, van der Wal, & Burt, 1994), producing a sequence where the background remains motionless. Our proposed process consists of three independent but closely related phases as shown in Figure 1. These phases are as follows:

- Motion Estimation
- Background Segregation
- Rudimentary Replication

MOTION ESTIMATION

Motion estimation is the process which generates the motion vector that determines how each motion prediction frame is different from the previous frame. In general there are following four cases of motion 1) Still camera, single moving object,

Figure 2. Motion vectors

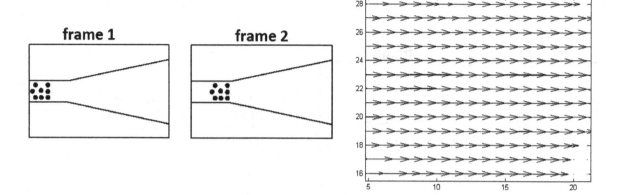

constant background 2) Still camera, several moving objects, constant background 3) Moving camera, relatively constant scene 4) Moving camera, several moving objects.

- **Computing Motion Vectors:** Motion vectors give the distance travelled by individual pixels in terms of their horizontal and vertical velocities. *A motion vector is the key element in the motion estimation process.* Motion Vectors can be used for determining any sort of motion in the video. This motion may be intentional or unintentional, i.e., jitter motion. This technique is also used in video compressions. In motion estimation optical flow is the methodology which is used to estimate motion in video subsequent frames.

The concept of motion vectors is illustrated in Figure 2, where the picture in the third right column is the corresponding motion vectors of the pixels from frame1 to frame2. Since all the pixels in frame1 move towards right so are the corresponding motion vectors.

- **Optical Flow Calculation:** Optical flow is a methodology to find how much two frames differ, i.e., how much motion is there between the two frames. Optical flow

has many different generic classes in which it can be categorized: 1) Matching Techniques: The principle is to divide the image into small blocks and to match them between two successive images based on similitude criterion. 2) Differential Techniques: Based on the hypothesis that the brightness of a particular moving point is constant in time. Based on extensive experiments, we have applied Lucas Kanade [LK] algorithm which belongs to differential technique for finding motion vectors.

Jitter in any video can be detected by using *motion vectors (LK algorithm)*. In case of jitterless video the corresponding motion vectors will be smooth and regular as the velocities of pixels lies within a certain range as shown in Figure 2 but in case of jittered video, the corresponding motion vectors will be very irregular as illustrated in Figure 3.

BACKGROUND SEGREGATION

Once the jitters are detected in the incoming video frames, the next task is to differentiate between an intentional and unintentional jitter. Background segregation is a simple and an efficient technique

Figure 3. Motion vectors (jittered)

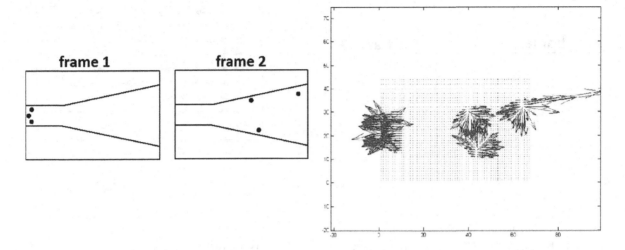

developed to differentiate between intentional and unintentional jerks.

Suppose a person is making a video, jitter can be introduced in one of two possible ways, either by his intentional fast movement of camera or by some unintentional push. The problem is to detect whether the jitter is intentional or unintentional so that only the unintentional jitters could be eliminated. The basic steps of this technique are:

- Detect the sequence number of the first jittered frame (This can be done using motion vectors, i.e., applying Lucas Kanade algorithm as described in section 3.1).
- Store previous two frames from the above specified frame sequence number let frame 1 and frame 2.
- The next task is to detect the foreground and background using frame 1 and frame2. This can be done by applying Lucas Kanade algorithm to these two frames. We consider pixels with reasonable velocities as foreground and remaining with negligible velocities as background.
- Save the background as a new image with foreground as zeros.

- Subtract this new image with upcoming frames and start a counter for counting the number of frames. Trace the minimum subtraction result and stop the counter. This minimum subtraction result shows the replication of background.
  - If minimum subtraction result is found then check
    - If the counter value is less than or equal to 15 then the jerk is considered to be *unintentional* and it should be operated.
    - If the counter value is greater than 15 then the jerk is considered to be an *intentional* jerk.
  - If minimum subtraction result is not found then it is also considered to be an *intentional* jerk but now in this case the cameraman is capturing a new scenario so that's why expected background does not replicate.

Based on experimental results and probabilistic theorems, in case of unintentional jitters background replicates after limited number of frames because cameraman immediately tries to focus its target. This technique is tested on two jittered

Figure 4. Intentional jittered video sequence

Figure 5. Background segregation result (count=25)

videos one with intentional jitter and the other with un-intentional jitter as shown in Figure 4 and Figure 6 respectively. In Figure 5, the intentional video sequence is operated and from the fig it can be seen that the background replicates after 25 frames so it is an intentional jitter.

In Figure 7, the un-intentional video sequence is operated and from the figure it can be seen that the background replicates after 13 frames so it is an un-intentional jitter.

Figure 6. Un-intentional jittered video sequence

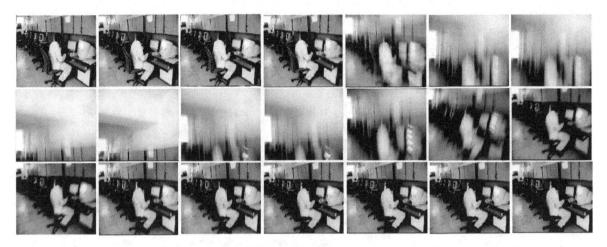

Figure 7. Background segregation result (count=13)

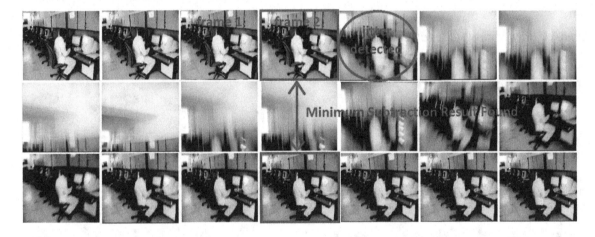

RUDIMENTARY REPLICATION

Background segregation provides us a path to discriminate between intentional and unintentional jitters. The next step is to eliminate only the unintentional jitters to stabilize the video. The major goal is to recover the lost information in the frame. Various techniques have been proposed. In Yasuyuki (n.d.), technique called motion inpainting is used for this purpose but the major drawback of this technique is that it is based on image inpaiting (Bertalmio, Sapiro, Caselles, & Ballester, 2000; Criminisi, Perez, & Toyama, 2003) which involves complex computation so

it is not efficient in video completion. In Litvin, Konrad, and Karl (2003), to fill the missing image areas a technique called mosaicing is being used. Although this technique is well suited for planar scenes but does not tackle the problem of non-planar scenes.

Jia et al. (2004) proposed a technique based on segmentation. The principle of the technique is segmenting the video in two layers: a background layer (static) and an object layer (moving). But the major drawback of this technique is that it is very time consuming as the moving object needs to be observed for a long time. Wexler et al. (2004) proposed a sampling based technique.

Figure 8. Rudimentary replication

Figure 9. Test case (jittered video sequence)

This approach when works correctly produces a very good result but the major drawback of this technique is that it is computationally intensive. Our proposed methodology *"Rudimentary Replication"* is based on motion vectors of individual pixels which are calculated by optical flow (Lucas Kanade Algorithm). Optical flow provides us the distance travelled by individual pixels between consecutive frames. In case of jitter, *there is irregular motion of pixels.* To recover the lost information, specific area is replicated from previous frame. The only overhead for this approach is of memory. But this technique is very cheap in the context of processing and fills the lost information in the jittered frame very precisely. The result of rudimentary replication is shown in the above Figure 8.

TESTING

The proposed system has been simulated using MATLAB and we found that more than 90% videos fall within aforementioned criteria. A test case (video sequence with an un-intentional jitter is shown below). The result shows the efficiency of our system. The processed (jitter-less) video has exactly the same quality as of input (jittered) video and that there is no loss of information in the processed video. Consider an input jittered video as shown in Figure 9. For explanation, frame numbers are written on the bottom right of each frame. Since the first phase of our project is to detect the jitters by using motion vectors. From Figure 9, it is clear that the jitter started from

Figure 10. Jittered motion vectors

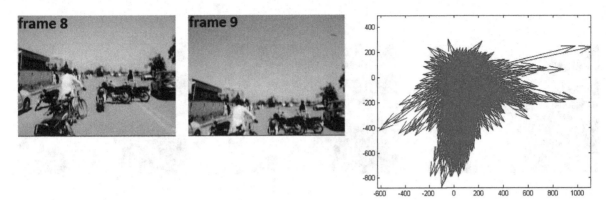

frame 9, the corresponding jittered motion vectors of frame 8 and frame 9 are shown in Figure 10.

From Figure 10, it is clear that the pixels of jerky frames have very high velocities so on these basis we have detected the jitters.

After the detection of jitters in the video, the next phase is to identify whether the jitters are intentional or un-intentional, i.e., applying *Background Segregation algorithm* . Storing frame 7 and frame 8 for extracting background and foreground. As explained in the article of Background Segregation that plotting the motion vectors of previous two frames from the jittered frame (i.e., in our test case frame 7 and frame 8) we can extract our required background and foreground. The pixels with negligible velocities are considered as *background* while those with

reasonable velocities as *foreground* as shown in Figure 11. Now we have to save this frame, i.e., frame 8 with background pixels as it is while zeros in place of foreground pixels. This new frame is shown in Figure 12. We have to perform subtraction between this new frame and the incoming frames so move from RGB to grayscale so that the processing time get reduced. The minimum subtraction result found between this new frame and frame 13, i.e., after 4 frames shown in Figure 13. Since the counter value, i.e., 4 lies in the range of un-intentional jitter so it is found that the jitter is un-intentional and it should be operated.

After the jerk is found to be an un-intentional, the next phase is to operate it so that the information is not lost. The next technique to fill missing area which appears as a compensation of jitter is

Figure 11. Extracting background

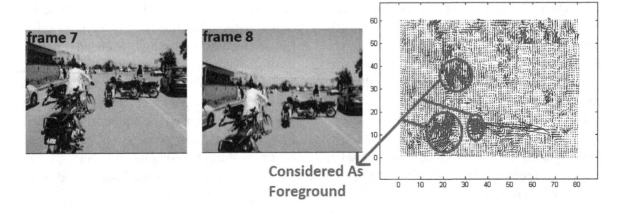

Figure 12. New frame in RGB and grayscale

Figure 13. Minimum subtraction result found (count=4)

Figure 14. Rudimentary replication

Figure 15. Processed video (jitter-less)

Rudimentary Replication where the required missed area is replicated from the previous frame. The results for the rudimentary replication are shown in Figure 14 and Figure 15. In Figure 14, black shaded region shows the required region to be replicated while Figure 15 shows the final output of our system. Figure 15 proves the efficiency of our system as there is no loss of information after removing the jitter and also the quality of video does not get reduced.

CONCLUSION

We have proposed an efficient, fast and a robust video stabilization system that produces stabilized output by removing jitters hence enhances the quality of a video. The three phases of the system are explained along with their real-world results. Motion Estimation is used to detect the presence of jitter in the incoming video. Then Background Segregation is used to identify either the jerk is intentional or un-intentional and finally if jerk is found to be un-intentional then Rudimentary Replication is being used to compensate the loss of information in the jittered frame. The proposed system has been tested on a wide variety of video clips to verify its effectiveness.

Video stabilization has very vast applications such as stabilizing videos made by mobile cameras and UAVs. Video stabilization is one of the most important enhancements in today's world. It will be useful to make the video quality better and let people enjoy multimedia world more.

REFERENCES

Bertalmio, M., Sapiro, G., Caselles, V., & Ballester, C. (2000). Image Inpainting. In *Proceedings of the SIGGRAPH* (pp. 417-424).

Canon Digisuper 100xs. (n.d.). *Product Manual.* Retrieved May 20, 2006, from http://www.canon.com/bctv/products/pdf/100xs.pdf

Criminisi, A., Perez, P., & Toyama, K. (2003). Object Removal by Exemplar-Based Inpainting. In. *Proceedings of the IEEE Conf. on Computer Vision and Pattern Recognition, 2*, 721–728.

Hansen, M., Anandan, P., Dana, K., van der Wal, G., & Burt, P. J. (1994). Real time scene stabilization and mosaic construction. In *Proceedings of the DARPA Image Understanding Workshop*, Monterey, CA (pp. 457-465).

iMultimedia (n.d.). *Use Image Stabilization – Gyroscopic Stabilizer*. Retrieved January 13, 2006, from http://www.websiteoptimization.com/speed/tweak/stabilizer

Irani, M., Rousso, B., & Peleg, S. (1994, June). Recovery of ego-motion using image stabilization. In *Proceedings of the IEEE conference on Computer Vision and Pattern Recognition*, Seattle, WA (pp. 454-460).

Jia, J., Wu, T. P., Tai, Y. W., & Tang, C. K. (2004). Inference of foreground and background under severe occlusion. In. *Proceedings of IEEE Conf. on Computer Vision and Pattern Recognition, 1*, 364–371.

Kimura, K. (1985). *Angular Velocity Measuring Instrument* (USP 2544646).

Litvin, A., Konrad, J., & Karl, W. C. (2003). Probabilistic video stabilization using Kalman filtering and mosaicking. In *Proceedings of the IS&T/SPIE Symposium on Electronic Imaging, Image and Video Communications* (pp. 663-674).

Morimoto, C., & Chellappa, R. (1996). Fast electronic digital image stabilization. In *Proceedings of the 13th International Conference on Pattern Recognition* (Vol. 3, pp. 284-288).

Robert, G. (n.d.). *VideoMaker Magazine The End Of ShakyCamera*. Retrieved January 13, 2006, from http://www.videomaker.com/scripts/article_print.cfm?id=9999

Ronchetti, M. (2010). A Different Perspective on Lecture Video-Streaming: How to Use Technology to Help Change the Traditional Lecture Model. *International Journal of Knowledge Society Research, 1*(2), 50–60.

Wexler, Y., Shechtman, E., & Irani, M. (2004). Space-time video completion. In. *Proceedings of the IEEE Conf. on Computer Vision and Pattern Recognition, 1*, 120–127.

Yasuyuki, M. (n.d.). *Full-frame Video Stabilization*. Beijing, China. *Microsoft Research Asia*.

This work was previously published in the International Journal of Knowledge Society Research, Volume 1, Issue 4, edited by Miltiadis D. Lytras, pp. 42-53, copyright 2010 by IGI Publishing (an imprint of IGI Global).

Chapter 21
A Change Management Framework to Support Software Project Management

Belinda Masekela
University of South Africa, South Africa

Rita Nienaber
University of South Africa, South Africa

ABSTRACT

In today's global marketplace, organizations are continually faced with the need to change their structures and processes to attain a competitive advantage. Implementation of new technology and information management systems results in inevitable changes in organizational procedures impacting on the people involved. Resistance to change may impact on this process and contribute to failure of this system. Managing change in an effective and efficient manner may negate this impact. This paper compiles a set of guidelines to support change which involves the incorporation of technology in an organization. These guidelines were mapped to a model, the GIC (Guidelines Implementing Change) model comprising all identified factors. These guidelines are utilized to guide the implementation of a new system, while simultaneously evaluating the success of these set guidelines. This research is cross disciplinary, affecting the areas of organizational behaviour, software project management, and human factors.

BACKGROUND

As the global marketplace becomes more competitive, organizations are increasingly utilizing software development to help them gain a competitive advantage. However, in spite of technological advances, the increased level of interconnectivity,

distribution and processing, creates vast challenges involving a wide spectrum of software-related activity management and organisational issues. In fact, complexities and risks of software project development continue to increase and drive software failure (Marchewka, 2003). Over the past years, the development of software projects have regularly failed to meet user expectations, were commonly delivered late, and mostly exceeded

DOI: 10.4018/978-1-4666-1788-9.ch021

the set budget. Much of this still holds true today, which is why these issues have to be addressed in concrete terms (Cokins, 2005).

Copious amounts of information on the management of change can be found in literature, indicating that change practitioners are nor failing due to a lack of information, but more likely they are failing to sort through all available information and extract fragments that are meaningful, useful and likely to be effective in the context of their own practice (Bodea et al., 2010). Since organisations continue to invest time and resources in strategically important software projects, the possibility of failure of the project should be minimised.

The field of SPM, with the focus specifically on the management of change, is receiving increasing attention and various methods and techniques are utilised to optimise the implementation of a new information system. The introduction of any information system causes change in the organization (Krovi, 1993). Literature reveals that it is inevitable that when an information system (IS) is successfully implemented in an organisation there will be some change to the organisation. Implementation of an IS has the potential to impact upon an organisation's structure, necessitating the redesign of business processes, individual tasks and job descriptions, as well as the attitudes of individual employees and the distribution of power (Sharma et al., 2010). User's working practises may also change as a result of this implementation – in ways that had not been expected (Doherty et al., 2003). Hence, with the implementation of an IS, users can expect to be affected by the changes introduced by the new system. A survey of the literature indicates that the human impacts of this trend are not negligible and could influence the outcome of the project (Chatzoglou & Macaulay, 1997; Doherty et al., 2003).

The aim of this literature study is twofold: To find evidence in the literature which attests to the positive relationship between effective change management and project outcome. Furthermore, the study seeks to formulate practical guidelines for incorporation into software project manage-

ment practises in order to maximise the likelihood of a positive project outcome. Thus the authors formulated a set of practical guidelines to guide the implementation of change and tested them against a measure of reality to determine if they would be applicable and effective in real-life situations. The authors explored the importance of managing the process of change during the implementation. The set of change management guidelines were compiled from existing literature and implemented on a case study reflecting a true-life situation. From these guidelines we compiled a model (GIC model) to support the process of change.

The first part of this study explores the impact of change management on project failure. This is followed by an investigation identifying the role-players in the change process and the possible reasons for resistance to change. The following section comprises a set of principles to underpin and support the process of change involving the incorporation of technology in an organization, compiled by the authors from literature. These guidelines were mapped to a model, the GIC (Guidelines Implementing Change) model comprising all identified factors. These guidelines are utilized to guide the implementation of a new system, and thus simultaneously evaluate the success of these set guidelines. The third section is devoted to a discussion of the implementation of these guidelines on a case study.

CHANGE AND PROJECT FAILURE

In today's world of globalisation and innovation, change is just about the only constant (Vales, 2007). According to the Standish group (2005), only 28% of projects succeeded, of which 23% failed and 49% were challenged. Those projects that were classified as challenged were completed and operational but they were either over budget, exceeded allocated time or they were delivered with fewer features and functions than what was originally specified.

Table 1. IT project reasons for success, failure, and challenges

	Reasons for success	Reasons for failure	Reasons for Challenges
1	Project team	Communication infrastructure	Requirements definition
2	Understanding user needs	Requirements definition	Handling change
3	Communication infrastructure	User involvement infrastructure	Communicaton
4	Requirements definition	Executive support	User involvement

Exploration of the literature yielded that there is no single cause of failure. Project failure is multifaceted and a variety of reasons can be attributed to it (2006; Schwalbe, 2009). The main reasons for failure, success and challenges cited in literature are shown in Table 1.

Table 1 reflects the problems IT projects face in South Africa, and shows that it the soft issues are clearly more problematic than standards and methodologies (Sonnekus & Labuschagne, 2003). Managing change is listed as one of the challenges to be addressed. Handling change refers to the process of executing changes in a planned and managed fashion. This consists mainly of models, methods, techniques, tools, skills and other forms of knowledge that go into responding to change in a thoughtful and systematic manner. Managing change is a complex process which entails managing the tension between security and insecurity (Clarke, 1994; Paper & Ugray, 2008; Bodea et al., 2010). The interested reader is referred to Paper and Ugray's publication for a more in-depth discussion on qualitative research, as this falls outside the scope of this study.

POOR MANAGEMENT OF CHANGE CAN LEAD TO PROJECT FAILURE

In the first section, it was shown that software development projects bring about change, which can have an impact on the people involved in the use of the system. *Change management* is the process that can be used to negate this impact as it assists people in transitioning to a new way of doing things. The aim is to assist personnel to adjust to the change and reflect on it in a positive light. However, if the change is not managed properly, it can be viewed negatively. This principle applies even in software development projects. If users are not assisted in adjusting to the change introduced by the development of an IS, they can react negatively to it. This could be because the do not understand what is going to happen or what is expected of them as participants in the change or they may even feel that their jobs are endangered by the introduction of a new system (Chatzoglou & Macaulay,1997). When users feel threatened, they react in a thoughtful and ingenious way by adopting counter implementation strategies in order to impede the development of the system (Chatzoglou & Macaulay, 1997). This impediment is a form of resistance towards the system. Users may resist a system for the following reasons (Kotter & Schlesinger, 1979):

- The users are innately conservative
- They do not see a need for the new system
- Uncertainty about the influence of the system afterwards
- They were not involved in the change,
- Resources have been redistributed,
- The change is not valid in the organisational context
- No support from management,
- The system itself is technically inferior

It is clear, then, that information systems are able to change existing power balances in the organization. This is noteworthy as very few authors in literature recognised power struggles as an issue of importance even though from

Table 2. Resistance to change

	Kotter & Schlesinger	Hirscheim & Newman	Clarke	Chatzoglou & Macauly
Attachment to old way of doing things	Afraid of losing old ways		Reluctance to let go	
Aversion to change	Low tolerance to change	Users innatively conservative	History of previous customs	
Change not applicable in organizational context	Belief that change will not benefit organization	The change is not valid in organizational context		
Benefits not clear	Belief that it will cost more than they will gain	See no need for a new system		
Insecurity			Threat to status, skills, power base, Fear of failure	Jobs endangered
Lack of support		No support from management	Fear of unknown	
Lack of understanding	Misunderstood the change	Uncertainty	Lack of information	Lack of understanding
Poor consultation and participation		Not involved in change		
Stress			Stress and anxiety	
Technical inferiority of solution		System is technically inferior		

personal observations and experience, it often plays a remarkable role in shaping the outcome of software development projects.

A summary of reasons identified for resistance to change are stated in Table 2.

Change management is not a distinct discipline with rigid, clearly defined boundaries. Rather, the theory and practice of change management draws on a number of social science disciplines and traditions (Kitchen & Daly, 2002). The change management process provides organisations with the ability to understand and better manage the realities in the face of change (McKeen & Smith, 2003). The process of change management usually involves 3 things (i) A programme designed to facilitate the transition between the beginning and end state; (ii) Specific actions taken by those responsible for implementing change; and (iii) a set of skills linked to these actions (Griffith, 2001). Role players that form part of the change management process include (McKeen & Smith, 2003) (Table 3).

Table 3. Role players in change management

Change agent	Someone who works cross functionally to manage and guide the process of change.
Change champion	Creates the strategy for change and offer ongoing guidance and support to those who are affected by the change
Change sponsor	Persons who initiates, legitimises, mobilise the change champions, and ensure alignment of the change with the organisational culture.
Change recipients	Stakeholders are the people who are affected by the change and whose involvement is key to it's success.

CHANGE MANAGEMENT PRINCIPLES

In response to the complexity involved in managing change as well as the high risk of failure, principles, guidelines and approaches have been proposed in the literature to assist practitioners in navigating the complex terrain of managing change (Kotter, 2002). The aim of this writing is to provide change management practitioners in the banking industry with an overview of specific guidelines. The authors compiled a set of principles from literature, categorized as: people involvement factors, relationship factors and factors pertaining to processes:

People Involvement Factors

1. **Use of change champions:** Change champions will endeavor to bridge the semantic and skills gap between the change agents and recipients of the change (McKeen & Smith, 2003). They will then be able to create a common understanding of the change thus making it easier for the recipients of such change to accept it.

2. **Use of skilled change agents to implement change:** Managing change is complex and the consequences of failure are noteworthy. Hence, it is important to use people with adequate skills and experience to run the implementation process (Cowley, 2007).

3. **Involvement of change recipients:** Insufficient user involvement has been cited as one of the reasons why information systems fail (Yeo, 2003). If employees are not involved in the change process, they are likely to have a limited understanding of the change that is to take place and how it will impact them. This view is affirmed by Vales (2007).

4. **Senior management involvement and visibility:** Senior management must express their commitment to the change publicly.

Relationship Factors

5. **Relationship & coalition building:** The most important change practice is personal contact (McKeen & Smith, 2003). Coalition-building: for the change to succeed, change sponsors need to rally the support of other influential leaders (McKeen & Smith, 2003).

6. **Partnership approach to diagnosing problems and finding solutions:** When going through a change process team work is crucial. Management should avoid the temptation to provide all the answers, but should allow employees to have an input (McKeen & Smith, 2003; Hernandez-Lopez et al., 2010).

7. **Informal authority in addition to formal authority and structures:** Informal authorities should be used to support change, i.e., the use of relationships (Cowley, 2007).

Process Factors

8. **Attainment of quick and visible results:** Implementation of the change should be fast and be highly visible as successful change boosts credibility (McKeen & Smith, 2003; Robertson, 2004). Large scale changes should thus be broken down into smaller deliverables which can be delivered iteratively.

9. **Creation of a vision:** The first step towards change is determining what needs to be done differently. Clearly communicating the vision, with emphasis on things such as usability and practicality for getting to the desired goal reduces the amount of difficulty involved in change because it makes change more attractive to the people involved (Robertson, 2004).

10. **Internal focus that takes into account external environmental factors:** Change management implies a continuous effort to understand external environmental factors

such as industry dynamics, whilst at the same time focusing on understanding the environment internal to the organisation (Kitchen & Daly, 2002).

11. **Balance hard and soft skills:** The information technology implementation should not focus too much on tactical issues but also recognise the people related issues (Robertson, 2004). To improve the chances of a successful implementation, there needs to be a balance between addressing the tactical issues as well as the people related issues.

12. **Regular, accurate and relevant communication:** Failure of communication lies at the heart of most botched programmes of organisation change (McKeen & Smith, 2003). More than that, communicating the need for change to those affected and how it can be achieved is absolutely essential for change to be managed successfully (Kitchen & Daly, 2002). Communication is regarded as a key issue in change programmes because it is used as a tool for announcing, explaining or preparing people for change and preparing them for the positive and negative effects of the impending change. Communication helps build motivation in people as it improves the awareness and understanding of the change impact as well as the potential benefits of the change.

13. **Publicising of successes:** The success of the change needs to be publicised. This encourages change recipients and reinforces the appropriate behaviours that are necessary to maintain the change going forward (McNish, 2002).

14. **Change recipient understanding of what is expected of them:** To avoid confusion and minimise the likelihood of resistance, affected staff should be well informed about what is expected of them in the new system (McNish, 2002).

15. **Understanding of the change and it's potential impacts:** Without a good understanding of the change and how it will impact the people and the organisation as a whole, devising a suitable strategy for executing the change is problematic. Careful studies should be made of the changes in practise that would be needed (Robertson, 2004) Also, change recipients will not be able to influence the nature of the change unless they have a good understanding of the business and where it is headed (McKeen & Smith, 2003).

16. **Commitment to the change from both change agents and change recipients:** The implementation team as well as the change recipients must be committed to the change for it to be successful (McNish, 2002). Commitment need to be cultivated within the organization. Vales proposed a change commitment curve to illustrate this process. Based on this curve, commitment is cultivated through the individual understanding of the reasons, the benefits of the change, what is expected of the individual, what the impact will be on the individual, the support mechanisms that will be available to assist them in transitioning to the new way of doing things.

By understanding the process that people go through to develop commitment to a certain change, change agents can increase the chances of the change succeeding by ensuring that all the information is available for the individual to progress through the change commitment curve.

17. **Reinforcement of change after it has been implemented:** When change has been implemented, there is still potential for failure in that things can revert back to the way they were before. To overcome this tendency to regress and to ensure that the change is sustained over a long period it is important to reinforce change through formal and

informal processes and structures (Cowley, 2007).

18. **Resistance must be proactive identification and managed:** Having defined change and established that change is inevitable, the next step is to understand what can be done to minimise the negative impact of such changes on users.

19. **Set of guidelines:** Literature recommends the use of specific, project oriented guidelines to direct activities and thus improve the likelihood of success in the implementation of a change (McNish, 2002; McKeen & Smith, 2003; Cowley, 2007). Guidelines are not prescriptive rules but rather parameters that provide direction when assembling a strategy for the implementation of change. These guidelines were mapped to the GIC (Guidelines implementing Change) model comprising all identified factors to support the process of change (Table 4).

Guidelines in Figure 1 were tested by implementing them on a true-life project in an organization.

A CASE STUDY IMPLEMENTING CHANGE: THE PROJECT DESCRIPTION

The project entails a large organization responsible for retail micro lending, ranging from R2000 to R100 000. It comprises a network of 200 branches with loans consultants and clients. This paper-based system had severe limitations, which resulted in unnecessary delays and affected the volume of work that could be undertaken by the division, as time was spent in physically relocating files and resources. To address these shortcomings a decision was made to introduce technology. A project team was assembled, workshops were held to document requirements for the new system. Once requirements had been documented, elaborated on and signed off by key stakeholders,

the requirements were prioritized in a forum that had representatives from all areas of the business. Thus a suitable technology solution, taking into account requirements, budget and time constraints was compiled, designed, coded and tested.

The solution was then deployed in the production environment following a very cautious approach, where the old manual process was run in parallel to the new automated process to ensure that the automated process worked well before all applications were switched over. Running the two processes in parallel also had the advantage of providing a smooth transition for work in progress, i.e., those applications that had been initiated (but not completed) before the automated process was implemented.

The envisioned solution would also automate menial tasks associated with processing applications thus leaving staff able to focus on value adding work and inadvertently increasing the divisional capacity to process increasing application volumes.

THE FORESEEN IMPACT OF THE CHANGE

Despite the caution with which the technology solution would be implemented, the people involved, namely clients, sales staff, operations staff, would still be impacted by this change. Both the staff and clients were likely to be significantly impacted by the upcoming changes. The automation would change their roles and the way they performed them. This left many staff feeling insecure in their jobs and it placed the organisation at risk of an increase in attrition rates (people resigning before they could be retrenched) and a loss of valuable experience and intellectual property. The challenge was great for management and the project team to allay the fears that had crept up.

The project team anticipated that the staff would not bring up any concerns / issues for discussion with management (especially if their

Table 4. Comparison of change management principles

Guidelines	Vales	McNish	McKeen & Smit	Cowley	Clarcke	Kotter & Schlesinger	Robertson	Chatzoglou & Mcacauly
Attainment of quick and visible results	X	x	x					
Creation of a vision			x		x			
Use of change champions	X	x	x					
Use of skilled change agents		x		x				
Involvement of change recipients	X					x	x	
Senior management involvement		x						
Relationship & coalition building			x	x	x			x
Partnership approach: problems and finding solutions		x	x		x			
Use of informal authority & formal authority and structures			x	x				
Internal focus that takes into account external environmental factors								
Balance hard and soft skills					x		x	
Regular accurate communication			x	x		x		x
Publicising of successes		x						
All parties (I e change recipients) should understand what is expected of them		x						
All parties should understand change and the potential impacts		x	x		x			
Commitment from both change agents and recipients		x						x
Reinforcement of change after it has been implemented				x	x			
Resistence to be identified and managed		x			x		x	
Use a set of guidelines		x	x	x				

Figure 1. Guidelines Implementing Change (GIC) model

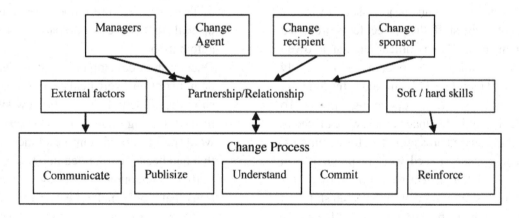

301

views opposed the upcoming change) for fear of losing their jobs but would remain unhappy with the change and perhaps even actively resist the change. Once the new system had been deployed, staff would also be afraid to ask for help if they were battling with a task because they do not want to be viewed as incompetent and hence singled out for retrenchment – in the event that it becomes necessary.

ACTIONS TAKEN TO MINIMISE THE FORESEEN IMPACT

The project team and the management and the project team decided that the only way to effectively minimise the human impacts brought about by the change would be to use their knowledge of their staff and put together an appropriate combination of change management strategies to assist the process of change.

The following interventions were put in place:

1. Staff representatives from a cross section of the organisation were involved in the joint application design (JAD) sessions in which the system requirements were elicited, to ensure that their needs were adequately catered for but also to ensure that staff participated in the debates that took place in shaping the requirements.

2. Taking into account the job insecurity felt by a lot of the staff, the project team proposed a means of communication that allowed staff to raise their concerns anonymously would facilitate dialogue and in the long run build buy in for the upcoming changes. To achieve this, feedback boxes were placed in all the shared areas for staff for comments. These issues raised were responded to in a newsletter. Effectively, this allowed for two way communication between staff and management but offered the staff security in anonymity.

3. A small group of staff was selected to be peer change champions (PCC). They were nominated by the staff themselves. The PCC would be an approachable advocate of the change, they would provide an empathetic ear and they would provide a non threatening platform through which staff members could influence the changes.

4. The PCC were also responsible for producing a fortnightly internal staff newsletter. Content of the newsletter covered progress updates on the project, responses to questions/concerns dropped in the feedback boxes as well as other topics of interest.

5. Towards the communication mechanisms discussed above, each manager scheduled a monthly informal chat with their staff. During the chats, management also made sure to reiterate their position on retrenchments, to allay the fears of job losses. This mode of communication was earnest and direct and it was helpful as a tool to build buy in.

6. To assist those members of staff who were not confident in their computer literacy skills, a set of computers was set up with a self training CD to explore and familiarise themselves with using a computer, in their own time, without being embarrassed about learning the basics aside some computers who may be more advanced. The availability of this infrastructure empowered them to up skill themselves in preparation for the automation

7. Once system development was underway, demonstrations were held every 6 weeks to showcase functionality of the new system to staff. During these demonstrations, staff would be introduced to any new functionality that had been incorporated into the system. Staff was encouraged to bring up suggestions that would make it easier for them to perform their jobs on the system, based on their knowledge of the work environment.

The sessions were used as a tool to communicate progress in a visual way, it was also used to build buy in from the staff as well as providing them an opportunity to influence the shape that the changes would take.

8. Once a working prototype of the new system had become available, a few computers were set up with the prototype. This prior interaction with the system provided a good basis for formal training as staff.

9. To maintain enthusiasm, a countdown to the implementation date was done. When key milestone were reached, small gifts with a meaning related to the change would be distributed to staff with an encouraging message. These gestures were small but very much appreciated by the staff.

10. In addition to the newsletter, important information relating to the project was posted on notice boards that were located in all the public areas.

11. As part of the project, a formal training program was devised to teach the staff how to use the new system.

EVALUATION OF THE CHANGE MANAGEMENT PRINCIPLES

Attainment of Quick and Visible Results

When defining the information system project, it was agreed that the project would be broken down into smaller deliverables. The advantages of this principle were the following:

- Delivering the system in a number of iterations would also enable incorporation of lessons learned into future iterations;
- The risk of functionality being rendered irrelevant and futile if it took too long to deliver was eliminated.

- The organisation needed to evaluate the financial benefits delivered by an iteration of the system before investing more funds into building more functionality
- Delivering 'bite size chunks' of the system would be less overwhelming for the change recipients and would be easier to manage for the change agents

Even though little emphasis was placed on change management as a reason for the iterative delivery of the system, Loans Inc, did act in accordance with this change management principle

Balance Hard and Soft Skills

The project management team selected to run this project were experts in the respective fields namely project management, information technology and human resource management. None of them was an expert in managing the impact of change on people. This was a shortcoming in ABCD Inc's criteria for selecting a project team. To ensure sufficient focus on change management, a change management expert should have been included in the project team. Despite the lack of change management expertise, the change project was still delivered successfully. This success can be attributed mainly to the sensitivity to issues affecting staff, as a result of the change. This balance between the hard and soft skills was of paramount importance in the successful delivery of the project.

Change Recipient Understanding of What is Expected of Them

To enable staff to understand the influence of the implementation, system demonstrations were used to paint a vivid picture of the future. By participating part in the requirements gathering sessions and receiving formal training, staff were further able to understand the roles they would play in the organisation, after the IS had been implemented.

It is the author's view that this function could be bettered by placing more direct focus on assisting staff to understand what was expected of them through measures such as redefining job profiles.

Commitment to the Change from Both Change Agents and Change Recipients

Members of the project team were selected on the basis of their expertise, as well as their attitude to change. This ensured that only people who were committed to the change were part of driving the change throughout the organisation. To cultivate commitment incentives for early delivery were built into the contract together with penalties for late delivery. This ensured that the vendor was committed and put in the necessary effort to deliver on time. Regular, relevant and open communication together with the chats with management was vital for staff to advance up the commitment curve proposed by Vale.

Creation of a Vision

The creation of a vision for this IS project was articulated verbally by the project sponsor, to all the affected employees and reinforced in the chats with management. Staff could form a dream about how they could best take advantage of the functionality to make their task performance more efficient. Not writing down the vision was a shortcoming because this approach left too much open for interpretation. Despite the shortcoming, the project was not compromised as it was still delivered successfully, even in the eyes of staff (Based on 360 recipients who gave feedback of the project).

Internal Focus That Takes Into Account External Environmental Factors

As part of the project process a SWOT analysis (strengths, weaknesses, threats, and opportunities) was done to identify areas that need focus. Also, a study of best practises was done on similar processes to establish how other organisations had approached similar challenges. In addition to that a competitor analysis was done to determine what competitors were doing to address problems similar to those that Loan Inc was trying to address. These analyses enabled the project team to form a view about the environment external to Loan Inc.

Involvement of Change Recipients

Various stakeholders were involved in project meetings and in requirements gathering workshops to provide feedback on how things could be improved. This involvement was instrumental in generating buy in for the project as this enabled staff to feel a sense of ownership towards the system. This sense of ownership also came through when technical problems arose with the system. Instead of assigning blame, staff members took ownership of working collaboratively with the technical team to ensure that the system was working as it should.

Partnership Approach to Diagnosing Problems and Finding Solutions

By presenting metrics that indicated the seriousness of the current situation as well as the best practise research and competitor analysis staff was supported to understand the situation. This improved the process to diagnose a problem and find a solution. Hierarchy and bureaucracy were set aside to make way for spirited debates among staff, the project team and management. These debates were very constructive as they generated solutions and ideas that improve the process of change.

Proactive Identification and Management of Resistance

In the planning phase of the project potential risks of resistance to the change was identified. The identified risk areas were documented and strategies were put in place to address those risks of resistance. The main strategy used to manage potential resistance was open communication. Having understood that the main reason for resistance was the fear of job losses following process automation, a strong message was sent out repeatedly through the various channels of communication, news letter, chats with management, change champions to let staff know that there were no intentions to retrench staff as applications volumes were increasing at a rate that justified hiring more staff even after the process automation.

Publicising of Successes

While the project was underway, completion of key milestones (requirements specification finalised, system development underway, etc) were publicised through the newsletter, notice boards and the monthly chats with management. This let staff know that they were a few steps closer to reaching the dream and it provided motivation to go on even when things got a little uncomfortable. The project sponsor personally thanked all contributors publicly. This gesture of thanks was very well received, to the extent that after the event, staff was motivated to get going with the enhancements to the system!

Regular, Accurate and Relevant Communication

Multiple channels of communication were used such as monthly chats with management, change champions, newsletter and notice boards. Feedback from the change recipients was obtained through the feedback boxes, the dialogue at the monthly chats as well as through the change champions.

Reinforcement of Change After it Has Been Implemented

A great shortfall in the ABCD Inc project was that there were no specific strategies put in place to reinforce the change after it had been implemented. The only thing that facilitated maintenance of the change was the reporting metrics that continued to show improvement as a result of the process automation, to the extent that people remained committed to working in the new way of doing things as they could see the good results for themselves.

Relationship and Coalition Building

The operations manager, who was also the project sponsor identified the sales manager, the technology executive as well as the CEO as key allies for ensuring that this project was successfully implemented. These parties were invited to all strategic meeting pertaining to the project, they were kept in the loop on the progress of the project and the operations manager ensured that he put in effort to maintain close relationships with these parties throughout the life of the projects.

Senior Management Involvement and Visibility

The sponsor of this IS project was so committed to this project to the extent that he attended all project meetings including weekly project update meetings and requirements gathering sessions (even though in Loans inc it was customary for management to attend only meetings in which high level decisions were made). He also did a walk about on the operations floor once a week and asked staff for their opinions on how things were going and what they believed needed to change. This level of involvement and visibility sent a clear message throughout the organisation that the project sponsor was committed to this change and he would do all he can to ensure it was implemented successfully.

Understanding of the Change and Its Potential Impacts

During the project definition stage, a detailed impact assessment was done on the change. This identified the stakeholders were and how each of them would be affected by the change. Once the impacts had been identified, mitigating actions were put in place to minimise the impact of the change on the identified stakeholders. Such mitigating actions included formal training for staff, as well as upgrading of information technology infrastructure. The one drawback to this process was that the impact assessment was not reviewed regularly; an impact matrix was drawn upfront and from there on, the impacts was dealt with as part of the risks and it is the author's belief that it would have been valuable to do so as each iteration is different to the next.

Use of Change Champions

Change champions bridged the divide between management and staff as they understood the terminology and reasoning used by management. They could also relate to the concerns and fears of the employees. By virtue of this dual understanding, they were able to facilitate developing a common understanding between the two parties whose views differ at the best of time. In this sense, the change champions provided a valid and useful perspective on the organisation during the period of change

Use of Informal Authority In Addition to Formal Authority and Structures

The change champions constituted a significant portion of the use of informal authority to muster support for the change. In addition to that, the labour unions represented in the organisation were approached and the idea of the change was sold to them – this was necessary as they had potential to put up significant resistance, if not bought into the change. The project sponsor used his influence in the executive committee to ensure that the project gained the priority required for resource allocation.

Use of Skilled Change Agents to Implement Change

The change agents used (part of the project team) were experts in the hard skills required (project management, system development etc) but none of them were skilled in managing the impact of technology change on people. On hindsight this was an immense shortfall in the change project as all change management activities were done 'blindly'.

Use of Guidelines

Aside from the best practise research, which focused on the technology implementation rather than change management practises, little effort was made to identify guidelines to follow in managing how this change affected people at Loans Inc. All the change management interventions that were put in place were done so intuitively, without guidelines or past experience to provide guidance. This was a major shortcoming.

CONCLUSION

This paper explores the management of change by using a set of guidelines or principles as set out in literature. It is clear from this research study that the process of change cannot be disregarded in an organization and needs to be specifically addressed to minimize the possibility of failure of the implementation of the new system.

In this paper we proposed an approach to implementing change to address these challenges. The GIC model was compiled to enhance the standard management of change practices and thus also to address challenges encountered due to the unique and changing environment of SPM. The GIC model is specifically tailored to address features driving failure. As is evident from this investigation, the results of using the GIC model, for the implementation of change in this case study, is that it is extremely suitable for handling complex and dynamically situations. We believe that our solution is significant, based on our experience in other fields that advocate management of change. This research is aimed at software project managers, software practitioners and software developers, but will also be beneficial to researchers working in the field of SPM. As the development of software projects supporting crucial business activities may be utilized to attain a competitive advantage for that organization, the successful implementation of the developed system is of utmost importance.

REFERENCES

Bodea, B., Dascala, M., & Coman, M. (2010). Quality of project management education and training programmes. *International Journal of Knowledge Society Research*, *1*(2), 13–25. doi:10.4018/jksr.2010040102

Chatzoglou, P. D., & Macaulay, L. A. (1997). The importance of human factors in planning the requirements capture stage of a project. *International Journal of Project Management*, *15*(1), 39–53. doi:10.1016/S0263-7863(96)00038-5

Clarke, L. (1994). *The essence of change* (pp. 39-43, 37-113). Upper Saddle River, NJ. Prentice Hall.

Cowley, B. (2007). Why change succeeds: An organizational assessment. *Organization Development Journal*, *1*(25), 25–30.

Doherty, N., King, M., & Al-Mushayt, O. (2003). The impact of inadequacies in the treatment of organizational issues in information systems development projects. *Information & Management*, *41*, 49–62. doi:10.1016/S0378-7206(03)00026-0

Griffith, J. (2001). Why change management fails. *Journal of Change Management*, *2*(4), 297–304. doi:10.1080/714042516

Hernandez-Lopez, A., Colomo-Palacios, R., Garcia-Crespo, A., & Soto-Acosta, P. (2010). Trust building process for global software development teams. A review. *International Journal of Knowledge Society Research*, *1*(1), 65–82. doi:10.4018/jksr.2010010105

Isabella, L. (1990). Evolving interpretations as a change unfolds: How managers construe key organizational events. *Academy of Management Journal*, *33*(1), 7–41. doi:10.2307/256350

Kitchen, P. J., & Daly, F. (2002). Internal communication during change management. *Corporate Communications*, *7*(1), 46–53. doi:10.1108/13563280210416035

Kotter, J. P. (2002). *The heart of Change*.

Kotter, J. P., & Schlesinger, L. A. (1979). Choosing strategies for change. *Harvard Business Review*, 106–114.

Krovi, R. (1993). Identifying the causes of resistance to IS implementation: A change theory perspective. *Information & Management*, *25*, 327–335. doi:10.1016/0378-7206(93)90082-5

McKeen, J. D., & Smith, H. A. (2003). *Making IT happen: critical issues in IT management* (pp. 75–90). New York: Wiley.

McNish, M. (2002). Guidelines for managing change: A study of their effects on the implementation of new information technology projects in organizations. *Journal of Change Management, 3*(2), 201–211.

Orlikowski, W. J. (1996). Improvising organizational transformation over time. *Information Systems Research, 7*(1), 63–92. doi:10.1287/isre.7.1.63

Paper, D., & Ugray, Z. (2008). Change Management: A Sensible Approach for IT Researchers. *Journal of Information Technology Case and Application Research, 3*(8), 1–8.

Robertson, J. A. (2004). *The critical factors for information technology investment success* (pp. 111–117). Johannesburg, South Africa: J A Robertson and Associates.

Scharma, R. S., Ng, E. W. J., Dharmawirya, M., & Samual, E. M. (2010). A Policy framework for developing knowledge societies. A review. *International Journal of Knowledge Society Research, 1*(1), 22–45.

Schwalbe, K. (2010). *Information Technology Project Management* (3rd ed.). London: Thomson Course Tech.

Sonnekus, R., & Labuschagne, L. (2003). IT Project Management Maturity versus Project Success in South Africa. *The Prosperus Report*.

The Standish Group International. (n.d.). *Latest Standish Group Chaos Report. Chaos Chronicle*s. Retrieved from http://www.standishgroup.com

Vales, E. (2007). Employees CAN make a difference! Involving employees in change at Allstate Insurance. *Organization Development Journal, 4*(25), 27–31.

This work was previously published in the International Journal of Knowledge Society Research, Volume 1, Issue 4, edited by Miltiadis D. Lytras, pp. 54-68, copyright 2010 by IGI Publishing (an imprint of IGI Global).

Chapter 22
Financial Needs for a Competitive Business Model in the Knowledge Society

David Castillo-Merino
Open University of Catalonia, Spain

Dolors Plana-Erta
Open University of Catalonia, Spain

ABSTRACT

This paper investigates the constraints for companies to innovate in order to be competitive in the knowledge society. Using a large and original data set of Catalan firms, the authors have conducted a micro econometric analysis following Henry et al.'s (1999) investment model and von Kalckreuth (2004) methodology empirically contrasting the relationship between firms' investment spread over time and their financial structure. Results show that it exits a positive and significant relationship between firms' investment shift and financial structure, emerging financial constraints for more innovative firms. Furthermore, these constraints are higher for micro companies and firms within the knowledge-advanced services' industry. Finally, the authors find that advanced ICT uses by more innovative firms allow them to reduce constraints of access to sources of finance.

INTRODUCTION

Under the assumption of imperfect capital markets, the access of firms to financial resources differs depending on the importance of information asymmetry, uncertainty and agency problems. These constraints generate a wedge between the costs of external finance and the opportunity costs of internal resources (von Kalckreuth, 2003). A critical consequence of this fact is that sources of finance do not fit with the neo-classical hypothesis (Modigliani & Miller, 1958). As they are no longer perfect substitutes, the amount of internally generated funds may matter to the firm's investment decision.

Concerning investment behaviour in firms, there is an increasing number of works that give evidence about the existence of financial

DOI: 10.4018/978-1-4666-1788-9.ch022

constraints for innovative firms[1]. This kind of constraints can be explained through the trade-off between the characteristics of investments in innovation, as they are risky, highly specific and showing cash flow returns in the long term, and the usual behaviour of financiers, which is characterised by a short term orientation and risk aversion. In addition, financial constraints are empowered by the existence of information asymmetries between managers and financing agents (Goodacre & Tonks, 1995). Despite of the empirical evidence available about the significant differences on the financial structure of innovative and non-innovative firms which explain that innovators are more likely to experience financial constrains (Fazzari et al., 1988), it has been demonstrated that successful innovative activity by firms allow them to obtain monopoly profits, which emerge as important internal resources avoiding firms' dependence of external financial sources and decreasing the scope of financial constrains (von Kalckeuth, 2004). Accordingly, firms' size and their adjustment capability (von Kalckreuth, 2006), the ownership of tangible assets, the existence of sustainable profitability rates, and their market position, can explain different intensity levels of financial constraints.

Within this framework, this paper aims to enlarge our understanding about the role of finance in the explanation of investment decisions in firms, the significant differences between financial structure of innovators and non-innovators, and the potential of ICT uses to overcome financial constraints inherent to innovative activities. To do that, we have divided the paper in four sections. Section II is focused on the literature review about the existent theoretical and empirical evidences in the relationship between innovation, finance and ICT uses. Section III presents the hypotheses, the methodology and the data set. Section IV contains our statistical test results. And, finally, Section V concludes the paper.

THEORETICAL FRAMEWORK: INNOVATION, FINANCE AND ICT USES

Investment decisions in innovative firms are influenced by financial structure. Empirical literature results in this field show that there are important constrains for financing innovative investments among companies. These constrains emerge for the lack of equilibrium between the economic traits of innovation and the economic behaviour of finance agents. As financial resources are not perfectly allocated among firms, differences between external resources cost and the opportunity cost of internal resources emerge. The different theories that try to explain this relationship argue that a firms' profitability (Henry et al., 1999), the disposal of free internal cash flow and the cost of external resources affects significantly the decision of investment in innovation.

Theories of capital structure, although they do not tend to focus directly on firms' technological traits, but are useful to identify the causes that may explain why more innovative firms use to have a particular financial structure and favour some particular sources of finance (Aghion et al., 2004).

FINANCIAL CONSTRAINS OF INNOVATORS' INVESTMENTS

The causes of financial constraints for innovative firms have been explained in the international literature through different approaches.

One approach emphasises information asymmetries between investors and firms' managers. Difficulties in assessing future cash flows from innovative activity generates the emergence of this lack of equilibrium and it can result in some positive net present value investments not being financed (Goodacre & Tonks, 1995). This situation reflects the effects of short-termism in capital markets (Innovation Advisory Board, 1990) and it originates out of the interaction of financing and investment decisions, as the suppliers of finance have less information available about the profitability of investment projects than firms' managers or entrepreneurs. Information asymmetries can be divided in two main situations (Laffont & Maskin, 1980): *i)* adverse selection, leaded by hidden information from managers to financiers; and *ii)* agency problems, leaded by managers' hidden actions.

Adverse selection leads to signalling problems (Myers, 1984; Myers & Majluff, 1984; Miller & Rock, 1985; Stein, 1989) that have as a consequence equilibrium points where there are under-investment decisions. For instance, under the assumptions of the most well-known signalling model, Myers' (1984) "Pecking Order" theory of capital structure, firms rank their financial resources, preferring the use of free internal sources first, then external debt and finally external new equity to fund investments, due to the effect of dilution costs. Thus, the inherent conflict of interest between equity and debt holders led to under-investment.

These adverse selection effects on investments are greater for more innovative firms, because they usually show higher levels of asymmetric information between insiders and outsiders, and, hence, dilution costs tend to be higher. Therefore, more innovative firms are likely to be more reluctant on external sources of funds, but are likely to favour debt over new equity among external resources of finance, in order to avoid the relatively high dilution costs (Aghion et al., 2004).

In his seminal work, Arrow (1962) recognized that the risk-shifting solutions to under-investment might lead to incentive problems. The trade-off between principal and agent utilities usually implies that adopted policies lead to a sub-optimal decision of investment according to firms' utility, preferring to promote short-term non-innovative investment projects as they are easier to be monitorized by owners and controlled by managers. In fact, all the different papers conducted in this field[2] adopt optimal contracts that results in an

allocation of financial sources that is bellow the first best.

Another approach focuses on bankruptcy costs (Brealy & Myers, 2003). These costs tend to be relatively lower in non-innovative firms, as they usually show a higher proportion of tangible capital among their assets, and higher in innovative firms, because they use to have a more important proportion of intangible assets. In this last case, for a given level of debt, the risk of bankruptcy may also be higher. This factor implies that more innovative firms are likely to be less reliant on external debt to fund their investments, in order to minimise their expected bankruptcy costs.

Finally, a third different approach emphasizes control rights (Hart, 1995). According to this theory, the lower the value of tangible assets inside a firm, the higher is the interest of outside investors on having control over the firm's decisions in order to satisfy their wealth constraints. This alternative theory of the pecking order also predicts that innovative firms will favour internal funds, in order to reduce the pressure of outside investors on control rights, but differently suggests that these firms will be likely to prefer new equity rather than debt among the external sources of finance.

ICT USES AND FINANCIAL CONSTRAINS

The use of digital technologies in managing and operating finance and investment in firms flow may lead to a reduction of the financial constraints that affect more innovative firms. Two are the main factors that explain this assumption.

On one hand, a direct effect. ICT uses for financing purposes may improve the information flow between managers and suppliers of finance, leading to a better equilibrium that reduces under-investment, based on a higher convergence of managers and financiers future clash flows' expectations. These dilution of information asymmetries can happen in two ways: *i)* through the interest of suppliers of finance to fund more risky and long-term investment projects under the assumption of a higher amount and quality of information available; and *ii*) through the use of digital technologies as a channel of signalling and monitoring investment projects, and, thus, avoiding the need to conduct short-term projects as a signal of better rates of firms' profitability.

On the other hand, an indirect effect. As it has been demonstrated in growth microeconomics (Bresnahan et al., 2002), when ICT adoption and use are well combined by firms with a suitable organizational structure and practice and with high labour skills, the advanced use of digital technologies arise as a source of firm's efficiency, contributing to explain the increase of labour productivity.

The main consequence of the abovementioned effects might be the reduction of financial constraints affecting more innovative firms, by the decrease of the amount of net positive investment projects remaining unfunded, and the short-termism of the suppliers of finance.

HYPOTHESES, METHODOLOGY AND DATA SET

Within this framework, we aim to verify a set of hypotheses:

- **H1:** Financial variables, measured by financial profitability, financial structure, cost of funds and internal free cash flow, is significant determinants of firms' investment levels.
- **H2:** Investment decisions in innovative firms are limited by financial constraints, showing a positive and significant relation between firms' financial structure and the investment in intangible assets.
- **H3:** Financial constraints can be explained by with firms' size, reflecting that the lower is a firm's size, the higher are the fi-

nancial constraints affecting its investment decisions.

- **H4:** Financial constraints affecting investment decisions in innovative firms are particularly higher in innovative services, due to a lower proportion of tangible capital among their assets compared to manufacturing industries.
- **H5:** Advanced ICT uses allow innovative firms to reduce their financial constraints affecting their investment decisions, as there is a decrease of the relationship intensity between financial variable and investment expansion.

Following Henry et al. (1999), we specify a general model that takes the following functional form:

$$\Delta I_i = \beta_0 + \beta_1 \Delta Rf_i + \beta_2 \Delta Ef_i + \beta_3 \Delta Cf_i + \beta_4 FT\_03_i + \beta_5 DEf\_01_i + \beta_6 CAj\_03_i + \mu_i$$

In order to contrast a relationship of causality, in the first place, we defined the following variables in Table 1.

In order to investigate the relationship between innovation and the determinants of firms' investment demand we use a direct approach by relying on explicit statements by the firms themselves. We are able to explore a micro data base of PIC (Project Internet Catalonia[4]) for 2001 and 2003 years. The sample was generated carrying out a survey by questionnaire[5] resulting on a representative sample of 2.038 Catalan firms, quoted by firms' size and economic sector[6].

Apart from its size, the data set has two relevant characteristics to our analysis. First, it contains many data on small firms, on which very little information is available from micro data sets usually based on quoted companies. Second, firms report on their innovation behaviour. They state whether or not a product innovation was achieved during the two past years and whether or not it was made on a technological basis.

Table 1. Definition of the variables of the model to contrast

Acronym	Name	Definition
Dependent variable		
ΔI_i	Variation of company's i total assets, exercise 2003 respect to exercise 2001.	
Financial independent variables		
ΔRf_i	Variation of company's i financial yield, 2003 respect to 2001.	The financial yield has been calculated as the quotient between the net result and the shareholders equity founds at the end of the year.[3]
ΔEf_i	Variation of company's i financial structure, 2003 respect to 2001.	The financial structure is the quotient between debt and shareholders equity at the end of the year.
ΔCf_i	Variation of company's i debt's cost, 2003 respect to 2001.	The debt is obtained as the quotient between financial expenses and the balance of debts with cost at the end of year.
FT_03_i	Cash Flow by unit sold generated by firm i, during the 2003 fiscal year.	It has been calculated as the quotient between the net result, adjusted by depreciation, allowances and working capital variation, divided by the net amount of revenues.
Real independents variables		
DEf_01_i	Company's i distance to technical efficiency frontier, 2001	This variable is measured by the average difference between the ratio of company's income by sales on assets and the maximum value of the ratio for the sample's set.
CAj_03_i	Company's i adjustment cost, 2003 respect to 2001.	It is measured through the ratio between the differential of the operating income by the differential of operational costs.

Source: Own elaboration.

In order to verify our hypotheses, we have divided the sample in two groups: *innovative firms* and the rest of the companies, which have been labelled as *non-innovative firms*. In order to identify these innovative firms, we have created a dichotomizing variable that:

- It takes value 1, when Catalan companies affirm that: a) has introduced some type of general innovation with the use of the ICT; b) has introduced some type of product innovation with the support of the ICT; and c) have introduced some type of innovation of process with the use of the ICT;
- And value 0 in the alternative case.

We also aim to verify that there is an inverse relationship between firms' size and the existence of financial constraints to finance investment growth. This inverse relation is fulfilled for the innovative companies as well as for the non-innovative companies. For this contrast, we have defined a variable measuring firms' size, which takes the following values:

- 1, when the company has 5 or less workers;
- 2, when the company has of 6-9 workers;
- 3, when the company has of 10-19 workers;
- 4, when the company has of 20-99 workers;
- 5, when the company has 100 or more workers.

We have checked the validity of this relationship by making an analysis of the variance between firm's size and investment behaviour. Then, we have contrasted it with our general model, but this time dividing the universe for each one of the dimensions significantly linked with assets variation.

In order to analyse the industry effect on the emergence of firms' financial constraints for investment, we have created a sector variable that takes the following values:

- 0 when the company belongs to the information industry;
- 1 when the company belongs to manufacturing industry; and
- 2 when the company belongs to the services industry.

Following the usual methodology, we have contrasted the effects of association between firms' investment and industry group by running our general model in a sample divided according to these three categories of economic activity.

And, finally, we want also to verify that advanced ICT uses allow innovative firms to reduce their financial constraints affecting their investment decisions. To reach this goal, we have divided the general sample in two groups, one of them conformed by those companies with ICT's low use and the other by companies that make an ICT's average or advanced use. Additionally to the general analysis for the Catalan company set, innovative and non-innovative companies have been also separated.

RESULTS

The explanation of firms' investment patterns can be address through a complementary approach: i) by analysing the contribution of real variables, including several hypotheses concerning companies' size, the emergence of sunk costs, the firm's distance to the technical efficiency frontier or some extern shocks; and ii) by considering the effect of firms' financial structure on investment decisions.

In this sense, we have conducted an analysis to demonstrate the significant effect of firms' access to financial resources on the explanation of investment growth, and to identify financial constraints affecting firms that develop innovative activities.

The results from the estimation of the general model (852 companies) by OLS, show that the expansion of firms' investment depends on their ability to obtain financial resources, either of in-

ternal resources, (i.e., the free internal cash flow that allow firms to face their financial necessities), or of external resources (new shareholders equity and liabilities). Indeed, as it can seen in Table 2, the coefficients β of our general model are significant and positive, showing a strong relationship between finance and investment demand in firms. Furthermore, the model has an explanatory capacity of 52%. In this sense, it is important to emphasize that more than 50% of companies' shift in investment is explained by the traits of their financial structure (ΔEf_i). In the global sample, the real variables we have defined, distance to the efficient frontier and adjustment costs, and are not revealed as significant in the explanation of investment changes in firms.

The second causal relation we set out to contrast is the emergence of financial constraints to satisfy the investment needs in innovative companies.

Firstly, we have verified, through an analysis of variance, the association between firms' investment, measured through the shift of the amount of total assets, and the innovating behaviour of Catalan companies.

Secondly, we have analysed this relationship with our general model, by sectioning, this time, the sample between non-innovators and innovators. The results of this analysis of the association between the investment's shift and firms' innovating behaviour, confirm the existence of the link between these two variables (investment decisions and innovative firms). The estimation of the coefficients β of our general model, now, nevertheless, for a sample of 517 innovative companies, allows us to verify the positive and significant relationship between innovative firms' investment and the variables measuring companies' financial structure, with a R^2 of 63% (Table 2). Therefore, and as it was expected, we have been able to obtain evidence about the relevant effect of financial resources on the growth of innovative firms' investment, as financial variables are also

Table 2. Determinants of the explanatory investment model in Catalan companies. 2001-2003 (model of multiple linear regressions; dependent variable: investment variation between 2003 and 2001)

		Values of β standardized					
Determinants of investment growth	Catalan firms. General case	Segmentation according to innovation degree:		Segmentation according to size and innovation degree:		Segmentation according to industry and innovation degree:	
		Innovative companies	Non-innovative companies	innovative micro companies	Non-innovative micro companies	Innovative of the sector services	Non-innovative micro companies of the sector services
(Constant)							(**)
ΔRf_i	0,167*	0,159*	0,138*	0,191*	0,151*	0,178*	0,106
ΔEf_i	0,607*	0,667*	0,225*	0,716*	0,368*	0,711*	0,246
ΔCf_i	0,202*	0,139*	0,254*	0,107*	0,328*	0,149*	0,311*
FT_03_i	0,204*	0,242*	0,066	0,266*	0,089	0,218*	0,097*
DEf_01_i	0,003	0,105*	-0,295*	0,111*	-0,387*	0,069*	-0,249*
CAj_03_i	-0,025	-0,018	-0,092	0,002	-0,201*	-0,019	-0,090
N	852	517	335	421	297	374	237
R^2 adjusted	0,522	0,628	0,195	0,732	0,328	0,701	0,229

* $\beta < 0,05$

** Nonsignificant constant

Source: Own elaboration.

in this analysis those independent variables with a greater explanatory weight.

In addition to these results, we have also analysed the financial determinants of investment in non-innovative firms, through a subsample of 335 companies. We have found that financial variables do show also for his type of firms a significant effect on the explanation of investment growth, but with a lower explanatory power than in the case of innovative firms, confirming that non-innovative companies are not showing financial constraints, as their investment decisions are not conditioned by the availability of free internal cash flow (FT_03).

When sectioning the general sample according to the innovating behaviour, the distance to the technical efficiency frontier (DEf_01), which is a relevant real variable, becomes significant in the explanation of companies' investment behaviour, emerging as an additional determinant for firms to conduct investment decisions. It's also important

to highlight that the effect of a firm's distance to the technical efficiency frontier on investment shift does not show the same pattern for innovative and non-innovative companies. In fact, this is a significant variable both for innovative and non-innovative firms, but with an opposite sign, reflecting a positive effect for innovative firms and a negative one for non-innovative (see Table 2). It can be explained by the fact that innovative companies usually need to reach high efficiency levels to assure increasing profitability rates and, thus, low efficiency levels act as a promoting factor for increasing investment demand. On the opposite side, non-innovative firms showing low levels of efficiency appear to have difficulties to undertake investment decisions.

Thirdly, we have empirically contrasted the relationship between firms' size and investment growth. As expected, we have found an inverse relationship between these two variables. And this inverse link is met in both cases, for innovative and non-innovative companies. Our analysis of contingencies corroborates the positive association between both variables. The estimation of the β coefficients in our general model allows us to verify the positive and significant relationship (with a R^2 of 73%) between investment shift in innovative micro-companies and firms financial structure. In this sense, we have found a positive and significant link (adjustment of 33%) between micro-firms investment and three out of four financial variables (Table 2). The comparison of the coefficients of the kindness of the adjustment demonstrates, this way, the high explanatory power of the financial variables in the analysis of the variation of the investment for the innovative micro companies.

Among the effects of real variables on the investment behavior of innovative micro-companies, we want to stress that the distance to the technical efficiency frontier (DEf_01) shows, as in the general case, a significant impact. And, as well as in the previous case, we have found and opposite sign when separating between innovative and non-innovative micro-companies, with a positive effect for the former case, and a negative impact in the second one.

Fourthly, we have analysed the complementarities between firms' financial structure and industry belonging on the explanation of investment growth. Here, we have demonstrated that the economic sector is another important determinant for a better understanding of firms' investment flows. The variance analysis corroborates the existence of different investment pattern depending on to which industry a company belongs. The estimation of β coefficients in our general model for this new firms' subsample, allows us to verify a positive and significant association (adjustment of 70%) between firms' investment variation and financial structure for those companies belonging to the service sector, evidencing the existence of financial constraints affecting investing decisions. Further, we have also found that innovative firms belonging to this industry show a higher level of

financial constraints that the non-innovative ones, as for this later case the relationship is positive and significant only for debt and internal free cash flow availability (Table 2). Thus, for this kind of companies, non-innovative firms belonging the service industry, financial constraints are not a so hard barrier to conduct investments than for their innovative counterpart.

Concerning the behaviour of real variables, we have found here exactly the same patterns as in the two previous cases: relevancy of the distance to the technical efficiency frontier (DEf_01), showing a significant effect on investment decisions for both innovative and non-innovative companies belonging to the service sector, but with an opposite sign: a positive link for innovative firms and a negative association for non-innovative ones.

And finally, we have aimed to analyse the relationship between the use of digital technologies (ICT) by companies and firms' financial cycle. Particularly, we have studied the contribution of productive ICT uses in the overcoming of firms' financial constraints affecting innovation investment decisions.

Linear regression results (see Table 3) for the Catalan companies set confirm the emergence of financial constraints for companies with ICT's low uses (N=563), so that their propensity to invest is conditioned by restrictions of access to financial founds, especially free internal generated cash flow, but also affecting those resources externally obtained through equity increase or leverage raise. In this subsample of companies, the technical efficiency gap (DEf_01) is not a driver for increasing investment. We have also found that those companies showing ICT's intensive (advanced and average) uses (N=289) are more likely to experience a decrease of their financial constraints for conducting investing strategies. This overcoming of financial handicaps is based on equity increases (Rf), by using new capital.

When focusing in innovative companies with ICT's low uses (N=296), along with financial structure, except for the debt cost (Cf), real vari-

Table 3. Explanatory model determinants of investment in Catalan companies according to ICT's uses, 2001-2003. (Model of multiple linear regressions; dependent variable: variation of the total assets between 2003 and 2001)

	Values of β standardized					
Determinants of investment	Catalan firms. General case		Segmentation according to the innovation degree:			
			Innovative companies		Non-innovative companies	
	ICT's Low uses	ICT's Advanced uses	ICT's Low uses	ICT's Advanced uses	ICT's Low uses	ICT's Advanced uses
(Constant)	(1)					
ΔRf_i	0,214*	0,051	0.256*	0,141*	0,022	0,144
ΔEf_i	0,509*	0,238*	0,781*	0,200*	0,623*	0,139
ΔCf_i	0,264*	0,639*	-0,013	0,386*	0,121*	-0,593*
FT_03_i	0,124*	0,095*	0,206*	0,076	0,245*	0,349*
DEf_01_i	-0,076*	0,042	0,201*	-0,334*	0,041	0,273*
CAj_03_i	-0,057	0,000	-0,122*	-0,096	-0,001	-0,197
N	563	289	296	267	220	68
R^2 adjusted	0,301	0,678	0,477	0,312	0,683	0,39

ables are significant determinants. However, in innovative firms with an ICT's intensive use (N=267) we have verified a high dependency on free internal cash flow generation (FT_03) for these firms to carry out investment projects, while the effect of the efficiency gap (DEf_01) does not explain an investment growth.

We can conclude, therefore, that the ICT intensive use by innovative companies allows them to reduce constraints related to obtaining the financial founds they need to carry out their investment projects.

CONCLUSION

Despite of the international consensus about the importance of firms' investment in intangible capital for promoting innovation processes and improving the sources of companies' productivity and competitiveness in a knowledge society (Sharma, 2010), there exist some constraints affecting the access by innovative companies to the financial resources they need to conduct their investments, and, thus, explaining the composition of their capital structure.

In this paper we have focused on the analysis of financial constraints affecting innovative firms' investment. On the basis of a representative sample of Catalan companies we have been able to verify that the assumptions set in the international literature are fulfilled, and that the relationship between financing and investment in companies is confirmed, so that, the existence of a positive and significant relationship between investment changes and firms' financial structure is demonstrated. In this sense, it is important to highlight that we have found empirical evidence about the fact that firms' financial structure, debt costs and internal free cash flow explain the scope and intensity of investment growth. Therefore, we have verified that financial constraints for the enterprise's investment do exist and, moreover, these constraints have an important weight in the investment patterns of innovative companies, due to the usual middle-term returns that characterise their investment activity.

It has been also empirically verified the existence of important financial constraints for investment decisions in micro companies and those belonging the services industry, being much higher than the average for innovative companies in these two subsamples. Therefore, middle-size and large firms, as well as information industry's and manufacturing companies do not show significant constraints to obtain resources for financing further investments.

Finally, and concerning the analysis of ICT uses effect on firms' investing behaviour, our results allow us to conclude intensive uses of digital technologies (companies with ICT's average and advanced uses) by innovative firms reduce, at° least partly, the well-known constraints of obtaining financial resources for further investment.

REFERENCES

Aghion, P., Bond, S., Klemm, A., & Marinescu, I. (2004). *Technology and Financial Structure: Are Innovative Firms Different?* Paper presented at the 6th Bundesbank Spring Conference Financing Innovation, Eltville, Germany.

Arrow, K. J. (1962). Economic welfare and the allocation of resources for invention. In Nelson, R. R. (Ed.), *The Rate and Direction of Invention Activity: Economic and Social Factors*. Princeton, NJ: Princeton University Press.

Bond, S., Elston, J. A., Mairesse, J., & Mulkay, B. (2003). Financial Factors and Investment in Belgium, France, Germany and the United Kingdom: A Comparison Using Company Panel Data. *The Review of Economics and Statistics, 85*, 153–165. doi:10.1162/003465303762687776

Bond, S., Harhoff, D., & van Reenen, J. (1999). *Investment, Financial Constraints and R&D in Britain and Germany* (Working Paper W99/05). London: The Institute for Fiscal Studies.

Brealy, R., & Myers, S. (2003). *Principles of Corporate Finance*. New York: Irwin/McGraw-Hill.

Bresnahan, T. F., Brynjolfsson, E., & Hitt, L. M. (2002). Information Technology, Workplace Organization, and the Demand for Skilled Labor: Firm-level Evidence. *The Quarterly Journal of Economics, 117*(1), 339–376. doi:10.1162/003355302753399526

Bundesbank, D. (2004). *Financial constraints for investors and the speed of adaptation: Are innovators special? (Discussion Papers Series 1: Studies of the Economic Research Centre No. 20)*. Deutsche Bundesbank.

CESifo. (2003, January). *On the German Monetary Transmission Mechanism: Interest Rate and Credit Channel for Investment Spending* (Working Paper 838). CESifo.

Chirinko, R. S., & von Kalckreuth, U. (2002, November). *Further Evidence on the Relationship between Firm Investment and Financial Status* (Discussion Paper 28/02). Economic Research Centre of the Deutsche Bank.

Constraints, F., & Adjustment, C. (2006). Evidence from a Large Panel of Survey Data. *Economic, 73*, 691–724.

Fazzari, S. M., Hubbard, R. G., & Petersen, B. C. (1988). Financing Constraints and Corporate Investment. *Brookings Papers on Economic Activity, 1*, 141–206. doi:10.2307/2534426

Goodacre, A., & Tonks, I. (1995). Finance and Technological Change. In Stoneman, P. (Ed.), *Handbook of the Economics of Innovation and Technological Change* (pp. 298–341). Oxford, UK: Blackwell Handbooks in Economics.

Hart, O. (1995). *Firms, Contracts and Financial Structure*. Oxford, UK: Oxford University Press. doi:10.1093/0198288816.001.0001

Henry, B., Sentance, A., & Urga, G. (1999). Finance, profitability and investment in manufacturing. In Driver, C., & Temple, P. (Eds.), *Investment, Growth and Employment. Perspectives for policy* (pp. 29–50). London: Routledge.

Holmstrom, B., & Ricart i Costa, J. E. (1986). Managerial incentives and capital management. *The Quarterly Journal of Economics*, 835–860. doi:10.2307/1884180

Laffont, J. J., & Maskin, E. (1980). The theory of incentives: an overview. In Hildenbrand, W. (Ed.), *Advances in Economic Theory* (pp. 31–94). Cambridge, UK: Cambridge University Press.

Miller, M. H., & Rock, K. (1985). Dividend policy under asymmetric information. *The Journal of Finance*, 40, 1031–1051. doi:10.2307/2328393

Modiglliani, F., & Miller, M. H. (1958). The cost of capital, corporation finance and the theory of investment. *The American Economic Review*, 48, 261–297.

Myers, S. C. (1984). The capital structure puzzle. *The Journal of Finance*, 39, 575–592. doi:10.2307/2327916

Myers, S. C., & Majluf, N. S. (1984). Corporate financing and investment decisions when firms have information that investors do not have. *Journal of Financial Economics*, 13, 187–221. doi:10.1016/0304-405X(84)90023-0

Ricart i Costa, J. E. (1989). On managerial contracting with asymmetric information. *European Economic Review*, 33(9), 1805–1830. doi:10.1016/0014-2921(89)90071-8

Sharma, R. S., Ng, E. W. J., Dharmawirya, M., & Samuel, E. M. (2010). A Policy Framework for Developing Knowledge Societies. *International Journal of Knowledge Society Research*, 1(1), 22–45.

Stein, J. C. (1989). Efficient capital markets, inefficient firms: a model of myopic corporate behaviour. *The Quarterly Journal of Economics*, 656–669.

Von Kalckreuth, U. (2003). Investment and Monetary Transmission in Germany: A Microeconometric Investigation. In Angeloni, I., Kashyap, A., & Mojon, B. (Eds.), *Monetary Policy Transmission in the Euro Area*. Cambridge, UK: Cambridge University Press. doi:10.1017/CBO9780511492372.012

ENDNOTES

[1] See Bond, Elston, Mairesse, and Mulkey (2003) for comparisons in Belgium, France, Germany and the United Kingdom; Bond, Harhoff, and van Reenen (1999), who were the first to undertake a detailed micro econometric comparison of firm investment behaviour in the United Kingdom and Germany; or von Kalckreuth (2003) and Chirinko and von Kalckreuth (2002/2003) for Germany.

[2] Such as the classical Works of Holmstrom and Weiss (1985), Holmstrom, Ricart, and Costa (1986) and Ricart and Costa (1989).

[3] We assume that the net amounts of the balance sheet at the end of period are representative of the average net amounts of the fiscal year.

[4] *The Network Company in Catalonia: ICT, Productivity, Competitiveness, Salaries and Performance in Catalonia's Companies*, funded by the Catalan Government. Available at URL: www.uoc.edu/in3/pic/eng/network_company.html

[5] The questionnaire, quite complex, includes 128 questions, as well as additional observations. The interviews, held with entrepreneurs or company directors who have a global vision of the whole activity, were generally well received and the collaboration of the

interviewed was high. In addition, we have completed the questionnaire information with economic and financial information available to the general public in the *Register Mercantile* (Mercantile Register), obtained through the SABI program.

6   In this sense, the analysis of more than 500 variables, forming a matrix of one million data about the Catalan firm, was carried out according to the common research methodology in social sciences; that is the frequency analysis, the contingency tables and the regression analysis, crossed with company sizes and economic sectors defined in the research.

Compilation of References

(1961). *Webster's New Collegiate Dictionary*. Springfield, MA: G. & C. Merriam Co. Publishers.

(2001). *Penguin*. The New PENGUIN English Dictionary.

9 Demetriadis, S., & Pombortsis, A. (2007). e-Lectures for Flexible Learning: a Study on their Learning Efficiency. *Educational Technology & Society*, *10*(2), 147–157.

AAE. (1981). *Academic American Encyclopaedia* (Vol. 5). Princeton, NJ: Cit-Cz, Arete Publishing Company Inc.

Abdel-Hamid, T. K., & Madnick, S. E. (1989). Lessons learned from modeling the dynamics of software development. *Communications of the ACM*, *32*(12), 1426–1438. doi:10.1145/76380.76383

Abelson, H. (2008). The creation of OpenCourseWare at MIT. *Journal of Science Education and Technology*, *17*(2), 164–174. doi:10.1007/s10956-007-9060-8

Abran, A., Khelefi, A., Suryn, W., & Seffah, A. (2003). Usability meanings and interpretations in ISO standards. *Software Quality Journal*, *11*, 325–338. doi:10.1023/A:1025869312943

Advances in Econometrics. (n.d.). *Stimulating and Analyzing Industrial Structure* (Vol. 10). *Association for Information Systems (AIS)*. Retrieved from http://home.aisnet.org/associations/7499/files/Index_Markup.cfm

Agarwal, R., & Prasad, J. (1998). A Conceptual and Operational Definition of Personal Innovativeness in the Domain of Information Technology. *Information Systems Research*, *9*(2), 204–215. doi:10.1287/isre.9.2.204

Aghion, P., Bond, S., Klemm, A., & Marinescu, I. (2004). *Technology and Financial Structure: Are Innovative Firms Different?* Paper presented at the 6th Bundesbank Spring Conference Financing Innovation, Eltville, Germany.

Al-adawi, Z., Yousafzai, Z., & Pallister, J. (2005). *Conceptual Model of citizen adoption of e-government*. Paper presented at the Second International Conference on Innovations in Information Technology.

AlAwadhi, S., & Morris, A. (2008). The Use of the UTAUT Model in the Adoption of E-government Services in Kuwait. In *Proceedings of the 41st Hawaii International Conference on System Sciences* (pp. 1-11). Washington, DC: IEEE Computer Society.

Albano, G., Gaeta, M., & Salerno, S. (2006). E-learning: a model and process proposal. *International Journal of Knowledge and Learning*, *2*, 73–88. doi:10.1504/IJKL.2006.009680

Albergaria Almeida, P. (2010). Scholarship of teaching and learning: an overview. *Journal of the World Universities Forum*, *3*(2), 143–154.

Albert, M. (2000). *Quantum mechanics*. New York: Dover Publications.

Albert, R., & Barabasi, A.-L. (2002). Statistical Mechanics of Complex Networks. *Reviews of Modern Physics*, *74*, 47. doi:10.1103/RevModPhys.74.47

Ali-Barbar, M., Verner, J. M., & Nguyen, P. T. (2006). Establishing and maintaining trust in software outsourcing relationships: an empirical investigation. *Journal of Systems and Software*, *80*(9), 1438–1449. doi:10.1016/j.jss.2006.10.038

Alier, M., & Barceló, M. (2005). An application of social constructionism and open source. In Mendez Villas, B., Gonzalz Pereira, J., & Mesa Gonzalez, J. A. (Eds.), *Recent research developments in learning technologies* (pp. 1170–1175).

Ally, M. (2008). Foundations of Educational Theory for Online Learning. In Anderson, T. (Ed.), *The Theory and Practice of Online Learning* (2nd ed.). Athabasca, CA: AU Press.

Almeida, P., Pedrosa de Jesus, H., & Watts, M. (2008). Developing a mini-project: students' questions and learning styles. *Psychology of Education Review, 32*(1), 6–17.

Almeida, P., Teixeira-Dias, J. J., & Medina, J. (2010). Enhancing the Scholarship of Teaching and Learning: the interplay between teaching and research. *International Journal of Teaching and Case Studies, 2*(3/4), 262–275.

Alsaghier, H., Ford, M., Nguyen, A., & Hexel, R. (2009). Conceptualising Citizen's Trust in e-Government: Application of Q Methodology. *Electronic. Journal of E-Government, 7*(4), 295–310.

Amaral, L. A. N., & Ottino, J. M. (2004). Complex networks - Augmenting the framework for the study of complex systems. *The European Physical Journal, 38,* 147–162.

Ambrosini, V., & Bowman, C. (2001). Tacit knowledge: Some suggestions for operationalization. *Journal of Management Studies, 38*(6), 811–829. doi:10.1111/1467-6486.00260

Anantatmula, V. S., & Stankosky, M. (2008). KM criteria for different types or organisations. *International Journal of Knowledge and Learning, 4*(1), 18–35. doi:10.1504/IJKL.2008.019735

Anderson, A. A. (n.d.). *Building a knowledge culture.* Retrieved September 2008 from www.robbinsgioia.com

Anderson, A. H., McEwan, R., Bal, J., & Carletta, J. (2007). Virtual team meetings: an analysis of communication and context. *Computers in Human Behavior, 23*(5), 2558–2580. doi:10.1016/j.chb.2007.01.001

Anderson, L. W., Krathwohl, D. R., Airasian, P. W., Cruikshank, K. A., Mayer, R. E., & Pintrich, P. R. (2001). *A taxonomy for learning, teaching and assessing: A revision of Bloom's taxonomy of educational objectives.* New York: Longman.

Antón, P., & Zubillaga del Río, A. (2005). *Teacher training for the deployment of ICT as a support to new models derived from the European Space of Higher Education (ESHE).* Paper presented at the First ICT meeting in the Spanish University at a Distance (UNED).

Aragonés, R., Saiz, J., Portero, A., Rullan, M., & Aguiló, J. (2006). Teaching Innovation Experience following European Space of Higher Education Guidelines in Digital Design Teaching. *Revista Latinoamericana de Tecnología Educativa, 2*(15), 203–222.

Arbaugh, J. B. (2004). Learning to learn online: A study of perceptual changes between multiple online course experiences. *The Internet and Higher Education, 7,* 169–182. doi:10.1016/j.iheduc.2004.06.001

Arias, M. (2003). *The European Higher Education Area: An opportunity for development through multi-disciplinary learning and technology.* Retrieved from http://www.usal.es/~ofeees/ARTICULOS/MarioAriasOliva%5B1%5D.pdf

Armstrong, D. J., & Cole, P. (2002). Managing distances and differences in geographically distributed work groups. In Hinds, P., & Kiesler, S. (Eds.), *Distributed Work* (pp. 167–186). Cambridge, MA: MIT Press.

Arora, A., & Gambardella, A. (2004). *The Globalization of the Software Industry: Perspectives and Opportunities for Developed and Developing Countries.* Washington, DC: National Bureau of Economic Research.

Arrow, K. J. (1962). Economic welfare and the allocation of resources for invention. In Nelson, R. R. (Ed.), *The Rate and Direction of Invention Activity: Economic and Social Factors.* Princeton, NJ: Princeton University Press.

Aubert, B., & Kelsey, B. (2003). Further understanding of trust and performance in vitual teams. *Small Group Research, 34*(5), 575–619. doi:10.1177/1046496403256011

Augar, N., Raitman, R., & Zhou, W. (2004). Teaching and learning online with wikis. In *Beyond the comfort zone: Proceedings of the 21st ASCILITE conference* (pp. 95-104).

Baars, B. J. (1997). *In the Theater of Consciousness. The Workspace of the Mind.* Oxford, UK: Oxford University Press. doi:10.1093/acprof:oso/9780195102659.001.1

Bagozzi, R. P., Davi, F., & Warshaw, P. (1992). Development and Test of a Theory of Technological Learning and Usage. *Human Relations*, *45*(7), 659–686. doi:10.1177/001872679204500702

Bagozzi, R. P., & Yi, Y. (1988). On the evaluation of structure equation models. *Journal of the Academy of Marketing Science*, *16*, 74–94. doi:10.1007/BF02723327

Bakry, S. H., & Al-Ghamdi, A. (2008, September). *A Framework for the knowledge society ecosystem: a tool for development*. Paper presented at Athens' Knowledge Society Summit.

Bakry, S. H. (2004, December). Development of e-government: A STOPE view. *International Journal of Network Management*, *14*(6), 339–350. doi:10.1002/nem.529

Bakry, S. H. (2005). *Transformation to the Knowledge Society*. Riyadh, Saudi Arabia: King Abdulaziz Public Library.

Bakry, S. H. (2008). *Knowledge Society Eco-System: in watching eyes and hopeful minds*. Riyadh, Saudi Arabia: King Saud University, Knowledge Society Program.

Bakry, S. H., & Alfantookh. (2009). Higher education for the 21st century: reviews and KC-STOPE views. *Evaluation in Higher Education*, *3*(2), 87–112.

Bakry, S. H., & Al-Ghamdi, A. (in press). *Cultural pluralism in the context of the knowledge society ecosystem: reviews and views*. Riyadh, Saudi Arabia: King Saud University. *Knowledge Society Program*.

Bandow, D. (2004). Time to create sound teamwork. *Journal for Quality and Participation*, *24*(2), 41–47.

Baqir, M. N., & Kathawala, Y. (2004). Ba for knowledge cities: A futuristic technology model. *Journal of Knowledge Management*, *8*(5), 83–95. doi:10.1108/13673270410558828

Barabasi, A.-L., & Réka, A. (1999, October 15). Emergence of scaling in random networks. *Science*, *286*, 509–512. doi:10.1126/science.286.5439.509

Barber, B. (1983). *The Logic and Limits of Trust*. New Brunswick, NJ: Rutgers University Press.

Barczak, G., McDonough, E., & Athanassiou, N. (2006). So you want to be a global project leader? *Research Technology Management*, *49*(3), 28–35.

Bauman, Z. (1999). *Modernidad líquida*. Buenos Aires, Argentina: Fondo de Cultura Económica.

Bauman, Z. (2006). *Vida líquida*. Barcelona, Spain: Paidós Iberica.

Bauman, Z. (2007). *Els reptes de l'educació en la Modernitat líquida*. Barcelona, Spain: Arcàdia.

Bearne, E. (2003). Rethinking literacy: Communication, representation, and text. *Reading Literacy and Language*, *37*(3), 98–103. doi:10.1046/j.0034-0472.2003.03703002.x

Beath, J., Katsoulacos, Y., & Ulph, D. (1989). Strategic R&D Policy. *The Economic Journal*, *9*(9), 74–83. doi:10.2307/2234071

Beaulieu, L. (1993). A Parisian café and ten prote-Bourbaki meetings: 1934-35. *The Mathematical Intelligencer*, *15*(1), 27–35.

Becker, K. (2007). Digital game-based learning once removed:Teaching teachers. *British Journal of Educational Technology*, *38*(7), 478–488. doi:10.1111/j.1467-8535.2007.00711.x

Beck, K. (1999). *Extreme Programming Explained: Embrace Exchange*. Reading, MA: Addison-Wesley Reading.

Belanger, F., & Carter, L. (2008). Trust and risk in e-government adoption. *The Journal of Strategic Information Systems*, *17*(2), 165–176. doi:10.1016/j.jsis.2007.12.002

Bell, M., & Farrier, S. (2006). Measuring Success in e-Learning - a Multi-Dimensional Approach. *Electronic Journal of e-Learning*, *6*, 99-110.

Bell, B. S., & Kozlowski, S. W. J. (2002). A typology of virtual teams. *Group & Organization Management*, *27*(1), 14–49. doi:10.1177/1059601102027001003

Bengtsson, M., & Eriksson, J. (2002). Stickiness and leakiness in inter-organizational innovation projects. In Sahlin-Andersson, K., & Söderholm, A. (Eds.), *Beyond Project Management* (pp. 81–107). Malmö, Sweden: Liber.

Bennett, E., & Maniar, N. (2008) *Are videoed lectures an effective teaching tool?* Retrieved May 15, 2009, from http://stream.port.ac.uk/papers

Beranek, P. G., & Martz, B. (2006). Making virtual teams more effective: improving relational links. *Team Performance Management*, *11*(6), 200–213. doi:10.1108/13527590510617774

Berg, B. (2004). *Qualitative Research Methods for the Social Sciences* (5th ed.). Boston: Pearson Education.

Berliant, M., & Fujita, M. (2007, November). *Knowledge creation as a square dance on the Hilbert cube* (MPRA Paper No. 4680). Retrieved from http://mpra.ub.uni-muenchen.de/4680/

Berner, E. S., & Adams, B. (2004). Added value of video compared to audio lectures for distance learning. *International Journal of Medical Informatics*, *73*, 189–193. doi:10.1016/j.ijmedinf.2003.12.001

Bertalanffy, L. (1969). *General System Theory: Foundations, Developement, Applications*. New York: George Braziller.

Bertalmio, M., Sapiro, G., Caselles, V., & Ballester, C. (2000). Image Inpainting. In *Proceedings of the SIGGRAPH* (pp. 417-424).

Bhat, J. M., Gupa, M., & Murthy, S. N. (2006). Overcoming requirements engineering challenges: lessons from offshore outsourcing. *IEEE Software*, *23*(5), 35–44. doi:10.1109/MS.2006.137

Bhattacharya, R., Devinney, T. M., & Pillutla, M. M. (1998). A Formal Model of Trust Based on Outcomes. *Academy of Management Review*, *23*(3), 459–472. doi:10.2307/259289

Bhide, A., & Stevenson, H. (1992). Trust, uncertainty, and profit. *Journal of Socio-Economics*, *21*(3), 191–208. doi:10.1016/1053-5357(92)90009-V

Biasiotti, M. A., & Nannucci, R. (2004). Teaching egovernment in Italy. In R. Traunmóller (Ed.), *Proceedings of the Third International Conference* (pp. 460-463). Zaragoza, Spain: EGOV.

Biggs, J. (1978). Individual and group differences in study processes. *The British Journal of Educational Psychology*, *48*, 266–279.

Biggs, J. (1999). *Teaching for Quality Learning at University*. London: SRHE and Open University Press.

Birkinshaw, J., & Sheehan, T. (2002, fall). Managing the Knowledge Life Cycle. *MIT Sloan Management Review*, 75-83.

Blackburn, S. (2008). *How are we to think about human nature?* Paper presented at Provost's Lecture Series On being human: 2007-2008, Duke University, Durham, NC.

Black, M. (1962). *Models and Metaphors*. Ithaca, NY: Cornell University Press.

Blanke, J., & Geiger, T. (2008). *The Lisbon Review 2008: Measuring Europe's Progress in Reform*. Washington, DC: World Economic Forum.

Blyachman, L. (2006). Innovation system as social institute of postindustrial information economy. *Problems of Modern Economics*, *3*(15). Retrieved from http://creativeconomy.ru/library/prd442.php

Bodea, C. (2007). An Innovative System for Learning Services in Project Management. In *Proceedings of 2007 IEEE/INFORMS International Conference on Service Operations and Logistics and Informatics*, Philadelphia. Washington, DC: IEEE.

Bodea, B., Dascala, M., & Coman, M. (2010). Quality of project management education and training programmes. *International Journal of Knowledge Society Research*, *1*(2), 13–25. doi:10.4018/jksr.2010040102

Bodea, C.-N., Dascalu, M., & Coman, M. (2010). Quality of project management education and training programmes. *International Journal of Knowledge Society Research*, *1*, 13–25.

Boehm, B., & Turner, R. (2003). Using risk to balance agile and plan-driven methods. *IEEE computer*, *36*(6), 57-66.

Boehm, B., Clark, B., Horowitz, E., Westland, C., Madachy, R., & Selby, R. (1995). Cost models for future software life cycle processes: COCOMO 2.0. *Annals of Software Engineering*, *1*(1), 57–94. doi:10.1007/BF02249046

Bond, S., Harhoff, D., & van Reenen, J. (1999). *Investment, Financial Constraints and R&D in Britain and Germany* (Working Paper W99/05). London: The Institute for Fiscal Studies.

Bond, S., Elston, J. A., Mairesse, J., & Mulkay, B. (2003). Financial Factors and Investment in Belgium, France, Germany and the United Kingdom: A Comparison Using Company Panel Data. *The Review of Economics and Statistics, 85*, 153–165. doi:10.1162/003465303762687776

Bontis, N. (2001). Assessing knowledge assets: a review of the models used to measure intellectual capital. *International Journal of Management Reviews, 3*(1), 41–60. doi:10.1111/1468-2370.00053

Bortz, J., & Lienert, G. A. (1998). *Kurzgefaßte Statistik für die klinische Forschung*. Berlin: Springer.

Brealy, R., & Myers, S. (2003). *Principles of Corporate Finance*. New York: Irwin/McGraw-Hill.

Bresnahan, T. F., Brynjolfsson, E., & Hitt, L. M. (2002). Information Technology, Workplace Organization, and the Demand for Skilled Labor: Firm-level Evidence. *The Quarterly Journal of Economics, 117*(1), 339–376. doi:10.1162/003355302753399526

Brew, L. S. (2008). The role of student feedback in evaluating and revising a blended learning course. *The Internet and Higher Education, 11*, 98–105. doi:10.1016/j.iheduc.2008.06.002

Brinkly, I. (2006, July). *Defining the knowledge economy*. London, UK: the Work Foundation. Retrieved September 2008 from www.theworkfoundation.com

Britannica. (n.d.). Retrieved October 2008 from www.britannica.com

Brown, B. W., & Liedholm, C. E. L. (2004). Student Preferences in Using Online Learning Resources. *Social Science Computer Review, 22*(4), 479–492. doi:10.1177/0894439304268529

Browne, C. (2001). *Saudie –Commerce Conference Lauded by Major Saudi Industry Experts, ITP*.

Bryan, C., & Clegg, C. (2006). *Innovative Assessment in Higher Education*. New York: Routledge.

Brzezinski, Z., (n.d.). *Will American superpower have a second chance* (Tech. Rep.). Duke University, Durham, NC.

Bubshait, A. A., & Farooq, G. (1999). Team building and project success. *Coastal Engineering, 41*(7), 34–38.

Bucklew, M., & Edvinsson, L. (1999). *Intellectual Capital at Skandia*. Retrieved November 26, 2006 from http://www.fpm.com/cases/el3.html

Buckley, J. (2003). E-service quality and the public sector. *Managing Service Quality, 13*(6), 453–462. doi:10.1108/09604520310506513

Buendia Garcia, F., & Hervas Jorge, A. (2006). *Evaluating e-learning platforms through SCORM specifications*. Paper presented at the IADIS Virtual Multi Conference on Computer Science and Information System (MCCSIS 2006).

Bundesbank, D. (2004). *Financial constraints for investors and the speed of adaptation: Are innovators special? (Discussion Papers Series 1: Studies of the Economic Research Centre No. 20)*. Deutsche Bundesbank.

Bürg, O., & Mandl, H. (2005). Akzeptanz von E-Learning von Unternehmen. *Zeitschrift für Personalpsychologie, 4*, 75–85. doi:10.1026/1617-6391.4.2.75

Burgos, D., Tattersall, C., & Koper, R. (2007). How to represent adaptation in e-learning with IMS learning design. *Interactive Learning Environments, 2*(15), 161–170. doi:10.1080/10494820701343736

Calvo de Mora, J. (2006). Teaching focused on students' work. *Revista de la Educación Superior, 128*. Retrieved from http://www.anuies.mx/servicios/p_anuies/publicaciones/revsup/index.html

Campbell-Kelly, M. (2003). *From airline reservations to Sonic the Hedgehog: a history of software industry*. Cambridge, MA: MIT Press.

Canon Digisuper 100xs. (n.d.). *Product Manual*. Retrieved May 20, 2006, from http://www.canon.com/bctv/products/pdf/100xs.pdf

Carmel, E. (1999). *Global Software Teams: Collaborating Across Borders and Time Zones*. Upper Saddle River, NJ: Prentice-Hall.

Carter, W. (1996). *Digital Designing with Programmable Logic Devices*. Englewood Cliffs, NJ: Prentice Hall. ISBN: 0133737217

Carter, L., & Bélanger, F. (2005). The Utilization of E-Government Services: Citizen Trust, Innovation and Acceptance Factors. *Information Systems Journal, 15*(1), 5–25. doi:10.1111/j.1365-2575.2005.00183.x

Case, J., & Marshall, D. (2009). Approaches to learning. In Tight, M., Mok, K. H., Huisman, J., & Morphew, C. C. (Eds.), *The Routledge International Handbook of Higher Education*. New York: Routledge.

Castells, M. (2000). *The Rise of the Network Society. The Information Age: Economy, Society and Culture* (*Vol. 1*). Malden, MA: Blackwell.

Castells, M., & Pekka, H. (2002). *The Information Society and the Welfare State. The Finnish Model*. Oxford, UK: Oxford University Press.

Catalyst IT. (2004). *Technical evaluation of selected portal systems*.

CESifo. (2003, January). *On the German Monetary Transmission Mechanism: Interest Rate and Credit Channel for Investment Spending* (Working Paper 838). CESifo.

Chan, C. C., Tsui, M. S., Chan, M. Y. C., & Hong, J. H. (2002). Applying the Structure of Observed Learning Outcomes (SOLO) Taxonomy on student's learning outcomes: An empirical study. *Assessment & Evaluation in Higher Education, 27*(6), 511–527. doi:10.1080/026 0293022000020282

Chatham, R. E. (2007). Games for training. *Communications of the ACM, 50*(7), 37–43. doi:10.1145/1272516.1272537

Chatti, M. A., Jarke, M., & Frosch-Wilke, D. (2007). The future of e-learning: a shift to knowledge networking and social software. *International Journal of Knowledge and Learning, 3*(4-5), 404–420. doi:10.1504/ IJKL.2007.016702

Chatzoglou, P. D., & Macaulay, L. A. (1997). The importance of human factors in planning the requirements capture stage of a project. *International Journal of Project Management, 15*(1), 39–53. doi:10.1016/S0263-7863(96)00038-5

Cheng, P., Choi, C. J., Chen, S., Eldomiaty, T. I., & Millar, C. C. J. M. (2004). Knowledge repositories in knowledge cities: institutions, conventions and knowledge sub-networks. *Journal of Knowledge Management, 8*(5), 96–106. doi:10.1108/13673270410558800

Chen, S. Y., Ghinea, G., & Macredie, R. D. (2006). A cognitive approach to user perception of multimedia quality: An empirical investigation. *International Journal of Human-Computer Studies, 64*, 1200–1213. doi:10.1016/j. ijhcs.2006.08.010

Chirinko, R. S., & von Kalckreuth, U. (2002, November). *Further Evidence on the Relationship between Firm Investment and Financial Status* (Discussion Paper 28/02). Economic Research Centre of the Deutsche Bank.

Chou, S.-W. (2005). Knowledge creation: absorptive capacity, organizational mechanisms, and knowledge storage/retrieval capabilities. *Journal of Information Science, 31*(6), 453–465. doi:10.1177/0165551505057005

Choy, S. O., & Ng, K. C. (2007). Implementing wiki software for supplementing online learning. *Australasian Journal of Educational Technology, 23*, 209–226.

Chua, B. B., & Dyson, L. E. (2004). Applying the ISO 9126 model to the evaluation of an e-learning system. In R. Atkinson, C. McBeath, D. Jonas-Dwyer, & R. Phillips (Eds.), *Beyond the comfort zone: Proceedings of the 21st ASCILITE Conference,* Perth, Australia (pp. 184-190).

Chubin, D. E., May, G. S., & Babco, E. L. (2005). Diversifying the Engineering Workforce. *The Journal of Communication, 94*(1), 73–86.

Chung, Q. B. (2005). Sage on the Stage in the Digital Age: The Role of Online Lecture in Distance Learning. *Electronic Journal of e-Learning, 3*(1), 1-14.

Civís, M., & Riera, J. (2007). *La nueva pedagogía comunitaria. Un marco renovado para la acción sociopedagógica interprofesional* (1st ed.). València, Spain: Nau Llibres.

Clarke, L. (1994). *The essence of change* (pp. 39-43, 37-113). Upper Saddle River, NJ: Prentice Hall.

Clarke, F., & Ekeland, I. (1982). Nonlinear oscillations and boundary-value problems for Hamiltonian systems. *Archive for Rational Mechanics and Analysis, 78*, 315–333. doi:10.1007/BF00249584

Clark, H. H. (1985). Language use and language users. In Lindzey, G., & Aronson, E. (Eds.), *Handbook of Social Psychology* (pp. 179–231). New York: Random House.

Clippinger, J. H. III. (1999). *The biology of business. Decoding the natural laws of enterprise*. San Francisco, CA: Jossey-Bass Publishers.

CMMI Product Team. (2006). CMMI for Development (Version 1.2) (Tech. Rep. No. CMU/SEI-2006-TR-008). Pittsburgh, PA: Carnegie Mellon University, Software Engineering Institute.

Codagnone, C., & Undheim, T.A. (2008). Benchmarking eGovernment: tools, theory, and practice. *European Journal of ePractice, 1*(4).

Cohen, D., & Prusak, L. (2001). *In good company how social capital makes organizations work*. Boston: Harvard Business School Press.

Coleman, J. S. (1990). *Foundations of social theory*. Cambridge, MA: Belknap Press of Harvard University Press.

Colesca, S. E. (2009). Increasing e-trust: a solution to minimize risk in the e-government adoption. *Journal of Applied Quantitative Methods, 4*(1), 31–44.

Colesca, S. E., & Dobrica, L. (2008). Adoption and use of e-government services: The case of Romania. *Journal of Applied Research and Technology, 6*(3), 204–217.

Collard, D., Girardot, S., & Deutsch, H. (2002). From the Textbook to the Lecture: Improving Prelecture Preparation in Organic Chemistry. *Journal of Chemical Education, 79*, 520–523. doi:10.1021/ed079p520

Collet, J. (2009). *El treball socioeducatiu en xarxa: una breu proposta de marc conceptual. Congrés de Formació per al Treball en Xarxa a la Universitat. Complexitat, corresponsabilitat i construcció del coneixement*. Retrieved from http://www.fbofill.cat/trama/pdfs/congres/marc_conceptual_treball_xarxacollet.pdf

Collier, P. (2007). *The Bottom Billion: Why the Poorest Countries are Falling and What can be done about it*. Oxford, UK: Oxford Univeristy Press.

Commission on Communication Education and Training. (2010). *The success of the Lisbon Strategy hinges on urgent reforms*. Retrieved from http://europa.eu/legislation_summaries/education_training_youth/general_framework/c11071_en.htm

Conceicao, P., Gibson, D. V., Heitor, M. V., & Stolp, C. (2003). Knowledge and innovation for the global learning economy: Building capacity for development. In Gibson, D. V., Stolp, C., Conceicao, P., & Heitor, M. V. (Eds.), *Systems and Policies for the Global Learning Economy* (pp. 11–43). Westport, CT: Praeger.

Connelly, C. E., & Kelloway, E. K. (2003). Predictors of employees' perceptions of knowledge sharing cultures. *Leadership and Organization Development Journal, 24*, 294–301. doi:10.1108/01437730310485815

Constraints, F., & Adjustment, C. (2006). Evidence from a Large Panel of Survey Data. *Economic, 73*, 691–724.

Contero, M., Naya, F., Company, P., & Saorín, J. L. (2006). Learning Support Tools for Developing Spatial Abilities. *International Journal of Engineering Education, 22*, 470–477.

Cooling, W. (2005). *All the colours of the earth*. Frances Lincoln Ltd.

Cope, B., & Kalantzis, M. (2000). *Multiliteracies: Literacy learning and the design of social futures*. London: Routledge.

Coppola, N. W., Hiltz, S. R., & Rotter, N. G. (2004). Building trust in virtual teams. *IEEE Transactions on Professional Communication, 47*(2), 95–104. doi:10.1109/TPC.2004.828203

CosmoCode. (n.d.). *Wikimatrix*. Retrieved July 5, 2010, from http://www.wikimatrix.org

Costa, A. C. (2003). Understanding the nature and the antecedents of trust within work teams. In Nooteboom, B., & Six, F. (Eds.), *The trust process in Organizations: Empirical Studies of the Determinants and the Process of Trust Development* (pp. 105–124). Cheltenham, UK: Edward Elgar.

Costa, A. C., Bijlsma-Frankema, K., & de Jong, B. (2009). The role of social capital on trust development and dynamics: implications for cooperation, monitoring and team performance. *Social Sciences Information. Information Sur les Sciences Sociales, 48*(2), 199–228. doi:10.1177/0539018409102408

Coward, L. A., & Salingaros, N. A. (2004). The Information Architecture of Cities. *Journal of Information Science, 30*(2), 107-118. Retrieved September 1, 2009 from http://zeta.math.utsa.edu/~yxk833/InfoCities.html

Cowley, B. (2007). Why change succeeds: An organizational assessment. *Organization Development Journal, 1*(25), 25–30.

Cramton, C. D. (2001). The mutual knowledge problem and its consequences in geographically dispersed teams. *Organization Science, 12*(3), 346–371. doi:10.1287/orsc.12.3.346.10098

Creed, W. E. D., & Miles, R. E. (1996). Trust in Organizations: A conceptual framework linking organizational forms, managerial philosophies, and the opportunity costs of controls. In Kramer, R. M., & Tyler, T. R. (Eds.), *Trust in Organizations: Frontiers of theory and research* (pp. 16–38). Thousand Oaks, CA: Sage Publications.

Criminisi, A., Perez, P., & Toyama, K. (2003). Object Removal by Exemplar-Based Inpainting. In. *Proceedings of the IEEE Conf. on Computer Vision and Pattern Recognition, 2*, 721–728.

Cummings, J. L., & Teng, B. S. (2003). Transferring R&D knowledge: The key factors affecting knowledge transfer success. *Journal of Engineering and Technology Management, 20*, 39–68. doi:10.1016/S0923-4748(03)00004-3

Cummins, J. (2000). Academic language learning, transformative pedagogy and information technology: Towards a critical balance. *TESOL Quarterly, 34*(3), 537–548. doi:10.2307/3587742

Curtis, B., Hefley, W. E., & Miller, S. A. (2001). *People Capability Maturity Model (P-CMM, Version 2.0) (Tech. Rep.)*. Pittsburgh, PA: Carnegie Mellon University, Software Engineering Institute.

Damian, D. (2007). Stakeholders in global requirements engineering: lessons learned from practice. *IEEE Software, 24*(2), 21–27. doi:10.1109/MS.2007.55

Dashti, A., Benbasat, I., & Burton-Jones, A. (2009, July 13-14). Developing trust reciprocity in electronic government: The role of felt trust. In *Proceedings of the European and Mediterranean Conference on Information Systems 2009*. Retrieved March, 25 2010, from http://www.iseing.org/emcis/EMCIS2009/ Proceedings/Presenting%20Papers/C16/C16.pdf

Das, T. K., & Teng, B. S. (1998). Between trust and control: developing confidence in partner cooperation in alliances. *Academy of Management Review, 23*(3), 491–512. doi:10.2307/259291

Davies, J. (2004). *Wiki brainstorming and problems with wiki based collaboration.*

Davies, F. D. (1989). Perceived usefulness, perceived ease of use and user acceptance of information technology. *Management Information Systems Quarterly, 13*, 319–339. doi:10.2307/249008

Davis, F. (1980). Perceived Usefulness, Perceived Ease of Use, and User Acceptance of Information Technology. *Management Information Systems Quarterly, 13*, 318–341.

Day, J., & Foley, J. (2006). Evaluating web lectures: a case study from HCI. In *Proceedings of CHI 2006 – Experience Report – User Centered Design for Learning and Education* (pp.195-200).

De Aguilera, M., & Mendiz, A. (2003). Video games and Education. Computers in Entertainment, 1(1).

De Burn, C. (2005). *ABC of knowledge management.* KMSL: Knowledge Management Specialist Library. Retrieved October 2008 from www.library.nhs.uk

de Catalunya, G. (2001). Law 6 stablishing University Spanish System. *Official Journal of the Spanish State, 307*, 49400–49425.

de Catalunya, G. (2003). Royal Decree 1125 establishing the European credit system and the system of qualifications in university degrees. *Official Journal of the Spanish State, 224*, 34355–34356.

De Feo, J. A., & Barnard, W. W. (2004). *Juran Institute Six Sigma: Breakthrough and Beyond: Quality Performance Breakthrough Methods*. New York: McGrawHill.

De Jong, T., & Ferguson-Hessler, M. G. M. (1996). Types and qualities of knowledge. *Educational Psychologist, 31*, 105–113. doi:10.1207/s15326985ep3102_2

De Pedro, X. (2006). Cómo evitar el 'café para todos' al evaluar trabajos en grupo, y de paso, estimular el aprendizaje reflexivo: resultados preliminares en el marco del proyecto awikiforum. In *Entorns col·laboratius per aprendre: comunitats virtuals d'aprenentatge.*

De Pedro, X. (2007). New method using wikis and forums to evaluate individual contributions in cooperative work while promoting experiential learning: results from preliminary experience. In *Wikis at work in the world: open, organic, participatory media for the 21st century* (pp. 87-92).

De Pedro, X. (2008). *Informe sobre wikis en educació per a la Universitat Oberta de Catalunya.*

De Pedro, X., Rieradevall, M., López, P., Sant, D., Piñol, J., Núñez, L., et al. (2006). Writing documents collaboratively in higher education using traditional vs. wiki methodology (i): qualitative results from a 2-year project study. In *Libro de comunicaciones del 4° congreso internacional de docencia universitaria e innovación.* Retrieved from http://cidui.upc.edu

De Pedro , X. (2006). Estimulación y evaluación del aprendizaje 'experiencial-reflexivo' del alumnado mediante la formulación explícita del tipo de contribuciones.

De Prada, E. (2006). Adapting to ECTS through the creation and use of a web page. *RELATEC, 5,* 235–249.

De Witt, C. (2005). E-Learning. In Hüther, J., & Schorb, B. (Eds.), *Grundbegriffe Medienpädagogik.* Munich, Germany: Köpäd.

DeMarco, T., & Lister, T. (1999). *Peopleware: Productive projects and teams.* New York: Dorset House.

Demirel, M. (2009). Lifelong learning and schools in the twenty-first century. *Procedia Social and Behavioral Sciences, 1,* 1709–1716. doi:10.1016/j.sbspro.2009.01.303

Derosa, D., Hantula, D. A., & D'Arcy, J. (2004). Trust and leadership in virtual teamwork: a media naturalness perspective. *Human Resource Management, 43*(2-3), 219–233. doi:10.1002/hrm.20016

Désilets, A., Paquet, S., & Vinson, N. G. (2005, October 17-18). Are wikis usable? In *Proceedings of the 2005 international symposium on Wikis* (pp. 3-15).

Devaraj, S., Fan, M., & Kohli, R. (2002). Antecedents of B2C channel satisfaction and preference: Validating e-commerce metrics. *Information Systems Research, 13*(3), 316–333. doi:10.1287/isre.13.3.316.77

Diamond, M. (2004). The usefulness of structured midterm feedback as a catalyst for change in higher education classes. *Active Learning in Higher Education, 5,* 217–231. doi:10.1177/1469787404046845

Diamond, R. (1989). *Designing and improving courses and curricula in higher education: A systematic approach.* San Francisco: Jossey-Bass.

Diaz Gibson, J., Civis Zaragoza, M., Longas Mayayo, J., & Murat, L. (2010). The study of educative network organizations in the city of Barcelona: The Nou Barris district. *International Journal of Knowledge Society Research, 1,* 26–37.

Dillenbourg, P. (1999). What do you mean by collaborative learning? In Dillenbourg, P. (Ed.), *Collaborative learning: Cognitive and Computational Approaches* (pp. 1–19). Oxford, UK: Elsevier.

Dirks, K. T., & Ferrin, D. L. (2001). The role of trust in organizational settings. *Organization Science, 12*(4), 450–467. doi:10.1287/orsc.12.4.450.10640

Dixon, N. (2000). *Common Knowledge: How Companies Thrive by Sharing What They Know.* Boston: Harvard Business School Press.

Dobson, M. (1999). Information enforcement and learning with interactive graphical systems. *Learning and Instruction, 9,* 365–390. doi:10.1016/S0959-4752(98)00052-8

Doherty, N., King, M., & Al-Mushayt, O. (2003). The impact of inadequacies in the treatment of organizational issues in information systems development projects. *Information & Management, 41,* 49–62. doi:10.1016/S0378-7206(03)00026-0

Dokeos CoolWiki. (n.d.). *CoolWiki extension for Dokeos LMS.* Retrieved July 5, 2010, from http://www.dokeos.com/extensions/index.php?section=tools&id=33

Dokeos Mediawiki. (n.d.). *Integration of Mediawiki in Dokeos.* Retrieved July 5, 2010, from http://www.dokeos.com/wiki/index.php/Integration_of_mediawiki

Dolfsma, W. (2006). Knowledge, the knowledge economy and welfare theory. In Dolfsma, W., & Soete, L. (Eds.), *Understanding the dynamics of a knowledge economy* (pp. 201–221). Cheltenham, UK: Edward Elgar.

Domsch, M., & Lidokhover, T. (2007). *Human Resource Management in Russia*. Cornwall, UK: MPG Books LTD.

Dougiamas, M. (1998). *A journey into constructivism*. Retrieved July 5, 2010, from http://dougiamas.com/writing/constructivism.html

Dougiamas, M., & Taylor, P. C. (2003). Moodle: Using learning communities to create an open source course management system. In *Proceedings of the EDMEDIA 2003 conference.*

Drucker, P. (1999). *Management Challenges for the 21st Century*. New York: Harper Business.

Duarte, D. L., & Snyder, N. T. (2006). *Mastering Virtual Teams* (3rd ed.). San Francisco, CA: Jossey-Bass.

Dumort, A. (2002). Guiding Principles of The Virtual European Space of Higher Education. *Revista Electrónica Teoría de la Educación, 7*, 185–197.

Dvir, R., & Pasher, E. (2004). Innovation engines for knowledge cities: An innovation ecology perspective. *Journal of Knowledge Management, 8*(5), 16–27. doi:10.1108/13673270410558756

Dyer, J. H., & Nobeoka, K. (2000). Creating and managing a high performance knowledge sharing network: The Toyota case. *Strategic Management Journal, 21*, 345–367. doi:10.1002/(SICI)1097-0266(200003)21:3<345::AID-SMJ96>3.0.CO;2-N

Educause Learning Initiative. (2005). *7 things you should know about... wikis.*

Edvinsson, L. (2000). Some perspectives on intangibles and intellectual capital. *Journal of Intellectual Capital, 1*(1), 12–16. doi:10.1108/14691930010371618

Edvinsson, L. (2003). The Intellectual Capital of Nations. In Holsapple, C. W. (Ed.), *Handbook of Knowledge Management 1 – Knowledge Matters*. Berlin: Springer.

Eisert, J., & Wilkens, M. (2000). Quantum Games. *Journal of Modern Optics, 47*, 2543.

Ekstedt, E., Lundin, R. A., Söderholm, A., & Wirdenius, H. (1999). *Neo-institutional Organising: Renewal by Action and Knowledge in a Project-intensive Economy*. London: Routledge.

El Sawy, O. A. (2003). The 3 Faces of IS Identity: connection, immersion and fusion. *Communications of the Association for Information Systems, 12*, 588–598.

El-Nasr, M. S., & Smith, B. K. (2006). Learning through game modding. Computers in entertainment, 4(1), 3B.

Elsas, A. (2003). Integration of e-government and e-commerce with web services. In R. Traunmuller (Ed.), *EGOV 2003* (LNCS 2739, pp. 373-376). Berlin: Springer.

Entwistle, N. J., McCune, V., & Walker, P. (2001). Conceptions, styles and approaches within higher education: analytic abstractions and everyday experience. In Sternberg, R. J., & Zhang, L. F. (Eds.), *Perspectives on Cognitive, Learning and Thinking styles* (pp. 103–136). Mahwah, NJ: Erlbaum.

Entwistle, N. J., & Peterson, E. R. (2004). Conceptions of learning and knowledge in higher education: relationships with study behaviour and influences of learning environments. *International Journal of Educational Research, 41*, 407–428. doi:10.1016/j.ijer.2005.08.009

Epstein, J. M., & Axtell, R. (1996). *Growing Artificial Societies*. Washington, DC: Brookings Institution Press.

Erdem, F., Ozen, J., & Atsan, N. (2003). The relationship between trust and team performance. *Work Study, 52*(7), 337–340. doi:10.1108/00438020310502633

Ergazakis, K., Metaxiotis, K., & Psarras, J. (2004). Towards knowledge cities: conceptual analysis and success stories. *Journal of Knowledge Management, 8*(5), 5–15. doi:10.1108/13673270410558747

Ergazakis, K., Metaxiotis, K., & Psarras, J. (2006). A coherent framework for building successful KCs in the context of the knowledge-based economy. *Knowledge Management Research & Practice, 4*(1), 56–59.

Erlach, C., Hausmann, I., Mandl, H., & Trillitzsch, U. (2002). Knowledge Master - a collaborative learning program for Knowledge Management. In Davenport, T. H., & Probst, G. J. B. (Eds.), *Knowledge management case book. Siemens best practices* (pp. 208–227). Erlangen, Germany: Publicis KommunikationsAgentur GWA.

Ertl, B., Kopp, B., & Mandl, H. (2005). Effects of an individual's prior knowledge on collaborative knowledge construction and individual learning outcomes in videoconferencing. In Koschmann, T., Chan, T.-W., & Suthers, D. D. (Eds.), *Computer supported collaborative learning 2005: the next 10 years* (pp. 145–154). Mahwah, NJ: Lawrence Erlbaum Associates.

Ertl, B., Winkler, K., & Mandl, H. (2007). E-learning - Trends and future development. In Neto, F. M., & Brasileiro, F. V. (Eds.), *Advances in Computer-Supported Learning* (pp. 122–144). Hershey, PA: Information Science Publishing.

Essomba, M. (Ed.). (2009). *Treball en xarxa a la formació dels professionals en educació. Col·lecció Finestra Oberta, 52*. Barcelona, Spain: Fundació Jaume Bofill.

Estallo, J. A. (1995). *Los videojugos. Juicios e prejuicios*. Barcelona, Spain: Planeta.

Europe's Information Society. (2010). *In context: ICT and Lisbon Strategy. Lisbon Review (2008)*. Retrieved from http://ec.europa.eu/information_society/eeurope/i2010/ict_and_lisbon.htm

European Commission. (2005). *The Business Case for Diversity. Good Practices in the Workplace*. Belgium: European Commission (ISBN 92-79-00239-2). Retrieved from http://ec.europa.eu/social/main.jsp?catId=370&langId=en&featuresId=25

European Information Society. (n.d.). Retrieved May 2008 from http://ec.europa.eu/information_society/index_en.htm

European Parliament. (2003). Decision No 2318 of the European Parliament and of the Council of 5 December 2003 adopting a multiannual programme (2004 to 2006) for the effective integration of information and communication technologies (ICT) in education and training systems in Europe (eLearning Programme). *Official Journal of the European Union. L&C, 327*, 45–68.

Ezechieli, E. (2003). *Beyond Sustainable Development: Education for Gross National Happiness in Bhutan*. Unpublished masters dissertation, Stanford University, Stanford, CA. Retrieved December 30, 2007 from http://suse-ice.stanford.edu/monographs/Ezechieli.pdf

Factbook, O. E. C. D. (2007). *Economic, Environmental and Social Statistics*. Retrieved August 20, 2007 from http://lysander.sourceoecd.org/vl=10624761/cl=11/nw=1/rpsv/factbook/

Fang, Z. (2002). E-Government in Digital Era: Concept, Practice, and Development. *International Journal of the Computer, the Internet and Management, 10*(2), 1-22.

Fazzari, S. M., Hubbard, R. G., & Petersen, B. C. (1988). Financing Constraints and Corporate Investment. *Brookings Papers on Economic Activity, 1*, 141–206. doi:10.2307/2534426

Fedorov, A. (2003). *Media Education and Media Literacy: Experts' Opinions*. Geneva, Switzerland: UNESCO.

Fetaji, B., & Fetaji, M. (2009). e-Learning Indicators: a Multi-Dimensional Model for Planning and Evaluating e- Learning Software Solutions. *Electronic Journal of e-Learning, 7*, 1-28.

Fey, A. (2002). Audio vs. Video: Hilft Sehen beim Lernen? Vergleich zwischen einer audio- visuellen und auditiven virtuellen Vorlesungen. *Lernforschung, 30*(4), 331–338.

Fishbein, M., & Ajzen, I. (1975). *Belief, attitude, intention, and behavior: An introduction to theory and research*. Reading, MA: Addison-Wesley.

Fitzpatrick, J. L., Sanders, J. R., & Worthen, B. R. (2003). *Program Evaluation: Alternative Approaches and Practical Guidelines*. Boston: Pearson.

Florida, R., & Gates, G. (2001). *Technology and tolerance: The importance of diversity to high technology growth*. Washington, DC: The Brookings Institution.

Foertsch, J., Moses, G., Strickwerda, J., & Litzkov, M. (2002). Reversing the lecture/homework paradigm using eTEACH web-based streaming video software. *Journal of Engineering Education, 91*(3), 267–274.

Fong, A. C. M., & Hui, S. C. (2001). Low-bandwidth Internet streaming of multimedia lectures. *Engineering Science and Education Journal, 10*(6), 212–218. doi:10.1049/esej:20010601

Font, A. (2003). *European Space of Higher Education (ESHE)*. Paper presented at the 9th Conference of Law Faculties Deans in the Spanish Universities.

Foray, D. (2006). Optimizing the use of knowledge. In Kahin, B., & Foray, D. (Eds.), *Advancing Knowledge and the Knowledge Economy* (pp. 9–15). Cambridge, MA: MIT Press.

Fornell, C., & Larcker, D. F. (1981). Evaluating structural equation models with unbearable and measurement error. *JMR, Journal of Marketing Research*, *18*, 39–50. doi:10.2307/3151312

FORTH. (2010). *Definitions & Glossary*. Hellas, Greece: Author.

Fountain, R. (2005). *Dossiers technopédagogiques: wiki pedagogy*. Retrieved July 5, 2010, from http://www.profetic.org/dossiers/dossier_imprimer.php3?id_rubrique=110

Fricke, R. (1997). Evaluation von Multimedia. In Issing, J. K., & Ludwig, P. (Eds.), *Information und Lernen mit Multimedia* (pp. 402–413). Weinheim, Germany: Beltz.

Fritze, Y., & Nordkvelle, Y. (2003). Comparing Lectures – Effects of the Technological Context of the Studio. *Education and Information Technologies*, 327–343. doi:10.1023/B:EAIT.0000008675.12095.7a

Fuchs, C. (2007). Towards a dynamic theory of virtual communities. *International Journal Knowledge and Learning*, *3*, 372–403. doi:10.1504/IJKL.2007.016701

Gallivan, M. J. (2001). Striking a balance between trust and control in a virtual organization: a content analysis of open source software case studies. *Information Systems Journal*, *11*(4,) 277-304.

García Manzano, A. (2006). *Blogs y wikis en tareas educativas*. Retrieved July 5, 2010, from http://observatorio.cnice.mec.es/modules.php?op=modload&name=News&file=article&sid=378

Garcia, A. C. B., Kunz, J., Ekstrom, M., & Kiviniemi, A. (2003). *Building a Project Ontology with Extreme Collaboration and VD&C (CIFE Tech. Rep. #152)*. Palo Alto, CA: Stanford University.

Gardner, H. (1993). *Multiple Intelligences: The Theory in Practice*. New York: Basic Books.

Gardner-Medwin, A. R., & Gahan, M. (2003). *Formative and Summative Confidence-Based Assessment* (pp. 147-155). Paper Presented at the 7th International Computer-Aided Conference, UK.

Gardner-Medwin, A. (1998). Updating with confidence: Do your students know what they don't know? *Health (San Francisco)*, *4*, 45–46.

Gareis, R. (2007). *Happy Projects!* Bucharest, Romania: ASE.

Garrety, C., & Schmidt, D. (2008). The evolution of digital storytelling: from enhanced oral tradition to genres for education. In K. McFerrin et al. (Eds.), *Proceedings of Society for Information Technology & Teacher Education International Conference 2008* (pp. 916-921). Chesapeake, VA: AACE. Retrieved from http://www.editlib.org/p/27289

Garrison, D. R., & Vaughan, N. D. (2008). *Blended Learning in Higher Education: Framework, Principles, and Guidelines*. San Francisco: Jossey-Bass.

Garrison, R., & Kanuka, H. (2004). Blended learning: uncovering its transformative potential in higher education. *The Internet and Higher Education*, *7*, 95–105. doi:10.1016/j.iheduc.2004.02.001

Gavari, E. (2006). Guiding Principles of The Virtual European Higher Education. *Revista Electrónica de Teoría de la Educación. Educación y cultura en la Sociedad de la Información, 7*(2), 185-197.

Gefen, D. (2002). Customer Loyalty in e-Commerce. *Journal of the Association for Information Systems*, *3*, 27–51.

Gefen, D., Karahanna, E., & Straub, D. (2003). Trust and TAM in online shopping: an integrated model. *Management Information Systems Quarterly*, *27*(1), 51–90.

Gefen, D., Karahanna, E., & Straub, D. (2003). Inexperience and experience with online stores: the importance of TAM and Trust. *IEEE Transactions on Engineering Management*, *50*(3), 307–321. doi:10.1109/TEM.2003.817277

Generalitat de Catalunya. (2003). Decree 325 approving Statutes of the University of Granada. *Official Journal of Andalusian autonomous region Government, 236*, 25745-25776.

Generalitat de Catalunya. (2003). Law 15 approving the Andalusian University System. *Official Journal of Andalusian autonomous regional Government, 251*, 27452-27474.

Georgina, D. A., & Olson, M. R. (2008). Integration of technology in higher education: A review of faculty self-perceptions. *The Internet and Higher Education, 11*, 1–8. doi:10.1016/j.iheduc.2007.11.002

Gersick, C. J. G. (1988). Time and transition in work teams: toward a new model of group development. *Academy of Management Journal, 31*(1), 9–41. doi:10.2307/256496

Giamouridis, A. (2006). Policy, Politics, and Social Inequality in the Educational System of Greece. *Journal of Modern Greek Studies, 24*(1), 1–21. doi:10.1353/mgs.2006.0004

Gibson, C. B., & Cohen, S. G. (2003). *Virtual teams that work: Creating conditions for virtual team effectiveness.* New York: Wiley.

Gibson, C. B., & Manuel, J. A. (2003). Building trust: effective muticultural communication processes in virtual teams. In Gibson, C. B., & Cohen, S. (Eds.), *Virtual teams that works: creating conditions for virtual team effectiveness* (pp. 59–86). San Francisco, CA: Jossey-Bass.

Gilbert, D., Balestrini, P., & Littleboy, D. (2004). Barriers and benefits in the adoption of e-government. *International Journal of Public Sector Management, 17*(4/5), 286–301. doi:10.1108/09513550410539794

Gillham, B. (2000). *Case study research methods.* London: Continuum.

Gilmore, D., & Bell, K. (2006). We are Family: Using Diverse Family Structure Literature with Children. *Reading Horizons Journal, 46*(3), 1–24.

Giordano, R. (2007). An investigation of the use of a wiki to support knowledge exchange in public health. In *Proceedings of the 2007 International ACM Conference on Supporting Group Work.*

Glowalla, U. (2004). Utility and Usability von E-Learning am Beispiel von Lecture-on-demand Anwendungen. In *Entwerfen und Gestalten.*

Goh, W. W., Dexter, B., & Murphy, W. D. (2007, March 14-16). *Promoting critical thinking with computer mediated communication technology.* Paper presented at the Sixth IASTED International Conference Web-Based Education, Chamonix, France.

Gold, A. H., Malhotra, A., & Segars, A. H. (2001). Knowledge management: an organization capabilities perspective. *Journal of Management Information Systems, 18*(1), 185–214.

Golembiewski, R. T., & McConkie, M. (1975). The centrality of interpersonal trust in group processes. In Cooper, C. L. (Ed.), *Theories of group processes* (pp. 131–185). New York: Wiley.

Goodacre, A., & Tonks, I. (1995). Finance and Technological Change. In Stoneman, P. (Ed.), *Handbook of the Economics of Innovation and Technological Change* (pp. 298–341). Oxford, UK: Blackwell Handbooks in Economics.

Goodman, P. S., & Leyden, D. P. (1991). Familiarity and group productivity. *The Journal of Applied Psychology, 76*(4), 578–586. doi:10.1037/0021-9010.76.4.578

Gorton, I., & Motwani, S. (1996). Issues in co-operative software engineering using globally distributed teams. *Information and Software Technology, 38*(10), 647–655. doi:10.1016/0950-5849(96)01099-3

Goulão, M. F. (2001). *Ensino aberto à distância: cognição e afectividade.* Unpublished PhD thesis, Open University.

Governing Council of the University of Granada. (2005). *Plan for Educational Excellence 05-08.* Retrieved from http://www.ugr.es/~vicinnova/plancalidaddocente05-08.html

Green, R. (2004). *Housing, Planning, Local Government and the Regional Committee: Social Cohesion; Sixth Report of Session 2003-2004.* Retrieved November 28, 2008 from http://publications.parliament.uk/pa/cm200304/comselect/cmodpm/45/45.pdf-Gupta, K. A., & Vijay, G. (2000). Knowledge flows within multinational corporations. *Strategic Management Journal, 21*, 473-496.

Griffith, J. (2001). Why change management fails. *Journal of Change Management, 2*(4), 297–304. doi:10.1080/714042516

Griliches, Z. (2000). *R&D: Education, and Productivity: A Retrospective.* Cambridge, MA: Harvard University Press.

Grundstein, M. (2009). GAMETH®: a constructivist and learning approach to identify and locate crucial knowledge. *Int. J. Knowledge and Learning, 5*(3/4), 289–305. doi:10.1504/IJKL.2009.031227

Guardado, M., & Shi, L. (2007). ESL students' experiences of online peer feedback. *Computers and Composition, 24*, 443–461. doi:10.1016/j.compcom.2007.03.002

Guégnard, C., Calmand, J., Giret, J.-F., & Paul, J.-J. (2008). Recognition of Higher Education Graduates' Competences on European Labour Markets. *Céreq –. Training & Development, 83*, 1–8.

Gunter, B. (2006). Advances in e-democracy. *Aslib Proceedings: New Information Perspectives, 58*(5), 361–370.

Gupta, M. P. (2004). *Promise of E-Governance: Operational Challenges*. New Delhi, India: Tata McGraw-Hill.

Gurtman, M. B. (1992). Trust, distrust, and interpersonal problems: a circumplex analysis. *Journal of Personality and Social Psychology, 62*, 989–1002. doi:10.1037/0022-3514.62.6.989

Haben, M. (2002). E-Learning in large German companies - most of the concepts are not effective. *Computerwoche, 30*, 12–16.

Haggie, K., & Kingston, J. (2003). Choosing your knowledge management strategy. *Journal of Knowledge Management Practice, 4*. Retrieved from http://www.tlainc.com/jkmpv4.tm

Hair, F. Jr, Anderson, R. E., Tatham, R. L., & Black, W. C. (1998). *Multivariate data analysis* (5th ed.). Upper Saddle River, NJ: Prentice Hall.

Halpern, D. (2005). *Social Capital*. Cambridge, UK: Polity Press.

Hamdouch, A., & Moulaert, F. (2006). Knowledge infrastructure, innovation dynamics, and knowledge creation/diffusion/accumulation processes: a comparative institutional perspective. *Innovation (Abingdon), 19*(1), 25–50. doi:10.1080/13511610600607676

Hancock, D. (2004). Cooperative learning and peer orientation effects on motivation and achievement. *The Journal of Educational Research, 97*(3), 159–166. doi:10.3200/JOER.97.3.159-168

Handy, C. (1995). Trust and virtual organizations. *Harvard Business Review, 73*(3), 40–50.

Hanlin-Rowney, A., Kuntzelman, K., Lara, M. E. A., Quinn, D., Roffman, K., & Nichols, T. T. (2006). Collaborative inquiry as a framework for exploring transformative learning online. *Journal of Transformative Education, 4*(4), 320–334. doi:10.1177/1541344606294820

Hansen, M., Anandan, P., Dana, K., van der Wal, G., & Burt, P. J. (1994). Real time scene stabilization and mosaic construction. In *Proceedings of the DARPA Image Understanding Workshop*, Monterey, CA (pp. 457-465).

Hansen, M. (1999). The search-transfer problem: the role of weak ties in sharing knowledge across organization subunits. *Administrative Science Quarterly, 44*(1), 82–11. doi:10.2307/2667032

Hansen, M. T., Nohria, N., & Tierney, T. (1999). What's your strategy for managing knowledge? *Harvard Business Review, 77*(2), 106–117.

Hardin, R. (1993). The street-level epistemology of trust. *Politics & Society, 21*(4), 505–529. doi:10.1177/0032329293021004006

Harhoff, D., & Küpper, C. (2002). *Akzeptanz von E-Learning. Eine empirische Studie in Zusammenarbeit von Cognos und dem Institut für Innovationsforschung, Technologiemanagement und Entrepreneurship*. Munich, Germany: INNOtec.

Harris, R. G. (2001). The knowledge-based economy: intellectual origins and new economic perspectives. *International Journal of Management Reviews, 3*(1), 21–40. doi:10.1111/1468-2370.00052

Harste, J. (2003). What do we mean by literacy now? *Voices from the Middle, 10*(3), 8–11.

Hart, O. (1995). *Firms, Contracts and Financial Structure*. Oxford, UK: Oxford University Press. doi:10.1093/0198288816.001.0001

Harvey, J., Oliver, M., & Smith, J. (2002). Towards effective practitioner evaluation. An exploration of issues relating to skills, motivation and evidence. *Journal of Educational Technology & Society, 5*, 3–10.

Hauschild, S., Licht, T., & Stein, W. (2001). *Creating a knowledge culture*. UK: McKinsey.

Hayes, M. H. (1998). Some approaches to Internet distance learning with streaming media. In *Proceedings of the Second IEEE Workshop on Multimedia Signal Processing*, Redondo Beach, CA.

Henninger, M., & Balk, M. (2001). *Integrative Evaluation: Ein Ansatz zur Erhöhung der Akzeptanz von Lehrevaluation an Hochschulen*. Munich, Germany: Ludwig-Maximilians-Universität.

Henry, B., Sentance, A., & Urga, G. (1999). Finance, profitability and investment in manufacturing. In Driver, C., & Temple, P. (Eds.), *Investment, Growth and Employment. Perspectives for policy* (pp. 29–50). London: Routledge.

Hense, J., & Mandl, H. (2006). *Selbstevaluation als Ansatz der Qualitätsverbesserung von E-Learning Angeboten*. Munich, Germany: Ludwig-Maximilians-Universität.

Herbsleb, J. D., & Moitra, D. (2001). Global software development. *IEEE Software*, *18*(2), 16–20. doi:10.1109/52.914732

Herminia, W. D. (2006). Play to learn exploring online educational games in museums. In Proceedings of International Conference on Computer Graphics and Interactive Techniques, Boston, Massachusetts. New York: ACM.

Hernandez-Lopez, A., Colomo-Palacios, R., Garcia-Crespo, A., & Soto-Acosta, P. (2010). Trust building process for global software development teams. A review. *International Journal of Knowledge Society Research*, *1*(1), 65–82. doi:10.4018/jksr.2010010105

Hilburn, T. B., & Humphrey, W. S. (2002). Teaching Teamwork. *IEEE Software*, *19*(5), 72–77. doi:10.1109/MS.2002.1032857

Hills, T. (2007). Is constructivism risky? Social anxiety, classroom participation, competitive game play and constructivist preferences in teacher development. *Teacher Development*, *11*(3), 335–353. doi:10.1080/13664530701644615

Hilt, V., & Kuhmünch, C. (1999). New Tools for Synchronous and Asynchronous Teaching and Learning in the Internet. In *Proceedings of ED-MEDIA* (pp. 975-980).

Hinds, P. J., & Bailey, D. E. (2003). Out of sight, out of sync: Understanding conflict in distributed teams. *Organization Science*, *14*(6), 615–632. doi:10.1287/orsc.14.6.615.24872

Hinds, P. J., & Mortensen, M. (2005). Understanding conflict in geographically distributed teams: The moderating effects of shared identity, shared context, and spontaneous communication. *Organization Science*, *16*(3), 290–307. doi:10.1287/orsc.1050.0122

Holland, C. P. (1998, April). The importance of trust and business relationships in the formation of virtual organizations. In *Proceedigns of the Organizational Virtualness 2nd*. International VoNet - Workshop.

Holmstrom, B., & Ricart i Costa, J. E. (1986). Managerial incentives and capital management. *The Quarterly Journal of Economics*, 835–860. doi:10.2307/1884180

Holton, J. A. (2001). Building trust and collaboration in a virtual team. *Team Performance Management*, *7*(3-4), 36–47. doi:10.1108/13527590110395621

Houghton, J., & Sheehan, P. (2000, February). *A primer on the knowledge economy*. Paper presented at the National Innovation Summit, Melbourne, Australia.

Huang, S.-Y., Chang, C.-M., & Yu, T.-Y. (2006). Determinants of user acceptance of the e-Government services: The case of online tax filing and payment system. *Government Information Quarterly*, *23*(1), 97–122. doi:10.1016/j.giq.2005.11.005

Humphrey, W. S. (1995). Introducing the personal software process. *Annals of Software Engineering*, *1*(1), 311–325. doi:10.1007/BF02249055

Humphrey, W. S. (1997). *Managing Technical People - Innovation, Teamwork, and the Software Process*. Reading, MA: Addison-Wesley.

Humphrey, W. S. (1999). *Introduction to the team software process*. Reading, MA: Addison-Wesley.

Hunt, D. P. (2003). The concept of knowledge and how to measure it. *Journal of Intellectual Capital*, *4*(1), 100–113. doi:10.1108/14691930310455414

Huntington, S. P. (1996). *The Clash of Civilizations and the Remaking of World Order*. New York: Simon & Schuster.

Huysman, M., & Wulf, V. (2004). *Social capital and information technology*. Cambridge, MA: MIT Press.

IDRC. (2007). *From e-Government to e-Governance: a paradigmatic shift.* Retrieved April 4, 2009, from http://www.idrc.ca/en/ev-115662-201-1-DO_TOPIC.html

iMultimedia (n.d.). *Use Image Stabilization – Gyroscopic Stabilizer.* Retrieved January 13, 2006, from http://www.websiteoptimization.com/speed/tweak/stabilizer

Information and Communication and Technologies Task Force. (2006). *UN Substantive session.* Retrieved from http://www.unicttaskforce.org/perl/documents.pl

International Project Management Association. (2006). *IPMA Competence Baseline.* Nijkerk, Netherlands: IPMA.

Irani, M., Rousso, B., & Peleg, S. (1994, June). Recovery of ego-motion using image stabilization. In *Proceedings of the IEEE conference on Computer Vision and Pattern Recognition*, Seattle, WA (pp. 454-460).

Isabella, L. (1990). Evolving interpretations as a change unfolds: How managers construe key organizational events. *Academy of Management Journal, 33*(1), 7–41. doi:10.2307/256350

ISCO. *Standard classification of occupations.* (n.d.). Retrieved January 14, 2010, from http://www.ilo.org/public/english/bureau/stat/isco/index.htm

Isiaka, B. (2007). Effectiveness of video as an instructional medium in teaching rural children agricultural and environmental sciences. *International Journal of Education and Development using Information and Communication Technology, 3,* 105-114

ISO (International Standards Organization). (1987). *Information Processing Vocabulary* (ISO 12382), Geneva, Switzerland.

ITU. (2007). *Measuring the information society: ICT opportunity index and world telecommunication/ICT indicators.* Geneva, Switzerland: ITU.

Jaeger, P. T., & Matteson, M. (2009). e-Government and Technology Acceptance: the Case of the Implementation of Section 508 Guidelines for Websites. *Electronic. Journal of E-Government, 7*(1), 87–98.

Janoff-Bulman, R. (1992). *Shattered Assumptions: Towards a new psychology of trauma.* New York: Free Press.

Jarvela, S., & Hakkinen, P. (2002). Web-based cases in teaching and learning-the quality of discussions and a stage of perspective taking in asynchronous communication. *International Journal of Interactive Learning Environments, 10,* 1–22. doi:10.1076/ilee.10.1.1.3613

Jarvenpaa, S. L., Knoll, K., & Leidner, D. E. (1998). Is Anybody Out There? The Antecedents of Trust in Global Virtual Teams. *Journal of Management Information Systems, 14*(4), 29–64.

Jarvenpaa, S. L., & Leidner, D. E. (1999). Communication and trust in global virtual teams. *Organization Science, 10*(6), 791–815. doi:10.1287/orsc.10.6.791

Jarvenpaa, S. L., Shaw, T. R., & Staples, D. S. (2004). Toward contextualized theories of trust: the role of trust in global virtual teams. *Information Systems Research, 15*(3), 250–264. doi:10.1287/isre.1040.0028

Jashapara, A. (2004). *Knowledge Management. An Integrated Approach.* Upper Saddle River, NJ: Pearson Education Limited.

Jeans, J. (1930). *The Mysterious Universe.* New York: Macmillan.

Jehn, K. A., & Shah, P. P. (1997). Interpersonal relationships and task performance: an examination of mediating process in friendship and acquaintance groups. *Journal of Personality and Social Psychology, 72*(4), 775–790. doi:10.1037/0022-3514.72.4.775

Jewitt, C. (2008). *Technology, Literacy and Learning: A Multimodal Approach.* New York: Routledge.

Jia, J., Wu, T. P., Tai, Y. W., & Tang, C. K. (2004). Inference of foreground and background under severe occlusion. In. *Proceedings of IEEE Conf. on Computer Vision and Pattern Recognition, 1,* 364–371.

Johnston, M. (n.d). *Good Governance: Rule of Law, Transparency, and Accountability.* Retrieved April 30, 2010, from http://www.unpan.org

Johnstone, A. H. (1991). Why is science difficult to learn? Things are seldom what they seem. *Journal of Computer Assisted Learning, 7,* 75–83. doi:10.1111/j.1365-2729.1991.tb00230.x

Johnstone, A. H. (1993). The development of chemistry teaching: a changing response to changing demand. *Journal of Chemical Education*, *70*(9), 701–705. doi:10.1021/ed070p701

Joia, L. A. (2006). A Framework for Developing Regional E-Government Capacity- Building Networks. *Information Technologies and International Development*, *2*(4), 61–73. doi:10.1162/154475205775249328

Joia, L. A. (2007). Knowledge management strategies: creating and testing a measurement scale. *International Journal of Learning and Intellectual Capital*, *4*(3), 203–221. doi:10.1504/IJLIC.2007.015607

Jonassen, D. (2006). Accommodating ways of human knowing in the design of information and instruction. *International Journal of Knowledge and Learning*, *2*(3/4), 181–190. doi:10.1504/IJKL.2006.010991

Jonassen, D. H., & Kwon, H. I. (2001). Communication patterns in computer-mediated vs. face-to-face group problem solving. *Educational Technology Research and Development*, *49*(10), 35–52. doi:10.1007/BF02504505

Jonassen, D., Davidson, M., Collins, M., Campbell, J., & Haag, B. B. (1995). Constructivism and computer-mediated communication in distance education. *American Journal of Distance Education*, *9*(2). doi:10.1080/08923649509526885

Jones, N. B., Provost, D. M., & Pascale, D. (2006). Developing a university research web-based knowledge portal. *International Journal of Knowledge and Learning*, *2*, 106–118. doi:10.1504/IJKL.2006.009682

Jones, O., & Smith, D. (1997). Strategic technology management in mid-corporate firm: The case of otter control. *Journal of Management Studies*, *34*(4), 511–536. doi:10.1111/1467-6486.00061

Joseph, R., & Kitlan, D. (2008). *Key Issues in E-Government and Public Administration*. Retrieved April 30, 2010, from http://old.igi-global.com/downloads/excerpts/reference/IGR5202_1YPRPC8baU.pdf

Jovanovic, M., Starcevic, D., Velimir, S., & Minovic, M. (2008). Educational Games Design Issues: Motivation and Multimodal Interaction (LNCS 5288, pp. 215-224). Berlin: Springer-Verlag.

Joy, S., & Kolb, D. A. (2009). Are there cultural differences in learning style? *International Journal of Intercultural Relations*, *33*, 69–85. doi:10.1016/j.ijintrel.2008.11.002

Kahin, B. (2006). Prospects for knowledge policy. In Kahin, B., & Foray, D. (Eds.), *Advancing Knowledge and the Knowledge Economy* (pp. 1–8). Cambridge, MA: MIT Press.

Kanawattanachi, P., & Yoo, Y. (2002). Dynamic nature of trust in virtual teams. *The Journal of Strategic Information Systems*, *11*(3-4), 187–213. doi:10.1016/S0963-8687(02)00019-7

Kanellopoulos, D., Kotsiantis, S., & Pintelas, P. (2006). Ontology-based learning applications: a development methodology. In *Proceedings of the 24th IASTED International Multi-Conference Software Engineering*, Innsbruck, Austria.

Karolak, D. W. (1998). *Global Software Development: Managing Virtual Teams and Environments*. Los Alamitos, CA: Wiley-IEEE Computer Society Pr.

Kauffeld, S., Brennecke, J., & Strack, M. (2009). Erfolge sichtbar machen: Das Maßnahmen-Erfolgs-Inventar (MEI) zur Bewertung von Trainings. In Kauffeld, S., Grote, S., & Frieling, E. (Eds.), *Handbuch Kompetenzentwicklung* (pp. 55–79). Stuttgart, Germany: Schäffer-Poeschel.

Kaufmann, D., Kraay, A., & Mastruzzi, M. (2007, July). *Governance Matters VI: Aggregate and individual Governance indicators 1996-2006* (World Bank Policy Research Working Paper 4280).

Kaywort, T. R., & Leidner, D. E. (2002). Leadership effectiveness in global virtual teams. *Journal of Management Information Systems*, *18*(3), 7–40.

Kellner, D., & Share, J. (2007). Critical Media Literacy, Democracy, and the Reconstruction of Education. In Macedo, D., & Steinberg, S. R. (Eds.), *Media Literacy: A Reader* (pp. 3–23). New York: Peter Lang Publishing.

Kelly, H. F., Ponton, M. K., & Rovai, A. P. (2007). A comparison of student evaluations of teaching between online and face-to-face courses. *The Internet and Higher Education*, *10*, 89–101. doi:10.1016/j.iheduc.2007.02.001

Kickmeier-Rust, M., Ebner, M., & Holzinger, A. (2006). Wikis: do they need usability engineering? In *M3 – Interdisciplinary aspects of digital media & education* (pp. 137-144).

Kimura, K. (1985). *Angular Velocity Measuring Instrument* (USP 2544646).

King, W. R. (2005). An androgogy model for IS and management education. *International Journal of Knowledge and Learning*, *1*(3), 186–209. doi:10.1504/IJKL.2005.007756

Kirkpatrick, D. (1994). *Evaluating Training Programs: The Four levels*. San Francisco: Berret-Koehler.

Kitchen, P. J., & Daly, F. (2002). Internal communication during change management. *Corporate Communications*, *7*(1), 46–53. doi:10.1108/13563280210416035

Klijn, E. H. (1996). Analyzing and Managing Policy Processes in Complex Networks: A Theoretical Examination of the Concept of Policy Network and Its Problems. *Administration & Society*, *28*(1), 90–119. doi:10.1177/009539979602800104

Klijn, E. H., & Koppenjan, J. F. M. (2000). Public Management and Policy Networks – Foundations of a Network Approach to Governance. *Public Management*, *2*(2), 135–158. doi:10.1080/146166700411201

KMSL (Knowledge Management Specialist Library). (n.d.). *NHS (National Library for Health)*. Retrieved October 2008 from http://www.library.nhs.uk/KnowledgeManagement/

Knyphausen-Aufseß, D., Smukalla, M., & Abt, M. (2009). Towards a New Training Transfer Portfolio: A Review of Training-related Studies in the Last Decade. *Zeitschrift für Personalforschung*, *23*, 288–311.

Kochova, S., & Sucharev, A. (2001). *India: head for the world leadership in the IT area. Government policy in the area of software development and its yields. Moscow, Russia*. Moscow: University press.

Koepp, M., Gunn, R., Lawrence, A., Cunningham, V., Dagher, A., & Jones, T. (1998). Evidence for striatal dopamine release during a video game. *Nature*, *393*, 266–268. doi:10.1038/30498

Koivula, N., Hassmén, P., & Hunt, D. P. (2001). Performance on the Swedish Scholastic Aptitude Test: Effects of Self-Assessment and Gender. *Sex Role, 44*(11/12).

Kolb, A., & Kolb, D. A. (2005). Learning styles and learning spaces: enhancing experiential learning in Higher Education. *Academy of Management Learning & Education*, *4*(2), 193–212.

Kolb, D. A. (1981). Learning styles and disciplinary differences. In Chickering, A. W.,(Eds.), *The modern American college*. San Francisco: Jossey-Bass.

Kolb, D. A. (1984). *Experiential Learning: experience as the source of learning and development*. Englewood Cliffs, NJ: Prentice Hall.

Kolb, D. A. (1999). *The Kolb Learning Style Inventory version 3*. Boston: Hay Resources Direct.

Kollias, A. (2007). *Framework for e- learning contents evaluation*. Heraklion, Greece: Foundation for research and technology.

König, J. (2000). *Einführung in die Selbstevaluation*. Freiburg, Germany: Lambertus.

Koshland, D. E. (2007). The Cha-Cha-Cha Theory of scientific discovery. *Science*, *317*, 761–762. doi:10.1126/science.1147166

Koskinen, K. U. (2003). Evaluation of tacit knowledge utilization in work units. *Journal of Knowledge Management*, *7*(5), 67–81. doi:10.1108/13673270310505395

Koskinen, K. U. (2004). Knowledge management to improve project communication and implementation. *Project Management Journal*, *35*(2), 13–19.

Koskinen, K. U. (2005). Learning that took place in office equipment retailers during a technological discontinuity. *International Journal of Learning and Intellectual Capital*, *2*(4), 408–421. doi:10.1504/IJLIC.2005.008100

Koskinen, K. U., & Pihlanto, P. (2006). Competence transfer from old timers to newcomers analysed with the help of the holistic concept of man. *Knowledge and Process Management*, *13*(1), 3–12. doi:10.1002/kpm.245

Kotter, J. P. (2002). *The heart of Change*.

Kotter, J. P., & Schlesinger, L. A. (1979). Choosing strategies for change. *Harvard Business Review*, 106–114.

Koufaris, M. (2002). Applying the Technology Acceptance Model and flow theory to online consumer behavior. *Information Systems Research*, *13*(2), 205–223. doi:10.1287/isre.13.2.205.83

Koutouzis, E., Bithara, P., Kyranakis, S., Mavraki, M., & Verevi, A. (2008). Decentralizing Education in Greece: In search for a new role for the school leaders. In *Proceedings of the CCEAM 2008 Conference*. Retrieved April 20, 2009, from http://www.emasa.co.za/files/full/H2.pdf

Kozma, R., & Russel, J. (2005). Modelling students becoming chemists: Developing representational competence. In Gilbert, J. K. (Ed.), *Models and modelling in science education: Visualization in science education*. Dordrecht, The Netherlands: Springer.

Kramer, R. M. (1999). Trust and Distrust in Organizations: Emerging Perspectives, Enduring Questions. *Annual Review of Psychology*, *50*(1), 569–598. doi:10.1146/annurev.psych.50.1.569

Kramer, R. M., & Cook, K. S. (2004). *Trust and Distrust in Organizations: dilemmas and approaches*. New York: Russell Sage Foundation.

Kramer, R. M., & Tyler, T. R. (1996). Whiter trust? In Tyler, T. R., & Kramer, R. M. (Eds.), *Trust in Organizations: Frontiers of Theory and Research* (pp. 1–15). Thousand Oaks, CA: Sage Publications.

Krathwohl, D. R. (2002). A revision of Bloom's taxonomy: An overview. *Theory into Practice*, *41*(4), 212–218. doi:10.1207/s15430421tip4104_2

Krauss, R. M., & Fussell, S. R. (1991). Perspective-taking in communication representation of others' knowledge in reference. *Social Cognition*, *9*(1), 2–24.

Kreijns, K., Kirschner, P. A., & Jochems, W. (2002). The sociability of computer supported collaborative learning environments. *Journal of Educational Technology & Society*, *5*, 8–22.

Kress, G. (2003). *Literacy in the New Media Age*. London: Routledge. doi:10.4324/9780203164754

Krovi, R. (1993). Identifying the causes of resistance to IS implementation: A change theory perspective. *Information & Management*, *25*, 327–335. doi:10.1016/0378-7206(93)90082-5

Krüger, M. (2005). Vortragsaufzeichnungen–Ein Querschnitt über die pädagogischen Forschungsergebnisse. In *Proceedings of the DeLFI Workshop*.

Kuznets, S. (1966). *Modern Economic Growth: Rate, Structure, and Spread*. New Haven, CT: Yale University Press.

Labbo, L., & Reinking, D. (1999). Negotiating the multiple realities of technology in literacy research and instruction. *Theory and Research into Practice*, *34*(4), 478–492.

Laffont, J. J., & Maskin, E. (1980). The theory of incentives: an overview. In Hildenbrand, W. (Ed.), *Advances in Economic Theory* (pp. 31–94). Cambridge, UK: Cambridge University Press.

Lage, M. J., Platt, G. J., & Treglia, M. (2000). Inverting the Classroom: A Gateway to Creating an Inclusive Learning Environment. *The Journal of Economic Education*, *31*(1), 30–43.

Lakkala, M. (2008). *The pedagogical design of technology enhanced collaborative learning*.

Lamnek, S. (2005). *Qualitative Sozialforschung*. Weinheim, Germany: Beltz.

Lankshear, C., & McClaren, P. (1993). *Critical literacy: Politics, praxis, and the postmodern*. Albany, NY: State University of New York Press.

Lau, E. (2004). Principaux enjeux de l'administration électronique dans les pays membres de l'OCDE. In *Revue Française d'Administration Publique* (Vol. 110, pp. 225–244). Paris: Icole Nationale d'Administration.

Lauer, T., Müller, R., & Trahasch, S. (2004). Learning with lecture recordings: key issues for end-users. In *Proceedings of the IEEE International Conference on Advanced Learning Technologies* (pp. 741-743).

Lau, H. Y. K., & Mak, K. L. (2005). A Configurable E-Learning System for Industrial Engineering. *International Journal of Engineering Education*, *21*, 262–276.

Lave, J., & Wenger, E. (1991). *Situated learning: Legitimate peripheral participation*. New York: Cambridge University Press.

Layne, K., & Lee, J. (2001). Developing fully functional e-government: A four stage model. *Government Information Quarterly, 18*(2), 122–136. doi:10.1016/S0740-624X(01)00066-1

Learnframe.com. (2005). *About e-learning.* Retrieved from http://www.learnframe.com/aboutelearning

Lee, S., Kim, I., Rhee, S., & Trimi, S. (2006). The role of exogenous factors in technology acceptance: The case of object-oriented technology. *Information & Management, 43*(4), 469–480. doi:10.1016/j.im.2005.11.004

Left, P. (n.d.). *Integrating Moodle and Mediawiki.* Retrieved July 5, 2010, from http://www.verso.co.nz/learning-technology/35/integrating-moodle-and-mediawiki/

Lehmann, K. (2004). *Innovation Diffusion Theory.* Retrieved April 3, 2010, from http://www.grin.com/e-book/80117/innovation-diffusion-theory Luo, G. (2009). e-government, people and social change: A case study of China. *Electronic Journal of Information Systems in Developing Countries, 38*(3), 1-23.

Leifer, R., & Mills, P. K. (1996). An information processing approach for deciding upon control strategies and reducing control loss n emerging organizations. *Journal of Management, 22*(1), 113–137. doi:10.1177/014920639602200105

Leland, C., Harste, J., & Smith, K. (2005). Out of the Box: Critical Literacy in a First-Grade Classroom. *Language Arts, 82*(4), 257–268.

Leslie, J. B., & van Velsor, E. (1996). *A look at Derailment Today: North America and Europe.* New York: SYMLOG Consulting Group.

Levin, S. A. (2003). Complex adaptive systems: Exploring the known, the unknown and the unknowable. *Bulletin of the American Mathematical Society, 40*(1), 3–19. doi:10.1090/S0273-0979-02-00965-5

Lewicki, R. J., & Bunker, B. B. (1996). Developing and maintaining trust in work relationships. In Tyler, T. R., & Kramer, R. M. (Eds.), *Trust in Organizations: Frontiers of Theory and Research* (pp. 114–139). Thousand Oaks, CA: Sage Publications.

Lewicki, R. J., McAllister, D. J., & Bies, R. J. (1998). Trust and Distrust: New relationships and realities. *Academy of Management Review, 23*(3), 438–458. doi:10.2307/259288

Lewin, R. (1999). *Complexity, life on the edge of chaos* (2nd ed.). Chicago: The University of Chicago Press.

Lewis, J. D., & Weigert, A. (1985). Trust as a social reality. *Social Forces, 63*(4), 967–985. doi:10.2307/2578601

Lewison, M., Flint, A. S., & Van Sluys, K. (2002). Taking on critical literacy: The journey of newcomers and novices. *Language Arts, 79*(5), 382–392.

Lincoln, Y. S., & Guba, E. G. (1985). *Naturalistic Inquiry.* Newbury Park, CA: Sage.

Lindsay, J. (2008). *Wikis that work. Practical and pedagogical applications of wikis in the classroom.* Retrieved July 5, 2010, from http://julielindsaylinks.pbwiki.com/Wikis-that-Work

Litvin, A., Konrad, J., & Karl, W. C. (2003). Probabilistic video stabilization using Kalman filtering and mosaicking. In *Proceedings of the IS&T/SPIE Symposium on Electronic Imaging, Image and Video Communications* (pp. 663-674).

Lizzio, A., & Wilson, K. (2006). Enhancing the effectiveness of self-managed learning groups: Understanding students' choices and concerns. *Studies in Higher Education, 31*(6), 689–703. doi:10.1080/03075070601004309

Locke, E. A., & Latham, G. P. (1984). *Goal-setting: A motivational technique that works.* Englewood Cliffs, NJ: Prentice-Hall.

Löfström, E., & Nevgi, A. (2008). University teaching staffs' pedagogical awareness displayed through ICT-facilitated teaching. *Interactive Learning Environments, 16*, 101–116. doi:10.1080/10494820701282447

Longàs, J., Civís, M., & Riera, J. (2008). Asesoramiento y desarrollo de redes socioeducativas locales. Funciones y metodología. *Cultura y Educación, 20*, 303–324. doi:10.1174/113564008785826330

Luhmann, N. (1986). The autopoiesis of social systems. In Geyer, F., & van der Zouwen, J. (Eds.), *Sociocybernetic Paradoxes* (pp. 172–192). Beverly Hills, CA: Sage Publications.

Lytras, M. D., Carroll, J. M., Damiani, E., & Tennyson, R. D. (2008). Emerging Technologies and Information Systems for the Knowledge Society. In *Proceedings of the First World Summit on the Knowledge Society,* Athens, Greece.

Lytras, M. D., & Pouloudi, A. (2003). Project management as a knowledge management primer: the learning infrastructure in knowledge-intensive organizations: projects as knowledge transformations and beyond. *The Learning Organization*, 10(4), 237–250. doi:10.1108/09696470310476007

Lytras, M. D., & Sicilia, M. A. (2005). The Knowledge Society: a manifesto for knowledge and learning. *Int. J. Knowledge and Learning*, 1(1/2), 1–11. doi:10.1504/IJKL.2005.006259

Machlup, F. (1962). *The Production and Distribution of Knowledge in the United States*. Princeton, NJ: Princeton University Press.

Mackey, M. (2002). An Asset Model of New Literacies. In Hammett, R., & Barrell, B. (Eds.), *Digital Expressions: Media Literacy and English Language Arts*. Calgary, Alberta, Canada: Detselig Enterprises Ltd.

Malhotra, Y., & Galletta, D. (1999). Extending the Technology Acceptance Model to Account to Account for Social Influence: Theoretical Bases and Empirical Validation. In *Proceedings of the 32nd Hawaii International Conference on System Sciences*.

Mandl, H., & Friedrich, H. F. (Eds.). (2005). *Handbuch Lernstrategien*. Göttingen, Germany: Hogrefe.

Mandl, H., & Hense, J. (2007). Lässt sich Unterricht durch Evaluation verbessern? In Schönig, W. (Ed.), *Spuren der Schulevaluation. Zur Bedeutung und Wirksamkeit von Evaluationskonzepten im Schulalltag* (pp. 85–99). Bad Heilbrunn, Germany: Klinkhardt.

Maness, J. M. (2006). *An evaluation of library instruction delivered to engineering students using streaming video*. Issues in Science and Technology Librarianship.

Mangione, G., Anna, P., & Salerno, S. (2009). A collaborative vision for generating available learning experiences. *Int. J. Knowledge and Learning*, 5(3/4), 306–317. doi:10.1504/IJKL.2009.031201

Mansell, R. (2002). From digital divides to digital entitlements in knowledge societies. *Current Sociology*, 50(3), 407–426. doi:10.1177/0011392102050003007

Manz, C., & Neck, S. (1997). Teamthink: beyond the groupthink syndrome in self-managing work teams. *Team Performance Management*, 3(1), 18–31. doi:10.1108/13527599710171255

March, J. G., & Olsen, J. P. (1994). *Rediscovering institutions: The Organizational Basis of Politics*. New York: Free Press.

Markkula, M. (2006). *Creating Favourable Conditions for Knowledge Society through Knowledge Management, eGorvernance and eLearning*. Paper presented at the FIG Workshop on eGovernance, Knowledge Management and eLearning, Budapest, Hungary.

Marshall, S. P. (1995). *Schemas in Problem Solving*. Cambridge, UK: Cambridge University Press. doi:10.1017/CBO9780511527890

Martins, L. L., Gilson, L. L., & Maynard, M. T. (2004). Virtual teams: What do we know and where do we go from here? *Journal of Management*, 30(6), 805–835. doi:10.1016/j.jm.2004.05.002

Marton, F., Dall'Alba, G., & Beaty, E. (1993). Conceptions of Learning. *International Journal of Educational Research*, 19(3), 277–300.

Marton, F., & Säljö, R. (1976). On qualitative differences in learning: I. Outcome and process. *The British Journal of Educational Psychology*, 46, 4–11.

Marton, K. (2007). *The great escape: Nine Jews who fled Hitler and changed the world*. New York: Simon & Schuster.

Massialas, V. (1981). *The Educational System of Greece*. Washington, DC: U.S. Government Printing Office.

Masterman, L. (1995). Media Education Worldwide: Objectives, values and superhighways. *Media Development*, 2, 37–51.

Matsuura, K. (2006). Knowledge Sharing – a powerful tool in the fight against poverty. *The Straits Times*, 27.

Mayer, R. (2008). Multimedia Literacy. In Coiro, J., Knobel, M., Lankshear, C., & Leu, D. (Eds.), *Handbook of Research on New Literacies*. New York: Lawrence Erlbaum Associates.

Mayo, M. J. (2007). Games for science and engineering education. *Communications of the ACM, 50*(7), 31–35. doi:10.1145/1272516.1272536

Maznevski, M. L., & Chudoba, K. M. (2000). Bridging space over time: Global virtual team dynamics and effectiveness. *Organization Science, 11*(5), 473–492. doi:10.1287/orsc.11.5.473.15200

Mbajiorgu, N., & Reid, N. (2006). *Factors Influencing Curriculum Development in Chemistry*. Hull, UK: Higher Education Academy Physical Sciences Centre.

McAllister, D. J. (1995). Affect- and Cognition-Based Trust as Foundations for Interpersonal Cooperation in Organizations. *Academy of Management Journal, 38*(1), 24–59. doi:10.2307/256727

McCall, M. (n.d.). *Leading the good life: lessons from the Greeks*. Paper presented at the Reunion Homecoming, Stanford University, Stanford, CA.

McCrohon, M., Lo, K., Dang, J., & Johnston, C. (2001). Video Streaming of Lectures Via the Internet An Experience. In *Proceedings of ASCILITE 2001 - The 18th Annual Conference of the Australasian Society for Computers in Learning in Tertiary Education,* Melbourne, Australia (pp. 397-405).

MCEETYA (Ministerial Council on Education Employment Training and Youth Affairs). (n.d.). *An education and training action plan for the information economy: Australia 2005-2007*. Retrieved September 2008 from www.mceetya.edu.au/aboutmc.htm

McIntosh, P. (1988). *White Privilege: Unpacking the Invisible Knapsack*. Retrieved from http://www.nymbp.org/reference/WhitePrivilege.pdf

McKeen, J. D., & Smith, H. A. (2003). *Making IT happen: critical issues in IT management* (pp. 75–90). New York: Wiley.

McNish, M. (2002). Guidelines for managing change: A study of their effects on the implementation of new information technology projects in organizations. *Journal of Change Management, 3*(2), 201–211.

Meltzer, D. E., & Manivannan, K. (2002). Transforming the lecture-hall environment: The fully interactive physics lecture. *American Journal of Physics, 70*(6), 639–654. doi:10.1119/1.1463739

Melville, D. (2009). *Report of an independent Committee of Inquiry into the impact on higher education of students' widespread use of Web 2.0 technologies*. London: Joint Information Systems Committee (JISC)

Merrick, K., & Maher, L. M. (2006). Motivated Reinforcement Learning for Non-Player Characters in Persistent Computer Game Worlds. In Proceedings of ACM Conference, Hollywood, California.

Meyerson, D., Weick, K. E., & Kramer, R. M. (1996). Swift trust and temporary groups. In Tyler, T. R., & Kramer, R. M. (Eds.), *Trust in organizations: Frontiers of theory and research* (pp. 166–195). Thousand Oaks, CA: Sage Publications.

Michael, Z. (2007). Creating a science of games. *Communications of the ACM, 50*(7), 27–29.

Miller, G. J. (1992). *Managerial Dilemmas: The Political Economy of Hierarchies*. New York: Cambridge University Press.

Miller, M. H., & Rock, K. (1985). Dividend policy under asymmetric information. *The Journal of Finance, 40,* 1031–1051. doi:10.2307/2328393

Mimirinis, M., & Bhattacharya, M. (2007). Design of virtual learning environments for deep learning. *Journal of Interactive Learning Research, 18*(1), 55–64.

Minović, M., & Štavljanin, V. (2006). MOBILE CLIENT FOR MOODLE CMS. In Proceedings of the International conference (IPSI 2006), Belgrade, Serbia.

Minović, M., Milovanović, M., Lazović, M., & Starčević, D. (2008). XML Application For Educative Games. In Proceedings of European Conference on Games Based Learning (ECGBL 08), Barcelona, Spain.

Minović, M., Štavljanin, V., & Vico, V. *(2007).* Educative game V-STRAT. *In* Proceedings of the International conference *(*SYM-OP-IS 2007*)*, Zlatibor, *Serbia.*

Minović, M., Štavljanin, V., Milovanović, M., Miroslav, L., & Milutinović, P. (2008). Game-Based Learning Environment. In Proceedings of the International conference(VIPSI 08), Bled, Slovenia.

Minović, M., Štavljanin, V., Starčević, D., & Milovanović, M. (2008). Usability issues of e-Learning systems: Case-study for Moodle Learning Management System. In Proceedigns of the OTM 2008 Workshops (LNCS 5333, pp. 561-570). Berlin: Springer-Verlag.

Modiglliani, F., & Miller, M. H. (1958). The cost of capital, corporation finance and the theory of investment. *The American Economic Review*, *48*, 261–297.

Moe, N. B., & Smite, D. (2008). Understanding lacking trust in global software teams: A multi-case study. *Software Process Improvement and Practice*, *13*(3), 217–231. doi:10.1002/spip.378

Mofleh, S., & Wanous, M. (1999). Understanding Factors Influencing Citizens Adoption of e-Government Services in the Developing World: Jordan as a Case Study. *Journal of Computer Science*, *7*(2), 1–11.

Mohrman, S. A., Cohen, S. G., & Mohrman, A. M. Jr. (1995). *Designing Team-Based Organizations, New Forms for Knowledge Work*. San Francisco, CA: Jossey-Bass.

Moller, K. (2002). Providing Support for dialogue in literature discussions about social justice. *Language Arts*, *79*(6), 467–476.

Monolescu, D., & Schifter, C. (2000). Online Focus Group: A Tool to Evaluate Online Students' Course Experience. *The Internet and Higher Education*, *2*, 171–176. doi:10.1016/S1096-7516(00)00018-X

Moodle. (2009). *Moodle development: wiki*. Retrieved July 5, 2010, from http://docs.moodle.org/en/Development:Wiki

Moodle. (2009). *Moodle docs - philosophy*. Retrieved July 5, 2010, from http://docs.moodle.org/en/Philosophy

Moodle. (2010). *Moodle forums thread about NWiki, and ouWiki*. Retrieved July 5, 2010, from http://moodle.org/mod/forum/discuss.php?d=89653

Moodle. (2010). *Moodle docs – pedagogy*. Retrieved July 5, 2010, from http://docs.moodle.org/en/Pedagogy

Moon, J.-W., & Kim, Y.-G. (2001). Extending the TAM for a World-Wide-Web context. *Information & Management*, *38*(4), 217–230. doi:10.1016/S0378-7206(00)00061-6

Moon, Y., Sánchez, T., & Durán, A. (2007). Teaching Professional Skills to Engineering Students with Enterprise Resource Planning (ERP): an International Project. *International Journal of Engineering Education*, *23*, 759–771.

Morales, P. (2008). *Corrección de las pruebas objetivas teniendo en cuenta el nivel de seguridad en las respuestas*. Retrieved January 1, 2010, from http://www.upcomillas.es/personal/peter/otrosdocumentos/NivelSeguridad.pdf

Moreno, R., & Mayer, R.-E. (2000). A Learner-Centred Approach to Multimedia Explanations: Deriving Instructional Design Principles from Cognitive Theory. *Interactive Multimedia Electronic Journal of Computer-Enhanced Learning, 2*.

Morgan, R. M., & Hunt, S. D. (1994). The commitment-trust theory of relationship marketing. *Journal of Marketing*, *58*(3), 20–38. doi:10.2307/1252308

Morimoto, C., & Chellappa, R. (1996). Fast electronic digital image stabilization. In *Proceedings of the 13th International Conference on Pattern Recognition* (Vol. 3, pp. 284-288).

Morin, E. (2004). *Introducción al pensamiento complejo*. Barcelona, Spain: Gedisa.

Morris, J. H., & Moberg, D. J. (1994). Work organizations as contexts for trust and betrayal. In Sarbin, T. R., Carney, R. M., & Eoyang, C. (Eds.), *Citizen Espionage: Studies in Trust and Betrayal* (pp. 163–187). Westport, CT: Praeger Publishers/Greenwood Publishing Group.

Morris, J. H., & Steers, R. M. (1980). Structural influences on organizational commitment. *Journal of Vocational Behavior*, *17*(1), 50–57. doi:10.1016/0001-8791(80)90014-7

Moser, R. (1997). A fantasy adventure game as a learning environment: Why learning to program is so difficult and what can be done about. In Proceedings of the (ITiCSE '97), Uppsala, Sweden. New York: ACM.

Murphy, J. (2005). *Beyond e-government - the world's most successful technology-enabled transformations, Executive Summary, MP Parliamentary Secretary Cabinet Office Report*. Retrieved from http://www.localtgov.org.uk

Mutc, A. (2003). Exploring the practice of feedback to students. *Active Learning in Higher Education*, *14*, 24–38. doi:10.1177/1469787403004001003

Myers, S. C. (1984). The capital structure puzzle. *The Journal of Finance*, *39*, 575–592. doi:10.2307/2327916

Myers, S. C., & Majluf, N. S. (1984). Corporate financing and investment decisions when firms have information that investors do not have. *Journal of Financial Economics*, *13*, 187–221. doi:10.1016/0304-405X(84)90023-0

Nahapiet, J., & Ghoshal, S. (1998). Social capital, intellectual capital and organizational advantage. *Academy of Management Review*, *23*(2), 242–266. doi:10.2307/259373

Nash, J. F. (1950). Equilibrium Points in N-Person Games. *Proceedings of the National Academy of Sciences of the United States of America*, *36*, 48–49. doi:10.1073/pnas.36.1.48

National Innovation Initiative Interim Report, Innovative America. (2004). Retrieved from http://www.goalqpc.com/docs/reports/NIIInterimReport.pdf

National Strategy on Information Society Development. *"e-Moldova".* (2003). Retrieved from http://www.mdi.gov.md/info21_en/

New London Group. (1996). A Pedagogy of Multiliteracies: Designing Social Futures. *Harvard Educational Review*, *66*(1), 60–92.

Newell, S., & Swan, J. (2000). Trust and inter-organizational networking. *Human Relations*, *53*(10), 1287–1328.

Newman, M. E. J. (2003). The structure and function of complex networks. *SIAM Review*, *45*(2), 167–256. doi:10.1137/S003614450342480

Nielsen, J. (2003). *Usability 101: Introduction to Usability.*

Nonaka, I., & Peltokorpi, V. (2006). Visionary knowledge management: the case of Eisai transformation. *International Journal of Learning and Intellectual Capital*, *3*(2), 109–209.

Nonaka, I., & Takeuchi, H. (1995). *The Knowledge Creating Company*. New York: Oxford University Press.

Nonaka, I., Toyama, R., & Konno, N. (2000). SECI, *Ba* and Leadership: A unified model of dynamic knowledge creation. *Long Range Planning*, *33*, 5–34. doi:10.1016/S0024-6301(99)00115-6

Nooteboom, B. (2002). *Trust: Forms, Foundations, Functions, Failures and Figures*. Cheltenham, UK: Edward Elgar.

Norris, P. (2000). *Digital Divide?* Retrieved March, 12, 2009, from http://ksghome.harvard.edu/~pnorris/acrobat/digitalch6.pdf

Nulty, D. D., & Barrett, M. A. (1996). Transitions in students' learning styles. *Studies in Higher Education*, *22*(3), 333–345. doi:10.1080/03075079612331381251

O'Donnell, M. (2006). Blogging as Pedagogic Practice: Artefact and Ecology. *Asia Pacific Media Educator, December*(17).

Obrenovic, Z., & Starcevic, D. (2004). Modeling multimodal Human-Computer interaction. *IEEE Computer*, *37*(9), 62–69.

Okubo, (2006). *R&D Satellite Account: Preliminary Estimates*. Washington, DC: Bureau of Economic Analysis.

Olssen, M., & Peters, M. A. (2005). Neoliberalism, higher eduction and the knowledge economy: From the free market to knowledge capitalism. *Journal of Education Policy*, *20*(3), 313–345. doi:10.1080/02680930500108718

Orlikowski, W. J. (1996). Improvising organizational transformation over time. *Information Systems Research*, *7*(1), 63–92. doi:10.1287/isre.7.1.63

Oshri, I., Kotlarsky, J., & Willcocks, L. P. (2007). Global Software Development: Exploring socialization in distributed strategic projects. *The Journal of Strategic Information Systems*, *16*(1), 25–49. doi:10.1016/j.jsis.2007.01.001

Oza, N. V., Hall, T., Rainer, A., & Grey, S. (2006). Trust in software outsourcing relationships: An empirical investigation of Indian software companies. *Information and Software Technology*, *48*(5), 345–354. doi:10.1016/j.infsof.2005.09.011

Panagis, Y., Sakkopoulos, E., Tsakalidis, A., Tzimas, G., Sirmakessis, S., & Lytras, M. D. (2008). Techniques for mining the design of e-government services to enhance end-user experience. *International Journal of Electronic Democracy*, *1*(1), 32–50. doi:10.1504/IJED.2008.021277

Paper, D., & Ugray, Z. (2008). Change Management: A Sensible Approach for IT Researchers. *Journal of Information Technology Case and Application Research*, *3*(8), 1–8.

Parisopoulos, K., Tambouris, E., & Tarabanis, K. (2009). Transformational Government in Europe: A Survey of National Policies. In *Proceedings of the Second World Summit on the Knowledge Society (WSKS 2009)* (pp. 462-471).

Parry, K. W. (1998). Grounded theory and social process: A new direction for leadership research. *The Leadership Quarterly, 9*(1), 85–106. doi:10.1016/S1048-9843(98)90043-1

Patel, H., & Jacobson, D. (2008). Factors Influencing Citizen Adoption of E-Government: A Review and Critical Assessment. In W. Golden, T. Acton, K. Conboy, H. van der Heijden, & V. K. Tuunainen (Eds.), *Proceedings of the 16th European Conference on Information Systems,* Galway, Ireland (pp. 1058-1069).

Pavard, B., & Dugdale, J. (2000, May 21-26). *The contribution of complexity theory to the study of sociotechnical cooperative systems.* Paper presented at the Third International Conference on Complex Systems, Nashua, NH. Retrieved from http://www-svcict.fr/cotcos/pjs/

Pavlou, P. A. (2003). Consumer Acceptance of Electronic Commerce: Integrating Trust and Risk with the Technology Acceptance Model. *International Journal of Electronic Commerce, 7*(3), 69–103.

Petty, R. E., & Cacioppo, J. T. (1981). *Attitudes and Persuasion: Classic and Contemporary Approaches.* Dubuque, IA: Wm. C. Brown Company Publishers.

Piccoli, G., & Ives, B. (2003). Trust and the unintended effects of behavior control in virtual teams. *Management Information Systems Quarterly, 27*(3), 368–395.

Pihlanto, P. (2000). *An actor in an individual situation: The holistic individual image and perspectives on accounting research* (Series Discussion and Working Papers 4). Turku, Finland: Publications of the Turku School of Economics and Business Administration.

Pihlanto, P. (2002). *Understanding Behaviour of the Decision-maker in an Accounting Context. The Theater Metaphor for Conscious Experience and the Holistic Individual Image.* Turku, Finland: Publications of the Turku School of Economics and Business Administration.

Pihlanto, P. (2009). *Decision-Maker in Focus. The Holistic Individual in the Theater of Consciousness.* Köln, Germany: Lambert Academic Publishing.

Pilatti, L., Audy, J. L. N., & Prikladnicki, R. (2006). Software configuration management over a global software development environment: lessons learned from a case study. In *Proccedings of the 2006 International Workshop on Global Software Development for the Practitioner International Conference on Software Engeneering,* Shanghai, China.

Pinto, J. K., & Kharbanda, O. P. (1995). *Successful Project Managers: Leading Your Team to Success.* New York: Van Nostrand Reinhold.

Pintrich, P. R. (2004). A conceptual framework for assessing motivation and self-regulated learning in college students. *Educational Psychology Review, 16*(4), 385–407.

Pintrich, P. R., Smith, D. A. F., Garcia, T., & Mckeachie, W. J. (1993). Reliability and predictive validity of the motivated strategies for learning questionnaire (MSLQ). *Educational and Psychological Measurement, 53,* 801–813. doi:10.1177/0013164493053003024

Pivec, M. (2007). Play and learn: potentials of game-based learning. *British Journal of Educational Technology, 38*(3), 387–393. doi:10.1111/j.1467-8535.2007.00722.x

Ploetzner, R., Bodemer, D., & Neudert, S. (2008). Successful and Less Sucessful Use of Dynamic Visualisations in Instructional Texts. In Lowe, R., & Schnotz, W. (Eds.), *Learning with Animation: Research Implications for Design* (pp. 71–91). New York: Cambridge University Press.

Poltrock, S. E., & Engelbeck, G. (1999). Requirements for a virtual collocation environment. *Information and Software Technology, 41*(6), 331–339. doi:10.1016/S0950-5849(98)00066-4

Porter, M. (1998). *Competitive Advantage: Creating and Sustaining Superior Performance.* New York: Free Press.

Porter, M. (1998). *The Competitive Advantage of Nations.* New York: Free Press.

Powell, W. (1996). Trust-based forms of governance. In Kramer, R. M., & Tyler, T. R. (Eds.), *Trust in Organizations: Frontiers of theory and research* (pp. 51–67). Thousand Oaks, CA: Sage Publications.

Powell, W. W., & Snellman, K. (2004). The Knowledge Economy. *Annual Review of Sociology*, *30*, 199–220. doi:10.1146/annurev.soc.29.010202.100037

Providers Edge. (2007). *Knowledge management and corporate culture*. Retrieved September 2008 from www.providersedge.com

Prowell, S. J., Trammell, C. J., Linger, R. C., & Poore, J. H. (1999). *Cleanroom software engineering: technology and process*. Reading, MA: Addison Wesley.

Putnam, R. D. (1993). *Making Democracy Work: Civic Traditions in Modern Italy*. Princeton, NJ: Princeton University Press.

Pyzdek, T. (2003). *The Six Sigma Handbook*. New York: McGrawHill.

Ramesh, B., Cao, L., Mohan, K., & Xu, P. (2006). Can distributed software development be agile? *Communications of the ACM*, *49*(10), 41–46. doi:10.1145/1164394.1164418

Ramsden, P. (1992). *Learning to Teach in Higher Education*. London: Routledge. doi:10.4324/9780203413937

Rauhala, L. (1988). Holistinen ihmiskäsitys (Summary: The Holistic Conception of Man). *Journal of Social Medicine*, 190-201.

Rauhala, L. (1986). *Ihmiskäsitys ihmistyössä* [The Conception of Human Being in Helping People]. 3rd ed. Helsinki, Finland: Gaudeamus.

Regis, E. (1991). *Who got Einstein's office?: Eccentricity and genius at the Institute for Advanced Study*. Reading, MA: Addison-Wesley.

Reinhardt, G., & Cook, L. S. (2006). Is This a Game or a Learning Moment? *Decision Sciences Journal of Innovative Education*, *4*(2). doi:10.1111/j.1540-4609.2006.00119.x

Reinmann-Rothmeier, G., Mandl, H., Erlach, C., & Neubauer, A. (2001). *Wissensmanagement lernen. Ein Leitfaden zur Gestaltung von Workshops und zum Selbstlernen*. Weinheim, Germany: Beltz.

Reisslein, J., Seeling, P., & Reisslein, M. (2005). Video in distance education: ITFS vs. web-streaming: Evaluation of student attitudes. *The Internet and Higher Education*, *8*, 25–44. doi:10.1016/j.iheduc.2004.12.002

Resnick, L. B., Levine, J. M., & Teasley, S. D. (Eds.). (1991). *Perspectives on socially shared cognition*. Washington, DC: American Psychological Association. doi:10.1037/10096-000

Rhodes, R. A. W. (1997). *Understanding governance - policy networks: Governance, reflexivity and accountability*. Buckingham, UK: Open University Press.

Rhodos, G., & Heidari, A. (1994). Research and Development Competition and Development of Market Structure. In Christopher, A. (Ed.), *Advances in econometrics*. Cambridge, UK: Cambridge University Press.

Ricart i Costa, J. E. (1989). On managerial contracting with asymmetric information. *European Economic Review*, *33*(9), 1805–1830. doi:10.1016/0014-2921(89)90071-8

Rico, R., & Alcover, C-M., Sanchez- Manzanares, M., & Gil, F. (2009). The joint relationships of communication behaviors and task interdependence on trust building and change in virtual teams. *Social Sciences Information. Information Sur les Sciences Sociales*, *48*(2), 229–255. doi:10.1177/0539018409102410

Ring, P. S., & Van de Ven, A. H. (1992). Structuring cooperative relationships between organizations. *Strategic Management Journal*, *13*(7), 483–498. doi:10.1002/smj.4250130702

Robert, G. (n.d.). *VideoMaker Magazine The End Of ShakyCamera*. Retrieved January 13, 2006, from http://www.videomaker.com/scripts/article_print.cfm?id=9999

Robertson, J. A. (2004). *The critical factors for information technology investment success* (pp. 111–117). Johannesburg, South Africa: J A Robertson and Associates.

Robinson, S. L. (1996). Trust and breach of the psychological contract. *Administrative Science Quarterly*, *41*(4), 574–599. doi:10.2307/2393868

Rocco, E. (1998). Trust breaks down in electronic context but can be repaired by some initial face-to-face contact. In *Proceedings of the SIGCHI conference on Human factors in computing systems*, Los Angeles, CA (pp. 496-502). New York: ACM.

Rodrigues, M. J. (2002). *The New Knowledge Economy in Europe: A Strategy for International Competitiveness and Social Cohesion*. Cheltenham, UK: Edward Elgar.

Rodrigues, M. J. (2003). *European Policies for a Knowledge Economy*. Cheltenham, UK: Edward Elgar.

Rodríguez, L. (2005). *Libro Blanco sobre los estudios de grado en Economía y Empresa. Aneca.* Retrieved January 10, 2010, from http://www.aneca.es/media/150292/libroblanco_economia_def.pdf

Rodriguez-Ortiz, G. (2003). Knowledge Management and Quality Certification in a Research and Development Environment. *Computer Science*, 89-94.

Rogers, E. M. (1995). *Diffusion of innovations* (4th ed.). New York: Free Press.

Romano, A., De Maggio, M., & Del Vecchio, P. (2009). The Emergence of a New Managerial Mindset. In Romano, A. (Ed.), *Open Business Innovation Leadership. The Emergence of the Stakeholder University*. UK: Palgrave Macmillan.

Ronchetti, M. (2003). *Has the time come for using video-based lectures over the Internet? A Test-case report.* Paper presented at CATE - Web Based Education Conference, Rhodes, Greece.

Ronchetti, M. (2003). Using the Web for diffusing multimedia lectures: a case study. In *Proceedings of ED-MEDIA* (pp. 337-340).

Ronchetti, M. (2009). Using video lectures to make teaching more interactive. In *Proceedings of the International Conference on Interactive Computer Aided Learning ICL-2009*.

Ronchetti, M. (2010). A Different Perspective on Lecture Video-Streaming: How to Use Technology to Help Change the Traditional Lecture Model. *International Journal of Knowledge Society Research*, *1*(2), 50–60.

Rousseau, D. M., Sitkin, S. B., Burt, R. S., & Carmerer, C. (1998). Not so different after all: a cross-discipline view of trust. *Academy of Management Review*, *23*(3), 393–404.

Saade, R., & Bahli, B. (2005). The impact of cognitive absorption on perceived usefulness and perceived ease of use in on-line learning: an extension of the technology acceptance model. *Information & Management*, *42*(2), 317–327. doi:10.1016/j.im.2003.12.013

Sabherwal, R. (1999). The Role of Trust in Outsourced IS Development Projects. *Communications of the ACM*, *42*(2), 80–86. doi:10.1145/293411.293485

Sagasti, F. (2004). *Knowledge and Information for Development*. Northampton, MA: Edward Elgar.

Sainsbury, E. J., & Walker, R. A. (2008). Assessment as a vehicle for learning: extending collaboration into testing. *Assessment & Evaluation in Higher Education*, *33*(2), 103–117. doi:10.1080/02602930601127844

Sajjapanroj, S., Bonk, C., Lee, M. M., & Lin, M. G. (2008). A window on wikibookians: surveying their statuses, successes, satisfactions, and sociocultural experiences. *Journal of Interactive Online Learning*, *7*, 36–58.

Sakai. (n.d.). *Sakai wiki tool (rwiki).* Retrieved July 5, 2010, from http://confluence.sakaiproject.org/confluence/display/RWIKI/Home

Salas, E., Sims, D. E., & Burke, C. S. (2005). Is there a "big five" in teamwork? *Small Group Research*, *36*(5), 555–599. doi:10.1177/1046496405277134

Säljö, R. S. (1979). *Learning in the learner's perspective. I. Some common-sense conceptions (Rep. No. 76).* Gothenberg, Sweden: University of Gothenberg.

Salmon, G. (2005). Flying not flapping: A strategic framework for e-learning and pedagogical innovation in higher education institutions. *ALT-J Research in Learning Technology*, *13*(3), 201–218.

Samarajiva, R., & Gamage, S. (2007). Bridging the Divide: Building Asia-Pacific Capacity for Effective Reforms. *The Information Society*, *23*, 109–117. doi:10.1080/01972240701224200

Sang, S., Lee, J.-D., & Lee, J. (2009). E-government adoption in ASEAN: the case of Cambodia. *Internet Research*, *19*(5), 517–534. doi:10.1108/10662240910998869

Sato, K. (1988). Trust and group size in a social dilemma. *The Japanese Psychological Research*, *30*(2), 88–93.

Sauer, C., Smith, C., & Benz, T. (2007). Wikicreole: a common wiki markup. In *Proceedings of the 2007 International Symposium on Wikis* (pp. 131-142). New York: ACM Press.

Schagaev, I. (1990). Yet Another Approach to Classification of Redundancy. In *Proceedings of the IMEKO Congress,* Helsinki, Finland (pp. 485-490).

Schagaev, I. (2001). Redundancy Classification For Fault Tolerant Computer Design. In *Proceedings of the 2001 IEEE Systems, Man, and Cybernetics Conference,* Tuscon, AZ.

Schagaev, I., & Buhanova, G. (2001, July). Comparative Study of Fault Tolerant RAM Structures. In *Proceedings of the IEEE DSN Conference,* Goteborg, Sweden.

Scharma, R. S., Ng, E. W. J., Dharmawirya, M., & Samual, E. M. (2010). A Policy framework for developing knowledge societies. A review. *International Journal of Knowledge Society Research, 1*(1), 22–45.

Schaumburg, H. (2008). *Die 5 Ws der Evaluaion von E-Learning.*

Schiller, S. Z., & Mandiwala, M. (2007). Virtual team research: an analysis of theory use and a framework for theory appropriation. *Small Group Research, 38*(1), 12–59. doi:10.1177/1046496406297035

Schnurer, K. (2005). *Kooperatives Lernen in virtuell-asynchronen Hochschulseminaren. Eine Prozess-Produkt-Analyse des virtuellen Seminars "Einführung in das Wissensmanagement" auf der Basis von Felddaten.* Munich, Germany: Department Psychologie, Institut für Pädagogische Psychologie. Ludwig-Maximilians-Universität.

Schöbel, M. (2009). Trust in high-reliability organizations. *Social Sciences Information. Information Sur les Sciences Sociales, 48*(2), 315–333. doi:10.1177/0539018409102416

Schön, D. (1998). *El profesional reflexivo. Cómo piensan los profesionales cuando actúan.* Barcelona, Spain: Paidos.

Schrire, S. (2006). Knowledge building in asynchronous learning groups: Going beyond quantitative analysis. *Computers & Education, 46*(1), 49–70. doi:10.1016/j.compedu.2005.04.006

Schuler, H., & Stehle, W. (1983). Neuere Entwicklungen des Assessment-Center-Ansatzes – beurteilt unter dem Aspekte der sozialen Validität. *Zeitschrift für Arbeits- und Organisationspsychologie, 27,* 33–44.

Schumpeter, J. (1961). *The Theory of Economic Development.* New York: Oxford University Press.

Schwaber, K., & Beedle, M. (2001). *Agile software development with Scrum.* Upper Saddle River, NJ: Prentice Hall.

Schwalbe, K. (2010). *Information Technology Project Management* (3rd ed.). London: Thomson Course Tech.

Schwartz, L., Clark, S., Cossarin, M., & Rudolph, J. (2004). Educational wikis: features and selection criteria. *International Review of Research in Open and Distance Learning, 5.*

Schweizer, K., Pächter, M., & Weidenmann, B. (2001). A field study on distance education and communication: Experiences of a virtual tutor. *Journal of Computer-Mediated Communication, 6.*

Scriven, M. (1980). *The logic of evaluation.* Iverness, UK: Edgepress.

Scriven, M. (1991). *Evaluation Thesaurus.* London: Sage.

Selber, S. (2004). *Multiliteracies for a Digital Age.* Carbondale, IL: Southern Illinois University Press.

Senge, P., Kleiner, A., Roberts, C., Ross, R. B., & Smith, B. J. (1994). *The Fifth Discipline Fieldbook: Strategies and Tools for Building a Learning Organization.* New York: Knopf Doubleday.

Serradell-Lopez, E., & Cavaller, V. (2009). National culture and the secrecy of innovations. *Int. J. Knowledge and Learning, 5*(3/4), 222–234. doi:10.1504/IJKL.2009.031197

Serradell-López, E., Jiménez-Zarco, A. I., & Martinez-Ruiz, M. P. (2009). Success Factors in IT-Innovative Product Companies: A Conceptual Framework. *Communications in Computer and Information Science, 49,* 366–376. doi:10.1007/978-3-642-04757-2_39

Sfard, A. (1998). On two metaphors for learning and the dangers of choosing just one. *Educational Researcher, 27,* 4–13. doi:10.2307/1176193

Shah, S. (2006). *The body hunters: Testing new drugs on the world's poorest patients.* New York: New Press.

Shapiro, A. M. (2004). Prior Knowledge Must Be Included as a Subject Variable in Learning Outcomes Research. *American Educational Research Journal, 41,* 159–189. doi:10.3102/00028312041001159

Shapiro, D. L., Sheppard, B. H., & Cheraskin, L. (1992). Business on a handshake. *Negotiation Journal, 8*(4), 365–377. doi:10.1111/j.1571-9979.1992.tb00679.x

Sharma, R. S. (2007). Value-Added Knowledge Management For Financial Performance: The Case of an East Asian Conglomerate. *The Journal of Information and Knowledge Management Systems, 37*(4), 484–501.

Sharma, R. S., & Azura, I. M. (2005). Bridging the Digital Divide in Asia - Challenges and Solutions. *International Journal of Technology. Knowledge and Society, 1*(3), 15–30.

Sharma, R. S., Ng, E. W. J., Dharmawirya, M., & Samuel, E. M. (2010). A Policy Framework for Developing Knowledge Societies. *International Journal of Knowledge Society Research, 1*(1), 22–45.

Sharp, H., Baddoo, N., Beecham, S., Tracy, H., & Robinson, H. (2009). Models of motivation in software engineering. *Information and Software Technology, 51*(1), 219–233. doi:10.1016/j.infsof.2008.05.009

Shaw, R. B. (1997). *Trust in the balance: building successful organizations on results, integrity, and concern.* San Francisco: Jossey-Bass.

Shih, H.-P. (2004). Extended technology acceptance model of Internet utilization behavior. *Information & Management, 41*(6), 719–729. doi:10.1016/j.im.2003.08.009

Shin, D., Yoon, E. S., Park, S. J., & Lee, E. S. (2002). Web-based interactive virtual laboratory system for unit operations and process systems engineering education. *Computers & Chemical Engineering, 24*, 381–385.

Shockley-Zalaback, P., Ellis, K., & Winograd, G. (2000). Organizational trust: what it means, why it matters? *Organization Development Journal, 18*(4), 35–48.

Siemens, G. (2005). Connectivism. A learning theory for the digital age. *International Journal of Instructional Technology & Distance Learning, 2*(1).

Singh, M., Sarkar, P., Dissanayake, D., & Pittachayawan, S. (2008). Diffusions of e-government services in Australia: Citizens' perspectives In W. Golden, T. Acton, K. Conboy, H. van der Heijden, & V. K. Tuunainen (Eds.), *Proceedings of the 16th European Conference on Information Systems,* Galway, Ireland (pp. 1227-1238).

Singh, V. (2007, December 28-30). Full Circle of Governance: How to Leverage Age Old Organic Structure of Governance. In *Proceedings of the 5th International Conference on E-governance,* Hyderabad, India. Retrieved November 28, 2009, from http://www.iceg.net/2007/books/3/2_281_3.pdf

Six, F. (2003). The dynamics of trust and trouble. In Nooteboom, B., & Six, F. (Eds.), *The trust process in organizations* (pp. 196–222). Cheltenham, UK: Edward Elgar.

Sloodle (Online). (2008). Retrieved from http://www.sloodle.org

Soete, W. D. (2006). *Understanding the Dynamics of a Knowledge Economy.* Cheltenham, UK: Edward Elgar.

Sonnekus, R., & Labuschagne, L. (2003). IT Project Management Maturity versus Project Success in South Africa. *The Prosperus Report.*

Sonntag, K.-H. (2002). Personalentwicklung und Training. Stand der psychologischen Forschung und Gestaltung. *Zeitschrift für Personalpsychologie, 2,* 59–70. doi:10.1026//1617-6391.1.2.59

Soong, S. K. A., Chan, L. K., & Cheers, C. (2006). Impact of video recorded lectures among students. In *Proceedings of the 23rd Annual Ascilite Conference: Who's learning? Whose technology?* (pp. 789-792).

Sorensen, E., & Torfing, J. (2004). *Making Governance Networks Democratic. Center for Democratic Network Governance.* Retrieved from http://www.ruc.dk/upload/application/pdf/7c331b9c/Working_Paper_2004_1.pdf

Sorrentino, R. M., Holmes, J. G., Hanna, S. E., & Sharp, A. (1995). Uncertainty orientation and trust in close relationships: individual differences in cognitive styles. *Journal of Personality and Social Psychology, 68*(2), 314–327. doi:10.1037/0022-3514.68.2.314

Squire, K., Barnett, M., Grant, J., & Higginbotham, T. (2004). Electromagnetism supercharged! Learning physics with digital simulation games. In Proceedings of the 2004 International Conference of the Learning Sciences, Santa Monica, CA. *Los Angeles:* UCLA Press.

Stark, R., & Mandl, H. (2002). *"Unauffällige", "Vorwissensschwache", "Unmotivierte" und "Musterschüler": Homogene Untergruppen beim Lernen mit einem komplexen Lösungsbeispiel im Bereich empirischer Forschungsmethoden*. Munich, Germany: Ludwig-Maximilians-Universität, Lehrstuhl für Empirische Pädagogik und Pädagogische Psychologie.

Steiner, B., Kaplan, N., & Moulthrop, S. (2006, June 7-9). When play works: Turning game-playing into learning. In Proceedings of (IDC '06), Tampere, Finland.

Stein, J. C. (1989). Efficient capital markets, inefficient firms: a model of myopic corporate behaviour. *The Quarterly Journal of Economics*, 656–669.

Stinchcombe, A. L. (1990). *Information and Organizations*. Berkley, CA: University of California Press.

Stockmann, R. (2000). Evaluation in Deutschland. In R. Stockmann (Ed.), *Evaluationsforschung. Grundlagen und ausgewählte Forschungsfelder* (pp. 11-40). Opladen, Germany: Leske + Budrich.

Strategy of the development of information society in the Russian Federation. (2007). Retrieved from http://www.kremlin.ru/text/docs/2007/07/138695.shtml

Stufflebeam, D. L. (1978). An introduction to the PDK book. Educational evaluation and decision-making. In Sanders, J. R., & Scriven, M. (Eds.), *Educational Evaluation: Theory and Practice* (pp. 128–150). Belmont, CA: Charles A. Jones Publication, Wadsworth Publishing Company.

Subirats, J., & Albaigés, B. (Eds.). (2006). *Educació i comunitat. Reflexions a l'entorn del treball integrat dels agents educatius. Col·lecció finestra oberta*. Barcelona, Spain: Fundació Jaume Bofill.

Suchan, J., & Hayzak, G. (2001). The communication characteristics of virtual teams: a case study. *IEEE Transactions on Professional Communication*, *44*(3), 174–186. doi:10.1109/47.946463

Svozil, K., & Wright, R. (2005). Statistical Structures Underlying Quantum Mechanics and Social Science. *International Journal of Theoretical Physics*, *44*(7), 1067–1086.

Sydow, J. (1998). Understanding the constitution of interorganizational trust. In Lane, C., & Bachmann, F. (Eds.), *Trust within and between organizations* (pp. 31–63). Oxford, UK: Oxford University Press.

Tait, H., Entwistle, N., & McCune, V. (1998). ASSIST: A reconceptualisation of the approaches to studying inventory. In Rust, C. (Ed.), *Improving student learning: improving students as learners*. Oxford, UK: Oxford Brookes University.

Tallent-Runnels, M.-K. (2005). The relationship between problems with technology and graduate students' evaluations of online teaching. *The Internet and Higher Education*, *8*, 167–174. doi:10.1016/j.iheduc.2005.03.005

Taweel, A., & Brereton, P. (2006). Modeling software development across time zones. *Information and Software Technology*, *48*(1), 1–11. doi:10.1016/j.infsof.2004.02.006

Taylor, S., & Todd, P. (1995). Assessing IT usage: The role of prior experience. *Management Information Systems Quarterly*, *19*(4), 561–570. doi:10.2307/249633

Taylor, S., & Todd, P. (1995). Understanding Information Technology usage: A test of competing models. *Information Systems Research*, *6*(2), 144–176. doi:10.1287/isre.6.2.144

Teekaput, P., & Waiwanijchakij, P. (2006). eLearning and Knowledge Management, Symptoms of a Reality. In *Proceedings of the Third International Conference on eLearning for Knowledge-Based Society*, Bangkok, Thailand.

Tennyson, R. D., Schott, F., Seel, N. M., & Dijkstra, S. (1997). Instructional Design: International Perspectives: *Vol. 2. Solving instructional design problems*. Mahwah, NJ: Lawrence Erlbaum Associates.

Teo, T., Srivastava, S., & Jiang, L. (2008). Trust and Electronic Government Success: An Empirical Study. *Journal of Management Information Systems*, *25*(3), 99–131. doi:10.2753/MIS0742-1222250303

Tergan, S.-O. (2004). Realistische Qualitätsevaluation von E-learning. In Meister, D., Tergan, S.-O., & Zentel, P. (Eds.), *Evaluation von E-Learning. Zielrichtungen, methodologische Aspekte, Zukunftsperspektiven* (pp. 131–154). Münster, Germany: Waxmann.

Tergan, S.-O., & Schenkel, P. (2002). Was macht Lernen erfolgreich? Evaluation des Lernpotenzials von E-Learning. In Hohenstein, A., & Wilbers, K. (Eds.), *Handbuch E-Learning*. Köln, Germany: Fachverlag Dt. Wirtschaftsdienst.

The Economist Intelligence Unit. (2009). *E-readiness ranking 2009*. Retrieved March 12, 2009, from http://www-935.ibm.com/services/us/gbs/bus/pdf/e-readiness_rankings_june_2009_final_web.pdf

The Networked Readiness Index. (2007-2008). Retrieved from http://www.weforum.org/pdf/gitr/2008/Rankings.pdf

The Standish Group International. (n.d.). *Latest Standish Group Chaos Report. Chaos Chronicle*s. Retrieved from http://www.standishgroup.com

Tobagi, F. (1995). Distance learning with digital video. *Multimedia, 2*(1), 90–93. doi:10.1109/93.368609

Toohey, S. (1999). *Designing Courses for Higher Education*. Buckingham, UK: The Society for Research into Higher Education & Open University Press.

Torralba, F. (2006). *La responsabilitat asimétrica dels agents educatius sustenta la pedagogía de la corensponsabilitat*. I Tribuna.

Treagust, D. (2007). General Instructional Methods and Strategies. In Abell, S. K., & Lederman, N. G. (Eds.), *Handbook of Research in Science Teaching* (pp. 373–392). Mahwah, NJ: Lawrence Erlbaum Associates Publishers.

Trigo, A., Varajão, J., Soto-Acosta, P., Molina-Castillo, F. J., & Gonzalvez-Gallego, N. (2010). IT Professionals: An Iberian Snapshot. *International Journal of Human Capital and Information Technology Professionals, 1*(1), 61–75.

Tsoukas, H. (1991). The missing link: a transformational view of metaphors in organizational science. *Academy of Management Review, 16*(3), 566–585. doi:10.2307/258918

Turner, R. J., & Simister, S. J. (2004). *Gower Handbook of Project Management*. Bucharest, Romania: Codecs Printing House.

Twitchell, D. P., Wiers, K., Judee, M. A., Burgoon, K., & Nunamaker, J. F., Jr. *(2005)*. StrikeCOM: A Multi-Player Online Strategy Game for Researching and Teaching Group Dynamics. In Proceedings of the 38th Hawaii International Conference on System Sciences.

UK-Idea. (n.d.). Retrieved October 2008 from http://uk-idea.co.uk/html/basics.htm

UNDP. (2007). *Human Development Report 2007/2008*. Retrieved December 12, 2007 from http://hdr.undp.org/en/media/hdr_20072008_en_complete.pdf

UNESCO. (2005). *From the Information Society to Knowledge Societies*. Paris: UNESCO Publishing.

UNESCO. (2007). *E-governance capacity building*. Retrieved April 23, 2009, from http://www.unesco.org/webworld/e-governance

United Nations Commission for Science and Technology Development (UNCSTD). Retrieved from http://www.unesco.org/webworld/telematics/uncstd.htm

United Nations. (2008). *UN e-government survey 2008: From E-Government to connected governance*. Retrieved April 23, 2009, from http://unpan1.un.org/intradoc / groups/ public/ documents/UN/ UNPAN028607. pdf

Usher, R. S. (1989). Locating experience in language: Towards a poststructuralist theory of experience. *Adult Education Quarterly, 40*(1), 23–32.

Valadas, S., Gonçalves, F., & Faísca, L. (2009). Approaches to studying in higher education Portuguese students: A Portuguese version of the approaches and study skills inventory for students. *Higher Education, 59*, 259–275. doi:10.1007/s10734-009-9246-5

Valentine, J. (1994). *One Dad, two Dads, Brown dad, Blue dads*. Los Angeles, CA: Alyson Wonderland.

Vales, E. (2007). Employees CAN make a difference! Involving employees in change at Allstate Insurance. *Organization Development Journal, 4*(25), 27–31.

Van de Ven, A. (1986). Central Problems in the Management of Innovation. *Management Science, 32*(5). doi:10.1287/mnsc.32.5.590

Venkatesh, V., & Davis, F. (2000). A theoretical extension of the technology acceptance model: Four longitudinal field studies. *Management Science, 46*(2), 186–204. doi:10.1287/mnsc.46.2.186.11926

Veron, D. T., & Blake, R. L. (1993). Does problem-based learning work? A meta-analysis of evaluative Research. *Academic Medicine, 68,* 550–563. doi:10.1097/00001888-199307000-00015

Vijayasarath, L. (2004). Predicting consumer intentions to use on-line shopping: the case for an augmented technology acceptance model. *Information & Management, 41*(6), 747–762. doi:10.1016/j.im.2003.08.011

Von Kalckreuth, U. (2003). Investment and Monetary Transmission in Germany: A Microeconometric Investigation. In Angeloni, I., Kashyap, A., & Mojon, B. (Eds.), *Monetary Policy Transmission in the Euro Area*. Cambridge, UK: Cambridge University Press. doi:10.1017/CBO9780511492372.012

Von Neumann, J., & Mongerstern, O. (1953). *Theory of games and econonmic behavior* (3rd ed.). Princeton, NJ: Princeton University Press.

Wang, K. T., Huang, Y.-M., Jeng, Y.-L., & Wang, T.-I. (2008). A blog-based dynamic learning map. *Computers & Education, 51,* 262–278. doi:10.1016/j.compedu.2007.06.005

Wangpipatwong, S., Chutimaskul, W., & Papasratorn, B. (2008). Understanding Citizen's Continuance Intention to Use e-Government Website: a Composite View of Technology Acceptance Model and Computer Self-Efficacy. *Electronic. Journal of E-Government, 6*(1), 55–64.

Warkentin, M. E., Sayeed, L., & Hightower, R. (1997). Virtual teams versus face-to-face teams: an exploratory study of web-based conference systems. *Decision Sciences, 28*(4), 975–996. doi:10.1111/j.1540-5915.1997.tb01338.x

Warkentin, M., Gefen, D., Pavlou, P. A., & Rose, G. (2002). Encouraging Citizen Adoption of eGovernment by Building Trust. *Electronic Markets, 12*(3), 157–162. doi:10.1080/101967802320245929

Wasserman, S., & Faust, K. (1996). *Social Network Analysis. Method and Applications*. Cambridge, MA: Cambridge University Press.

Wauters, P., Nijsken, M., & Tiebout, J. (2007). The user challenge: benchmarking the supply of online public services. In *Proceedings of the 7th measurement*. European Commission. *World Economic Forum (WEF)*. Retrieved from http://www.weforum.org/en/index.htm

Weinberger, A. (2003). *Scripts for computer-supported collaborative learning*. Munich, Germany: Department Psychologie. Ludwig-Maximilians-Universität.

Westbrook, V. (2006). The virtual learning future. *Teaching in Higher Education, 11*(4), 471–482. doi:10.1080/13562510600874276

Wexler, Y., Shechtman, E., & Irani, M. (2004). Space-time video completion. In. *Proceedings of the IEEE Conf. on Computer Vision and Pattern Recognition, 1,* 120–127.

Wikipedia. (n.d). *Management*. Retrieved October 2008 from http://en.wikipedia.org/wiki/Management

Wikipedia. (n.d.). *Acquisition*. Retrieved September 2008 from http://en.wikipedia.org/wiki/Knowledge_Acquisition_and_Documentation_Structuring

Wikipedia. (n.d.). *Francis Bacon*. Retrieved August 2008 from http://en.wikipedia.org/wiki/Francis_Bacon

Wiley Media. (n.d.). *What is knowledge management*. Retrieved June 2008 from http://media.wiley.com/product_data/excerpt/51/18411270/1841127051.pdf

Williams, J. B., & Jacobs, J. (2004). Exploring the use of blogs as learning spaces in the higher education sector. *Australasian Journal of Educational Technology, 20*(2), 232–247.

Williams, M. (2001). In whom we trust: group membership as an affective context for trust development. *Academy of Management Review, 26*(3), 377–396. doi:10.2307/259183

Wittke, A., & Granow, R. (2007). *Why German universities choose Moodle instead of Sakai*.

Wolf, M. (2004). *Why Globalization Works*. New Haven, CT: Yale University Press.

World Bank Knowledge Assessment Methodology. (2007). Retrieved April 1, 2008 from http://web.worldbank.org/WBSITE/EXTERNAL/WBI/WBIPROGRAMS/KFDLP/EXTUNIKAM/0,menuPK:1414738~pagePK:64168427~piPK:64168435~theSitePK:1414721,00.html

World Bank. (2000). *Attacking poverty: opportunity, empowerment, and security.* Retrieved from http://siteresources.worldbank.org/INTPOVERTY/Resources/WDR/overview.pdf

World Bank. (2006). *Where is the Wealth of Nations? Measuring Capital for the 21st Century.* Washington, DC: The International Bank for Reconstruction and Development/The World Bank.

World Bank. (n.d.). *Knowledge Assessment Method (KAM).* Retrieved May 2008 from http://www.worldbank.org/kam

World Economic Forum. (2006). *The Global Competitiveness Report 2006-2007.* Retrieved August 10, 2007 from http://www.weforum.org/en/initiatives

World Economic Forum. *Global Information Technology Report.* (2007-2008). Retrieved from http://www.insead.edu/v1/gitr/wef/main/analysis/choosedatavariable.cfm

World Ranking for Capacity for Innovation, Global Information Technology Report. (2007-2008). *Availability of latest technologies Index.* Retrieved from http://www.insead.edu/v1/gitr/wef/main/analysis/showdatatable.cfm?vno=1.42

World Ranking for Companies Spending on R&D, Global Information Technology Report. (2007-2008). *Capacity for Innovation Index.* Retrieved from http://www.insead.edu/v1/gitr/wef/main/analysis/showdatatable.cfm?vno=8.2&countryid=552

World Summit on the Information Society (WSIS). (n.d.). Retrieved from http://www.itu.int/wsis/index.html

Wu, A. (2003). Supporting electronic discourse: Principles of design from a social constructivist perspective. *Journal of Interactive Learning Research, 14*(2), 167–184.

Wu, I.-L., & Chen, J.-L. (2005). An extension of Trust and TAM model with TPB in the initial adoption of online tax: An empirical study. *International Journal of Human-Computer Studies, 62,* 784–808. doi:10.1016/j.ijhcs.2005.03.003

Yamagishi, T., & Yamagishi, M. (1994). Trust and commitment in the United States and Japan. *Motivation and Emotion, 18*(2), 433–465. doi:10.1007/BF02249397

Yasuyuki, M. (n.d.). *Full-frame Video Stabilization.* Beijing, China. *Microsoft Research Asia.*

Yeganeh, B., & Kolb, D. (2009). Mindfulness and experiential learning. *OD Practitioner - Journal of the Development Organization Network, 41*(3), 13-18.

Yi, M., Jackson, J., Park, J., & Probst, J. (2005). Understanding information technology acceptance by individual professionals: Toward an integrative view. *Information & Management, 43*(3), 350–363. doi:10.1016/j.im.2005.08.006

Yin, R. K. (2003). *Case study research: Design and methods* (3rd ed.). Thousand Oaks, CA: Sage.

Young, A., & Norgard, C. (2006). Assessing the quality of online courses from the students' perspective. *The Internet and Higher Education, 9,* 107–115. doi:10.1016/j.iheduc.2006.03.001

Zack, M. H. (1999). Developing a Knowledge Strategy. *California Management Review, 41*(3), 125–145.

Zafiropoulos, K., Karavasilis, I., & Vrana, V. (in press). Exploring E-governance by Primary and Secondary Education Teachers in Greece. *International Journal of Electronic Democracy.*

Zand, D. E. (1972). Trust and Managerial Problem Solving. *Administrative Science Quarterly, 17*(2), 229–239. doi:10.2307/2393957

Zand, D. E. (1997). *The Leadership Triad Knowledge, Trust and Power.* New York: Oxford University Press.

Zhang, D., Zhu, L., Briggs, L. O., & Nunamaker, J. F. Jr. (2006). Instructional video in e-learning: Assessing the impact of interactive video on learning effectiveness. *Information & Management, 43,* 15–27. doi:10.1016/j.im.2005.01.004

Zucker, L. G. (1986). Production of trust: Institutional sources of economic structure. In Staw, B. W., & Cummings, L. L. (Eds.), *Research in organizational behavior* (pp. 1840–1920). Greenwich, CT: JAI Press.

Zupancic, B., & Horz, H. (2002). Lecture recording and its use in a traditional university course. In *Proceedings of the 7th Annual Conf. on Innovation and Technology in Computer Science Education ITiCSE '02* (pp. 24-28). New York: ACM.

About the Contributors

Miltiadis D. Lytras has co-edited/co-edits, 25 special issues in International Journals (e.g. *IEEE Transaction on Knowledge and Data Engineering, IEEE Internet Computing, IEEE Transactions on Education,Computers in Human Behaviour*, etc.) and has authored/[co-]edited 12 books (e.g. *Open Source for Knowledge and Learning Management, Ubiquitous and Pervasive Knowledge Management, Intelligent Learning Infrastructures for Knowledge Intensive Organizations* and *Semantic Based Information Systems*). He is the founder and officer of the Semantic Web and Information Systems Special Interest Group in the association for information systems (http://www.sigsemis.org). He serves as the (Co) Editor-in-Chief of 12 international journals (e.g. *International Journal of Knowledge and Learning, International Journal of Technology Enhanced Learning, International Journal on Social and Humanistic Computing, International Journal on Semantic Web and Information Systems, International Journal on Digital Culture and Electronic Tourism, International Journal of Electronic Democracy, International Journal of Electronic Banking and International Journal of Electronic Trade) while he is an associate editor or editorial board member of seven more.*

* * *

Abdulkader Alfantookh is the Deputy Minister of Higher Education for Planning and Information in the Kingdom of Saudi Arabia. He is also an Associate Professor of Computer Science, College of Computer and Information Sciences, King Saud University. He received his PhD in 1995 from Illinois Institute of Technology, USA. His current research is mainly concerned with IT governance and security; and the development of higher education.

Patrícia Almeida is currently a researcher at the Research Centre for Didactics and Technology in Teacher Education (CIDTFF), at the University of Aveiro, in Portugal. She holds a Ph.D. in Science Education. Her main research interests are classroom based, looking at how questions promote creativity, active learning, critical thinking, and the understanding of students' learning process in science. Currently she is also interested on learning styles, new learning and teaching approaches, and linking teaching and research in Higher Education as a means of enhancing the scholarship of teaching and learning. She is the author of papers and chapters of books in the field of questioning, learning styles and science education.

David Avison is Distinguished Professor of Information Systems at ESSEC Business School and visiting professor at Brunel University. He was President of the Association of Information Systems (AIS) 2008-9. He is joint editor of the Information Systems Journal. So far, over twenty-five books are to his credit including the fourth edition of the well-used text Information Systems Development: Methodologies, Techniques and Tools (jointly authored with Guy Fitzgerald) and most recently the text Information Systems Project Management (with Reza Torkzedah). He has published a large number of research papers in learned journals, edited texts and conference papers. He was Chair of the International Federation of Information Processing (IFIP) 8.2 group on the impact of IS/IT on organisations and society. He has been program chair, conference chair and general chair of several conferences including ICIS and IFIP. He researches in the area of information systems development and more generally on information systems in their natural organizational setting, in particular using action research and case study, though he has also used a number of other qualitative research approaches.

Saad Haj Bakry is Professor of Information Networks at the College of Engineering, King Saud University. He received his PhD in 1980 from Aston University in Birmingham, England; and he is a Chartered Engineer and a Fellow of the Institution of Engineering and Technology, UK. His current research is mainly concerned with network planning and design optimization; IT governance and security policies; and the development of the knowledge society.

Chinthaka Balasooriya is a lecturer at School of Public Health & Community Medicine, University of New South Wales, Australia. In his current position, he facilitates scenario groups in all courses of Phase 1 in the undergraduate medicine program, and teaches clinical skills to medical students at the Clinical Skills Centre. He is also a convenor of the Society & Health B course of the undergraduate medicine program, and a Portfolio Advisor for College C of Phase 1 medical students. He holds his PhD in Medical Education from University of New South Wales. He has obtained his bachelor's degree in Medicine and in Surgery from University of Colombo, Sri Lanka. His ongoing research aimed at further exploring the small group learning process.

Constanta-Nicoleta Bodea is a professor of project management and artificial intelligence at the Academy of Economic Studies (AES), Bucharest, Romania. She directs a Masters Program in Project Management, and is the head of the Economic Research Department at AES. She is the chair of the "334 Technical Committee - Continuing Education Standards" at the Romanian Association for Standardization - ASRO, president of the Project Management Romania Association (since 2000), chair of the Education & Training Board of the International Project Management Association - IPMA (since 2007), project manager of more than 20 R&D and IT projects in the last ten years, contributor and author of 11 books and more than 50 papers on Project Management, Information Systems, and Artificial Intelligence, being Honored by IPMA with the *Outstanding Research Contributions* (2007).

David Castillo-Merino is a Senior Lecturer at the Economics and Business Department of the Open University of Catalonia (Spain). He is also associate professor at the Economics and Business Departament of the Pompeu Fabra University and has been visiting professor at University of Paris-Sud and at the University of Barcelona. His work combines professional and academic activities. His main research fields are elearning, firms' intangible investment and productivity, and corporate finance, in which he has participated in some European research projects and published several books and papers in national and international journals. He is a research member of the New Economy Obsevatory (ONE), a consolidated research group focused in the analysis of companies' transformations by the use of information and communication technologies.

Melania Coman has a Master Degree in Project Management from the Academy of Economic Studies (AES), Bucharest, Romania (2008), a Bachelor Degree in International Business, awarded by Transilvania University, Brasov, Romania (2003), a Quality Assurance and Internal Audit Certificate, awarded by The Institute for European Studies and Management (2005) and she is a Certified Project-Management Associate, since 2008. Member of the Romanian Association of Project Management, she is currently a senior consultant in project management and structural funds.

Maria Dascalu has a Master Degree in Project Management from the Academy of Economic Studies (AES), Bucharest, Romania (2008) and a Bachelor Degree in Computer Science from the Alexandru-Ioan Cuza University, Iasi, Romania (2006). She is a PhD student in Economic Informatics at the University of Economics, combining her work experience as a programmer with numerous research activities. Her research relates to computer-assisted testing with applications in e-learning environments for project management. Her interests are algorithm design, web technologies, artificial intelligence, IT project management, project management methodologies, risk management, e-learning systems and knowledge management. Maria Dascălu is a Certified Project Management Associate (2008). Currently, she is conducting a research stage at the University of Gothenburg, Sweden.

Craig Deed is currently Senior Lecturer, Course Coordinator for the Graduate Diploma of Education (Secondary) and Bachelor of Physical and Outdoor Education (4th Year) at La Trobe University (Australia). His current research interests include engaging students through innovative pedagogy, student agency in contemporary school contexts, and self-regulation of learning behaviour and boys and education. He is widely published in the fields of meta cognition, self motivation and leaning and new technologies.

Katharina Ebner has been a scientific assistant, professorship for Work and Industrial Psychology, at the Universität der Bundeswehr München since 2007. She is responsible for designing, implementing, managing and evaluating the university's student coaching. With a diploma in psychology granted by the Ludwig-Maximilians-Universität München in 2003, and as former Business and Psychology student of the University of Hartford (USA), she completed her professional education by certifications as systemic Business Coach and competency-based Career Counselor. Her research contributes to the theory and evaluation of causes and effects of coaching as tool for professional and personnel development especially in the younger adult age.

Anthony Edwards is currently Director of HEFCE programmes at Liverpool Hope University (UK). His current research interest includes innovation and creativity and the history of technology. He is widely published in the fields of using new technology to promote creativity and the history of technical education. He is current working on a new book exploring the contemporary issues generated because of the growing use of technology in education.

Bernhard Ertl is senior researcher at the Universität der Bundeswehr München. He has realized several research projects in the context of gender in computer and science teaching which includes projects with national and EU funding, e.g. SESTEM *(Supporting Equality in Science Technology and Mathematics related choices of careers)*, PREDIL *(Promoting Equality in Digital Literacy)* and *"Comparative study on gender differences in technology enhanced and computer science learning: Promoting* *equity*". A further focus of research is on issues like video-mediated learning, Internet collaboration and online-courses with a particular focus on the support of collaborative knowledge construction by the methods of scripts and structured communication interfaces. He recently edited books about E-collaborative knowledge construction and Technologies and Practices for Constructing Knowledge in Online Environments. Bernhard Ertl earned his Diploma in computer science from the Ludwig Maximilian University Munich in 1998 and his Doctorate in education 2003. From 1999 to 2006, he was researcher at the Department Psychology of Ludwig Maximilian University of Munich and worked with Professor Heinz Mandl in DFG-funded research projects focusing on collaborative learning, e.g. "*Collaborative Learning in Graphics-enhanced Tele-learning Environments*" and "*Collaborative Knowledge Construction in Desktop Videoconferencing*".

Jordi Díaz Gibson is a Professor of Education at Ramon Llull University. His research is focused in Educational networks, social capital and the pedagogical use of ICT in schools. He is developing a PhD around the definition of a methodological model of educative networking focused on experiences in Spain, United States and Sweden.

I. González is a Lecturer at the Business Administration Department of the Open University of Catalonia (Spain). PhD in Business Administration (Accounting and Finances speciality) for the University of Valladolid (Spain) and eMBA for the European School of Businesses of Madrid (Spain). She has worked as a Manager at several companies linked to the Public Administration, as well as a Strategy Consultant. Her lines of investigation revolve around two areas: Management Accounting - the system of process management - and innovation in e-learning. She has written several articles, having presented communications in national and international Congresses.

Janette Hughes is assistant professor in the Faculty of Education at the University of Ontario Institute of Technology. Her research interests are in new literacies in general, with particular emphasis on digital literacies.

M.ed Ioannis Karavasilis is the Administrator of Administration of Primary Education of Serres, Greece. He is a teacher and he holds a master degree in administration of education. Currently he is PhD student in the Department of International and European Studies, University of Macedonia. He is the author of one book and has published many articles. His research interests include e-governance practices, TQM and reform of education.

Kathy Kikis-Papadakis received her PhD in Educational Planning and Evaluation (area of investigation: Employability and Language Training of Minority Groups in the USA). Since then she held the post of leading the section of bilateral cooperation at the Hellenic Ministry of Research and Technology and taught at the Department of Philosophical and Social Science at the University of Crete. Since 1993 she is leading the Educational Research and Evaluation Group at the Institute of Applied and Computational Mathematics at FORTH. Her research interests are in the study of impact of technology enhanced learning, both from an effectiveness and innovation introduction perspectives, and on the socio-cultural aspects of learning. Specific areas of interest include gender and mathematics and curriculum development for teachers' professional development. She has extensive experience in RTD management with focus on innovation in learning at various educational levels. All of her research work is supported from competitive grants (National and Community levels) and focuses in the area of educational policy, evaluation and gender equity issues in learning and working.

P. Lara is a Director of Innovation and Senior Lecturer at the Information and Communication Department of the Open University of Catalonia (Spain). His main research lines are innovation products and management, information electronic systems and elearning. He is a Research Member of SCIMAGO Group about scientific information in CSIC and also Research Member of eLearnCenter.

Umar Manzoor is a PhD Student in Computer Science at the School of Computing, Science and Engineering. He received his Masters in Computer Science from National University of Computer and Emerging Sciences (NUCES). In 2006, he joined the Computer Science group at NUCES University as a Lecturer and promoted after as Assistant Professor. Currently, he is involved in development of autonomous framework using cognitive agents for network monitoring and management. He has published extensively in the area of Multi-Agent Systems, which appeared in conferences such as Springer Lecture Notes in Computer Science, IEEE International Conference on Intelligent Agents, Web Technologies and Internet Commerce and journals such as Expert systems with applications, Journal of Network and Computer Applications.

Mariana Martinho holds a Master in Science Communication and Education and is currently a Physics and Chemistry teacher at the Escola EB 2,3/S de Oliveira de Frades, in Portugal. Her research interests include gender differences in science education, classroom questioning and new teaching and learning approaches in Higher Education.

Belinda Masekela completed her BSc Hons at the University of South Africa (UNISA) during 2008. She is working as Product Manager at Nedbank Ltd. Her research interests span Software Project Management and Change Management.

Jordi Longás Mayayo is a Professor of Pedagogy, and academic director of the masters degree in Social and Community Pedagogy at Ramon Llull University. He is a city council advisor in the creation of Local Educative Networks referred to scholar success in several cities in Catalonia, Spain. He has several publications concerning school organization, kindergarten management, school-work transition, tutorship and educative networks.

Ana Mª López Murat is a Social worker and researcher member of Social Pedagogy and Informational and Communication Technologies (PSITIC), at Ramon Llull University. Specifically, her research is centred in Community development and Educational networks in Spain and Paraguay.

Samia Nefti is currently a Senior Lecturer at the School of Computing, Science and Engineering. She holds a Doctorate in Computer Science from Paris XII, France. In 1999, she joined the Computer Science group at Liverpool University as a Senior Research Fellow and after as Lecturer at Salford University. She is the head of the intelligent systems group within Salford's 6* rated Informatics Research Institute. She has twenty years experience in the field of cognitive modeling, machine learning, focused on Neural-Fuzzy based predictive modelling for embodied agents. She has been invited recently to present a global lecture "Shangh'AI" on Cognitive systems. She has published extensively in the above areas, which appeared in journals such as IEEE Transaction on Fuzzy Systems, Expert systems with applications, Journal of Intelligent and Robotics Systems and recently edited a book on "Advances on cognitive systems". She is IEEE member, Chartered member of BCS and active member of the European Network for the Advancement of Artificial Cognitive Systems.

Rita Nienaber received a PhD Computer Science degree from the University of South Africa (UNISA) in 2008. She has presented research papers at international and national conferences focusing on software project management. She was appointed as senior lecturer at Unisa from 1998, and teaches undergraduate, as well as post graduate courses. Her research interests are Software Project Management, Risk Management, Change management, E-learning and Outcome Based Education.

Dolors Plana-Erta is a Lecturer at the Economics and Business Department of the Open University of Catalonia (Spain). Her research field is focused on management and corporate finance, in which she has written several articles, having presented communications in some Congresses. She is a research member of the New Economy Obsevatory (ONE), a consolidated research group focused in the analysis of companies' transformations by the use of information and communication technologies.

Lorayne Robertson is assistant professor and Program Director in the Faculty of Education at the University of Ontario Institute of Technology. Her research interests include digital literacy, critical literacy and media literacy.

E. Serradell-Lopez is a Senior Lecturer at the Business Administration and Management Department of the Open University of Catalonia (Spain). His work combines professional and academic activities. His main research lines are elearning, corporate culture, intangibles and product innovation and ICT applications in management. He is a Research Member of IN3 that conducts cutting-edge research on the interaction between information and communication technologies, society, economy and culture and also Research Member of eLearnCenter, an e-learning research, innovation and training centre, focusing on higher education and lifelong learning.

José Joaquim Teixeira-Dias is professor of molecular physical chemistry at the Chemistry Department of the University of Aveiro, Portugal, and is responsible for teaching Elements of Physical Chemistry (first semester) and General Chemistry (second semester) to first year students of Science and Engineering courses at the University of Aveiro. His current research interests lie in cyclodextrin-micelle interactions and in the learning and teaching of chemistry to university students. He has been awarded by the Science Council the designation of Chartered Scientist, and is Fellow of the Royal Society of Chemistry (Chartered Chemist).

Vasiliki Vrana is a mathematician and holds a PhD in Computer Sciences, Aristotle University of Thessaloniki, Greece. She is an education consultant in secondary education and she teaches information systems at the Department of Business Administration, Technological Education Institute of Serres, Greece. Her research interests include the study of web 2.0, of IT in tourism and hospitality industries and e-governance. She has published one book and many articles in international and Greek journals.

Kostas Zafiropoulos is an Assistant Professor at the Department of International and European Studies, University of Macedonia. He holds a PhD in applied statistics and has published articles in international and Greek journals. He is the author of three books about marketing research and research methodology (in Greek). His research interests include sampling and data analysis and research methods.

Mireia Civís Zaragoza holds a PhD in Community education, and is experienced in social and scholar pedagogy. She is a Professor of Education, Pedagogy and also of a Masters degree in Social and Community Pedagogy at Ramon Llull University. She is an active researcher with several publications in the creation of Local Educative Networks, communitarian educative projects, educational city projects, citizen participation and educative coresponsibility.

Aljona Zorina is a PhD student of ESSEC Business School in Paris. In 2009 she presented a paper at the World Summit on the Knowledge Society (WSKS 2009) and this paper was developed from that conference publication. Aljona's research in the methods and strategies for sustainable knowledge society development started during her undergraduate and Master studies in Belarus, where she has had several publications on the topic. In 2007 one of Aljona's works was a prize-winner of the annually competition organized by Nikolay Federonko Interantional Foundations for Economic Research and guided by the Russian Academy of Science.

Index